🔥 THE EAST-WEST CENTER—officially known as the Center for Cultural and Technical Interchange Between East and West—is a national educational institution established in Hawaii by the U.S. Congress in 1960 to promote better relations and understanding between the United States and the nations of Asia and the Pacific through cooperative study, training, and research. The Center is administered by a public, nonprofit corporation whose international Board of Governors consists of distinguished scholars, business leaders, and public servants.

Each year more than 1,500 men and women from many nations and cultures participate in Center programs that seek cooperative solutions to problems of mutual consequence to East and West. Working with the Center's multidisciplinary and multicultural staff, participants include visiting scholars and researchers; leaders and professionals from the academic, government, and business communities; and graduate degree students, most of whom are enrolled at the University of Hawaii. For each Center participant from the United States, two participants are sought from the Asian and Pacific area.

Center programs are conducted by institutes addressing problems of communication, culture learning, environment and policy, population, and resource systems. A limited number of "open" grants are available to degree scholars and research fellows whose academic interests are not encompassed by institute programs.

The U.S. Congress provides basic funding for Center programs and a variety of awards to participants. Because of the cooperative nature of Center programs, financial support and cost-sharing are also provided by Asian and Pacific governments, regional agencies, private enterprise and foundations. The Center is on land adjacent to and provided by the University of Hawaii.

East-West Center Books are published by The University Press of Hawaii to further the Center's aims and programs.

PROPAGANDA AND COMMUNICATION IN WORLD HISTORY

PROPAGANDA AND COMMUNICATION IN WORLD HISTORY

VOLUME III

A Pluralizing World in Formation

edited by

Harold D. Lasswell
Daniel Lerner
Hans Speier

AN EAST-WEST CENTER BOOK 乑
Published for the East-West Center by
The University Press of Hawaii
Honolulu

"Must Science Serve Political Power?" by Harold D. Lasswell, reprinted with permission from *American Psychologist* 25 (February 1970): 117–123.

"The Social Effects of Communication Technology," by Herbert Goldhamer, reprinted by permission of The Rand Corporation.

"Social Science and the Collectivization of Hubris," by Joseph J. Spengler, reprinted with permission from the *Political Science Quarterly* 87 (March 1972): 1–21.

"The Emerging Social Structure of the World," by Alex Inkeles, *World Politics* 27, no. 4 (copyright © 1975 by Princeton University Press): 467–495. Reprinted by permission of Princeton University Press.

Library of Congress Cataloging in Publication Data
Main entry under title:

A Pluralizing world in formation.

   (Propaganda and communication in world history ;
v. 3)
   Includes index.
   1.   Communication—Political aspects—Addresses,
essays, lectures.   2.   Power (Social sciences)—
Address, essays, lectures.   3.   Equality—Addresses,
essays, lectures.   4.   Underdeveloped areas—Communication.   5.   Communication—Social aspects.   6.   Social
structure.   I.   Lasswell, Harold Dwight, 1902–
II.   Lerner, Daniel.   III.   Speier, Hans.   IV.   Series.
HM258.P74   vol. 3   301.14   79–21108
ISBN 0–8248–0507–0

These three volumes are dedicated to
    JEAN LERNER
our indispensable collaborator
who, with insight, skill, and good cheer,
did whatever needed to be done
through the years of these studies

CONTENTS

VOLUME I: The Symbolic Instrument in Early Times

VOLUME II: Emergence of Public Opinion in the West

THE ENLARGING SYMBOLIC OF THE MODERN WEST

THE SYMBOLIC IN WORLD REVOLUTIONARY PROCESSES

PREFACE

The final volume of *Propaganda and Communication in World History* deals with the contemporary world situation. A salient feature is the technology that makes operative the first "world communication network." Just two centuries ago the American Declaration of Independence justified itself in terms of "a decent respect for the opinions of mankind." Only in the past decade, however, has the technology of satellites produced a functioning global network that is instantaneous, simultaneous, and continuous.

This achievement has not met with universal enthusiasm. The phrase "cultural imperialism" has come into vogue among those who fear the intrusion of more developed countries (MDC) into less developed countries (LDC) via this network. The specter of "direct satellite broadcasting" has led to a humiliating defeat of American proposals for a free flow of information in the UN and UNESCO. These controversies over international and intercultural communication signal wide and deep differences in social and political values around the world.

The conflicts between old and new values can best be presented, for nonpartisan purposes, in terms of a "multivalue context." As some of these conflicts stem from the relationship between knowledge and power, Lasswell opens the volume with the crucial question: "Must science serve political power?"

Wiesner, a major figure in developing the highly visible technologies that have shaped the world image of contemporary
America, then assesses the often troubled "marriage of science
and government."

Inasmuch as MDC-LDC relations over the past quarter century usually have turned upon "development" (the current
LDC version of the old MDC idea of "progress"), Spengler addresses the central problem of "rising expectations: frustrations." This problem is central for communication as well as for
economics. For it is communication that has led the peoples of
LDC to expect more of the good things of life than their poor
economies can provide. Despite such epithets as "materialism"
and "consumerism" invoked by the ideologues of traditional
values, the imbalanced Want:Get Ratio that turns rising expectations into frustrations in LDC is a key problem in our contemporary world.

"The Multivalue Context" concludes with two chapters that
go to the core of the present conflict between old and new values. Traditional societies evolved lifeways based largely upon *respect* for those in ascribed roles of social superiority, for example, elder males. Contemporary society stresses the values of
freedom and *equality,* which provide opportunities for any and
all (in principle) to rise to positions of achieved superiority. Killian analyzes the characteristics and consequences of this "respect revolution," primarily with respect to race relations.
Rogow then traces the deep transformation of traditional values
of "love and intimacy" as diffused through the mass media.

The second part of this volume surveys "The Multivariate
Process" of world communication today by dealing with four
main elements in the classic paradigm of communication research. Pool deals with content, Davison with channels, Martin
with audiences, Schramm with effects. Goldhamer supplements
these chapters with an analysis of a distinctively contemporary
problem: the social effects of advanced communication technology.

The concluding part on "The Symbolic Instrument" looks
back at recent trends as a source of some future propects for
communication. Rolle explores "the historic past of the unconscious" with an eye to present transformations of character and
personality. Spengler considers "the hubris of social science" so

that awareness of past errors may help to improve future efforts. Inkeles outlines "the emerging social structure of the world" as the context for future communication. Lasswell then brings the work to a final focus on "the future of world communication and propaganda."

It remains for the editors to thank all those who have made contributions to this long and laborious effort. For us it has been a rich learning experience. We trust it will prove so for our readers as well.

Postscript. As this final volume goes to press, we pay tribute to our senior coeditor, the late Harold Dwight Lasswell. His passing is a great loss to all students of communication and to the world of scholarship in general. His memory and his legacy will enrich many generations yet to come.

D. L.
H. S.

THE MULTIVALUE CONTEXT

1

MUST SCIENCE SERVE POLITICAL POWER?

HAROLD D. LASSWELL

At least one fundamental statement about our time arouses little disagreement: The science-based technology of Western European civilization is moving toward universality. Almost everything else is open to debate. For instance, is the man of knowledge taking over the seats of the powerful? Will he? Should he? Such questions give new vitality to talk of professional ethics, or the social responsibility of science, or the control of education and research.

That political power is affected by knowledge and that political power affects knowledge is no revelation. The interesting problem is the timing of two-way effects. Until recently it could be held that knowledge affected power more slowly than power affected knowledge. A substantial change in the map of knowledge would first alter many less comprehensive maps. Then technology changed, altering the composition and experience of groups. The resulting changes in the direction and intensity of demand affected public policy. Political decisions, in contrast, have often had immediate consequences for knowledge. If proposed appropriations are voted yes or no, everyone—researcher, teacher, or student—adapts as well as he can.

Today's timing is different because the structural position of science is different. The impact of new knowledge on public policy is almost instantaneous, thanks to the many institutions that specialize in science or government, or mediate between the two. A huge communication network interconnects laboratories, observatories, field stations, and libraries in universities, industries, and governments. Revised matter-of-fact expectations, such as comprise the map of knowledge, promptly change expectations about the future of all concerned. As a result policies are modified: Scientists suddenly see new lines of research, technologists recognize promising lines of development, investors see new investment opportunities, officials perceive new ways of affecting national security (or insecurity). Given the position of science in American or Soviet society, the chain runs from innovations in the map of knowledge to projections of the future, to evaluations of alternative policy objectives and strategies, to demands for decision, to the making of decisions, to further changes in perspectives, behavioral operations, and aggregate structure.

SCIENCE, MILITANCY, AND OLIGARCHY
Despite the remarkable, even explosive, expansion of knowledge, and its global diffusion, it must be conceded that, up to the present, *the aggregate impact of the scientific revolution has failed to revolutionize the basic structure of world politics.* The relations of the United States, Soviet Russia, and mainland China, to say nothing of the middle-sized and smaller powers, are constrained as usual by the expectation of violence. The expectation of violence contributes to, and is in turn sustained by, the division of the globe into apprehensive or threatening powers in an arms race of unexcelled magnitude and danger. This divided and militant structure of the world political arena preceded the era of science, and has succeeded thus far in subordinating the institutions of knowledge to its perpetuation.

We take note of another fact about the social consequences of science. It is often pointed out that *knowledge is more commonly used for the relative benefit of the few than for the benefit of all.* This is most obvious in the contrast between the suburban ghettos of the prosperous and the poverty-stricken ghettos of urban and rural slums.

How can we account for the historic subordination of knowledge to the institutions of war and oligarchy? Certainly there is no lack of hortatory rhetoric on the part of eminent contributors to knowledge celebrating the latent universality of the fruits of knowledge for all mankind, or the fraternal unity of all who contribute to a verifiable map of nature, man, and society.

PAROCHIALIZATION

Up to the present a root difficulty appears to be that *however universal the manifest content of scientific propositions, or the procedures by which they may be verified, they are parochially introduced.* Their diffusion or restriction is heavily dependent on the characteristics of the parochial environments in which they appear. The response of each environment depends on the expectations of advantage or disadvantage that would follow from expediting or interfering with the global spread or techno-logical application of new knowledge. It is a matter of everyday experience that most individuals and organizations are not in-terested in the advancement of knowledge as an end in itself either for themselves individually or collectively. They are con-cerned not with enlightenment as a scope value but as a base for obtaining wealth, power, respect, health, and other valued out-comes. In a world divided by the institution of war the support for science depends in no small measure on the expectation that scientific knowledge will contribute to the power needed to throw off the domination of imperial states and to achieve a level of modernization that will prevent the reimposition of direct or indirect rule from outside. Among the superpowers and the older industrial nation-states science is cultivated to provide the muscle that is presumably required to maintain freedom from enforced subordination to outside control.

The institution of war is expressed and sustained by drawing scientists into a coalition with political leaders, military officers, administrative officials, factory managers, and other significant participants in the power process. In socialist-communist hierar-chies the coalition mates are the top leaders and bureaucrats of the monopoly party (or political order), the political police, the army, the official departments and agencies. In bodies politic having more co-archic traditions and procedures, much more prominence is given to the leaders of private industry, competi-tive political parties, pressure groups, and mass media of com-munication. The military-industrial complex is no respecter of popular distinctions between forms of industrial society.

INNER STRUCTURE OF KNOWLEDGE
INSTITUTIONS

Why science works for power can be better understood if we examine the inner structure of knowledge institutions themselves. We recognize that scientists differ from one another in the intensity of their commitment to fundamental theory. At one limit are those who specialize on the principal contours of the map of nature, man, and society; at the other are routineers who fill in detail. The former are oriented toward enlightenment. Typically their skills include techniques of theory formation and procedures of primary observations directed to novel possibilities. Those who fill in detail are more characteristically equipped with skills adapted to purposes other than fundamental enlightenment. The implication is that as the pursuit of verifiable knowledge grows in importance in society and research institutions expand, the percentage of those who are mainly concerned with fundamental enlightenment diminishes (toward an unknown limit) in comparison with those who are satisfied to exercise their skill in the service of other purposes. As the knowledge institutions expand, they reach a level at which they recruit personnel from all save the most humble strata of society. Hence the personnel of science increasingly come from those who share the conventional culture, which means that knowledge is seen as instrumental to value outcomes other than the pursuit of enlightenment.

The consequence for the subserviency of science to political power, or to other "practical" values, is evident. Those who, in effect, "have skill, will move" make themselves understood and available to the demands of decision makers at every level. These are the mid-elite and rank and file of science and scholarship. From them are recruited the thousands who cement the interdependence of science and the established structure of society. In the aggregate they contribute more directly to the service of war and oligarchy than to world security and the welfare of the whole community.

It is true that from its broadly based supply of manpower the scientific establishment does succeed in developing a relatively small and highly respected elite whose members are oriented toward knowledge as an end in itself, or as an end that ought to be employed for the benefit of the whole nation of man rather than its parochial subdivisions. Many members of this elite are specialized to operations whose working techniques are less than usually dependent on the empirical data collected by the individual investigator, or on immediate applications. Included are many mathematicians, logicians, linguists, and related theorists who are less firmly embedded than their colleagues in the constraints of a localized environment.

HIGHLY CAPITALIZED SCIENCE

The dependence of science on the social environment is emphasized by the transformation from the early age of handicraft science to the present era of highly capitalized science. The flow of assets for research and education depends on sustaining a structure of expectation in the environment that "knowledge pays." Hence the internal structure of knowledge institutions changes in ways that enable them to draw upon the environment. In the subculture of science those most directly responsible for these expectations are those who mediate between the institutions of knowledge and other institutions. They include heads of laboratories, department chairmen, deans, presidents, popular professors, many trustees, public relations and development officers, alumni secretaries, and the officers and staffs of professional associations.

The participation by scientists in the decision processes of society goes much further than in representing the case for the support of science. The fact is that the decision processes of modern and modernizing powers are deeply permeated by men of knowledge. The proposition is true even when you eliminate the lawyers and theologians, and count only physicians, scientists (physical, biological, behavioral), and engineers, or those who have received college or professional training. It is true of many political leaders, government officials, and military officers in industrial and industrializing countries.

All this has happened, yet the institutions of war and oligarchy continue. Evidently, we can have scientists in government without having government for science or man. Along the path that leads from an early training in science toward political leadership or government service the individual learns the conditions of survival in the arenas of power. He learns to negotiate behind the scenes and to propagandize in public places. The outcome is a present politician and an ex-scientist, a man who has learned to survive by coming to terms with the militant structure of world power and the typically oligarchical structure of internal politics.

VISIBILITY AND VULNERABILITY

The bearing of this evolution on the future of science in society is far from trivial; for science has grown strong enough to acquire visibility, and therefore to become eligible as a potential scapegoat for whatever disenchantment there may be with the earlier promises of a science-based technology. Even today there is much articulate disenchantment that goes beyond the traditional resistance of feudal elites to industry and science-based technology. If the earlier dream was a rising tide of production, the later reality also includes the social costs of polluted air, water, and soil. If the earlier hope was the abolition of disease, the current reality includes the discovery of pharmacological side effects that threaten life and health. If the earlier dream was safety and security for all, the current reality is the augmented peril of nuclear or biological destruction. If the earlier dream was that latent capabilities would be identified and matured into socially useful skills, the present reality includes augmented public and private forces of organized militancy, criminality, and delinquency. If the earlier vision was that destructive limitation on the growth of love and dedication would be dissolved by knowledge-guided socialization, the current reality is a very considerable demand to dominate, or to withdraw, to nonparticipate, to self-segregate, to celebrate alienation from collective life. If the earlier promise was that knowledge would make men free, the contemporary reality seems to be that more men are manipulated without their consent for more purposes by more techniques by fewer men than at any time in history.

Are we, in fact, in another period in which the faiths, beliefs, and loyalties of a once-progressive evolution have so weakened the bonds of public and civic order that massive seizures of destructive rage at the humiliations imposed on human dignity will once more disrupt the nonviolent processes of change, and reinstate the turbulence of a time of trouble, a rebarbarization of civilized centers, and another collapse of a discredited system of militancy and oligarchy? The verdict may be that whom the historical process would destroy it first must make strong enough to achieve a visibility sufficient to arouse false hopes, while remaining weak enough to acquiesce and connive in the frustration of their potential—thus for science and scientists.

CURRENT PROPOSALS •

It must not be supposed that all men of knowledge, and notably scientists, are happily reconciled to the contemporary situation. Many of them resent the degree to which their knowledge builds political power for others, or accumulates wealth for others, while leaving them to enjoy an advisory status quo and a fluctuating income from charitable gifts or bureaucratic salaries. In our society more specialists are taking steps to work for themselves rather than for others. They often use the corporate device of limited liability to set up profit or nonprofit companies in the hope of benefiting from entrepreneurial gains. Consultants and consulting firms often take their compensation in the form of stock, enabling them to share the appreciating assets of a successful enterprise.

Another and often closely connected source of dissatisfaction is the resentment among scientists of the degree to which they seem to be working for the benefit of an oligarchy instead of contributing directly to mankind. Many of them are searching for forms of scientist and user cooperatives that pool knowledge and technical know-how in laboratories that generate products and services for the general welfare.

These sentiments cut across the parochial lines of communist-socialist or liberal-capitalist economies and policies. Do we, in fact, stand at the beginning of a movement that could transform the role of science? What if every university or every professional specialty had exclusive claim to the discoveries and inventions of its members so that an increasing share of the applications of knowledge would flow to the man of knowledge? Would he work directly to spread the benefits from science to raise the aggregate level of regional and national welfare, to call a halt to the diseconomies of environmental loss, and especially to undermotivation for the use of human resources? In a word, would the scientist work more directly for man?

We are not without historical precedents of at least limited relevance. Some monasteries—Buddhist, Muslim, Christian—have sustained their rituals, their charities, and their scholars by marketing alcohol or other commodities. A modern university occasionally supplements its income from the proceeds of a patent or copyright pool. It is not inconceivable that associations of scholars might publish all the textbooks and reference works in their field, and design and manufacture educational (and hopefully interesting) games and school equipment. The school of architecture and planning might design cities.

More than this, associations of scientific planners might take the lead in developing a transnational chain of cooperatively organized cities intended to aid in the formation of a new world community within the framework of the old. Perhaps cities can be built on old or new islands or space platforms for people who "opt out," as far as possible, from the arms race. Perhaps great enterprises for the development of resources can create nonsegregated communities in the present waste regions of the earth (the deserts, the polar lands). Once constituted, such centers could reach well beyond their nominal boundaries and provide educational, scientific, recreational, and medical facilities for many more people than they would accommodate as permanent residents.

ARE SCIENTISTS LIKE EVERYBODY ELSE?

It is not too difficult for us to identify some of the factors that explain why proposals of this kind have made relatively modest headway. For instance, there is fear of their implications for the internal policy process of professional associations and universities. Any multiplication of entrepreneurial functions would multiply administrative staffs and presumably alter the balance of impact on decision. It is feared that those who engage in the activities that bring in the most money would insist on increasing their weight in the decision process. Many are apprehensive that conflicts would both proliferate and intensify over the identity of acceptable outside contractors; the salaries and conditions of work of researchers, teachers, administrators, and students; the allocation of resources for expansion in the physical, biological, and cultural sciences. One can envisage interuniversity competition to attract the big money makers (as well as grant swingers), or to set up new splinter associations in order to improve the "take" by the professional skill groups in relatively short supply. Also, it is not difficult to imagine competing horizontal unions appealing separately to younger, middle, or older faculty members, or to recent or older students, and confronting one another as collective bargainers. As the knowledge institutions extend transnationally it is not absurd to predict the accentuation of cleavages among rich and poor and according to traditional identities of tribe, language, race, or nation. In a word, the pessimistic expectation has been that a scientist or any other man of knowledge will act like everybody else, especially if he (or his spouse) thinks that he has a chance to get a bigger piece of pie somewhat nearer than the ever-receding sky.

Let us grant that this conventional wisdom has more than a grain of truth as a description of the past. Will it necessarily be true tomorrow? Is it to be asserted as beyond dispute that scientists and institutions of knowledge will continue to fail to identify and to serve common interests within the field of science and humanity?

COGNITIVE MAPS AND PROCEDURES

Perhaps, as some colleagues suggest, the challenge actually calls for a basic reconsideration of the character of the cognitive map for which it is appropriate for science to take responsibility. The proposition is that the fragmented cultivation of skill for opportunistic purposes is not enough. It does not automatically trigger an invisible hand that redraws and improves the contours of the general map of knowledge. A truly comprehensive cognitive map would include the significant future as well as the salient past. The inclusive map becomes known, not only by the piecemeal splitting of the pebbles on the beach, but by identifying the changing contours of sea and shore. The proposition is that at any slice of time these aggregate contours are the principal realities of nature, life, and culture. They are also the entities that in the past we have been least successful in identifying, explaining, or managing. It may be that as we adopt methods appropriate to discovering the congregation of cycles that define the reality of the moment, we learn how to modify their future timing by feeding their symbolic representations back into the intelligence flow of the moving present.

If attention is to be directed to the relevant cognitive context, appropriate institutions must be invented or adapted to the purpose. Luckily, we are not without guidance in this matter. For example, we are accustomed to the planetarium technique of providing a selective audiovisual experience of the past and future of the earth and its environment. We are capable of adapting the technique to the presentation of equally inclusive and selective maps of the past and prospective succession of biological forms. It is entirely possible to apply the planetarium technique to depictions of the past, prospective, and preferred sequences of value priorities and institutions in the social process of the earth, the hemisphere, the region, and the neighborhood.

It is not difficult to see how these contextual techniques can be adapted to the task of providing a regular means of giving consideration to the social consequences and the policy implications of knowledge. Such a function can be performed by a continuing seminar concerned with a provisional and changing map of the past, present, and future of science and man. Whatever the specialists represented, the practice of sharing, evaluating, and contributing to an inclusive map keeps alive the latent embers of concern for the knowledge enterprise as a whole.

Here is a means of examining the historical trends, conditioning factors, and future projections of the impact of knowledge on the use or abuse of human and environmental resources, on the institutions of war and peace, of production and distribution, of safety and health, of education and family life, of social caste and class, of ethical or religious responsibility, and of the future of science and scholarship themselves.

We recognize the possibility of feeding into a perfected network of interconnected seminars and planetaria the results obtained by the most sophisticated simulations of past and future (area by area, component by component).

Such changing cognitive maps can be used to initiate and guide the formation of research policy by identifying the zones of neglect or duplication. These presentations can release creative policy proposals for the future structure and functioning of universities, the professional associations, and communities at every level.

COMMON VERSUS SPECIAL INTERESTS

Furthermore, these continuing seminars can be incorporated explicitly into the whole complex decision process of professional associations, universities, and other knowledge institutions. These primary centers of cognitive orientation provide at least a partial answer to the challenge issued to men of knowledge by the conventional wisdom that the scientist and the scholar are as incapable as other men of discovering and pursuing enlightened common interests. You recognize the jibe: If men of knowledge cannot run themselves, how can they expect to continue to be taken seriously by the rest of the community as advisers or leaders? The argument is that if we cannot find criteria and procedures for discovering how, within the community of science and scholarship, common interests can overcome special interests, we cannot be trusted to clarify common interests in the wider community.

As indicated before, the possibility is not to be overlooked that the task of eliciting and evaluating the policy objectives and alternatives open to professional associations, universities, and other knowledge institutions will bring about a progressive improvement in fundamental cognitive maps and in the scientific process itself.

Furthermore, we can think in terms that include continuously expanding arenas of cognitive and policy operations. They may well begin inside knowledge institutions, and then proceed to the decision processes of mixed-knowledge and other institutions at national, subnational, and transnational levels. Certainly if political power is to be shaped and shared outside the limits of oligarchy, and if coercive authority is eventually to be supplanted by a voluntary civic order, it is fairly clear that the members of the body politic must have the means of keeping their cognitive maps adapted to the discovery of valid *common* interests, and of mobilizing dispositions to do what is necessary to overcome the dominance of *special* interests. In the circumstances of today's world, men of knowledge, especially men of science, can participate, as many of us are already doing, with the victims of urban blight and total neglect in a mutually illuminating search for the timing of the policy objectives and strategies that overcome these discriminations. Specialized men of knowledge, in cooperation with neighbors in the opulent suburbs, can search for the cues that release latent dispositions to overcome indifference to, or satisfaction in, the plight of others. In conjunction with the peoples affected, scientists can strive to identify the timing of the acts most likely to close the frustration gap that separates the multitude in underdeveloped nations from their newly awakened hopes. Most challenging of all, perhaps, is the possibility of continuing efforts to discover the timing of options that tame and redirect the militantly competitive elites of the opulent and knowledgeable powers, and to integrate a system of world public order that serves, not merely the minimum requirement of security, but the optimum potentials of man and his resources.

Such techniques as the planetarium, the continuing seminar, and continuous planning and appraisal are capable of being adapted to the needs and interests of human beings, whether or not they are highly specialized in the conventional institutions of knowledge. These procedures can be institutionalized as we perfect our knowledge of timing to match motivation. These instruments can give realistic help in overcoming the sense of indignity and injustice that so permeates the lives of modern men. Men do not need to live as resentful pawns in a game that no one bothers to explain. It is feasible for everyone to achieve some understanding of the whole chessboard of nature, life, and culture; to acquire some awareness of the rules of the game; to see where he can win or lose by abiding by the rules; or how he can most effectively act to change the rules.

CAREER PATTERNS

The discovery of how to navigate through the future calls for the perfecting of institutions of knowledge that are as yet poorly adapted to the knowledge of time or the timing of knowledge. The individual man of science may continue to devote himself mainly to the exercise of the competence for which he is trained; or he may complicate the pattern of his career by life plans that combine specialized activity with varying degrees of role playing in the decision processes of public and private institutions. In any case he can make these continuing policy judgments for himself, and in conjunction with others, with higher hopes of realism and relevance if he engages in recurring reappraisals of cognitive maps that display the social consequences of knowledge for the aggregate shaping and sharing of valued outcomes, and the readjustment of social institutions.

It is to be noted that cognitive maps are not restricted to representations of social, biological, and physical environments.

Many procedures have been invented by which the individual and hence each member of a group can reedit his cognitive map to include a more disciplined image of himself, of his value priorities, assets, and potential strategies for independent or collective policy formation and execution. The members of continuing seminars may include intervals of intense exposure to specific procedures designed to allow predispositions to come to the surface. The reference is to such procedures as depth interviewing, sensitivity training, aptitude and attitude testing, and pharmapsychic responses (to name a few).

CONCLUSION

The conclusion is that science and scientists in the aggregate need not serve political power in the future as they have in the past. It is possible to weaken and eventually to overcome the parochialisms of perspective that have restricted the universalization of science and laid scientists open to the charge of giving disproportionate service to militancy and oligarchy. By working together inside the institutions of knowledge, and as participants in public associations, men of knowledge can assist in modifying the traditional reliance of society on coercive political power. They can do so in the course of discovering how to obsolesce the institutions of militancy and oligarchy and to cultivate institutions of civic order. In the civic order there is reliance on active consent to the common interest in cultivating knowledge as a major expression of man and as an instrument of service to the nation of man.

Yes, scientists can serve science and commonwealth—whether as scientists or ex-scientists. It can be done by perfecting the institutions by which the cognitive maps that refer to the future as well as the past are corrected by continual feedback about the content and timing of knowledge of nature, life, and culture.

2

THE MARRIAGE OF SCIENCE AND GOVERNMENT

JEROME B. WIESNER

Relationships between science and government are, at the moment, in a state of rapid change. We have arrived at today's situation without having planned the existing relationships, much less desired them, so that future developments also may well have the character of a "random walk"—partially dependent on historical accidents and to a considerable degree dependent on the nature of the political process. To imagine how these developments might evolve, it may be useful to review a bit of the recent history of science in the federal government.

Those of us who have been involved in the problems of the interaction of science and technology and the federal government believe that there are actually two sets of problems: those of the impact of science on policy, and those of the impact of policy on science. They may interact; for example, if the president is unhappy about what he perceives to be the scientist's attitude about a policy, it may affect his attitudes toward and policies for science. But, on the whole, the two are quite different problems.

From a broad perspective, it is clear that the most crucial problems are those of the impact of science (more precisely, science-based technology) on policy. In the modern world, technology is the most dynamic force at work, and it poses an ever-increasing number of problems not only for our government but for every government. The most dramatic example, of course, is found in defense policy, but one sees the impact of technology also in most questions of international relations and in many domestic problems such as the energy problem and the urban crisis. So, in a sense, it is fair to say that nearly all governmental activity today is a response to technology and its impact on society.

This country came out of World War II having discovered that organized scientific efforts could have a tremendous impact on society. The radars of the Radiation Laboratory and the atomic bombs of the Los Alamos Laboratory were two prize examples of what science could accomplish. Of course, some of the industrial enterprises—like the Bell Telephone System and the General Electric Company—had discovered the power of organized research long before World War II, but there was not the general appreciation of the power of applied research that existed after the war. As the war ended, an effort was undertaken, first by interested persons in the Defense Department, later in other branches of the government, to provide support for research on the general assumption that good basic research would be good for the country, and particularly good for the national defense effort. The Office of Naval Research was created to sponsor such work, to be followed by the establishment of a whole series of other governmental institutions for supporting research (primarily through the Defense Department and the Atomic Energy Commission). As the cold war became tense, there was little need for justification of the individual undertakings. At that time, the Defense Department was able to request support for research and development and get almost anything it wanted with very little need to justify its expenditures. It is a surprising thing that, given such permissiveness, so much of the work turned out to be very good. Of course, by today's standards the budgets were quite small.

If you put aside the moral question of association with the Defense Department, which has been the object of so much campus concern in recent years, then, from the point of view of a university administrator, the Defense Department was an almost ideal agency to deal with, as it left program direction and program choices entirely up to the university.

In contrast with that is the fact that, if you want to make a modest change in the direction of a project sponsored by a civilian agency (for example, the National Institutes of Health), you would have to write to Washington for permission, and if you want to spend more than a limited amount of money on a piece of equipment, you likewise have to ask for permission. So, purely from the point of view of intellectual freedom and also freedom from red tape, the Defense Department has been an extremely good sponsor for scientists doing basic research. The Atomic Energy Commission was similarly skillful in its supervision of its external research activities.

Unfortunately, benign support of basic research was not the primary mission of the Department of Defense. Its primary technical mission was to develop a great technological capability to counter perceived Soviet threats. To counter Soviet bombers, we developed an air defense system, and then the Russians developed ballistic missiles. Then we had to develop both missiles and antimissile systems, and the Soviets responded to these with their own new programs. The result was that we had, speeding along in parallel on both sides, a growing and accelerating nightmare of interactions between the Soviet Union and the United States. This process—an endless arms race, going faster and faster, growing larger and larger, and becoming costlier and costlier—in the end generated some major problems for this country and for the world that we have not been able to deal with.

During the early part of this period (say, from 1946 to about 1952), there was little recognition among White House staff of what was happening, and particularly of the interactive nature of the problem. Most of the decision making was in the Defense Department, which was not much different from a typical university department in that it asked for support for everything that its members conceived of. The difference was that a university department received support for a number of years. This process was tolerated until expenditures reached the point where they undermined President Eisenhower's ability to balance the budget. More or less at the same time, President Eisenhower and some of his aides began to realize that the more money they spent on defense, the more dangerous the world seemed to become. For a while, this was thought to be just a consequence of incompetence in the Pentagon. So, beginning in 1954, there was developed a series of studies associated with the White House (in which I took part) to find out how better to manage Pentagon technical programs.

Unfortunately, enough incompetence was found to disguise the real problem. We found that there was a lack of hard technical assessment on which to base judgments about weapon systems, and we developed a conviction that the Defense Department was scattering its efforts much too widely. We concluded, at that time, that good management might in fact make it possible to achieve a substantial degree of security based on real military superiority.

We failed to catch on then to the fact that, at least in part, we were running an arms race with ourselves. The United States is a country in which we publish everything almost as fast as we do it. It is a necessary part of our system. (In fact, in the military field we usually publish our intention before the fact in order to get money from the Congress.) We were, therefore, actually giving the Soviet Union an enormous amount of technical guidance. This is not generally recognized, but I think it was a very important fact in the period I am discussing.

This no doubt still is the case: the Soviet Union now is working hard to reproduce our Multiple Independently Targeted Re-entry Vehicle (MIRV), and we are moving into high-accuracy counterforce weapons that no doubt they also will want—at least they will after Pentagon officials have touted such weapons for a few more years. At any rate, after two or three years of trying to apply the cure of better technical management, which we thought would improve the Defense Department programs, the situation seemed to get only worse.

During this period, however, President Eisenhower began to recognize that there was value in independent scientific advice. To provide him with such advice, a committee was set up under the director of the Office of Defense Mobilization. This committee was the predecessor to the president's Science Advisory Committee. (It is clear that science here meant mostly defense technology.) In 1957, the president asked this group to take an in-depth look at some of the major defense problems troubling him, particularly the problems of civil defense and active defense for the country. I became deeply involved in this effort. In the course of these studies many of us came to recognize what was articulated to us by the president himself, when we talked to him at the end of our year-long study, as the futility of the arms race. "This is all kind of foolish," said the president. "You can't have that war. You can't make a strong enough defense to protect the people, and there won't be enough bull-dozers to scrape the bodies off the streets. You have to see whether you can't find a way to stop the arms race. You fellows are working on the wrong problems."

We reminded him that we were working for him and that his question to us had been quite explicitly, "Can you build a defense system for the country that would protect us in the event of a nuclear war?" Our reply was, "We don't think so, at least not all of the people." By spending a lot of money you could protect some of the people, but, if you were unwilling to accept 20 or 30 or maybe even 70 million casualties after you had spent an enormous sum like $100 billion for defense, then there could be no defense.

"Why don't you work on the problem of disarmament? Nobody in the government wants to help me with disarmament," the president asked, in a poignant plea. "The AEC has their thing, and the Defense Department has their thing, why don't you fellows worry about this problem?" We said we would.

All this took place in August 1957, just before the first flight of Sputnik. While we were still reeling from having spent a year "working on the wrong problem," the Russians launched their satellite. Once again, the president turned first to the agencies that had the responsibility for the problem, to the National Science Foundation and to the navy, which together were re-sponsible for something called Vanguard. He asked them to ex-plain what had happened and what was its significance. But he soon recognized that he was not getting explanations, just defenses. At that point he remembered there was a group called the president's Science Advisory Committee. I do not think it had met with him during the previous two years, except to dis-cuss the defense studies I mentioned, but he called the group in and asked us whether we could explain Sputnik and its signifi-cance.

His experiences, as I stated above, led President Eisenhower to realize that he was a captive of the operating agencies, and that he needed a continuing independent source of information about science, its impact on the government, and what his choices were if he were to have any hope of controlling the government.

In November 1957, he asked James R. Killian, president of M.I.T., to be the full-time special assistant for science and technology as a means of dealing with this problem. At the same time, the Science Advisory Committee was reconstituted and made directly responsive to the president. As the new entity operated and gained experience, it became a self-starting operation in the sense that it no longer waited for presidential directives (although it was responsive to them), but looked around for problems and then suggested to the president areas of study and investigation.

This new activity represented a true watershed in the relationship between scientists and the political process, particularly at the presidential level, for it brought a continuing scientific voice and concern into the highest level of the government. In contrast, I recall having an occasion to see Oliver Buckley, one-time president of the Bell Telephone Laboratories, who was a science adviser in the Truman administration. Buckley had an office in a corner room in the Executive Office Building (an office that later was mine for a while), which surveyed the big White House lawn. "Oliver," I asked him, "what do you do here?"

"I see the president every day," he replied.

"You do?" I responded, somewhat surprised.

"Yes," he said, pointing to the lawn. "Mr. Truman takes a walk out there."

He went on to explain that, in fact, he did not do very much. "If you're an adviser," he declared, "you don't give advice unless you're asked."

This attitude changed under President Eisenhower. Dr. Killian and the Science Advisory Committee became an active force, seeking out problems, trying to identify in advance areas where something that was being done or not being done, inside the government, or was emerging in science or technology, would pose a serious policy question for the government.

The two major areas, at the start, obviously were space (which had been the cause of all the embarrassment to the country) and defense. Sputnik represented a double-edged threat. The public still may not appreciate the full extent of the shock Sputnik created in inner circles. It was an obvious political embarrassment, which made most uninformed people (including a very large segment of our own population) think that the Russians suddenly had become much stronger technologically and militarily than the United States and that we faced an immediate threat. It also upset the predictions that informed people had made concerning the time when the Soviets were likely to possess ballistic missiles, because it was obvious that they could not have launched Sputnik without a truly powerful rocket.

The reaction was, therefore, a double one. First, how to get a more effective space program; second, how to close the so-called missile gap. On the basis of the best intelligence estimates we had at that time and the schedules of our own rocket programs, it was believed by almost everyone that by 1959 or thereabouts the Soviet Union would have a large ballistic missile force, whereas we would have none. Hence, there would be a missile gap. This would have made the U.S. strategic air force and air defense systems extremely vulnerable. Consequently, we put a very high priority on trying to accelerate our missile and space programs. The Science Advisory Committee worked hard on those programs for several years, to the neglect of the problem that the president had asked us to work on—the disarmament issue.

On the subject of disarmament, the Science Advisory Committee was able to deal with only two major issues during this period. In the spring of 1958, we began to work on the technical facts concerning a nuclear test ban, and shortly thereafter, following some correspondence between President Eisenhower and Chairman Khrushchev, we were asked to consider the question of what might be done to reduce the dangers of surprise attack. In the process of examining these two issues, we discovered that the federal government, with the exception of the State Department, was monolithically opposed, just as the president had said, to all disarmament efforts. Officials always posed the problem in terms of the threat to national survival; by coincidence it also tended to be a threat to the bureaucratic health of the agencies involved. So the Science Advisory Committee was forced to develop its own competence (in terms of consultants and staff experts) in the disarmament field, and, for a number of years (roughly, 1958 through 1961), it was *the* expert technical and policy group advising the president on disarmament matters. During this period it had by all odds the most comprehensive understanding of disarmament problems that existed within the government. The committee was involved in every discussion of whether the United States could afford to indulge in test-ban treaties, weapons limitations, inspections, and the like.

Through these experiences, those of us who were involved began to recognize that something was deeply wrong with the organization of the federal government and some of its agencies, such as the Defense Department. Why, for example, should one have to deal in the White House, as we were forced to do, with the basic technical questions that determined whether the United States should build a nuclear-powered aircraft? On most defense and nuclear issues the president could not count on getting a sensible policy position out of any part of the government other than the White House staff, that is, the Bureau of the Budget or the Science Advisory Committee. To correct this, a new technical office called the Office of the Director of Defense Research and Engineering was created in the Defense Department, and, until it became swamped by the Vietnam War, the D.D.R.& E. succeeded in doing much of the analysis of military-technical problems that previously had been done by the White House staff.

The establishment of the D.D.R.& E. within the Pentagon created a responsible group of policy makers who could rise above the old interservice rivalry problems. Under the old system, we always could predict exactly what the three services were going to say in any given situation; for example, the air force on nuclear-powered submarines. The air force would say exactly what you would expect it to say, given its commitment to maximizing air force programs. The two services that said you should not do something were more right than wrong. But because the system consistently worked that way, there was not much useful information for the president in any Joint Chiefs' recommendation. The navy always was for nuclear-powered submarines; the air force always was for nuclear-powered aircraft; the army always was for portable nuclear power plants that could run in the Arctic. There always would be a two-to-one vote against any of these, or almost any other, proposals. We did not realize how favorable a situation this was. It gave the secretary of defense and the president a great amount of latitude to make their own decisions. After Secretary McNamara succeeded in reorganizing the Pentagon, the three members of the Joint Chiefs realized that unless they voted together they would not get anything. Suddenly there were three-to-nothing votes in favor of everything! This did not convey much information, either, and it was much tougher to deal with.

Up to this point, I have concentrated on military matters because they presented the overriding issues for the president during the period when I was involved. But other agencies presented similar problems. For example, the water quality program of the Department of Health, Education, and Welfare required a considerable White House effort during my term as special assistant.

The role of the Science Advisory Committee thus evolved into a kind of counterbalance to other government agencies. President Kennedy once suggested to a newspaperman that although the Science Advisory Committee seemed to be an anomaly, in that it cut across many agencies, its value was that it kept the government from going all one way. It was the only body that had this effect. It played this role in a great variety of fields besides defense and space; it did so particularly in education, and, after Sputnik, especially in scientific and technical education.

At any rate, this system worked well as long as three conditions existed: (1) we knew—or thought we did—that our task was to work primarily with national security problems; (2) the cost of research was tolerable, so that those who were involved did not worry too much about costs; and (3) the arrangement had the confidence of the president. These conditions changed with time, however. First, as the Soviet Union began to open up a little bit, and we began to explore many of the issues that separated us, we began to be less fearful of the threat the Soviets posed. Many of us became convinced that the USSR was not singlemindedly devoting all its efforts to preparing for an attack on the United States so that it could dominate the world. Second, it became clear that, even if Russia decided to attempt such an attack, it did not have the capability to succeed; and it appeared that Russia would not be able to acquire such a capability, no matter how hard it tried.

Thus, the Science Advisory Committee's concern with defense problems became less acute, and it was able to spend more and more time trying to find alternative forms of ensuring our national security. This involved a closer examination of what the Pentagon was doing and how its large sums of money were being used. A number of other national problems began to be recognized, as the almost paranoid preoccupation with national security waned. In retrospect, we see that it had caused our leaders to overlook a number of growing social problems for so long that they had become almost unmanageable. Among these problems were the deterioration of the cities; the problems of our minorities; failures in the educational system; and environmental problems.

Unfortunately, we did not know how to respond to these problems, for we had not been working on them; we had not done the experimentation necessary to be prepared to tackle them. Also, many people in the Congress had come to regard research and development (R&D) funds—spent in some areas of the country, particularly the east and west coasts—as sure sources of economic input. A serious pork barrel problem developed. The Pentagon and other agencies had been free to spend the money where and in any way they pleased, because of the national security aspect of their work. When that consideration did not exist, members of the Congress began to insist upon wider geographic distribution of R&D money more than, or at least as much as, upon the achievement of technical goals. Given the power balances that regulate our federal government, it was possible for interested persons in Congress to push through a number of programs designed to achieve a more uniform distribution of R&D activities around the country.

One of these programs was designed to create "centers of excellence" in parts of the country where none existed. The concept was a workable one as long as the nation was committed to a budget for R&D that was able to grow at a rate of 10 to 15 percent per year. With such growth, as new institutions developed there were adequate funds to support them. But, just as this new program was indeed getting under way, the costs of the

Vietnam War and the financial demands of urban and other domestic needs began to rise steeply. At the same time, campus protest against the Vietnam War and against defense research in the universities appeared and congressional enthusiasm for support of university research began to decline. Thus, the growth pattern that had existed up to this point changed. At the same time there developed both a levelling off in support for existing programs and a need for more support for a whole series of new institutions that had just been created. This development exacerbated what in any case would have been a serious financial problem, so that today many research projects are badly underfunded.

Many of the present difficulties in science-government relationships exist because up to this point, we did not adequately think through science management mechanisms. During Killian's, Kistiakowsky's, and my own regimes as science adviser, we thought about the question of how to establish priorities, if they should be needed, among scientific activities. But we all resisted setting priorities, except implicitly. I took the position that I could not do so because I did not know how. For example, I felt I was unable to judge the priorities between molecular biology and high-energy physics, at least in any dollar terms. I was unwilling to do this, although we did try to understand how one would if it became necessary.

The country probably is now at the stage where it is necessary to establish at least some priorities. We are going to be forced to face up to priorities between some programs and some institutions. In one sense, we have already done so, although not very effectively, by budget restraints, and this is one of the reasons we are in trouble. Fortunately, despite all of the rhetoric to the contrary, there does remain in this country a belief that knowledge based upon education and research is essential to the solution of most of our major problems. There is an intuitive belief, a feeling that perhaps research similar to that which helped so much in the defense area will help with our serious social problems. But in fact we do not know how to go about relating the research to the problems. In the health field, for example, for quite a long time we have funded a vast amount of basic research in biology and medicine. Yet now there is a general feeling in the Congress and in the top levels of the administration (among the people who are being asked to continue this support) that the investment has not paid off. Here is, I think, one of our communication failures, for the people who are beginning to doubt the wisdom of large-scale fundamental research in the life sciences do not understand how basic knowledge is put to work. Frequently it must first permeate the information base of scientific workers, and only then does it contribute to the solution of specific problems. Government officials tend to expect a payoff on a short time scale, and though this sometimes occurs, it is the exception not the rule. The payoff more often comes from the painstakingly built broad base of understanding. Beyond this—and I think that it is the key problem—these officials do not adequately understand the interrelationship between basic research, that is, the creation of new knowledge, and its utilization. In most of the social areas the link between new knowledge and its employment is inadequate and the processes by which the government tries to stimulate it do not seem to work. In fact, I am convinced that we do not know how to put new knowledge to work except through the medium of the industrial firm. That is why our efforts otherwise to stimulate civilian technology have been so unsatisfactory.

The public, as well as most of our political decision makers, seems to believe that if you discover something, it will automatically be put to work. Now, this is not true even in those fields where it is easy for private enterprise to pick up a new idea and exploit it, for the time constants for the exploitation of a new idea are long and the costs of industrial development and marketing are great. In fields where there is no process through which ideas are picked up and rushed through the development and production stages, and then put to work, the situation is much more unsatisfactory, chaotic, and haphazard. In particular, in the health field, whether a scientific discovery becomes used often depends on the chance that some individual will be greatly interested in a problem to which the discovery is relevant. Until very recently, for example, a serious imbalance existed between the amount of fundamental biological research being done and the work under way to try to apply that knowledge to the prevention or cure of cancer. One can say the same thing about a number of other diseases. The response should be not to stop the basic research, which was the Nixon administration's response, but rather to try to do something about the important transitional step that is missing. Although there is some effort along this line, I think it is far from adequate.

The same is true in the field of education as well as in urban affairs, housing, and most of the other social problem areas. Researchers are just beginning to recognize that in these fields the practical tasks are far more complex than the problems involved in designing and building a radar or a computer. These tasks involve interactions between people; they also involve a kind of moving target. If an engineer working on a radar gets to a certain point and decides to go home that night, when he comes back the next morning the problem is just where he left it. With any complicated social problem, one is racing against a continuously changing set of relationships in an infinitely complex world. One can never be sure that any data collected, any experiment made at one place at one time, has any relevance to the next set of problems, or possibly even to the same problem at a later time.

Thus, while theories are desirable, much more common sense, that is, educated intuitional common sense, is desperately needed here. To some degree this applies in all those fields that we want to work in now: how to understand the impact of science and technology on society; how to make the world a more decent place; how to ensure that we are not going to suffocate from the air we breathe or die from the water we drink, or that we won't be blown up by the huge stockpiles of plutonium that the nuclear energy program will create.

We also face the problem of scale. I can think of no major social problem which a civilian agency has tackled with resources or a time perspective that matched the scale of the problem in the same way that the Pentagon tends to match the resources to the task at hand. Despite all the concern about the cities, no one has faced such basic questions as: What will it actually take to meet our urban needs? What kinds of research teams? How long will it take? How much money? Rather, research has been undertaken in response to individual, and usually small, research proposals from investigators in many separate institutes and universities. This approach does generate knowledge, but it is not a program and it may never meet the need!

The same is true of our R&D efforts in most other domestic areas. Programs are the aggregate of many individual studies directed and integrated by a program officer in Washington who cannot bring about a truly interactive, creative relationship between the individual investigators. These officials fail to recognize that the informational short circuit they create eliminates the possibility of interaction among the working scientists; the result is that true programs fail to develop. As applied programs in the areas of the environment, energy, medical care, productivity, materials, transportation, and the urban setting generally become more urgent, it will be recognized that the grant system of supporting individual investigators, so ideal for supporting basic research, is totally inadequate for solving major problems.

These problems are built into the way we now run our civilian research programs and explain, at least in part, why we are not now able to mount effective programs. We will not be able to do so until the agencies are prepared to support a few major centers to bring together the many aspects of a problem.

The Congress presents yet another problem with regard to coordinated technical programs: its structure makes coordination difficult. The Congress operates through committees, usually one for each department of the executive branch (Defense; Health, Education, and Welfare; Interior; and so on) plus some general committees such as the Ways and Means Committee and the Appropriations Committee. These committees decide what they are willing to support within the agencies for which they are responsible. So, whenever a broad problem arises that spans several departments, it is more or less impossible to create a unified program in the executive branch and then to get support for it in the Congress. This is another of the difficulties in most of the domestic fields where several agencies are involved; it has been impossible to create a coherent set of programs to deal with them. There is another problem from the point of view of the welfare of science: some of the most important agencies are the responsibility of committees that are relatively uninterested in research. Congressional committees not surprisingly span a spectrum of competences and motivations; at one extreme are those who are quite perfunctory in their behavior. If they have any motivating principles, these stem pri-

marily from budgetary considerations, that is, how to save
money. At the other extreme there is the Joint Committee on
Atomic Energy, which regards itself as the sponsor and
protector-advocate of governmental atomic energy programs for
both military and peaceful uses. In the Joint Committee on
Atomic Energy, which I believe is the only joint committee that
has responsibility for an agency of the government, the House
and Senate team up to sponsor programs, so the committee itself becomes an extremely powerful lobby. In fact, on occasion
it has essentially run the Atomic Energy Commission.

In contrast, in a sense, the National Science Foundation
reports to a group called the Independent Offices Committee.
This is more or less a housekeeping agency for all the independent offices. It is hard to be the advocate for a widely diverse
group of activities, so all the committee shows any enthusiasm
for is saving money. Year after year, the president requests, for
the National Science Foundation, more money than the Congress grants, because NSF has no strong congressional constituency.

In more general terms, one could go so far as to say there is no
broad constituency in the Congress for general technological
programs, for health research, or for educational research. In
any event, the Congress is not properly organized to deal with
these problems and, despite all the efforts that have been made
in recent years to set up oversight committees that could interre-
late programs, little progress has been made in this regard.
When space was "*the* thing," a new committee, called the
Science and Astronautics Committee, was created in the House.
Science was put in as something of an afterthought, but, as
space became less exciting to the country and the Congress, the
committee began to take the science half of its charter more
seriously. In particular, Representative Emilio Z. Daddario (formerly Democratic representative from Connecticut) thought
that he could use the committee as an integrating and correlat-
ing device for science programs. When no one else cared, he got
permission to form a subcommittee (called Science, Research,
and Development) on science policy, enlisted some of his more
receptive colleagues, commissioned several reports, quietly ran
through a series of hearings, and built up an understanding of
what was wrong with the way in which the Congress deals

with science problems. Under Daddario, that subcommittee assumed leadership in dealing with the problems of research and development. Daddario gave up his seat to run (unsuccessfully) for governor of Connecticut in 1970, but until then, the subcommittee had hoped to evolve into something of an R&D authorization committee, like the committees for specific programs such as defense. Although that is not likely to occur, the subcommittee has been allowed to do much general good for science.

There is an analogous situation in the Senate, which has no authorization committee for R&D. There, the staff of the Labor and Welfare Committee, to which the National Science Foundation reports, has persuaded Senator Edward Kennedy to try to create an authorization committee for NSF. This effort has been reasonably successful. Nonetheless, in neither house of Congress is there yet a mechanism for integrating science affairs. At the moment, the situation is unpredictable; it depends on the whims of individuals and on the relationships of people in the agencies with the committees. (This material was prepared before the new Office of Technological Assessment was created by the Congress. This new office may, to some extent, be able to help the Congress coordinate science and technology programs, though that is not its purpose.)

My final point concerns the problem of relating research to practical problems, whatever the field: health, defense, urban affairs, or any other. There is, at the moment, no single place in the government, except the White House, where the programs can be brought together, and they are not in fact brought together effectively there.

White House coordination occurs in the annual budget decision process, in the year-round activities of the Office of Management and Budget, and, for technical matters, through the efforts of the Office of Science and Technology. For a long time, the Office of Management and Budget (called the Bureau of the Budget until 1970) was the one place in Washington where people worried about interactions and interrelationships of programs. Only in the budget process are serious efforts made to bring things together. Unfortunately, that process is so rapid and conducted under so much pressure that it is impossible to be thoughtful or careful about the results: even if you do not have the necessary facts, you have to make decisions. When I was working in the White House, the budget had a firm deadline of 20 December at which time it went to the printer. In preparation, the budget went through a number of cycles. The agencies would begin working on the budget fourteen months earlier. The process would start in the Bureau of the Budget, whose director would provide the president with an estimate of revenues and foreseeable expenditures (most of the federal budget is controllable and predictable) and with suggestions regarding the adjustable requests from the agencies.

Together the bureau and the agencies would make tentative assignments, including funds for whatever new programs the president wanted. They would try to hold the existing agencies to their previous year's budgets, plus inflation, and try to put into new programs whatever increases in revenues were anticipated. I never realized until I worked in the White House how little free maneuverable money the president actually has at his disposal. At that time, the national budget was about $100 billion. (Today it is more than double that sum.) When one added up all the fixed costs—such as for agricultural support programs, veterans' benefits and interest payments, and manpower—the total came to more than $60 billion. The programs that the president had some possibility of influencing—though obviously he could not greatly influence them—totaled about $40 billion. The research and development budget that I was concerned with accounted for approximately $16 billion of that. Although $16 billion does not seem very large as compared with the total of $100 billion, it was a large portion of the $40 billion that could be maneuvered. This explains, of course, why even small items in the budget receive so much scrutiny.

In any event, the guidelines would go out in October, and in March the White House would expect to receive the proposed budgets from the agencies. Most agencies would send back a requirements budget about 40 percent higher than the president's guidelines. The Bureau of the Budget and my office then would go to work on each budget, to understand the pieces of it; and, in the process, we would negotiate away some of the 40 percent over guidelines. This process took most of the spring and summer. In the end the two groups, the Bureau of the Budget and the Office of Science and Technology together, worked on the technical programs of particularly recalcitrant agencies such as the Defense Department. We did this by a series of discussions with the agency heads and their senior officers regarding specific budget proposals, in an effort to get them to cut back their requests to the proposed levels. Up to a point, it was just a matter of how extravagantly the agency wanted to live, but frequently, the difficult problems turned out to be ones that required resolution of basic policy. Thus, finally, there would emerge some unresolvable issues that were taken to the president for decisions. For example, the cancellation of the Skybolt missile required major changes in the U.S. policy with regard to supplying the United Kingdom and France with assistance in the construction of Polaris-armed submarines and missiles.

Another example, and perhaps the most difficult issue I faced during my term as special assistant, related to the fallout shelter program. In 1962, the Pentagon was strongly in favor of a large-scale shelter program, whereas my office and the Bureau of the Budget were equally committed against one. This program involved a number of serious policy questions, including large expenditures, the need to convince the public of an immediate danger that was not apparent, and housing policy. We argued about the shelter question for many months. Finally, in the fall, as the budget was being finished, we went to Cape Cod for several days and spent the entire time, morning till night, going through the budget issues one at a time with the president until he understood each one and made a decision. After a day of discussing the massive shelter program, President Kennedy decided against it.

Because these issues were brought up in the context of the budget, however, many important questions were never asked, much less answered. These questions, relating to the context in which the things fit, frequently were more important than the budget question. Several health programs, for example, which were started because they were felt to be desirable, were handled as budget problems. Nobody ever asked whether there were enough doctors or hospitals to meet the commitments that were being made, because no one had studied the questions adequately enough to know that the question mattered. This whole area of predicting or forecasting the consequences of new programs, particularly those involving new technology, has not been dealt with adequately in the past, and the government still is not prepared to deal with such issues properly. There is now an effort in Congress, initiated by Representative Daddario, to establish a technological forecasting capability for the Congress.

The Technological Assessment Act of 1972 (P.L. 92–484) established an Office of Technological Assessment (OTA) for the Congress as an aid in identification and consideration of existing and probable impacts of technological applications, and to develop other coordinate information to assist the Congress. To carry out the assigned functions of OTA, the legislation specified eight specific activities:

1. Identify existing or probable impacts of technology or technological programs;

2. Where possible, ascertain cause-and-effect relationships;

3. Identify alternative technological methods of implementing specific programs;

4. Identify alternative programs for achieving requisite goals;

5. Make estimates and comparisons of the impacts of alternative programs;

6. Present findings of completed analyses to the appropriate legislative authorities;

7. Identify areas where additional research or data collection is required to provide adequate support for the assessments and estimates described above;

8. Undertake such additional associated activities as the appropriate authorities specified . . . may direct.

The OTA consists of a Congressional Board; a director, a deputy director, and other employees; and a Citizens' Advisory Council. The board consists of six senators and six representatives and the director as a nonvoting member. The Advisory Council consists of ten private citizens and, in addition, the director of the Congressional Research Service of the Library of Congress and the comptroller general of the United States. The office began to function in the spring of 1974 when Congress provided funds for its operation. Congressman Daddario, having previously retired from the House, was named director and Senator Edward Kennedy became chairman of the board. The OTA staff has undertaken a number of studies requested by the

Congress and is hard at work on efforts to define the scope and limits of its assignment as well as to develop adequate processes and methodology for its operation.

During the initial period of OTA's existence it has been swamped by requests for studies ranging over the full spectrum of congressional activities, many of them much broader than technological assessments and some involving technology only in the most tangential sense. On the other hand, some requests are for purely technical studies not involving assessment of the application of a development. For example, the OTA's first study, now completed, was on the bioequivalence of certain types of drugs. The report that resulted discussed in great detail the many scientific questions involved but did not examine the deeper issues that grow out of the study: that is, could the government, in its payment for drugs, insist on the least costly product that qualified chemically and, if so, what would be the consequences to the drug industry? Such questions, which must be faced, are perhaps best resolved in the context of a congressional hearing rather than by means of a study. The OTA study provided the technical foundation for a sound congressional airing of the question. Perhaps this will always be OTA's most important function.

When I was special assistant to the president for science and technology, I tried to present the president with the broadest range of possibilities to maximize his freedom of choice. Doing so sometimes meant opening up options that the departments involved preferred to rule out. This was a continuation of the mode of operation that developed under President Eisenhower's leadership and was particularly important in the national security area, as I indicated above.

The Congress has always been a leader in such domestic areas as health and welfare, where information was available. But it has been extremely hesitant to challenge or lead in highly technical fields such as defense or arms control, where its members felt they were inadequately informed. Perhaps as the competence of OTA increases, Congress will develop truly independent leadership in those important areas as well.

I hope that the OTA will persuade organizations like the National Academy of Sciences and the National Academy of Engineering as well as university groups to study specific problems for the OTA (for example, the supersonic transport). As yet, we do not have the ability to make good forecasts or even to bring up all the various questions that ought to be reviewed. The development of capability for technology assessment is one of the most important steps we can take for the better management of our society.

As defense technology comes to be regarded as less overriding and civilian technology is given higher priority, we see that the government is increasingly unable to cope with the urgent problems. With the demise of the special assistant for science and technology and of the president's Science Advisory Committee, the president has little or no help in recognizing or understanding the problems in which science and/or technology play a key role. So, these problems are neglected or at best are handled in a piecemeal fashion. The limping energy research and the diffuse health care system are but two examples of such matters. It is hoped that with the coming of a new president and administration this serious gap can be eliminated. The House Science and Astronautics Committee is preparing legislation that would establish a new presidential-level science organization. If passed by the Congress and accepted by the president, this would create the opportunity for dealing with society's complex technological problems.

Even with a presidential-level mechanism, many of our problems will be difficult to manage, for they are complex and involve technical, social, and political issues that have no simple answers. The answers depend, in fact, on our social goals and objectives, which are hardly simple or ever defined. Nonetheless, we have little choice; our future welfare depends upon the aggressive development of appropriate technologies in a wide range of fields, many of them dependent upon wise leadership and support from the society at large.

3

RISING EXPECTATIONS: FRUSTRATIONS

Joseph J. Spengler

> As he is happiest whom very little contents, so the great and ambitious are most miserable—their happiness demands a vast accumulation of blessings.
>
> La Rochefoucald

> At the rate of progress since 1800, every American who lived in the year 2000 would know how to control unlimited power.
>
> Henry Adams

> 2,000 Dollar Monthly Retirement Is Eyed
> *Durham Morning Herald,* 25 June 1972

> The higher the human intellect rises in the discovery . . . of aims, the more obvious it becomes that the final aim is beyond its reach.
>
> Tolstoy, *War and Peace*

This chapter deals with the interrelations of rising expectations in the realm of human affairs and frustrations associated with unsatisfied or disappointed demand flowing out of these expectations. Although confidence in the realization of expectations may be conditioned by the state of the physical world environing an individual, this confidence is necessarily less strong than that attached to the belief that so-called physical laws will rule in the future as in the past. The first three of the following sections are devoted to the analytical framework employed, and later sections to past, present, and prospective circumstances affecting expectations, the degree of their realization, and possible sources of frustration. It will become apparent that the subject of this chapter is of quite modern vintage in that it could command little attention so long as men assumed, much as did Plato, that each generation would live amid conditions essentially the same as those governing the lives of their fathers.[1]

Two quotations, one from T. R. Malthus's *Essay on Population,* formulated nearly 175 years ago, and the other from a recent study, reflect the issue here under analysis and the changes in its character. Wrote Malthus, by no means an optimist:

> This habit of expecting too much, and the irritation occasioned by disappointment continually give a wrong direction to their efforts in favour of liberty and constantly tend to defeat the accomplishment of those gradual reforms in government and that slow melioration of the condition of the lower classes of society which are really attainable.[2]

Malthus's notion of expectations was congruent with reality,[3] departure from which gives rise to dilemmas. An example is described by Aaron Wildavsky. He has in view a dilemma facing today's so-called elites, sprung largely from classes emerging since Malthus wrote, and now, as Hofstadter suggests, reflecting disappointment at the political legacy of the past:

> Dissemination of the idea that man has to be creative at a time when so many have been exposed to higher education gives rise to expectations that cannot be met. New creations can only become the property of the few; if all are "original," none are. There is an immense contradiction between the pressures on the educated to find new forms of expression, and the common perception of originality as something rare and unusual. The result is widespread anger at a system that denies special status to its system of aspiring elites.[4]

The treatment of expectations, together with reactions to them, may be organized in terms of the paradigm underlying the work of which this chapter is a small part: (1) The economic expectations under consideration have their origin in the examples of others, in environmental situations, in individual experience, and in a variety of visual, auditory, and tactile stimuli that denote, connote, or suggest objects of desire; they are reinforced by opinion makers and propagators, today more than in the past when means of communication were inferior, information was less, affected populations were much smaller, and societies probably were less "other-directed."[5] (2) The content of relevant information flowing from the points of origin to the subjects destined to be influenced ranges from the very general to the quite specific, from what is designed to influence individuals to that which, however influential, is an unintended by-product of other activities. (3) Those exposed to the information and stimuli consist of individuals and categories of individuals, only some of whom are deliberately selected to receive information and stimuli individually or en masse. Most of the information and stimuli are incident, much as is rain, on anonymous "addressees." (4) Only "information" originating with advertisers and others engaged in "selling" may be described as policy-oriented. (5) Changes in expectations are influenced (pace McLuhan) in only a minor degree by techniques designed for this purpose; the changes flow rather from the general socioeconomic environment to which consumers are exposed. (6) Expectations generate feedbacks; while these may reinforce the trend in expectations, they can end in frustrations not easily resolved, with the result that the generation of expectations must be brought into equilibrium with realities.

Rising expectations, it will be shown, constitute an essentially modern phenomenon, one destined, however, to persist for several decades. Throughout most of man's history, expectations were in equilibrium with realities, held there in part by a widespread opinion, articulated in proverb, verse, and philosophical dictum to the effect that for most men this-worldly prospects were slim. Moreover, most individuals in comparison with today's Americans resembled pre–Green Revolution grain as compared with today's; insensibility to stimuli was high, serving to cushion the impact of recurring adversity even as does today's "culture of poverty" and (as William James observed) as did yesterday's poverty.

It is not clear what determinants of rising expectations were most significant, at least initially. Our information is limited and, as Barbara Tuchman remarked in another connection, a great change sometimes is less noticeable to the eyewitness than to history. Three determinants seem, however, to have played a major role in shaping the course of expectations; namely, improvement in channels and means of communication, increase in social and geographical mobility, and the direction and rate of invention and innovation (especially since "invention of the method of invention" in the nineteenth century).[6] In the present century, World Wars I and II and their corollaries have contributed greatly by destroying power- and class-structures the world over and thereby undermining constraints upon the forces of the twentieth century. Impending on the horizon is mind-management through widespread directed use of drugs as well as through control of mass media.[7]

DEMAND; FRUSTRATION

We use here concepts defined with sufficient rigor to facilitate discourse, but not with so great specificity that much of what is of concern is excluded by definition. After all, insofar as man's affairs and responses are fuzzy, somewhat fuzzy terminology may be indicated.[8]

We conceive of economic demand in a somewhat different sense from that signified by an individual or a group (à la Marshall) function, or from that represented by a macroeconomic demand function. Frustration is conceived of as an individual manifestation; it can, however, assume a quasi-group or mob form when many individuals, who, qua individuals, are subject to frustration, become aware that other individuals are experiencing similar feelings. Then each individual's attitudes tend to be reinforced as he becomes aware that others share his attitude. Accordingly, aggregate frustration will tend to exceed that associated with a group of individuals, each of whom remains unaware of his neighbor's feelings.[9] Bandwagon-like shifts in public attitude may be associated with a general becoming aware by many an individual of his neighbor's attitude.

Of special concern here is the tendency for the frustration that an individual may associate with unsatisfied economic demand to exceed in amount or intensity that which is strictly related to his *economic* demand functions. An individual is a member of a number of subsystems, as Parsons, Pareto, and others have pointed out.[10] He does not, nor is he likely to be able to, distinguish sharply between frustration of purely economic origin and much frustration of noneconomic origin. Wants or demands originating in any one subsystem (say, economic) spill over into other subsystems, with the result that frustration associated with unsatisfied economic demand usually is of multisystem origin and impact. It is theoretically possible, of course, to transform any one kind of demand into other kinds—not linearly and without limit, but curvilinearly and within a definite range. Indeed, every mode of conduct-determining and hence variable demand, economic or otherwise, reflects, or is in response to, some form of scarcity, that is, a state in which less is available at zero "price" than is wanted at that price. Scarcity may consist in that of goods and services or in that of power—indeed, in that of whatever men find desirable as well as divisible, transferable, and utilizable by an individual.

In view of what has been said, it is advisable, when dealing with frustration of economic demand, that demand be defined rather broadly, since those experiencing frustration are likely, though they implicitly define it broadly, to view it in economic terms. Indeed, for purposes of the present chapter, the object of demand may be viewed as reflecting an individual's welfare function, that is, as representing the collection of diverse goods, services, and satisfactions which he seeks and considers to be within reach.

In keeping with this view, most if not all social sciences, or modes of social inquiry, are derivatives of forms of scarcity, and social science in general is a derivative of the scarcity of that which men want. Each social science is concerned with the response of the individual, reacting individually or in temporary or permanent association with others, to some form of scarcity. For example, economics deals with man's response to the scarcity (that is, nonsuperabundance) of goods and services; political science, with his response to inequality in the interpersonal distribution of power; and so on. The "immediate objects of law are the creation and protection of legal rights," derivatives of scarcity, whereas the concern of jurisprudence is the means by which law subserves its purposes.[11] The current widespread interest in exchange reflects increasing recognition of the fact that concern with scarcity underlies social science and that exchange is man's principal utility-increasing and hence scarcity-reducing mechanism.[12] Not only can exchange increase utility and diminish consciousness of scarcity within one subsystem (for example, the economy); it may also, if it is extended to inter-subsystem relations, facilitate intersubsystem substitution that further augments utility and eases overall consciousness of scarcity.

EXPECTATIONS; RISING EXPECTATIONS

Here, only economically oriented expectations are under consideration, even though these are not independent of noneconomic change. Indeed, since expectations relate to options in the future and since options are conditional as well as interrelated,[13] it may be said that at any time an individual's behavior is conditioned by a somewhat unstable set of expectations, some of which are economically oriented and in a measure dependent upon particular members of this set. Accordingly, complete explicitness of denotation is difficult if not impossible to achieve.

Individual aspirations (or changes in taste), issuing as they do from a variety of sources, generate activity suited to their realization if this appears to be in reach. Welfare then is conditioned by the individual's ability to realize his aspirations[14] as well as by his environment, which governs the number, kind, interrelation, and cost of the things to which he aspires.

In what follows we are concerned with the expectations of communities of men rather than with those of the individual as such, and with the longer run rather than the immediate chain of aspiration $\rightarrow$ incentive $\rightarrow$ satisfaction (or frustration). Accordingly, we shall treat economically oriented expectations, e, as functionally related to average income, y, and to other relevant variables, V_i. For the level of income y not only reflects man's past ability to realize expectations and conditions his current ability to do so; it also gives release to what were latent or suppressed expectations. Although e relates to the future and hence is most closely associated with anticipated future values of y, we may make $e = f(y, V_i)$ on the supposition that y will be expected to continue to grow as in the recent past. We may then suppose that $e' = f(y', V_i)$, where e' and y' denote the rates of growth of e and y. We may also write $E = e'/y'$, where E denotes elasticity of expectations. Then $E \gtreqless 1$, and expectations may be defined as elastic, inelastic, or *rising* accordingly as the value of E exceeds, falls short of, or equals 1. Here the term *rising* is arbitrarily restricted to situations in which $E = 1$. Presumably, changes in V_i will account in the main for deviations in the value of E from 1.

As noted above, we shall usually treat e, e', y, y', and V_i as descriptive of the behavior of a community of individuals, each of whom is reacting to his own y, y', and V_i. Accordingly, E is likely to be affected if there is change in the variance about the average values descriptive of the community, or in the distribution either of overall income or of the impact of conditions included under V_i. E will increase also if a belief develops that in the future y' will increase, for then the current value of e' will rise more than the immediately anticipated value of y'. A change in the composition of expectations may also modify E. Thus if, as in the nineteenth century, expectations consist more largely of goods highly elastic in supply, E may rise. The converse also holds; thus when incomes rise beyond a certain level, much greater stress may be put upon wants that draw on resources very limited in supply (for example, suitably situated space) and/or give rise to diseconomies of consumption and adverse externalities.

Rising expectations in the sense of aspirations to continuing improvement, or to anticipation of it, do not constitute a novel phenomenon. Over the centuries small segments of the populations of nations have been motivated by the prospect of improved economic circumstances.[15] But rising expectations in the sense of a widely held and essentially mass outlook constitute a modern phenomenon, mainly of nineteenth-century origin and twentieth-century fruition, a concomitant of the acceleration of material change, of change sometimes at a rate that not only divides generations but also separates the late from the early periods of the life of the individual.[16]

Expectations are subjective phenomena, though largely of social origin. They are readily converted into effective demand as long as those with new perspectives derived from their social environment have disposable funds or their equivalent.[17] They were never so inelastic, therefore, as was assumed by many pre-1700 and some later writers who sought thereby to justify holding down wages. There may, of course, be a "revolution of declining expectations," as well as the now overpublicized one of "rising expectations"; such reversals attended disappointment at the (expected) failure of the "UN Development Decade."[18]

Indeed, because expectations are subjective and hence flexible, they can fairly easily be modified in the face of frustration consequent upon nonrealization of aspirations and adjusted downward in keeping with realities.

Expectations, being subjective in character, are also somewhat free of constraints imposed by such conditions as underlie "probability" defined in terms of "frequency theory." Expectation denotes a subjective attitude toward the future, especially toward particular segments of the future with which anticipated events or streams of events are associated. One may form particular opinions respecting the likelihood that some event or stream of events will emerge within a designated time interval. At issue, however, is the rational belief one may attach to the coefficient of certainty that is associated with this opinion. Such belief varies with individuals, for they differ in respect of knowledge, constitution of the mind, and so on. "What we know and what probability we can attribute to our rational beliefs is, therefore, subjective in the sense of being relative to the individual."[19] Man acts on the basis of the probable, though he may, as Adam Smith observed, overestimate what is probable, given the "natural confidence which every man has more or less, not only in his own abilities, but in his own good fortune."[20] Such seeming overestimates can at times prove self-confirming,[21] or eventuate in income and wealth differences that reflect not "acts of God" but differences in the tastes of individuals for risk;[22] they also give rise to misfortune and disappointed hopes.

Even if we define expectations in economic terms, we must allow for the dependence of economic expectations upon the past and prospective course of noneconomic as well as of economic events. For example, in Athens prior to Plato's ascendancy, there was some belief in progress, past and prospective, according to plays of Euripides and Sophocles.[23] When a society is static, encased in fixed social dimensions subject only to irregular short-run variation, earthly expectations will remain correspondingly static and unchanging, particularly if other-worldly concerns predominate as they did in Europe until (after 1300) the Renaissance weakened their hold and subsequently (after 1500) the ideal of material happiness became ascendant.[24] Illustrative of a static society in microcosm is the village, a social system of which the nineteenth-century Indian village—traditional, self-sufficing, self-perpetuating, unchanging—was a prototype.[25] Destruction of this homeostatic social organism reinforced changes in man's expectations respecting the future. The forces that undermined the village served also to destabilize other formerly static social structures. Societal metabolism, formerly conducive to social heterogeneity, now made for social homogeneity. That spirit of egalitarianism which eventually pervaded pluralistic societies and accentuated intergroup conflict did not emerge until later, however.

The impact of specific changes upon expectations is not always easy to assess, in part because they may produce several effects. Since expectations are subjective in character, they reflect not events as such but man's perceptions of events. Moreover, changes must be great enough and continuous enough to impress these qualities upon man's perceptions. As almost invariably there are in a community levels or thresholds of sensitivity, below which insensitivity rules, new stimuli must be powerful enough to transcend such thresholds if they are to reorient man's behavior and view of the future.

Illustrative of diverse effects are those associated with changes in life expectancy. On the one hand, life expectancy did not greatly depress potential productive power per capita, even though before 1800 it generally was not more than 30–35 years at birth. Since heavy mortality was concentrated among the young, adults dominated populations. Given a male life expectancy at birth of only 25.3 years, life expectancy at ages 25, 30, and 60, respectively, would approximate 27.7, 25, and 10 years; with male life expectancy at birth around 30 years, the corresponding expectancies would approximate 30, 27, and 10.8 years. Given a male life expectancy at birth of 25 years and a male stable population growing at 5 per 1,000, about 51 percent of the males would fall in the age group 20–65. This percentage would become about 52, with life expectancy at birth near 30 years. Normally, therefore, there was not a "shortage" of manpower unless parasitical use was made of it, a use fostered by modes of conducting war and government.[26]

On the other hand, low life expectancy at birth entailed omnipresence of death and perhaps of morbidity as well. For, with life expectancy at birth at 25–30 years, male deaths in a stationary population would run 40–33 per 1,000 and surround the living with two to three or more times as many deaths as that to which we today are accustomed. About half of those born would have died by the close of their tenth year, and 50–60 or less out of 100 reaching age 20 would attain age 60. This high mortality, together with considerable illness and recurring pestilence, war, and food shortage, did make for depressed states of affairs.[27] At the same time high mortality, by offsetting natality, made for a very low rate of population growth, and this in turn was favorable to continuation of a hierarchial form of society, a form unfavorable to rising expectations when population grows very little. This state of affairs was reinforced by the shortness of the time horizon animating human decisions when the probability of death, especially among the young, was high and not easily counterbalanced by institutional arrangements.

Though expectations are subjective and hence may, in individual instances, tend to become inflated, there was little basis for widespread rising expectations prior to the nineteenth century. Chiefly responsible for their absence was the failure of incomes to rise regularly and enough from year to year to make many persons sufficiently conscious of an improvement in economic conditions to infer that such improvement would continue. That not much was expected from growth is suggested by the inclination of authors of Utopias to stress redistribution rather than growth. There was little or no basis, therefore, for pre-1800 writers or individuals to assume much increase or accelerating increase in the income of individuals. It is doubtful whether, in a world generally short of public information relating to price and income behavior, the typical individual would be sensible of a 0.25–percent-per-year increase in average income in *addition* to such small increase as was associated with his acquisition of seniority and experience in his line of activity.[28] After all, an increase of 0.25 percent per unit per year increases income only slightly more than 10 percent in forty years. Even so, had such an increase persisted over the seven-hundred-year interval between A.D. 1000 and 1700, average income would have been nearly six times as high in 1700 as it was in the year 1000, when presumably average income in Western Europe was in the neighborhood of subsistence or not much above it. Yet in 1700, average income in advanced countries probably was not much more than double or treble subsistence, if that. In England and Wales, increase per decade in real output per head between 1700 and 1785 averaged out at only 2.5 percent though this rate rose to about 9 percent in the next fifteen years.[29] Had the latter rate persisted, it might have generated a state of rising if not accelerating expectations.

It is true, as a rule, that tastes, aspirations, and expectations common in the upper or middle reaches of somewhat pyramidal societies tend to influence some individuals situated in the lower reaches of such societies. It can happen, of course, that tastes flow from the lower reaches of a society, from the proletariat, to the upper reaches, sometimes with the ultimate result that the power of the latter is undermined.[30] The former movement is the more probable. It underlies what Duesenberry has called "demonstration effect." He observes that "the consumption pattern of the moment is conceived of not as part of the way of life, but only as a temporary adjustment to circumstances. We expect to take the first available chance to change." This makes it easy to increase consumption as income increases, but does not explain why, with income fixed and a balance having been reached between consumption and saving and then undergirded by habit, this "habit pattern can be broken without a change in income or prices." The stimulus that breaks the habit pattern consists in "contact with superior goods," usually repeated contact that produces invidious comparisons and a "feeling of dissatisfaction" with one's own goods.[31] This demonstration effect, together with dynamic technology and improved remuneration of labor, in turn helps to define the norms of poverty and hence its extent, norms that not only move upward but can significantly affect social policy.[32]

The explanation just put forward depends not only upon the state of the means of communication, but also upon change in the average income of at least one category of the population; for such change typically is a prelude to the acquisition of goods, the "sight" of which in turn motivates their consumption by those whose income has not risen. For the production of new types of goods usually is a concomitant of increase in income, at least in the sense of the derivation of greater utility or service than formerly out of given sets of inputs. In the absence of such increase in income, consumption patterns become stable in the several categories composing a population, and these patterns in turn form an equilibrium no longer very susceptible of modification. Under such circumstances expectations become virtually stationary. As a rule, a dynamic source of change is essential to the elevation of the level of expectations. Even then the social structure must be somewhat open, allowing a degree of upward mobility; barriers to mobility tend to stifle expectation of improvement in the population thereby affected.

Parallel to the case just described is that involving the transmission of tastes from one country to another and the generation there of demands whose satisfaction is seldom realizable. Let R designate a rich country and P a poor country. Modern means of communication serve to acquaint many people living in P with the mode of living and tastes characteristic of many inhabitants of R. The transmission of tastes in question may be reinforced by occasional experience on the part of inhabitants of P with manifestations of these tastes by inhabitants of R who are in contact with inhabitants of P who reside in P or in R. In general, however, inhabitants of P lack the means wherewith to satisfy demands originating in R and hence tend to experience dissatisfaction.

Returning to the impact of rising income upon expectations, it is to be noted that rising income may prove a necessary though not a sufficient condition for the generation of rising expectations. Recall our earlier formulations $e' = f(y', V_i)$ and $E = e'/y'$, and let y' arbitrarily designate the rate of increase in both y and average output. Suppose that the value of E begins to fall after having been in the neighborhood of 1.0; this could reflect the state of V_i or a change in V_i. Thus, a fall in E may reflect a failure in the composition of output to change as required, a failure in output to grow in variety as well as quantity; for with V_i constant, failure of composition of output to change makes the utility of output less than it otherwise would have been.

What has been said may be illustrated. Suppose that a community produces and consumes only one product, A, and that average output of this product increases until everyone's desired daily requirement is realized with two hours of work per day. Then, as no more A is wanted, average income expressed in terms of A is stationary and nonaugmentable, and so is aggregate output in the absence of population growth, though increasing output of A per man-hour does increase income in terms of A plus leisure. If, however, a new product, B, not substitutable or only partly substitutable for *A*, is introduced, the level of average satisfaction will rise even though leisure per day is reduced, through substitution of leisure time for *B*. While the economy is adapting to the introduction of *B*, average income will be rising and expectations may rise also among those who do not initially share in the availability of *B* but expect to do so. Eventually, everyone's daily requirement of *A* and *B* will be met, and the balance of the community's time will be devoted to nonwork or leisure. It is possible, therefore, in the absence of population growth and of sufficient variety in the goods and services susceptible of production, that the growth of aggregate product in terms of *A*, *B*, and so on, will come to a halt, limited by lack of demand as a result of the nonsubstitutability at the margin of leisure for product.

Continuation of rising expectations, of $E = 1$, thus may depend upon continuation of increase in the variety of output as well as upon increase in output per head, upon a sufficiency of new-product–producing rather than of labor-displacing inventions and innovations. Usually, of course, increases in variety and of output per head take place together, since innovation gives rise to each. Indeed, in the absence of invention and innovation, increase in average output could come to a halt, as then it might be possible to increase and use "capital," that is, agents complementary to labor, up to the point where no more could profitably be used jointly with labor.[33] The decision to produce or not to produce more turns also, of course, upon the demand for leisure and the economic conditions under which recreation is available.[34] We shall touch later upon leisure, time-cost, and other factors.

Innovation is the main source of new products. Schumpeter rightly observed:

> We will, throughout, act on the assumption that consumers' initiative in changing their tastes—i.e., in changing that set of our data which general theory comprises in the concepts of "utility functions" or "indifference varieties"—is negligible and that all change in consumers' tastes is incident to, and brought about by, producers' action.

He went on to argue that while some changes could be produced in tastes by leaders of fashion and by demand creators (for example, advertisers) as well as by increase in population and producers' goods, these changes would be relatively unimportant. Whence invention and innovation constituted the principal source of new products and changes in tastes.[35]

Expectations may cease to rise for reasons relating to demand as well as to supply. Should the economy assume the form of a circular flow society, or stationary state,[36] expectation would cease to rise and would become constant. Expectations may also become constant, even though the limits of production have not been reached, if the physical and time-consuming costs of consuming goods and services exhaust the capacity of individuals to augment their rate of consumption.

EXPECTATIONS AND FRUSTRATION

Frustration, as has been implied, may be generated in one of two main ways. First, it may prove impossible to satisfy growing demand for particular goods or services. Second, what was supposed to be demand may be satisfied formally but not substantively because that which seems to match the requirements of expressed demand fails to do so. To these sources a pre-1800 writer might add a source that we ignore, namely, complete satiety.

Frustration of the first sort may develop in both advanced and underdeveloped countries. In an advanced country, with $e' = f(y', V_i)$ and $E = e'/y'$, change in V_i may increase E, with the result that the now inflated expectations cannot be satisfied so long as y' remains at its current level. Again, the value of e may be governed by the current and hence prospective rate of growth, y', of average personal income, y, whereas the capacity of the individual to satisfy his expectations is roughly fixed by the rate of growth of posttax or *disposable* income. Accordingly, if the ratio of *disposable* to *personal* income continues to fall and expectations are not adjusted to this fall,[37] frustration develops. For what the government supplies is an imperfect substitute for what most consumers prefer. A partial parallel to this situation is that characteristic of the underlying population of the Soviet Union and its satellites. Here overall average output continues to rise much faster than permissible consumption, demand for which rises both with output and with stimuli from the West.

The first type of frustration is destined to grow in intensity in underdeveloped countries except insofar as the sense of frustration produces an antidotal feedback, a response more limited in an underdeveloped than in a developed country by an individual's lack of economic autonomy.[38] There changes in y and y' are not so likely to match increases in e and e' associated with changes in conditions included under V_i. For, while the economic distance separating underdeveloped from advanced countries is very great and very unlikely to be eliminated, the corresponding communications distance is much shorter and hence surmountable in large measure. Modern means of communication transmit the tastes and life-styles in one country to the inhabitants of another, with the result that many of these inhabitants aspire to live as do those in advanced countries. This is not possible, however, for many of those residing in underdeveloped countries. A hypothetical example makes this clear. Suppose that average income in advanced country A is ten times that in underdeveloped country U. Suppose further that income grows 2 percent per year in U and only 1 percent per year in A. Then, as the following hypothetical data suggest, much more than a century must pass before U closes in on A. Although the relative spread between A and U diminishes, the absolute spread is destined long to increase. Whence expectations in U tend to rise relatively rapidly, fed both by internal progress and by external stimuli. Meanwhile capacity to match expectations lags, with the result that frustration increases.

| Year | Comparative growth | | Difference |
	A	*U*	
0	10.0	1.0	9.0
50	16.4	2.9	13.5
100	27.0	7.2	19.8
200	72.9	52.4	20.5

The second type of frustration may prove characteristic of developed countries. In these countries, we may suppose, expectations do not outstrip income and may even expand less rapidly than income because of physical and temporal constraints on consumption and hence on the growth of demand. Meanwhile, many persons may find that, even though their incomes have increased more rapidly than their expectations, attainment of demand-satisfaction proves disappointing in that they fail to

realize the degree of satisfaction or euphoria upon which they
had counted. For in wealthy societies only a small fraction of
that which is acquired or consumed produces Pavlovian quies-
cence; most products may be described as enveloped in subjective states of mind that are prone to change as anticipation of
their attainment is succeeded by their acquisition—to change
ranging from reinforcement to dissipation of the state associated with anticipation.[39] Moreover, this tendency to disappointment may be intensified if many members of a community experiencing somewhat parallel disappointments become
cognizant of one another's experience, as, for example, have
overly indulged upper–middle-class youth.[40]

Fixity of supply may strongly reinforce both causes of frustration and give rise to interclass conflict, as it will impinge most
heavily upon lower-income groups. For goods and services are
divisible into two categories, those sufficiently augmentable to
surfeit man's want of them, at least in the absence of population growth, and those whose supply finally cannot be made to
keep pace with demand. The latter category is subdivisible into
two subcategories. The first includes those made up in relatively
large measure of not very augmentable agents, such as recreation based upon seashore, park areas, suitably situated space,
and so on. Demand for these rises as man's income rises, but, as
supply cannot grow at the same rate, price must rise and preserve balance between what is wanted and what is available. Accordingly, many will find their wants increasingly unsatisfied.
Second, as Keynes argued,[41] humans have need for whatever
makes them feel superior to their fellows, and this need is insa-
tiable "for the higher the general level, the higher still are
they." In sum, as incomes rise and the first category of wants is
more completely satisfied, increments in productivity and buying power are directed to the second category. Yet demand for
neither of these subcategories can be satisfied. Accordingly,
frustration rises, market allocation fails to satisfy, class struggle
is intensified, and some sort of rationing or collective allocation
becomes necessary.

LOOKING BACKWARD

Having roughly conceptualized and illustrated the subject of
this chapter, we may now look at the past, then at the "modern

period'' running from, say, the onset of the Industrial Revolution to the present, and finally at what may be in prospect. Our information bearing upon conditions obtaining prior to the eighteenth century is limited in amount and largely literary in origin. It reflects the fact that though man's real history has long been largely one of hunger and misery, his history as prepared by historians was long confined in the main to the affairs of the ruling circles.[42] Yet, had more of the ancient and premodern authors been acquainted with poverty, as was Hesiod, earliest Greek economist, they might have been pressed by scarcity, as was this eighth-century–B.C. farmer, to recognize resulting problems of choice and resource-allocation and to discuss the impact upon man's expectations of his passage out of a mythical Golden Age.[43]

As has been suggested above, conditions compatible with the emergence of rising expectations did not come generally into existence until the nineteenth century. It may be said, however, that the Age of Discovery lifted men's horizons and helped give release to output-increasing change. It should be noted, of course, that concern with the future, though a necessary condition, is not a sufficient basis for rising expectations. For such concern may be transcendentally or spiritually rather than materially oriented; desire for escape from the present may, as Toynbee has shown, assume a number of forms other than the rising material standard stressed by present-day futurologists.[44]

Prior to the modern era a number of conditions were inimical to rising expectations: (1) attitudes toward nature and environment; (2) degree to which economic activity is Faustian; (3) rigidity of social structure; (4) very low rate of population growth; (5) unawareness of economic change and absence of belief in progress and of inclination to foment it; and (6) poor means of communication.

1. So long as nature is looked upon as essentially immutable and hence as constituting a fixed environment to which man must adjust, as he cannot modify it to his advantage, so long will man's expectations in general tend to be stationary except as they occasionally may be influenced by variability or declension of his social or physical environment.[45] Such an essentially pessimistic outlook seems to have been common in premodern times, in part on philosophical grounds and in part because in a

world largely rural, nature predominated over man's social environment. Philosophical and related conditions also may have had a bearing.[46] It is the approach of the engineer that is best suited to make nature subservient to man's needs, even when potentially relevant scientific findings originate with nonengineers. Though it is true that man has been able over the centuries to produce considerable change in his physical environment, only within the past century has he come to take it for granted that his physical environment usually can be bent to his service.[47]

2. Those engaged in agricultural activities long believed themselves possessed of very limited capacity to improve the performance of nature. This outlook, though gradually weakened even before the Age of Discovery, must have been partially dissipated by the discovery of America and its doubling of "the potential vegetable sources of the known world."[48] It gave way to a progressive outlook with the "grass revolution" and the transformation of European agriculture in and after the eighteenth century.[49] Land long remained, much as in the ancient world,[50] the main form and object of investment. The smaller number engaged in various other undertakings seem in time to have found themselves in more Faustian milieux, exposed to challenges and problems associated with differences in practices, culture, and customs, and hence sensible of the need to be flexible in their operations.[51] For, as Sorokin observed in a different connection, the persons and groups earliest and most exposed to new cultural values, practices, and so on are the most congenial to change, at least initially. Representative of these persons and groups are merchants, missionaries, scholars, scientists, adventurers, and so on.[52] Accordingly, as commerce increased and with it the number of potential bearers of novel values and practices, outlooks became more dynamic and more oriented to what the future might have in store.[53]

3. Other conditions given, a relatively rigid social class structure conduces to constant expectations unless forces are at work that, so to speak, continually lift the social pyramid to ever-higher welfare levels. Rigidity of class structure varied somewhat with country and with the degree of political stability. Though ancient Athens may not have been typical, with only one person in seven unfree and with a corresponding theory of government,

it was more representative of the earlier Mediterranean world than of that in the days of Imperial Rome after the ancient world had, in Clark's terms, "crossed the threshold which separates the free man from the serf, commercial economy from the 'natural economy,' contract from status."[54] Typical of a rigid scheme of social organization was the medieval conception of "the body social."[55] Representative of this conception is the commonwealth, described by twelfth-century John of Salisbury as analogous to the human body. Corresponding to the head of this body is the prince, who is subject only to God, and who is assisted in governance by a variety of personnel (senate, governors, judges, officials, and financial officers) who correspond to various organs of the body and who, along with the prince, are supported by "the husbandmen [who] correspond to the feet, which always cleave to the soil, and need the more especially the care and foresight of the head. . . . The higher members shield the lower, and the lower respond faithfully and fully in like measure to the just demands of the superiors. . . . [In this] sort of reciprocity . . . each regards his own interest as best served by that which he knows to be most advantageous for the others." Of workers he wrote:

> Those are called the feet who discharge the humbler offices, and by whose services the members of the whole commonwealth walk upon solid earth. Among these are to be counted the husbandmen, who always cleave to the soil, busied about their plough-lands or vineyards or pastures or flower-gardens. To these must be added the many species of cloth-making, and the mechanic arts, which work in wood, iron, bronze, and the different metals; also the menial occupations, and the manifold forms of getting a livelihood and sustaining life, or increasing household property, all of which, while they do not pertain to the authority of the governing power, are yet in the highest degree useful and profitable to the corporate whole of the commonwealth. All these different occupations are so numerous that the commonwealth in the number of its feet exceeds not only the eight-footed crab but even the centipede, and because of their very multitude they cannot be enumerated; for while they are not infinite by nature, they are yet of so many different varieties that no writer on the subject of offices or duties has ever laid down particular precepts for each special variety. But it applies generally

to each and all of them that in their exercise they should not transgress the limits of the law, and should in all things observe constant reference to the public utility. For inferiors owe it to their superiors to provide them with service, just as the superiors in their turn owe it to their inferiors to provide them with all things needful for their protection and succour.[56]

This conception of order was in keeping with the philosophy of St. Augustine and its emphasis upon order directed against anarchy and the allegedly irrational behavior of history and intended to support progress toward Christian good.[57] It probably implies, as St. Augustine held, that virtues not be made the servants of bodily pleasure.[58]

The medieval conception of order continued to find expression even in the Elizabethan world, for, though it was being undermined by growing trade and commercialism, it lent intellectual support to the ruling circles and, given their disregard of the medieval principle of reciprocity, to the police-state despotism of the Tudors.[59] The social position of the mercantile class, especially that of large-scale traders, was somewhat better than it had been in the medieval period, especially in Italy, while that of the working class was no better.[60] Only as the social structure declined in rigidity, and as status relationships gave place to contractual ones, was there enough opportunity open to the less privileged to allow some to anticipate improvement in their situations.

Although the actual social order resembled the models described by political philosophers, the allocation of social stations in keeping with such models was not wholly acquiesced in. There were many internal disturbances, in which peasants and workers occasionally participated, some triggered by economic dissatisfaction, reinforced always, Sorokin concluded, by an unsettling of the social or cultural system.[61] Even so, the continual presence of an image of a quite fixed social order bearing the imprint of approval of the dominant classes served to stifle expectations that otherwise might have come to life.

4. Population growth may or may not significantly affect expectations; it is likely to do so, however, if it affects the rate of increase of per capita income, or if it contributes to the destruction of a social structure that makes for virtually stationary ex-

pectations. Until the advent of modern times, social structures often were quite fixed and allowed little social mobility when sociopolitical conditions were stable and numbers and technological conditions changed very little; then socioeconomic conditions approximated those characteristic of a stationary state and the number of persons newly entering a socioeconomic category amounted to replacements of those removed by death, disability, or withdrawal. When, on the contrary, population grows significantly and place-seekers exceed place-vacaters, pressure is put upon the social structure to expand and absorb this excess. In consequence, the social structure will have to be reorganized, or, as Plato proposed, introduced elsewhere by colonists from the community suffering population pressure.

The slowness with which population grew when it grew at all indicates both a lack of demographic pressure upon rigid social structures and a failure of the food supply to increase notably and carry numbers to higher levels at which they might remain virtually stationary (for example, in China). This slowness is suggested both by available empirical evidence and by inference from hypothetical data and information relating to epidemic disease and famine. At the beginning of the Christian Era the world's population numbered 210–250 million, with something like 34 million in Europe, at least 138 million in Asia, perhaps 30 million in Africa, and additional numbers in the Americas and Oceania; it was not much larger a thousand years later, totaling perhaps 275 million. Numbers began to grow after A.D. 1000, especially in Europe where they increased slightly more than 1.75 percent per decade from 1000 to 1300 compared with slightly more than one percent in the world as a whole. Following the Black Death, which reduced Europe's population by about three-eighths in the fourteenth century, world population resumed its former rate of growth, increasing slightly more than 1 percent per decade from 1450 to 1650, between 3 and 4 percent per decade from 1650 to 1750, and somewhat more than 4 percent from 1750 to 1850. The rate was higher in Europe than in Asia in the nineteenth century, but lower in the present century; it has been much higher in the Western Hemisphere than in the world as a whole.[62]

Turning to hypothetical data characteristic of a stable population, we find that, even given a life expectancy of only 25 years at birth, a birth rate of a little more than 40 (that is, a Gross Reproduction Rate of roughly 2.8–3.0) will yield a surplus of births over deaths, and that with life expectancy of 30 years, a birth rate of about 38 will increase numbers about 0.5 percent per year. Upon the ascent of life expectancy to 35 years, a birth rate of slightly more than 29 (that is, a G.R.R. of slightly more than 2.0) will yield a surplus over deaths.[63] Accordingly, in the absence of unusual adverse events, populations would grow markedly in time even at low annual rates of increase—for example, about 30 percent per century if population increased about 0.25 percent per year. That numbers did not grow as much as 2.5 percent per decade over long periods of time must have been largely the result of recurring excessive mortality associated not only with epidemic disease but also with famine, usually local in incidence but easily resulting if yields of produce were quite low even when times were good.[64] Death, as Fourastié has pointed out, was at the center of life even as the churchyard was at the center of the village.[65] What he said of the eighteenth century was applicable in medieval and ancient times as well; thus in ancient Attica as in Carthage, males fortunate enough to survive to age 20 suffered a uniformly high death rate, with the result that by age 60 only about one-fifth of those reaching 20 still survived, a figure below that suggested by current hypothetical life tables.[66]

It should be noted, of course, that fertility often, if not as a rule, fell short of its practical maximum, which we may put at, say, a Gross Reproduction Rate of around 3.5. Institutional, class-structural, mortality, and health conditions were mainly responsible.[67] In Europe, J. C. Russell concludes, loss of control over population, theretofore held within the confines of subsistence, came in the wake of the Black Death, which caused a loss of a third or more of the population in the lands afflicted.[68] Removal of institutional controls on fertility made possible a higher rate of natural increase than would have resulted under favorable conditions, given institutional controls over marriage, and so forth.[69]

5. If technological conditions begin to change, an initially stable social structure may change even if, as is unlikely, population changes very little.[70] For expectations may rise as technological conditions and socioeconomic options improve.

Rising expectations presuppose the presence of a well-founded belief in man's improvability and improvement, a belief nourished by awareness of technological change. Even though there be as yet too little favorable change to inspire in men belief in continuing change, it is possible to lay a theoretical groundwork for rising expectations. The theory of cumulative progress constituted such groundwork, for it ran counter to theories of cyclical change or continuing retrogression and rested belief in continuing improvement upon a regularly operating law.[71] This theory took belief-shaping and conduct-determining form in the seventeenth and eighteenth centuries, especially in France, where, as in England, confidence in science was growing. Not only was there taking place what Whitehead in another connection called a mating of professionalism with progress.[72] A rational rather than a merely empirical underpinning also was being given to the belief in progress.[73] Illustrative is Adam Smith's dynamic theory of the division of labor, theretofore mainly a limited model of specialization. Malthus's emphasis upon the finiteness of man's economic universe prompted inquiry on the part of his critics into theoretical factors countervailing finiteness and thus indirectly stimulated concern with "progress."

It is not surprising, in view of what has been said, that the expectations of most men manifested little tendency to rise above a stationary level before the late seventeenth or early eighteenth century. For, even though scattered individuals, members of ruling or trading circles, might sense prospective improvement of their affairs, their outlooks did not influence others. At times, of course, cults remindful of the "cargo cult" may have generated hopes of improvement, but these occultish hopes could not persist.[74] In contrast, prophecies usually embody forecasts of deteriorating conditions.

6. An epidemiological model could be employed to represent the role of communications media in the generation of rising expectations. One requires sources of infection with new tastes and rising expectations and vectors to carry the infection to those who are uninfected but not immune to infection. The function of vector is performed by means of communication—by infected migrants, the press (especially the penny press when incomes are relatively low),[75] radio, television, and so on. Since

the capacity of vectors to overcome distance remained small until the present century, vectors could function effectively only in areas where population was concentrated, mainly in larger towns and cities, and these in general did not environ large fractions of the population of countries until the nineteenth century.[76] One may infer that the impact of a "demonstration effect" could not become powerful until in the nineteenth century even though noninfected populations were marked by little immunity to new tastes.[77]

Perhaps most important of the socioeconomic complexes unfavorable to the emergence of rising expectations was the very low rate of technical progress, the low rate of improvement in economic output, and the prevalence of aspiration-depressing and essentially hopeless poverty. Turning first to poverty, counterpart to wasteful consumption by the wealthy, two of Finley's observations regarding the ancient world retain considerable validity.

> The ancient world was very unambiguous about wealth. Wealth was a good thing, a necessary condition for the good life, and that was all there was to it. There was no nonsense about wealth as a trust, no unconscious guilt feelings, no death-bed restitutions of usury. . . . There was never the slightest danger in antiquity that the lower classes would be anything but poor, and it did not matter much if some of them, notably the citizens of the capital cities, were industrious or not. They provided neither the products nor the profits. These came from peasants and from dependent labour, and their industriousness was secured by ways which had nothing to do with wages or technology.[78]

Under these circumstances, it was observed long before modern scholars began to write of a "culture of poverty" that the poor were without aspiration for more than immediate satisfaction of elementary needs.[79] That the surfeit of the few was at the expense of the many, though in varying degree from one country to another, probably continued to hold until modern times. About 1370, William Langland wrote: "Some laboured at ploughing and sowing, with no time for pleasure, sweating to produce food for the gluttons to waste."[80] Four centuries later, Adam Smith wrote: "All for ourselves, and nothing for other people, seems, in every age of the world, to have been the vile maxim of the masters of mankind."[81] Under the feudal system of his day, Langland implies, cultivators could not benefit from an abundance of uncultivated land.[82] Indeed, as Alfred Marshall implied in another connection, the common man could hardly aspire until a system of contract had replaced the system of status.[83]

Until considerable economic power had passed into the hands of the bourgeoisie, those possessed of politico-economic power were animated, as a rule, by values and concerns unfavorable to technological progress and the productive use of capital. Hence, though capital was potentially available, even in antiquity and the Middle Ages,[84] technological progress received little stimulus from those with means, nor did the latter invest their considerable actual or potential surplus in productivity-increasing instruments, preferring instead to expend their incomes upon retainers and upon unproductive durables.[85] Indeed, only as the bourgeoisie increased in relative number, initially in Italian cities, did the propensity to save and invest *productively* become ascendant, and thus indirectly increase economic opportunity open to cultivators and casual workers. The growth of the bourgeoisie in number was associated with the growth of towns and cities, for the impact of a bourgeois business-like approach to agriculture was associated with investment in land on the part of those with urban business experience.[86] The gradual improvement in economic conditions, though subject to fluctuation, was associated with increase in the number of bourgeoisie, bearers of a material or "sensate" culture, as Sorokin observed.[87] His findings also suggest that the number of technological as well as related scientific discoveries steadily grew after the early sixteenth century.[88] Preconditions to the emergence of rising expectations were slowly taking shape.[89] There was no basis, however, for rising expectations before the late eighteenth century, or for a widely held way of life based upon confidence in the steady improvement of man's economic lot, before the nineteenth century.

EIGHTEENTH CENTURY AND AFTER

England's economic and political development in and after the eighteenth century exemplifies the gradual emergence of rising expectations as incomes began to rise and society became more open and mobile. In the relation of this emergence both to earlier changes and to the progress of that transformation labeled the Industrial Revolution, England's experience illustrates this slow gestation of growing expectations. By 1750 average English income, somewhat above the 1700 level, approximated £70 with 1950 purchasing power; this figure in 1950 was nearly 3 times that then realized in India, about 2⅓ times that attained in Nigeria, and only ⅓ below that of Brazil. The English average, in 1750 as in 1700, approximated the Dutch average and appreciably exceeded the French average. Even though the 1750 average exceeded the 1700 average, Phyllis Deane concludes that "it is fair to say that before the second half of the eighteenth century people had no reason to *expect* growth." Such growth as took place was "painfully slow or spasmodic" and "readily reversible."[90]

Deane and Cole found little basis for "much improvement in average English standards of living" between the fifteenth century and the close of the seventeenth century when Gregory King made his well-known estimates. "King lived in a world in which economic change, outside the cataclysms produced by famines and epidemics, was generally small, slow and easily reversed."[91]

> The beginnings of sustained economic growth can be traced to the middle of the eighteenth century when the overall rate of growth seems to have risen to near 1 percent per annum from probably not more than 0.3 percent per annum. At this stage, however, the expansion of the economy was apparently swamped by the growth of population which also dates from slightly before mid-century. There is little evidence of an appreciable acceleration in the long-term rate of growth of real incomes per head until the last two decades of the eighteenth century, when the average rate of growth seems to have approached 1 percent per annum. The acceleration which then took place was significant . . . it marked the beginning of a more or less continuous upward trend. The rate of growth continued to accelerate into the nineteenth century, slackened in mid-century, recovered to record heights and then slackened again at the beginning of the twentieth century."[92]

Although the Industrial Revolution eventually transformed the economy and society of Britain, it was the product of a complex of complementary changes continuing over a sustained period of time. It may be described as evolving in keeping with Adam Smith's view of economic progress as associated with continuing division of labor and the circumstances conducive to this change. Not only was Smith sanguine about the future, even to the extent of anticipating (at least metaphorically) a "sort of wagon-way through the air";[93] he also drew attention to progress in the past.[94] He found the limit to economic expansion in the finiteness of available agricultural land, as did the classical school and its successors, underestimating, as did many of his successors, man's capacity to press back the limits of environment through recourse to direct or indirect replacement of scarce elements in this environment.

After presenting a summary of the leading theories put forward to account for the Industrial Revolution, R. M. Hartwell concludes:

> The various "forces making for growth" in the eighteenth century were not autonomous variables, but rather manifestations of growth itself; this seems to have been particularly true of capital formation, innovation and population growth. Does this mean that changing human attitudes, in particular the development of a rational ethic about wealth, and the emergence of business enterprises motivated by profit-making (and, thus, the willingness to take risks), were the promoters of the industrial revolution? We cannot say; but, again, it is reasonable to argue that because the profit-motive depended on the possibility of making profits, this possibility was created by the economic changes of the eighteenth-century. . . . Could [the industrial revolution] not be the culmination of a most unspectacular process, the consequence of a long period of slow growth?[95]

The forces that transformed the structure of Britain's economy between the early eighteenth and mid- or late- nineteenth century became operative on the Continent as well; some were of indigenous and some of external origin. There, as in England, the transformation proceeded slowly, initially in France and then elsewhere.[96] As it progressed, however, and the economic structure changed, the rate of growth of average income rose to levels much above those obtaining at the start.[97] The aggregate rate of growth fluctuated, of course, sometimes slowing down notably, as in late Victorian Britain; a result, some have held, of a failure of demand to expand rapidly enough, and, others have held, of an insufficiently elastic supply of resources.[98]

In the nineteenth century, expectations eventually began to grow faster than income.[99] Various forces, besides increase in income and wages, sustained when they did not accelerate living standards. Growth of population probably increased the pressure on many individuals to consume,[100] a pressure intensified by the increasing concentration of the population.[101] Innovation and invention increased output per head and augmented the number and variety of products, making many available at prices well within the reach of wage earners. Moreover, some inventions increased man's physical mobility (steam and electric railways, motor cars, air carriers) and gave him ready access to ever-larger areas of supply (for example, motor and rail transport), or made him aware of how others lived (for example, newspapers, magazines, motion pictures, radio, television).[102] In the United States in particular, the impact of income levels, high already by 1860,[103] was accentuated by forces more powerful than elsewhere. Most Americans believed "in the power of the individual to alter his lot" and move up the economic ladder. The country's culture was thing-oriented and much influenced by women who associated prestige as well as utility with consumables and who were increasingly interested in entering the labor force. Work became less burdensome, with the result that the pain cost of products fell. The aspiration to consume therefore grew in strength as the opportunity to satisfy it improved for women as well as for men.[104]

In the past, multiplication of wants came in the wake of augmentation of average output and income, together with multiplication of contemporary contacts and increase in the flow of stimuli from ever more diverse means of communication. Even though resources increasingly were devoted to want stimulation, the line of causation ran, and was believed to run, from supply to demand, with the result that the value of $E = e'/y'$ tended to remain in the neighborhood of 1.0. Today, by contrast, considerable support is commanded by the belief that the line of causation runs strongly also from demand to supply. This belief derives support from the growing importance of *discretionary income* and time, and from the increasing emphasis being placed upon the alleged responsibility of the state for the generation of demand both by financing more and more wants and by subsidizing markets on employment-creating grounds. Expectations are likely to be affected accordingly, with the result that $E > 1$ either because changes in V_i as well as y' affect e', or because heavy taxation reduces the ratio of disposable to personal income and thereby limits the purchasing power and hence the capacity of many persons to satisfy their expectations.

The steady growth of consumption in quantity and variety has interacted with a continuing devolution and diffusion of political power. The nineteenth and twentieth centuries have witnessed a redistribution of power, from those with property and the control of decisions to those with relatively limited means and little power of decision, from the once dominant male element to the female element, and from those in the middle and upper age groups to the young and often the quite young.[105] This power has become reassembled in new bodies, mainly in worker organizations, now bent upon wage increases far in excess of productivity, with the result that inflation is proceeding at unprecedented rates and the discipline of the market has been undermined, destined to be reinforced or replaced by collective controls.

Many factors have contributed to this devolution. Currently, and in recent times, the emergence of professional specialization and institutional compartmentalization, together with professional and sectoral autonomy, has weakened when it has not destroyed the bonds that formerly gave societies a sense of unity and totality, meanwhile dissipating institutional controls and elevating emotionalism.[106] Earlier the Industrial Revolution as well as the development of mass armies adapted to mass slaughter[107] greatly augmented the utility of the common man. In time, also, the spread of education, together with increase in both the requirements of many employments and the incomes of the underlying population, strengthened the common man's economic and social position. Important, too, has been a steady increase in the number of intellectuals, many of whom, as J. A. Schumpeter has emphasized, are hostile to the current political and economic power structure. ''Unlike any other type of society, capitalism inevitably and by virtue of the very logic of its civilization creates, educates and subsidizes a vested interest in social unrest."[108] As a result, the capacity of modern democratic societies to support political and economic order has been undermined.

The devolution of power proceeded at varying pace in America, in Britain, and on the Continent. The stick was slow to be replaced by the carrot, even in Europe.[109] Writing in the 1850s, Nassau Senior, probably the father of the economy-promoting expenditure tax, observed: "A tranquil, unadvancing, indolent, but frugal and contented poverty, with little to hope, but still less to fear, is the state of the great mass of the inhabitants of continental Europe." Far less frugal were the English. "When wages are high, they work fewer hours and inhabit better houses" and spend prodigally any remaining "superfluity." "When wages fall" they work harder and economize. "When their earnings become insufficient for a maintenance, they throw themselves on the parish."[110] Senior's successors were more disturbed than he at the lack of participation of the common man in economic progress under the dominance of what Barbara Tuchman has called "the patricians."[111] Britain's common man, often poor in an age of accelerating change,[112] was "with almost no effective access to government."[113] Writing in 1909, G. F. G. Masterman indicated that four-fifths of Britain's population were "more or less effectively excluded from the British political community of which they were nominally members." Eleven years later, after the First Modern Peloponnesian War, J. M. Keynes described Britain's laboring classes as "accepting a situation in which they could call their own very little of the cake that they and Nature and the capitalists were cooperating to produce."[114] Under the corroding impact of this war, writes Tuchman, "illusions and enthusiasms possible up to 1914 slowly sank beneath a sea of massive disillusionment," with "humanity's major gain" consisting in "a painful view of its own limitations"—limitations of which Rudyard Kipling had warned Britain in 1897 in his prescient "Recessional."[115]

One outcome was increase in the momentum toward democracy, slowly growing since its origin early in the nineteenth century. "The poor have become less poor, more articulate, more politically active, their demands in Britain (as elsewhere) have risen steadily and steeply, along with those of nearly all classes of society."[116] Eventually, though poverty still persisted, pretax income inequality began to decline.[117] A trend seemed to have set in that foreshadowed J. M. Keynes's optimistic forecast of the Englishman's prospective lot.[118]

Democracy, as has been suggested, was embedded early and deeply in the culture of America, far more than elsewhere, and there it continued to grow, in a social atmosphere rendered congenial by abundance of land, scarcity of manpower, reverence for religion, and the absence of a dominating elite, though endangered, De Tocqueville believed, should a tyrannical majority emerge.[119] In consequence the common man shared more equitably in economic improvement, except in occupations crowded with immigrants or adversely affected by cultural residues of a slave economy. Indeed, it probably was comparison of America with Europe that led Simon Nelson Patten to infer that a "pleasure" economy had replaced a "pain" economy.[120] Far less optimistic, of course, was Matthew Arnold, disturbed at what he thought he saw in Britain and America, namely, the disintegration of modern society "into its component classes, each of which presumes to consider its interests of paramount importance, and to act as though it were 'a center of authority.'"[121] Aversion of anarchy therefore called for a unifying "culture."[122] Arnold's reaction to the changes under way, though unique in form, had a variety of parallels, such as the reaction of John Ruskin.

CURRENT SITUATION

The situation depicted in earlier sections has been projected into the future by Alvin Toffler, in his account of accelerating change and the replacement of "permanence" by "transience," "novelty," "diversity," and taxation of the limits to man's adaptability, with the result that "strategies for survival" become essential.[123] Earlier it was indicated that frustration arises (1) if $E > 1$, that is if expectations continue to grow more rapidly than capacity to satisfy them; or (2) if man becomes disenchanted with components of demand, D, because they fail to yield anticipated services and satisfaction, given the resource, physical, and time costs involved.[124]

For purposes of exposition, we may write $D = I + C + G$, where D denotes aggregate demand, I denotes investment required to maintain C and G, C denotes goods and services absorbed by consumers, and G those absorbed by governments in the form of consumer-oriented goods and services, G_c, and non-consumer-oriented products, G_n. Then the rate D' at which D can grow is fixed by the rate S' at which S grows, where S denotes the flow of inputs, of goods and services, available for transformation into C and G and hence over time also into I, the requirement of which derives from the volume and rate of growth of C and G. We may also let D'_e designate the rate of increase in D_e, when D_e denotes aggregate demand as implied by a community's conduct-determining expectations. So long as $E = 1$, D_e and D'_e will not deviate greatly from D and D', which in turn must approximate S and S'. Then, though the wants of men generally will exceed what they have, the pace of their growth will correspond quite closely to the pace at which men increase their power to supply wants. Frustration, while always present in some degree, will not grow at a pace making for socioeconomic disturbance.

Prior to 1914, D_e tended to grow as did S, since causation ran predominantly from supply and availability to demand. Should D_e increase, this increase could be met out of the normal increase in S, product of past increase in I and in human capital, invention, and so on. If ΔD began to exceed ΔS, as in time of war, C would be reduced through taxation or inflation. As a rule, increase in G would be associated mainly with increase in G_n; for so long as social philosophy and the limitedness of the common man's political power remained unfavorable to increase in G_c, it did not increase notably. Over the past half century, especially after World War II, however, causation began to flow increasingly from demand to supply, with both G_n and G_c subject to more rapid increase than S. This presented no problem in times of underuse of capacity, as in prosperous 1929 when S was still susceptible of considerable increase,[125] but it constituted a threat to the growth of C and a potential source of conflict between recipients of G_n and G_c and between recipients of components of G_c.

The pressure to increase C has been rising faster than the disposable income available for C, though associated in part with the rate of increase in total income. Increase in C is not likely to be retarded by dissatisfaction with the results of not very well informed expenditure of *discretionary* income upon products novel to the purchaser, nor by the irregular development of leisure-favoring innovations, nor as yet by the increasing degree to which the products of American industry prove defective and impose unanticipated time and physical costs on consumers.[126] Reorganization of American society in ways allowing much more outdoor and participatorial recreation and activity will increase the demand for leisure and leisure-oriented resources, many of which will prove inelastic in supply. In general, for a variety of reasons, some historical, aspirations continue to rise, feeding on themselves and on persisting optimism regarding the course of prospective income, especially in Europe and the United States,[127] and contributing to unprecedented inflation.

It is, however, the severing of the constraints that formerly subordinated the rate of growth D' and D'_e to the rate of growth S' of S that constitutes a major source of unsatisfied demand and consequent frustration. Increases in both G_n and G_c have pressed G upward. Developed countries, especially the United States, have assumed large military defense and related (for example, space, foreign aid) burdens. Even if, as Britain's experience portends, dissatisfaction with the results of international expenditure may prompt its limitation,[128] other categories of G_n are destined to grow rapidly. Among these are the cleaning up of an increasingly polluted environment; law enforcement; large expenditure for rehabilitation of urban structures rendered obsolete and unviable by technological change, neglect of finance and transport, the dissolution of racial, ethnic, and similar barriers, and the growing breakdown of urban government and order; rehabilitation of the nation's habitat; and so on. H. and M. Sprout conclude: "We doubt that any political community, even the most productive and affluent, can evade or avoid these issues that are everywhere implicit in the dilemma of insufficient resources to cover rising and proliferating demands and commitments."[129]

Elsewhere they observe: "There appear to be grounds for querying whether any society . . . can long pay the price of competition for global political and military primacy without progressively eroding and eventually destroying the material and moral supports upon which national power and influence ultimately depend."[130]

Growth of pressure to increase G_c expenditures is likely even

though taxation for this purpose may be resisted. Such pressure
has many sources. It will arise from the efforts of weak local governments to placate public employees ever ready to strike and
interrupt essential services. It will continue to flow, in populist
societies, from governmental efforts to elevate expenditure on
the part of those in lower-income groups,[131] from efforts to relieve "intractable poverty in the midst of affluence." Pressure
to spend will be sustained by measures dealing with environmental rehabilitation, "urban decay, suburban sprawl, disorder
in the schools, crime in the streets, vocational displacement,
and other evidences of a society in deep trouble." Politicians
may, of course, hesitate to impose heavier taxes for fear of running counter to the American dream of "endlessly expanding
affluence." But they will be confronted not only by the demands described but also by the inflexibility of governmental
budgets at every level, with built-in and growing commitments
(for example, social security, veterans' benefits, retirement pen-
sions, and grants for public assistance) destined to absorb ever
larger revenues.[132] The conditions described vary in perceived
intensity by country; in general, welfare aspirations of countries, as reflected in poverty norms, are correlated with per capita income levels by country but in differing degree.[133]

Should the Congress (or other national legislature) hesitate to
increase tax revenue in keeping with growing expenditures, it
will have to fall back upon deficit financing. Indeed, this is inevitable, for, as Von Justi implied in 1766 and Colin Clark and
others have insisted, there is a limit to the fraction of national
income that a democratic state can appropriate in peacetime
without generating inflation and accentuating intergroup conflict associated with attempts to increase G and hence D faster
than S. Illustrative is conflict between those under, say, age 60
who pay the rising monetary bill and those over age 60 who are
beneficiaries of various, ever more costly security and welfare
programs.

Pressure to increase G_c and, in some measure, to elevate minimum wages above levels commensurate with the economic employment of less productive workers, is accentuated by the
growing belief that, despite the persistence of marked income
inequality and the inference that income structures are not very
modifiable,[134] poverty can be abolished through governmental

measures. This belief tends to be strong in societies made up of a plurality of groups with diverse incomes and planes of living and yet permeated by an ideology of egalitarianism; it tends to flourish as well in democracies large enough to permit concentration of considerable power in the hands of those animated by egalitarian sentiments. In general, "awareness of rapid economic progress increases the dissatisfaction of those who do not participate in it," among them the poor who "feel discriminated against and alienated" and hence "demand and press for immediate change in their situation."[135] Increasing the *absolute* content of lower-level incomes and of "poverty"-level benchmarks does not dissipate the influence of "demonstration effects" in societies largely emancipated from a deadening "culture of poverty."

Pressure to increase G may give rise to a paradox. On the one hand, economists and others recognize that the efficiency with which an economy embodying a price system, free competition, and contract can function depends upon the state's ensuring order and compliance with essential rules and thereby preventing destructive conflict among those with diverse interests.[136] Such action by the state is essential also to preservation of confident expectations that political and related essential forms of stability will persist.[137] On the other hand, if control of a state, initially powerful enough to sustain the hegemony of price, competition, and contract, passes into the hands of those bent upon accentuating the growth of G, this passage can produce disorder that weakens *gemeinschaftliche*, or communal ties, essential to the stability of *gesellschaftliche*, or purely economic relationships.[138]

When D threatens to exceed S, initially at the expense of I and in favor of G, the need to ration output will arise if the price system is prevented from restoring equilibrium between D and S. Competition among groups for greater shares in G unaccompanied by offsetting decreases in C also produces intergroup conflict and weakens ties that bind individuals together in a community. This outcome is likely in large states in which interindividual points of contact and sources of potential conflict are numerous.[139] Such conflict may result from a people's unwillingness to accept rationing solutions achievable either through price competition or under workable rules prescribed by agencies of the state. Though this type of conflict tends to be horizontal in character, it may be accentuated by vertical conflict associated with rapid rates of technical and other progress differentially incident on the age and occupational categories composing a population.

Illustrative of vertical conflict is that associated with the so-called generation gap. The socioeconomic status of a member of the labor force may be determined by his fund of experience or by his fund of recently developed and hence novel knowledge. Whereas experience tends to be correlated with age, novel knowledge tends to be associated with youth. Accordingly, in a relatively static society, considerable advantage lies with age whereas in a society subject to a high rate of technological and related change, considerable advantage lies with younger cadres. The resulting redistribution of power and influence can produce conflict, for instance, when increase in G_c for the benefit of older persons (for example, social security) is concomitant with $D' > S'$. The resulting impact may be expressed in terms of sets. Let g_1 designate the set of values, concerns, and so forth of Generation 1, and g_{15} the set of those of Generation 15. Then the set formed by the intersection of sets g_1 and g_{15} and hence representing values and concerns common to generations G_1 and G_{15} may be relatively large or small. In a society subject to a slow rate of change the area lying within the intersection will be very large relative to that lying in g_1 and g_2 but outside the intersection. If, however, the rate of change is high and if in addition there is conflict arising out of scarcity, the area within the intersection will be relatively small. Moreover, if this area is unduly small, ties of reciprocity will be reduced in number and the community will be weak, too weak perhaps to resolve conflicts easily.

Preservation of balance between D' and S' is prevented by current monetary policy flowing from an initial disparity between D and S. Balance results automatically when an economy is completely competitive, monetary policy consists in measures allowing the stock of money to grow at about the same rate as output,[140] and governmental undertakings are not financed through resort to inflation-generating means. Today, however, pressure upon G, especially upon G_c, together with changes accentuating rise in aspirations,[141] makes for imbalance and increase in frustration. For the governmental apparatus has lost the will to confine D' within bounds set by S', and there currently exist no other forces strong enough to bring about balance. Dissatisfaction associated with the lag of S' behind D' is accentuated, of course, by a growing awareness of deterioration in the quality of S, together with increase in the time and physical cost of consumption, a cost reinforced by shoddiness of output in a malfunctioning economy.[142] Inquiry into the future therefore entails inquiry into the mechanisms that can bring S' and D' into balance, into the forces making for convergence and divergence of S and D, and the probable behavior of each of these sets of forces.

THE FUTURE

There are two limits to the growth of S: (1) man's external environment, and (2) the morphology of the society he creates to facilitate the growth of S, presumably to satisfy D.

1. No society or its economy, be it national or metanational, is a closed, self-sustaining system;[143] each is parasitic on the physical world environing it and imposing constraints that optimistic futurologists neglect. In short, the homosphere (including man's economic universe) is finite, resting as it does both on elements that are fixed in amount and on elements that are subject to increasing entropy and decline in actual or potential usefulness. Accordingly, man's capacity to increase output per head depends ultimately upon the degree to which the rate of population growth can be reduced to the zero level and more abundant components of man's physical environment can be substituted for less abundant and hence limiting components. It is now recognized not only that continued exponential growth is impossible but also that environmental limits are closing in on man and compelling him to reassess his future options and prospect.[144] It is also recognized that technological offsets to the limitedness of some utilizable elements, together with economic growth, give rise to costs that have been neglected in the past.[145]

2. How a society and its economy are organized conditions the rate of growth of S and sets limits to S'. Furthermore, whether this organization be optimum or suboptimum, frustration and conflict arising out of failure of S to keep pace with D

may reduce the rate of growth of S and thus intensify frustration, at least in the short run.

Although all constraints of the sort included under limit 1 retard growth of S in general, some of these constraints become conspicuous in advanced countries. For as incomes rise and *discretionary* time or leisure per head increases, the desired rate of consumption of some of the elements especially limited in availability will increase rapidly (for example, various forms of recreational and other suitably situated space). Consciousness of scarcity will grow, therefore, with increase in the relative and absolute number of people who, as they become sated with goods and services in very elastic supply, turn for additional satisfaction to goods and services in quite inelastic if not fixed or diminishing supply. Frustration at inability to satisfy demand for such goods and services will probably become most pronounced among those lacking property in the sources of these products.

Because this inelasticity of supply is encountered in many countries, conflict in the wake of this scarcity is experienced at the international level as well as at the domestic level. Within countries it will originate in the uneven incidence of the scarcity of goods and services in inelastic supply and in disagreement regarding the impact of pollution and related controls upon the growth of average income. At the international level corresponding conflict will arise, for here as within countries, dependence upon the price system to ration what is scarce will be resisted, as will stringent controls upon pollutants and environmental deterioration.

One may argue that, as a rule and in the longer run, equilibrium tends to emerge and persist in a closed society—in the present case, that which we have called S and D tend to move into equilibrium, in terms of both the aggregate quantity and the composition of S and D. For example, D and D' may adjust downward in keeping with S' because of change in V_i, essentially a collection of intervening variables, or because disappointment at the content of S when actually realized makes for that downward adjustment of expectations. Frustration will then abate insofar as it is associated with inability to realize expectations of the sort here under discussion.

When societies are open to the inflow of stimuli from other

societies, the tendency to equilibrium is weakened, though not necessarily eliminated. Then D'_e is governed by external as well as internal forces, whereas S' depends in the main upon internal conditions. Even so, those residing in relatively low-income countries and hence resembling members of relatively low-income classes in advanced countries are quite aware of the smallness of the probability that any one individual can realize inflated expectations. They may change their perceptions of what is possible as a result, even though the international income structure may no longer continue to diverge as in the past century.[146] For even then it is not likely to be expected to converge rapidly enough to warrant hope in the realization of anything like international economic equality.

As has already been suggested, adjustments reducing disparity between D' and S' and thereby abating frustration are of both accidental and designed origin. For example, changes in consumption patterns may serve to decelerate the rate of increase in expectations. An individual may be viewed as endowed with a budget made up of a fixed quantity of time convertible into work or nonwork, together with physical energy and perhaps some purchasing power in addition to that for which he can exchange some of his time. This endowment of time, energy, and unearned purchasing power he may allocate in any one of a large number of ways, some of which are insensitive to the forces producing rising expectations and/or frustration. Widespread reorientation of consumption patterns can, therefore, greatly weaken the sources of rising expectations and frustration, even as many philosophers have contended or urged. It is unlikely, of course, that the condition of the typical individual will approximate that of the wantless Abyssinian prince described in Samuel Johnson's *Rasselas:* "That I want nothing, or that I know not what I want, is the cause of my complaint."[147]

Changes in consumption patterns may affect S' and thus make for increase or decrease in disparity between D' and S'. For example, such changes may shift inputs to sectors in which output per head grows less rapidly; a case in point seems to be the service sector, which by 1980 is expected to engage at least two-thirds of the labor force compared with about half in 1947. It is possible that increasing separation of ownership, together

with top- and lower-level management, from the underlying
work force in both goods and service industries may increase
alienation of workers from employers,[148] reduce the concern of
workers to perform well, and thus increase malfunction in production and products. Today "consumerism" and self-service
constitute responses to products of alienation. Indeed, the four-
day week is defended on the ground that, on the other three
days, the consumer can function as Mr. Fixit and repair the
shoddy products of a malfunctioning economy.

Increase in the value attached to time, whether as leisure or as
a complement to consumption, also may reduce the rate of
growth both of commercial output per worker per year and of
the demand for that output. It is to be expected that an ever-
larger fraction of the increase in his productivity per hour will
be "consumed" in the form of time devoted to purposes other
than employment for pay. Not only does the demand for leisure
increase with rise in income and decline in the cost of commercial recreation;[149] it also increases as the pattern of consumption
becomes more oriented to goods and services to which time is
highly complementary and as the pattern of living increasingly
entails planned use of scarce time.[150] Increase in the physical
cost of consuming commercial products also will decrease the
rate of growth of demand for them.

The course of E is conditioned not only by the degree to
which S' keeps pace with D' but also by variation in the want-
satisfying power of S, components of which may differ notably
in respect of their want-satisfying power. The want-satisfying
power of ΔS depends in large part upon the extent to which ΔS
is transformed into ΔC of such composition as matches the composition of the increment in wants associated with the increase
in purchasing power accompanying the transformation of ΔS into ΔC. As a rule, the relative want-satisfying power associated
with an increment in ΔS will correspond to $\Delta C/(\Delta C + \Delta G)$ and
hence tend to diminish with increase in $\Delta G/(\Delta G + \Delta C)$. Moreover, since G_c tends to be more substitutable for C than is G_n,
increase in the ratio G_n/G will further depress the want-satisfying power of ΔS, some of which is transformed into G_n and/or
G_c. In view of what has been said, it is inferable that E is more
likely to approximate 1.0, or, given appropriate changes in V_i,
fall short of 1.0, if the ratio $\Delta C/(\Delta C + \Delta G)$ approximates 1.0.

If, on the contrary, this ratio falls quite short of 1.0, E will tend to fall, since the capacity of the economy to produce want-satisfaction will not keep pace with e and y. The magnitude and the significance of $C/(C + G)$ will be conditioned by the order of values insofar as consumer sovereignty and freedom of choice rule.

It has been argued that though expectations may rise at an accelerating rate, equilibrating forces usually keep the rise in line with the economy's capacity to support it. Converging forces swamp those conducive to divergence. It is always possible, of course, that in the short run, departures from equilibrium will provoke not a compensatory response but a yet further movement from equilibrium and thus possibly set in motion a cumulatively disequilibrating process.[151] In the end, however, though after a long and system-changing time, the forces making for convergence will become ascendant, since persistence of divergence-producing forces eventually must destroy the community or social body within which they have escaped control. Then restoration of order becomes a primary objective and this presupposes as a precondition the return of balance between expectations and capacity to satisfy them.

Whether such a destructive process is under way in the United States and other Western democracies is uncertain. Overloading economies is already leading to inflation; for, although satisfaction of aspirations, moral[152] and nonmoral, absorbs excessive inputs, politicians increasingly are engaged in bribing the electorate[153] with such satisfaction, at the expense of all elements vulnerable to plucking. The destructive process is fed—sometimes through deification of the lawyers' *adversary* principle—by growth of specialization of all sorts and hence increase in the number of contact points at which the economic network is subject to threat of disruption, especially after much of the power to exercise duress or force has passed from the state to special-interest groups (for example, trade unions, professional and business associations). Moreover, populations are splitting up into groups after the manner of a collapsing assembly of units constituting what had been a functioning empire, with each group bent upon seeking differential advantage or support of its already acquired advantage, even as Hobbes foresaw and to the same effect.[154] Dissolution of what had been a network of reciprocity knit together by exchange and other mechanisms is hastened with the gradual passage of the apparatus of state under the partial control of the inept, the parasitical, the lumpen intelligentsia, and with the accompanying dissipation both of community-preserving social-psychological ties and of security-conserving forces. To such process there is little general alertness[155] until division and polarization have reached a critical point. Then an order-promising movement may come into being and, with military assistance, seize control of the apparatus of state and dislodge those who, as Socrates warned, define as good that which the populace momentarily seems to want.

What the future holds in store is hidden. For futurologists' forecasts of the future tend to neglect both the social orders and limitations arising from man's physical and internal environments. If we assume, with MacIver and Page, that there are three social orders, "the order of values or the cultural order, the order of means or the utilitarian order, and the order of nature on which man's valuations and man's devices alike depend,"[156] then it is change in the first of these orders that is most difficult to project. Yet it is this order that in the long run determines the selection of objectives for whose realization the utilitarian order supplies the means. As a rule, therefore, given environmental limitations, it will be within the order of values that correctives for imbalance between expectations and the means to their satisfaction will originate, whether in the form of increase in S and the degree of equality with which it is distributed, or in the form of downward revision of D'_e. That adjustment is most likely to originate in the order of values is inferable also from the fact that this order is susceptible of greater, more varied, and more rapid change than are the other two orders; for the order of values is subjective and hence relatively free of constraints encountered in the other two orders. For this reason also the order of values is less susceptible of successful computerization, simulation, and projection than are the other two orders.

CONCLUSION

Rising expectations and frustration are modern phenomena, hardly two centuries old. Disparity between expectations and capacity to satisfy them has tended to become pronounced only in the present century, with the weakening if not the complete destruction of the link running *from* growth in capacity to growth of expectations. This weakening has been associated with growth of the political power of the underlying population and the steady increase in the economic and the social role of the populist or democratic state—a state with too much capacity to promise and distribute but with too little capacity to preserve the hegemony of the market and the price system. More generally, this weakening has been associated with reduction in the role of homeostasis-producing agents and their replacement by arbitrary, uncoordinated, interest-group–dominated instrumentalities that now threaten the continuity of truly democratic forms.

Solution consists in increasing the role of homeostasis-producing agencies and in limiting the role of interventionist agencies to dissolution of concentrations of laboristic and industrial-commercial power not conducive to economies of scale and to the performance of functions that clearly lie outside the capacity of the private sector and of lesser jurisdictional components of the polity.

NOTES

1. See, for example, A. N. Whitehead, *Adventures of Ideas* (New York: Macmillan, 1933), chap. 6, esp. pp. 116–118. Cf. J. M. Keynes, *Essays in Persuasion* (New York: Harcourt, Brace and Co., 1932), pp. 360–361.

2. T. R. Malthus, *Essay on Population,* Everyman Ed. (New York: Dutton, n.d.), pp. 194–195.

3. Congruence with reality entails "conformity with general natural laws" and with existence of "a discernible path by which the expected state of affairs, labelled with a future date, could, without breach of these laws, be attained from the existing situation within 'the available time.' " See G. L. S. Shackle, *The Nature of Economic Thought* (Cambridge: Cambridge University Press, 1966), p. 78.

4. Richard Hofstadter, *The American Political Tradition and the Men Who Made It* (New York, Knopf, 1948). The following quotation is from Aaron Wildavsky, *The Revolt Against the Masses* (New York: Basic Books, 1971), p. 45; see also p. 44 on the conflict between the wants of the masses and the wants of the environmentalist elite.

5. David Riesman's "other-directedness" is more prevalent in "achieving" than in other societies, D. C. McClelland suggests in *The Achieving Society* (New York: Van Nostrand, 1961), pp. 190–203.

6. This phrase is A. N. Whitehead's, in his *Science and the Modern World* (New York: Macmillan, 1947), p. 141.

7. See, for example, H. J. Schiller, "Mind Management: Mass Media in the Advanced Industrial State," *Quarterly Review of Economics and Business* 11 (1971):39–52. A number of pieces on the possible future role of drugs have appeared in *The Futurist* in recent years.

8. Cf. Alfred Marshall's approaches in his *Principles of Economics* (London: Macmillan & Co., 1961); this is a variorum edition with annotations by C. W. Guillebaud.

9. Cf. N. S. Timashef's analysis of "power structure" in his *An Introduction to the Sociology of Law* (Cambridge: Harvard University Press, 1939), pp. 184–187. Reinforcing transpersonal links increase as $[(n-1)\ (n-2)/2]$ where n denotes the number of members of a group each of whom initially experiences frustration.

10. See, for example, Talcott Parsons and Neil Smelser, *Economy and Society* (Glencoe, Ill.: Free Press, 1956); V. Pareto, *The Mind and Society* (New York: Harcourt Brace, 1935).

11. T. E. Holland, *The Elements of Jurisprudence,* 12th ed. (New York: Oxford University Press, 1917), p. 80; see also Timashef, *Introduction to the Sociology of Law,* esp. pt. 1.

12. See Peter M. Blau, *Exhange and Power in Social Life* (New York: Wiley, 1964); also my "Allocation and Development, Economic and Political," in Ralph Braibanti, ed., *Political and Administration Development* (Durham: Duke University Press, 1969), pp. 588–637, esp. 632–637.

13. Exercise of an option always imposes choice and cost in the sense of alternative options foregone.

14. See, for example, R. S. Weckstein, "Welfare Criteria and Changing Tastes," *American Economic Review* 52 (March 1962):133–153; also W. P. Strassmann, "Optimum Consumption Patterns in High-Income Nations," *Canadian Journal of Economics and Political Science* 28 (August 1962):364–372.

15. For example, even before the medieval urban renaissance, Christian merchants found "an almost limitless source of recruitment" in the agricultural population whence "there emerged everywhere individuals driven to seek a livelihood, and even wealth, by their enterprising spirit and by their shrewd ability to profit by circumstances." See H. van Werocke's account of the rise of towns in *The Cambridge Economic History of Europe* (Cambridge: Cambridge University Press, 1963), vol. 3, chap. 1, p. 11.

16. Somewhat indicative is Henry Adams's account of his life in relation to changing times in *The Education of Henry Adams,* (New York: Random House, 1931); also Whitehead, *Science and the Modern World,* p. 282, and Keynes, *Essays in Persuasion,* pp. 360–361, 364–370.

17. See Maurice Halbwachs, *L'évolution des besoins dans les classes ouvrières* (Paris: Félix Alcan, 1933), pp. 150–151.

18. Keith Irvine, "Revolution of Declining Expectations," *The New Leader,* 20 November 1967, pp. 13–14. See also Philippe de Seynes, "Prospects for a Future World," *International Organization* 26 (Winter 1972):1–17.

19. J. M. Keynes, *A Treatise on Probability* (London: Macmillan & Co., 1921), p. 18, also chaps. 2, 26. On expectation and subjective belief, see Nicholas Georgescu-Roegen, *Analytical Economics* (Cambridge: Harvard University Press, 1966), chap. 6, esp. pp. 258–263.

20. Adam Smith, *The Wealth of Nations* (New York: Random House, 1937), p. 107.

21. A. O. Hirschman, "The Principle of the Hiding Hand," *Development Projects Observed* (Washington, D.C.: Brookings Institution, 1967), chaps. 1, 2.

22. See Milton Friedman, "Choice, Chance and the Personal Distribution Of Income," *Journal of Political Economy* 61 (August 1953):277–290.

23. E. A. Havelock, *The Liberal Temper in Politics* (London: Jonathan Cape, 1957), chap. 3, also p. 405 and chap. 13. See also St. Augustine's *The City of God* (New York: Random House, 1950), bk. 22, chap. 24.

24. J. U. Nef, *The Conquest Of The Material World* (Chicago: University of Chicago Press, 1964), pp. 67–69, and 215–239 on the impact of the Reformation. See also G. Le Bras's account of medieval conceptions of economy and society in *The Cambridge Economic History of Europe* (Cambridge: Cambridge University Press, 1963), vol. 3, chap. 8.

25. See Karl Marx and F. Engels, *The First Indian War of Independence 1857-1859* (London: Lawrence and Wishart, 1959), pp. 18–19; G. G. Coulton, *Medieval Village, Manor, and Monastery* (New York: Harper, 1961); G. Myrdal, *Asian Drama* (New York: Random House, 1968), chaps. 22, 23.

26. See, for example, M. I. Finley, "Technical Innovation and Economic Progress in the Ancient World," *Economic History Review* 18 (August 1965): 43–44; A. E. R. Boak, *Manpower Shortage and the Fall of the Roman Empire in the West* (Ann Arbor: University of Michigan Press, 1956).

27. Sylvia Thrupp describes the period from 1349 to the 1470s in England as "the golden age of bacteria." See "The Problem of Replacement Rates in Late Medieval English Population," *Economic History Review* 18 (August 1965):118. K. F. Helleiner describes the unfavorable economic impact of the Black Death and its sequelae in his "Population Movement and Agrarian Depression in the Later Middle Ages," *Canadian Journal of Economics and Political Science* 15 (August 1949): 368–372. See also Helleiner's chapter in *The Cambridge Economic History of Europe* (Cambridge: Cambridge University Press, 1967), vol. 4, pp. 1–95.

28. On the role of threshold in choice, see Georgescu-Roegen, *Analytical Economics,* p. 151 and passim.

29. Phyllis Deane and W. A. Cole, *British Economic Growth 1688-1959* (Cambridge: Cambridge University Press, 1962), p. 80. Average income was, however, more than double subsistence.

30. For historical instances, see Arnold Toynbee, *A Study of History* (London: Oxford University Press, 1939), vol. 5, pp. 459–489. See also R. S. Berman, *America in the Sixties: An Intellectual History* (New York: Free Press, 1968).

31. J. S. Duesenberry, *Income, Saving and the Theory of Consumer Behavior* (Cambridge: Harvard University Press, 1949), pp. 26–28. See also Weckstein, "Welfare Criteria," pp. 137–143.

32. Koji Taira, "Consumer Preferences, Poverty Norms, and Extent of Poverty," *Quarterly Review of Economics and Business* 9 (1969):31–44, esp. 32–34, 40–41, 44.

33. See my "Product-Adding versus Product-Replacing Innovations," *Kyklos* 10 (1957):249–277.

34. See, for example, J. D. Owen, "The Demand for Leisure," *Journal of Political Economy* 79 (1971):56–76; S. B. Linder, *The Harried Leisure Class* (New York: Columbia University Press, 1970). See also Georgescu-Roegen, *Analytical Economics,* pp. 343, 352, 377, 387–390, and *The Entropy Law and the Economic Process* (Cambridge: Harvard University Press, 1971), pp. 285, 288–291.

35. Joseph A. Schumpeter, *Business Cycles* (New York: McGraw-Hill, 1939), vol. 1, chap. 3, esp. pp. 72–75.

36. Cf. Joseph A. Schumpeter, *The Theory of Economic Development* (Cambridge: Harvard University Press, 1934), chap. 1. on "the circular flow of economic life."

37. In the United States the ratio of *disposable* to *personal* income fell from 0.97 in 1929 to 0.91 in 1951 and 0.87 in 1971.

38. Within limits, frustration when tolerable facilitates learning, See "Healthy Frustration," *Time,* June 5, 1972, p. 61.

39. As Charles Dickens observed in his novel *Great Expectations:* "Probably every new and eagerly expected garment ever put on since clothes came in, fell a trifle short of the wearer's expectation" (chap. 19). In life it is often the hunt rather than catching the quarry that is the more pleasurable.

40. See note 9 and text above.

41. Keynes, *Essays in Persuasion,* pp. 365–368.

42. See my "World Hunger: Past, Present, Prospective," *World Review of Nutrition and Dietetics* 9 (1968):1–31, esp. 1–4. We know the kings, statesmen, writers, thinkers, etc., "and yet we do not know whether all our ancestors had enough to eat." So writes Peter Laslett in *The World We Lost* (London: Methuen & Co., 1965), p. 127.

43. B. J. Gordon, "Aristotle and Hesiod: The Economic Problem In Greek Thought," *Review of Social Economy* 21 (1963):147–156.

44. See Toynbee, *Study of History,* vol. 6, passim.

45. That man's physical environment was subject to decline was a common belief, one held by Plato (*Timaeus,* 23–25, *Critias,* 108–121) and Cicero (in "The Dream of Scipio"), among others.

46. See, for example, P. A. Sorokin, *Social and Cultural Dynamics* (New York: American Book Co., 1937), vol. 2, chap. 3, and vol. 4 (1941), pp. 221–222; Oswald Spengler, *The Decline of the West* (New York: Knopf, 1939), vol. 2, pp. 89–92, 96, 449n., 504–505.

47. See, for example J. S. Berliner, "The Feet of the Natives Are Large," *Current Anthropology* 3 (February 1962):47–62.

48. *The Cambridge Economic History of Europe* (Cambridge: Cambridge University Press, 1967), vol. 4, chap. 5.

49. Ibid., vol. 6, chap. 6; V. G. Simpkhovitch, *Toward the Understanding of Jesus* (New York: Macmillan, 1937), pp. 140–165; C. P. Timmer, "The Turnip, the New Husbandry, and the English Agricultural Revolution," *Quarterly Journal of Economics* 83 (1969):375–395; E. L. Jones, "The Condition of English Agriculture, 1500–1640," *Economic History Review* 21 (1968):614–619.

50. Finley, "Technical Innovation and Progress," pp. 29–45, esp. 36–39.

51. Oswald Spengler contrasts what he calls the Faustian outlook with alternative outlooks in *Decline of the West,* esp. in vol. 1, chap. 6, and vol. 2, chap. 14.

52. Sorokin, *Social and Cultural Dynamics,* chap. 5, esp. pp. 227–234. Oswald Spengler, writing in 1914–1917, identified "the entrepreneur, the engineer, and the factory-worker" as the fountains of the "economy of the machine industry" (*Decline of the West,* chap. 2, p. 504.)

53. As early as 1525, 2–3 million of western Europe's 60–70 million people were engaged in industry, and others in trade. Nef, *Conquest of the Material World,* p. 69.

54. Colin Clark, *The Conditions of Economic Progress,* 3rd ed. (London: Macmillan & Co., 1957), pp. 652–684, esp. p. 684. On democratic Athens, see A. H. M. Jones, *Athenian Democracy* (Oxford: Blackwell, 1957), chap. 4, esp. pp. 76–81.

55. See, for example, R. W. Southern, *The Making of the Middle Ages* (London: Hutchinson, 1956), chap. 2.

56. From *Politcraticus,* trans. J. Dickinson (New York: Appleton, 1927).

57. C. N. Cochrane, *Christianity and Classical Culture* (London: Oxford University Press, 1944), pp. 242, 245, 483–484; St. Augustine, *City of God* (New York: Random House, 1950), bk. 14, chap. 13, pp. 690–693.

58. St. Augustine, bk. 5, chap. 20. St. Augustine would have approved J. K. Mehta's suggestion that "nobler and superior" wants be "employed to kill the baser and inferior wants," and thus facilitate "elimination of wants" by arousing or creating "superior wants." *A Philosophical Interpretation of Economics* (London: Allen & Unwin, 1962), pp. 66–67.

59. See E. M. W. Tillyard, *The Elizabethan World Picture* (New York: Random House, n.d.), chaps. 2, 7; D. L. Stevenson, ed., *The Elizabethan Age* (New York: Fawcett, 1967), pp. 15–20, 58–91.

60. Stevenson, *Elizabethan Age,* pp. 44–48.

61. Sorokin, *Social and Cultural Dynamics,* vol. 3, chap. 14, esp. pp. 198–506, also chap. 13 for a statistical summary of internal disturbances in Europe. On peasant revolts, see Coulton, *Medieval Village,* chaps. 11, 16, 23–25, app. 37.

62. For estimates of population, see W. S. and E. S. Woytinsky, *World Population and Production* (New York: Twentieth Century Fund, 1953), pp. 33–34; M. K. Bennett, *The World's Food* (New York: Harper, 1954), p. 9; J. D. Durand, "The Modern Expansion of World Population," *Proceedings of the American Philosophical Society* 111 (1967):136–159; United Nations, *The Determinants and Consequences of Population Trends,* ST/SOA/Ser.A/17 (New York: United Nations, 1953), chap. 2, esp. p. 11; C. Cipolla, *The Economic History of World Population* (London: Pelican Books, 1962). Colin Clark puts world population at 256, 280, 384 and 427 millions as of A.D. 14, 1000, 1200, and 1500, respectively; see his *Population Growth and Land Use* (London: Macmillan & Co., 1967), chap. 3.

63. Based on tables in A. J. Coale and Paul Demeny, *Regional Model Life Tables and Stable Populations* (Princeton: Princeton University Press, 1966). Colin Clark puts at 0.3 percent per annum "the rate of natural increase of an agricultural community under medieval conditions" (*Population Growth,* p. 83).

64. For brief accounts, see the articles on "Black Death," "Communicable Diseases, Control of," "Epidemic," and "Famine" in *Encyclopedia of the Social Sciences* (New York: Macmillan, 1930–1931), vols. 2, 4–6. See also K. F. Helleiner's splendid account of Europe's population from the Black Death to the eve of the "vital revolution," in *The Cambridge Economic History of Europe,* vol. 4 (Cambridge: Cambridge University Press, 1967), chap. 1.

65. J. Fourastié, "De la vie traditionelle à la vie tertiaire," *Population* 14 (1959):417–132.

66. Jones, *Athenian Democracy,* pp. 82–83. According to hypothetical life tables prepared by A. J. Coale and Paul Demeny, the Western Model suggests that of 100 males reaching age 20, 39 reach age 60 when life expectancy at birth is 30.08 years, and 33 when it is 25.26 years. The Southern Model suggests 42 survivors when life expectancy at birth is 24.66 years, and 48 when it is 29.33 years. Computed from Coale and Demeny, pp. 4, 6, 658, 660.

67. See, for example, Clark, *Population Growth,* chaps. 1, 2.

68. J. C. Russell, "The First Loss of Control over Population in Europe," paper presented at the meeting of the Population Association of America, Toronto, April 1972. See also his *Medieval Regions and Cities* (Bloomington: Indiana University Press, 1972).

69. Colin Clark's estimates suggest that increase per decade of Europe's population approximated 3.6 percent in 1200–1340, 2 percent in 1500–1600, and 2.4 percent in 1600–1700. *Population Growth,* p. 97.

70. Technological change in times past made for increase in population capacity and hence in numbers.

71. See G. H. Hildebrand's introduction to *The Idea of Progress: A Collection of Readings,* selected by F. J. Teggert (Berkeley: University of California Press, 1960), chap. 8; and J. B. Bury, *The Idea of Progress* (New York: Dover, 1955).

72. "In the past, professionals have formed unprogressive castes. The point is that professionalism has now been mated with progress." See Whitehead, *Science and the Modern World,* pp. 294–295.

73. The rational-empirical problem was discussed by A. B. Wolfe in "Is There a Biological Law of Population Growth?" *Quarterly Journal of Economics* 41 (August 1927):557–594.

74. See Weston La Barre's interesting "Materials for a History of Studies of Crisis Cults: A Bibliographic Essay," *Current Anthropology* 12 (February 1971):3–44.

75. See, for example, N. E. Himes, *Medical History of Contraception* (Baltimore: Williams & Wilkins, 1936), chap. 10, on "democratization by publicity." Somewhat pertinent is my "Notes on the International Transmission of Economic Ideas," *History of Political Economy* 2 (1970):133–151.

76. See, for example, Deane and Cole, *British Economic Growth,* pp. 7–11; A. F. Weber, *The Growth of Cities in the Nineteenth Century* (New York: Macmillan, 1899).

77. Methodologically relevant is A. R. Omran, "The Epidemiologic Transition: A Theory of the Epidemiology of Population Change," *Milbank Memorial Fund Quarterly* 49 (1971):509–538.

78. Finley, "Technical Innovation and Economic Progress," pp. 31–32, 43. Cf. A. L. Basham, *The Wonder That Was India* (New York: Grove Press, 1954), p. 215, on early Indian dread of poverty and the desirability of wealth, a point of view encountered in the Middle East as well.

79. See, for example, my *Indian Economic Thought: A Preface to Its History* (Durham: Duke University Press, 1971), pp. 42–46. On the "culture of poverty," see Oscar Lewis, "The Children of Sanchez, Pedro Martinez, and La Vida," together with comments on Lewis's work, in *Current Anthropology,* 8 (December 1967):480–500. See also Simon Nelson Patten, *The Development of English Thought* (New York: Macmillan, 1899), pp. 6–10, 23–25, and *Essays in Economic Theory,* ed. R. G. Tugwell (New York: Knopf, 1924), pp. 337–338.

80. William Langland, *Piers the Ploughman* (Baltimore: Penguin, 1970), p. 25. Shakespeare wrote in similar vein when he had a poor citizen exclaim in *Coriolanus:* "What authority surfeits on would relieve us . . . the leanness that afflicts us, the object of our misery, is as an inventory to particularize their abundance; our sufferance is a gain to them" (act 1, sc. 1).

81. Smith, *Wealth of Nations,* pp. 388–389.

82. He observed that the plague had greatly reduced the income of parish priests, but he said nothing of the availability of untilled land and a consequent improvement in the lot of cultivators who were poverty-ridden in comparison with those who "chose to live by trade" or with lawyers "pleading their cases for as much money as they could get. Never once did they open their mouths out of love for our Lord." Langland, *Piers the Ploughman,* pp. 26, 27, 31, also p. 26 on the "greed" of "Doctors of Divinity." See also Southern, *Making of the Middle Ages,* chap. 2; a serf "did not know today what he would have to do tomorrow" (p. 107).

83. "Hope and ambition, and some scope for the play of free competition, are conditions—necessary conditions so far as we can tell—of human progress." A. C. Pigou, ed., *Memorials of Alfred Marshall* (London: Macmillan & Co., 1925), p. 238, also 82–83.

84. Finley, "Technical Innovation and Economic Progress," pp. 32–41, also p. 45 on the degree of progress, and pp. 44–45 on the unfavorable impact of the servile or slave status of labor upon artisanry. Cf. Pigou, *Memorials,* pp. 82–83. On waste of potential capital in the Middle Ages, see G. C. Coulton, *Medieval Panorama* (New York: Meridian Books, 1955), pp. 493, 511–512, 654–655, 759–760. Presumably, even with a very low average income, 5 percent might assume the form of capital and increase average output perhaps 0.25–0.5 percent per year, enough to increase average output 30 or more percent per century, perhaps enough to quadruple average output in five centuries. On capital formation in England in the late seventeenth century see Deane and Cole, *British Economic Growth,* chap. 8.

85. As Milton Friedman has noted, "Savings may well have been at least as large a fraction of income in the Middle Ages as in major part, took the form of cathedrals, which, however productive of ultimate satisfaction and of social security in more than one sense of that term, were not productive of wordly goods. . . . Perhaps the crucial role that has been assigned instead to the factors determining the form in which wealth is accumulated." *A Theory of the Consumption Function* (Princeton: Princeton University Press, 1957), p. 236.

86. On the development of urban classes in and after the late Middle Ages, see *The Cambridge Economic History of Europe,* vol. 3, chaps. 1, 3, 6. Cf. Adam Smith, *Wealth of Nations,* bk. 3, chap. 4.

87. Sorokin, *Social and Cultural Dynamics,* vol. 3, chap. 8.

88. Ibid., vol. 2, chap. 3, esp. pp. 134–140, 150.

89. On the concept of preconditions, see W. W. Rostow, ed., *The Economics of Take-Off into Sustained Growth* (New York: St. Martin's Press, 1963).

90. Phyllis Deane, *The First Industrial Revolution* (Cambridge: Cambridge University Press, 1965), pp. 5–7, 10–11. Cf. Simon Kuznets, *Economic Growth and Structure* (New York: Norton, 1965), pp. 176–194.

91. Deane and Cole, *British Economic Growth,* p. 38.

92. Ibid., p. 285. Except for the two World War periods, the annual rate of growth per head, though fluctuating, generally exceeded 1 percent after the end of the eighteenth century. Uncertainty attends estimates of population change in eighteenth-century England and Wales, though not enough to modify the findings. See Larry Neal, "Deane and Cole on Industrialization and Population Change in the Eighteenth Century," *Economic History Review* 24 (1971):643–647; and Cole's rejoinder, ibid., pp. 648–652.

93. Smith, *Wealth of Nations,* p. 305.

94. Ibid., pp. 70, 73–74, 89–90, 200, 202, 205–206, 327–329. See my "Adam Smith's Theory of Economic Growth," *Southern Economic Journal* 25 (1959):397–415; 26 (1959):1–12.

95. R. M. Hartwell, "The Causes of the Industrial Revolution: An Essay in Methodology," *Economic History Review* 18 (August 1965):180. Under the heading of "forces making for growth" are included improved organization and technology, expanding resources and population, invention and its diffusion, growing demand, changes in society and its values, but "no great acceleration in capital formation." On the interaction of the Industrial Revolution and population growth, see J. R. Hicks, *Value and Capital* (Oxford: Clarendon Press, 1948), p. 302.

96. See *The Cambridge Economic History of Europe,* vol. 6 (1966), esp. chap. 1; William Woodruff, *Impact of Western Man* (New York: St. Martin's Press, 1967).

97. Simon Kuznets, *Modern Economic Growth* (New Haven: Yale University Press, 1967), esp. pp. 64–65, 352–353; and *The Economic Growth of Nations* (Cambridge: Harvard University Press, 1971), esp. p. 24. On underdeveloped countries see Kuznets, "Problems in Comparing Recent Growth Rates for Developed and Less Developed Countries," *Economic Development and Cultural Change* 20 (1972) :185–209.

98. D. N. McCloskey, "Did Victorian Britain Fail?" *Economic History Review* 23 (1970):446–459. On annual average income and the decline in its rate of increase after the 1880s, see Deane and Cole, *British Economic Growth,* pp. 329–331, also 282–284. The role of demand is stressed by Angus Maddison in *Economic Growth In The West* (New York: Twentieth Century Fund, 1964).

99. On changes in family living, see Faith M. Williams and C. C. Zimmerman, *Studies of Family Living in the United States and Other Countries,* U.S. Department of Agriculture Miscellaneous Publication no. 223 (Washington, D.C.: 1935); C. C. Zimmerman, *Consumption and Standards of Living* (New York: Van Nostrand, 1936), esp. chaps. 12–19; Hazel Kyrk, *A Theory of Consumption* (Cambridge, Mass.: Houghton Mifflin, 1923), chaps. 8–10, on the origin of living standards. See also J. F. Dewhurst et al., *America's Needs and Resources* (1955) and *Europe's Needs and Resources* (1961), both ¬ublished by the Twentieth Century Fund, New York.

100. The populations of North America and of Europe and the Soviet Union increased, respectively, about 75 and 230 millions between 1800 and 1900 and about 147 and 282 millions between 1900 and 1970.

101. In 1920 about 30 percent of the population in the developed world lived in places of 20,000 or more inhabitants; in 1960, 46 percent. The corresponding percentages for the underdeveloped world are 7 and 17. These figures and those in the preceding footnote are from United Nations publications. On the growth of cities, see also W. S. and E. S. Woytinsky, *World Population and Production,* chap. 4. In 1800, 3 percent of Europe's, 6.1 percent of Asia's, and 1.3 percent of the world's population lived in cities of 100,000 or more; the corresponding figures in 1930 were 29, 6, and 11 (ibid., p. 118).

102. On some of the forces at work, see D. E. Robinson, "The Importance of Fashions in Taste to Business History: An Introductory Essay," *Business History Review* 38 (1963):5–36, and "Fashion Theory and Product Design," *Harvard Business Review* 36 (1958):126–138; Leo Moutin, "The Sociology of Gastronomy," *European Community,* November 1967, pp. 10–13.

103. See E. W. Martin, *The Standard of Living in 1860* (Chicago: University of Chicago Press, 1942).

104. The factors mentioned are discussed by Ruth Mack in "Trends in American Consumption and the Aspiration To Consume," *American Economic Review* 46 (May 1956):55–68; see also Robert Ferber's comments in the same issue, pp. 84–86. Cf. W. L. O'Neill, *Women at Work* (Chicago: Quadrangle, 1972).

105. See, for example, Herbert Moller, "Youth as a Force in the Modern World," *Comparative Studies in Society and History* 10 (1967–1968): 237–260.

106. See A. C. Zijderveld, "Rationality And Irrationality In Pluralistic Society," *Social Research* 37 (1970):23–47; also R. Dahrendorf, *Class and Class Conflict in Industrial Society* (London: Routledge & Kegan Paul, 1963). See also, on the effects of decline in size of community, J. B. Quandt, *From the Small Town to the Great Community* (New Brunswick: Rutgers University Press, 1970).

107. See E. M. Earle, ed., *Makers of Modern Strategy* (Princeton: Princeton University Press, 1943), chaps. 3–5. Today, by contrast, civilians seem destined for mass slaughter by remotely controlled vehicles of destruction.

108. Joseph A. Schumpeter, *Capitalism, Socialism, and Democracy* (New York: Harper, 1942), p. 146, also pp. 143–155 and chap. 11.

109. More reliance was placed on the stick in Asia than in Europe. "The bamboo is the great moral panacea of China" observed an anonymous author in the *Edinburgh Review* in 1810; see vol. 16 (August 1810):488.

110. Nassau Senior, *Industrial Efficiency And Social Economy,* ed. S. L. Levy (New York: Holt, 1928), vol. 2, pp. 190–191, also p. 222 on tax. On p.

272 he said of the English: "The millions whom we have crowded into densely-peopled districts, are accustomed not merely to prosperity, but to constantly advancing prosperity." More symbolic of the situation of the common man in Senior's day is an account of his friend, financier Bingham Baring, who was struck on the hat with a stick by a nineteen-year-old ploughboy, for which offence the latter was hanged shortly thereafter. See S. L. Levy, *Nassau W. Senior, the Prophet of Modern Capitalism* (Toronto: Ryerson Press, 1943), p. 137.

111. See Barbara W. Tuchman, *The Proud Tower* (New York: Macmillan, 1966), esp. chap. 1; J. E. Cairnes, *Some Leading Principles of Political Economy Newly Expounded* (New York: Harper, 1874), pt. 2, chap. 5, secs. 6–9; G. Wallas, *The Great Society* (London, 1914), chap. 1; S. G. Checkland, *The Rise of Industrial Society in England, 1815–1885* (New York: St. Martins Press, 1965), and "Growth and Progress: The Nineteenth-Century View in Britain," *Economic History Review* 12 (August 1959):49–62; also G. W. Young, *Victorian England: Portrait of an Age* (London: Oxford University Press, 1961).

112. Barbara Tuchman describes 1890–1914 as "the culmination of a century of the most accelerated rate of change in man's record" (*Proud Tower*, p. xiv). Henry Adams observed in 1904 that there was in effect a "law of acceleration" that within a generation "would require a new social mind," one that "would need to jump" (*Education of Henry Adams*, chap. 24, p. 498).

113. Harold and Margaret Sprout, "The Dilemma of Rising Demands and Insufficient Resources," *World Politics* 20 (1968):664–693, 672.

114. Ibid., p. 673. The Sprouts cite many works, among them G. F. G. Masterman's *The Condition of England* (London, 1909) and Keynes's *The Economic Consequences of the Peace* (New York, 1920).

115. Tuchman, *Proud Tower*, p. 463. Confirmation of Kipling's pessimistic forecast is found in Joel H. Wiener, ed., *Great Britain: Foreign Policy and the Span of Empire*, 4 vols. (New York: McGraw-Hill, 1972), covering 1689–1971 and with an introduction by J. H. Plumb.

116. H. and M. Sprout, "Dilemma."

117. "The relative distribution of income, as measured by annual income incidence in rather broad classes, has been moving toward equality, with these trends particularly noticeable since the 1920s but beginning perhaps in the period before World War I." See Kuznets, *Economic Growth and Structure*, p. 260, also p. 275; also Clark, *Conditions*, chap. 12.

118. J. M. Keynes, *Essays in Persuasion* (New York: Harcourt Brace, 1932), pp. 358–374. "Assuming no important wars and no important increase in population, the *economic problem* may be solved, or at least be within reach of solution, within a hundred years. This means that the economic problem is not—if we look into the future—*the permanent problem of the human race*" (p. 366).

119. See Alexis de Tocqueville, *Democracy in America,* trans. Henry Reeve (London: Saunders and Ottey, 1836), passim; J. S. Schapiro, "Alexis de Tocqueville, Pioneer of Democratic Liberalism in France," *Political Science Quarterly* 57 (1942):545–563. On the development of American theory and practice of democracy, see, besides the many works of Richard Hofstadter, C. A. Beard and Mary Beard, *The Rise of American Civilization* (New York: Macmillan, 1930), chaps. 16, 22, and passim; and V. L. Parrington's literary history, *Main Currents in American Thought* (New York: Harcourt Brace, 1930).

120. S. N. Patten, *Development of English Thought,* pp. 6–10, 23–25; and *Essays in Economic Theory,* ed. R. G. Tugwell (New York: Knopf, 1924), pp. 337–338.

121. W. S. Knickerbocker, in his introduction to Arnold's *Culture and Anarchy* [1869] (New York: Macmillan, 1938), p. xix. See especially chaps. 2–3.

122. Ibid., chaps. 4–6 and conclusion.

123. Alvin Toffler, *Future Shock* (New York: Random House, 1970).

124. Parallel is what Lionel Trilling calls "the disenchantment of our culture with culture itself," manifest in the hostility of much literature to modern civilization. See his *Beyond Culture* (New York: Viking, 1965), p. 3. Cf. also R. S. Berman, *America in the Sixties;* and J. L. Dillard, *Black English* (New York: Random House, 1972).

125. See, for example, H. G. Moulton, *Income and Economic Progress* (Washington, D.C.: Brookings Institution, 1935); this was the last of a series of studies of America's capacity to produce and consume in 1929.

126. "Only an innovation in supply, such as the automobile, the radio, TV, or fractional horsepower motor could stimulate sufficient demand to shift the average propensity to consume leisure to significantly higher levels." So concluded George Fisk in *Leisure Spending-Behavior* (Philadelphia: University of Pennsylvania Press, 1963), p. 194. See also G. Katona, B. Strumfel, and E. Zahn, *Aspirations and Affluence* (New York: McGraw-Hill, 1971), pp. 10, 60–62, 65–68, 217 on discretionary buying, pp. 107, 109–112 on leisure and spending, and chap. 9 on the degree to which leisure in the form of early retirement is based on retirees' optimistic notions of what their incomes will be in retirement.

127. Katona et al., *Aspirations and Influence,* passim.

128. "The British Empire was maintained as long as lowly folk in the United Kingdom and in the colonies could be controlled and kept working at relatively low cost in money and violence. The British Empire became progressively insupportable as rising demands within Britain and resistance to imperial rule in the colonies coincided with escalating costs of maintaining Britain's historic role in international politics." H. and M. Sprout, "Dilemma," p. 692. See also Wiener, *Great Britain.*

129. H. and M. Sprout, "Dilemma," p. 693.

130. Harold and Margaret Sprout, "National Priorities: Demands, Resources, Dilemmas," *World Politics* 24 (1972):317.

131. Around 1960, the fifth of the population ranking lowest in income received only about 4 percent of pretax income in developed countries; the lowest two-fifths, 15 percent. See Kuznets, *Economic Growth and Structure,* p. 289. In 1970, about one person in eight lived below the "poverty level" in the United States. U.S. Bureau of Census, *Current Population Reports,* series P–60, no. 81, November 1971, p. 2.

132. See H. and M. Sprout, "National Priorities," pp. 305–309, 315.

133. Taira, "Consumer Preferences," pp. 37–38, 42–44. In Western Europe, declared family needs vary with international differences in income by country, but not in quite the same degree. See the Gallup Survey reported in *European Community,* April 1972, p. 10. On American aspirations, see A. H. Cantril and C. W. Roll, Jr., *Hopes and Fears of the American People* (New York: Universe Books, 1971).

134. See, for example, V. Pareto, *Cours d'économie politique* (Lausanne, 1896–1897), pp. 957–962, 994, 1008, 1012. In advanced countries the average income of the highest fifth of income receivers is about twelve times that of the lowest fifth. Kuznets, *Economic Growth and Structure,* p. 289.

135. Katona et al., *Aspirations and Affluence,* p. 14, also pp. 22–23, 196–200.

136. See Talcott Parsons, *The Structure of Social Action* (New York: McGraw-Hill, 1937), esp. pp. 89 ff., 151–152, 165, 235–241, 314–316, 337, 402, 718, 767–768.

137. Cf. Talcott Parsons, *Sociological Theory and Modern Society* (New York: Free Press, 1967), pp. 15, 187–188.

138. See Parsons, *Structure,* pp. 686–694.

139. See note 9 above.

140. See, for example, Milton Friedman, "Monetary Policy," *Proceedings of the American Philosophical Society* 116 (June 1972):183–196.

141. See, for example, Katona et al., *Aspirations and Influence,* pp. 11–13, 41–73, 165–201.

142. On time cost, see S. B. Linder, *The Harried Leisure Class* (New York: Columbia University Press, 1970), chaps. 1–3 on time and 4–5 on services. Complaint about the quality of life in the United States is reported in the Institute for Social Science *Newsletter* (University of North Carolina at Chapel Hill), spring 1972, p. 3.

143. See, for example, Georgescu-Roegen, *Entropy Law,* chap. 10.

144. For example, D. H. Meadows and associates, *The Limits to Growth* (New York: Universe Books, 1972). On limiting factors, see also Georgescu-Roegen, *Analytical Economics,* chap. 10; Bentley Glass, *The Timely and The Timeless* (New York: Basic Books, 1970), pp. 67–75.

145. See, for example, E. J. Mishan, *The Costs of Economic Growth* (New York: Praeger, 1967).

146. See L. J. Zimmerman, *Poor Lands, Rich Lands: The Widening Gap* (New York: Random House, 1965), chap. 2.

147. F. Y. Edgeworth suggested that some individuals have "greater capacity for happiness" than others. *Mathematical Psychics* (London: Kegan Paul, 1881), pp. 56–82.

148. It is now proposed to utilize drugs to induce "bliss" and do away with alienation. W. O. Evans, "Mind-Altering Drugs and the Future," *The Futurist* 5 (June 1971):101–104.

149. Owen, "Demand for Leisure."

150. See, for example, Linder, *Harried Leisure Class.*

151. See, for example, A. J. Lotka, *Elements of Physical Biology* (Baltimore: Williams and Wilkins, 1925), chaps. 21–22. See also Sorokin, *Social and Cultural Dynamics,* vol. 4, chap. 14.

152. M. Polanyi has noted that "our age overflows with inordinate moral aspirations." *Personal Knowledge* (Chicago: University of Chicago Press, 1958), p. 142.

153. See, for example, Robert Dahl, *A Preface to Democratic Theory* (Chicago: University of Chicago Press, 1956), p. 68. Cf. Socrates' observation in *Gorgias,* 502.

154. See my "Return to Thomas Hobbes?" *South Atlantic Quarterly* 68 (1969): 443–453. Cf. J. G. Gurley, "The Future of American Capitalism," *Economics and Business* 12 (1972):7–18.

155. It is doubtful that Kipling, at the time he wrote his ominous "Recessional" in 1897, really anticipated advent of the sunset of Britain's empire within a half century. A prescient Henry Adams did not foresee 1939 and the final collapse of West European world hegemony.

156. R. M. MacIver and C. H. Page, *Society* (New York: Rinehart, 1949); R. M. MacIver, *Social Causation* (New York: Ginn, 1942).

4

THE RESPECT REVOLUTION: FREEDOM AND EQUALITY

Lewis M. Killian

The themes of freedom and equality have been easy to discern in revolutions around the world for at least three centuries. These themes have had diverse referents. "Freedom" or "liberty" has meant liberation from feudal or monarchic despotism; from the rule of alien dynasties; from the despotism of economically powerful classes; and, more recently, from colonialism. It has signified freedom for nationalities, as in the case of the Poles and the Vietnamese; for ethnic, class, or sexual categories —black slaves, exploited workers, and oppressed women; and for individuals without regard to group identity, as the historic concept of "civil rights" implies. "Equality" has included among its referents equal participation in the political process; equitable treatment before the bar of justice; equal opportunity for access to education, work, medical services, public accommodations, and, broadly, to all the resources that make for material welfare. Freedom usually is weighted with political connotations, and equality, particularly since the elaboration of socialistic doctrines, with economic ones.

Liberty and equality are the best remembered, most often repeated parts of the great slogan of the French Revolution of 1789. The rallying cry in its totality was triadic, however: "Liberté, Egalité et Fraternité." The third term of this revolutionary formula may be taken to connote a social and psychological dimension that complements the political and economic ones. In the French Revolution itself the notion of "fraternity" was related to the concept of "the people," which, in turn, was integral to the novel, emerging spirit of nationalism. In conjunction with liberty and equality it implied not only the redistribution of political power and economic wealth but also a new source of pride, dignity, and respect: the "people-state," in which the "subject" became the "citizen."[1]

Thus even long-finished revolutions that may be viewed, in the broad sweep of history, as primarily political or economic had their social and psychological aspects. It is difficult to study the history of any revolution without concluding that, however much they might have emphasized their demands for political democracy or economic relief, the participants were also seeking *respect* for themselves and for the group in which they found their identity. In the revolutionary movements of the latter half of the twentieth century, the theme of respect has become the dominant one, in comparison with liberty and equality. It is inescapably evident that there is a spirit of revolution among the affluent, not just among the hungry. Yet even where revolutions are still closely related to economic deprivation, the theme of respect receives primacy in the ideology. Thus Adolf Gilly, an ideologist of revolutions in modern underdeveloped countries, declares, "The essence of revolution is not the struggle for bread, it is the struggle for human dignity."[2] The theme of respect, dignity, or pride plays a prominent part in both the rhetoric and the dynamics of such diverse movements as anticolonial movements in Asia, Africa, and Latin America; French Canadian nationalism; the Black Power movement ("Black is beautiful"); the defensive mobilization in the United States of ethnic groups that had seemed well along the road to assimilation; the rebellion of young people in what they often designate a "search for identity"; and the Women's Liberation movement.

Obviously this psychological dimension was present in revolutions of the past. It is equally evident that political power and economic welfare have not disappeared as important goals in modern revolutions. But the quest for identity and pride has achieved a new and greater importance in the motivation of modern revolutionaries and in the ideologies through which they justify their movements. Furthermore, the rise to prominence of this theme has its roots in both the successes and the failures of earlier revolutions, which gave rise to such phenomena as representative government, the doctrine of human rights, individualism, nationalism, egalitarianism, monopoly capitalism, socialism, imperialism, and racialism. Finally, the meaning of dignity as a revolutionary motive has undergone significant transformation in a world in which nationalism is no longer the wave of the future, as it was in the eighteenth century, and is viewed by many thinkers as a legacy of the past.

REVOLUTIONS AND SOCIAL CHANGE

The concept *revolution* has been used loosely up to this point, encompassing a wide variety of social movements. Some are easily recognized, in retrospect, as political revolutions; others would be classified by various analysts as reform movements or even social trends. Political scientists and historians who focus on political rather than social history endeavor to trace the careers of revolutions as specific historical episodes that culminate in the creation of a new political system through illegal means. Many include violence as an essential ingredient of their definition. Scholars who attempt to identify the revolutions they study in terms of temporally delimited political struggles recognize, however, that far-reaching, fundamental changes in social structure, in the economic system, and in dominant values usually accompany revolutionary transfers of political power. Moreover, they are constantly plagued by the difficulty of specifying the time when a revolution begins. Often the people who are making a revolution are not aware of what they are about, at least until their movement reaches the stage of irreconcilable confrontation with the established government. Just when any specific revolution "began" is always an elusive question.

Since specific revolutions are so often like the highly visible centers of vast social storms that are long in forming and extensive in their consequences, it is not surprising that "revolution" continues to be used to characterize profound but broad and sweeping social trends. This usage, while violating the criteria by which political revolutions are defined, is congenial to many social scientists and social historians. The Industrial Revolution is as well established in the conventions of historical analysis as are such political events as the French, American, Russian, and Chinese revolutions. The Cuban, Egyptian, and Algerian revolutions are modern instances of political revolutions but, in 1964, "a meeting of 32 noted social critics produced a policy statement entitled 'The Triple Revolution' . . . to call attention to changes in our society which were so revolutionary in magnitude that the society's current response to them was proving totally inadequate."[3] The composers of this statement identified three contemporary revolutions, in warfare, cybernation, and human rights. These technological, economic, legal, and value changes obviously are related to the social problems, the social discontent, and the social unrest that manifest themselves in multifarious ways not only in the United States but around the world. Comparable changes during earlier eras have been the soil out of which new human aspirations, collective strivings, and demands for structural changes in societies have grown. It seems that social changes that are collectively defined as generating social problems and social unrest are likely to be characterized by the term "revolution."

The concept of *social unrest* as elaborated by Herbert Blumer offers a means for reconciling the inconsistency between divergent uses of the concept "revolutionary," and between "revolutions" and "revolution." Blumer proposes that social unrest "signifies a rejection of the authoritative character of some portion of the social order and hence a reaching out for a new social arrangement."[4] Its primary significance lies in the fact that "it is a process by which people redefine or recast their world and so prepare themselves to act toward the world." He observes, "In the intricate interplay of factors in the formation of social unrest people come to revise the way in which they see given social objects and values, social practices, institutional arrangements, systems of authority, authoritative figures, and the social order itself. Parallel to such redefinitions people form new conceptions of themselves."[5]

Blumer argues that social unrest may eventuate in any of five lines of resolution: (1) an accommodated acceptance of established social arrangements; (2) a flight from these arrangements; (3) the creation of a transcendental world of belief that overshadows the existing order; (4) a resort to a life of hedonistic satisfaction within this order; or (5) collective and aggressive protest against established social relations.[6] Obviously, political revolutions constitute a subtype of only the last of these "lines of resolution." Hence, while specific, political revolutions may grow out of antecedent periods of social unrest, revolution as a condition analogous to social unrest is far more frequent and widespread than are revolutions as forms of resolution. The content and form of social unrest in a given society during a particular era do not dictate that it will eventuate in collective, aggressive protest, but this is always a possibility. To the extent that the definitions developed through social unrest in different societies are similar, some conclusions about the "spirit of revolution" in a given era may be derived despite differences in the lines of resolution. In short, we are not forced to await the verdict of history that a political revolution did occur before identifying the social-psychological beginnings that might lead to such a denouement. Ideas may be revolutionary without leading to revolutions. In both accomplished revolutions and in early stirrings of unrest, the way in which people are recasting their image of the world and their relationship to it may be discerned. Analysis of the themes of political revolutions that confront the governments of some nation-states may sensitize us to potentially revolutionary themes in other societies in which the threat of revolution appears remote.

THE REVOLUTIONARY SPIRIT

The Age of Enlightenment was also an Age of Revolution. The philosophical abstractions of Hume, Locke, Voltaire, Rousseau, Jefferson, and Paine were translated, however imperfectly, into action in the French and American revolutions. During the eighteenth century, even before modern developments in rapid communication, ideas flowed back and forth across continental frontiers, the English Channel, and the broad Atlantic Ocean. In the next century the spirit of nationalism helped inspire a virtual epidemic of revolutions in Europe and Latin America. In the twentieth century the teachings of Marx, Lenin, and, later, Mao, Che Guevara, and Frantz Fanon have been quoted by revolutionaries around the world. Although in ancient and medieval times movements that might be identified as revolutions may have been isolated from each other both geographically and ideologically, developments in science and technology brought an end to this isolation of revolutions. As early as the eighteenth century, diverse revolutions began to be marked by a kindred revolutionary spirit. The extent to which the world of the discontented has been made yet smaller is epitomized by the fact that the works of an otherwise obscure black psychiatrist and Algerian revolutionist, Frantz Fanon, translated from the French, have become "must" reading for poor blacks in the inner cities of the United States.[7] In the age of television, not only battles between national armies but the violence of revolutionary commandos and urban insurrectionists may be brought into the living rooms of millions of people.

If indeed there is a revolutionary spirit that is reflected in both political revolutions and social unrest in the waning years of the twentieth century, it is the aspiration for respect. As has been suggested above, this social-psychological dimension of liberty and freedom was coupled with the political and economic dimensions in earlier revolutions. It is a new revolutionary spirit, however, insofar as it has come to overshadow the political and economic dimensions both as one of the causes of social unrest and as a justification for collective protest.

It must be emphasized that what is being indentified here as the revolutionary "spirit" or "theme" is not to be taken as signifying the *cause* of revolution. Social discontent, social unrest, and collective protest reflect dissatisfaction with many features of the existing social order. Revolutionary manifestos usually include a catalogue of specific grievances. The overreaching theme of the movement constitutes a collective definition of the nature of the general problem. It denotes a conception of the character of the opposition as distinguished from its specific misdeeds. It also implies, however vaguely, the nature of the solution. The revolutionary spirit is typically expressed in slogans, which are not only shouted by rioters in the streets but are also manipulated by intellectuals as they construct the ideology of the movement.

The revolutionary spirit, not springing directly and automatically from specific grievances but emerging in a process of communication, is susceptible to communications from other social situations that may appear quite discrete and even dissimilar.

That the specific forms of oppression may not be identical is of little consequence to discontented people in different societies; they are still able to define the general nature of the oppressive forces in the same way. Thus the revolutionary spirit of a given era may be widely diffused in the form of slogans or overarching modes of analysis, as in the characterization of the plight of blacks in both Africa and the United States as consequences of "colonization."

POLITICAL LIBERTY, ECONOMIC WELFARE, AND RESPECT IN PAST REVOLUTIONS

The great, classical revolutions of the seventeenth and eighteenth centuries, the English, American, and French, are variously classified as "political," "democratic," "republican," and "bourgeois" revolutions. The central question each posed was, Who shall govern? They created models for popular government that, despite their obvious imperfections, have been praised by their inheritors and emulated by revolutionary movements in other lands, despite obvious dissimilarities in their situations. The French Revolution, in particular, symbolized the wedding of ideas of democracy with the spirit of nationalism in the concept of the people-state.

Economic historians, in attempting to sustain their thesis that the search for material welfare underlies all historical upheavals, have reminded us of numerous forms of economic deprivation existing prior to these revolutions. To demonstrate the existence of poverty, exploitation, and concentration of wealth in certain classes in any prerevolutionary period poses no great challenge. Yet it is recognized that the classic revolutions of Europe and America were bourgeois revolutions. It was in analyzing the background of the French Revolution that de Tocqueville advanced one of the first formulations of what has become familiar as "relative deprivation" and "the revolution of rising expectations." His observation that "the Revolution, though sponsored by the most civilized classes of the nation, was carried out by its least educated and most unruly elements" adumbrated another important generalization about social movements.[8] The fact that the most depressed classes may be vitally involved does not signify that they are the population segments most likely to initiate revolutions, or that their very real deprivation is somehow the true cause of revolutions. Nor did the success of these revolutionary movements benefit the lower economic classes nearly so much as it did the more affluent segments who not only had found reasons for discontent but also had felt strong enough to challenge the holders of political power.

Despite the diversity of the social, economic, and political strains that may have predisposed individuals of different classes to join in collective protest against old regimes, the slogans "liberty" and "equality" were rallying cries for all of them, and these slogans had very clear political referents. Regardless of their specific grievances—social, political, or economic—an overriding feature of life for the vast majority of people in western Europe in the eighteenth century was the feeling that they had no control over the governmental processes that determined their fate. Where vestiges of clerical power survived, the clergy appeared unresponsive to popular influence, torn in their allegiance only by the struggle between pope and king. To the extent that the nobility retained a share of power, their possession of it was validated by heredity. De Tocqueville said of pre-revolutionary France, "The nobility had deliberately cut itself off both from the middle class and from the peasantry . . . and had thus become like a foreign body in the State."[9] Where monarchy had become absolute, royal despots, benign or not, were separated from the people by the doctrine that they derived their power from God and not at all from their subjects. By their own definition they were alien to the people, not part of them. In many cases, royal dynasties were alien in a more literal sense: they were foreigners in parts of their own domains. Revolutionaries in France denounced Marie Antoinette as "the Austrian woman"; American rebels ascribed unwarranted significance to the fact that George III was "German."

The revolutionary spirit of political democracy came to be joined with another new theme—nationalism. Rupert Emerson had said of the emergence of the people-state, "The French Revolution presented the challenge . . . of a state which was no longer the king but the people, and thrust across the face of Europe the power of a nation in Arms."[10] After Napoleon's imperial dream was shattered, nationalism survived as a legacy of the French Revolution and continued as a theme of revolutions throughout the nineteenth century.

The revolutionary tradition that received collective definition in the English, American, and French revolutions of the seventeenth and eighteenth centuries thus centered on two concepts that were predominantly political in tone: democracy, the right of the people to govern themselves, even if through a constitutional monarchy or a republican government; and nationalism, the right of the people to collective self-determination of the nation-state that would constitute the political boundaries of their society. As late as the termination of World War I in the Treaty of Versailles, some of the peoples of Europe still were demanding the extension of the principle of self-determination to themselves, and Woodrow Wilson saw national self-determination as an integral part of his goal "to make the world safe for democracy."

The achievement of political liberty and equality freed "the people" from the oppression and superiority of "higher orders" that claimed legitimacy through heredity or divine sanction. The fraternity of the nation-state bound all, from king or president to commoner and manual laborer, into a political unit in which all were equal in basic civil rights. At the same time that governments became, however incompletely, more responsive to the will of the people, the sense of respect underwent a transformation. The notion of the "rights of man" carried with it a corollary, "the dignity of man." To be a citizen rather than a subject implied a new self-conception, a source of self-esteem, that could cut across differences in socioeconomic status. The power and the glory of the nation-state, now perceived as a natural and mystical union of the people, became a wellspring of pride for even the most lowly placed patriot.

But freedom and equality were not, it is evident, distributed uniformly among the people. Inequality and injustice have continued to exist after every revolution. Different orders, particularly the bourgeoisie, benefited unequally from the political revolutions; moreover, democracy and nationalism facilitated the rise of the middle class and the growth of industrial capitalism.

The Industrial Revolution gave rise to new social classes and set the stage for a new form of social conflict, capital versus labor. Modern socialism developed as an ideology in response to this peaceful, technological "revolution." It must not be forgotten, however, that the growth of nationalism was as much a feature of the nineteenth century as was the spread of political democracy and the development of industrial capitalism.

A second wave of European revolutions in 1848 still shared the political definition of freedom and equality formulated in the "classic revolutions." The work of political liberation remained far from complete even after these revolutions, but a new revolutionary spirit became the dominant tone. Economic oppression came to be seen as even more important than political tyranny as a barrier to freedom and equality. With the elaboration and spread of socialistic doctrines the economic connotations of freedom and equality surfaced.

What Engels and Marx observed in England was a state that was the most advanced of the new people-nations in political democracy and in industrial capitalism and yet was marked by inequality, particularly in the economic realm. The transfer of government from kings and nobles to the people, as the nation, had not ended oppression there or in countries that had experienced violent revolutions. Certainly the lower classes of nations that had experienced political revolutions sensed that, no matter what the degree of political success, none of them had ushered in the promised utopia. Inequality and oppression still existed, but Marx and his followers gave them a new name: exploitation. The "oppressors" no longer were identified as an alien group who set themselves apart from the people by the very way in which they claimed the right to rule. Instead, the exploiters were politically of the people but separated from them economically by ownership of property. Political democracy did not produce liberty and equality as long as it was combined with capitalism. The former leaders of the people in the battle against hereditary privilege now were the enemies of freedom, of economic equality, and of respect. Yet there was no single, universal trend from dominance of the political theme to that of the economic. The Russian Revolution of 1917, although led by self-proclaimed Marxists, was not truly Marxist in character. It was soldiers and peasants, not an industrial proletariat, who were the troops of the revolution, and they were, in the last analysis, revolting against hereditary privilege, not capitalism.

The significance of fraternity, as embodied in the nation-state, also was reshaped by the winds of socialist doctrine. Emerson notes that during the era of political revolutions, before 1848, "the national principle was itself a revolutionary one, intimately bound up with the democratic aspirations of the masses for whom the troublesome bourgeoisie appeared as self-appointed spokesman."[11] Now the economic interpretation of injustice cast nationalism in the role of an enemy of freedom and equality. Even the people-state, dominated by the capitalistic class, was an instrument of exploitation. The "fraternity" of the new revolutionary spirit was expressed in the slogan, "Workers of the world, unite!" Less than a century after the French Revolution seemed to usher in an age of nationalism, the internationalism of the working classes was proclaimed as the next objective in the world's quest for utopia.

The ideal of national self-determination continued to coexist with the revolutionary myths of socialism. To the Marxist ideologist, the bourgeois class was the obdurate defender of nationalism, as the state, under its control, had become the instrument of exploitation. The proletariat, victims of capitalism and its logical enemies, also proved unable to free themselves of the bonds of nationalism, even while they mouthed the slogans of international communism. The collapse of the Second International with the outbreak of World War I dashed the hopes of Marxist leaders that nationalism had lost its allure for the working class. History was to show that the nationalism born at the end of the nineteenth century would gain even greater vitality during the twentieth, despite both its bloody consequences and the challenge of new ideologies.

The clash of nations in arms in the First World War appeared to many observers as a sign that nationalism had become essentially a destructive and oppressive force. Although Wilson still sought to extend the democratizing effects of nationalism through the principle of self-determination, he dreamed of a new level of political unity, expressed in the idea of the League of Nations. The aggressive nationalism of Germany, Italy, and Japan, threatening the entire world during the second Great War, marked the failure of the League of Nations but did not destroy the dream of "one world." The horrors of that war, culminating in the dropping of the first atomic bomb by the nation that proclaimed itself the champion of democracy, lent greater strength to the conviction that unrestrained nationalism would lead to death, not to freedom and equality. The United

Nations nevertheless constituted a parliament of independent nations, and the superpowers that created it retained an iron grip on their national sovereignty through the veto. Yet this newest world organization, with its declaration of the universal rights of man, represented the second attempt during the twentieth century to usher in an age of internationalism. At the same time, the ideology of international socialism continued to offer its challenge to the value of nationalism despite the very obvious vitality of nationalistic sentiments in socialist societies. The conflict between Tito and Stalin and, later, the rivalry between the USSR and the People's Republic of China were clear indications that socialism in practice fell far short of the internationalism that its theory proclaimed.

Despite the reality of technological progress and the illusions of political and economic progress, the second half of the twentieth century has not appeared to be a period of peace and social order. Movements of protest continue to erupt in every quarter of the globe, emphasizing the old themes of liberation from political repression, relief from economic inequality, and the right to self-government. The theme of nationalism, rather than diminishing, appears in a revitalized form. Peace between nations is disrupted by "wars of national liberation," with the insurgents praising socialism and denouncing capitalist imperialism. The internal order of self-proclaimed democratic nations is threatened by movements that are labeled "nationalistic," black nationalism in the United States being the prototype. The concept of the Third World suggests a rejection, by peoples still striving for respect, of the internationalist dreams of both the communist powers and the "free world." The resurgence of ethnicity among the relatively affluent descendants of poor immigrants in the United States suggests that neither the dream of one world nor that of "one nation, indivisible" satisfactorily embodies the theme of fraternity. The politically oppressed and the economically deprived experience discontent that seems to have obvious sources. But today, as in the past, beyond liberty and affluence lies *respect*. The quest for respect is dominant in the revolutionary spirit of the modern era.

RESPECT AND ANTICOLONIALISM

The revolutionary doctrines of democracy, nationalism, and then socialism were born in Europe. They were quickly carried to other continents by European settlers, particularly to North America where the American Revolution preceded the French. With the aid of industrial capitalism the new nation-states were able to extend their power and influence to all the inhabited continents. The political revolutions spanning the period from the American to the Russian Revolution made anachronisms of emperors, but they did not bring an end to imperialism. National imperialism supplanted dynastic imperialism.

To the peoples of "the world beyond Europe" the onward march of nationalism, even that of the democratic nations, appeared in the dominant guise of colonialism. The armies, the missionaries, the investors, the administrators, the technicians, and the merchants of the imperialist nations invaded their lands and disrupted their distinctive, traditional patterns of existence. Even in cases where white European colonists achieved political emancipation in the name of democracy, the benefits of their revolutionary movements were not extended to the natives. Thus Pierre Van den Berghe characterizes not only the Republic of South Africa but also the United States, during most of its history, as "*Herrenvolk* democracies," parliamentary regimes "in which the exercise of power and suffrage is restricted, *de facto,* and often *de jure,* to the dominant group."[12] Naked political domination by aliens prevailed in the colonial possessions of the great powers. Although at Versailles the principle of self-determination was being extended to numerous European nationalities, the colonies of the defeated Germans and Turks were treated almost as spoils of war. Mandated territories under the League of Nations remained, de facto, in colonial bondage. Economic imperialism and "gunboat diplomacy" kept even nominally independent nations, such as China and Cuba, in a semicolonial status. The policy of white European and American governments toward these subordinate peoples was that while democracy would be good for them, they were not yet ready for self-government. Under even the most benevolent colonialism, government was of and for the people, but not *by* them.

Politically, colonialism, no matter what its form, still incorporated the hierarchical principle against which millions of white Europeans had rebelled. Individual civil liberties were modified to secure the safety and freedom of members of the colonial ruling class and to prevent the development of subversive movements. Suffrage was nonexistent or was differentially extended to strata defined by the colonial government. The most ambitious effort to extend political democracy to colonized peoples was the French assimilationist policy of incorporating some of its colonies into metropolitan France and conferring equal rights of citizenship upon the colonists. Yet even then European and native colonists were elected to separate "colleges" in the Assembly, with different powers. Frantz Fanon wrote bitterly in 1959: "In the French National Assembly eighty Algerian deputies have seats. But today this serves no purpose."[13] Algeria ended as a model not of national assimilation but of successful anticolonialist revolt.

Even where nations appeared politically independent or where colonial powers attempted to combine democracy with imperialism, economic exploitation loomed as a barrier to equality. In the "banana republics" of Latin America and the European quarters of Asian cities the disparity between the wealth of the colonizers and the poverty of the masses of the colonized made inequality visible. In a world in which the nationalism and industrial capitalism of Europe and North America had extended far-reaching imperialist tentacles, a wide range of non-European peoples perceived themselves as sharing a common plight. The cry of the natives of the Portuguese colony of Mozambique, "Strangers, get out!" was part of a chorus that included the demands of citizens of supposedly independent nations in South America and the Caribbean, "Yanqui, go home!" Discontent linked to political domination, where it clearly existed, and to economic exploitation, was traced with growing conviction to yet a third factor that is inescapably linked with the theme of respect: race. As George Lensen expressed it:

> In the 1940's and 1950's the people of the world beyond Europe found a common denominator in anticolonialism and, because colonialism had been predominantly Western, in anti-Westernism. Many Westerners would have slept less soundly had they been aware of the intensity with which the majority of mankind hated their white skin. The fact that discrimination was not peculiar to the West did not blot out the memory of personal and national humiliation suffered at the hands of white sahibs.[14]

While the political and economic tones remain strong in the chord that rallies modern people to movements of protest and revolution, the psychological note of respect has become dominant. The ideologists of anticolonialism continue to decry political oppression and economic exploitation. They make it clear, however, that no amount of freedom and equality, political and economic, can be sufficient without the eradication of psychological colonialism.

In lands in which national economic freedom requires dismantling the superstructure of Western capitalism, some form of socialism offers itself as the only feasible course. Marx remains an important prophet for their revolutionary leaders. But it is the spirit of the early Marx, who wrote of alienation as the laborer's loss of his sense of self through loss of control of his work, and of psychologists and philosophers concerned with the selfhood of the individual, that leavens the modern tradition of revolution more significantly than does the economic theory of *Capital*. The rise to prominence in the twentieth century of the varieties of psychoanalytic theory and of existentialist philosophy presaged the emergence of a new revolutionary spirit.

The appeal of the psychological dimension of this spirit is symbolized by the fact that a psychiatrist, Frantz Fanon, became in his short lifetime one of the foremost ideologists of the Third World. His book *The Wretched of the Earth* is characterized by its American publishers as "a manifesto for the Third World"; in 1972 it was listed by a black bookstore owner in Chicago in a "must" reading list for blacks in the United States. It is an analysis, against the background of the Algerian war of national liberation, of how colonized people must go about achieving decolonization, creating a nation, overcoming the pitfalls of the "neocolonialism" of the native bourgeoisie, and creating a national culture. The nation is to Fanon, the psychiatrist, not an end in itself, politically or economically. It and the struggle for its creation are the vehicle for the psychological redemption of oppressed individuals. He totally rejects Europe and condemns it for its crimes, "of which the most horrible was committed in the heart of man, and consisted of the pathological tearing apart of his functions and the crumbling away of his unity."[15] His analysis is self-consciously Marxist, but he goes beyond Marx because of the importance he sees in race. Thus he declares, "In the colonies the economic substructure is also a superstructure. The cause is the consequence; you are rich because you are white, you are white because you are rich. This is why Marxist analysis should always be slightly stretched every time we have to do with the colonial problem."[16] At the outset, he proclaims his concern with a goal that is more psychological than it is political or economic. Thus of decolonization he says, "At whatever level we study it . . . decolonization is quite simply the replacing of a certain 'species' of men by another 'species' of men. Without any period of transition, there is a total, complete, and absolute substitution. It is true that we could equally well stress the rise of a new nation, the setting up of a new state, its diplomatic relations, and its economic and political trends."[17]

It is in Fanon's first book, *Black Skin, White Masks: The Experience of a Black Man in a White World,* that he states most directly his conception of what revolutionary wars of national liberation are, and should be, about. His theme, he says, is "the disalienation of the black man."[18] Disalienation, the achievement of respect, is not something that can be gained by the granting of freedom and equality, political and economic, by the oppressors, for the problem has become that the oppressed is his own oppressor. Fanon reflects the fact that the psychologists have joined the philosophes and the political economists in the academy of revolutionary philosophers when he writes:[19]

> The analysis that I am undertaking is psychological. In spite of this it is apparent to me that the effective disalienation of the black man entails an immediate recognition of social and economic realities. If there is an inferiority complex, it is the outcome of a double process:
>   –primarily, economic:
>   –subsequently, the internalization—or better, the epidermalization—of this inferiority.

Earlier he says, "At the risk of arousing the resentment of my colored brothers, I will say that the black is not a man. . . . I propose nothing short of the liberation of the man of color from himself."[20]

In his prescription for how this liberation is to be achieved,

Fanon emphasizes two factors: violence and nationalism. His words on the functions of violence for the individual and for the emerging nation give a new and chilling connotation to the revolutionary themes of respect and fraternity. "At the level of individuals," he says, "violence is a cleansing force. It frees the native from his inferiority complex and from his despair and inaction; it makes him fearless and restores his self-respect."[21] Of the effect of the violence of wars of national liberation on the collective level, he writes:

> The mobilization of the masses, when it arises out of the war of liberation, introduces into each man's consciousness the ideas of a common cause, of a national destiny, and of a collective history. In the same way the second phase, that of the building-up of the nation, is helped on by the existence of this cement which has been mixed with blood and anger.[22]

Certainly violence is not new to revolutions, and it has been shown that in the classic political revolutions the idea of the nation has been closely linked with both fraternity and democracy. The violence of modern revolutions in the Third World still could be viewed as only incidental to the task of achieving freedom and equality, and colonial nationalism might be viewed as simply an extension of the spirit of nationalism to the world beyond Europe.

But the sort of analysis of revolutionary nationalism that Fanon presents, and the fact that colonialism has been so closely correlated with the intrusion of the white race and the imposition of Euro-American culture, both suggest that this new round of revolutions can be better understood if the focus is on the psychological dimension rather than on the political or economic. Rupert Emerson suggests:

> To people emerging from imperial overlordship the major immediate contributions of nationalism are a sense of independent worth and self-respect and a new social solidarity to replace the traditional bonds. It is the sword and shield of those who are achieving independence. From being "natives" they rise to the honorable title of nationals. Through national self-assertion they achieve the spiritual satisfaction of demonstrating that they can make their own the forms on which the superior powers pride themselves.[23]

As Emerson is careful to point out, colonial nationalism does not reject the material welfare that Western culture offers, despite the fact that this nationalism is accompanied by the glorification of a real or mythical national heritage. As in earlier revolutions, the leaders in this new round have not come from the most depressed classes. Fanon did not live out his life as a pidgin-speaking black laborer in Martinique; he went to France as a young man to study medicine. His *Black Skin, White Masks* is to a large extend a cry of protest evoked by the discovery that in continental France, the homeland of which he was officially a citizen, he was not a Frenchman but a Negro.

In an earlier period the rising bourgeoisie in France and colonial America were distressed that they did not have political power. Where hereditary status was important, they also did not receive a full measure of respect. The desire to become citizens instead of subjects encompassed both of these sources of discontent. Today the subject who is also a "native" in the colonial situation experiences the lack of respect in a more acute way, particularly as he acquires the culture of the West. A large proportion of nationalist leaders in Asia and Africa received their advanced education in Europe or the United States, where they not only acquired Western skills but were exposed to the ideology of democracy and nationalism that is the residue of the classic revolutions. Emerson noted, "Having come to intimate acquaintance with the West, the nationalist leaders found peculiarly humiliating their rejection as equals by the Westerners who had taken over their countries."[24]

The Western nations also "exported revolution" in another significant way. In such initiatives as organizing and supporting guerrilla movements in countries occupied by the Germans and Japanese during World War II, the anti-Axis allies took some steps toward implementing the principle proclaimed in the Atlantic Charter of 1941: "The right of all people to choose the form of government under which they will live." It should not be forgotten, for example, that the United States, under the leadership of Franklin D. Roosevelt, supported Ho Chi Minh in his early struggles against both the Japanese and the French. The motives for these initiatives were mixed, including both genuine allegiance to Wilsonian principles and the desire to hasten the defeat of the Axis powers. Of even greater import is that after the war some of these guerilla movements continued as insurgent revolutionary movements that eventually came to define their erstwhile sponsors as opponents. Despite the verbal trappings of Marxism and the fact that most modern revolutions propose to inaugurate some variety of socialism, the revolutionary outbreaks since World War II have been more nationalist than socialist. The communist dream of international socialism has been overshadowed by nationalist aspirations. The dream of one world symbolized by the United Nations must, at the least, be deferred until the nonwhite peoples of the world feel that they can sit in its councils with a dignity that is no longer dimmed by the shadow of white colonialism. The persistent struggle of Yugoslavia to maintain its national identity in the shadow of Russian power, and the abortive revolts of the Hungarians and the Czechs, show that even in countries where socialism has been accepted the striving for respect as nations continues. The North Vietnamese leaders of their war of national liberation have consistently emphasized their intention to remain independent of both their Chinese and Russian supporters, even though they regard the white capitalist power, first of France, then of the United States, as the principal affront to their dignity. In the modern revolutionary era respect is tied even more closely to psychological identity than it is to political freedom or economic equality. Fraternity, as a source of collective pride and individual respect, stands today more than ever before as a significant element of the triadic slogan "Liberty, Equality and Fraternity."

THE RESPECT REVOLUTION IN THE UNITED STATES

The insurgent nationalism of peoples striving to overcome the heritage of colonialism has been analyzed as a symbol of the importance of respect in the modern spirit of revolution. Even in some newly created nations, the quest for respect as nationals must compete with other group loyalties, which often give rise to even newer nationalist movements. R. L. Sklar has observed, "Tribalism is the red devil of contemporary Africa."[25] Ironically, he then proceeded to argue that the assumption was questionable. His article, published in 1966, was entitled "The Contribution of Tribalism to Nationalism in Western Nigeria."

Only a few years later the tribal and religious loyalties of the Ibo peoples almost destroyed the new nation of Nigeria. The Bengali Muslims united with their co-religionists in the western portion of British India to create an independent Pakistan, but two decades later their own tribal loyalties and pride resulted in revolution and the creation of Bangladesh.

Movements of collective protest that reflect the spirit of the respect revolution are not confined, however, to the natives of areas emerging from colonial domination and seeking to achieve national independence, unity, and pride. Indeed, the term *tribalism* recently has come to be applied to divisive trends in societies in which democracy and nationhood appeared to have been firmly established and deeply cherished. Thus an editorial in the *New York Times* of 26 November 1972 lamented, "The fall of Premier Gaston Eyskens's Belgian Government after ten months in office provides another grim reminder that tribalism and ethnic fragmentation are in ascendancy in nearly every section of our world. It was the old feud between Flemings and Walloons that upended Mr. Eyskens as it had so many of his predecessors."[26] A few weeks earlier the veteran black civil rights leader Bayard Rustin had deplored the Black Power movement in these words: "By drawing a shell of race sensitivity around blacks, black power has infected the rest of society with what might be described as a 'new tribalism'."[27] Harold Isaacs has characterized the return to intraethnic solidarity as "the retribalization of American society."[28]

A kinship between the open insurgency of the natives of many developing societies and the social movements of some population segments in affluent, developed nations is suggested also by the frequent reference to these movements as "nationalistic." Black and Chicano nationalism in the United States, French-Canadian nationalism, and Croatian nationalism in Yugoslavia all denote tendencies toward differentiation, pluralism, or even separatism rather than strivings toward integration within the bonds of the nation. In the United States pluralistic goals are competing with assimilationist goals in the minds of racial and ethnic groups with a vigor that threatens the ideal of "one nation, indivisible." The sons and daughters of people who desperately wanted to be viewed as "Negro-Americans" now demand that they be called "Black Americans," "Afro-

Americans," or even simply "Blacks." The grandchildren of immigrants who wished to divest themselves of the stigma of being "hyphenated Americans" are beginning to place a new emphasis on their Italian, Polish, Jewish, or Mexican heritage.

In the case of black, Indian, and Mexican Americans, there is enough evidence of persistent political and economic inequality to suggest that political and economic goals would suffice to explain their continuing protest. Even then, there is so much evidence of progress that many analysts feel compelled to fall back on the concepts of "relative deprivation" and "the revolution of rising expectations" to explain the vigor of collective protest among these groups. Harder to account for is the fact that the ideology of the black protest movement has shifted so markedly away from integration as a goal. Even more perplexing is the resurgence of emphasis on ethnic identity among more affluent and powerful white groups. It may be postulated that it is the nature of the nationalism that grew out of the American Revolution that produced conditions conducive to the current trend toward pluralism. The manner in which the ideal of democracy was implemented in practice, and those changes that are vaguely subsumed under the notion of "mass society," have combined with the nationalism of 1776 to produce what Orin Klapp has called "the incredible rebellion."[29] Klapp includes in this rebellion not only protests of "the economic and political have-nots" but the "hippie rebellion" and movements of the radical right, rooted in the middle classes. Why does the beacon light of equal, "first-class" citizenship, defined by the Bill of Rights and subsequent amendments to the Constitution, shine less brightly than it once did for so many Americans?

THE MAKING OF THE "AMERICAN"

The Revolution of 1776 started out as a movement of the diverse inhabitants of thirteen separate English colonies to gain rights that certain of them claimed as British subjects. It was transformed into a war to create a new nation. It culminated in the formation of a politically unified republic with a constitution that codified the ideas of democracy derived from the philosophy of the Enlightenment.

Like other colonial revolutions, this one created not only a nation but the idea of a new type of being, the "American."

Although in prerevolutionary times the term "American" may have differentiated the colonial Englishman from his fellow citizen in the homelands, the inhabitants of the colonies were not all Englishmen. They were a diverse lot differentiated by varieties of European culture, by religion, by language, and, in the case of the Africans and Indians, by race. The dominant group, politically and economically, however, was comprised of people who considered themselves "British." A little-known aspect of this early American pluralism is described in Glenn Weaver's account of the long controversy of Benjamin Franklin with the Pennsylvania Germans.[30] The great patriot mistrusted both the business ethics and the political loyalty of these peaceable settlers, who were inclined more toward the pacificism of the Quakers than to the aggressive expansionism of the English-speaking farmers and merchants who were in constant conflict with the Indians and the French. Franklin not only saw the Germans as a political bloc with interests inimical to those of the English colonists, but also bitterly disparaged their non-English ways.

The outbreak of conflict with the British army created a new axis of identity. The British became the enemy, and the English loyalists were despised as Tories. Those inhabitants of the colonies who supported the Revolution were transformed into "patriots" and "Americans" whatever their origin. Thus Weaver observes:

> During the eighty-four years of Franklin's lifetime the Pennsylvania Germans had undergone a long process which had made "Americans" of them. From a timid, misunderstood, and misunderstanding national minority they had become accepted by English-speaking Americans, and although they succeeded in preserving much of what was good in their own culture, they came to accept the dominance of the English element in what is "American." The Germans and Franklin, in the course of long association, had come to stand on the common ground of American nationality.[31]

This common ground, for all its promises of freedom and equality for men of all conditions save slaves and Indians, nevertheless had firm roots in English culture. At the time of the very birth of the nation there emerged the theme of assimilation that Milton Gordon has called "Anglo-conformity." Gordon says of the founding fathers: "There is no reason to suppose that they looked upon the fledgling country as an impartial melting pot for the merging of the various cultures of Europe or as a new 'nation of nations,' or as anything but a society in which, with important political modifications, Anglo-Saxon speech and institutional forms would be standard."[32]

And standard they became, notwithstanding their modification through years of separation from "Mother England" and the infusion of successive waves of non-English immigrants into the population. One of the important implications of democracy throughout the history of the United States has been that every individual citizen should enjoy the opportunity to become as free and as equal as any other American, but at the price of giving up any obtrusively "un-American" values and ways, no matter how prized. As Gordon noted, acculturation has been a two-way process to a significant extent only in the area of religion, and then only in respect to the three principal faiths brought from Europe.[33] For members of the colored races, Americanization has been a chimerical goal and an unreasonable demand, for the unspoken modifier of the label "American" is "white." Traditionally, differences from the ideal of the white, culturally Anglo-Saxon, Protestant, Catholic, or Jewish American have been sources of embarrassment or even shame, not of pride. The respect revolution in the modern United States is, in part, a reaction to Anglo-conformity.

During the tumultous decade of the 1960s the "incredible rebellion" included among its targets not merely the so-called WASP but the "middle-class white American." Values characterized as middle-class were denounced not only by many blacks but by white college students from middle-class families. Yet for an ever-increasing proportion of the population to see themselves as comfortably ensconced in an almost universal middle-class would seem to represent the fulfillment of the promise of equality contained in the concept of a democratic, "open-class" society. The notion of the allocation of civil and political rights on the basis of social class is as repugnant to the professed ideals of American democracy as is their allocation on the basis of race, religion, or national origin. Why, then, should encouragement to move upward in class status be perceived as an oppressive demand rather than as a valuable opportunity?

The perceptive analysis by T. H. Marshall of citizenship and social class in Britain serves well to explain this anomaly.[34] As their English cousins were to do by successive acts of reform over a period of two centuries, the founders of the American republic sought through the Constitution to abolish the vestiges of a class system based on a hierarchy of hereditary status. As Marshall contends, citizenship as ''a status bestowed on those who are full members of a community'' undermined the inequality of the medieval class system.[35]

Marshall saw citizenship as evolving over three centuries in the Anglo-Saxon world. At the forefront of development in the eighteenth century were civil rights, involving the freedom of the citizen; in the nineteenth, political rights to equal participation in government; and in the twentieth, social rights, aimed at the abatement of economic inequality and its social concomitants. Achievement of social rights might even involve the abridgement of traditional ''freedoms,'' as laws restricting the powers of employers and of the freedom of the *individual* worker to contract for his labor outside the framework of collective bargaining made evident. By the dawn of the twentieth century the realities of inequality in politically democratic societies had made evident the ultimate contradiction between freedom and equality as absolutes, long pointed out by philosophers.

Marshall expressed this contradiction in saying, ''In the twentieth century, citizenship and the capitalist class system have been at war.''[36] This was a second type of class, different from the medieval or feudal type. ''Class differences are not established and defined by the laws and customs of society . . . but emerge from the interplay of a variety of factors related to the institutions of property and education and the structure of the national economy.''[37]

Implementation of the spirit of social rights, primarily through the economic nexus, did not eradicate class inequality although it alleviated its harshest material consequences. It reduced the proportion of the population who experienced abject poverty, unrelieved by systematic public aid. In raising the wage levels of those workers protected by union power or minimum wage laws, it made upward mobility a continuing reality for millions of workers and their children. At the same time, the technology of mass production brought a vastly increased range of products into the reach of people no longer forced to display the uniforms of low status at all times. Under this type of class system, Marshall says:

> Class cultures dwindle to a minimum, so that it becomes possible, though admittedly not wholly satisfactory, to measure the different levels of economic welfare by reference to a common standard of living. The working classes, instead of inheriting a distinctive though simple culture, are provided with a cheap and shoddy imitation of a civilization that has become national.[38]

Thorstein Veblen foresaw the effects of this ideal of an equally accessible, national culture, with its emphasis on individual mobility, in his concept of "conspicuous consumption." Even in a theoretically egalitarian society, material possessions not only served an economic, welfare function but also possessed a psychic significance. The sociologist Michael Lewis has described a further consequence of the growing importance of this psychic function: the development of the "status-market." This, he says, "is a device that caters to widespread aspirations for individual mobility by literally *selling* the illusion of personal success without regard to the quality of actual individual achievements."[39]

Here was not only a new structure of opportunity but also a new demand for conformity. For nearly two centuries in the United States, the seemingly endless reaches of the frontier and the constant expansion of commercial and industrial capitalism lent luster to opportunity and softened the harshness of the demand for upward mobility. Even the early ethnic groups— Germans, Scotch-Irish, French Huguenots, and others—found ethnic as well as class assimilation made easier by the reality of opportunity in the young nation, and many disappeared into an undifferentiated category of (white) "old Americans" that spanned the whole class structure. That their gains were often paid for with the labor and the blood of Indians, blacks, Mexicans, and Chinese was glossed over or justified in the name of "national progress." After the Civil War the growth of industry and the cities made "the immigrant experience" of new white ethnic groups amenable to interpretation as proof of the genuine "openness" of American society.

The pressure for upward class mobility differed from that for Anglo-conformity, for its weight was felt not only by the ethnic and racial minorities but also by those Americans who fit, by ascription or achievement, into the white dominant group. In some respects it bore even more heavily on them. Popular racism might offer a ready explanation of the failure of blacks or Mexicans to move up in the de facto class system that existed in America despite the rhetoric of egalitarianism and the absence of an institutionalized class system. Even after the spread of scientific theories of racial equality in intellectual circles, white liberals could find an explanation for racial inequality that did not challenge the premise that the nation was essentially egalitarian. This was the emphasis on the prejudice and discrimination of individual bigots, particularly those concentrated in the South, as the prime cause of the various forms of deprivation suffered by blacks.

Such explanations were not so easily accepted in the case of the nonachieving white, particularly after so many white ethnic groups seemed to climb out of their early minority status, proving that even the despised greenhorn could succeed in America if he worked hard. Neither racial inferiority nor race prejudice served to explain the poverty of the white person who failed to be upwardly mobile in a society that offered opportunity for all. Some personal, moral defect must account for his "failure," for his uncouth culture and his poverty. This attitude was adumbrated in the widely felt contempt for "po' white trash" in the antebellum South, which unabashedly denied freedom and equality to blacks while claiming that slavery created even greater opportunities for whites. It was found to be still strong in a southern community long after slavery had been abolished. Davis and Gardner, in *Deep South,* found the "lower-lower" class of whites characterized as "shiftless," "immoral," and "no-count" even by "upper–lower-class" whites who felt that they themselves, even though poor, were still "striving."[40] Lewis concludes that, even in an affluent America committed, since 1932, to the philosophy of the welfare state, the stigmatization of poverty continues as an "unapplauded" consequence of the credo of egalitarianism combined with the fact of inequality. He observes:

> We interpret the indicators of poverty in terms of our assumptions
> about opportunity and just reward; and we therefore conclude that

these indicators mean that the poor are poor because of their ineptness, their laziness, and their general lack of moral fiber.[41]

Thus, in view of the pressure for middle-class conformity and
upward mobility, one of the most remarkable aspects of the
"incredible rebellion" is the rejection by such a wide variety of
discontented Americans of the symbols of "middle America."
It is not just that many blacks have stopped straightening their
hair and have started to defend as virtues what were traditionally viewed as the pathological traits of lower-class black culture:
"street language," soul food, bizarre dress styles, and even the
one-parent family. Even a short tour of an Ivy-league campus
confronts the visitor with hundreds of white youth who, regardless of background, seem to have adopted both the dress of the
poor and the language of the tavern brawler. The professed
"career" plans of many emphasize their wish to avoid the very
routes to "success" that their parents fought to follow. The traditional values of Americans who have prided themselves not
only on the symbols of their success but on their moral respectability repeatedly are affronted by Americans asserting their right
to be different rather than their desire to conform to these
values. This is, in essence, a new version of the quest for respect.

THE SIGNIFICANCE OF THE BLACK REVOLUTION

This new revolutionary spirit is manifest in diverse movements
and obviously has multifarious roots. Ralph H. Turner has proposed that the unifying theme in current conceptions of injustice is "violent indignation . . . over the fact that people lack a
sense of personal worth—that they lack an inner peace of mind
which comes from a sense of personal dignity or a clear sense of
identity."[42] This is, obviously, another statement of the theme
of respect. He finds the new views this theme expresses most
fully embodied in the doctrines propounded by the youthful
constituents of the New Left. Prior to, and strongly influencing,
the New Left, however, were the tumultuous events of what has
come to be identified as "The Negro Revolt" or "The Black
Revolution." Blacks have suffered deprivation in the areas of
political freedom, economic equality, and respect longer and
more severely than has any other segment of the American population. The "race problem" has been the most visible and per-

sistent domestic issue throughout the life of the republic. It may be postulated that the Civil Rights movement of the 1950s was the catalyst that stirred up and shaped the new sense of injustice as experienced by many other groups. Most important, in the career of the black protest movement, from victory in the school desegregation decision of 1954 through the civil rights phase to the present phase of black nationalism, may be clearly seen the interaction of the political, the economic, and the psychological aspects of freedom and equality.

The overthrow of the judicial principle of "separate but equal," with the accompanying denunciation by the Supreme Court of the injurious effects of segregation by race on "the hearts and minds" of black children, appears on superficial examination to address itself primarily and directly to the issue of respect. In actuality, the spirit in which the crucial cases were brought by the NAACP and the justifications used by the Court in its decisions bore a much closer relationship to the older concepts of individual civil liberties and equal opportunity than to the new theme of respect or dignity. Removal of the stigma of segregation was an instrument for maximizing these rights rather than an end in itself. The right that was affirmed was the right to equal educational opportunity unimpeded by differences in race, not the right to equal respect regardless of racial identity. The central question before the Court was, in its words, "Does segregation of children in public schools solely on the basis of race, even though the physical facilities and other 'tangible' factors may be equal, deprive the children of the minority group of equal educational opportunities?"[43]

In framing their answer (that "to separate them from others of similar age and qualifications solely because of their race generates a feeling of inferiority as to their status in the community that may affect their hearts and minds in a way unlikely ever to be undone") the justices relied heavily on social science evidence demonstrating this psychological damage.[44] Denying the conclusion of an earlier Court, in *Plessy* v. *Ferguson*, that laws requiring separation of the races "do not necessarily imply the inferiority of either race to the other," the Supreme Court of 1954 said, in effect, that to remind a person of his blackness was, in the United States, to make him feel inferior. It was to this implication that black nationalists later were to take exception, contending that it is *who* raises the question of race, and to what end, that is crucial rather than the fact of separation itself.

The famous *Brown* decision of 1954 also reflected the philosophy of opportunity for individual social mobility in the discussion of the importance of public education as a right of citizenship in the political community. After having reviewed the rather insignificant status of public education at the time of the adoption of the Fourteenth Amendment, Chief Justice Warren declared, "Today, education is perhaps the most important function of state and local governments."[45] He went on to say, "In these days, it is doubtful that any child may reasonably be expected to succeed in life if he is denied the opportunity of an education."[46] If, as has been argued above, "success" in the American tradition actually meant Anglo-conformity, then a question remained as to whether even unsegregated, equal education could offer a route to success for the black child so long as blackness was not accorded respect. This was another question that black nationalists were to raise as they rejected the goal of integration during the next decade.

There is a significant contrast between the liberal-humanitarian overtones of the Court's decision in 1954 and the direct consideration of the question of respect in the famous dissent of Justice Harlan in the case of *Plessy* v. *Ferguson,* in 1896.[47] It is important to remember that this case did not directly concern the opportunity of children to acquire the prerequisites for upward mobility in a white-dominated society. The issue in question, segregation in public transportation, might seem almost trivial in comparison with the value of education in a technological society. Yet, as Harlan perceived quite clearly at a time soon after the institution of slavery had been declared illegal, an issue more basic than the opportunity to *prove* one's personal worth was at stake. He recognized the social-psychological implications of the segregation law that the majority of the Court voted to uphold. So, without discussion of the intrinsic importance of public transportation and without recourse to social science evidence, he went to the heart of the issue of respect:

The arbitrary separation of citizens, on the basis of race, while they are on a public highway, is a badge of servitude wholly inconsistent

the civil freedom and the equality before the law established by the
Constitution.[48]

Elsewhere he said:

> What can more certainly arouse race hate, what more certainly
> create and perpetuate a feeling of distrust between these races, than
> state enactments, which, in fact, proceed on the ground that col-
> ored citizens are so inferior and degraded that they cannot be al-
> lowed to sit in public coaches occupied by white citizens?[49]

Thus Harlan enunciated, far in advance of his times, the
principle that freedom and equality included the right not to be
humiliated in a society supposedly dedicated to the principle
that "there is in this country no superior, dominant, ruling
class of citizens."[50]

While insisting that the Reconstruction amendments to the
Constitution did, quite literally, make the Constitution color-
blind and remove the basis for legal distinctions based on race,
this amazingly prescient jurist was not blind to the realities of
the American system of class and caste. While he denied the
power of the government to stamp a badge of inferiority on any
class of persons, he bluntly described the inferiority of blacks in
what remained a white society despite the extension of full citizenship to them. So he declared:

> The white race deems itself to be the dominant race in this country.
> And so it is, in prestige, in achievements, in education, in wealth
> and in power. So, I doubt not, it will continue to be for all time, if
> it remains true to its great heritage and holds fast to the principles
> of constitutional liberty.[51]

This remarkable and seemingly inconsistent statement suggests that although Harlan acted as a "strict constructionist" in
dissenting from the majority, he did not believe that the law
could ever give blacks a full measure of equality and respect.
Even though the Constitution might guarantee the free and
equal enjoyment of civil rights by blacks, and though it could
not be used to humiliate them, it could not confer prestige or
power on them.

The *Brown* decision of almost a century later, with its emphasis on education as a primary and essential qualification for so-

cial mobility, implied an assumption that the law could be instrumental in doing just this. Many blacks and their white liberal allies perceived this ruling as opening the way to Anglo-conformity and assimilation to a color-blind "middle America" through the removal of the barrier of racial segregation. With this handicap removed, thousands of blacks would rise to the level of their individual abilities and aspirations, becoming like middle- or upper-class white Americans in all but the physically identifying marks of race. These, supposedly, would come to be regarded as inconsequential, if not totally ignored, by both whites and blacks. "Blackness" as a personal characteristic would become only an unpleasant historical memento of the shameful years of slavery and then of segregation. "Nonwhite" Americans henceforth would be freed from the prison of color.

A modern black American revolutionary, James Boggs, has succinctly characterized this spirit in which the "integrationist" interpretation of the Constitution was initially acclaimed as revolutionary but subsequently reevaluated by the ideologists of Black Power:

> Sometimes a revolution starts because the people believe that the country in its present form can do more for them than it is already doing. So they go out and ask for these things which they call their rights under the system. If they get these rights and don't press for more, then the country has made a social reform. But if they don't get what they believe are their rights and they continue to fight for them, they begin to make a revolution.
>
> In the United States, following the Supreme Court decision of 1954, the Negro proceeded to do just this. They began demanding the rights which they felt the country had admitted were theirs and which many Negroes felt could easily be granted under the Constitution. But in the period since 1954, Negroes have found that every institution in the country, from the Constitution on down, cannot guarantee or give them the rights they are entitled to. . . . The myth that American democracy protects the rights of Negroes has been exploded.[52]

Despite evidence from public opinion polls that the majority of black Americans still respond favorably to the symbol "integration"; despite the continued emphasis of the NAACP on

the implementation of desegregation laws; despite denunciations of what they perceive as "black racism" by Negro leaders
such as Bayard Rustin, A. Philip Randolph, and Kenneth
Clark, the emergence of the Black Power movement is an historical reality. Activists whose behavior reflects their spirit have,
since 1964, precipitated most of the confrontations that have
shaped the public image of the racial crisis. Its ideologists, appearing first as brash challengers to the immensely popular
Martin Luther King, Jr., succeeded in putting the defenders of
integration as the paramount goal on the defensive. Its slogans
—"Black Power," "Black is beautiful," and "What time is it?
Nation time!"—drowned out the loving, harmonious refrain,
"Black and white together, we shall overcome!"

The story of the rise of the Black Power movement has been
told many times. Briefly, three factors contributed to the disillusionment of an indeterminate number of blacks, including
some of the most dedicated young civil rights workers, with the
strategy of interracial cooperation. First, even with the law on
the side of blacks and against segregation, white resistance to
change proved more adamant and pervasive than liberal optimism had predicted. Massive resistance emerged in the South.
Blacks perceived the efforts of the federal government to overcome this resistance as halting and half-hearted. When the civil
rights struggle moved into the North with an attack on de facto
segregation in schools, housing, and employment, white
resistance appeared. As during the period following the end of
Reconstruction in 1876, blacks again questioned the depth of
the commitment of white Americans to the ideals of democracy
when the color line seemed threatened. Not moral suasion, not
appeals to a legal structure that was controlled by whites, but
the development of *power* to demand change gained favor as
the requisite for achieving freedom and equality.

Second, as the legal barriers to black progress were partially
and imperfectly stripped away, the extent to which the white
dominance that Justice Harlan had described so frankly was
based on the structure of the economy became evident. The unemployment and underemployment that oppressed the residents of the burgeoning "black ghettos" of the North and
West caused a shift in attention from the segregation laws of the
South to the nationwide pattern of subtle, institutionalized discrimination. The conflict between political democracy and capi-

talism, so well analyzed by T. H. Marshall, was emphasized by an increasing number of black ideologists as more important than the contradiction between the "general valuations" reflected in the Declaration of Independence and the "specific valuation" underlying white supremacy that Myrdal had described as "An American Dilemma."[53] Whether blacks could hope to move up even in a politically democratic American system came under question. One black writer, Robert L. Allen, expressed this doubt.

> The argument for democratization of the American social system assumes that there is still room in the political economy for black people. But this overlooks, for instance, the fact that black unemployment normally is double the rate for whites, and in some categories it runs at several times the white jobless rate. The jobs which black workers do hold are largely the unskilled and semiskilled jobs which are hardest hit by automation. Government-sponsored retraining schemes are at best stopgap measures of limited value. . . . Integration thus fails, not because of bad intentions or even a failure of will, but because the social structure simply cannot accommodate those at the bottom of the economic ladder. Some individuals are allowed to climb out of deprivation, but black people as a whole face the prospect of continued enforced impoverishment.[54]

Drawing on the analogy of the plight of colonized peoples of Africa and Asia, Allen declared that black America is being transformed into a neocolonial people, which he characterized as follows:

> Under neocolonialism an emerging country is granted formal political independence but in fact it remains a victim of an indirect and subtle form of domination by political, economic, social, or military means. Economic domination usually is the most important factor, and from it flow in a logical sequence other forms of control.[55]

From this mode of analysis it is clear that the welfare implications of freedom and equality remain strong in the new ideology of black nationalism. The economic distress that the black population experiences so disproportionately even after numerous federal court decisions and two major civil rights laws, those of 1964 and 1965, has led to a muting of the political strains in their demand for liberty and equality.

Of greatest interest here is the third factor contributing to the diminishing appeal of integration as a goal. This is the attitude expressed in the notion of black nationalism and the revival of the concept of pluralism among black spokesmen. The pluralism of which they speak ranges from a voluntary and partial sort of separatism in which blacks would have the choice of segregating themselves in both private and public activities and yet would not be compelled to do so; through a form of political pluralism within the framework of the nation, with black-governed cities, a separate black political party, proportional representation, and such devices as the already extant congressional Black Caucus; and finally, to proposals for the formation of an independent black nation on the North American continent. These varied lines of activity have numerous political and economic implications, such as a political strategy based on the idea that the black vote can hold the "balance of power," black economic cooperatives, control of "community" schools, and the development of "Black Studies," but underlying all of them is a turning away from the value of becoming an undifferentiated part of the American nation.

This theme is not new in movements of black protest in America. Part of the motivation for its revival lies in despair over the possibility of making the United States, with its history of white dominance, truly color-blind. After pointing out that nationalism and separatism have been "ever-present undercurrents in the collective black psyche," Allen observed:

> In periods of social crisis—that is, when repression and terror are rampant or hopes of progress have been dashed—the resulting suspicion that equal participation is impossible becomes a certainty. Nationalist leaders and intellectuals come to the fore and assert that not only is racial integration not possible, it is not even *desirable*. Such an eventuality, they contend, would destroy the group's distinctive culture and its sense of ethnic identity.[56]

A critical question is whether the present thrust toward pluralism and black nationalism is just another temporary resurgence of an undercurrent, or whether it presages the dominance, for a longer, indeterminate time, of the theme of respect. That the latter may be the case is suggested by the fact that blacks see the United States as entering a second Reconstruction era within a span of a century, by the doubt as to whether the American economy still offers the same opportunity for economically depressed groups to move up that it once did, and by the growing sense among black Americans that they are part of a Third World that is colored, not white.

In their effort to formulate an ideology of Black Power in the book by that title, Stokely Carmichael and Charles V. Hamilton compare the experiences of blacks in America with those of colonized natives in Africa.

> In a manner similar to that of the colonial powers in Africa, American society indicates avenues of escape from the ghetto for those individuals who adapt to the "mainstream." This adaptation means to disassociate oneself from the black race, its culture, community and heritage, and become immersed (dispersed is another term) in the white world.[57]

This opportunity they define as degrading and dehumanizing to blacks, teaching the subject "to hate himself and to deny his own humanity."[58] As an alternative they call for a new black consciousness, "a sense of peoplehood: pride, rather than shame, in blackness, and an attitude of brotherly, communal responsibility among all black people for one another."[59]

Here, once again, the theme of respect is tied to the value of *fraternity*. Earlier in his career as the prophet of the Black Power movement, while he was still working through the Student Nonviolent Coordinating Committee, Carmichael had made it clear that he was calling for a psychological revolution as well as a political and economic one. He wrote in 1966:

> The need for psychological equality is the reason why SNCC today believes that blacks must organize in the Black community. Only black people can convey the revolutionary idea that black people are able to do things themselves. Only they can help create in the community an aroused and continuing black consciousness that will provide the basis for political strength.[60]

Long after this first hero of the Black Power movement had lost his position of eminence, other "soul brothers" and "sisters" were playing variations on the same theme. In essence, this is the theme that black people in America can gain political and economic liberty and equality only if they first come to regard their blackness with pride and force white people to view it with respect. Moreover, pride and respect can be created only through collective efforts and group power, not through individual achievements evaluated from the perspective of Anglo-conformity and middle-class values.

It is the separatist and collectivist implications of black nationalism that are most perplexing and disturbing to all except those blacks who have committed themselves fervently to its philosophy. To whites who cling to an attitude of white supremacy, the comforting thought that blacks do indeed want to be separate is overshadowed by the fear that a black community that is not only separate but powerful will threaten their own power and privilege. To white liberals, dedicated to integration, the call for black pride and black power is even more distressing. It challenges the liberal tenet that race as a highly salient determinant of identity is a lamentable aberration, neither supported by science nor justified by the liberal-humanitarian creed that is the legacy of the Enlightenment. They cannot come to terms with what seems to them the faulty logic of conceding the right of blacks to segregate themselves while denying the right of whites to exclude them. So profound has been the influence of white domination in American society that it is difficult for whites to understand how black Americans might give higher priority to achieving pride in their blackness than to sharing the company of white Americans like themselves or to striving to win the material rewards that the society offers as prizes in the status race.

Even white radicals who are contemptuous of the values of "middle America" and define American society as sick and corrupt find themselves discomforted when they try to form alliances with militant black nationalists. The weight of the black experience in America causes the black radical to think of himself first as black and only secondarily as radical, so he sees the world through different eyes than does his white radical ally. There exists a somewhat different priority of issues, and there is a lurking fear that in any brave new world in which blacks do not have a veto power they once again may find themselves in a subordinate position.

Many blacks who have been victims of segregation and are veterans of the struggle against it perceive tremendous dangers in the ideology of black nationalism, whatever form it may take. Those who cling to a faith in the possibility of individual

mobility in an American class system freed of the artificial barrier of race see the cultivation of black pride and black ethnic
identity as a poor and fraudulent substitute for the acquisition
of individual skills for competition in the status race. Black
leaders like Bayard Rustin, who proclaim the need for a more
socialistic economy in the United States, fear that black nationalism will divide blacks from what they regard as their most important allies, the white working class. Both types see any advo-
cacy of black separatism as playing into the hands of their old
antagonists, the segregationists.

Although both present momentous challenges to white supremacy, black nationalism is more revolutionary than is integration. One self-proclaimed black revolutionary, James Boggs,
sees integration as not truly revolutionary at all:

> The first thing that every revolutionist has to be clear about is that
> integration is not in itself a revolutionary concept. It means assimi-
> lation into the system rather than a radical transformation of that
> system on the basis of new values and new methods. The only thing
> that has made integration seem revolutionary up to now is the way
> it has been resisted by whites, and particularly by those whites who
> have most benefited from it—the former immigrants.[61]

The respect revolution among blacks is profoundly revolutionary in that it demands that white Americans desist from the
game of proclaiming that the Constitution is color-blind while
the actual workings of the covert class system exert pressure for
conformity by all to white middle-class standards. It demands
open recognition of, and respect for, differences, particularly
those imposed by accident of birth. This acceptance of differences as an ineradicable aspect of a heterogeneous nation implies that every citizen must be accorded not only political freedom and economic welfare but also personal respect, regardless
of race and whether or not he demonstrates his right to this respect by achievement. To bring this about in a society in which
to be unconditionally "American" is to be white and to be
black is a handicap to be overcome may seem an impossible
dream. It is a dream for which countless blacks are striving,
however, as is evident from their ever more frequent assertion of
blackness in their dress, their hair-styles, their music, their art,
and their patterns of association.

There has been a close and complex relationship between socioeconomic class and race in the history of the United States, both during and after the era of slavery. For nearly a century after emancipation, most blacks found themselves trapped in a socioeconomic status that was grossly inferior in wealth, power, and prestige. During this time the promise was held out, even in the South, that when and if, despite segregation, they proved themselves qualified to enter the mainstream of American life, the barriers of race would be dropped. This was the dream that Booker T. Washington accepted as valid when he urged blacks to devote themselves to proving they could be good citizens and good workers in order to gain the respect of their white fellow citizens. This was implicit in Gunnar Myrdal's "theory of cumulation," holding that every time a black could take advantage of the slightest relaxation of prejudice and discrimination to improve his condition, there would be a payoff in a further relaxation of the barriers because of his demonstration that the popular stereotypes were wrong.[62] Even while appealing to Myrdal as an authority, however, the Supreme Court declared in 1954 that this promise of achievement of equality through gradualism was false because segregation itself erected an insuperable psychological barrier to achievement. Following the reversal of the "separate but equal" principle, many formal barriers to individual mobility and equality of opportunity were lowered, even though slowly and reluctantly. Then blacks began to discover that the winning of the full rights of citizenship through achievement still remained of critical importance to them.

It became inescapably evident that although individuals might be perceived by whites as exceptions, blacks still were perceived as a group. Centuries of discrimination had given them the collective character of a lower-class group. Their rapidly increasing aggregation in the slums of the central cities made their inferior, disadvantaged position in the status system even more visible. Shackled by the history of discrimination and by the inherited badge of membership in a group that always had been on the bottom, they still felt the traditional American pressures for conformity and upward mobility.

Those individuals who could somehow take advantage of the new opportunities that were opened to them by the Civil Rights movement could enjoy their achievements to some extent. They could begin to receive rewards that previously had been arbitrarily denied them. They might even be welcomed and sought after as neighbors, employees, and students. Yet three shadows still dimmed their enjoyment of their progress. One was the fear that they might be only "token blacks," that their actual achievements and qualifications might not be proportionate to the rewards they received. Another was the consciousness that behind them still stood the mass of "unqualified," nonachieving blacks. Experience taught that if many of their brothers and sisters sought to follow on the trails they had blazed, the barriers quickly would go up again. Moreover, their own tenuous integration would be endangered because the controversy over how many and what kind of blacks would enter a neighborhood, a school, a faculty, or a work force would restore an acute awareness of race even in their own interaction with whites who had accepted them. Finally, they were forced to live with the knowledge that in a society that had piously proclaimed that equal opportunity at long last was available to all without regard to race, their own success could be used as weapons for the condemnation of the larger number of their fellows who had not made such progress. Their success could be taken as evidence that the opportunities indeed were real; if others had not taken advantage of them, was this not proof that they simply had not tried hard enough?

Thus even for successfully upward-mobile blacks, achievement of respect in terms of the standards of a white society proves to be a risky endeavor. So long as American society is not color-blind in truth rather than in theory, the individual black cannot divest himself of his black identity even if he desires to do so; his fate remains bound up to some extent with the lot of his fellow blacks who have not climbed as high as he. Not only from frustrated blacks on the streets of the ghettos but from black intellectuals commanding high salaries in prestige universities has come an increasing chorus of demands for compensatory programs to produce "equality of results" instead of "equality of opportunity"; for the recognition of group rights as well as of individual rights; for "reparations" to redress the grievances and hardships generated by past discrimination; and for a new respect for blackness even when it might be accompanied by cultural differences that appeared to be lower-class or even "un-American."

Actions taken by some blacks in the spirit of black pride and black power, some calculated in advance and others erupting spontaneously, struck the larger American society with a dramatic and far-reaching impact. The defiant, collective action of blacks in spontaneous urban insurrections, carefully planned demonstrations of the right to self-defense by the Black Panthers, and the seizure of university buildings by black students with "nonnegotiable demands" not only captured the attention of the mass media and their audience but, in some cases, actually won concessions. Despite widespread condemnation of these activities as "violent" and "illegal" there was also an extensive public attempt to explain them by defining them as social protest expressing resentment at genuine grievances. As Ralph Turner has pointed out, one consequence of such a definition is that even those who see themselves as targets of the attack may respond with an offer of conciliation involving "a generous interpretation of the trouble-makers' activities, acknowledging their grievances, admitting fault. . . ."[63] Martin Oppenheimer has suggested that even as governmental agencies, federal, state and local, made preparations further to prevent or suppress such collective protest, they adopted a companion strategy of "domestic pacification" designed to ameliorate the conditions that presumably gave rise to such protest.[64] This strategy and the publicity surrounding it gave credence to the belief that collective defiance of the authorities did indeed "work." The nonviolent but disruptive protests of the Civil Rights movement earlier had produced the same kinds of results, including the passage of the Civil Rights Act of 1964 and the Voting Rights Act of 1965. Although the majority of black leaders were in agreement that all the programs of domestic pacification fell far short of correcting the injustices to which they were addressed, there developed among white Americans a widespread belief that blacks were receiving not just overdue justice but favored treatment, particularly from the federal government.

At the same time, the inflammatory, antiwhite rhetoric of the most radical black nationalist leaders and the well-publicized personal violence against whites of a minority of blacks added to the fear and hostility that the more massive protests had engendered. Distrust of the ability and even the will of the police to protect the average white citizen from the violence of the black protest was reflected in the purchase of guns by some white suburbanites. In some urban neighborhoods white vigilante patrols were organized. Although these were not admitted by the members to be antiblack forces, they most often arose in areas that were contiguous to concentrations of poor blacks. Furthermore, many of the white neighborhoods were inhabited predominantly by members of white ethnic groups who themselves only recently had climbed out of poverty and the slums. It was not only the occasional depredations of black criminals that these people feared, however. They were afraid also that large numbers of lower-class, "not-qualified" blacks would invade their neighborhoods and their children's schools. Many of these white people expressed liberal sentiments in regard to the equal treatment of blacks in the abstract, and their actions toward individual, middle-class blacks were friendly and receptive. David Danzig has aptly characterized their new crisis:

> The white liberal . . . who—whether or not he has been fully conscious of it—has generally conceived of progress in race relations as the one-by-one assimilation of deserving Negroes into the larger society, finds himself confused and threatened by suddenly having to come to terms with an aggressive Negro community that wishes to enter it *en masse.*[65]

The folklore of the American experience and, for whites, the reality of a competitive status system have placed maximum emphasis on individual rights, individual opportunity, and individual achievement. In its emphasis on pride and respect, the black revolution is a revolt against this sort of individualism. Fearful that "first-class citizenship" has been extended to their people just at the time when opportunities to gain economic equality through individual striving are diminishing; reminded all too frequently that individual achievement does not completely erase the stigma of blackness; heartened by gains in power and prestige won by the participants in the respect revolution abroad, the ideologists of black nationalism have called on their followers to win respect through fraternity

This spirit has proved to be contagious. The model of black collective protest, with its evidence of success, invited imitation by other minorities who still suffered economic deprivation as well as psychological degradation. For members of groups who were enjoying hard-won status gains but felt insecure in their possession of them, communal black militancy suggested a model of defense. Finally, the spirit of the new tribalism fell on a society that was receptive to it because so many of its members were asking anew the question "Who am I?"

THE CRISIS OF IDENTITY

The same social changes that free the individual from what are felt as repressive forces may, at the same time, uproot him from familiar anchorages. Social mobility provides the individual with a sense of having achieved equality on a new and higher level of a vaguely defined but always challenging status ladder. To move up requires sacrificing the sense of place that even a lowly status may offer; the insecurity and discomfort of the nouveau riche has long been noted by observers of the human condition. It is not surprising that in a society in which, in the name of liberty and equality, there has been unrelenting pressure for mobility and conformity, the crisis of identity and the problem of alienation should emerge as central issues of our time. Both are related to the fact that in a population of mobile, striving individuals there are many who find the achievement of a secure sense of personal worth an ever-elusive goal.

Hosts of sociologists, psychologists, historians, and journalists have designated a variety of developments as causes of the crisis of identity. The physical mobility that has been correlated with social mobility and made possible by developments in transportation has torn individuals out of the intimate, if confining, bonds of the small community and the extended family. Work, mechanized and bureaucratized, has ceased to be a satisfying central life interest for many Americans. What some observers have said of factory workers might also be said of workers in a wide variety of occupations and professions:

> Other observers of factory life have made it abundantly clear that most workers are not happy in their jobs, that they feel trapped and degraded by their working conditions, that they have a powerful desire to escape from the factory, and that what drives them on is the incessant demands of our consumption economy.[66]

What historically have been two of the most important sources of meaning for the individual, religion and nationalism, also have lost much of their potency in modern America. Religion, on the one hand, has been assaulted by the forces of rationalism and science, so that both the comforts it offered and the demands it imposed lost their mystical, compelling force. On the other hand, it has had to compete with the frantic pursuit of leisure-time activities, particularly during weekends, that modern technology and the consumption economy have made more accessible for even the moderately affluent citizen.

Patriotism, the individual manifestation of nationalism, has always been intimately connected with evidence of national power in foreign relations and, particularly, with victory in war. The effects of intergroup conflict in heightening in-group solidarity and providing meaning for the individual have, in the past, been inescapably apparent. The war against fascism and Japanese imperialism was, however, the last war that could serve for the people of the United States as a great crusade, unifying the nation in the name of patriotism and in a quest for righteous victory. The threat of nuclear, total war made it impossible to romanticize warfare any longer. The prediction that in such a conflict there would be no victor and perhaps no survivors destroyed the illusion that national power and individual dedication could lead to victory. Then came the long and, to many people, senseless conflict in Indochina to strip away the myths of the role of the United States as the defender of freedom. It was not that all Americans came to deny the justification in terms of necessity for the presence of American military might in Southeast Asia, but that the justification offered became increasingly that of the national interest rather than of the extension of liberty and equality. What is important is that the flag, symbol of the nation, was transformed from a unifying into a polarizing symbol. The display of the flag, even as a decal pasted on a car window, became more common, but its display became as much a gesture of defiance of domestic critics of the nation's actions as it was a proclamation of loyalty. On the other side, denunciation and even desecration of the flag increased in frequency. It, the national anthem, the uniforms of servicemen, and military installations, from air bases to ROTC buildings, became for many Americans symbols of an aggressive, imperialist, and racist nation that had betrayed the ideals on which it was founded.

All these influences fell with especially heavy impact on the youth of the nation. If they came from disadvantaged families, especially if they were not white, they found it difficult to enter the world of work and to find what little meaning it might offer. For the better part of the decade of the 1960s it was they who faced the prospect of fighting in Vietnam without even the assurance of a hero's welcome if and when they returned. To a greater proportion of the young people than ever before in the history of any society, going to college appeared as a not only desirable but necessary step toward achieving respect and a sense of self-worth as well as material well-being. Once in the university, however, many of them felt it to be an impersonal, degrading milieu, an institution insensitive both to their personal, psychic needs and to the critical problems of the society. It is because of their manifestations of discontent that Ralph Turner sees this age group as the leaders in the respect revolution, generating a new conception of injustice:

> This new conception is reflected in a new object for indignation. Today, for the first time in history, it is common to see violent indignation expressed over the fact that people lack a sense of personal worth—that they lack an inner peace of mind which comes from a sense of personal dignity or a clear sense of identity.[67]

This new conception arises particularly among the young people of the contemporary era, Turner argues, because:

> The problem of alienation and the sense of worth is most poignantly the problem of a youthful generation with unparalleled freedom and capability but without an institutional structure in which this capability can be appropriately realized. Adolescence is peculiarly a "non-person" status in life. And yet this is just the period in which the technical skills and the new freedom are being markedly increased. The sense of alienation is distinctively the sense of a person who realizes great expectations for himself yet must live in a non-status.[68]

But, he adds, this is not exclusively a problem of youth, for there are other segments of the population that experience their own crises of identity:

> Today alienation is understandable to other groups than youth. The new sense of injustice can become the leaven for vast social changes

because adults, the elderly, minority groups and other organizable segments of society can see many of their own problems in the terms set forth by youthful activists.[69]

The great variety of movements emphasizing the theme of identity that have sprung up in the past few years reveals that the search may take many forms. Some forms are highly individualistic, although they may involve cults of people who seek in the same way. The individual may attempt to "find his real self" through highly private psychic experiences induced by drugs or by meditation. "Dropping out" of the conventional structures of the society and "doing one's own thing" constitute other forms of striving to find meaning and a sense of self-worth in a world that destroys these very values by its pressures for conformity.

Other forms of seeking reflect the ancient Christian concept of losing one's life in order to find it, signifying the achievement of a meaningful identity through submission to, and immersion in, a group. Many movements that have arisen as responses to the identity problem of modern society are explicitly religious. There has been a Pentacostal revival within the framework of many of the established churches, both Protestant and Catholic, in the United States as well as in Latin America. The so-called Jesus movement among American youth addresses itself directly to loss of religious faith, to joy through community, and to peace of mind. Competing with these Christian movements are numerous varieties of Eastern religions, such as Zen Buddhism and Hare Krishna. Blacks led the way, however, in the contemporary search for identity through religion. The Nation of Islam, or Black Muslim movement, burst upon the American scene in the early 1950s not only as a distinctive religious sect but as the precursor of the subsequent revival of ethnic nationalism among blacks.

The ideology and rigid religious discipline of the Nation of Islam proved to be remarkably successful in engendering a sense of self-worth and pride in the small minority of blacks who could accept them. At the same time, they discouraged many potential followers from being converts and kept the sect from developing the sort of mass following that Marcus Garvey and Martin Luther King, Jr., had enjoyed. Yet the nationalism of the Black Muslims, and particularly the speeches and writings of their one-time member Malcolm X, contributed significantly to laying the base for the search for identity through the revival of ethnicity.

The flowering of the Black Power movement following Stokely Carmichael's exhortations during the "Meredith march" through Mississippi in 1965 reflected the secularization of the black nationalist gospel that the Black Muslims had already been preaching. As indicated above, the various manifestations of this new spirit among blacks served to sensitize the members, particularly the younger ones, of other minority groups. The Chicano movement developed among Mexican-Americans, with their Brown Berets organization presenting a public image analogous to that of the Black Panthers. A spokesman for this organization, after quoting the old saying "White is Right, Brown can just stick around, but Black must go back," made explicit the kinship between the two movements:

> No, our black brothers will not go back and Hell, no, we will not just stick around. We will act like a thorn in the establishment's side. That is the kind of sticking we will do. The Brown Berets have done more to shake up the establishment than any group could accomplish in three centuries. The Brown Berets have led the March for Liberation: liberation for our people, La Raza Unida, through Chicano Power.[70]

The cry for "Red Power" arose among some segments of the American Indian population, along with denunciations of older, assimilationist Indians as "Uncle Tomahawks." An Indian scholar and Pulitzer Prize winner, N. Scott Momaday, has expressed the spirit of his peoples' participation in the respect revolution:

> We have robbed the Indian of his pride. He has been a prisoner of war for generations and we have not let him forget it. We've made him dependent on the generosity of the white man spiritually, psychologically, and often materially.[71]

Momaday went on to advocate the cultivation of respect among Indians.

> The whole concept of education can be changed so that the objective is to instill within the Indian a pride in being what he is. He can

be taught his own history, which has never been done before. He can be educated into the conviction that his way of life is intrinsically valuable, and valuable to the dominant society.[72]

Mexican-Americans, Indians, and Puerto Ricans, who also developed their own form of nationalism, shared with blacks the disadvantage of suffering material deprivation and political powerlessness; so the older political and welfare themes remained strong for them even as the new emphasis on dignity and respect was asserted. In the case of the Puerto Ricans, nationalist organizations often developed partly out of fear that better-organized, militant blacks would gain an advantage over them in the cities they both inhabited.

Japanese-Americans are a nonwhite minority who, despite their history of political persecution from the end of the nineteenth century through the period of World War II, have been remarkably successful in achieving success as measured by white, middle-class norms. Yet many of their younger members also have found American pressures for Anglo-conformity distressing and success on its terms degrading. A young Japanese-American, Daniel Okimoto, clearly sees the influence of the Black Power movement:

> No longer apologetic about being members of a minority nor eager to discard their past, many college-age nisei today are rebelling against remnants of racism and old Oriental stereotypes, and are aggressively raising a cry for Yellow Power. . . . The new ethnic consciousness and defiance against racial prejudice owes much to the Black Power movement which, by boldly challenging the status quo, brought vividly to light conditions of injustice that confront all minorities. . . . Borrowing the insights and even some of the rhetoric of the blacks, the Asian-American movement represents a sharp divergence from the old pattern of silence and passivity.[73]

All of these minorities are defined with increasing frequency by their nationalist leaders as part of the Third World. One of the major targets of criticism by "Third World Alliances" has been a vaguely defined "middle-class white America," its values, its economic advantages, and its political dominance. But by mid-century this middle-class America encompassed numerous members of white ethnic groups that, within the memory of the older generation, had been economically disadvantaged minorities, low in prestige, and struggling to gain some measure of political power. As recent research has shown, they have not disappeared into a "melting pot America" but, in comparison with nonwhite minorities, have been highly successful in taking advantage of the educational and economic advantages that the course of Anglo-conformity offered. Through the successes of the American labor movement, in whose battles they played a heroic part, they gained a measure of job security unprecedented in the nation's history. Much of this security rested, of course, on an almost monopolistic control of entry into organized occupations, and on the ability of the unions to keep wages abreast of prices in the inflationary spiral of the economy. They became an important segment of the consumer market, and they treasured the material possessions they could amass as important signs of their individual success and self-worth. Most importantly, the failure of so many members of the disadvantaged, nonwhite minorities to achieve comparable upward mobility could be taken as evidence of their own moral superiority and as proof that devotion to the work ethic did pay off both in material welfare and in prestige.

The demands, backed up by disruptive, extralegal tactics of the insurgent blacks and other nonwhite minorities gravely threatened their new-found but tenuous sense of economic security. Demands for compensatory treatment in the form of "quotas" in employment threatened their jobs; demands for greater welfare benefits promised to increase their tax load. In his campaign for reelection in 1972, President Nixon and his advisers, guided perhaps by the strategy of George Wallace, played on these fears by emphasizing his devotion to the work ethic. At the base of the Statue of Liberty, the president uttered words of fulsome praise for those immigrants who had proved by their hard work and success that opportunity was abundant in America for those who were willing to take advantage of it.[74] Unmentioned was the fact that while the lady of the statue faced east, inviting Europe to send its "tired, its poor, its huddled masses" to the land of opportunity, blacks in the South were captives in a system of tenant farming that amounted to a new form of slavery. The ancestors of the "welfare loafers" in the black ghettos had worked longer and harder for lower wages than had even the immigrants exploited in the sweat shops, on the docks, and in the mines and mills of the North, but without the opportunity to pull themselves out of their lowly state by organizing unions, accumulating capital, or developing powerful political machines. By the time that blacks, Mexican-Americans, Puerto Ricans, and Indians were offered the opportunity to move up in the system, they found themselves confronted with a technology that was reducing its need for new workers through automation and a labor force that was highly organized and strongly resistant to sharing its hard-won advantages with new groups that demanded "instant equality" and made explicit a philosophy of "group rights."

It was the justifications advanced for compensatory treatment, group rights, and equality of results that dealt the sharpest blow to the pride of the white ethnic groups. Their material symbols of status were denigrated by the attack on the allegedly materialistic values of the white middle-class. The argument that the ability to acquire these symbols was not the consequence of individual moral superiority but was a combination of luck and collusion, and hence was undeserved, struck at the very heart of the sense of self-worth of these upwardly mobile whites. Furthermore, it was not just angry black nationalists but radical white intellectuals who argued that special, compensatory treatment was justly deserved by individuals simply on the basis of their membership in oppressed minorities, not on the basis of individual achievement. The so-called welfare ethic and the principle of group rights seemed to be about to sweep away the work ethic and the principle of equal opportunity for individuals.

In reaction to these threats, a new tribalism began to appear in the ranks of those ethnic groups that had long striven to become "standard Americans" and to transform their diverse cultural backgrounds into quaint but insignificant reminders of a past that was no longer a compelling force in their lives. Even Jews who could not abide the extreme nationalism of Meier Kahanes's Jewish Defense League felt the need to revive a defense of their Jewish heritage in the face of the angry attacks on their group by black nationalist leaders. An Italian-American Anti-Defamation League emerged, even though under dubious sponsorship, to demand that stereotypes of Americans of Italian descent be censored as strictly as were stereotypes of blacks. An

Alliance of Ethnic Groups held its first annual meeting to consider the problems that a variety of white ethnic groups saw confronting them in the new, polarized America that black power had brought into being. A writer of Slovak descent, Michael Novak, felt impelled to write a book on the rise of the white ethnic groups in America.[75] He said of himself, "I am born of PIGS—those Poles, Italians, Greeks, and Slavs, non-English-speaking immigrants, numbered so heavily among the workingmen of this nation."[76] He went on to express the anguish experienced by the white ethnic groups in the face of the sympathetic response of white liberals to the demands of the non-white minorities:

> In particular, I have regretted and keenly felt the absence of that sympathy for PIGS that simple human feeling might have prodded intelligence to muster: that same sympathy that the educated find so easy to conjure up for black culture, Chicano culture, Indian culture, and other cultures of the poor.[77]

In asserting the value of reexamining the worth of his own ethnicity and of the preservation of diversity in the American nation, Novak concluded:

> Yet it does not seem evident that by becoming more concrete, accepting one's finite and limited identity, one necessarily becomes parochial. It seems more likely that by each of us becoming more profoundly what we are, we shall find greater unity, in those depths in which unity irradiates diversity, than by attempting through the artifices of the American "melting pot" and the cultural religion of science to become what we are not.[78]

RESPECT AND THE NEW NATIONALISMS

Despite the existence of its covert class system, the United States has from its founding held out to all of its citizens the promise of equality in civil rights, in political power, in economic welfare, and in personal dignity and respect. Yet the actual workings of the system, with its combination of political democracy and economic capitalism, have caused all of these, and particularly respect, to be unevenly distributed. The pressures for Anglo-conformity and for middle-class achievement as prerequisites for respect have been greater than the opportunity for all citizens, particularly those not of white skin, actually to disappear into the "one nation, indivisible," that the theme of assimilation in a "melting pot America" implies. It is not new for blacks, the minority that has always found achievement of this goal most dubious, to turn their backs on the attainment of equality through sameness and to demand respect for their differences. The most recent resurgence of the spirit of black nationalism has come at a time when opportunities for individual achievement seem to many to be diminishing and when the search for identity and respect reflects a pressing need among many segments of the population. The respect revolution, manifest in the United States in a variety of new "nationalisms" and in the revival of ethnicity as a salient characteristic even for moderately affluent, acculturated citizens, is not likely to be evanescent. Instead, it promises to usher in extensive changes in the social and political structure of the nation.

The new tribalism of the respect revolution should not be mistaken for a mere extension of the political and economic revolutions of the past, as represented by the American Revolution, the new federalism that followed the crushing of the Southern Secession movement, the successes of the labor movement, and the welfare philosophy of the New Deal. The nationalism that was new and democratic in spirit at the founding of the nation has failed to satisfy the quest for identity and respect of citizens of diverse backgrounds who, though declared equal before the law, still have found themselves individually and collectively stigmatized when they failed to forge ahead in the highly competitive, individualistic status race into which they are forced by the combination of political democracy and capitalism. No new internationalism has arisen to satisfy their quest for identity, so there is a growing trend toward the achievement of respect through the glorification of subnational reference groups.

This new "internal nationalism," emphasizing cultural, ethnic, and even racial differences, shares in the revolutionary tradition of respect manifest in the emerging nations of the world beyond Europe. Communication between nationalist leaders of the colored minorities and people whom they regard as their compatriots in the Third World shapes and lends strength to the respect revolution within the United States. At the same time, it brings them into sharp conflict with the dreams and promises of an older form of nationalism that sought to create an illusion of homogeneity in one of the most heterogeneous societies in the world—and failed.

As a new sense of injustice has arisen among peoples who consider themselves psychologically dispossessed, there have been new and different stirrings of conscience even among those whom they deem to be the oppressors. Despite the many failures of the organization, the ideology of the United Nations does symbolize a new commitment in principle to the further extension of freedom and equality in the world. In the councils of the United Nations, the "developing" nations have achieved some new measure of respect, and their aspirations for independence, welfare, and dignity have received a hearing. At one of its most recent conferences, in July 1972, UNESCO called together experts to consider the concepts of "race, identity, and dignity." These experts focused their attention on the significance of separatist movements among racial and national groups.[79] Even the manifestations of conflict between various parties—black nationalists and the police, Quebecois separatists and the Canadian government, Palestinian guerrillas and Israeli nationals—have caused the quest for respect of numerous, diverse groups to penetrate the consciousness of a large segment of the world's population. The mass media, particularly television aided by satellite communication, convey the jarring impact of struggles for dignity into the homes of the most secure citizens of the most powerful nations. For while newspapers, radio, and television can only report the onus of political repression and the pangs of hunger, they effectively convey the sense of urgency felt by those who seek respect.

NOTES

1. See Carl Wittke, ed., *Democracy Is Different* (New York: Harper and Brothers, Publishers, 1941), p. 16.

2. Adolf Gilly "Introduction" to Frantz Fanon, *A Dying Colonialism,* trans. Haakon Chevalier (New York: Grove Press, 1965), p. 12.

3. Robert Perrucci and Mark Pilisuk eds., *The Triple Revolution: Social Problems in Depth* (Boston: Little, Brown and Co., 1968), p. vii.

4. Herbert Blumer, "Social Unrest and Collective Protest," unpublished paper made available by courtesy of the author, p. 8.

5. Ibid., p. 36.

6. Ibid., p. 41.

7. " 'Must' Reading Listed for Blacks," *Springfield* (Mass.) *Daily News,* 30 August 1972, p. 9.

8. Alexis de Tocqueville, *The Old Regime and the French Revolution,* trans. Stuart Gilbert (Garden City, N.Y.: Doubleday & Co., 1955), pp. 206–207.

9. Ibid., p. 204.

10. Rupert Emerson, *From Empire to Nation* (Cambridge: Harvard University Press, 1967), p. 190.

11. Ibid., p. 191.

12. Pierre Van den Berghe, *Race and Racism: A Comparative Perspective* (New York: John Wiley & Sons, 1967), p. 29.

13. Frantz Fanon, *A Dying Colonialism* (New York: Grove Press, 1965), p. 27.

14. George E. Lensen, *The World Beyond Europe* (Cambridge: Riverside Press, 1960), p. 182.

15. Frantz Fanon, *Wretched of the Earth,* trans. Constance Farrington (New York: Grove Press, 1968), p. 315.

16. Ibid., p. 40.

17. Ibid., p. 35.

18. Frantz Fanon, *Black Skin, White Masks: The Experience of a Black Man in a White World* (New York: Grove Press, 1967), p. 38.

19. Ibid., p. 13.

20. Ibid., p. 10.

21. Fanon, *Wretched of the Earth,* p. 94.

22. Ibid., p. 93.

23. Emerson, *Empire to Nation,* p. 380.

24. Ibid., p. 207.

25. R. L. Sklar, "The Contribution of Tribalism to Nationalism in Western Nigeria," in Immanuel Wallerstein, ed., *Social Change: The Colonial Situation* (New York: John Wiley & Sons, 1966), p. 290.

26. *New York Times,* 26 November 1972, p. 8.

27. Bayard Rustin, "Black Power's Legacy," *Newsweek,* 13 November 1972, p. 19.

28. Harold Isaacs, unpublished remarks at Faculty Seminar on Comparative Ethnic Relations, Smith College, December 1969. See also "Changing Arenas and Identities in World Affairs," chapter 14 of volume II of this work.

29. Orin Klapp, *The Collective Search for Identity* (New York: Holt, Rinehart and Winston, 1969), p. 47.

30. Glenn Weaver, "Benjamin Franklin and the Pennsylvania Germans," in Leonard Dinnerstein and Frederich C. Jaher, *The Aliens* (New York: Appleton-Century Crofts, 1970).

31. Ibid., p. 89.

32. Milton Gordon, *Assimilation in American Life* (New York: Oxford University Press, 1964), p. 90.

33. Ibid., pp. 109–110.

34. T. H. Marshall, *Class, Citizenship and Social Development* (New York: Anchor Books, 1965).

35. Ibid., p. 92.

36. Ibid., p. 93.

37. Ibid., p. 94.

38. Ibid.

39. Michael Lewis, *Urban America: Institutions and Experience* (New York: John Wiley & Sons, 1973), p. 191.

40. Allison Davis, Burleigh Gardner, and W. Floyd Warner, *Deep South* (Chicago: University of Chicago Press, 1941).

41. Lewis, *Urban America*, pp. 194–195.

42. Ralph H. Turner, "The Theme of Contemporary Social Movements," in Jerome Rabow, ed., *Sociology, Students, and Society* (Pacific Palisades, Calif.: Goodyear Publishing Co., 1972), p. 590.

43. *Oliver Brown et al.* v. *Board of Education of Topeka, Shawnee County, Kansas, et al.* United States Supreme Court, 17 May 1954, 347 U.S. 483.

44. Ibid.

45. Ibid.

46. Ibid.

47. *Plessy* v. *Ferguson.* United States Supreme Court, 1896, 163 U.S. 537.

48. Ibid.

49. Ibid.

50. Ibid.

51. Ibid.

52. James Boggs, *Racism and the Class Struggle* (New York: Monthly Review Press, 1970), pp. 22–23.

53. Gunnar Myrdal, *An American Dilemma* (New York: Harper and Brothers, 1944).

54. Robert L. Allen, *Black Awakening in Capitalist America* (Garden City, N.Y.: Anchor Books, 1970), pp. 3–4.

55. Ibid., p. 14.

56. Ibid., p. 89.

57. Stokely Carmichael and Charles V. Hamilton, *Black Power* (New York: Random House, 1967), p. 30.

58. Ibid., p. 31.

59. Ibid., p. viii.

60. Stokely Carmichael, "What We Want," *New York Review of Books,* 22 September 1966, p. 5.

61. Boggs, *Racism*, p. 34.

62. Myrdal, *American Dilemma*, pp. 1065–1068.

63. Ralph Turner, "The Public Perception of Protest," *American Sociological Review* 34 (December 1969):829.

64. Martin Oppenheimer, *The Urban Guerrilla* (Chicago: Quadrangle Books, 1969), p. 157.

65. David Danzig, "The Meaning of Negro Strategy," *Commentary*, February 1964, pp. 42–43.

66. Eric and Mary Josephson, eds., *Man Alone* (New York: Dell Publishing Co., 1962), p. 24.

67. Turner, "The Theme of Contemporary Social Movements," p. 590.

68. Ibid., p. 593.

69. Ibid., p. 594.

70. "Brown Berets," in George E. Frakes and Curtis Solberg, eds., *Minorities in California History* (New York: Random House, 1971), p. 158.

71. N. Scott Momaday and Jose Colmenares, in Frakes and Solberg, *Minorities*, p. 186.

72. Ibid.

73. Daniel Okimoto, *American in Disquise* (New York: Walker-Weatherhill, 1971), pp. 146–147.

74. Robert B. Semple, Jr., "President Scores 'Welfare Ethic'—Labor Day Speech Backers of Policies That Threaten 'Work Ethic'," *New York Times,* 4 September 1972, p. 1.

75. Michael Novak, *The Rise of the Unmeltable Ethnics* (New York: Macmillan Co., 1972).

76. Michael Novak, "White Ethnic," *Harper's,* September 1971, p. 44.

77. Ibid., p. 46.

78. Ibid., p. 50.

79. "Final Report," Meeting of Experts on the Concepts of Race, Identity and Dignity, 3–7 July 1972. (Paris: United Nations Educational, Scientific and Cultural Organization, 17 November 1972).

5

LOVE AND INTIMACY: MASS MEDIA AND PHALLIC CULTURE

Arnold A. Rogow

Evidence is accumulating that the mass media have a major share in transforming the socialization process in advanced industrial societies, and that this change in the priority and interpretation of values carries with it a widening circle of consequences for the relationship between man and his political, economic, and social institutions. These transformations have come to the surface most rapidly in American society, where the mass media have attained phenomenal strength. Evidently the competing institutions of family and neighborhood have been relatively weaker in the United States than in less industrialized economies.

Until recent years the principal thrust of the mass media was in substantially the same direction as the values and value interpretations transmitted through the home, school, church, and neighborhood. It is presumably safe to assert that exposure to newspapers and magazines had an *exaggerating* effect on certain norms, especially those that presented success as wealth. It is trite to emphasize the influence of advertising in stimulating demand for consumption. As long as economic opportunities were perceived as open, advertising was a potent incentive to production for immediate or more remote consumer goals.

The author notes that, with permission, he has drawn freely on research studies jointly prepared with Harold D. Lasswell on Sex and Politics in American Society (in manuscript).

As advertising increased, appeals to family love and loyalty were attached to consumption opportunities across the board. How can affection be demonstrated? By an endless stream of commodities and services. Advertisers learned the strategy of the snob appeal. You expressed your love by enhancing the prestige of the loved one, and this concurrently improved your own respect position. You aspired to a house in a prestige neighborhood; you belonged to a prestige church; you joined prestige clubs; your children went to prestige schools; and of course you drove a prestige car, dressed the family in prestige clothes, entertained the relatives in prestige restaurants, took the family to prestige resorts on prestige vacations.

The family appeal would lead to disease and death insurance (artfully labeled health and life insurance). And the family might pay off in politics if a healthy brood of bright-eyed sons and daughters were available for display, and a beautiful, talkative, and discreet hostess-wife did her part.

News selection automatically chose the stories and the pictures that confirmed the advertiser's pitch directly. The media and the merchants were partners in an open conspiracy to demonstrate the "obvious" and to imply that that "bitch-goddess success" really was a goddess after all.

Even in the days of print there were counterimages to the ruling image, and articulate counterideologies to the established myth. Some culture heroes seemed to get on without a family, although not necessarily without a lover. There were grumpy clergymen who condemned luxury and spoke well of pain; and there were prophetic Marxists who forecast a secular hell for the propertied classes. There was an underground literature of pornography, blasphemy, and crime.

With the advent of "yellow journalism," a bridge was built to the day of film, radio, and television; and especially to the television epoch. The discrepancies in outlook and impact began to multiply, and socialization changed. The crisis surfaced in the 1960s and future implications are obscure.

Socialization is the social process by which private motivations are channeled into acceptable public acts. Relatively undifferentiated impulses are restructured into personality structures that conform, in the main, to the requirements of the established culture. The practices of culture are themselves in flux. However, the flux is less rapid than the alterations through which an individual passes on his way from infancy, through childhood and juvenility, to adolescence, young adulthood, maturity, and late adulthood. The relative stability of the socializing process is a result of the flow of value indulgences and deprivations. In general, compliance with culturally accepted ways of talking and doing is rewarded, and noncompliance is punished. As the child develops he "internalizes" most of the norms of the culture.

To understand the "socialization crisis" in U.S. society we must bear in mind a general model that emphasizes some of the principal features of earlier America. In the beginning American society was rural and agrarian; it has become urban and industrial. The farm family was a basic unit of production, and sexual norms were adapted to the procreation of farm hands and in general to the management of sexuality in ways that did not interfere with the conduct of agriculture. As urbanization and industrialization cut down the importance of the family as a unit of production, large families ceased to be obvious economic assets. Meanwhile, public policy was relatively successful in excluding children and young people from early involvement in mines and factories. In a dynamic technoscientific civilization education was cultivated as a crucial means of personal advancement. The consequences of these changes were cumulative in the sexual sphere: for married partners the tie between sexuality and procreation was attenuated; for young people the postponement of entry into the market and the deferment of marriage meant that permissible modes of sexual conduct were severely curtailed. At this stage of the evolution of industrial society young people were for many years excluded from adult forms of participation in production, in family formation, or in sexual expression.

The deprivations imposed upon the young were much more comprehensive than those in the sphere of physical sexuality. In the interest of acquiring skill the younger generation was consigned to prolonged juvenility. They were respected for their *potential* contribution, to be made after years of education. Meanwhile they did not receive the evidence of respect obtained by those who performed needed chores on the family farm or who brought home pay from a man's job in industry. The community respected education at the lower levels enough to make it free; they did not respect it sufficiently to pay the adolescent and the young adult for undertaking a responsible role in society. Scholarships continued to have an ambivalent meaning: sometimes they were "charity"; sometimes a recognition of merit. In any case young people were kept in a state of prolonged dependence on parents who were becoming less dependent on children for immediate income or ultimate social security.

The problems of the young in the United States have recently been exacerbated by the communications revolution, which, as indicated above, is largely managed by private interests that depend on the marketing of articles of general consumption. Media specialists have perfected the program techniques of the massive sexual tease. Equally the ethos of the market, the sale of affection, the depersonalization of human relations have been first legitimized then lionized by the media. It has become the accepted pattern to "keep one's cool" emotionally but not physically. This means the acceptance of the physical without any valuation of the partner for anything but market "performance." The emphasis is constantly on "technique" rather than on sharing or mutual development.

All this might suggest that while sex is increasingly sought everywhere, it is found nowhere, and indeed there are good reasons to think that although Americans may be copulating more than ever before, they are enjoying it less. If the reports of psychotherapists are any guide, the sexual malfunctions of impotence, frigidity, and premature ejaculation have been increasing, and even more striking is evidence that many young men in their twenties, to all appearances healthy and normal, are finding themselves invariably or frequently impotent. Psychiatrists are not certain how general this phenomenon is, or what the causes may be, but one explanation, according to Dr. George L. Ginsberg of the New York University School of Medicine, is that the "average expectable sexual behavior" of young women who have ceased to be inhibited or passive is experienced by their male partners as "threatening." Where once women were sexually undemanding and indifferent to their lack of response, says Dr. Ginsberg, they now insist on "sexual performance" from their boy friends, thereby making them anxious and impotent.[1]

But why should a young man feel threatened by his girl friend's demanding sexual satisfaction? One possible reason is the emergence in America of phallic culture, by which is meant a culture whose sexual ethic regards women and men as primarily outlets for gratification.[2] The emphasis of such a culture is less on the mutuality of sexual pleasure than on self-satisfaction, and, even where "performance" is valued, it is valued not because it enables one's sexual partner to experience orgasm but because of the associated narcissism and opportunities for exhibitionism. The entire body, being viewed and treated as essentially a phallus, is endlessly anointed, stroked, groomed, and decorated; the cathexis of the body as phallus is the main reason for the proliferation of body conditioning centers and spas where the body is reverentially treated, and massage, the bath, and exercise take on some of the aura of religious rituals.

Sex in the phallic culture is, therefore, somewhat impersonal and promiscuous; as in the movie *Carnal Knowledge,* which could well serve as a documentary study of phallic culture, scoring becomes an end in itself, whether or not one keeps a record on slides of the body count. Since the dimensions of the sexual organs are of particular importance, great value is attached to being "well endowed" or "well hung." Nor are sexual tastes and preferences unaffected. With the erotic focus on the self, foreplay, oral-genital-anal contacts, and mutual masturbation are increasingly substituted for intercourse as primary sources of gratification, and because there is a strong sadistic and masochistic component, painful sensations are not infrequently associated with pleasure. The paraphernalia of sex in phallic culture abounds with gadgets and devices designed to ward off the always present threat of impotence and frigidity: mirrors, vibrators, special lotions and ointments, aphrodisiacs, pot.

Even if all goes well, the experience of orgasm in phallic culture often is a disappointing one, and here again it is instructive to hear from psychiatrists that many of their male and female patients complain of feeling "letdown" or unsatisfied after intercourse. Apparently many men who are disappointed in this fashion experience some degree of anxiety or depression, and often there is irritability and restlessness as well. As a consequence, not long after intercourse there may be resort to masturbation, but this may only add a feeling of guilt to the existing anxiety or depression. In effect, so male and female patients report, that deep, satisfying orgasmic experience, about which they have read and heard so much, and which some individuals seem easily to experience, has eluded them.

It is easy to dismiss this as the result of having seen too many movies where the hero and heroine thrash around ecstatically in the throes of orgasm.[3] Yet it remains true, in phallic culture, that whole books and numerous magazine articles stress the importance of full and complete orgasm without always making it clear that there are many varieties of orgasm, and that all persons are not equal in orgasmic capacity. Perhaps because it is erroneously assumed that ejaculation and orgasm are identical, the question of male orgasm has received much less attention than the question of female orgasm.

In the germinal sense, phallic culture began when sexual intercourse became freed of any necessary connection with marriage and procreation, or, to put it another way, phallic culture originated with the discovery that sexual pleasure was an end in itself and not merely a means to an end. But in its mature form phallic culture is founded on the peculiarly American tendency to treat sex as totally separate from personality, that is, from affective involvement. As psychologist Rollo May, in positing a "new Puritanism," has suggested, the typical sexual relationship in America is characterized by a "state of alienation from the body, separation of emotion from reason, and use of the body as a machine." Doubting that there is any less guilt, loneliness, and frustration in contemporary America than there was at an earlier time, May argues that we have simply reversed the Victorians who "sought to have love without falling into sex; the modern person seeks to have sex without falling into love."[4] May, like theologian Harvey Cox and other critics of the sexual values espoused by *Playboy, Penthouse,* and similar magazines, regards much of the sexual revolution as, in essence, antisexual because of the treatment of sex as a consumer goods commodity that is promoted and sold much like any other consumption product. From Cox's point of view, a *Playboy* cartoon in which a young man, as he is about to have intercourse with a girl, asks, "Why speak of love at a time like this?" must be regarded as an expression more of reaction than of revolution.

While the divorce of sex from personality can be observed in many areas of social life, perhaps nowhere is it more perfectly expressed than in the Miss America contests that began in 1921. Designed to promote Atlantic City, New Jersey, as a resort, the Miss America competition by its success has spawned not only the Miss Universe, Miss U.S.A., and Miss Black America contests, but also the assorted queens of businessmen's conventions and football bowl games. Contestants are said to be of "good moral character," and sponsors, sensitive to certain criticisms, have alleged that the girls must demonstrate a skill or talent. Apparently this requirement is satisfied by demonstrating an ability to sew clothes or play "Abide with Me" on the piano. But the winners are usually described only in terms of 36–24–35 or thereabouts. Rarely is the public supplied with anything more than the names, ages, hometowns, and measurements of the rivals.

The numerous sex manuals and guides, by focusing on the purely physical aspects of sexual behavior, also contribute to the tendency to detach sex from any affective involvement. Beginning with the Kinsey reports of 1948 and 1953,[5] the behavioral scientists, in particular, have been guilty of depersonalizing sex by treating it as almost entirely a stimulus-response phenomenon. Kinsey himself, in tabulating the frequency of orgasms no matter how achieved, was inclined to regard all "outlets" (a remarkable expression in itself) as essentially equal, thereby implying that there were no important differences between sexual intercourse and masturbation in terms of sexual satisfaction.[6]

The Kinsey tradition continues in the more recent investigations of William H. Masters and Virginia E. Johnson, but the Masters-Johnson approach to sexual behavior is even more impersonal and detached. Whereas Kinsey based his findings on what was reported by volunteer respondents, Masters and Johnson have devised elaborate techniques for measuring orgasmic response in a variety of situations. In their first book, *Human Sexual Response,* the result of an eleven year inquiry into the anatomy and physiology of sexual response, Masters and Johnson and their associates reported in detail the orgasmic experience of 382 women and 312 men, mostly between the ages of twenty-one and fifty, almost all of whom were paid volunteers.[7] The total of more than ten thousand orgasms, of which three-quarters were experienced by females, were recorded by camera, electrocardiographs, electroencephalographs, and other devices while the volunteer subjects were engaging in coition and masturbation. The conclusions in *Human Sexual Response,* tending to confirm what had long been known about physiological aspects of sexual experience, nevertheless were given extensive coverage in every major newspaper, and the book itself was widely reviewed; the *New York Times,* for example, devoted forty-one column inches to the book, including a two-column article about it on the front page of the second section, 18 April 1966.[8]

Unlike Kinsey, Masters and Johnson have long been interested in sexual malfunctions such as impotence, premature ejaculation and inability to ejaculate, frigidity, vaginismus (involuntary spasm of the muscles at the entrance to the vagina, thus preventing entrance of the penis), and painful intercourse. In *Human Sexual Inadequacy,* their second book published in 1970, they reported the results of eleven years of work on these problems, during which they treated 510 married couples and 57 single persons, all but 3 of whom were men. The immediate and five-year follow-up results were impressive: the overall success rate was a striking 80 percent, with primary impotence (men who had never experienced intercourse) accounting for the highest failure rate, or 40.6 percent, and premature ejaculation, the least important, for 2.7 percent. Failure was defined as the inability to achieve orgasm during the two-week treatment period, or as a return to the sexual malfunction within a period of five years after treatment.

Certainly these results are impressive, but again it should be noted that the Masters-Johnson approach to sex is to treat it as almost entirely a physiological and nonaffective response to a variety of stimuli. This emphasis is reflected even in the clinical setting; since they will not administer sexual therapy to persons without partners, "carefully screened female volunteers" were selected to work with the single men. Couples saw the therapists one hour or more each day, seven days each week for two weeks, during which the emphasis was on uninhibited communication and mutual participation. In keeping with the assumption that sexual satisfaction is always a stimulus-response outcome unless there is blocking, inhibition, or anxiety, separately or in combination, at some point in the sequence, the couple was gradually led to maximize their "sensate pleasure" in each other's bodies through tactile explorations. Toward this end the entire sensory apparatus of touching, feeling, hearing, tasting, and smelling was enlisted, and it was only when the therapists were convinced of the probability of successful intercourse that the couple was permitted to make the attempt.

As might have been expected, the sexual therapy techniques of Masters-Johnson Reproductive Biology Research Foundation have been widely copied, and almost as widely distorted. Many sex therapy clinics, in fact, are designed not to remedy sexual malfunctions in a relationship but to compensate for them or provide substitutes in the form of extramarital experiences. Thus there are nude encounter groups specializing in massage and other kinds of body exploration, and clinics where the "therapy" is supplied by surrogate sexual partners. Whether or not many such clinics are hardly more than disguised houses of prostitution, frequently the surrogate partners are former prostitutes who are paid well for their services. In at least one New York sex therapy center, the therapists themselves, who mainly are psychiatrists or psychologists, function as surrogate partners, while in other centers, therapists and their patients are encouraged to observe each other performing sexual acts.

In effect, the sex therapy centers, and phallic culture in general, tend to eliminate distinctions between what is public and what is private, just as they make it difficult to determine which behavior falls on the side of exhibitionism and which on the side of voyeurism. In the name of sexual liberation from inhibition and repression, all sexuality is deemed to be of public interest, and all citizens are at once both participants and observers, exhibitionists and voyeurs. Thus in phallic culture no biography, even of the most scholarly type, will be regarded as complete or "thorough" unless the author has discussed in detail the sexual life of his subject or, if factual information is lacking, has speculated at length about it. A female anthropologist who has done a study of aboriginal culture will be shown in a provocative pose on the book's dust jacket; the jacket photo of a young and pretty ethnologist will display her in shorts and a halter. Advertisements for novels increasingly will feature photos of authors made to look as sexually enticing as possible if they are women, or, if they are men, as rugged and handsome as the photographer's art will permit. In phallic culture, everyone is or must appear to be an object of sexual desire.[9]

Since celebrities, almost by definition, thrive on exposure and a willingness to exhibit themselves, they usually offer no objection to having their sexual lives become public property; perhaps this is particularly the case if they are persons of uncertain achievement whose celebrity status derives not from any accomplishment but from the space accorded them in the mass media. Prior to the emergence of phallic culture there were relatively few magazines publishing intimate information about the private lives of well-known individuals. The most successful ones, such as *Confidential,* were based on the formula that in every celebrity's life there is a secret vice, aberration, weakness, or departure from the moral norm about which many people would like to know, presumably because such knowledge satisfies the desire to see the famous, powerful, and rich reduced to the common condition of mankind, and also provides vicarious relief for lives that are drab and mediocre. Thus it was possible to read articles in the so-called scandal magazines about the alleged adulteries, promiscuities, alcoholism, homosexuality, and illegitimate children of a large number of Hollywood personalities.

In recent years, the *Confidential* formula has been adapted to a large number of general circulation magazines and newspapers, where, in the guise of a "profile" or "close-up," the private lives of celebrities are written about at length. For example, the "profiles" in the "Sunday Drama Section" of the *New York Times* invariably discuss the marital, drug, and drinking problems, if any, and the current sexual liaisons of "profile" subjects. Magazines such as *Good Housekeeping, Ladies Home Journal,* and *McCall's* regularly publish articles about the private lives of the Leonard Bernsteins, the Nelson Rockefellers, Princess Margaret and Lord Snowdon, the Shah of Iran and Queen Saroya, in addition to pieces about leading actors and actresses. John J. Miller, a widely read syndicated newspaper columnist, has made a career of reporting the fistfights, "emergency operations" (that is, abortions), and underworld connections of celebrities, in addition to their extramarital affairs, paternity suits, drunken episodes, and the like.[10]

For the most part, these stories are rarely challenged in the

courts, and when they are it is rare for the court to rule in favor
of the plaintiff. In a case brought against now-defunct *Look*
magazine in 1957, Frank Sinatra, at that time the leading *per-
sona* of many "profiles" and "close-up" articles, disputed
"the right of the press to report publicly the personal or private
lives of celebrities, as distinguished from their professional activity." *Look* "welcomed" the challenge as an "ideal test
. . . if the press is to be restricted as to facts it can publish about
such a public personality, it is important that the limits be
clearly defined."

Sinatra's suit was settled out of court, but by now it is clear
that *Look*'s position, implying that "public personalities" are
entitled to much less privacy than ordinary citizens, has been accepted by most courts and, needless to say, almost all magazine
editors. But, quite apart from the legal issues, it could hardly be
otherwise in phallic culture, considering the supreme importance the culture accords to sexual performance. Indeed, the
impact of the sexual revolution is such that what used to be regarded as loose and promiscuous behavior is now viewed as sexual emancipation or enlightenment, and those once stigmatized as tarts and gigolos are now admiringly referred to as
"swingers." It follows that the male and female sex symbols in
society must be capable, or appear to be capable, of outstanding
sexual achievement, and this in turn requires open and frequent
evidence in the mass media that they are "making out." Hence
subsequent articles about Sinatra, depicting at length his numerous romances with leading actresses, did not occasion response from the singer other than satisfaction, with the result
that by his retirement in 1970, he had been accorded the supreme accolade of phallic culture. He had become not merely
the chief male celebrity, or the leading "swinger," but, as the
New York Post put it, a "happening."

The Sinatras of real life have their counterparts in popular
novels, and here, too, the isolation of sex from other personality
components, which is the central feature of phallic culture, can
be seen in the treatment of love. Prior to World War II, love in
best-selling novels usually was depicted in romantic terms,
which is to say that the lovers in these novels were drawn to each
other by something more than the purely physical, clinical aspects of sex. Frequently the occurrence of the sexual act itself

was hinted at rather than made explicit, and where the sexual relationship was described, as in *For Whom the Bell Tolls* or *Anthony Adverse,* it was done with tenderness and romantic feeling.[11]

The clear tendency of much current fiction is to treat sex in purely clinical terms and to emphasize deviant practices such as rape, incest, and homosexuality. Even in the work of distinguished writers, such as Mary McCarthy, John Updike, and Philip Roth, the reader is better informed about the sexual experiences of the leading characters than about any other aspect of their lives or personalities. In Mary McCarthy's *The Group,* to take one instance, there are episodes of defloration and lesbianism, and although the people in the novel live together in and out of wedlock, marry and divorce, bear children, have jobs, even commit suicide, what is most vivid is their sexual behavior depicted at length and in careful detail. In *The Group* as in other novels, any emotion corresponding to love or affection, respect, and tenderness is subsidiary to sexual desire, or altogether absent.

But sexual desire itself may be muted, as in the novels of John O'Hara where sexual intercourse is without passion and sometimes almost as if the couple were bored by the whole business. Much of the copulation in contemporary fiction is casual and totally lacking in commitment, the result of chance encounters in bars, hotels, offices, planes, ships. What seems to matter is the sexual act itself, reduced to its simplest fundamentals, namely, the achievement of orgasm or "climax." Frequently a relationship proceeds to this as expeditiously as possible, with a minimum of characterization and of description of setting and scenery. We hear only of the physical and/or sexual attributes of the couple as they proceed to an orgasm free of psychological or emotional nuances. In O'Hara novels, which express a literary mastery of this orgasmic style, even conversation is reduced to the barest essentials.

Given the clinical emphasis of phallic culture, one begins to think of one's own autobiography as a sex drama that can be performed in front of a live audience; a husband's depiction of his wife's orgasm becomes simply another instance of life imitating not so much art as living theater.[12] Popular books and movies, such as *Last Tango in Paris* starring Marlon Brando, begin to resemble pornography, and pornographic works take on some of the attributes of an art form. Hence the necessity to make further distinctions, as between ''hard-core'' and ''soft-core'' pornography and between ''X''- and ''R''-rated movies. What was formerly pornographic in the art world and bought and sold behind the scenes is now relabeled erotic and becomes a legitimate subject for gallery exhibitions. Off-Broadway theater simulations of sex acts and nude shows presented in cellar cabarets to select audiences now move to big midtown playhouses and ultimately are performed nationwide by touring companies; *Deep Throat* is shown in Princeton, New Jersey. Phallic culture, in other words, inevitably gives rise to pornographic imperialism, the expansion of which is marked by a horizontal movement toward the mass audience, and an upward thrust toward acceptance as a genuine aesthetic experience.

Contributing to the rise of phallic culture is a basic change that has taken place in the practices by which the young are provided with basic enlightenment about the roles they are supposed to play in society. Where once there was a long and clearly defined time in youth during which one learned the etiquette and rules by which one would be expected to live and by means of which one could cope with one's developing sexuality, now no such period exists. Almost from the time a child can walk and talk, more accurately from the time he or she can turn on a television set, children are bombarded with sexually charged matter. Toys, television, advertisements, clothes, and most particularly records and news media all contribute to the pressure that brings children of today into adolescence with a veneer of sophistication that is no thicker than tissue paper. No doubt it is to the credit of those who survive such a beginning that they mature at all, and one cannot help wondering whether the failure to develop into adults capable of giving and receiving affection can be attributed in no small measure to the brutal confrontation between the myths of the sexual communication industry and the realities of everyday social life. The demands for immediate gratification that the society generates cannot be satisfied at anything near the rate necessary to keep everyone happy, nor would it necessarily be a good thing if they could.

One way to describe the changing trends in socialization is to say that family norms of right and wrong (rectitude), which are negatively sanctioned by acts of punishment and feelings of guilt, are replaced by the style-norms of the commercial entertainment industry, which are negatively sanctioned by expressions of contempt and feelings of shame. In terms of value-institution analysis these shifts can be perceived in several dimensions. Dominant impacts on socialization pass from an institution primarily specialized to affection to an institution of fun (well-being and wealth), the commercial entertainment and merchandising industry. The family transmits enlightenment about society, and takes special responsibility for eliciting behavior that conforms to the norms of rectitude and for generating a conscience that uses feelings of moral integrity and of guilt to sustain the norms. The mass media branch of the commercial entertainment and merchandising industry takes special responsibility for selling commodities and services, and incidentally it trains the young to accept changing styles of sexual and affectionate conduct and hence to feel pride (positive self-respect) in being "with it" and shame in being out of it.

Further exploring the shift from rectitude-based norms to norms founded on fun and fashion (well-being, respect), it is well to remember that a unified code of responsible conduct regarding love and sex is more a matter of doctrine than behavior in American or in western European society. When the peoples of Asia, Africa, and the Pacific Islands are added to the picture, and when the practices of the past are taken into account, no one can fail to recognize the great variety of ties that have bound different modes of sexuality with different expressions of affection. Evidently the explosive development of a mass communications industry in the United States, an industry that has remained relatively free of political censorship, has allowed the new technology to be exploited in the main for economic purposes.

It is obviously impossible for any social institution, and particularly for a major structure of communication, to operate in a social vacuum. This is demonstrated in all the chapters of the present work. It is no surprise to find that familial and educational institutions have been affected. What will puzzle future interpreters, perhaps, is the seeming passivity with which these traditional strongholds of the socialization process—the family and school, to which we might add the church—allowed their functions to be appropriated to such an extent by the mass media–commercial entertainment–merchandising industry.

Many psychologists, psychiatrists, and social scientists are in substantial accord in presenting the often-destructive consequences of an appeal to guilt as the supreme negative sanction of sexual norms, and hence by extension to other norms in a culture in which rectitude values are emphasized. They stress the self-righteousness, self-confidence, and inflexibility of rectitude-oriented persons. Much of this seems to stem from incipient guilt at recurring sexual impulses, and from the relief from self-condemnation by the device of projecting blame onto public objects. Hence autopunitive tendencies that otherwise might contribute to severe depressions are directed away from the self toward an "other." Is the implication that as shame is substituted for guilt, the internal tensions generated within personalities become less malignant?

In attempting to answer this question we distinguish between the potential significance of respect deprivations and the *actual* magnitude of such factors in the history of American society. There are no grounds for asserting that, in general, shame is less intensively deprivational than guilt. Psychiatric and anthropological data seem to show that both deprivations can be equally devastating. Our problem is whether a shift from rectitude to respect in this specific context is *in fact* more or less conflict-generating in regard to sexuality.

Viewed in historical depth, rectitude has been utilized by ecclesiastical authorities to control sexuality and also to benefit from the role of the church in alleviating the guilt generated by either overt or fantasied sexual acts. Hence the symbolic source of sexual practices endorsed by ecclesiastical authorities has been trans-empirical (Divine Will). Theologians have elaborated the chains of doctrine that connect the imputed source with explicit norms and applications. After the Reformation the number of competing ecclesiastical authorities increased as religious denominations became more numerous. More individuals accepted religious doctrines whose teachings in regard to sexual gratification might be either more or less deprivational than the Roman Catholic church of the early sixteenth century. Individuals often withdrew from organizations based on divine revelation and joined associations that asserted a metaphysical source of authority. Individuals also joined associations that purported to derive their norms from neither source (for example, ethical culture societies).

The obvious results of the fractionalizing trend are these: (1) guilt-generating norms in reference to sexuality, with the exception of an overreactive minority, have relaxed; (2) many new norms have been developed in the sphere of respect that are prescribed by the leaders of fashion (personal style), and enforced by feelings of embarrassment (shame) referred to above. The leaders of personal style are the popular heroes of the mass media, who compete with one another to navigate the largely unknown sea of vague predispositions (including the sexual) of young and old.

What, then, is the significance of these factors for frustration, self-deprivation, and politics? The guilt generated by sexuality is most intensely felt by those who have been exposed in early life to social environments in which older—that is to say, obsolescing—norms of a restrictive character were sought to be imposed. Subsequently, the norms might be vigorously rejected, an act that usually was accompanied and strengthened by the rejection of other patterns of traditional culture. However, the relatively rigid self-system could not shed its fundamental mode of seeking to solve its problems. Hence the erratic and extreme political positions taken up by ''authoritarians of the Left'' and ''authoritarians of the Right'' who succeed in utilizing the public objects of politics to reduce inner turmoil without becoming alienated from earlier codes.

In a society of accelerating diversity of role and heightened mobility among roles, the substitution of shame and pride for guilt and self-righteousness cannot fail to affect many institutions, including the political process. When personal style in sexuality, as in other life situations, depends on fashion models who gain visibility through the mass media, the expectation is that conceptions of politics will spread in the same way. For instance, the norms of family, student, and work groups will become more changeable and diverse. The formation of coalitions among the leaders of territorial and pluralistic groups will be favored by the increased openness of response.

In recent years depth psychologists who are concerned with

the emerging culture of highly industrialized societies have identified a socialization process that is closely entwined with the outlook disseminated through the many channels at the disposal of those who operate an opulent economy. A deprivation of love is indifference. Indifference is conveyed not by hatred, but by withdrawal and impersonality. If sexual blocking is accompanied by indifference, and indifference is the pattern incorporated by the self in dealing with the self, the personality that results differs from the guilt-ridden or shame-driven model. The individual is deeply alienated from himself, treating his sexual impulses with relative indifference. Will the individual be unconcerned with people, and at home only with abstractions and with ''things''? Will such a person adopt defense mechanisms that draw intensity from subterranean sexual impulses while operating with detached ruthlessness if circumstances catapult him into a ruling role?

It has been suggested that a fundamental source of difficulty in an ''affluent'' society is the lack of intensely expressed love by the primary socializers. The analysis is that with affluence the mother is permissive and evasive in dealing with the child, finding it easier to achieve conformity by the use of bribery than by facing the emotional turmoil of suppressing the child's demands and of giving genuine and intense love as a reward for the renunciation of unacceptable forms of gratification. The political implication is that young people in an affluent society become alienated from lack of properly timed frustration combined with love; hence they continue to pursue ego gratifications with no firmly organized self-system that identifies with the value position and prospects of large groups in society. The classical picture of personality growth as outlined by Freud emphasized the Oedipal situation, whose fundamental feature is the acceptance of frustration in the immediate context, and the incorporation of models that permit eventual gratifications to become acceptably specialized as to object choice and strategy of expression. The frustration is bearable because in return for love the completion of disapproved acts is relinquished. The hypothesis outlined above alleges that affluent societies incapacitate their rulers, their most privileged classes, from achieving their potentialities for responsible participation in decision.[13]

Absence of ''successful'' frustration (that is, renunciation combined with affirmative evaluations of the self) leads to "acting out," and acting out adds to the difficulties of collective action. Any failure to achieve a self that includes identification with the aspirations of the body politic is a danger to the integrity of the commonwealth. It diminishes the chances of orderly agreement, and increases the strength of factors that provoke coercion.

The self-indulgent mother presumably perceives herself as permissive in a sophisticated and self-fulfilling manner, and as a source of "things" that gratify the child and contribute to the material richness of the environment that challenges his skill and enlightenment. It is a chilling thought that she has failed as a meaningful source of affection and that this failure lets loose in our dangerous world a growing contingent of thing- and power-oriented persons whose capability for love and loyalty is deeply damaged.

The implication of the changes in love and intimacy, and in the socialization process of a technoscientific society, is not that the mass media of communication are solely responsible for what has happened. It would be untenable to affirm, on the contrary, that an institution of such pervasive scope can be regarded as free of impact on matters that receive cumulative attention. At the very least it is credible to affirm that the mass media act as accelerators and resonators of market initiatives and preferences in a high-consumption economy. The traditional institutions of love and intimacy are exploited and attenuated by the pervasive propagandas of goods and services. Small wonder that a widening span of disassociation separates affection from sexuality, and substitutes the strategy of bribery, even in the home, for the intensities of the emotional confrontations required for achieving a postphallic approach to life.

NOTES

1. George L. Ginsberg, *New York Times,* 15 March 1972. Formerly, Dr. Ginsberg reported, "patients with impotence were, for the most part, married men who gradually began to abandon sexual activity with their wives after a period of more successful functioning. They complained that the excitement

had passed, and that their wives no longer provided the variety in sexual practices they craved. Impotence was accompanied by minimal anxiety; they
usually had conscious fantasies about the secretary at work, the girl next door,
etc., and felt confident that novel objects or practices could revive their interest.''

2. The term *phallic* is borrowed from psychoanalytic usage, but is not used
here in precisely the same way. In psychoanalysis, phallic refers to the stage of
psychosexual development that follows the anal phase. It is characterized by a
heightened awareness of and interest in the penis or phallus of the male child
(usually at ages three to five), and the clitoris of the female. Masturbation is
common, as are pleasurable sensations associated with urination.

3. I am speaking of mass audience movies, not pornographic fare, where,
as in the love scene between Karen Black and Jack Nicholson in *Five Easy
Pieces,* the moment of climax is marked by visual and sound effects as dramatic as those that accompany depictions of battle scenes. The fantasy elements in
cinema orgasms have been too little noted by critics and viewers. Novelists,
too, have been prone to this kind of exaggeration. In J. P. Donleavy's *The
Onion Eater* (Penguin, 1972) for example, one of the female characters
achieves orgasm simply by being touched on the inside of her arm ''by the
elbow.'' The hero has three testicles, while in Donleavy's *A Singular Man*
(Penguin, 1966) the central male figure's penis is unusually large.

4. Rollo May in *Saturday Review,* 26 March 1966.

5. Alfred C. Kinsey, *Sexual Behavior in the Human Male* (1948) and *Sexual Behavior in the Human Female* (1953), both published by W. B.
Saunders Co. in Philadelphia.

6. Nothing said here is intended to minimize the fact that the Kinsey studies were significant pioneering contributions to knowledge. The point is that
they did not deal with aspects of sexual behavior other than physical, thus
denying, in effect, their importance.

7. William H. Masters and Virginia E. Johnson, *Human Sexual Response*
(Boston: Little, Brown and Co., 1970).

8. Despite the statement by the book's publisher that it would be of interest primarily to physicians, the book was on the *New York Times* best-seller
list for thirty-two consecutive weeks following publication. The two Kinsey reports had been best sellers also, although they, too, had been billed as being
of interest primarily to physicians and marriage counselors. Since publishers
are not known for their naiveté, the hypocrisy of the initial statement deceived
no one.

9. While it is conventional practice for paperbacks and record albums to
feature nude female models on their covers, even if the material within originated with Thomas Mann or Mozart, a recent innovation in the record field is
the nude appearance of the performing artist. Outstanding examples include
front views of John and Yoko Lennon on an album released in Britain al-

though not in the United States, and a back view of Joni Mitchell on the inside jacket of one of her records. The dust jackets of recent books by Mickey Spillane feature photographs of his wife, nude.

10. Techniques of snooping and spying have been transformed in recent years by a revolution in electronic gadgetry that has effectively destroyed what remained of privacy in and out of the bedroom. No doubt most of the eavesdropping devices—a microphone hidden in the martini olive, a tape recorder concealed in the attaché case, and so forth—are used for purposes of business espionage, but it is probable that these and other devices are coming into extensive use for personal and social entertainment. Magazines such as *Esquire* have advertised "The Snooper—World's Only Private Listening Device," guaranteed to pick up normal conversations at a distance of five hundred feet. A New York firm specializes in one-way bedroom and bathroom mirrors that can be seen through from one side, and wall-attachment listening gadgets that can pick up whispered conversations in the next apartment.

11. It is arguable that the character of hard-core pornography has also changed with the emergence of phallic culture. For example, in *Fanny Hill,* first published in 1748, the kindness and thoughtfulness that Fanny's successive lovers display for her sensibilities as well as erogenous zones almost justify characterizing the book as a novel of manners and courtly behavior.

12. In an article about his release from prison after having served an eight-month sentence, *Eros* publisher Ralph Ginzburg writes of his reunion with his wife: "Wordlessly, we undressed. . . . I was overwhelmed by the lush relevation of things about her that are precious to me: a certain look in her eyes, the conformation of her hands, the smell of her hair, the curve of her hip. . . . Lost to all reason and restraint, we made love. The force of our orgasm shattered the damming walls of anxiety . . . at the moment when the tidal wave of my wife's sexual passion burst through, all her other passions flooded close behind" (*New York Times Magazine,* 3 December 1972).

13. See Alexander Mitscherlich, "Changing Patterns of Political Authority: A Psychiatric Interpretation," in Lewis Edinger, ed., *Political Leadership in Industrialized Societies: Studies in Comparative Analysis* (New York: John Wiley & Sons, 1967); also Harold D. Lasswell, "Political Systems, Styles and Personalities," in Edinger, *Political Leadership.*

THE MULTIVARIATE PROCESS

6

THE LANGUAGE OF POLITICS: GENERAL TRENDS IN CONTENT

ITHIEL DE SOLA POOL

This summer I read, in a little counterestablishment magazine, a definition of politics as the giving of old answers to new questions.

That is not a bad definition for an activity that can still find in Aristotle and Plato most of its current formulations. But like any aphorism, it is, at best, a half-truth. Modern behaviorist political scientists prefer to replace vigorous aphorisms with statements of the form: "on the one hand this and on the other hand that." They prefer to measure the relative power of each opposing factor. So be it with the balance between what is old and what is new.

Our topic here is political symbols, and our purpose is to assess the relative weight of the old and the new in them.

Twenty years ago, in 1951, I published a series of studies, the RADIR symbol studies,[1] dealing with trends in political symbols over a sixty-year period, 1890–1950. It was a content analysis. The methodology was primitive by contemporary standards. Harold Lasswell and Daniel Lerner drew up a list of some four hundred key political terms and we measured their appearance in the editorials of the top prestige papers in the United States, Great Britain, France, Germany, and Russia. About half of the terms were country, regional, and ethnic names, the other half such conceptual symbols as DEMOCRACY, LIBER-

TY, COLLECTIVE SECURITY, WAR, PEACE, and PRIVATE PROPERTY. No rigorous criterion for inclusion or exclusion of terms was made explicit. An attempt was made to include all the words that seemed intuitively to be key political symbols that had been used over a substantial period of time and in more than one country's editorials. The coders were urged to note important symbols that were missing from the original list, and those words were added to the list.

I have no inclination to defend this methodology beyond asserting that it produced a list reflecting the best judgment of a panel of conscientious, informed judges.

Now twenty years have passed, one-third of what then seemed to be the long sweep of "the revolution of our time." It is interesting to look back over these twenty years and ask how has political language changed. What new symbols have come along that we would have to include today were we to repeat the content analysis and that then we missed as not important or that did not exist in 1950?

To replicate the RADIR study we would have to count symbols in five prestige papers for the past twenty years. That would be a major undertaking, costing several tens of thousands of dollars. We have not done that, but I have taken the first few preliminary steps. I have reexamined the symbol list in the same way as we originally constructed it, considering what changes would now be required, and I have pretested the new suggestions against a small sample of editorials from 1969–1970.

I am, therefore, in no position to say anything as yet about trends in frequencies. I must limit myself in this chapter to the question of what symbols may be new.

A priori, one might expect a vast change in our political language. Clearly, we are living in a society that is changing as never before. There may be differences of opinion as to the nature of the revolution, but it is hard to deny that we are living in a revolution. Many social phenomena show an exponential growth curve with doubling times between seven and fifty years. The world's population doubles in roughly every half century, the gross national product in roughly every twenty years, the number of scientists in about fifteen years, and the destructiveness of weapons and war also in about fifteen years. Libraries and book production also double in size about every fifteen to twenty years.

That means that most of what is around us, in area after area, is new:

More than half of all products in supermarkets did not exist a decade ago.[2]

Half of all the people who have ever walked on the face of the earth are alive today.

Eighty-seven percent of the scientists who have ever lived are alive today.

Similarly, more than half the books that have ever appeared have been published since 1950.

Similar figures could be given for all the paintings, all the musical compositions, all the poems, all the inventions, all the picket lines, and all the propaganda pamphlets, if we had the data to calculate the number.

Under such circumstances, there would be reason to expect that political language is changing with comparable rapidity. Occasionally, one hears comments to that effect. A popular type of article in the mass media these days is one on the new language of the hip generation. There is no doubt that in well-defined in-groups of young people, slang (to use an old-fashioned word) changes with a rapidity that immediately distinguishes the informed, "in," conforming group member from others who may have been skilled users of the argot as recently as two years before. That is not a new phenomenon. There has always been a radical chic along with fads in popular culture. That the code words in these private languages wear out faster than ever before is likely, but something we do not know for sure.

More interesting, however, is the degree and rate with which these private argots are absorbed into the established political language. This happens in several ways.

1. It happens when the counterculture becomes so strong that the Establishment has to talk about it and needs a name to apply to it. Sometimes the established language applies a derogatory name which the dissidents do not use for themselves, for example, Viet Cong, which was a deprecatory term for Vietnamese communists, not used by them. More often the group's

own self-designation, or at least one of them, is adopted into the accepted language, for example, Bolshevik, New Left, and hippie.

2. Argot also is absorbed in the manner of restriction by partial incorporation when the establishment, or a part of it, adopts a dissident political symbol to represent its own values. At an earlier period (as the RADIR studies showed) DEMOCRACY was a symbol so assimilated. More recently, ECOLOGY, POLLUTION, RELEVANCE, ALIENATION, PROTEST, DISSENT, and THIRD WORLD have shown signs of becoming normal vocabulary.

In any case, it is the elite vocabulary, in the editorials of prestige papers, not the changing argots of countercultures, that the RADIR project studied. The papers we content-analyzed included the *New York Times, London Times, Izvestia, Frankfurter Zeitung,* and *Le Monde.* In looking at the last twenty years, we want to ask, therefore, what new key symbols have entered the standard political vocabulary, not what has entered the argots of special groups.

When I started writing this chapter, as a first step I asked colleagues what trends in political symbolism they observed. A common answer was to note a rise in rudeness. From where my informants sat, they may have been right. Civility perhaps has been a casualty of the new politics among the academic intelligentsia. But in the worldwide rhetoric of established regimes, the 1960s were an era of politeness as compared with that of Hitler and Stalin. A rise in rudeness is not a trend that appears in the prestige press.

One finding of the RADIR study that we might test against the past twenty-year experience is that persistent changes in political symbolism occur surprisingly slowly. The earlier study would suggest that changes in language do not fit the model that applies to inventions, science, libraries, and population. Let us review what we found in the original study about the extent of change from 1890 to 1950.

We found that short-term fluctuations in symbolism often were marked but that the basic political vocabulary, around which the fluctuations swung, changed only slowly. For example, the two world wars and the rise of nazism each quickly produced a characteristic rhetoric that came and went. In the whole

TABLE 6–1.
Amount of Change as Shown by Index Used in 1950 Study

	Change From			
	Pre–World War I to 1920s	1920s to early 1930s	Early to late 1930s	Late 1930s to Post–World War II
United States	40	9	6	111
Great Britain	40	10	14	65
France	63	12	56	139
Russia	2306	70	116	160
Germany	–	29	110	–

SOURCE:
   The Prestige Press: A Comparative Study of Political Symbols (Cambridge: M.I.T. Press, 1970).
NOTE:
   Index based on chi-squares.

sixty years in the four countries studied, only the Russian Revolution produced an extensive and abrupt change in vocabulary that then persisted. In the *London Times* the cumulative change in symbolism from before World War I until after World War II as measured by the index of change used in that study is only slightly more than the short-run changes in the decade from the late 1930s to the late 1940s. In the *New York Times* the same is true. In the French papers the short-run fluctuations are greater, but the cumulative change for the sixty years is no greater. (These points are documented in table 6-1, drawn from the original RADIR studies.)

Among nontrivial changes in key political symbols that persisted once the change had occurred, the following were noted in the original study. In England, the replacement of the Liberal party by the Labour party as the recognized voice of the left was accompanied by a decline in the frequency of such terms as REFORM, RADICALS, LIBERALISM, and PROGRESS, and in the increased incidence of SOCIALISM, NATIONALIZATION, and TRADE UNIONS. In the United States, there was one major and persistent change in political vocabulary in the *New York Times* editorials over the sixty-year period. The change was a reflection of America's increased involvement in a warlike world. For example, the four symbols that rose most from before World War I to after World War II were PEACE, WAR, ARMAMENTS, and SECURITY.

Only in Russia did political language change drastically in the sixty years till 1950, and that change was not just in 1917. The changes were summarized in our early study. First, the Revolution brought a whole new vocabulary to the fore. Words like SOVIET, BOURGEOISIE, PROLETARIAT, COMMUNISM, BOLSHEVISM, RED, and COUNTERREVOLUTION that had been part of the specialized vocabulary of small sects were adopted into the establishment vocabulary in the Soviet Union, and as a result also into the vocabulary of the capitalist establishment papers in the West. Most of this new vocabulary persisted or increased in use up to 1950, but not all. Some of the more technical jargon such as PROLETARIAT began to give way to more familiar, old-fashioned terms such as WORKERS or MASSES. More important, patriotic symbolism began to displace Marxist symbolism. Terms like PATRIOTISM, FATHERLAND, and STATE were all along as prominent in *Izvestia* as they had been in its Czarist predecessor, became more prominent in the 1930s, became the dominant symbols during World War II, and remained so afterward.

Although such changes indeed were taking place, the striking dominant fact is basic continuity of political vocabulary from 1890 to 1950.

One thing that Table 6-1 does suggest, but only suggest, is that the rate of change in political symbolism may have been growing. In three of the four countries represented, the last period showed the largest change. It is certainly not surprising, and perhaps not indicative of any trend, that in the United States, Britain, and France the changes that spanned wars were larger than successive peacetime changes, nor that the changes spanning World War II were greater than those spanning World War I. But there are enough clues of a trend of accelerating change to make that hypothesis an important candidate for testing in later data. Is the persistence of basic political symbolism that we found in 1950 going to continue?

For 1970 we proceeded roughly as in the original study, first intuitively considering what terms should be placed on a list of key symbols. Then we checked that list for omissions in a sample of editorials. Later, we hope to do a quantitative replication to test frequencies of the new and old terms.

There are few obviously new terms. For example, the country and minority name lists, which I have not reproduced, now would include Tanzania, Laos, Vietnam, United Arab Republic, and Ibo among many new names. Those changes, however, we shall skip as of less theoretical interest. We shall limit ourselves to new conceptual terms.

There was a list of 199 conceptual symbols whose incidence was tabulated in the original study.[3] Ask yourself what additional terms would have to be added in 1970. That is what I have done by myself, with a graduate political science class, with my colleagues in the original study, and with expert informants in Europe and America.

The result is 101 new candidates for inclusion on the list. Grouping these tells us a lot about the politics of the last two decades. With a certain number of arbitrary decisions they fall more or less naturally under nine topics:

Terms related to	Number of candidate terms considered for addition
The bipolar world conflict	26
Developing nations	12
Communist ideology	8
Dissent	16
Individuals in relation to society	15
Life style	6
Welfare	5
Technology	6
Ecology	7
	101

Before presenting these nine groups, two minor points about procedure must be clarified, that is, the problem of synonyms and the problem of old terms whose meaning may have changed.

Synonyms: Keep in mind that our original content analysis was in four languages. Clearly by a symbol we mean a meaning unit, not a typographical one. AMERICA and USA were the same symbol. We even coded leaders such as the president under the country name. And we grouped certain closely related concepts. So now, too, when we add the new organizations of European integration we treat them all as one symbol. EMERGING NATIONS and NEW STATES are for us one symbol, as in some language other than English they may be.

Changing meanings: To cope with this problem we will list below, in a column parallel to the new terms, other terms that one might have expected to find on a list of current jargon, but that already appeared on the list in 1950. In many instances we note a change in the connotations, and sometimes in the denotations of those words. That second list is suggestive rather than exhaustive, for any term on the old list might in the current usage have a somewhat different implication than it did in the past. The usefulness of the second list is to save the reader from searching two hundred terms to spot obviously important and changing current terms that would otherwise seem to be omitted.

With that much introduction let us examine the nine lists of new terms. The number of new terms in list 1 reflects the pervasiveness of war and bipolar struggle in the past two decades. More than a quarter of the listed new symbols deal with that domain.

What is more, there is hardly any item on that list that is of dubious importance. BRINKSMANSHIP is arguable. If we do a content analysis in all five countries for each year in the two decades, it is very likely that BRINKSMANSHIP would not appear in the sample or would do so only a few times. But every other word on the list has been in the focus of attention for at least several years and in more than one country.

PEOPLE'S DEMOCRACY is an interesting special case. Both PEOPLE and DEMOCRACY were on our 1950 list, but the whole in this instance is not the sum of the parts. In our original list we felt it necessary to list BOURGEOIS DEMOCRACY as a separate symbol from DEMOCRACY. Clearly the same applies here; PEOPLE'S DEMOCRACY must be treated as a new symbol.

List 2 reflects another of the dominant political forces of our time, the emergence of the Third World.

Of the ten symbols on the list, only two, RISING EXPECTATIONS and the IBRD, might turn out to be infrequent. On the other hand there are several symbols that already would have been coded if one used the 1950 list, but in ways that would miss their new meaning. To code NEOCOLONIALISM under COLONIZATION, PAN-AFRICAN under AFRICA, NEGRITUDE under NEGRO, would miss much of what is essential. At least NEOCOLONIALISM is both new enough and frequent enough to be a necessary addition to the 1950 list.

LIST 1.
Symbols Related to Bipolar Conflict

New Symbols	Related Words on Old List
Referring to alliances and organizations:	
FREE WORLD	PEOPLE'S DEMOCRACY
COMMUNIST BLOC, WARSAW PACT,	
COMECON	COMMUNISM (WORLD)
NATO, ATLANTICISM	
COMMON MARKET, OEEC, OECD,	
COAL–STEEL COMMUNITY, M.L.F.	EUROPE
SEATO, CENTO, ANZUS	
OAS, ALLIANCE FOR PROGRESS,	
INTER–AMERICAN BANK	SOUTH AMERICA
IRON CURTAIN	
SATELLITE NATIONS	COLONIES
Referring to balance of power:	
BIPOLAR	AMERICA (includes ANTI–AMERICA)
MULTILATERAL	USSR (includes ANTI–SOVIET)
SUPERPOWERS	
PEACEFUL (COMPETITIVE)	
COEXISTENCE	PEACE
CONVERGENCE	
DÉTENTE, DISENGAGEMENT	ISOLATIONISM
SUPRANATIONALISM, REGIONALISM,	
INTEGRATION	INTERVENTIONISM
CONTAINMENT	
COLD WAR	
Referring to war:	
ATOMIC, NUCLEAR POWER, NUCLEAR	DISARMAMENT (includes ARMS
BLACKMAIL	CONTROL)
DETERRENCE	COLLECTIVE SECURITY
BRINKSMANSHIP	
MISSILE GAP	
LIMITED WAR	REVOLUTION, COUNTER-
TOTAL WAR	REVOLUTION, CIVIL WAR,
	INSURRECTION (includes
	INSURGENCY PACIFICATION,
	COUNTERINSURGENCY
ESCALATION	
GENOCIDE, WAR CRIMES	

Besides war and the emerging nations, a third great source of vocabulary for current politics is radical ideology. From 1917 till World War II, it was Moscow from which the new concepts came, and indeed, as we noted above, Moscow was overwhelmingly the major source for the whole world of whatever new ideological vocabulary persisted. But since 1950 very few of the new symbols have come from there. We have made a perhaps

LIST 2.

Symbols Related to Developing Nations

New Symbols	Related Words on Old List
THIRD WORLD	NEUTRALISM (includes NONALIGNED)
EMERGING NATIONS, NEW STATES	
MODERNIZATION	NEGRO (includes NEGRITUDE)
DEVELOPMENT, UNDERDEVELOPMENT, LDCs	AFRICA (includes PAN-AFRICANISM)
NATION BUILDING	
INDUSTRIALIZATION	
INDEPENDENCE	
PANCHA–SILLA	
RISING EXPECTATIONS, DEMONSTRATION EFFECT	
IBRD, UN DEVELOPMENT FUND	
NEOCOLONIALISM	IMPERIALISM
	COLONIZATION
FOREIGN AID	

somewhat arbitrary distinction between symbols related to communist ideology and other symbols of dissent. Eight terms are included in the first column of list 3, but of them only five are derived from Soviet output.[4] REVISIONISM and CULTURAL REVOLUTION are terms given most currency by the Chinese, and NEW LEFT by revisionists. The term LIBERALIZATION also might be included here, but has instead been included on list 5 (shown and discussed below) dealing with the relation of the individual to society. However one makes these more or less arbitrary marginal decisions, it is clear that the intellectual sources of dissident symbolism clearly have shifted.

The term NEW LEFT might well have been included on the list of terms related to dissent. With it or without it, that list reflects a much more lively seedbed of ideas today than do the publications of the established communist regimes.

The prototypic terms in list 4 are PROTEST and DISSENT. Those are not new terms, but in the past they were more or less colorless verbs. As nouns with high valence they need to be added to a list of contemporary political symbols.

The valence of most of the symbols on list 4 reflects the widespread assumption among contemporary intellectuals that it is somehow more sophisticated and moral to criticize the institutions than to justify them. In most contemporary discussion of the subject in this country (not, of course, in the Soviet Union),

LIST 3.
Symbols Related to Communist Ideology

New Symbols	Related Words on Old List
REVISIONISM	COMMUNISM
SECTARIANISM	SOCIALISM
VOLUNTARISM	REVOLUTION
STALINISM, DESTALINIZATION	
COLLECTIVE LEADERSHIP	
CULT OF THE INDIVIDUAL	
CULTURAL REVOLUTION	
NEW LEFT	

LIST 4.
Symbols Related to Dissent

New Symbols	Related Words on Old List
DISSENT, PROTEST, MILITANT	REFORM
CONFRONTATION	
DISRUPTION	
NONVIOLENCE, CIVIL DISOBEDIENCE	RESISTANCE
HIPPIE, BEATNIK, YIPPIE, COUNTER-CULTURE	
CHANGE	PROGRESSIVE
CRITICAL (KRITISCHE)	
CONSCIOUSNESS (e.g., REVOLUTIONARY CONSCIOUSNESS)	
LIBERATION, NLF, WARS OF NATIONAL LIBERATION, WOMEN'S LIB.	REVOLUTION, LIBERTY, CIVIL WAR (includes INSURGENCY, GUERRILLA WAR)
GLEICHBERECHTIGUNG	EQUALITY
EXTREMISM	RADICAL
MCCARTHYISM	
THE ESTABLISHMENT	AUTHORITY (includes AUTHORITARIAN)
CO-OPTION	
BLACK POWER	RACISM
BLACK MUSLIMS, BLACK PANTHERS	NEGRO (includes BLACK)

the proper role of the journalist is said to be to expose abuses rather than to build national or social cohesion. Similarly, the proper role of the intellectual is said to be that of social critic, not aide and adviser to men of power. From Plato and Kautilya through Machiavelli and since, there has been a rival view that perceives of intellectuals as guides to princes, but today it is more popular to see them as exposers of princes. What little justification is given for this postulated norm is the cliché that "this is a bad society."

It is not for us here either to support or to criticize this particular value-judgment. It is enough to take note of it as an unexamined article of faith, the power of which in the contemporary world is demonstrated by the vocabulary on list 4. Only two of the terms on the list carry a negative effect toward dissent, namely, DISRUPTION and EXTREMISM.[5] There are three words on the list that refer not to the dissidents but to their opponents, but in all three cases with negative effect: MCCARTHYISM, THE ESTABLISHMENT, and CO-OPTION.

HIPPIE and earlier BEATNIK are ambivalent terms, used with pride by those they describe, but by most of society as terms of abuse.

For the rest, however, the terms of dissent are terms with positive affect. Some of them are infrequently used, but when used they justify dissent. NONVIOLENCE, CIVIL DISOBEDIENCE, CHANGE, and LIBERATION are all rallying symbols for their advocates.

LIBERATION and GLEICHBERECHTIGUNG (translatable as "redress of inequality") are both activist variants on words that already existed on the old list. LIBERTY is a long-established symbol, but the newly popularized symbol LIBERATION implies a positive act to overcome existing oppression. EQUALITY also is a long-established symbol, but GLEICHBERECHTIGUNG implies a positive act to overcome existing inequality. The activist terms are sufficiently different from their counterparts and sufficiently prominent in current rhetoric so that they should be considered as new key symbols.

LIBERATION has, of course, its various special forms: NATIONAL LIBERATION as in "wars of——" and "——Front." And now there is WOMEN'S LIBERATION, given that highest testimony of acceptance that any symbol can have, namely, a nickname, "WOMEN'S LIB."

Perhaps ANTIAUTHORITARIANISM and also AUTHORITARIANISM should be added to the list. These words, when they previously occurred, were coded with the term AUTHORITY, one of the words on the old list. But clearly the meaning has changed. AUTHORITY was a slowly vanishing symbol of the right, referring favorably to legitimacy, not a term that referred unfavorably to a rigid oppressive style of personal relationship. Whether we choose to treat this as a change of valence

LIST 5.
Symbols Relating the Individual to Society

New Symbols	Related Words on Old List
ALIENATION	
PRIVACY	
PLURALISM	
PARTICIPATORY (e.g., DEMOCRACY)	
POWER TO THE PEOPLE	
COMMITMENT	
EXISTENTIALISM	
RELEVANCE	
CONFORMITY	
CREDIBILITY GAP	
REPRESSION, REPRESSIVE TOLERATION	
DROP–OUT, COP–OUT	
LIBERALIZATION (e.g., ABORTION LAWS or EROSION OF DICTATORSHIPS)	ORDER (including LAW AND ORDER)
ANTIINTELLECTUALISM	CIVIL RIGHTS
SEGREGATION, DESEGREGATION, APARTHEID	BILL OF RIGHTS (including HUMAN RIGHTS)

and of connotation or as a new term is an arbitrary matter. There has been change.

One might also make a case for treating the words INSURGENCY, COUNTERINSURGENCY, and GUERRILLA WAR as new key symbols, for as particular phonemes they are newly fashionable; but they are not new words, and when they occurred in the past they were coded under their then more usual synonyms, REVOLUTION, CIVIL WAR, and COUNTERREVOLUTION. It is hard to argue that the change is anything but verbal.

Similarly the term BLACK is newly popular but a synonym for NEGRO on the older list. BLACK POWER, BLACK MUSLIM, and BLACK PANTHER, however, clearly are newly popularized concepts. POWER in this sense perhaps deserves to be singled out as a generalized radical concept quite apart from its particular usage with BLACK. The more general usage, PEOPLE'S POWER, appears on the next list.

The next list of new symbols, list 5, also is closely related to social dissent. It consists of terms that deal with the relation of the individual to society.

What these terms seem to have in common is a view of the individual as a potential victim needing to be protected from an oppressive society. REPRESSION, ALIENATION, SEGREGA-TION, CONFORMITY is what he suffers. POWER, PRIVACY, PARTICIPATION is what he needs. COMMITMENT, RELE-VANCE, PLURALISM, LIBERALIZATION may get him there.

Aside from EXISTENTIALISM and Marcuse's causuistry of REPRESSIVE TOLERATION, few of these words are new. Some are newly politicized. PRIVACY was not recognized as a right in common law precedents. Only since a law review article by Louis Brandeis has it gradually acquired legal recognition in this country. Currently, discussions of computers, consumer credit, and social science research use that symbol continuously. By now it clearly belongs on any list of rights.

Other terms on the list such as ALIENATION and PARTICI-PATION are old in political theory but recent in popularized rhetoric. A few of the other terms have been political symbols for a long time and might even have been oversights from the 1950 list, but now clearly are important. Among them are PLURALISM, POWER TO THE PEOPLE (recall ''all power to the Soviets''), and LIBERALIZATION.

Both the latter terms are examples of what we called activist variants on old terms. Power has long been a political symbol, though so general a term as not to have entered our 1950 list. PEOPLE'S POWER, STUDENT POWER, WORKER'S POWER (the latter admittedly an older expression) all suggest an aggressive demand to do something. So, too, LIBERALIZA-TION (like LIBERATION) is not just a verbal variant of the philosophical concept of LIBERTY, but rather implies more by way of action, even if less by way of ultimate achievement.

REPRESSION certainly is not a new concept. In 1950 we would have coded the various references to oppression and repression under TYRANNY or DICTATORSHIP. However, the term REPRESSION, like COMMITMENT, RELEVANCE, and CONFORMITY, has acquired a popular propaganda life of its own. In contrast to the common words of the language, which they originally were, these terms have become symbols that are used chiefly by adherents of a particular ideological position. They are words whose very usage is a flag signaling the speaker's point of view. They are words that at least started their life as key political symbols in social criticism from the left.

LIST 6.

Symbols Related to Personal Life-Style

New Symbols

LIFE–STYLE
GENERATION GAP
COMMUNE
DRUGS, ADDICTION
ABORTION
UP TIGHT

In exactly the same way LAW AND ORDER consists of every-day words but has been adopted as a flag by the right.

On the other hand, CREDIBILITY GAP is not everyday language, but jargon. What is interesting about that symbol is that it belongs to a class of terms all of which use the same new metaphor, GAP, that is, a difference of rates in a process of development. That is a highly sophisticated concept that could be natural only to people in a post-Newtonian world of change. The MISSILE GAP, the GENERATION GAP, the DOLLAR GAP, the CREDIBILITY GAP, and the REVOLUTION OF RISING EXPECTATIONS all involve the same metaphor or conception.

GENERATION GAP belongs to the next list of symbols (list 6) that refer to LIFE-STYLES. The life-styles that have become political issues in the last decades represent dissident views of the role of the individual in society. The terms on this new list tend, therefore, to come from the same realms of discourse as do the two preceding lists, those on dissent and on the role of the individual.

Perhaps the most significant thing about the list of symbols of life-style is that these terms are political symbols at all. They refer to behavior in the most private parts of life, but they also have become part of public political discourse. None of the terms on our 1950 list had that character. Not that there were no issues then about private behavior, including free love, Prohibition, and similar matters. Perhaps a retrospective content analysis would show our 1950 list to have had omissions. What we can safely say, however, is that in 1970 a political symbol list that failed to include terms referring to issues about life-styles would be untenable.

Most of the lists we have looked at so far have had a distinc-

LIST 7.
Symbols Related to Welfare Goals

New Symbols	Related Words on Old List
WELFARE STATE	THE COMFORTABLE LIFE (includes AFFLUENCE, ECONOMY OF ABUNDANCE)
PLANNING, PLANNED ECONOMY	
DISADVANTAGED	
POVERTY, HUNGER, THE POOR	
CHRISTIAN DEMOCRACY	

tively radical flavor. Except for the terms referring to the cold war, most of the terms so far were radical at least in origin, though many eventually were picked up for partial incorporation into the mainstream of language. Richard Nixon talks about POWER TO THE PEOPLE. Nonetheless, the predominant effect, usage, and reference of the terms on lists 3 to 6 are clearly to the left. We now move into some terminology of a more moderate character.

It is significant of something about our era that when we look at the symbols that relate to welfare goals (list 7) we find the key terms to be in the vocabulary of governments as much as in the vocabulary of movements of dissent. In the United States, we find that the New Deal, the Fair Deal, and the Great Society promoted PLANNING, the WELFARE STATE, the attack on POVERTY, and aid to the DISADVANTAGED.

Elsewhere around the world, (inter alia in Chile, Venezuela, France, Italy, and Germany) moderate Catholic parties, generally labeled CHRISTIAN DEMOCRATIC, moved AUTHORITY, and antiatheism to moderate policies of reform and welfare.

The list of symbols for welfare goals is not a list of terms that are the *exclusive* prerogative of the middle. On the contrary. These are terms used by dissidents, too. The point seems to be that in the post-1950s world they are consensus terms, used with much the same affect by all but the extreme right.

Incidentally we include CHRISTIAN DEMOCRACY on our symbol list but not GREAT SOCIETY or the earlier NEW DEAL because our principle is to include symbols whose usage spans periods and locations. We do not include terms, important as they may be, whose usage was in only one particular time

LIST 8.

Symbols Related to Technology

New Symbols

AUTOMATION
CYBERNETICS
URBANIZATION
TECHNOCRACY
COST–EFFECTIVENESS, SYSTEMS
    ANALYSIS
SPACE, MOON

LIST 9.

Symbols Related to Ecology

New Symbols

ECOLOGY, ENVIRONMENT
POLLUTION
CONSERVATION
BLIGHT, DECAY (URBAN)
QUALITY OF LIFE
CONSUMERISM
POPULATION, POPULATION PLANNING,
    OVERPOPULATION, BIRTH
    CONTROL, CONTRACEPTION,
    PLANNED PARENTHOOD,
    ABORTION

and place. NEW DEAL was a political term for the United States in the 1930s. CHRISTIAN DEMOCRACY, on the other hand, shows evidence of becoming a more widespread phenomenon in Western Europe.

The symbols in lists 8 and 9 relate to technology and pollution. Given the vast impact of science on the modern world, those lists may seem small ones, and still so even if we add several terms from the list referring to war. Outer SPACE and the MOON as well as CYBERNETICS and AUTOMATION have become political issues, but perhaps not proportionately to their role in society.

Note, however, that the 1950 list did not have even a single such term. URBANIZATION already was a major fact of life in the nineteenth century. TECHNOCRACY had been a fly-by-night movement in California in the 1930s. CONSERVATION was, of course, a respectable political movement going back to the Theodore Roosevelt era. But none of those terms could have been justified as major world political symbols in 1950. No scientific term had entered the arena of politics strongly enough to cause us to include it in our list at that time.

The rise of attention to science-related issues clearly is a dramatic change. It can be illustrated by an anecdote. In 1970, a mere two years after the publication of the new edition of the *International Encyclopedia of the Social Sciences*, I had reason to seek a review of the social science literature on pollution. Somewhat to my surprise, that entry was listed in the *Encyclopedia* index. Turning to *P,* I found the article. It was an article by the anthropologist Mary Douglas dealing with taboos around the world regarding women after menses and childbirth. That was what pollution meant in 1968.

In summary, what can we say from looking at the new symbols of politics from the past twenty years?

One major change, the last one discussed, is the emergence of science as a political issue and as a source of political language.

A second major change is the fertility of antiestablishment dissent as a source of political vocabulary, and its emphasis on vocabulary referring to life-styles and the relation of the individual to society. In contrast to the situation in the three previous decades, in which communist regimes in power generated widely accepted new jargon, in these last two decades it has been the dissident intelligentsia expressing their generalized alienation that has created the new vocabulary of protest.

A third major force on political vocabulary has been the ever-present threat of war. The largest single source of new symbols has been the bipolar power struggle.

The next step in this research is to test (by counting) the hypotheses just noted, and to test them in the five countries of our earlier study. Counting is important, particularly to test one additional hypothesis that is suggested, but only suggested, by our present results. At the start of this chapter we found that until 1950 political vocabulary had been a surprisingly stable social phenomenon in the prestige papers of the major powers. We also found a few clues in the 1890–1950 data to indicate that the rate of change was perhaps beginning to grow. In our preliminary study of 1950–1970 we find much evidence of change.

The evidence is in the form of an extraordinary number of

important new terms. Even if only half the new symbols that we have listed turn up with any frequency in the editorials of the prestige papers, when we actually count, then this clearly will be evidence of increasingly rapid change in political vocabulary. Is language joining science, invention, production, and many other social phenomena on a curve of exponential change? If so, that could have profound implications for the politics of the future. Our generation already has the experience that the technology and skills we learn in school are not the technology and skills needed in our more mature years. Are we entering an era in which it becomes increasingly true that the concepts and ideologies into which we are socialized in our postadolescent years will no longer be relevant to our years of maturity? If so, the consequences for the age and character of political leaders, and their capability of bridging various gaps to their followers, are very severe. Alienation, conflict, and future shock may be increasingly fed by accelerating change in one more aspect of society, the symbolic one. Perhaps political language is entering into a process of accelerating (and maybe exponential) change.

NOTES

1. Republished as *The Prestige Press: A Comparative Study of Political Symbols* (Cambridge, Mass.: M.I.T. Press, 1970).

2. For rates of change, see: Derek Price, *Big Science, Little Science* (New York: Columbia University Press, 1963), pp. 6–7; Bruce Russett, *Trends in World Politics* (London: Macmillan & Co., 1965), pp. 7 ff.; Pitrim Sorokin, *Social and Cultural Dynamics* (Boston: Horizon Books, 1957); Alvin Toffler, *Future Shock* (New York: Random House, 1970), p. 71; J. C. R. Licklider, *Libraries of the Future* (Cambridge, Mass.: M.I.T. Press, 1965), p. 15; *UNESCO Statistical Yearbooks.*

3. Cf. my *Prestige Press,* Appendix A.

4. Inclusion of the terms STALINISM and DESTALINIZATION needs some explanation. In the 1950 study we avoided using such symbols coined from names of men. MARXISM was one exception, CHRISTIANITY another, for in both instances the term has come to have an objective meaning going well beyond its manifestation in one man. But Leninism, Trotskyism, Hitlerism, etc., were not included; we felt that they could easily be coded under more general terms such as communism and nazism. In replicating the same procedures we have declined to list Maoism or Keynsianism as new terms. However, since the XXth Party Congress it seems hard to exclude

STALINISM from the list of key terms, and similarly MCCARTHYISM on a later list. We feel that STALINISM needs to be treated as a common noun because it refers to much more than Stalin's personal actions and it is hard to identify a general term of which STALINISM is but a special case; certainly DESTALINIZATION did not mean either COMMUNISM or ANTICOMMUNISM.

5. MODERATE appeared on the old list; so did RADICAL; but EXTREMISM did not.

7

THE MEDIA KALEIDOSCOPE: GENERAL TRENDS IN THE CHANNELS

W. Phillips Davison

"Who says what in which channel to whom with what effect?" This formula for describing the communication process, suggested by Harold D. Lasswell in 1948, immediately raises another question: How can one describe a single component in the process without reference to the others? The answer is that one cannot; all are interrelated. Nevertheless, for analytical purposes it is often useful to examine each component separately, recognizing that it not only influences, but is influenced by, all the others.

To describe a communication channel, one must take into account five dimensions:

Diffusion. How widely is it available?

Control. Who determines the content flowing through it?

Social functions. What role does it play in the society?

Individual functions. How does it serve the individual?

Physical characteristics. What are its costs, capabilities, and so on?

Just as the components of the total communication process are interrelated, so are the dimensions of the subsystems that constitute the channel. The degree of availability or dispersion of a channel has a bearing on its control, its functions, and its size or other physical aspects. Experimental radio broadcasts in the early part of the twentieth century contrast in all these respects with the highly developed network operations of today. Changing control of channels similarly may affect its diffusion, functions, and physical development, as frequently can be seen when a government takes over any medium from private interests. Analogous statements can be made about the effects of changes in the public or private functions served by a medium or in its physical characteristics or capabilities: a change in one is likely to affect all.

Any survey of trends in communication channels will be incomplete, as relatively little is known about some of their dimensions in all parts of the world and about all of them in some parts of the world. The situation is further complicated by the fact that channels interact; the characteristics of any will be affected by the presence of others, and even less is known about the nature of this interaction. We are aware that the advent of television has affected radio, magazines, newspapers, books, recordings, and even public meetings and interpersonal conversations, but we can describe these effects only in gross outline and with the aid of generous speculation. We face similar problems in describing the impact of existing channels on the development of television.

Let us look briefly at each of the dimensions listed above.

Voluminous data on the diffusion of communication channels are available, but there are large gaps in these data and comparisons over time and between areas are difficult. We should be able to list all the daily newspapers in the world. But what is a daily newspaper? Must it appear seven days a week, six days, five days? Does a newspaper printed on both sides of a single sheet belong in the same category with one of ninety-six pages? How does one count a paper that is equipped with its own masthead and perhaps a few columns of original material, but whose content otherwise is identical with that of another paper? Television or radio broadcasting stations are somewhat easier to count, but some of them operate twenty-four hours a day and some of them only a few hours; some have very high power and some low power; some rebroadcast material prepared elsewhere and some originate most of their own. Are all these of the same genus? Such problems are reflected in most media statistics. The editors of UNESCO's *World Communications* caution the user: "Statistics are not always strictly comparable, mainly because of lack of uniformity in national definitions and classifications.''[1] They also note that it is often difficult to pin down the exact date to which each statistic applies. Nevertheless, at least a rough and serviceable description of the diffusion of the mass media throughout the world can be given.

The same is not the case when it comes to quasi–mass communication and interpersonal communication.[2] We know very little about the incidence of public meetings and other quasi-mass events throughout the world, although in this respect the communist countries have kept better records than have noncommunist countries. Even less is known about interpersonal communication, although it may constitute the most important sector of the total communication network. Do Burmese communicate with each other more than do Swedes? And how much of this communication in both cases is redundant or repetitive? With what content does it deal? To what extent and in what ways is it related to the channels serving mass publics? When it comes to quasi–mass and interpersonal communications we are forced to rely mainly on speculation, although there are some scattered shards of information in the literature. For instance, we know quite a lot about the role of interpersonal communication in diffusing word about important news events to the American public.

Who determines what content flows through all these channels? Obviously, those who control or own the channels do so. But this answer is as unsatisfactory as it is equivocal. What we really are interested in is how decisions about content are made, and in specifying the forces that influence what is actually communicated. From the viewpoint of content determination, channels can be ordered within a spectrum: at one end are media whose content is determined entirely by the interests of the communicator; at the other end are those whose content is determined entirely by the audience. Most media fall somewhere between these two extremes. An example of communication content controlled entirely by the communicator is provided by the crank newsletter, or by the person who says exactly what he feels or thinks, regardless of whom he is talking to. The audience plays no role in determining content. At the other extreme is the politician who will tell people whatever they want to hear, or the publisher who will print anything that will sell.

In such cases, the audience decides. Media that are operated for profit tend to be located toward the audience end of the continuum, since they depend for their existence on satisfying public demands. Media that are subsidized, whether by governmental or private interests, are mostly located toward the other end of the continuum, as their viability does not depend on conforming with mass taste. Most subsidized media do, however, take the desires of their audiences into account, even though less weight may be attached to these desires than to the policy or ideology of the sponsor; and the content of most profit-seeking media is influenced at least to some degree by the interests or ideology of the owners, even though these rarely can be given full rein.

There are many configurations of sponsor and audience interest. In some instances, the interests of the sponsor and those of the audience are almost identical. This presumably would be the case with a medium that is dedicated to improving public health. In other instances, the sponsor also may constitute the audience. This could be true of a house organ that is published by an organization for its own members. When several media are competing for the attention of the same public, popular desires are likely to be given more weight in the determination of content; when one sponsor has a monopoly or near monopoly of communication channels in a given area, the media may be able to pay less regard to audience interests and still show a profit. Economic forces thus may give an "advantage" to either the sponsor or the audience.

The bargaining process that results in adjustment of audience and sponsor interests does not take place in a vacuum. It is influenced by journalistic standards, governmental regulations, advertisers, and pressures of many types. In some countries, journalists, publishers, or other communicators have drawn up standards that are enforced by sanctions imposed by the group. These standards set limits to what the media may provide, regardless of the wishes of the individual sponsor or the audience he serves. Film codes and press councils are among the instrumentalities involved in this kind of regulation. Professional standards informally adopted by journalists and enforced by peer group pressure also influence media content. Advertisers may play a part in shaping decisions about media content, and organized groups such as printers may refuse to handle certain types of material, thus limiting categories of content that may flow through the channel in question.

Most governments employ a variety of devices to influence communication channels. These may include laws regarding libel, protection of honor, or censorship; economic pressures such as discriminatory taxation or rationing of film stock or newsprint; licensing of individual journalists or media; restrictions on access to information; preparation of handouts; subsidies or special privileges for individual media; and threats of various kinds to media or journalists. When a government or ruling political party is itself in full control of a channel, it usually has no need to resort to these devices.

Some of the same pressures may be applied by nongovernmental interest groups or even individuals. Journalists may be threatened or bribed; interest groups may assist the media in gaining access to information or make it difficult for them; they may bring economic suasion to bear by giving or withholding advertising, and so on. A mild form of pressure is exercised in some countries by the practice of offering prizes to journalists for the "best" story of a given type. In the United States, prizes are offered by medical groups, trade groups, industrial organizations, and a variety of civic organizations. The Cigar Institute, for example, has offered annual prizes for the best news pictures showing a cigar. Many journalists feel that the existence of such prizes does in fact influence their coverage.[3] Counterpressure is exerted by prizes conferred on journalists by other journalists, such as the Pulitzer Prizes and the Sigma Delta Chi awards. This latter category of prizes serves to reinforce group norms and standards among journalists.

According to Western standards, a press is "free" when it is subject to a minimum of economic, political, or other pressures, that is, when bargaining between the communicator and his audience is not influenced by other considerations. The Freedom of Information Center at the University of Missouri has compiled a list of twenty-three types of pressures, and has rated the press of most countries according to the degree to which it is subject to these.[4] When judged by these standards, the press in most countries of Europe and North and South America is relatively free, whereas in most communist and underdeveloped countries of Africa and Asia the press is relatively more controlled, although there are several exceptions in both these categories.

Freedom of the media is not directly related to quality or responsibility. Under conditions of freedom an audience may demand, and a communicator may provide, a diet of sensation, half-truths, and trivialities. Conversely, a controlled channel may contribute to the realization of beauty, social justice, peace, and other highly prized values. The advantages of uncontrolled channels are that communicators are assured the opportunity of presenting a wide variety of information to any who will give their attention, and audiences that demand media of quality and responsibility will get at least some. When channels are not free, some would-be communicators are prevented from reaching the public, the range of ideas that can be presented in the media is limited, and audience desires may or may not be taken into account.

Regardless of the manner in which channels are operated or controlled, they must perform a number of sociopolitical functions if the society in which they are located is to survive, and if they themselves are to survive. The three basic functions have been described by Lasswell as providing surveillance of the environment, linking the parts of a society together so that it can function as an organism, and transmitting the social inheritance from one generation to another.[5] The surveillance function involves providing many varieties of social units, and the nation itself, with information about the external situation. Business organizations have to keep informed about the availability of raw materials and markets, the activities of their competitors, and governmental regulations that may affect them; governments require a vast amount of information about the situation at home and abroad in order to form and implement policies; and so on. Nearly all larger social organizations rely at least in part on the mass media to provide them with necessary information about the environment; smaller groups may rely on person-to-person channels, although their need for surveillance of the environment is qualitatively the same.

Social linkage is provided by communication in social units of all sizes. In a factory, channels from management to the labor force carry instructions and exhortations; labor to management communications include suggestions and complaints; interdepartmental messages keep one part of the organization informed of what is going on in other parts. These internal communications enable decisions to be made and implemented, with each element of the organization doing its part. A similar process can be observed in whole nations. Hans Speier has described the political order as a pyramid, in which the ruling elite communicates downward to the subelite and the mass, while the subelite and mass also may communicate in an upward direction to the rulers. Communications from the citizens to their government may be thought of as public opinion, which itself has been formed by lateral communication among the citizens.[6] Communication also links together the various parts of the economic system, so that producers know what consumers need, consumers know where to find what they want, jobs and job-seekers can locate each other, and so on. Without mechanisms for this exchange, the division of labor in a society will remain rudimentary, and a complex economic order cannot operate.

The nature of political and economic systems plays a large part in determining the kinds of differentiated channels that emerge, and the efficiency with which these channels function helps to determine the nature of the political and economic systems. The economic historian Harold A. Innis has noted that ancient empires which devoted great energy to raising monuments of stone and kept their records on clay tablets, tended toward decentralization and hierarchical types of institutions, while those that emphasized the use of lighter materials, such as papyrus or parchment, were likely to be more centralized and to give greater emphasis to commerce.[7] In early-modern times, as trade quickened and centralized banking developed, the requirements of merchants and bankers for information about events in many countries was one of the stimuli giving rise to modern newspapers.[8] The mass media are an essential tool for providing social linkage in a complex society.

Transmission of the social inheritance is a third basic function that communication provides for society. Much of this communication takes place on a person-to-person basis in school or in the home, but in complex societies the mass media also play a role. They channel specialized information to individual parts of large educational systems, they help to familiarize each generation with basic skills, and they reinforce common values. For a channel to exist it must be able to provide a service to the society; and if social needs change then the structure and/or content of the channel also will change.

At the same time, the channels must serve individual needs as well. Even a communication with potential social value will not receive attention if people find it irrelevant, cannot understand it, are bored by it, or regard it as offensive. Individuals rely on the channels for four principal types of information: instrumental information, which tells them how to do something they wish or find advisable to do; information for social exchange, which provides them with content for conversation with others; reassuring information, which equips them with a mental picture of the world in which they live and usually confirms their attitudes and sterotypes; and entertainment, which enables them to relax and sometimes to forget. Communication channels may be thought of as a link between the individual and the world around him, enabling him to know about phenomena that he cannot perceive directly.

The distribution of individual needs influences the demands that people make on the channels. In societies where most people are engaged in specialized occupations, the demand for specialized instrumental information will be correspondingly great; those who live in traditional societies are likely to require reassurance that their religions and values are indeed correct and to resent dissonant information; those who are concerned with fads and fashions will rely on the media for conversational currency; and so on. The manager or operator of a channel who can find an unfulfilled need and find a way of satisfying it will achieve fame, financial success, or both.

Each channel has a particular set of physical characteristics that give rise to certain capabilities. These characteristics and capabilities are well known, at least on a superficial level. A printing press usually is fairly heavy and may be of moderate cost or very great cost, depending on the performance one demands of it. For printed materials to reach a wide audience some kind of transportation system is necessary. Unless heavy reliance is placed on pictorial or diagrammatic content, print can reach directly only those who are literate. Radio transmitters are rather cheap or rather expensive, depending on their power; but inexpensive receivers can be constructed, including those that are battery operated. Thus radio can reach illiterate people in areas that are not supplied with electric current. A list of commonly known media characteristics and capabilities could be extended to great length, but to little purpose.

The more esoteric physical properties of the media are often important, but are the province of technicians. Certain types of paper and batteries stand up better in hot, humid climates than do others. Radio reception varies markedly in reach and quality, depending on where one is situated on the globe. For details as to such characteristics one must consult the appropriate experts.

All five dimensions of communication channels that have been mentioned can be used as a basis for categorizing them. They may be widely available or scarce; they may be "free" or controlled; they may be vehicles for political propaganda or may serve other functions; people may use them for entertainment, information, or other purposes.

Channels are most commonly classified by physical characteristics. Thus, when we think of newspapers, magazines, radio, television, films, museums, libraries, or public meetings, we usually conjure up an image of a printed page, a sound coming from a radio receiver, a picture on a television tube, a motion picture theater, a building full of statues or paintings, one or more rooms filled with books, or a large hall with a public address system. These physical characteristics are also the basis for other, more specialized, classification schemes that depend on the interests of particular groups of people. Entrepreneurs or governments, for instance, may be primarily interested in the amount of investment required to establish a channel: how much equipment does it require, and how expensive is this equipment? Operators and creative personnel usually think in terms of skills: schools of communication customarily divide their offerings into print, broadcast, and speech, and may introduce further subdivisions focusing on film, the arts, or other branches. Those who use media to transmit ideas are interested in how much it costs to reach a certain number of people, what socioeconomic levels a medium appeals to, and how fast it can report or react to events. Psychologists are concerned with the ways different channels convey meaning, whether by visual or

auditory stimuli or through a combination of sensory perceptions. Governments may look at media from the standpoint of
ease of control: print can be easily censored; shortwave radio is
difficult to stop at national boundaries.

Students of communication generally classify channels according to the number of people they can reach, which in turn
is determined largely by their physical characteristics. At one
pole are the mass media, usually led by radio or television; at
the other pole are the point-to-point and person-to-person
channels, including telephone and personal conversation. Mass
communication is characterized by a high degree of standardization of messages transmitted to a heterogeneous audience,
and by a limited degree of feedback from the audience to the
communicator. Interpersonal communications are nearly always
specially designed for a single individual or group, feedback is
immediate and constant, and there is a high degree of interaction between the communicator and his audience. Menzel has
suggested that in between these polar types an intermediate
form that might be called ''quasi–mass communication'' could
be usefully distinguished. It shares some of the characteristics of
both mass and interpersonal communication, but is identical
with neither. Messages are partially standardized and partially
tailored to the individual audience, there is some immediate
feedback, and the degree of interaction between communicator
and audience can vary widely. Examples of quasi–mass communication are afforded by the political speaker, who gives slightly
different versions of the same talk to a series of audiences, by
the lecturer in the classroom, or by the salesman who approaches a number of prospects with variations on the same
basic themes. Quasi–mass communication of a political nature
is most highly developed in communist countries, where large
numbers of political agitators, centrally directed, expound pre-
established points to their audiences, but then try to respond to
questions posed by individuals.

Any attempt to describe trends in communication channels
should take account of changes in these five dimensions over
time, yet it is impossible to do so in any detail. Our record
keeping is too inaccurate and incomplete, and the variations
among channels in different countries and even within countries introduce inordinate complexities that make generaliza-

tions of limited value. Nevertheless, it is possible to give an approximate picture of gross trends in the three major politico-economic divisions of the world: the industralized democracies, the developing nations, and the communist states.[9] Some of these observations are based on very incomplete evidence or tenuous extrapolations, and can be accepted only pending more exact statements.

THE INDUSTRIALIZED DEMOCRACIES

If one selects the ten most populous democratic states with per capita incomes of more than $1,000 in 1968, one emerges with the list shown in table 7–1. This table immediately makes one important trend clear: since the end of the Second World War all of these countries have become media-saturated, or nearly so. By "saturation" we refer to a condition where people have access to any media to which they would like to have access. If they do not buy more newspapers or see more motion pictures, it is primarily because they do not wish to do so, rather than because these or other media are in short supply or because people cannot afford them. The United States was the first to become saturated; the others followed rapidly. Italy may not yet be completely saturated with radio and television receivers, but is close to it.

Each channel follows a different curve. The curve tends to be approximately the same for each country but reaches its high or low point in a different year, those countries with a higher per capita income usually being a little "ahead" of those with a lower per capita income. Copies of newspapers per thousand population remain about the same, or decline slightly, during the period under consideration, as the saturation point had already been reached before 1948. Radio and television receivers show a rapid rise, radio preceding television by a decade or more. Cinema attendance falls, as television lessens the demand for motion pictures. The overall trend is for the number of newspaper titles to decline slightly, relatively minor fluctuations in numbers reflecting differing conditions in different countries.

Some figures on media diffusion give grounds for speculation that cannot be answered without investigation of the situation in individual countries. For example, why did the number of

TABLE 7-1.

Media Diffusion in the Ten Most Populous Industrialized Democracies, Selected Years (ordered by per capita income)

		Daily newspapers	Newspapers per 1,000 population	Radio receivers per 1,000 population	Television receivers per 1,000 population	Cinema attendance per annum	Radio transmitters	Television transmitters
United States	1948	1,780	354	481	53[a]	22	2,909[a]	106[a]
	1958	1,745	327	949	239	12.5	3,717	562
	1968	1,749	309	1,417	408	7	—	—
Australia	1948	53	432	251	—	25	153[a]	—
	1958	53	381	222	73	14	163	6
	1968	60	363	171	184	3	—	—
Canada	1948	111	245	143	—	17	194[a]	—
	1958	106	232	582	189	11	275	52
	1968	113	212	666	290	5	—	—
West Germany	1948	162	—	104	—	—	—	—
	1958	473	300	278	61	14	312	162
	1968	403	328	477	248	3	—	—
France	1948	166	282	148	—	9	60[a]	—
	1958	130	246	239	30	9	51	34
	1968	113	251	308	180.5	4	—	—

Netherlands	1948	133	280	169	—	8	13[a]	—
	1958	65	264	271	47	6	9	4
	1968	91	301	248	208	3	—	—
United Kingdom	1948	122	600	227.5	10	29	88[a]	2[a]
	1958	114	573	288	194	14.5	68	29
	1968	106	488	316.5	279	4	—	—
Japan	1948	130	—	92	—	7	136[a]	—
	1958	97	398	159	36	12	297	68
	1968	171	492	255	208	3	—	—
Belgium	1948	46	338	123	—	16	8[a]	—
	1958	39	383	272	43	8	12	4
	1968	54	285	332	195	4	—	—
Italy	1948	98	99	48	—	13	34[a]	—
	1958	107	107	123	36	15	538	269
	1968	88	112	222	151	11	—	—

SOURCES:
Statistical Yearbook (New York: Department of Economic and Social Affairs, Statistical Office of the United Nations, 1950, 1960, and 1969); *World Communication: Press, Radio, Film, Television* (Paris: United Nations Educational, Scientific and Cultural Organization, 1951).

NOTES:
The years given are approximate: 1948 may refer to 1946, 1947, or 1948; 1958 to 1956, 1957, or 1958; 1968 to 1966, 1967, or 1968.
[a]These data, taken from the latter source, are for 1948, 1949, or 1950.

radio receivers per thousand population in Australia decline from 1948 to 1968, when it rose sharply in every one of the other industrialized democracies? Is this phenomenon an artifact of the system whereby the official number of receivers is derived from the number that have been officially licensed by the authorities? Can it be explained by policies of the Australian Broadcasting Commission? Did television in Australia somehow compete with radio more than it did in other industrialized democracies?

Proprietorship of the mass media in these states tended to become more concentrated during the period under study, and the types of pressures on media operators shifted somewhat. One pattern for radio and television is that of monopolies controlled by some variety of public, nongovernmental body, on which a variety of interests in addition to that of the government are represented. This is true of both media in Belgium, West Germany, and Italy; and is the case with radio in the United Kingdom and with television in Canada. A second pattern is one of mixed control, with some broadcasting being conducted by private commercial interests under governmental license, which operate beside stations controlled by public corporations or other quasi-official bodies. Both radio and television show this "mixed" pattern in Australia and Japan, while "mixed" radio systems operate in Canada and "mixed" television is found in the United Kingdom. France is the only one of the large industrialized democracies where radio and television are in the hands of the government; and the United States is the only one where both media are predominantly in private, commercial hands. Radio and television in the Netherlands are controlled by private, noncommercial foundations, several of them reflecting the interests of religious groups.

Summarizing trends in noncommunist nations, Wilson P. Dizard concludes that since 1954, when a commercial television enterprise was authorized to compete with the state-chartered British Broadcasting Corporation, the tide has run in the direction of loosening direct governmental controls over television. He notes that "there is no country in the world where television systems operate in political opposition to the government."[10] Television thus has become either primarily a governmental spokesman, ordinarily with some limitations on governmental prerogatives, or else a "common carrier," open at least to some extent to all major interest groups. There are no television stations anywhere under the control of an opposition political party. Radio, on the other hand, can show at least a few stations that are primarily spokesmen for commercial, political, or religious interest groups, primarily in the United States.

At the same time, the political opposition has lost much of its control of the mass press. There are still some newspapers in the industrialized democracies that reflect the view of political parties, and in some cases are directly controlled by them, but they have declined since World War II in both numbers and circulation. *L'Humanité,* the central organ of the French Communist party, fell from a circulation of approximately 500,000 in 1946 to about 180,000 in the late 1960s. In Italy, where numerous dailies published by political parties flourished before the rise of Mussolini, only two out of the thirteen largest papers were identified with political parties in 1968, nearly all the rest being classified as "general information newspapers" and one as a sports newspaper. A report on the West German press, published in 1970, observes that the political party press that had become a major feature of the Weimar Republic did not develop again after the war. A few local and regional dailies identified themselves with the views of one or another political party, but "recently the readership has begun to turn away from these so-called 'quasi–party newspapers' also; they are ceasing to appear or else abandon their political tendency."[11] The trend away from newspapers identified with political parties and toward a "general information" press started even earlier in Great Britain and the United States.

The tendency of daily newspapers to become common carriers of information has been occasioned not only by popular changes in taste but by the rapidly increasing costs of operation, which have forced publishers to appeal to as many readers and advertisers as possible. The cost factor has led also to newspaper chains and consolidations, some of them not immediately apparent. Thus, the *Handbuch der Weltpresse* notes that there are today really only 73 separate daily newspapers in France, the remainder being "satellites" of larger organs, and estimates that by 1975 there will be only about 40. Development of the satellite press has reached a high point in West Germany. The

Handbuch der Weltpresse lists more than 350 newspapers, each of which has a separate name, that are largely identified with 67 "parent" papers.[12] A somewhat similar development has taken place in Japan, where the giant *Asahi Shimbun* has five branches in five major cities and issues more than 100 editions, most of them designed for particular localities. The other four large Tokyo newspapers follow a similar procedure.[13] In English-speaking countries newspaper chains have become more and more prevalent. Each newspaper in a chain usually retains its local editorial staff, but all share a common top management. By 1967, 871 American dailies belonged to newspaper chains, as opposed to 560 in 1960 and 153 in 1920. The average chain in the United States still is rather small, consisting of 5 papers; in terms of number of titles, the largest chain in the United States, and probably in the world, is owned by Lord Thompson of Fleet, the Canadian newspaper magnate. The Thompson Organization, Ltd., as of about 1968, controlled approximately 34 newspapers, 65 magazines, 6 book publishing houses, 2 television stations, and several print shops in Great Britain; about 40 newspapers and 8 radio stations in Canada; 25 newspapers in the United States; and a sprinkling of newspapers, periodicals, and television enterprises in the rest of the world.[14]

The picture that emerges is one of press, radio, and television proprietorship concentrated in fewer and fewer hands. This development has caused alarm among those concerned with the future of freedom of information, but its actual effects are difficult to demonstrate. Some students have pointed out that large industrial interests already own a substantial sector of the mass media in the United States, and ask what happens when the information network is dominated by the very same institutions that it is supposed to monitor in the public interest, and to which it is supposed to provide a counterbalance.[15] The question is a good one, but it is difficult to show empirically that industrial interests indeed have used the mass media to further their other financial or political goals, for example, to sell arms and munitions to governments. There are no systematic content studies bearing directly on this point, although there is indication that television stations in the United States that are owned by networks provide broader public affairs coverage and carry more controversial programs than do independently owned stations. This would suggest that financial strength is likely to be an asset when it comes to preserving freedom of information, and that a threat to this freedom arises when media are financially weak. If a commercial interest were to operate a newspaper or a broadcasting station at a financial loss, covering its deficit from profits made elsewhere, there might be greater cause for alarm although even then the case would not be clear. The *Frankfurter Zeitung,* one of the great liberal newspapers of Weimar Germany, was subsidized for years by industry, but remained an example of outstanding independent journalism up to the time of the Nazi takeover.

Despite the trend toward consolidation in the "general" mass media, nearly all audiences in the industrialized democracies are assured of access to a variety of competing sources of news and entertainment. The compact geography and highly developed transportation systems of Western European countries make it possible for national media to compete with each other in most areas of the country. The same is true in Japan. Furthermore, local newspapers supplement national newspapers in most cities of the industrialized democracies, and a variety of radio and television stations can be received in nearly all areas. In the United States, only forty-five cities supported competing local dailies in 1969, but most towns with only one newspaper were within the circulation areas of newspapers in larger urban centers nearby.[16] Circulation of national news magazines in cities that are more than seventy-five miles from a major urban center tends to be about two-thirds higher than in cities that are closer to another larger metropolitan area.[17] This would suggest that people in more "isolated" cities consciously seek out additional sources of information. Furthermore, 97 percent of all television households in the United States can receive three or more stations; two-thirds have access to more than five.[18] Accessibility to numerous radio stations is even more widespread. Thus it would appear that the fears of those who see concentration of ownership as depriving audiences in the industrialized democracies of access to competing sources of information are groundless.

Nevertheless, critics of ownership concentration in the news media are dissatisfied on at least three scores. Even when they concede that corporation A and corporation B are competing for the same audience through their respective publishing and broadcasting enterprises, what difference does this make if the two corporations are very similar in the makeup and philosophy of their controlling interests and professional personnel? There can be little real competition on the level of ideas between Tweedledum and Tweedledee. Second, while there may be some competition for audiences of national and international news, what about local news? An audience may have access to several competing news media, but it is likely that only one or two of these will have facilities for maintaining a close watch on city hall. Third, competition for national and international news audiences is more apparent than real, as this news is dominated by a handful of wire services. Nearly all newspapers and broadcast enterprises in the United States rely mainly on the Associated Press or the United Press, or both, for most such news. AP serves approximately 9,000 newspapers and broadcast stations in about 100 countries, and UPI has some 7,500 clients worldwide. International News Service, which formerly competed with the other two agencies, was forced by economic problems to merge with the United Press in 1958, forming the UPI. Of the three other worldwide agencies, Reuters (Great Britain), Agence France Presse, and TASS (Soviet Union), each dominates in its respective homeland and certain foreign areas, although they compete for clients in many countries. In addition, each of the other major industrialized democracies has a national news service that dominates as far as national news is concerned.

During the period under consideration, there thus appears to be a trend in the industrialized democracies toward greater concentration of power in the hands of those who control and operate the general news services. Faced with ever-larger news enterprises, many of them with a monopoly on the local level, the individual news consumer has less bargaining power than before.

There does, however, appear to be a contradictory trend insofar as the publication of periodicals and books and the production of motion picture and television films is concerned. Records in this area are poorly kept, and exact comparisons among various years are difficult. Nevertheless, the number and circulation of specialized magazines, books, and films appear to be increasing in most if not all the industrialized democracies, whereas general-circulation magazines and films tend to decline in numbers and relative influence, probably as a result of competition by television. Books, of course, have always been a specialized medium.

In the United States, a substantial number of large-circulation general magazines have disappeared since World War II, including *Coronet, Woman's Home Companion, Colliers,* and the *Saturday Evening Post.* At the same time, magazines appealing to specialized population groups, or dealing with specialized subjects, have gained large circulations. These include *Psychology Today, TV Guide,* and *Playboy.* During the past decade, about 700 new magazines were started in the United States, although approximately one-fourth of them soon went out of business.[19] The *Standard Periodical Directory 1970* lists more than 53,000 current publications appearing in the country. These include not only magazines but newsletters, house organs, yearbooks, and 328 major city dailies. Suburban, weekly, and small daily newspapers are excluded. A rough breakdown of these periodicals according to subject categories appears in table 7-2. This breakdown, of course, tells us more about the variety of *interests* that are served than about the number of individuals who make use of these periodicals. It is probable, for instance, that more people read the 273 entertainment magazines than read the 1,407 journals devoted to natural science. And it is probable that the 746 periodicals devoted to sports have a wider audience than the 2,201 that serve the education industry. Nevertheless, it is clear that enormous diversity is present, and that the individual who makes use of the periodical literature can find a wide range of information and views. And most of these periodicals, even though they do not deal with the day's news, contain information of news value. The man who reads about the generation gap in his newspaper, for instance, may gain a different slant on the same issue by looking at his alumni magazine. Foreign affairs are discussed at length in political science journals, current business developments are analyzed in management and banking periodicals, and so on. Thus the periodical press offers a counterweight to the concentration of proprietorship in the newspaper and

TABLE 7-2.
Major Categories of U.S. Periodicals, 1970 (excluding newspapers)

Trade periodicals (advertising, building and construction, drugs and pharmaceuticals, etc.)	10,451
College and alumni	4,502
House organs	3,787
Applied science and engineering	3,160
Social science (including political science and world affairs)	2,725
Medicine, hospitals, and nursing	2,315
Religion and theology	2,321
Education and school administration	2,201
Agriculture, forestry, fisheries, livestock	1,625
Natural science	1,407
Libraries and bibliography	1,317
Law and law enforcement	1,263
Business and management (including personnel)	1,150
Ethnic and black-oriented periodicals	1,139
Labor and union affairs	1,067
Banking and finance	998
Hobbies	948
Literature, poetry, and linguistics	777
Sports	746
Clubs: social, fraternal, and service	732
History and geography	657
Public management and planning	645
Health	607
Literary and political reviews	557
Social services and welfare	526
Insurance	482
Military and naval affairs	414
Music and music trades	385
Travel	359
Comics	305
Entertainment and romance	273
Conservation	264
General interest and home	173
Youth	162
Philosophy	117
News magazines	26

SOURCE:
Adapted from *Standard Periodical Directory* (New York: Oxbridge Publishing Company, 1970).

broadcast industries. Whether it is an *adequate* counterweight, we don't know.

Total circulation of periodicals in the United States seems to have increased sharply during the past few decades. Comprehensive figures are not available, but detailed records are kept with respect to magazines that sell advertising and belong to the

Audit Bureau of Circulation. According to the Magazine Publishers' Association of America, in 1940 there were 95.8 ABC magazines for each hundred adults in the country. By 1960, the figure had increased to 153.7 magazines per hundred adults, and by 1968 it was 169.1.

There is a similar proliferation of periodicals in all the industrialized democracies, although it is not clear whether all of them have experienced the same trend away from general-circulation magazines and toward those that serve specialized interests that has been observed in the United States. The *Handbuch der Weltpresse* does, however, note that a similar trend appears to have started in England.[20]

Another counterweight to concentration is provided by the book industry. Table 7–3 shows the broad trends in the five most populous industrialized democracies during the two decades in question. In all of them, there has been a rapid rise in the total number of titles published, far outstripping population increases during the same period. All of them except the United Kingdom show a growth in relative attention to the social sciences, and all except Japan register a decline in the proportion of titles devoted to literature and the arts. Again, it is clear that an enormous amount of background information about current affairs, as well as about almost every other subject, is available to the individual in book form, and that this information has at least the potential of offering an alternative to the picture of the world presented by newspapers and broadcast media.

It is sometimes objected that both periodicals and book-publishing houses, just as newspapers and broadcasting enterprises, are being bought up by larger interests, are being formed into chains, or are being incorporated into multimedia combinations. Such developments indeed can be observed in most of the industrialized democracies, but as yet do not seem to have appreciably diminished the capability of magazines and books to introduce ideas that deviate from those current in the general media. The field of periodicals is so broad, and new periodicals are so relatively easy to bring into existence, that no single combination has succeeded in dominating more than a small sector of the market. Although there are quite a few publishers who own magazine chains in the United States, and the Springer

TABLE 7–3.

Book Production in the Five Most Populous Industrialized Democracies, Selected Years

		Total titles	Percent pure science	Percent applied science	Percent social science	Percent geography and history	Percent art and literature
United States	1953	11,022	6	14	10	9	43
	1959	14,876	7	14	9	14	42
	1968	26,384a	8	14	21	11	30
West Germany	1947	8,612	3	15	18	4	31
	1959	16,532	7	14	26.5	13	25
	1968	30,223	7	9	31	10	22
France	1949	9,908	8	—b	12	14	—b
	1959	12,032	7	18	9	11	42.5
	1967	19,021	9	18	19	11	40
United Kingdom	1950	17,072	4.5	17	15.5	8	43
	1959	20,690	7	17	17	10	40
	1966	28,789	11	17	14	35	12
Japan	1959	24,152	4	12	12.5	5	29
	1968	31,086	6	19	23	8	31.5

SOURCE:
Statistical Yearbook (New York: Department of Economic and Social Affairs, Statistical Office of the United Nations, 1951, 1960, and 1969).

NOTES:
a In addition there were 12,449 federal government publications (4,487 books and 7,962 pamphlets) and 20,414 university theses for which subject categories were not available.
b The combined art and applied science total is 2,269, or 23 percent.

concern in Germany and Hachette in France both bring out a
number of large-circulation entertainment magazines, there are
vigorous and independent journals of opinion in all the industrialized democracies. Furthermore, trade union publications,
academic publications, and specialized publications of most
types are difficult to form into chains. For one thing, they are
likely to be unprofitable. Books, also, resist being brought into
line with a given editorial policy, even when several publishing
houses may be controlled by the same interests. By their very
nature books are a communication between author and reader
that must retain a certain individuality. There are, of course,
organization-produced books that appeal to millions of readers
of childrens' stories, detective stories, or adventure yarns. A few
texts are produced for captive audiences in schools. But most
books, those with both large and small editions, retain a personal quality, because (as opposed to the situation in most other
mass media) the reader retains enormous bargaining power as
opposed to the communicator and the book must appeal to
him. It is perhaps symptomatic of the trade book that some of
the largest and most conservative publishers in the United
States have made strenuous efforts to obtain titles written by
radical authors. They sell well.

While retaining their individuality, books and magazines
achieve a multiplier effect through the frequency with which
they are used as source materials by the general mass media, and
through their ability to provide subject matter for quasi–mass
communication and personal conversation. A large number of
newspaper and broadcast stories originate in book and magazine publication, and the frequency with which a book that
almost nobody has read can become subject matter for conversation throughout a country or throughout the world has often
been noted.[21]

Film production has become markedly less concentrated since
World War II. Prior to about 1950, Hollywood dominated the
world market. Its relative decline in influence after that time
was the result in part of a consent decree of 1946, which forced
studios to divest themselves of distribution and exhibition
facilities, in part of the rapid rise of television, and in part of
the growth of film production in other countries. By the 1960s,
the era of the independent producer had arrived in the United

States, and in other democracies motion picture theaters tended to show pictures produced in a variety of countries. American production still dominates the American market, although the proportion of foreign films has increased sharply since World War II, but in other industrialized democracies the market tends to be more evenly divided. Between 1950 and 1965, for instance, approximately 7,000 entertainment films were shown in the Federal Republic of Germany. Of these, 20 percent were produced in West Germany, 12 percent in France, 8 percent in Italy, 9 percent in England, 41 percent in the United States, and the remainder in more than ten other countries.[22] During the period studied, the proportion of U.S. films fell from about one-half in 1949–1952 to about one-third in 1961–1964. The proportion of the film market occupied by U.S. films in other non–English-speaking industrialized democracies tends to be considerably less, especially as many countries impose a legal limit on the number of foreign films that can be shown. Under these conditions diversity of film sources is assured, and the viewer retains substantial bargaining power vis-à-vis the producer. He can choose among a wide variety of products, and by his behavior at the box office cause some to be financial successes and others to be financial failures.

Viewing the mass media as a whole in the industrialized democracies, one can conclude that control is sufficiently diversified to ensure a balance of power between operators and consumers. Although there are substantial concentrations of power that favor the operators in the mass press, and broadcasting is sometimes government-dominated, at least a partial counterweight is offered by more specialized media in conjunction with informal channels. The general media, and especially the wire services, have partially compensated for the mass media imbalance by their willingness to act as ''common carriers'' and serve as channels for ideas representing a wide spectrum of views. Nevertheless, the preponderance of control of the general mass media by either big business or big government suggests the desirability of searching for ways in which further diversification can be assured.

The sociopolitical functions of the mass media in the industrialized democracies have often been a subject for speculation and impressionistic judgment, but there is a notable absence of precise information about trends.

As far as surveillance of the environment is concerned, the media in all democracies keep a watch on government, but how close a watch is difficult to determine. Nor do we know whether press criticism of government has increased or decreased during the period under consideration. It is probable, however, that other aspects of the surveillance function have received more attention. In the United States, at least, both general and specialized channels have shown a growing concern with activities of business corporations and with the condition of the environment. The fact that 264 periodicals can be classified as principally devoted to "conservation" may be indicative of this trend.

A tendency toward centralization of attention, if not of actual power, in each of the industrialized democracies also has been noted. This has been hastened by the centralized nature of broadcasting systems, especially television. In parliamentary democracies, for example, elections tend to be seen as a contest between two or more political leaders, even though the actual election outcome depends on the fate of hundreds of contenders for parliamentary seats campaigning in individual constituencies. The mass media have pitted the Social Democratic leader against the Christian Democratic Union leader in recent West German elections, and ran Heath against Wilson in the 1970 British election, although in no case did the voters have to make a direct choice between any two of these men. In both France and the United States, the ability of the president to command a national audience via television has been seen as strengthening the executive power as against that of the legislature.

The coordination function of communication channels in the industrialized democracies is clear, but again, trends are difficult to discern. It is generally accepted that advertising enables the industrial and commercial sectors to operate on the basis of a mass market, and it may be that the increasing amounts spent for advertising have worked in favor of large producers and against the smaller ones, thus favoring commercial concentration. The channels also have enabled political groupings of all shades to form, function, and compete for power, although as a rule those groups tending toward the center seem to enjoy an advantage.

In this connection, political advertising in American electoral

contests, and the role of specialists in advertising and public relations, have attracted increasing attention in recent years. It
seems fairly certain that the enormous cost of this advertising,
especially for television time, has worked to the disadvantage of
candidates and parties with relatively modest financial resources. Nevertheless, the extent of this disadvantage is not
known. There seems to be no correlation between the amount
spent for political advertising and the outcome of an election.
Among twenty-six leading ''television'' candidates in the U.S.
congressional elections of 1970, for instance, there were thirteen
winners and thirteen losers.[23] Some students of communication
have speculated that there is a basic minimum of publicity that
a candidate must have in order to succeed, but after that the in-
cremental advantage given by political advertising rapidly levels
off. A specialist in political advertising expressed somewhat the
same idea when he remarked that half of what his candidate was
spending on publicity was wasted, but he didn't know which
half.

The education function of the mass media in the industrialized democracies is equally difficult to characterize over time.
During the past two decades public communication has increasingly played a role in formal schooling, and it has often been
noted that children gain much of their knowledge of the world
outside their homes and communities through television, but
the impact of these developments has not been satisfactorily
measured. There has been increasing concern about the effects
of portrayals of violence in the mass media, but the magnitude
and character of the relationship between violent behavior and
violent content has remained a subject for debate. Whether the
mass media have increasingly debased popular tastes and
lowered the general cultural level, or have raised them, likewise
has been a subject for continuing controversy.

Record keeping about functions performed by the mass
media for the individual is only slightly better. These functions
enable him to exist and sometimes to prosper in a highly complex society: they help educate him for a role and a specialization, they tell him what to buy, and they offer him a basis on
which to make political choices. They also offer him entertainment, relaxation, and reassurance, and provide him with ideas
he can use in social relations with his fellow men; conversation
in the industrialized democracies depends heavily on media

content. "Have you read any good books lately?" "Did you see 'Bonanza' last night?" Each individual extracts from the general media what he needs, or what he can use, and tends to ignore the rest. In addition, he consults the specialized media for information that applies more specifically to himself. A list of books or periodicals published in any country having a free press offers a key to the informational wants and needs of the literate population of that country. Indeed, it is surprising that students of communication have not applied themselves more to the analysis of such lists. The breakdown for U.S. periodicals offered in table 7–2 above is a gross one, and incorporates numerous submerged problems of classification and definition. Nevertheless, it provides a fairly accurate mirror of the interests and needs of individuals in American society. Large groups of publications are devoted to the professions: law, science, medicine, education, military specialties, theology. Even more are concerned with commerce, business, banking, agriculture, labor, and skilled crafts. Several categories serve the needs of entertainment and relaxation: sports, hobbies, comics, and romance. Some help people fulfill their needs for sociability, and keep them in touch with their clubs, colleges, churches, and other institutions. A large number of house organs serve to keep their readers informed about what goes on in the organizations for which they work; others provide guidance for political attitudes and action. No major sector of individual interest or activity is neglected.

One could look at the same list of periodicals to see what it reveals about the sociopolitical functions of mass communication. Clearly, some categories serve the maintenance of the economic order; others the political and cultural orders. Many periodicals help to provide identity to ethnic or youth groups. Some publications might be regarded as having little social value, but even these probably would not lack a social function. Comics, for example, although bought and read for purposes of entertainment and relaxation, might serve functions of avoiding social unrest, introducing semiliterate people to the world of print, or inculcating the values of the larger society. Periodicals may also, of course, be dysfunctional, as when they divert people from attention to their jobs or glorify cruelty or violence.

An analysis of book titles published in a given country during a specified period similarly would provoke insights about individual and social functions that were being served. Since book readers in most countries make up a rather small proportion of the population, however, the analysis would apply only to limited, but important, sectors of the society.

The social functions of entertainment films are more difficult to isolate. A student of films in West Germany found a relationship between West German rearmament in the 1950s and the incidence of "war films" in West German theaters. During the period 1949–1952, only 3 percent of all films had war as a principal theme. This proportion rose steadily until it reached 10 percent in the 1957–1960 period, and then fell to 6.5 percent in 1961–1964.[24] But these data are difficult to interpret. Most of the films in question were of American origin, and it may have been coincidence that they reached the German market at the same time that German rearmament was proceeding. Entertainment films certainly serve to teach people to be consumers, and they are powerful exponents of certain goals and values, but their relationship to specific social institutions is difficult to unravel.

Films are more valuable for the insight they give into the world of fantasy, and may be studied to find out to what daydreams millions of moviegoers are exposed.[25] Yet even here we cannot be sure of the extent to which films reflect the fantasies of the cinema patron, as opposed to the extent to which he finds enjoyable a fantasy of the movie makers. The analysis of films shown in West Germany suggests that the latter often may be the case. Of 3,286 principal characters in a random sample of films during a fifteen-year period, 15.7 percent were artists (writers, singers, dancers, painters, and the like). Other principal categories included police and private detectives (9.4 percent), military personnel (8.1 percent), and professional criminals or prostitutes (6.9 percent).[26] These proportions clearly have no relationship to the occupational distribution of any population, and not even to the aspirations of any population. The preoccupation with artists does suggest that film makers share one characteristic with the rest of us: they find themselves a fascinating subject matter. But most of all, they want to tell a good story.

The relatively recent trend toward making films for smaller, more specialized audiences (one of the unintended benefits that television conferred on the motion picture industry) may make analysis of movies more revealing as far as functions for the individual and society are concerned. Indeed, someday it may be possible to derive an index of public concern with specific social problems from studies of film content and box office statistics.

As far as the physical capabilities and characteristics of the mass media are concerned, two almost opposed trends can be noted. One is for the necessary facilities to become more complex and expensive, and at the same time able to reach ever-larger audiences. The other is the increasing capability of mass media to address more and more specialized groups.

Rising costs have been largely responsible for the large number of newspaper consolidations in the industrialized democracies, at the same time that publishers without extensive financial backing are unable to enter the field. Similarly, the expense of television production has forced the growth of networks. Each new refinement, whether color television or computerized typesetting, requires more capital investment. Costs of radio broadcasting and of magazine and book publishing also have risen, although at a more modest rate. The net effect of increased expenses has been to limit new entrants into the field of the general media and somewhat to restrict those going into the specialized media. In the case of government-operated or publicly controlled television systems, the effect has been to encourage the acceptance of advertising to cover a part of the costs.

At the same time it has become technically feasible for many of the mass media to cultivate specialized audiences, and to tailor material especially for them. The growth of cable television in the United States presents the possibility that many more television channels will become generally available. Some of these channels, at least, may be used to serve specialized audiences. Large newspapers more and more are developing local editions that contain information aimed at residents of specific subareas. Mass magazines have adopted the practice of splitting their press runs so they can appeal to regional or even local advertisers. Some AM and a large proportion of FM radio stations have found audiences among ethnic groups, youth, rock music enthusiasts, or classical music listeners. Several all-news stations have proved profitable. Specialized periodicals have become more so, as audiences grew to a point where they could offer sufficient support. Book publishers place less emphasis on the novel that appeals to the general reader and give more attention to yachting enthusiasts, suburban gardeners, and armchair political critics. Film producers think in terms of the rebellious young or the nostalgic middle-aged, but not both in the same film.

Looking into the future, students of communication sometimes anticipate the day when each person will print his own newspaper on his home facsimile receiver, programming his computer to select only those stories that will interest him most. He will choose from a wide assortment of cassettes to structure his television viewing according to his individual preferences. He still will make use of the specialized media, but increasingly will rely on centralized data banks to deliver to him on order those articles and books, or selections from them, that are likely to satisfy his needs.

This vision of the future probably is misleading, as it ignores the necessity that the media also must perform socially integrative functions if society is to to be held together. Nevertheless, the capacity for developing individualized mass communications is growing, and the extent to which such capacity can be used to serve social as well as individual functions will play an important part in determining the future course of the industrialized democracies.

THE COMMUNIST NATIONS

Nations whose leaders adhere to the principles of Marxism-Leninism are highly diverse as to the stage of their economic development, and are fairly diverse in the ways in which they apply their political principles. Nevertheless, in all of these nations the mass media are more strongly influenced by the policies of the rulers than is the case in the industrialized democracies. This influence can be seen in the degree of diffusion of the media, the extent of state or party control, the functions that the media serve for the society and the individual, and even in the physical characteristics of some of the media.

Degree of mass media diffusion in communist societies in large measure depends on the resources, in terms of money and personnel, that the leaders choose to allocate to development of information channels. As various communist countries have followed different economic plans at different times, trends are not easy to discern, even within a single country. This difficulty is enhanced by the partial character of the media statistics available, and the conflicting statistics that are presented by different sources.

Some of the surface trends seem to resemble those in the industrialized democracies; others differ markedly. As shown in table 7-4, numbers of radio and television receivers per thousand population increased in all the countries listed during the period studied. Cinema attendance tended to fall off after 1960, except in mainland China, Rumania, and the Soviet Union. On the other hand, the number of daily papers and the numbers of copies available per thousand population show no consistent trends. There seems to have been a tendency to increase the number of copies available per thousand, but the magnitude of the increases varied greatly. East Germany, for instance, reported almost four times as many newspaper copies available in 1968 as in 1959, whereas Czechoslovakia showed about a 50 percent increase and Rumania about a 15 percent increase. The number of newspaper titles fluctuates, but no more so than in some of the democracies shown in table 7-1. What is noteworthy, however, is the small number of daily newspapers relative to population, and their high average circulation. This pattern holds for all the communist countries listed except Yugoslavia, where the press is subject to controls that are mild in comparison with those in the other states. The norm in communist nations appears to be for the rulers to decide how many papers are needed and what the press run of each should be. A student of communications in mainland China speaks of the seemingly arbitrary distribution of media in that country, noting that total newspaper circulation was rapidly forced up to 30 million in 1958 and then declined steadily for a number of years, with the number of titles also diminishing.[27]

As in the industrialized democracies, the number of periodical and book titles published in communist countries appears to have increased rapidly during the past twenty years. Periodicals appearing in the Soviet Union, for instance, jumped from a little more than 2,000 in 1955 to more than 5,000 in

TABLE 7-4.
Media Diffusion in the Ten Most Populous Communist Countries, Selected Years (ordered by per capita income)

		Daily newspapers	Newspapers per 1,000 population	Radio receivers per 1,000 population	Television receivers per 1,000 population	Cinema attendance per annum	Radio transmitters	Television transmitters
Hungary	1948	40	109	51	—	5	—	—
	1958	22	124	211	5	13	—	—
	1968	26	205	245	136	8	—	—
East Germany	1948	39[a]	—	153	—	—	—	—
	1958	37	118	311	34	16	—	1
	1968	40	445	348	250	6	—	—
USSR	1948	—	158	59	—	6	—	—
	1958	472	151	190	17	16	—	—
	1968	620	305	357	112	20	—	—
Czecho-slovakia	1948	20	193	188[a]	—	9	15	—
	1958	17	189	—	38	14	—	—
	1968	28	283	266	188	8	—	—

Poland	1948	32	125	36	—	4	—
	1958	42	142	168	8	7	—
	1968	43	199	174	105	5	—
Rumania	1948	—	—	16	—	—	—
	1958	33	132	101	1	6	—
	1968	46	158	153	56	10	—
Yugoslavia	1948	17	80	16	—	4	—
	1958	21	59	71	1	6	—
	1968	23	83	157	64	5	—
China	1948	—	10	—	—	—	—
	1958	392	9	—	—	—	—
	1968	—	—	—	—	6	—

SOURCE:

Statistical Yearbook (New York: Department of Economic and Social Affairs, Statistical Office of the United Nations, 1950, 1960, and 1969); *World Communication: Press, Radio, Film, Television* (Paris: United Nations Educational, Scientific and Cultural Organization, 1951).

NOTES:

The years given are approximate: 1948 may refer to 1946, 1947, or 1948; 1958 to 1956, 1957, or 1958; 1968 to 1966, 1967, or 1968. No data were available for North Vietnam or North Korea.

aThese data, taken from the latter source, are for 1948, 1949, or 1950.

TABLE 7-5.
Periodicals in East and West Germany, 1963

	East Germany	West Germany
Total periodicals	501	7,120
Specimen subcategories		
Religion, theology, church	34	695
Art and culture	21	272
Child rearing, education, youth	40	305
Sports	13	296

SOURCE:
   Bundesministerium für gesamtdeutsche Fragen, *SBZ von A bis Z* (Bonn: Deutscher Bundes-Verlag, 1965), p. 493. This source adds that most periodicals in East Germany are given a monopoly position in their respective fields.

1968, and total periodical circulation rose from 361 million to 2.4 billion.[28] Although the number of titles is not directly comparable with the number of periodicals in the United States, because of differing definitions of a "periodical," it seems probable that the number in the United States is several times larger, reflecting a policy decision in the Soviet Union as to which titles could be considered necessary. Thus, there are two major popular magazines for women in the USSR—*Rabotnitsa* [Woman worker] and *Krestyanka* [Peasant woman]—with circulations of about 10 million and 5.4 million, respectively,[29] whereas in the United States more than six major publishers and a host of minor ones compete for the attention of women readers. An even more graphic illustration is provided by a comparison between the numbers of specialized journals in East and West Germany as of 1963, shown in table 7-5. Although the population of West Germany is more than three times as great as that of East Germany, it is apparent that the number of titles per individual in the former is far greater than in the latter.

   When it comes to books, on the other hand, it is probable that the European communist countries publish about the same number of titles in proportion to population as do the industrialized democracies. Major categories of book titles published during three years of the period under study are shown in table 7-6. The large number of titles appearing in the Soviet Union is striking, as is the high proportion of titles categorized as "applied science." These accounted for nearly half of the Soviet production for 1959 and 1968, and for well over a third of total

TABLE 7–6.
Book Production in Selected Communist Countries, Selected Years

		Total titles	Percent pure science	Percent applied science	Percent social science	Percent geography and history	Percent art and literature
East Germany	1949	—	—	—	—	—	—
	1958	7,101	7	20	20	10	29
	1968	5,568	7	15	31	7	24
USSR	1949	—	—	—	—	—	—
	1959	69,072	5	49	18	18	27
	1968	75,723	9	44	23	3	13
Poland	1949	4,602	9	23	24	5	28
	1959	6,613	11	29	19	6	27
	1968	9,361	9	36	20	6	20
Rumania	1945	2,700	7.5	19	24	12	22
	1959	5,290	4	33	30	2	27
	1968	7,032	6	38	22	3	26
Yugoslavia	1949	3,528	10	22	32	3	21.5
	1959	5,060	7	15	31	4	31
	1968	9,586	7	12	40	4	32

SOURCE:
Statistical Yearbook (New York: Department of Economic and Social Affairs, Statistical Office of the United Nations, 1951, 1960, and 1969).

production in all five states taken together during the same years.

Both the Soviet Union and mainland China supplement the mass media by large-scale use of quasi–mass communication, and China has made extensive use of traditional forms as well. In both countries thousands of political agitators, recently supplemented in the Soviet Union by the slightly more expert *politinformator,* conduct meetings in collective farms, factories, and communities, exhorting their audiences to greater productivity and explaining the latest policies of the leadership.[30] The Chinese communists have trained and dispatched large numbers of drama groups and storytellers throughout the countryside, and party workers have taught inspirational songs and poems to millions. A 1964 report mentions that more than 4,000 spare-time storytellers were active in countries and towns on the outskirts of Shanghai, and 813 storytellers were trained in one county alone during 1962–1963. In another area, some 80,000 people learned to sing songs entitled ''Obey Only the Party'' and ''Chairman Mao Is Really Great'' during 1961. The number of professional drama groups increased from about 1,000 in 1949 to more than 3,500 ten years later, and they were supplemented by far larger numbers of amateurs.[31] Apparently, use of traditional channels of communication is increasing as modern mass media develop.

Nearly all mass media in communist countries are under the direct or indirect control of the Communist party, but the degree of direction that is exercised varies greatly. Yugoslavia is classified by the Freedom of Information Center of the University of Missouri as having a ''transitional'' press, neither completely controlled nor mostly free. Hungary is classified as having a press that is subject to ''medium controls,'' along with such countries as Senegal, Egypt, and Syria. The press of all other communist countries is seen as ''controlled to a high degree,'' although within this category the controls in Poland are considerably less stringent than those in North Korea or Albania. The relative freedom of the media in Yugoslavia is further suggested by the way in which statistics regarding the development of her press and book publishing tend to follow the pattern of the Western European democracies more than the pattern of the European communist states.

The tendency in most communist countries seems to be for greater consideration to be given to the desires of the audience than previously was the case. During Stalin's rule in the Soviet Union, mass communications were structured principally to please the political elite; little attention was given to the needs or tastes of the masses. A report on books published in East Germany speaks of titles being ground out "according to plan," regardless of whether anybody wanted to read them.[32] Following Khruschev's denunciation of Stalin in 1956, greater efforts were made in the Soviet Union and throughout Eastern Europe generally to give the media wider appeal.[33] These efforts included public opinion polls on reactions to the press and broadcasting in Yugoslavia, Hungary, Poland, Czechoslovakia, and the Soviet Union itself. A related tendency, especially in Yugoslavia, was to place more emphasis on the ability of print media to operate with balanced budgets. This placed more bargaining power in the hands of the newspaper or magazine buyer.

It may be that similar tendencies are at work in mainland China, Albania, North Korea, and North Vietnam, but if so they are not noticeable. All these states emphasize the use of the mass media for persuasion, but the alternatives available to the individual if he is not persuaded are undesirable in the extreme. As A. Doak Barnett points out in the case of Communist China, persuasion is backed by the overwhelming coercive power of a highly centralized state and party bureaucracy, so that the responsiveness of the masses is scarcely voluntary.[34] The bargaining power of the individual member of the audience vis-á-vis those who control the mass media in these countries is so weak that he cannot even safely withhold his attention, let alone express dissenting ideas.

The basic social functions served by the media in communist states are similar to those served by mass communication in the industrialized democracies, but the communist media are concentrated to a far greater extent on advancing purposes defined by the party and state. The press does exercise surveillance of the environment, but there are some things it cannot criticize or even mention. It fulfills a coordinating function, but mainly for approved groups and activities. It is a powerful force in formal and informal education, but its educational efforts are centrally directed.

All channels of communication are used to bring instructions from those in authority to the masses, to inform people how to do the jobs called for in economic or political plans, and to inculcate approved norms and values. The purpose of the popularly written and illustrated Soviet magazine for women, *Rabotnitsa,* for example, has been defined as the "cultural and political education of working women and housewives and their mobilization to fulfill the tasks established by the Communist Party."[35] The media in communist states also serve to enable organizations of many kinds to keep their membership together, recruit new members, explain their purposes, and otherwise to function in an orderly manner. Publications that amount to trade journals and house organs are common. But whereas in the democracies trade journals and house organs are oriented primarily toward voluntary associations or toward individual crafts and professions, in communist states these publications are more likely to be oriented toward members of organizations created by the party or state: collective farms, state factories, or party subunits. In 1965, for instance, there were 6,253 newspapers in the Soviet Union, including those that appeared fewer than five times a week. Of these, 2,769 were factory organs and 2,954 were organs of cities or districts. There were in addition 1,434 newspapers published by collective farms.[36] Very few served purely private associations, such as churches. Many scientific publications, on the other hand, tend to fulfill substantially the same functions as they do in democratic states.

Emphasis on books in the applied sciences suggests the importance placed on economic development tasks in communist states. In 1968 the Soviet Union was by far the world's leading publisher in this field. And in 1962, the mass-circulation Peking *People's Daily* published a serialized translation of *The Art of Scientific Investigation,* by William I. B. Beveridge of Cambridge University, the first book of its kind to be so treated in the Chinese communist press.[37]

The primary sociopolitical functions served by the media in communist states are thus to solidify the power of the ruling elite, to condition the masses to accept centralized direction, and to aid in the fulfillment of economic, social, and political plans. The degree to which the media are constrained to devote themselves to these functions varies considerably from state to state, with mainland China and those countries aligned with her showing the greatest concentration of purpose, while Yugoslavia and Hungary are at the other end of the spectrum.

Communist states have made extensive use of the device of conducting "campaigns" to further specific objectives. During the course of these campaigns, the mass media are mobilized and combined with several forms of person-to-person communication in an effort to enlist the energies of all members of the population. Mainland China has made the most frequent use of this technique. Frederick T. C. Yu has identified almost one hundred mass exercises of this nature in China that took place from 1949 to 1959. They included such diverse objectives as the suppression of counterrevolutionaries, studying Mao's works, and encouraging deep plowing and dense planting. In one campaign, all residents of the village studied (and presumably all villages) were required to attend numerous mass meetings and discussion groups, special wall newspapers and posters were prepared, a special motion picture was shown in a nearby town and attendance was mobilized, a "cultural station" was set up where people could read newspapers, books, and magazines that were not normally available, four loudspeakers in the village square broadcast material in support of the campaign starting at 6:30 A.M., and all work was suspended for three days so that everyone could attend meetings.[38]

Functions that the media perform for individuals in communist nations are similar to those noted in the democracies, but the degree to which various functions are served differs significantly. In particular, there is a tendency for less entertainment material to be available, with the result that the relatively small proportion of content that can be used for relaxation is eagerly seized upon. In the Soviet Union and the European communist states there has been, however, a trend toward the supply of more material that can be used for entertainment, even though much of this also contains purposive political content. Newspapers and periodicals include more pictures and show a more attractive makeup. Films and television programs that are not overtly didactic increasingly can be found. One popular Moscow evening paper, *Vechernya Moskva,* has an almost "Western" appearance, although the *Handbuch der Weltpresse* lists it as

being published in an edition of only 225,000.[39] It is perhaps
noteworthy that movie going in the Soviet Union is more prevalent than in any other major country of the world, even
though television also is highly developed there. One might
speculate that Soviet citizens flock to the cinema to find entertainment that television does not offer.

Even more important is the degree to which the individual
relies on the media to keep informed about party and governmental policies. Whereas in the industrialized democracies the
audience for political information varies in size and attention
from issue to issue, and often is rather small, the individual in
communist nations finds it prudent to know what current
policies are, in order to make the correct response when called
upon. To refuse to expose oneself to the mass media is regarded
as antisocial behavior. Indeed, one of the complaints made
about hippies in the Soviet press has been that they do not read
newspapers or listen to the radio.

Most media in all countries share similar physical characteristics, but again, the communist states have tended to favor
those with certain capacities. Wired radio, in particular, has
been used to a massive extent in mainland China and the Soviet
Union, and a large proportion of receivers are of this kind, offering set owners a limited choice of broadcasting stations, or
even only one station. This gives central authorities a greater
opportunity to supervise what is heard than in the case of non-
wired receivers. A Chinese periodical observed in 1959:

> The wired broadcasting network in the suburb of Shanghai is an ef-
> fective weapon for the county office of the Party to command pro-
> duction, arrange work and carry out Communist ways of education.
> The station is also a part of the cultural life of the masses. The wired
> network's main duty is to serve the central task of production and
> policy of the Party.[40]

In recent years, the proportion of wired radio receivers in the
Soviet Union and Communist China appears to have decreased,
giving listeners a wider choice of programs.

The capability of radio loudspeakers to reach large masses in
public places also has been exploited in communist states. In
some cases, large crowds are assembled to hear certain broadcasts; in others, the broadcasts reach only those who happen to

be present, for example, in public marketplaces and railroad stations. As with wired radio, this capability makes possible controlled exposure, but it is valuable also because of its low cost per listener. When large numbers of people cannot afford to purchase radios, or none are available for purchase, loudspeakers offer a cheap alternative service. Although no hard statistics are available, it seems probable that the use of radio loudspeakers has decreased during the period under study, as more individual receivers have come on the market.

Wall newspapers and posters also have been favored in communist countries, especially mainland China and the Soviet Union, probably in part because of their physical characteristics. They are cheap to produce, require little equipment, and can deal with highly specialized matters. Some are hand-lettered and illustrated with snapshots or line drawings. Mark W. Hopkins speaks of five hundred thousand of them being regularly produced in the Soviet Union, most of them publications of a local party unit, youth group, or labor union.[41] Wall newspapers were particularly prevalent in China during the Maoist cultural revolution; since then their frequency seems to have declined.

THE DEVELOPING COUNTRIES

If we select the ten most populous nations with per capita incomes of less than $500 per year (excluding communist countries), we arrive at the list shown in table 7–7. Most of these nations, especially India and Brazil, have large modern sectors within their societies. In some, such as Nigeria and Indonesia, the absolute size of the modern sector is small. Statistics regarding information media in these countries are likely to be less reliable and more incomplete than those in more highly developed nations. Nevertheless, several characteristics stand out. The most striking of these is the explosive diffusion of radio during the past two decades, together with the fact that the market for radio is far from saturated. Thailand achieved a level of eighty-two receivers per thousand people toward the end of the 1960s, higher than the level in any of the other nine countries, but even there it is clear that many people do not have easy access to radio broadcasts. Television had scarcely started to grow at the end of the period under consideration. There were

TABLE 7-7.
Media Diffusion in the Ten Most Populous Developing Countries, Selected Years (ordered by per capita income)

		Daily newspapers	Newspapers per 1,000 population	Radio receivers per 1,000 population	Television receivers per 1,000 population	Cinema attendance per annum	Radio transmitters	Television transmitters
Brazil	1948	220	31	51	—	3	—	—
	1958	290	63	64	—	6	593	6
	1968	241	36	—	—	3	—	—
Turkey	1948	72	15	12	—	1	—	—
	1958	116	32	42	—	—	5	—
	1968	472	45	74	—	—	—	—
Thailand	1948	30	4	—	—	1	—	—
	1958	30	4	4	—	—	20	1
	1968	22	22	82	6	—	—	—
United Arab Republic	1948	55	18	12	—	2	—	—
	1958	50	25	32	—	3	32	6
	1968	12	—	—	13	2	—	—
Republic of Korea	1948	—	—	10	—	1	—	—
	1958	42	57	16	—	1	13	—
	1968	42	75	74	3	6	—	—

Philippines	1948	20	25	4	—	1	—	—
	1958	19	19	13	—	1	—	—
	1968	23	27	—	5	—	—	2
Indonesia	1948	—	—	2	—	1	—	—
	1958	95	11	7	—	3	31	—
	1968	85	7	13	—	—	—	—
Pakistan	1948	35	2	1	—	—	—	—
	1958	79	9	3	—	1	9	—
	1968	95	18	9	—	2	—	—
India	1948	300	6	1	—	1	—	—
	1958	465	9	4	—	3.5	29	—
	1968	636	13	14	—	4	—	—
Nigeria	1948	—	—	—	—	—	—	—
	1958	20	8	2	1	—	—	—
	1968	24	7	—	—	—	—	—

SOURCE:
Statistical Yearbook (New York: Department of Economic and Social Affairs, Statistical Office of the United Nations, 1950, 1960, and 1969).
NOTE:
The years given are approximate: 1948 may refer to 1946, 1947, or 1948; 1958 to 1956, 1957, or 1958; and 1969 to 1966, 1967, or 1968.

appreciable numbers of sets in the United Arab Republic, Thailand, and the Philippines, but these were concentrated in the major cities and scarcely touched the traditional societies throughout the back country. The number of newspapers per thousand people increases steadily from decade to decade in India, South Korea, Pakistan, Turkey, and probably in Thailand and the United Arab Republic, but in other developing countries this statistic wildly fluctuates or declines. Declines may be the result of increasing population with no increase in resource allocation, or they may be the result of political censorship that makes newspapers less interesting. One constant, however, is the relatively large number of dailies and the low average circulation. South Korea has more dailies than East Germany; Turkey far more than Poland; India more than the USSR. But most of these dailies are economically weak. They represent the diverse political and group interests among the modern sector of the population; they do not penetrate deeply into the masses.

Cinema attendance statistics are very incomplete, but suggest a trend toward increasing patronage. Comparative figures for two or more decades are available in seven cases, and in four of these there is a sharp rise. Where cinema attendance declines, a major reason is probably a stable or decreasing supply of cinema seats (or of mobile projectors) in the face of a rising population. This is suggested by table 7–8. Thus, when the number of seats declines or does not keep up with population increase, attendance per thousand declines. We can assume that people in developing countries would like to see more films if they had the opportunity.

In the face of the weakness of the mass media in developing societies, traditional person-to-person and quasi–mass communication networks are strong. Except in the relatively small modern sectors, usually in and around the capital, villages and small areas are almost self-contained units as far as exchange of information is concerned. There are exceptions, to be sure. The developing countries are extremely diverse. In Egypt, for example, well-organized local groups of the ruling political party provide a communication network that links the center with the villages. By and large, however, the gaps between the modernizing elite and the tradition-bound people, and between both and the traditional elite, are large ones.[42]

TABLE 7–8.
Per Capita Annual Cinema Attendance and Seats Per 1,000 Population in Selected Developing Countries, Selected Years

Year	Brazil		Egypt		India		South Korea	
	Attendance	Seats	Attendance	Seats	Attendance	Seats	Attendance	Seats
1948	3	20	2	10	1	4	1	3
1958	5.7	27	2.9	13	3.5	6	0.9	8
1968	3	22	2	5	4	7	6	14

SOURCE:
Statistical Yearbook (New York: Department of Economic and Social Affairs, Statistical Office of the United Nations, 1950, 1960, and 1969).

Most analyses of mass communication in developing countries focus on what the media are *not* doing, how they could be strengthened, and the tasks they might perform if they were stronger. To quote a noted anthropologist from India, "Mass communication is as yet a largely untried weapon in underdeveloped societies."[43] Yet, obviously, the media perform extremely important functions for the modern sectors of these societies, much as they do in the industrialized democracies: they monitor the activities of governments, and criticize government when they are allowed freedom to do so; they enable what is sometimes very vigorous political and economic activity to be carried on, linking the political and economic leadership to the relatively small but highly significant attentive public; and they are increasingly used for purposes of mass education.

Statistics on book publication in five developing countries, as shown in table 7-9, suggest both the relatively small absolute number of those who make use of the specialized mass media and also some of the social functions that these do and do not perform. The figures are very incomplete, but three features stand out that distinguish them from similar statistics from either the industrialized democracies or the communist countries. One is that the rate of increase (where comparative figures are available) is very slow. Another is the small percentage of publishing effort devoted to applied science; one must assume that most books of this type are imported. Third is the relatively large proportion of books classified as "social science." Indeed, if one were to characterize our three groups of countries by their book publishing, one would have to say that the industrialized democracies were principally concerned with art and literature, the communist countries with applied science, and the developing countries with social science.

We do not know exactly what books are classified as "social science"; to find out, a content analysis of titles and subtitles would be necessary. But it is probable that this category includes mainly publications on the overwhelming social problems with which the developing countries are faced: education, poverty, minorities, national identity, and the like. If this is correct, then we can assume that these specialized mass media are performing a very important social function by focusing the attention of the elite on these problems, and by helping to coordinate efforts to overcome them.

TABLE 7-9.

Book Production in Selected Developing Countries, Selected Years

		Total titles	Percent pure science	Percent applied science	Percent social science	Percent geography and history	Percent art and literature
Turkey	1950	1,859	6	18	38	11	18
	1958	3,925	5	17	23	9	26
	1968	5,492	5	18	31	5	21
Thailand	1950	—	—	—	—	—	—
	1959	1,081	2	2	11	8	16
	1968	1,364	1	10	27	8	17
Pakistan	1950	—	—	—	—	—	—
	1959	—	—	—	—	—	—
	1967	3,312	3	5	20	5	32
India	1950	—	—	—	—	—	—
	1959	11,979	8	5	25	7	38
	1968	11,413	5	6.5	31	8	36
Nigeria	1950	—	—	—	—	—	—
	1959	—	—	—	—	—	—
	1968	1,004	1	5	73	2	4

SOURCE:
Statistical Yearbook (New York: Department of Economic and Social Affairs, Statistical Office of the United Nations, 1951, 1952, 1960, and 1969).

In at least two respects, the mass media may be dysfunctional for developing countries. As Daniel Lerner has pointed out, they can help to unbalance the Want : Get Ratio by arousing expectations that the economy is unable to satisfy. Teaching a man to read, or making it possible for him to buy a radio or go to the movies, is a formula for discontent when there is no way for him to satisfy his aspirations for the life he learns about through the mass media.[44]

Second, growth of the mass media in developing countries may contribute to what has been called the "knowledge gap." People who already know more tend to learn more from the communications to which they are exposed.[45] Increasing the supply and quality of the mass media therefore tends to benefit disproportionately those who are already in the modern sector of a society, and traditional sectors are thereby increasingly disadvantaged.

Mass communications in developing countries *should be* a chief advocate of national development programs and a force for unity. As yet, only radio has developed sufficiently to make its voice heard beyond the sectors that are already modern; the other mass media are struggling. They have made progress in some states, but in most cases are far from being equal to their task.

As far as the individual is concerned, mass media in developing countries perform much the same functions in the modern sector as they do in communist countries or industrialized democracies. For the masses who are exposed to them, especially to radio, they are primarily a form of entertainment and a source of information to use in conversation. The problem for those who wish to use the media as a constructive force in national development is to find ways that development messages can be mixed with entertainment so that the former will gain attention and acceptance. It is surprising that experience gained by commercial advertisers in the industrialized democracies has not been more widely used to solve this problem in developing areas. The traditional villager is just as reluctant an audience for a development message as is the Western television viewer for the commercial that interrupts his program. Neither will tolerate a long break in the entertainment program, but both are likely to give their attention for thirty seconds.

For the leaders of developing countries, the most salient physical characteristic of the mass media is their expense. Those who would establish modern broadcasting stations and printing plants have to compete for very scarce funds with advocates of more schools, highways, or national defense. In this competition the mass media rarely fare well.

INTERNATIONAL COMMUNICATION CHANNELS

The past two decades have seen an explosive growth in international communication. Statistics for various channels during this time period are even more sparse and unreliable than those regarding communication in individual states, but those figures that are available all point in the same direction. With regard to person-to-person international communication, for instance, UNESCO found that the number of foreign students at institutions of higher education in 45 countries increased from 107,000 to 191,000 between 1955 and 1961. Between 1956 and 1964, the number of teachers and researchers crossing the Atlantic in both directions jumped from 10,000 to 30,000. During approximately the same period the number of international nongovernmental organizations listed in the *Yearbook of International Organizations* grew from approximately 1,100 to more than 1,900.[46] We know that interpersonal channels of these types directly foster other forms of international communication: letter writing, and reading of foreign books, magazines, and newspapers, even though comprehensive figures are not available.

Increases in international short-wave broadcasting have been even more striking. As shown in table 7–10, the large nations have devoted more and more attention to this activity, and by the late 1960s were broadcasting thousands of hours per week in scores of languages. But short-wave broadcasting has not been monopolized by powerful countries with worldwide interests. Smaller states and the developing countries also are playing a more active part. Although table 7–10 presents figures for only a few of the medium-sized nations and developing countries, the short-wave efforts of these states taken together are far greater than those of the largest broadcasters: the Soviet Union, the United States, and mainland China. The voice of West Germany, in particular, recently has become one of the most pervasive in the world airways; England and France continue to be active in short-wave broadcasting; and there is scarcely a nation, no matter how poor, that does not beam some programs abroad.

Governments appear to have devoted increasing energy to international radio in recent years. Certainly this has been true in the case of the United States. In 1952, the International Information Administration devoted $20 million to foreign broadcasting, and by 1968 the figure had almost exactly doubled.[47] Even so, the rate of increase in the U.S. effort is far slower than that of many other countries.

Another index of the growth of international communication is the increase in activity of foreign governments and governmental agencies in sponsoring publicity in the United States. During the period 1955–1959, an average of 12,600 pieces of political propaganda distributed by U.S. agents of foreign principals were filed each year with the U.S. Department of Justice, as required by the Foreign Agents Registration Act of 1938. In 1969, 14,300 pieces were filed. The number of agents (mainly organizations) registered increased from 271 at the end of 1954 to 434 in 1959 and to 450 in 1969. The number of individuals involved in the publicity activities of these agents grew from 2,000 to 2,500 between 1959 and 1969.[48] All indexes of international communication that can be located appear to point upward.

Sociopolitical functions performed by these rapidly rising streams of information exchange have not been systematically studied. One can assume that a major effect will be to speed up the process of cultural diffusion and borrowing. Hadley Cantril, after studying human aspirations in fourteen countries at different stages of development all over the world, concluded that everywhere "the potentialities and possibilities of a good life are defined in Western terms," and that more and more people were hoping for technological advances that would make their lives easier and speed improvements in their standards of living.[49] It may be that international communication is gradually decreasing the psychological distance between the various peoples of the world, although of this we cannot be sure. One student who observed the impact of Radio Moscow broadcasts on groups of American students, found that the effects de-

TABLE 7-10.

Trends in Short-wave Broadcasting in Selected Communist Countries, Industrialized Democracies, and Developing Countries, Selected Years

	1950		1960		1970	
	Hours per week	Languages	Hours per week	Languages	Hours per week	Languages
Hungary	27	6	105	8	158	7
USSR	193	9	879	41	1,621	76
China	35	6	426	19	847	33
United States	405	24	730	34	1,454	34
West Germany and West Berlin	—	—	20	5	733	27
Netherlands	150	7	265	6	308	8
Brazil	212	3	151	7	—	—
Nigeria	130	5	642	8	120	4
Spain	63	12	123	20	329	6

SOURCES:
O. Lund Johansen, ed., *World Radio Handbook for Listeners, 1950–1951* (Copenhagen, 1950); *World Radio Handbook: Radio-Television, 1960* (Copenhagen, 1960); *1970 World Radio-TV Handbook* (Copenhagen, 1970).

NOTE:
In this table Spain was added as an example of an authoritarian country.

pended on the prior attitudes and expectations of those in the audience.[50] Exposure to messages from abroad may cause some people to become less favorable to the message source. One important function that international communication certainly does perform is to enable international organizations of both a governmental and a private nature to develop and grow. And it certainly raises the level of information in each country about other countries.

Some international channels are used mainly by governments to further national purposes. This is especially the case with short-wave radio, which almost entirely is sponsored or conducted by governments. At least three major purposes are served: to promote tourism, trade, and investment; to keep in touch with national minorities or ideological sympathizers abroad; and to present governmental positions on major international issues. All three of these purposes involve building goodwill among foreign audiences.

The Foreign Agents Registration Section of the U.S. Department of Justice has noted that the largest category of foreign publicity agents to come to their attention is composed of governmental information and tourist offices, many of which seem to be interested in promoting trade and investment as well as tourism. Some of the short-wave broadcasts beamed from abroad to this country also are frankly aimed at encouraging commercial interchange.

Languages used by foreign nations in their short-wave schedules suggest the importance attached to keeping in touch with emigrants. Mainland China broadcasts to nearly all the world in standard Chinese; the Netherlands has almost as complete coverage in Dutch. Nigeria's short-wave broadcasts in Hausa may have the same purpose, as well as West Germany's extensive German-language programs.

The short-wave broadcasts of some countries suggest that political purposes dominate. Albania, for instance, is one of the world's leading short-wave braodcasters, airing 138 different programs daily in 17 languages.[51] Yet Albania does not encourage foreign tourism or investment, and there are few Albanians in other countries, which leads one to believe that the primary purposes of the broadcasts must be political. The United States, the Soviet Union, and mainland China clearly have worldwide political interests that are served by broadcasting. Their attention to rather exotic languages otherwise would be difficult to explain. The Soviet Union, for example, directs programs to Africa in Bambasu, Foula, Hausa, Lingala, Malagay, Shona, Somali, and Zulu, as well as in Arabic and Swahili. It appears probable that one of the primary functions of broadcasting by communist countries is to acquaint affiliated or sympathetic political groups abroad with the current line of thinking in Moscow or Peking.

One unintended outcome of short-wave broadcasting may be the spread of English as an international language. The pattern for most non-English-speaking nations is to devote the largest number of hours to programs in their own languages, but for English to be the language that is used next most often. English-speaking nations naturally tend to use their own language for most broadcasts, the second language being determined by their purposes and their geographical position in the world.

In view of the limited amount of information about the actual effects of short-wave broadcasting, it may be that part of the money devoted to it is wasted. For some countries, it may be primarily a status symbol, serving to massage the egos of the elite. To this extent, it is probably dysfunctional for the nations concerned.

As far as the individual is concerned, one of the principal functions of international communication is to maintain family ties and keep friendships alive, although no quantitative data are available. In a study of the American short-wave audience of the 1960s it was found that about a third of regular listeners tuned in to a station in a country where they had personal ties of some kind. They listened to news broadcasts, but also to sports, music, and special features.[52] Many international letter writers and travelers, as well as readers of foreign publications fall into this group.

Other individuals are involved in international communication because of their interest in world affairs. About two-thirds of American short-wave listeners fall into this category. They listen primarily to Radio Moscow, Radio Havana, Radio Canada, and the BBC. Often, they are dissatisfied with American news media, or are suspicious of them, and would like to hear another point of view. Such listeners make up only a small proportion of the American public, although the group is numerically rather large, comprising several hundred thousand and possibly as many as a million people. About half of them also read the English-language publications that are distributed by other governments, such as *Soviet Life* or *China Reconstructs*.

A third major function of international communication for the individual is to help him in his job. Those who study abroad, or who read foreign publications, often do so to obtain information that will be useful to them professionally. This is true not only of students, teachers, and newsmen, but also of scientists, engineers, and physicians. People in developing countries most frequently need information from abroad to do their jobs, but this is increasingly true in the industrialized nations also.[53]

Finally, international communication may provide entertainment for the individual. This has been true of foreign motion picture films, which have occupied a large share of the market in most countries during the past twenty years, and more recently of television programs. A number of international magazines have jumped the language barrier by publishing special editions for other countries (for example, *Realités* and the *Reader's Digest*) but as yet the print media have played a relatively small role in the entertainment field. In view of the difficulties of reception, short-wave radio can scarcely be regarded as a medium that is conducive to entertainment or relaxation, except in small doses, but international radio hookups and rebroadcasts for sporting or musical events have increased during the past decades and probably will continue to do so.

Two physical aspects of the mass media are of particular relevance to international communication: the degree to which they are dependent on language for the transmittal of meaning, and the degree to which they are subject to control at national borders. Short-wave radio jumps national borders with ease, but is heavily dependent on language. Motion picture film is less dependent on language, but is relatively easily excluded by any government that wishes to do so. Publications occupy an intermediate position in both respects. A newspaper or magazine, especially if profusely illustrated, can be appreciated by someone who is not fluent in the language of publication, although he must have some knowledge of it. And printed media in small numbers can filter across most national borders, even though their distribution on a large scale can be prevented.

During the past two decades there seems to have been a slight lowering of both barriers. Most countries that as of 1950 tried to exclude communications from abroad have become somewhat more permissive, or much more permissive. Jamming of short-wave radio broadcasts is now rare, and a wider assortment of publications is available throughout Eastern Europe, although mainland China, North Korea, and North Vietnam still are highly restrictive. The growth of English as an international language has reduced the language barrier for the relatively few educated elite in many countries, but it would be presumptuous to assume that English could ever become a second language for mass audiences in non-English-speaking countries, particularly with the ridiculous grammar and spelling from which it now suffers.

It is because of the stubborn character of linguistic and political barriers that the imagination of many students of international communication has been captured by the possibilities of television broadcasting via satellite. Technically, at least, satellite broadcasts could be available relatively soon to anyone with a receiver. And these broadcasts could be structured so as to convey most of their meaning through visual images, or they could carry subtitles in several languages. The political and technical difficulties of achieving a worldwide satellite broadcasting system are enormous, but it may be that someone writing about trends in communication channels from 1970 to 1990 will record progress in this respect as one of the main developments of the period.

NOTES

1. UNESCO, *World Communications: Press, Radio, Television, Film* (Paris, 1964).

2. I am indebted to Herbert Menzel of New York University for the concept of quasi–mass communication. This concept will be discussed in more detail below.

3. David Zinman, "Should Newsmen Accept PR Prizes?" *Columbia Journalism Review* 9 (Spring 1970).

4. Freedom of Information Center, University of Missouri, Report no. 166, August 1966, and Report no. 181, May 1967.

5. Harold D. Lasswell, "The Structure and Function of Communication in Society," in Lyman Bryson, ed., *The Communication of Ideas* (New York: Harper, 1948).

6. Hans Speier, *Social Order and the Risks of War* (New York: George W. Stewart, 1952), pp. 323–324.

7. Harold A. Innis, *Empire and Communications* (London: Oxford University Press, 1950).

8. Wilhelm Bauer, *Die Oeffentliche Meinung in der Weltgeschichte* (Potsdam: Akademische Verlagsgesellschaft Athenaion, 1929).

9. A fourth category is sometimes recognized. This consists of countries organized along authoritarian lines where democratic institutions are weak and power is concentrated in a few hands. Most countries that satisfy these conditions, however, either fall into the developing category or, as in the case of Greece, have wavered between authoritarianism and democracy.

10. Wilson P. Dizard, *Television: A World View* (Syracuse, N.Y.: Syracuse University Press, 1966), pp. 105–106.

11. Henk Prakke et al., *Handbuch der Weltpresse* (Cologne and Opladen: Westdeutscher Verlag, 1970), vol. 1, p. 124; for the French and Italian press, see pp. 165 and 264.

12. Ibid., vol. 2, pp. 45–50.

13. Ibid., vol. 1, pp. 275–276.

14. See Bryce W. Rucker, *The First Freedom* (Carbondale, Ill.: Southern Illinois University Press, 1968); also Prakke, *Handbuch der Weltpresse,* vol. 1, p. 192.

15. Herbert I. Schiller, *Mass Communications and American Empire* (New York: Augustus M. Kelley, 1969).

16. Charles S. Steinberg, *The Communicative Arts* (New York: Hastings House, 1970), p. 62.

17. From a study by the Bureau of Advertising, American Newspaper Publishers' Association, 1966.

18. Steinberg, *Communicative Arts,* p. 144.

19. Ibid., p. 92.

20. Prakke, *Handbuch der Weltpresse,* vol. 1, p. 196.

21. I would cite here Lasswell's characterization of an influential book— obscure, ponderous, little-read—if I could find it.

22. Martin Osterlund, *Gesellschaftsbilder in Filmen* (Stuttgart: Ferdinand Enke Verlag, 1970).

23. *New York Post,* 5 November 1970.

24. Osterlund, *Gesellschaftsbilder in Filmen,* pp. 204, 219.

25. Martha Wolfenstein and Nathan Leites, *Movies: A Psychological Study* (Glencoe, Ill.: Free Press, 1950).

26. Osterlund, *Gesellschaftsbilder in Filmen,* pp. 93–94.

27. Alan P. L. Liu, "Mass Communication and Media in China's Cultural Revolution," *Journalism Quarterly* 46 (Summer 1969):315–316.

28. Mark W. Hopkins, *Mass Media in the Soviet Union* (New York: Pegasus, 1970), p. 226.

29. Ibid., p. 227.

30. Hopkins, *Mass Media,* pp. 309–310; Liu, "Mass Communication," p. 319.

31. Alan P. L. Liu, *The Use of Traditional Media for Modernization in Communist China* (Cambridge, Mass.: Center for International Studies, M.I.T., 1965).

32. Bundesministerium für gesamptdeutsche Fragen, *SBZ von A bis Z* (Bonn: Deutscher Bundes-Verlag, 1965), p. 450.

33. Hopkins, *Mass Media,* p. 308.

34. A. Doak Barnett, "A Note on Communication and Development in Communist China," in Daniel Lerner and Wilbur Schramm, eds., *Communication and Change in the Developing Countries* (Honolulu: East-West Center Press, 1967), pp. 232–233.

35. *Spravochnik zhurnalista,* p. 120, quoted by Hopkins, *Mass Media,* p. 228.

36. Prakke, *Handbuch der Weltpresse,* vol. 1, p. 504.

37. Alan P. L. Liu, *Book Publishing in Communist China* (Cambridge, Mass.: Center for International Studies, M.I.T., 1965), p. 22.

38. Frederick T. C. Yu, "Campaigns, Communications, and Development in Communist China," in Lerner and Schramm, *Communication and Change,* pp. 195 ff.

39. Prakke, *Handbuch der Weltpresse,* vol. 1, p. 504; vol. 2, p. 185.

40. Quoted by Alan P. L. Liu, *Radio Broadcasting in Communist China* (Cambridge, Mass.: Center for International Studies, M.I.T.), p. 48.

41. Hopkins, *Mass Media,* p. 204.

42. S. C. Dube, "A Note on Communication in Economic Development," in Lerner and Schramm, *Communication and Change,* pp. 94–95.

43. Ibid., p. 96.

44. Daniel Lerner, in Lerner and Schramm, *Communication and Change,* pp. 312 ff.

45. P. J. Tichenor, G. A. Donohue, and C. N. Olien, "Mass Media Flow and Differential Growth in Knowledge," *Public Opinion Quarterly* 34 (Summer 1970).

46. Robert C. Angell, *Peace on the March: Transnational Participation* (New York: Van Nostrand Reinhold, 1969), pp. 34, 53, 131. Angell has compiled numerous other statistics, nearly all pointing in the same direction.

47. Overseas Information Programs of the United States, Report (no. 406) of the Committee on Foreign Relations, U.S. Senate, 15 June 1953 (Hickenlooper Committee), p. 79; USIA Appropriation Hearings for Fiscal Year 1970, House of Representatives Subcommittee on Departments of State, Justice, and Commerce, pp. 430–431.

48. Report of the Attorney General to the Congress of the United States on the Administration of the Foreign Agents Registration Act of 1938, as Amended, for the Period 1 January 1955 to 31 December 1959 (Washington, D.C.: U.S. Department of Justice, June 1960); Report for the Calendar Year 1969 (Washington, D.C.: Government Printing Office, 1970).

49. Hadley Cantril, *The Pattern of Human Concerns* (New Brunswick, N.J.: Rutgers University Press, 1965), p. 313.

50. Don D. Smith, "Some Effects of Radio Moscow's North America Broadcasts," *Public Opinion Quarterly* 34 (Winter 1970–1971).

51. The 1970 *World Radio-TV Handbook* does not give the length of Albanian broadcasts, as it does in the case of most other countries. Nevertheless, if one assumes that programs average only one half-hour each, the total weekly broadcast time would be about five hundred hours.

52. Don D. Smith, "America's Short-Wave Audience," *Public Opinion Quarterly* 33 (Winter 1969–1970).

53. The writer is conscious of having made direct or indirect use of the work of at least half a dozen foreign scholars in writing this chapter. If he had been able to make use of the work of additional foreign scholars, it presumably would have been a better chapter.

8

THE MOVING TARGET: GENERAL TRENDS IN AUDIENCE COMPOSITION

L. John Martin

AUDIENCE CONCEPT AND MASS SOCIETY

Concept of the Public

Since the beginning of communication, the concept of audience has existed in one form or another. Communication, which involves a transmitter and a receiver, by definition requires an audience. The audience may comprise a single recipient or a multiplicity of recipients. It is reasonable to assume that man has always been conscious of the audience status of others in his environment, whether or not he was able to articulate their "reactive other" relationship to himself.

The concept of audience is, however, a sounding board concept that involves a directed message emanating from some source to a particular target, plus feedback from that target. There are other ways of looking at people in the aggregate. There is the target concept, in which major emphasis is placed on the proper mix of individuals for a particular message or treatment. During and after treatment, the target becomes an audience. There is also the concept of public, which acquires meaning in the context of a common bond of opinion, behavior, or power. Publics are numerous and changing in any society, and their members can and generally do belong to several at any given time. Publics are potential audiences to which a ruler or leader might appeal. But even without communicating with them, he is generally conscious of their status as a potential "reactive other" with power to limit his actions. Recognizing the potential force that inheres in publics, leaders throughout history have consciously or unconsciously treated them as audiences to be manipulated through communication.

The concept of public is closely tied to public opinion. In fact, a public really does not exist conceptually without some common attitudes, beliefs, or values that serve to cement individuals in a group together. It is in the manifestation, distribution, sensing, and measuring of opinion in a public that the concept of public has changed down the ages, although this may not have been too apparent to social philosophers until recent times. For Plato, the public was an undifferentiated mass of citizens in which there resided some power about which Plato was quite ambivalent. There is an element of truth in the principle that the multitude should be supreme, he said in book VII of *The Republic*. Yet he also believed that rulers are qualified because of their superior knowledge, and that it would be superfluous for them to consult public opinion. Aristotle disagreed about the relative wisdom of a ruler and his people. The collective wisdom of a people is superior even to that of the wisest lawgiver, he taught, as one person's knowledge supplements that of another.

Aristotle interjected a new thought, however. Although he retained the concept of an amorphous will, his analysis led him to conclude that there was more than one public, whose separate cohesions were the result of certain common objectives and, by implication, values. In book VI of his *Politics,* Aristotle speaks of "two classes out of which a state is composed—the poor and the rich." He sees a dichotomy between numerical and proportionate equality. True democratic justice, he says, requires that all should count equally, "for equality implies that the poor should have no more share in the government than the rich, and . . . that all should rule equally according to their numbers."

Until the seventeenth century, little further progress was made in the analysis of publics. For the Roman and the medieval British scholar and philosopher, the people manifested their common will through the law and through their leaders. Marsilio of Padua in the thirteenth century agreed with the pre-

vailing sentiment that the community is absolutely omnipotent
—*vox populi, vox dei,* as the Romans put it—but, like Aristotle,
he saw society as being composed of a number of classes or
parts, such as soldiers, officials, and priests, and both their
number and quality must be taken into account, he said.[1]
Others thought of the public merely as a political power that
either could be exploited or had to be taken into account, depending on the purpose and viewpoint of the writer. Thus the
seventeenth-century Spanish philosopher and jurist Francisco
Suarez, speaking as a protagonist of the church, said that political power was an inherent property of the community, and that
it was the right of the church to divine and interpret that power.
On the other hand, Machiavelli, advising his prince, told him
that the public was a monolithic force that the ruler had to endeavor to manipulate by exploiting the desire for security in the
masses. Machiavelli understood, however, that the masses were
made up of individuals and that government is founded on the
weakness and insufficiency of individuals unable to protect
themselves against one another's rapacity without the support
of the state. He said that the power of the ruler is based on just
this fear of anarchy among his subjects. Yet he did not go beyond this analysis of what constituted the cement that turned
individual members of the populace into a powerful force
which, in turn, gave power to the state and to its ruler.

In the seventeenth century, John Locke added a new dimension to the study of publics. In "An Essay Concerning the True
Original, Extent and End of Civil Government," he wrote that
"when any number of men have, by the consent of every individual, made a community, they have thereby made that community one body, with a power to act as one body, which is only
by the will and determination of the majority. For . . . it is necessary the body should move that way whither the greater force
carries it, which is the consent of the majority." Locke had
faced the problem of a public, or body politic, formed into a
single society under a single government yet made up of individual wills, by positing a consensus in which "every
man . . . puts himself under an obligation to everyone of that
society to submit to the determination of the majority."[2]

Three quarters of a century later, Jean-Jacques Rousseau was
to distinguish in *The Social Contract* between "the will of all

and the general will. The latter is concerned only with the common interest, the former with interests that are partial, being itself but the sum of individual wills."[3] By the "general will" Rousseau understood the arithmetic sum of wills, that is, the sum of the positive and negative wishes of the people with sign taken into account. This net sum of wills or opinion amounts to the same thing as the majority opinion of Locke, except that Rousseau with his neat French logic saw individual wills of the minority canceling out a similar number of wills among the majority, leaving an unopposed set of wills that he calls the general will. He failed, however, to explain how the will of these residual few can be equated with the will of the public as a whole. Elsewhere he implied that the general will was the majority will, but at the same time he rejected majority rule.

Rousseau also wrestled with the problem of subgroups within the public. Unlike Aristotle, however, he does not let himself get caught in the dilemma of numerical versus proportionate equality. His arguments are not unlike those of the modern statistician discussing homogeneity within a sampling cluster. He says: "When intriguing groups and partial associations are formed to the disadvantage of the whole, then the will of each of such groups is general only in respect of its own members, but partial in respect of the State. *When such a situation arises, it may be said that there are no longer as many votes as men, but only as many votes as there are groups.*"[4] Ideally, in Rousseau's view, each member of a public should express his own opinion rather than that of a group he belongs to. Groups play havoc with the concept of the general will, Rousseau thought, and he would have preferred the state, or the public, not to be fragmented into subgroups. But if these had to exist, they should be large, few, and of about equal size.

As the republican and democratic ideas of the late seventeenth and early eighteenth centuries began to come to fruition in the latter part of the eighteenth century, the question of quality versus quantity, first raised by Aristotle, began to acquire new significance. The controversy manifested itself in two forms. There were those, like Edmund Burke, who thought of the public as delegating its powers to its elected leaders, who, being better informed than their constituents, were guided solely by their intellect and conscience. This argument was rejected by others. Thomas Jefferson, for example, was more concerned about responsive government that served the majority will than about a stable central government. "The generalizing and concentrating all cares and powers into one body . . . has destroyed the liberty and the rights of men," he wrote.[5] Another form of the controversy was between those who believed that opinion within the public ought to be weighted according to its quality and those who believed in simple majority rule. Thus John Adams wrote that "the people of all nations are naturally divided into two sorts, the gentlemen and the simple men." And, "Every democracy . . . has an aristocracy in it as distinct as that of Rome, France, England."[6] On the other hand, Thomas Paine championed the sovereign will of the common man as expressed through a simple majority.

The Industrial Revolution focused attention on a new phenomenon. The masses concentrated in urban centers, invested with at least philosophical sovereignty, became the objects of study by the new sociologists. August Comte, the father of sociology, saw the individual as the product of his environment, with values similar to the publics (or institutions) to which he belongs. These publics, according to the nineteenth-century sociologists and social psychologists influenced by Comte, had metaphysical qualities that made them different from the sum total of the individuals they comprised. The French writer Gustave LeBon singled out the crowd for special study, thus distinguishing between the metaphysical and the physical public. LeBon conceived of a crowd as a group of people who, under the influence of certain psychological forces, think and behave as a unit, as a "single being." LeBon believed that in a crowd a collective mind temporarily is formed that differs essentially from the minds of the individuals comprising it. Similar views were held by the English psychologist William McDougall, who spoke of the group mind. Other group phenomena studied were the herd and the mob. In *Instincts of the Herd in Peace and War,* the British sociologist Wilfred Trotter spoke of the herd that, like a flock of sheep, follows its leader. The herd's influence over its members is irresistible, according to Trotter. It was the French social psychologist Gabriel Tarde who first called attention to the difference between the crowd and the public. In *L'Opinion et la foule,* he pointed out that whereas the crowd depends on physical contact, the public through the printed word has "contagion without contact."

By the turn of the twentieth century, thoughtful writers like James Bryce had decided that it was futile to try to describe, delimit, or categorize publics in terms of individuals. It made more sense to think of them in terms of the opinions they held in common. At least by implication, Lord Bryce suggests that a public is made up of all those who are giving their attention to public questions. And in this there is little difference between the commercial or professional classes and the "humbler" classes, the educated and the uneducated. Similarly, the American political scientist A. Lawrence Lowell, writing in 1913, approached the problem of what constitutes a public not by counting heads but by focusing on the cement that bound them together into a single unit. Publics that neither have a common perception of a problem nor are willing to submit to a majority will might as well belong to different commonwealths. Using a different tack, Harold D. Lasswell in 1935 showed that publics could be identified in terms of the symbols that united them. "We identify with others (a process which is not necessarily accompanied by acute self-awareness) by perceiving that they are from the same college, the same town, the same country; that they admire the same politicians."[7]

Thus, finally, we have arrived at a modern definition of public which, according to Herbert Blumer, refers to a group of people "(a) who are confronted by an issue, (b) who are divided in their ideas as to how to meet the issue, and (c) who engage in discussion over the issue."[8] W. Phillips Davison adds that while individuals in a public do not know one another, they "have formed beliefs concerning each other's attitudes on a particular subject and modify their behavior in accordance with these beliefs."[9]

Through a series of metamorphoses, the concept of public has developed from the idea of an amorphous, mystical force inherent in all states. Early concerns were with the manifestation, distribution, and locus of opinion and power within a given public. The cynosure was the public, and the philosopher went in search of its opinions and power. Definitions went through cycles of singleness and multiplicity of wills. In the nineteenth century it looked as though the concept had reverted to its original, mystical form as a monolithic force. Then, in the twentieth century, there was a change of focus. Attention turned from the public to opinions. The question changed from What opinions do publics spawn? to What publics swarm to or are united by particular opinions or symbols?

Concept of the Target

The public, we have said, cannot exist conceptually without the cementing bond of common attitudes, opinions, beliefs, or values. A target cannot exist unless there are purposive messages emanating from a motivated source. The concept of target in communication and propaganda is by no means a new one, although purposive targeting of messages for maximum effect is a product of the scientific age. Subsumed is the ability to segment a public into subgroups that have certain predetermined qualities, to recognize and isolate the members of the subgroup, and to reach them with a directed message. As publics grow and disperse, targeting requires more and more sophisticated media and an ever-increasing amount of information about the component members of the public.

The military has long been the target of psychological warfare. The Chinese are said to have used various propaganda devices to deter or to frighten enemy soldiers. The target concept doubtless was present when Rab-shakeh, emissary of the Assyrian King Sennacherib, visited the Israelite King Hezekiah in the eighth century B.C. and demanded his surrender. General Rab-shakeh, we are told in the Bible, taunted the representatives of Hezekiah for trusting the staff of the Egyptian pharaoh, "this bruised reed." The Israelites were concerned about the impact Rab-shakeh's words might have on the soldiers within earshot on the walls of the city and asked the Assyrian to speak in the Syrian language, "for we understand it; and talk not with us in the Jews' language in the ears of the people that are on the wall." But Rab-shakeh countered that his master had sent him to speak to the men on the wall rather than to the representatives of the king. Then he "cried with a loud voice in the Jews' language. . . . Thus saith the king. Let not Hezekiah decieve you: for he shall not be able to deliver you out of his hand."[10] Hessian mercenaries during the American Revolution were told by the English that Americans were cannibals who would torture them and eat them alive. The Americans, in turn, offered the mercenaries freedom of worship and other immunities plus fifty acres of land if they chose to leave the armies of His Britannic Majesty.

By the nineteenth century, attention had turned to subverting the civilian population. Revolution had become the order of the day, and Napoleon's soldiers were sent into battle with slogans of *guerre aux chateaux, paix aux chaumières!* appealing to the masses to overthrow the aristocracy.

It was not until World War I, however, that propaganda was bureaucratized and made the full-time responsibility of a governmental department. With its institutionalization, propaganda was systematically analyzed and the concept of targets and targeting inevitably became a conscious reality. After the war, institutionalized propaganda continued as a peacetime activity by such revolutionary elements as the Bolsheviks. Naturally, their activities were viewed with great alarm by the established powers. In 1918, Bukharin, member of the Politburo, the Communist party, and the Comintern, announced: "The program of the Communist Party is the program not only of liberating the proletariat of one country; it is the program of liberating the proletariat of the world, for such is the program of the 'International Revolution.' "[11] The Comintern then proceeded to target its propaganda to the workers of the world.

Since then, most governments have added a propaganda arm, some in the guise of culture, most in the form of press relations. The more sophisticated carefully target their output; all have learned the cost-benefit of selective communication. Furthermore, as we shall see, domestic political propaganda and commercial propaganda also have undertaken selective targeting in an effort to increase their effectiveness.

Concept of the Audience

It is but a small step from the target concept to the audience concept. Intrinsic in the concept of the target is a directed message and a defined and delimited destination. The concept of audience involves *communication* with a target. Now communication is, as Colin Cherry has said, a social function. "Communication means a *sharing* of elements of behavior, or modes of life, by the existence of sets of rules."[12] It can be thought of also as "the procedures by which one mind may affect another."[13] Both definitions assume a dyadic system comprising a source and a receiver who "depend on each other for their very definition. You cannot define a source without defining a receiver. You cannot define a receiver without defining a source."[14]

Public, target, audience—all are receivers in this system. But conceptually the audience is the only receiver that embraces the entire communication process. The audience is a dynamic entity with which one communicates. Individuals in the public have a common bond among themselves. The audience has a bond with the source of a message. One can *speak at* a public or a target. We communicate with an audience because we expect, demand, or fear feedback. A public or a target may be passive. If an audience is "passive" it is communicating something.

The concept of audience, as we have said, has existed since the dawn of human history, at least in retrospect.[15] Every time someone speaks or manipulates any symbols, whether verbal or nonverbal, he assumes or envisions an audience, either present or prospective. For gregarious man, life would be untenable without an audience. Even the hermit communes with God or nature for his audience.

Two factors have increased the importance of the audience in recent times. The first is the physical factor of the development of mass communication. With the invention of the various mass media, audiences could grow in size and could be dispersed over vast areas. The second is the philosophical development that came with the Age of Enlightenment. The democratic concepts advanced in the eighteenth century linked ruler and ruled, at least theoretically, in an inseverable communication system. Even the recidivism of twentieth-century dictatorships failed to break down the communication system completely. Audiences did not relapse into target status, that is, they were closely watched for reaction and feedback by despotic rulers who claimed a symbiotic relationship with the people.

It is in the context of a mass audience—mass in the sense of numbers and dispersion of people, and audience in terms of a dyadic relationship between source and recipient—that propaganda as a form of public communication becomes meaningful. The term itself first came into use in the seventeenth century, when Pope Gregory XV founded the Sacre Congregatio de Propaganda Fide to do missionary work abroad. Originally, of course, the spreading of the faith may have been peremptory and one-sided. The recipients were mere targets whose acceptance of the message was enforced by the sword. Propaganda before the eighteenth century did not necessarily, therefore, have its modern meaning of influencing the attitudes and thereby the behavior of people in the interest of some particular cause. Attitudinal influence involves communication, a jockeying for an intellectual advantage. This, in turn, means that the target recipient is being treated as an audience whose reactions are relevant. It was only when the originator of a message felt that it made a difference how his message was received that propaganda in its present-day sense developed into an important, daily activity.

The mass media, as we have said, caused audiences to grow and democratic philosophy caused them to become important. By the mid-twentieth century, however, an anomalous situation had developed. Audiences lost their exclusivity. It is hard to feel important if everyone is equally important and "everyone" is counted in the millions. Numerous studies have shown that group cohesiveness and satisfaction are inversely related to the size of the group.[16] Furthermore, the larger the community, the more heterogeneous its population and the less effective communication becomes when it is addressed through a single message to an undifferentiated audience.[17]

The critical mass is reached in communication when the efficiency of a message drops below a tolerable level by tuning out a large proportion of the audience. At this point the originator of the message discovers that he can increase his efficiency by composing a different message for different segments of his public. Targeting communication is intuitive, as every politican knows. But the successful politician has learned to analyze the composition of his audience so that he can pick his targets systematically for maximum effectiveness and efficiency.

AUDIENCE COMPOSITION AND DEVELOPMENT OF THE MASS MEDIA
Oral Communication and the Consensual Imperative

It was the impact of the mass media in a world that is paying increasing attention to its masses (if not to the individuals who comprise them) that, ironically, led to the segmentation or fragmentation of audiences. If we look back to the period before the mass media, the age of oral tradition, communication was simple, direct, and homogeneous. In oral systems, messages emanated from a known source to a known audience. While it is true that this enables the originator of the message to tailor his communication to his particular target according to the interpersonal situation involved, it is also true that when it comes to messages of importance to the community, consensus is demanded and achieved. Deviant behavior is not tolerated in face-to-face groups. "That individuals tend to conform to the norms of the [small] group is one of the best documented generalizations in the small group literature," according to Sidney Verba.[18] And this is true both in primitive and in modern societies, in ongoing and in experimental groups.

Messages in oral systems would tend to be prescriptive rather than descriptive or exploratory, Daniel Lerner concluded after a study of communication systems and social systems. "In oral systems, public information usually emanates from sources authorized to speak to their place in the social hierarchy, i.e., by status rather than skill criteria. . . . News is less salient than 'rules' which specify correct behavior toward imminent events."[19] The audience, therefore, is expected to provide consensual feedback. Not only is there pressure to conform—and this leads to more communications being directed at deviants than at nondeviants—but each individual member of the audience experiences internal pressure which helps to reduce the unpleasant sensation of what Leon Festinger terms "cognitive dissonance," as well as the empty feeling of being isolated from the group.

The mass media have by no means eliminated oral traditions. Even mass education and general affluence made it possible and meaningful to put the necessary artifacts of mass communication into the hands of all members of the public, the psychological frame of mind would be lacking. The mass media are too impersonal for general acceptance in most societies. "Only in a society with an unusually high degree of mutual trust in interpersonal relationships," writes Ithiel de Sola Pool, "would people accept statements regardless of source. In most societies facts must be validated by an in-group authority before they can be considered credible. Word of mouth is therefore more trustworthy than written sources.''[20] Dependence on the mass media is the outgrowth of a highly industrialized and commercialized, scientifically based free enterprise system. Such a system would be impossible without some centralized source of accurate information, written with a minimum of prescription and a maximum of description.

Yet even in the most exemplary of such systems—for example, the system in the United States—all the evidence points to audiences being influenced primarily by face-to-face communication, much as they are in traditional societies with oral systems. Paul Lazarsfeld and his associates found in a study of the 1940 presidential elections that "more people put reliance upon their personal contacts to help them pick out the arguments which are relevant for their own good in political affairs than they do in the more remote and impersonal newspaper and radio.''[21] From this and numerous other studies there developed a theory that communication flows in two (later it was suggested several) steps from the mass media through opinion leaders to their followers. The determination that personal influence through oral communication is more effective and more frequent than is communication through the mass media has been substantiated among groups as disparate as villagers in India with low literacy and American doctors with high.[22]

Certain generalizations may, therefore, be made about oral communication and the composition of audiences:

1. The face-to-face group demands a consensual audience, especially on matters important to the group.

2. Oral communication, it would seem, is an important if not essential step in effective communication.

3. Oral communication remains the only trustworthy communication in most systems.

Since traditional societies depend largely on oral communication systems, audience groups in these societies tend to be consensual and homogeneous. Elements that for a variety of reasons —mainly economic, religious, and ethnic—have deviated in any important respect from the consensus generally have broken away completely and formed their own audience groups. Leaders in traditional societies tend to by polymorphic, a term used by Robert K. Merton to mean that they exert influence in a number of areas.[23] Age, position, and family confer leadership status, and the composition of audience groups of traditional leaders coincides with the total community or public.[24]

Modern societies continue to form face-to-face audience groups, but these are flexible and fluctuating. Opinion leaders specialize, which means that an individual necessarily finds himself in a number of different audience groups, for modern life tends to be complex. Continued membership in these groups requires conformity, as it does in the more all-encompassing traditional society. But there is greater tolerance of limited nonconformity, depending on the educational level of the group, and on other marks of sophistication such as multigroup membership.

Printed Communication and the Fragmentation of Audiences

The invention of printing with movable type more than any other factor cut audiences from their moorings at the dock of the message source. The communication process now could be consummated outside the oral range of the communicator. This had a number of important implications. Print, as Marshall McLuhan has pointed out, extended and amplified man's voice and other human functions, accelerating technological change.[25] As people spread out spatially, they continued to maintain communication contact through the printed media so that they remained part of the same audience group for communication purposes. This made it possible for them to maintain the same or similar value systems, attitudes, and beliefs. Besides increasing the size of the basic audience group, dispersion within the range of printed communication made it possible for people to specialize in economic production and in other ways (because they were closer to exploitable resources) without losing their desire or ability to cooperate. Cooperation is, however, the hallmark of an advanced society. It involves "performance of acts for the welfare of a unit larger than the individual or the family," and we are told by anthropologists such as Margaret Mead that the concept of cooperation in less developed areas is understood only in the context of the family or village.[26] Such a narrow view greatly hampers development even at the agricultural level. Yet all cooperation among human beings requires at least some degree of communication. Furthermore, as Karl W. Deutsch points out, "the richer their cooperation in producing tangible goods and services, in developing highly organized societies, and in developing and sharing intangible treasures of knowledge, art, and values, the greater their need for rich, varied, quick, and accurate communication."[27] And it was such communication that was ushered in by the printed media.

The printed media also led to fragmentation of and diversity among audience groups. If oral communication exacted consensus, the impersonality of cold print permitted, if it did not invite, diversity. The sociologist Ferdinand Tönnies saw the close personal ties of the community (he called it *Gemeinschaft*) in his German homeland change with industrialization, the division of labor, and increased specialization into a looser *Gesellschaft* in the 1880s. Instead of a personal bond, the *Gesellschaft* was based on a contractual arrangement that gives only grudgingly. Thus, largely through the impact of the printed media, a system of competitive relationships developed, in which each individual seeks to maximize his profits and to minimize his contribution to society.[28]

With the stratification of society, too, came the problem of different levels of education and comprehension. The idea that the mass media can cater to a mass society is illusory. The communication needs of a mass society are so varied that specialization in content, detail, style, level of sophistication and technicality become inevitable. This means a multiplicity of specialized audience groups. The need for validation and interpretation is not eliminated. As we said above, all audience groups still require oral reinforcement by opinion leaders. But the printed media have created the possibility of greater diversity among audience groups and hence have led to greater numbers of audience groups, each group containing one or more of the elements that make up modern mass society.

Electronic Communication as a Centripetal and Centrifugal Force

If the printed media liberated the audience in the communication model, the electronic media, in a certain sense, dragged them back again. Some years ago, Gerhart D. Wiebe put for-

ward the idea that people perceive things at various levels of viv-
idness. He suggested that the same event may be viewed in an
intimate frame of reference and in a distant frame of reference.
The former involves informal, face-to-face relationships, the
consciousness of a "responsive other," and the presence of a
sensitive and rather intuitive system of ethics. The latter lacks
all these. In the distant frame of reference it is possible for a person who could not find it in him to stand by and see someone
starving, to accept as an abstraction that thousands of flesh-and-
blood people in some distant country are dying of starvation—
or in his own country, for that matter. Print, according to
Wiebe, "with its double system of symbols, tends to be perceived in the distant frame of reference." But radio, and even
more so television, "can create the illusion of experience within
one's intimate world."[29] Wiebe shows how the Army-McCarthy
hearings were brought into the intimate frame of reference for
those people who saw them on television.

Rulers were not slow in seeing the potential of the electronic
media as a propaganda tool. Morroe Berger quotes Radio Bagh-
dad as announcing after the Iraqi revolution of 1958: "Thus the
Radio was the midwife by whose hands the republic came to
life. . . . And from the first moment the radio and television
have guarded the beloved republic and have gone hand in hand
with it and step by step through the stages of its progress."[30]
What the electronic media have done is to re-create the consensual audience but on a much larger scale. Where face-to-face
contact was lost, it was regained through voice and image, approximating oral communication of traditional society without
losing the much greater coverage of modern society.

It is not suggested here that the electronic media are more
persuasive or more effective than other media. Most communication specialists believe that the media differ markedly from
one persuasive task to another, but that although there is some
evidence that the more intimate the frame of reference, the
more effective the medium,[31] this cannot be proved conclusive-
ly because of the difficulty of experimentally controlling the
many variables. What I *am* saying is that the electronic media
have provided a potential for enlarging the audience groups
fractured by the printed media.

Radio and television thus exercise a centripetal force on far-flung audiences. At the same time, however, these media serve as a centrifuge in that they tend to polarize audiences. The larger the audience to which a medium caters, the more difficult it becomes to span its taste criteria. Ithiel Pool notes that "the mass media in a stratified society inevitably have the problem of vulgarity in a particularly acute way. They can avoid vulgarity by pretending they are addressing their most cultured superiors. This results in media which use only the highest form of the language and which are not understood by the bulk of the population."[32] The same is true at the other extreme, where elite audiences complain that programming is directed at the lowest common denominator.

AUDIENCE TRENDS AND EDUCATION

The accident of birth may at one time have been the most important disjunctive factor in the composition of groups. Freeman and slave, feudal lord and vassal, even rich man and poor were each born to his estate with little chance of ever escaping it. But in the past century the most important basis for segmentation and segregation of publics, targets, and audiences has been education. Education, naturally, has brought with it a number of blessings, and this is not intended to be a criticism of it. Seymour Martin Lipset point out that evidence from numerous countries indicates that "the most important single factor differentiating those giving democratic responses [to questions regarding ethnocentrism and multiparty systems] from others has been education."[33] Its virtues are too obvious to mention. But from the point of view of parsimony and efficiency, education has tended to fragment rather than to unify audiences.

Economic factors dichotomized publics back in the days of Aristotle, as we saw above. But for purposes of communication and propaganda, they still could remain in the same audience without too much of a strain. It was education that interjected distinctions that rapidly broke up audiences into an ever growing number of categories. This did not cause people at the lower levels of education to expose themselves to less communication or even to different media, using the term media in its classificatory sense. On the contrary, there is some evidence that the overall *amount* of exposure to the media in general is only slightly higher at the upper levels of education, at least in the United States.[34]

Where education plays an important role, however, is in what is read, viewed, or heard, both in terms of type of publication or program and in terms of specific content. Alfred O. Hero found, for instance, on the basis of secondary analysis and after consulting a number of studies, that "there is virtually no overlap in frequent readership between critical magazines of the *Harper's, New Republic,* and *The Reporter* genre and such periodicals as *Coronet, Charm, Glamor, Playboy, American Legionnaire, Elks Magazine, Modern Screen, True Story,* and *Confidential.*"[35] There also is no doubt that education is positively and strongly correlated with the *number* of media a person is exposed to. Two American studies illustrate this adequately despite inordinate discrepancies in their findings. One study was done in a large Midwestern city by the research division of Batten, Barton, Durstine and Osborn advertising agency in 1957; the other was a nationwide study by the Survey Research Center at the University of Michigan in 1958. Both are based on probability samples.[36]

	Uses four or five media (BBDO)	Uses four media (SRC)
Grade school	11%	30%
Some high school	12	48
Completed high school	19	64
Some college	26 ⎱	70
Completed college	32 ⎰	
	(N=2,678)	(N=1,919)

The situation is similar in other countries, only more extreme.[37] Furthermore, a person who tends to use one medium more than the average is likely to use all media to a greater extent. This would tend to put him in a larger number of audience groups.

Lord Bryce once said that though public opinion grows, it is also made. "There is not merely the passive class of persons; there is the active class, who . . . aspire to create and lead opinion."[38] Now if anything tends to create "active rather than passive habits of obtaining information," it is education,[39] and, conversely, education tends to create communicators. In fact, U.S. election surveys have given strong evidence that education is associated with political motivation and that the more highly educated are more likely to seek the role of opinion leader.[40] It has been shown also that lower-class groups will tend to select the better-educated among themselves as their leaders.[41]

Education, therefore, has stratified society, creating various levels of audience groups. These levels not only attend differentially to communication messages and, potentially, to propaganda, but also serve as entry points to less-motivated strata of the public. This is another way of suggesting a multistage flow of communication.

We have been talking about education as though it were a self-evident concept. Actually, most sociological studies treat it as an isomorph of formal schooling, that is, number of years in school, as this provides an interval scale, spurious though it is, and makes statistical manipulation easier. In this chapter we have been using the term to mean a broadening of what Kurt Lewin called the "life-space" by developing proficiency in several skills, the learning of a variety of traditions and ethical precepts, and either direct or indirect acquisition of a body of theory about physical and social relationships. These types of education are often acquired without formal schooling and are just as conducive to segmentation of audiences as is the formal type.

In developing countries, however, probably even more than in advanced societies, formal schooling ipso facto leads to audience stratifications. In her sociological study of India, Kusum Nair found that education of the formal type was creating new problems in rural areas. "Generally, the educated son of a peasant, though he may own sufficient land, seeks alternative avenues of work which he considers to be less difficult, more pleasant and more dignified, even though his income from them may be lower than what he could earn if he worked on the land. Indeed he prefers to remain idle rather than work on the land, because that to him is wholly incompatible with education."[42] On the other hand, the Arab world has discovered, as have Western societies before it, that "with the rapid expansion of compulsory primary education in the last decade, it is possible that middle-class status is no longer automatically assumed by secondary school graduates but that it now takes a university degree to confer that position."[43] One of the curious things noted by Edward Shils about the educated class in developing countries is that as a state progresses economically and socially, there is a tendency for intellectual classes to grow larger and to splinter into their several professional and specialized categories. However, "this incorporation of the intellectuals into their own societies [and hence their own audience groups] will depend to a large extent on the establishment of an equilibrium between the demand for and the supply of intellectuals. If there always is such a surplus of university and college graduates that their salaries are low and many of them have to take posts which they regard as unsuitable, the process of incorporation will be obstructed."[44]

AUDIENCE SEGMENTATION IN MODERN PROPAGANDA
Audience Groupings in Domestic Political Propaganda
So far we have been dealing with audiences in general and with the conceptual framework within which people in the aggregate may be analyzed. What follows are three sections of applied audience analysis. The first considers the grouping of audiences in domestic politics to maximize support, to permit greater specificity in campaign issues, and to minimize inevitable intergroup conflicts. The second relates to the segmentation of audiences in modern commercial propaganda or advertising. The third involves some of the policy considerations in targeting for international political propaganda.

Obviously, there are differences from country to country in useful audience groupings for purposes of domestic politics. The groupings vary according to political system, sociocultural patterns such as class, caste and religion, size and topography, distribution of wealth, ethnic composition, and generally the historical accidents and traditions of the country. Probably there are no two politically autonomous entities about which one can make generalizations as to relevant audience groupings in the political power structure. The complexity of the groupings depends on all the factors mentioned. It might be interesting to attempt to give weights to the various factors, yet I know of no published work that has suggested a method for ranking these variables according to their relative importance in segmenting the population for political purposes.

In the final analysis, each individual forms a separate audience group when it comes to satisfaction as a "political animal." The fact that he can be satisfied at all is the result of the varying salience of his needs. Because political man is willing to compromise differentially on his perceived needs, he is able to associate himself with other individuals in groupings that form relevant political audiences. Politicians, in turn, are able to appeal to relatively large political groupings by manipulating the issues.

The mark of a good politician, charismatic leader, campaign manager, or dictator is his ability to mold large numbers of small groups into large groups and rally them around a small number of issues or, on occasion, even a single issue. When there are too many issues, there are too many parties (as in France or Israel) that later must be brought together through compromises by ranking issues according to their salience and pertinence for the party and bartering away the demands of lesser concern. The groups who know their problems will receive short shrift tend to be indifferent to politics as a general rule. Thus, researchers have found there is remarkable similarity in most European and many other countries in the groups that tend to participate in elections. They are the middle-aged, better-educated, married, urban men who tend to have relatively high status and to be members of organizations.[45] Only about 20 to 40 percent of the electorate feel they have any impact at all on their government; the rest are indifferent about politics.[46]

Politicians probably always have intuitively tailored their message to the audience they happened to be addressing. But the systematic effort to seek out audiences of particular composition is a recent phenomenon in political campaigning facilitated by modern communications. The a priori determination that such demographic characteristics as age, sex, education, income, geographic region, and urban-rural dichotomies may be fruitful indicators of voting behavior probably antedated public opinion polling, but by only a few years. The ability to test such hypotheses was a necessary concomitant of any theorizing about or activity among the various population groups. In the 1920s, social scientists such as Harold F. Gosnell, Stuart A. Rice, Charles E. Merriam, Claude E. Robinson and others began comparing the voting behavior by demographic characteristics for which aggregate data were available. Because these groups were easily identifiable and because both census and later survey data were readily accessible, these groups became the special targets of political propaganda.

Their recognition as special audiences was not automatic, however. Women, for example, were long ignored. In his book *Political Behavior,* subtitled *The Heretofore Unwritten Laws, Customs, and Principles of Politics as Practiced in the United States,* Frank Kent wrote in 1928: "Rule 8. Don't worry about the Women—if in the eight years they have had complete political equality with men any one in politics has discovered a key to the woman vote—a sure way of lining it up—they have kept it a profound secret. And that is because there is no such thing. As a matter of fact there is absolutely no rule for dealing with women in politics which will not work just as well half the time if reversed."[47] Similarly, making special appeals to blacks and to young people is a phenomenon of the 1960s, although various ethnic groups have long been wooed as separate entities.

Besides such idiosyncratic groupings as sex, age, and race, there are the socio-cultural-economic groupings represented by religion (in the sense of church membership), socioeconomic status, occupation, urban or rural residence, and geographic region. Finally, there are certain attitudinal-behavioral self-alignments that have formed useful and at times basic criteria for audience groupings, including party of choice, liberal-conservative dichotomies, religious versus secular, and intellectual as against anti- or non-intellectual elements. Politicians today appeal to each of these groups differentially if they must, although in an age of electronic communication they search for a formula that will encompass all these groups in the same message without insulting any particular group or leaving one dissatisfied.

Computer simulations of the electorate have attempted to use such breakdowns of the publics in as many relevant components as possible without overtaxing the computer, but more especially the programmer or the end-user of the data. The results are applied to both prognostic and diagnostic—that is, policy-making and evaluation—needs. The Simulmatics project initiated at M.I.T. in 1959 by William McPhee, Ithiel de Sola Pool, and Robert Abelson reduced data from commercial and academic surveys covering 85,000 respondents to a 480 by 52 matrix by using six available audience characteristics: party, region, religion (combined with race), sex, city size (including rural), and occupation (covering socioeconomic status).

The realities of political campaigning, however, involve recognition of a number of both formal and informal groupings that cross most of these demographic attitudinal lines. No politician can ignore the various labor, business, professional, and agricultural organizations. These are occupational groups with considerable political and economic power.[48] They include such large organizations as the National Association of Manufacturers, the U.S. Chamber of Commerce, the Committee for Economic Development, the AFL–CIO, the Farmers Union, the Grange, and the Farm Bureau; such professional organizations as the American Medical Association, the American Bar Association, the National Education Association, and the American Federation of Teachers; such elements of the military bureaucracy as the American Legion and the Veterans of Foreign Wars, or the civil bureaucracy represented by the National Federation of Federal Employees and various postal unions. Then there are the social and political action groups like the League of Women Voters, the Americans for Democratic Action, and the John Birch Society; groups based on religious denominations like the Anti-Defamation League, the National Catholic Welfare Conference, and the American Friends Service Committee; ad hoc groups like Antiwar New Mobilization Committee, the Princeton Plan, and the Amendment to End the War in Southeast Asia Committee.

Until the 1950s it was conceivable that separate appeals to different population elements and power groups might go unnoticed by the others, so that for a brief period of about thirty years politicians were able to a minor extent to exploit population cleavages. Network television has made this all but impossible. Party strategists must count on any gains with one group being offset by losses with other groups. Thus one Republican strategist has suggested writing off blacks and parts of the Northeast and the Pacific Northwest, and working toward a majority Republican party based in the heartland, the South, and California.[49] Such ruthless decisions probably will have to be made in the future, as it will be increasingly difficult for a politician to appear to be all things to all men.

On the other hand, there is much evidence that party and group affiliations per se are giving way, at least at the national level, to considerations of personal competence of the candidate and his stand on specific issues. This probably is because the voter today is much better informed about candidates and issues than ever before and need not fall back on group affiliations to help him decide how to vote.[50] Under these circumstances, new group and audience alignments will develop, probably along paternalist-liberalist, centralist-decentralist, conformist-nonconformist lines.

Most of the above discussion has dealt with political audience groups in the United States, although *mutatis mutandis* the situation is not too dissimilar in other countries. There are differences, however. Britain, for example, unlike many other parts of the world, does not have a peasant or farm labor class. It employs only one man in twenty in agriculture.[51] Class, on the other hand, is a much more important audience component in Britain than, say, in the United States. Although class is based largely on occupation and education in Britain, it has important social undertones such as family background, accents, manners, and the particular school a person went to. Social mobility is increasing in Britain, and some claim that it is greater than in other European countries, especially France and Italy, "yet for the time being, the social structure of Britain retains its traditional façade. New members are introduced, on an individual basis, into a compact and well-integrated upper middle class group."[52]

While class and occupational loyalties play an important role in Britain and the European continent, family and tribal loyalties still tend to be the most influential in the Near East, as do caste loyalties in India. This situation is rapidly changing with increased education and communication.

What seems fairly obvious is that political audiences group themselves along communication lines. Individuals make political decisions on the basis of the detail of information available to them and the amount of influence they sense they can exert. The family, tribe, caste, occupation, class, or party may be the best line of communication to some. These also may provide the greatest detail on political issues important to the individual. With better communication, the individual is exposed to a political figure in person and to the issues that the politician stands for. Paradoxically, this closer involvement on the part of the citizen tends to reduce the number of issues, for issues proliferate along with audience characteristics. The individual is forced to rank-order his concerns and to make a number of compromises. It should be remembered in this context that issues on which everyone agrees cease to be issues.

From the point of view of audience composition, it looks as though political alignments of the future will be around issues and charismatic and competent leaders rather than group affiliations. The basis for such adherences being reactive rather than structural, it will be increasingly difficult to develop objective criteria for predetermined audiences. It is not inconceivable that conformities in politics—and, therefore, audiences—will group themselves increasingly on psychological rather than sociological or biological lines, so that common values forged through physical contiguities and shared adversities will control our political alignments.

Audience Groupings in Commercial Propaganda
Many learned arguments have been put forward distinguishing between propaganda and advertising, and, with a larger number of variables, between these two and education. The major difference between propaganda and advertising is in message content. The concept of audience, however, is the same for both. Once again, marketing, and hence communication behavior related to it, has always had to be discriminating. You couldn't sell purple robes to a pauper or a chariot to a foot soldier.

This was just as true in the days before mass sales and advertising. Promotion through the mass media goes back to the beginning of the eighteenth century. But so long as the mass media were few and nonspecialized, advertising itself had to be undifferentiated. As the number of readers increased it was possible to cater to their special needs, and publications addressed to a farm audience or a female audience began to appear early in the nineteenth century. The advertising or marketing audience thus became coterminous with the audience of the particular medium in which the advertisement appeared. Further proliferation and specialization of media made it possible to reach highly idiosyncratic audiences.

In a controlled economy, targeting of advertising messages through specialized media is as far as audience segmentation is likely to go. But competition and prosperity tend to lead to further segmentation of the market by personality types.[53] The man who has everything is willing to pay a little more to get just what he wants, as Wendell R. Smith noted in a 1956 trailblazing article on market segmentation. And from the point of view of industry, "many companies are reaching the stage in their development where attention to market segmentation may be regarded as a condition or cost of growth. Their *core* markets have already been developed on a generalized basis to the point where additional advertising and selling expenditures are yielding diminishing returns. Attention to smaller or *fringe* market segments, which may have small potentials individually but are of crucial importance in the aggregate, may be indicated."[54]

In its search for marginal markets, industry found that certain needs cut across the traditional demographic and social class categories, although the differences between the various personality groups were not as large as the differences between age, sex, and social class groups.[55] From a research point of view, however, it made more sense to segment one's audience for communication purposes in terms of its needs and values than in terms of traditional demographic methods, and market researchers began to emphasize the new segmentation principles in their presentations and conferences in the mid-1960s.[56] In this context, it was pointed out also that heavy users of a product seemed to have lower than average brand loyalty; that heavy users of one product were different in their media habits from heavy users of other products, and they were not necessarily the same individuals, either; that heavy product users were not necessarily heavy media users; and that the individual who does most of the buying in a heavy user household is not necessarily the one who is most exposed to the media in which it is advertised.[57] Hence it was important to devise audience categories that differentiated not merely in terms of demographic and social class characteristics but also in terms of psychological attributes. Leo Bogart, of the Bureau of Advertising of the American Newspaper Publishers Association, suggests that people follow three major purchase patterns—repetitive, emotional, and logical—which break down along psychological rather than demographic lines. Anxieties over schools, taxes, and the draft may be more pertinent in determining audience categories than are such classical factors as city size, income, and sex.[58] "A media vehicle may have an audience that is highly concentrated in a certain income or age sector of the population and still fall far short of giving the advertiser adequate coverage of that sector. It may be more efficient for him to use a vehicle that has a more diversified audience, yet which also covers his desired specialized target more completely," Bogart argues.[59]

This categorization of audiences in terms of personality values–product usage is analogous to the attitudinal-behavioral breakdown we found in political propaganda, although marketers have carried their probings further than have the politicians. It is now investigating the interaction between an individual's self-image and the symbolic value of products. "Firms can and should identify and/or segment their markets in terms of differentiated self-concepts," one article urges.[60] Such approaches will lead to the atomization of audience groupings, but only in the sense that it will liberate the individual from the constrictions of his somatic statistics and place him with his spiritual peers in more appropriate audience categories as his tastes dictate. Another development will result in examining and grouping individuals in terms of their actual or potential attitude-behavior rather than dismembering them as intermittent "exposees" of the mass media. The former approach uses as the unit of measurement the individual calibrated in terms of a subjective inclination vis-à-vis a particular product, person, or construct. In the latter approach, the unit of measurement is an exposure calibrated in terms of a particular medium in space and time.

Audience Groupings in International Propaganda

International propaganda became a potential tool of diplomacy with the appearance of nations and, hence, the need for diplomacy. In essence, international propaganda is nothing but purposive communication at the international level. But while ad hoc international propaganda was feasible from the start of internation intercourse, anything more systematic and continuous had to await the invention of a nonphysical means of transmission, in other words, the electronic media. Oral communication and the printed media ran the risk of fairly easy physical apprehension. Radio was the ideal instrumentality of the international propagandist. With the invention of radio and the cheap wireless receiver, the international propagandist could address himself to a receptive audience without fear of his own physical detention or of the censorship of his message. True, his message could be electronically jammed—but only at great cost and inconvenience, and at the risk of helping the propagandist and hurting the jammer's own cause. Other inhibiting methods have included the confiscation of sets, adjusting sets so that they would receive only certain signals, and the use of wired receivers. Once radio had developed into an important medium of domestic communication, external propaganda became an impurity one had to put up with if one wanted any mass communication at all. Not that attempts to discourage or to prohibit exposure to foreign propaganda were dropped altogether. They just were not very successful in those countries and among those people who had cause to seek it out.

For a variety of reasons, but mostly because modern means of communication made further attempts at exclusion futile, propaganda of one friendly state in the territory of another was permitted with only minor restrictions after World War I. Low-key cultural and information centers, specializing in the teaching of languages, literature, and the fine arts, were set up by France, Britain, and the Soviet Union, mainly in Europe and Latin America.[61] Later, in the 1920s and 1930s, other colonial and major powers began a variety of propaganda activities, notably in countries within their spheres of influence. The United States was a late arrival among these.

The early cultural efforts obviously were intended as a public relations gesture by resident commercial interests of the countries engaged in the propaganda. Thus, both the *Alliance Française* and the British Institutes (later the British Council) were inspired and sponsored by French and British residents, respectively, in European and Latin American countries. Both received subsidies from their home governments. The targets were members of the middle and upper-middle classes with whom French and British entrepreneurs were interested in doing business.

Radio propaganda was a different proposition. With the exception of the USSR, the major purpose of early foreign broadcasting was to keep in touch with expatriates in distant colonies and to provide them with approved news and interpretations of the mother country and the world. The Netherlands inaugurated its overseas broadcasting service in 1927, followed by France in 1931 and Britain in 1932. Germany began to broadcast to *Auslandsdeutsche* in 1933, Italy to Italians in South America and North Africa in 1935. The United States entered the race in 1939 with broadcasts to the Western Hemisphere. In all cases up to the mid-1930s, broadcasting was in the mother tongue and there is little doubt that expatriates were the prime targets. But in the second half of the decade, as the world raced toward another war, the targets changed almost overnight. In 1936 France initiated its foreign-language broadcasts, starting with German, ostensibly to Alsatians but probably to Germans in all of Germany. The following year, Italy began broadcasting in eighteen languages, including Arabic to the Near East, evoking a British protest. The Anglo-Italian Accord of 1938 provided, among other things, that Italy would refrain from attempting to undermine the British position in the Arab world. Britain, however, decided it could not stay out of the propaganda war and began broadcasting in foreign languages, including German and Italian, the same year. When war broke out the following year, the BBC had programs in sixteen languages.

The Communist Propaganda Audience. The Russians were the first to use radio for international propaganda, and their targets were neither expatriates nor colonials. Toward the end of World War I and in the early 1920s, they broadcast revolutionary appeals to the workers of the world in English, German, Polish, Finnish, and Estonian, among other languages. When the countries concerned protested, the Russians claimed they were broadcasting to national minorities within the Soviet Union. Similar revolutionary broadcasts to proletarians all over the world were transmitted by Béla Kun, the Hungarian communist leader, after World War I. Strong protests were voiced to Hungary by Austria and Switzerland. The British Parliament took up the matter of the English-language broadcasts of Radio Moscow. But it was soon discovered that only the most expensive receivers could pick up the Moscow signal, and the broadcasts ceased to be taken seriously.

Soviet propagandists sought to reach "the masses" as their major target. This was in keeping with communist doctrine and made good sense to party workers, for they looked upon the masses as the chief source of power. But what did the term "masses" mean? Lenin wrote: "The meaning of the term 'masses' changes in accordance with the character of the struggle. . . . During our revolution there were occasions when several thousand workers represented the masses. . . . When the revolution has been sufficiently prepared the term 'masses' acquires a different meaning."[62] During its conflict with the bourgeoisie, says the Communist Manifesto, the proletariat that forms the mass base is forced to organize itself as a class. As civilized society, according to communist doctrine, is divided into irreconcilably antagonistic classes, the masses form one of these classes and the function of communist propaganda is to exploit the permanent and reliable tensions that exist between the proletarian class and the bourgeois class of capitalists, their henchmen, retainers, and dependents.

The prime target, therefore, was this "exploited" class that could include different elements of the population at different times and in different countries. Other audiences were the natives of colonies and of semifeudal and underdeveloped countries. They, too, were disaffected and vulnerable targets of communism.

In effect, therefore, the targets of communist propaganda are all those alienated elements of the public that are looking for an antipodal banner to which to rally so that they can work out their resentments against the establishment. This is considered to be the magnetic power of communist propaganda, as a Soviet writer frankly puts it in discussing its strengths: "While Communist propaganda, appealing to the broad masses, speaks the language of the masses, expresses ideas, sets goals and defends interests vital to the masses, it is a completely different, directly opposite goal which is pursued by bourgeois propaganda, appealing to the masses with ideas foreign to them."[63] An enormous amount of sociological research has been done in the United States, this writer says, to prove that classes have been eliminated in that country, that workers are really capitalists, and that everyone belongs to some sort of "average class." "The ugly reality which is the real face of America," he says, is impossible to conceal, and hence "the failure of attempts by American foreign propaganda to 'sell' their false myths to the young emerging nations who have turned from the capitalistic path of development and who have censured . . . the regime of crying social contrasts, racial oppression and piratic imperialism which in fact is the U.S."

Although the disaffected masses form the ultimate target of communist propaganda, Lenin recognized that without a dozen or so of talented leaders, no class in modern society is capable of conducting a determined struggle.[64] This small core of "professional revolutionaries" must keep in contact with the masses, exploiting their dissatisfactions. "We must train our . . . practical workers to become political leaders . . . able at the right time to 'dictate a positive program of action' for the discontented students, for the discontented Zemstvo councilors, for the discontented religious sects, for the offended elementary school teachers, etc.," wrote Lenin.[65] These trained revolutionary party workers then were another important propaganda target besides being a propaganda source.

Finally, communist propagandists believe in working through existing organizations, which Lenin found more economical and effective than trying to form complete communist organizations from scratch. Workers' organizations, the unions, were thought to be the most obvious organized groups into which the party could infiltrate and work. "The Communists have no fear of the largest workers' organizations which belong to no party," the second International Congress said, "even when they are of a decidedly reactionary nature (yellow unions, Christian associations, etc.). The Communist Party carries on its work inside such organizations and untiringly instructs the workers." Besides the mass organizations of workers, including cultural, fraternal, sport, and unemployed associations, communist propaganda was directed at and through various "front" organizations, such as the World Peace Council and federations of students, teachers, news media workers, and other professionals.[66]

To sum up, therefore, we find that communist doctrine, and more especially the practices and guiding policies of the Soviet Union, calls for a target or audience structure shaped like an inverted pyramid. All-encompassing at the top is the universe of disaffected individuals who, according to communist dogma, tend to be the downtrodden masses of "toilers," feudal peons, colonials, and other denizens of underdeveloped countries— clearly a majority of the world's population. Conceptually lower but subsumed within this majority are the discriminated-against racial, ethnic, social, and other minorities who are not a part of the established "capitalist conspiracy." Marxist-Leninist theory specifies three additional groups that often are susceptible to revolutionary propaganda. These are the armed forces, young people, and intellectuals, although Lenin considered intellectuals as unreliable because of their propensity toward "abstract morality and justice."[67] In trying to reach these three audience groups, communist propaganda generally works through the next level, which comprises a variety of importuning and denunciatory groups, in which the propaganda target is the leadership. The communist objective here is to exploit the common bond of grievance that has attracted individuals to membership in the organizations. Finally, at the pyramid's nadir is the small nucleus of trained agitators, an audience of faithful party workers, often referred to as a "fraction." It is these workers who carry out the decisions of the party. Fractions exist at all levels of the party hierarchy.

I am not suggesting that communist propaganda ignores other demographic and functional groupings in its output. The Overstreets point out that it exploits "the interest of women, for example, in not having their men go to war; of religious groups in promoting world peace; of college students in not having their lives interrupted by military training."[68] Nor does communist propaganda ignore influentials in all walks of life, especially in the developing countries. As a representative of the Voice of America stated in testifying before a Senate subcommittee, "Class broadcasting—to government officials, politicians, newspaper editors and college students—is practicable and essential in all areas. These are the classes which control or most powerfully influence the internal and external policies of the country. They are the principal target of both VOA and the Communist radio."[69] In fact, one unpublished study by the Bureau of Applied Social Research at Columbia University reported in 1962 that most publications of the U.S. Information Service in India were not aimed at a definable audience, whereas Soviet publications were more differentiated, in sharper focus. They "not only had a definite audience in mind, but different Soviet publications were aimed at different audiences."

Regardless of group or class, however, communist propaganda tends to address itself to audiences that are disaffected in some way or other within that group, except that it assumes that every member of what it vaguely describes as "the masses" is exploited and hence disaffected.

The Nazi Propaganda Audience. The concept of the audience in nazi propaganda is considered here not because it differed markedly from the audience concept in communist propaganda nor because it was a highly successful formula, but because Nazi Germany itself was essentially the product of propaganda: it was the first country to develop an effective worldwide propaganda operation, and it put tremendous resources into its unique propaganda organization. It provoked, inspired, or forced others to follow its example in instituting or strengthening their own propaganda activities.

The ideal nazi propaganda audience was the undifferentiated mass, preferably the crowd. Hitler reveled in the spoken word, and he put his greatest emphasis on oratory before large crowds. "The mass meeting is necessary," he wrote, "if only for the reason that in it the individual, who in becoming an adherent of a new movement feels lonely and is easily seized with fear of being alone, receives for the first time the pictures of a greater community, something that has a strengthening and encouraging effect on most people."[70] Goebbels, too, believed that "revolutionary movements are not the work of great writers but of great orators. It is a mistake to assume that the written word is more effective because it reaches, through the daily paper, a wider public. . . . The spoken word influences by word of mouth a hundredfold and sometimes a thousandfold."[71] Goebbels developed an army of party speakers, graded by ability and personality. The stars were the "Reich speakers," whose names were printed in large letters on the posters that advertised meetings. At the next level were members of speakers' squads, with specialized experience in addressing audiences of a particular composition, such as peasants, industrialists, or professionals. Then came a level of regional orators known as *gau* speakers. Finally, party propaganda headquarters also controlled a panel of specialized speakers who were experts in a particular field such as foreign affairs or the Jewish question.

The anomaly of the nazi system was that although its philosophy was elitist, its field of operation was totally mass-oriented.

Both Hitler and Goebbels believed that society was made up of a mass of uninformed people whose political decisions could easily be controlled. "The rank and file are usually much more primitive than we imagine," Goebbels wrote. "Propaganda must be essentially simple."[72] And Hitler said that "all propaganda has to be popular and has to adapt its spiritual level to the perception of the least intelligent of those towards whom it intends to direct itself. Therefore its spiritual level has to be screwed the lower, the greater the mass of people which one wants to attract."[73] That Hitler was more concerned about the undifferentiated mass audience than about possible intellectual elements that might be included in its composition is evident from such statements as the following: "For I must not measure the speech of a statesman to his people by the impression which it leaves in a university professor, but by the effect it exerts on the people."[74]

Although both communism and national socialism saw their source of power as stemming from the masses, the nazi philosophy was disdainful of their intellectual capacities and for that very reason appealed directly to them whereas communism, which, at least overtly, did not look upon the masses as simpleminded, believed in a multistep flow of propaganda through highly trained and motivated elite cadres. The difference may have been the result of the necessarily clandestine nature of communist organization in many parts of the world, whereas Hitler could operate out in the open; but mainly it was a difference in philosophy. Nazi ideology, like that of the communists, stressed the importance of leadership. But in Germany, leaders were people you made propaganda about, not to. Goebbels made heroes out of men like Field Marshal Rommel, although in the privacy of his diary he was furious about German leaders whose conduct in public made it difficult for him to ask the masses to follow them blindly.

On the other hand, nazi propaganda was also directed at targets of opportunity, such as foreign students in Germany. But this was not part of a conscious effort to segment the public into homogeneous audience groups. The propaganda messages themselves may appear to have been target oriented, as when German broadcasts attempted to pit political parties, social and economic classes, ethnic groups, or isolationists and interventionists against each other. But this was a haphazard effort, often contained in the same broadcast or article with no consistent policy of targeting. So that while the rightist Fichte League, a publicly supported organization engaging in cultural propaganda in foreign countries, was encouraged to make lists of "important people," these then were supplied with the same pamphlets that the league was instructed to leave "lying about in factories, schools, banks, trams, and cafés, quite casually." And in dealing with "important people," the league followed Hitler's injunction that propaganda to the masses be limited "to a very few points": "Never give them more than one [pamphlet] at a time," wrote Theodor Kessemeier, head of the league, to his "foreign correspondents."[75]

The British Propaganda Audience. Unlike the Germans and the Russians, the British had to maintain rather than to develop their world power in the post–World War I era that saw the rise of institutionalized international propaganda. The British were appealing not to publics that already had national allegiances of their own, but mainly to peoples who were economically, if not culturally, tied to the British Empire. As already stated, the early British propaganda efforts were directed mainly at expatriates, an elite group that tended to be more British than were their compatriots in the mother country. To these were added loyal natives, generally middle-level and senior civil servants and military officers. This was a stratum of society that was educated in English-speaking missionary and secular schools and occasionally in England. More often than not, they spoke English in their homes and were steeped in English literature and culture, since they coveted for themselves and for their children the high-paying and prestigious governmental jobs that were open only to people with such backgrounds.

This was the original composition of the audience of the British Broadcasting Corporation and the British Council, the two major propaganda instrumentalities of Great Britain. The British were frankly elitist from the start. They catered to the head on the assumption that the body and the tail would follow. If they failed to follow, the British administered the whiplash rather than propaganda blandishments. So much for policies and operations within the empire.

Britain also paid some attention to countries outside her empire, as for instance in Latin America, where Britain had sizable investments. British Institutes (later the British Council) had started operations there in the early 1920s, and even prior to that in the Mediterranean area. But these were not particularly influential or large-scale. As British Ambassador to the United States John Freeman told a conference of UPI editors in Bermuda on 8 October 1969, "about the degree of effectiveness of British influence on world events prior to 1939—no doubt it was considerable. But outside the colonial empire it was probably more limited and more haphazard than most of us now think we remember."

Having started an elite-oriented propaganda program, Britain never deviated from it. In the years immediately after World War II, an official report on *The Strategy of Political Warfare* stated that "the most effective means of communication is to provide respected leaders of opinion (generally local) with the relevant facts, objectively presented, leaving them to draw the right conclusions and to publicize them."[76] BBC officials, speaking of listeners in the Far East, told Ralph K. White, then with USIA, that "it is better to be above their heads than below." And, "we make few concessions to popular tastes" in Germany. "We try to be above the average German station, which is pretty low."[77]

The British had no illusions about the size of their audience. The statement on strategy of political warfare referred to "that (almost certainly) minute section of the population which has both the desire and the opportunity to listen to foreign broadcasts." It went on to "assume that listeners are for the most part either officials or technical personnel (military and civilian) whose duties provide them with ready-made opportunities—e.g., monitors, radio operators and the like."

Besides concentrating on an audience of well-educated opinion leaders, the British directed their propaganda at "those elements whose defection to the Communist cause would represent a substantial gain for that cause." Here they recognized that it was pointless to try to go after "hard-core" communists in the free world, and a waste of effort to reach elements that already were anticommunist. It would be most profitable to try to stiffen "the resistance to current Communist propaganda themes and political devices of those who are most susceptible to its influence," the statement read. "In other words . . . the neutralists, the left-wing lunatic fringe, the politically innocent, and those (e.g., the extreme nationalists) who think they are clever enough to make use of Communism for their own purposes."

In the early 1950s, an Independent Committee of Enquiry chaired by the Earl of Drogheda was set up in England "to assess the value, actual and potential" of British overseas information work and to advise on the relative importance of different methods and services in different areas and circumstances. The Drogheda committee recommended that British propaganda continue to concentrate on "the influential few."[78] Ten years later, a second committee, chaired by Lord Plowden, reiterated the recommendation.[79] And in July 1969, Sir Val Duncan's Review Committee on Overseas Representation 1968–1969 reemphasized that "there can be no hope of reaching mass audiences effectively from within the limited resources available to the overseas information services. Our efforts should be directed towards the influential few."[80]

The Duncan report spelled out in detail why it recommended that British propaganda concentrate on a limited target audience: "Although the transistor radio audience is growing rapidly in Asia, Africa, and Latin America we nevertheless take the view that political motives for a direct interest in Britain on the part of mass audiences will diminish, as Britain's political influence in these areas is reduced, and her military forces are withdrawn." It felt there still would be residual interest in Britain, but that "the BBC's external services will have the greatest effect upon the educated and professional classes, for whom English will often be the main lingua franca; these classes will have a broad interest in the whole range of subjects affecting their countries, and will therefore take an interest in their countries' relations with Britain." The committee recommended that major emphasis should be placed on English-language rather than on vernacular broadcasts, for "foreign language broadcasts are less likely to attract the influential few—i.e., those whom we most rely on to see that Britain's political and commercial case does not go by default."[81]

On the other hand, the committee recommended that broadcasts in the vernacular continue in two areas. These areas are

Eastern Europe and the Arab Near East. Eastern Europe, it said, "is one area where we are, exceptionally, concerned with a large audience with whom there are clear political reasons for maintaining contact." These are the many people who are "out of sympathy with various aspects of Communist life and are eagerly seeking some communication and understanding with Western Europe." Arabic was recommended "for the rather different reason that Arabic is the lingua franca in a fairly concentrated area and one which is of considerable importance for British interests . . . English is perhaps not used by the influential few to the same extent as in some other areas."[82]

Similarly, the committee recommended that the British Council concentrate its efforts on the educated classes to ensure that "many educated overseas citizens will develop and retain a special and friendly interest in Britain."[83] Furthermore, "it has to be recognized that it is not possible to reach the mass of potential English students."[84]

Indubitably, therefore, Britain was banking on its continued snob appeal for its audience. The British did not and do not seek out their audience. They expect to get, and there is evidence that they do get, an audience that seeks them out. They are discriminating in the selection of their audiences, not by artificially or arbitrarily excluding anyone, but by maintaining such high standards in their programming that only those with the best brains and highest motivation are attracted.

The Propaganda Audience of the United States. Communism sought to bring about a proletarian revolution. Its propaganda appeal was to the proletariat of the world. Nazism strove to boost the German *Herrenvolk,* using the tactics of a Joshua or a Genghis Khan to drive terror into the heart of any would-be opponent. Thus, while communist propaganda asks its audience to join the group, the audience of nazi international propaganda tended to comprise those who were asked to stand aside and remain neutral or to submit. Britain's foreign propaganda before World War II tried to hold an empire together. Unlike both communist and nazi propaganda, which were talking mainly to outsiders, asking them to come in and stay out, respectively, the British were talking to insiders, members of the family, so to speak. Since the war, the major emphasis of British propaganda has been on trying to get people to continue to look to Britain for economic and moral leadership. The relationship between Britain and its audience, however, is becoming less and less clear.

The international propaganda of the United States invites people to look to it for leadership. But like Britain since the war, the United States does not state with any great clarity what its relationship is to its audience. This fuzziness about the locus of the audience vis-à-vis the United States and the direction in which it is expected to move weakens the impact of U.S. propaganda. There is evidence that overt behavior demanded of the audience leads to greater attitude change,[85] and that the impact of propaganda is enhanced when a specific role is assigned to an audience.[86] U.S. propaganda objectives and themes seldom indicate clearly what the relationship is between the audience and the United States, and all too often they are no more than an exposition of American philosophy or an attack on the philosophy of the opposition rather than a call to action.[87]

From the start, U.S. external propaganda, like that of Britain, has been addressed to an elite audience. Unlike Britain, however, the United States makes a great effort to seek out its audience ''by the book'' and makes a great issue of targeting for effectiveness. This started out as a financial necessity for the United States. Its interests and its responsibilities were global, yet the funds it was willing to allocate to its information and cultural programs were limited. It was forced, therefore, to be selective in its targets. Thus, when the Senate Subcommittee on Overseas Information Programs under Senator Bourke B. Hickenlooper asked the International Information Administration (predecessor of USIA) whether its propaganda did not go over the heads of many to whom it was directed, the agency responded: ''While in isolated instances this may be true, it is probable that the criticism is based on a misunderstanding of the question to whom is IIA addressing itself. Due to limited resources, IIA has necessarily had to address itself in every country to a limited group of politically significant leaders. IIA recognizes the need to reach the general population of many important countries, but has not had the resources to undertake such a program.''[88] In fact, in answer to another question, the IIA, then a part of the State Department, said that ''if resources were made available IIA would agree that it should attempt to reach the lowest third of the population in many important countries.''

On the other hand, it is not clear whether the agency was thinking of limited funds alone when it agreed that target countries and groups ought to be differentiated and pinpointed, and that ''the importance of each group must be properly weighted, and the most money should be devoted to reaching the key countries and groups. Hard-core communists should not be a target group as they are hard to reach and change.'' Arguments over mass versus class have been persistent in the U.S. government over the years. At the same Senate hearings on overseas information programs, Lloyd A. Free, then a public affairs officer in Italy, told Senator Alexander Wiley that it was important to get ''a clear understanding of what target groups . . . you want to work on.'' He opposed trying to reach ''a lot of nice middle-class people who are already with us and who do not have too much influence with anybody, and that means that you are devoting all these resources in terms of cost to a group of individuals which do not include the people of influence that you are after.'' Yet sixteen years later, a task force of senior U.S. Information Agency officers wrote that ''some members of the group believe that the Agency is losing sight of its obligation—as stated in PL 402—to reach public opinion abroad. Recognizing that the Agency cannot reach everyone, they still feel that it should aim for as broad an audience as it has the capability of reaching effectively; in their view, present Agency directives focus too narrowly on elite leadership groups.''

Whether driven by financial necessity or by the inexorable findings of communication studies, the U.S. propaganda program was keyed to definite targets. In the early days the argument tended to be mostly that the agency ''could not afford to send a penny postcard to every Indian,'' and besides, most Indians would not have the slightest knowledge of or interest in the United States and its activities, being concerned only about ''gut issues.'' By the 1960s, the argument had changed. ''Opinion leaders'' and ''influentials'' were the key words. At least in most countries, USIA was interested in the power-elite and decision makers, and in the ''comers'' among young people. The ''limited funds'' argument no longer was important in the minds of most of the top-echelon officers in the agency: else how does one explain the insistence on including only members of the target audience reached, in the measurement of the effectiveness of Voice of America broadcasts? No additional costs were involved in reaching nontarget listeners, who often greatly outnumbered target elements.

During the latter part of the 1960s, prompted by the Planning-Programming-Budgeting System (PPBS) that had become the rage in the federal government, this elite audience was further broken down into what turned out to be mainly occupational groups. Thus the target groups for 1970 were:

Government and political leaders
The academic community
Military officers
Traditional leaders
Communication and media leaders
Professional leaders
Creative and intellectual leaders
Entrepreneurs, businessmen, and managers
Labor leaders
Agricultural leaders

Women leaders and youth leaders, targets in previous years, had been dropped as being too general. In not every country were all these groups included, and in some it was found to be necessary to include additional categories. Thus *campesinos* (peasants) were part of the target in certain Latin American countries, as were religious leaders in certain Asian and Latin American countries, and practically the entire population was included in Vietnam and Thailand. There was some concern at the policy level because public affairs officers were taking their target categories too literally. "Almost invariably," complained a task force examining the preparation of Country Plan Program Memoranda, or CPPM, an annual plan of operations prepared by each country public affairs officer, "posts have adopted the CPPM Handbook's illustrative list of occupational groups as their own means of target group classification. The Working Group believes that classification of target groups must be more flexible, and should not be limited to set occupational categories." Posts occasionally overlook important "agents of change," the task force pointed out. "More attention should go to the roles individuals play in the communication process; these may cut across occupational categories, and may vary with the socio-economic structure of a given country."[89]

The reason posts hewed to the guidelines set out by the handbook was obvious. If they failed to do so, officers responsible for planning at the area level or the agency level found it difficult to make cross-country comparisons. Yet whatever comparisons *were* made were spurious, for the categories were neither qualitatively nor quantitatively comparable. As one public affairs officer put it, perhaps overdramatizing his point, "my primary target is made up of exactly four senior military officers."

The federal government's emphasis in the latter half of the 1960s on PPBS necessarily resulted in an emphasis on numbers, for the weighting of audience members in terms of their importance to the accomplishment of the mission was too difficult a problem for several hundred agency officers to agree on. Qualitative judgments were excluded as much as possible, although quantitative judgments had to be retained for lack of any harder figures. Earlier methods of assessment had permitted more subjective evaluations. "Teaching English to the Prime Minister of a closed Society individually and at great relative expense may be justified," one directive stated; "teaching English in Scandinavia at minuscule cost per individual would be unnecessary and unproductive." A return to more subjective criteria of audience selection for U.S. propaganda is probable, however. Also one may expect a greater personalization of propaganda effort and segmentation of the audience in terms of its relationship to the communicator.

Any comparison of the day-to-day output of a handful of international propagandists, including the four we have looked at, might lead one to the conclusion that we are straining over Tweedledum and Tweedledee. A scanning of the mailing lists might strengthen this suspicion. They were probably purchased from the same mailing list compiler or, even more likely, copied from the same directories. Is there a difference, then, after all? The answer is yes, obviously there is a difference. True, there are certain titular leaders in all countries who are on the pro forma mailing lists of every foreign information service and cultural center. These, like the parents of the fiancée, must be acknowledged if not wooed by all parties, even though everyone knows that their alignment is preordained by their country's ideology. The real propaganda targets, on the other hand, are determined by the political ideology of the propagandist, which underlies its concept of audience. In the 1962 USIA-sponsored Bureau of Applied Social Research study, for example, it was found that "U.S. materials were directed at upper class business and professional groups. And these already were favorably disposed toward the U.S. Soviet publications, on the other hand, were aimed at the wider, middle and lower class element." The conclusion drawn with respect to India was that the U.S. "target audience contains those people with whom we [the United States] have had the most success in the past, while the Communists appeal to those sub-elites among whom *they* have found most followers." This is good politics because it is successful politics. It is also the stuff that political philosophy is made of, for it would be futile to develop an ideology that appeals to no one. If, therefore, there is any trend in audience composition in international propaganda, the trend is inextricably tied to the political philosophy of the propagandists.

NOTES

1. George H. Sabine, *A History of Political Theory* (New York: Henry Holt & Co., 1937), p. 297.

2. *Social Contract: Essays by Locke, Hume, and Rousseau* (New York: Oxford University Press, 1948), p. 57.

3. Ibid., p. 193.

4. Ibid., p. 194, italics added.

5. Thomas Jefferson, *Writings*, H. A. Washington, ed. (Washington, D.C., 1853–1854), vol. 3, p. 451.

6. John Adams, *Works: With a Life of the Author*, C. F. Adams, ed. (Boston, 1850–1856), vol. 2, p. 516.

7. Harold D. Lasswell, "Nations and Classes: The Symbols of Identification," in Bernard Berelson and Morris Janowitz, eds., *Reader in Public Opinion and Communication*, 2d ed. (New York: Free Press, 1966), p. 31.

8. Herbert Blumer, "The Mass, the Public, and Public Opinion," in Bernard Berelson and Morris Janowitz, eds., *Reader in Public Opinion and Communication*, 2d ed. (New York: Free Press, 1966), p. 46.

9. W. Phillips Davison, quoted in H. Laurence Ross, *Perspectives on the Social Order* (New York: McGraw-Hill, 1968), p. 499.

10. II Kings 18.

11. U.S. Department of State, *Papers Relating to the Foreign Relations of the United States (1923)* (Washington, D.C.: Government Printing Office, 1938), vol. 2, p. 769.

12. Colin Cherry, *On Human Communication* (New York: M.I.T. Press, 1961), p. 6.

13. Claude E. Shannon and Warren Weaver, *The Mathematical Theory of Communication* (Urbana: University of Illinois Press, 1964), p. 3.

14. David K. Berlo, *The Process of Communication* (New York: Holt, Rinehart and Winston, 1960), p. 108.

15. In this context, we are not concerned with the *word* "audience," which, as Leo Bogart has suggested, originated with the theater. The term was later applied to motion pictures and, in the mid-1930s, to the printed media. See Leo Bogart, "Is It Time to Discard the Audience Concept?" *Journal of Marketing* 30 (January 1966):47–54.

16. David Krech, Richard S. Crutchfield, and Egerton L. Ballachey, *Individual in Society* (New York: McGraw-Hill, 1962), p. 459.

17. See Terry N. Clark, "Power and Community Structure: Who Governs, Where, and When?" in Edgar F. Borgatta, ed., *Social Psychology: Readings and Perspective* (Chicago: Rand McNally, 1969), pp. 523–538.

18. Sidney Verba, *Small Groups and Political Behavior* (Princeton: Princeton University Press, 1961), p. 22 and citations on p. 23.

19. Daniel Lerner, *The Passing of Traditional Society* (Glencoe, Ill.: Free Press, 1958), p. 55.

20. Ithiel de Sola Pool, "The Mass Media and Politics in the Modernization Process," in Lucian W. Pye, ed., *Communications and Political Development* (Princeton: Princeton University Press, 1963), p. 242.

21. Paul F. Lazarsfeld, Bernard Berelson, and Hazel Gaudet, *The People's Choice* (New York: Columbia University Press, 1948), p. 155.

22. See Everett M. Rogers, *Diffusion of Innovations* (New York: Free Press, 1962), pp. 208–253.

23. Robert K. Merton, *Social Theory and Social Structure* (New York: Free Press, 1957), pp. 413–415.

24. See Lerner, *Passing of Traditional Society*, pp. 185–186.

25. Marshall McLuhan, *Understanding Media: The Extensions of Man* (New York: McGraw-Hill, 1965), pp. 101–102.

26. See *Cultural Patterns and Technical Change* (New York: Mentor [UNESCO], 1955), pp. 182–184.

27. Karl W. Deutsch, *Nationalism and Social Communication* (Cambridge: M.I.T. Press, 1966), p. 91.

28. Ferdinand Tönnies, *Community and Society (Gemeinschaft und Gesellschaft)*, trans. and ed. Charles P. Loomis (East Lansing: Michigan State University Press, 1957), p. 65.

29. Gerhart D. Wiebe, "A New Dimension in Journalism," *Journalism Quarterly* 31 (Fall 1954):411–420.

30. Morroe Berger, *The Arab World Today* (New York: Anchor Books, 1964), p. 402.

31. See Joseph T. Klapper, *The Effects of Mass Communication* (New York: Free Press, 1960), pp. 106–112.

32. Pool, "Mass Media and Politics," p. 244.

33. Seymour Martin Lipset, *Political Man: The Social Bases of Politics* (New York: Anchor Books, 1963), pp. 39–40.

34. Paul F. Lazarsfeld and Patricia Kendall, "The Communications Behavior of the Average American," in Wilbur Schramm, ed., *Mass Communications* (Urbana: University of Illinois Press, 1960), p. 432. See also Merrill Samuelson, Richard F. Carter, and Lee Ruggels, "Education, Available Time and Use of Mass Media," *Journalism Quarterly* 40 (Autumn 1963):491–496, 617.

35. Alfred O. Hero, *Mass Media and World Affairs* (Boston: World Peace Foundation, 1959), p. 50.

36. Ben Gedalecia, *The Communicators* (New York: BBDO, 1957); Survey Research Center, University of Michigan, *The Public Impact of Science in the Mass Media* (Ann Arbor: Survey Research Center, Institute for Social Research, 1958), p. 17.

37. The author bases this view on familiarity with a large number of studies as a former head of media research in the United States Information Agency.

38. Gedalecia, *The Communicators,* p. 17.

39. Angus Campbell, Gerald Gurin, and Warren E. Miller, "Television and the Election," in Daniel Katz et al., eds., *Public Opinion and Propaganda* (New York: Dryden Press, 1954), p. 289.

40. Angus Campbell, Philip E. Converse, Warren E. Miller, and Donald Stokes, *The American Voter* (New York: Wiley, 1964), pp. 252–253.

41. William Kornhauser, *The Politics of Mass Society* (New York: Free Press, 1959), p. 57; see also Bernard R. Berelson, Paul F. Lazarsfeld, and William N. McPhee, *Voting* (Chicago: University of Chicago Press, 1954), p. 112.

42. Kusum Nair, *Blossoms in the Dust* (New York: Frederick A. Praeger, 1962), p. 196.

43. Berger, *Arab World Today,* p. 255.

44. Edward Shils, "The Intellectuals in the Political Development of the New States," in Louis Kriesberg, ed., *Social Processes in International Relations* (New York: Wiley, 1968), pp. 186–187.

45. Lipset, *Political Man,* pp. 187–191.

46. Ibid., pp. 293–294.

47. Frank Kent, quoted in Harwood L. Childs, *An Introduction to Public Opinion* (New York: Wiley, 1940), p. 99.

48. See R. Joseph Monsen, Jr., and Mark W. Cannon, *The Makers of Public Policy: American Power Groups and Their Ideologies* (New York: McGraw-Hill, 1965).

49. See Kevin P. Phillips, *The Emerging Republican Majority* (New Rochelle, N.Y.: Arlington House, 1969).

50. See Walter De Vries and Ithiel de Sola Pool, *Strategies in the New Politics* (Washington, D.C., Acropolis, 1971).

51. The proportion is about the same in the United States.

52. Jean Blondel, *Voters, Parties, and Leaders* (Baltimore: Penguin Books, 1963), pp. 43–44, also 21–48.

53. Morris J. Gottlieb, "Segmentation by Personality Types," in James U. McNeal, ed., *Dimensions of Consumer Behavior* (New York: Appleton-Century-Crofts, 1969), pp. 135–145.

54. Wendell R. Smith, "Product Differentiation and Market Segmentation as Alternative Marketing Strategies," *Journal of Marketing* 21 (July 1956):7.

55. Gottlieb, "Segmentation," p. 142.

56. For an illustration of how market segmentation works, see Daniel Yankelovich, "New Criteria for Market Segmentation," *Harvard Business Review,* March-April 1964, pp. 83–90.

57. Study by Dik Warren Twedt using the *Chicago Tribune* consumer panel on eighteen product categories, quoted by Leo Bogart, *Strategy in Advertising* (New York: Harcourt, Brace and World, 1967), p. 197.

58. Ibid., pp. 209, 211.

59. Ibid., p. 213.

60. Edward L. Grubb and Harrison L. Grathwohl, "Consumer Self-Concept, Symbolism and Market Behavior: A Theoretical Approach," in James U. McNeal, ed., *Dimensions of Consumer Behavior* (New York: Appleton-Century-Crofts, 1969), p. 72.

61. Actually, the first publicly supported, secular cultural organization was established in 1883. It was the *Alliance Française,* which is still functioning in a number of countries.

62. Quoted in Harry and Bonaro Overstreet, *What We Must Know About Communism* (New York: Pocket Books, 1961), p. 54.

63. Nikolay Ivanovich Zhiveynov, *Operation "PW": The "Psychological Warfare" of the American Imperialists,* privately translated (Moscow: Publishing House of Political Literature, 1966), chap. 1.

64. V. I. Lenin, quoted by Wilbur Schramm, "The Soviet Concept of 'Psychological' Warfare," in *Four Working Papers on Propaganda Theory* (Washington, D.C.: Institute of Communications Research, University of Illinois [for USIA], 1955), p. 105.

65. V. I. Lenin, *Selected Works* (New York: International Publishers, 1935–1938, 1943), vol. 2, p. 103.

66. See Evron M. Kirkpatrick, *Year of Crisis* (New York: Macmillan Co., 1957), pp. 41–43.

67. H. and B. Overstreet, *What We Must Know,* pp. 171–186.

68. Ibid., p. 161.

69. *Overseas Information Programs of the United States,* Hearings Before a Subcommittee of the Committee on Foreign Relations, United States Senate, 83rd Congress, 1st Session, 6 March through 13 May, 1953, p. 1310.

70. Adolf Hitler, *Mein Kampf,* trans. sponsored by John Chamberlain, S. B. Fay, et al. (New York: Reynal & Hitchcock, 1939), p. 715.

71. J. P. Goebbels, quoted in Derrick Sington and Arthur Weidenfeld, *The Goebbels Experiment* (New Haven: Yale University Press, 1943), p. 33.

72. Louis P. Lochner, *The Goebbels Diaries* (New York: Doubleday and Co., 1948), p. 56.

73. Hitler, *Mein Kampf,* p. 230.

74. Ibid., p. 477.

75. Quoted in Sington and Weidenfeld, *Goebbels Experiment,* p. 86.

76. Quoted by Wilbur Schramm, "Notes on the British Concept of Propaganda," in *Four Working Papers on Propaganda Theory* (Washington, D.C.: Institute of Communications Research, University of Illinois, 1955), p. 77.

77. Ibid., p. 79.

78. Published April 1954, Cmd. 9138.

79. "Report of the Committee on Representational Services Overseas," February 1969, Misc. no. 5, 1969.

80. Cmd. 4107, p. 98.

81. Ibid., p. 103.

82. Ibid., p. 104.

83. Ibid., p. 110.

84. Ibid., p. 109.

85. See William J. McGuire, "Inducing Resistance to Persuasion," in *Advances in Experimental Social Psychology* 1 (1964):191–229.

86. See Charles A. Kiesler, Barry E. Collins, and Norman Miller, *Attitude Change* (New York: Wiley, 1969), p. 115.

87. For a statement of USIA objectives during the Kennedy administration, see Thomas C. Sorensen, *The Word War* (New York: Harper & Row, 1968), p. 145.

88. *Overseas Information Programs,* p. 1081.

89. Report of PPBS Working Group, 19 June 1969. Incidentally, Lloyd Free served as a consultant to this group.

9

THE EFFECTS OF MASS MEDIA IN AN INFORMATION ERA

WILBUR SCHRAMM

EMERGING PATTERNS OF AN AGE

Every man tends to see his own time as a turning point in history. Yet, those of us who study human communication find reason beyond the fact that the twentieth century is *our* age to focus upon it as a time of fundamental change in the long history of man's ways of relating symbolically to his fellow men.

Twice in the last five centuries communication technology has changed so spectacularly that it affected all human life. When printing from movable metal type came into wide use in Western Europe in the fifteenth and sixteenth centuries, it assured that virtually all communication over long distances and long times would be in a linear, verbal, silent code, and thereby set a pattern for coding experience and abstracting reality. Because this was such an efficient procedure, it brought with it broad participation in politics and government, political revolution, widespread public education, the growth of science and industry, and an enormous widening of horizons.

When film and electronic communication came into use in the latter nineteenth and early twentieth centuries, the imbalance of print was partly restored. Once again the human voice rather than merely its printed symbols could be recorded and transported, and the abstraction of reality coding in print could be supplemented by the readily transmittable sight of reality, in

still or moving pictures, in black and white or in color. The social effects of these changes upon the life habits of people are
readily apparent, but we are still assessing the full impact upon
percepts and values.

What has happened to human communication since the
film-electronic revolution has been less remarkable for its technology than for its social changes, although the computer,
which dates from the mid-century, promises to be the chief
communicating machine of the late twentieth century. The fact
that the computer may assume such importance is itself an indication of what is happening, for this is essentially an instrument
to store, retrieve, and manipulate an enormous mass of data
with a speed and efficiency otherwise unachievable. The computer stands, in the history of communication technology, with
a line of receiver-related as against a line of sender-related instruments. The latter line is dedicated to circulating more information faster and more widely; it is represented by fast printing
and duplicating, swift photo-typesetting, telegraph, telephone,
radio and television broadcasting, broad-band cable, communication satellites, waveguides, communication on laser beams,
and the like. The receiver-related line has lagged behind; it includes libraries, summary news services, information catalogues, abstracting services, microfiche, recording devices, and,
recently, the computer.

The inevitable result of swifter technological growth in the
one line than in the other was that there would be *too much* information to be handled efficiently. With more research results
at hand than ever before, the scientist, the physician, the engineer, and the teacher could not be sure of finding what they
needed when they needed it. The layman, with more news and
entertainment at hand than ever before, could not be sure of
finding what most interested *him* when he wanted it. The history of communication technology and its related developments
in recent decades, therefore, has been a contest between these
two kinds of technologies, one controlled by the sender, the
other by the user. And the significance of the computer is that it
can handle a tremendous amount of information, sort it out,
work with it, and produce any part of it in a form acceptable to
a user, on command.

We therefore are seeing a phenomenon in society that reflects communication technology but goes far beyond it. We are seeing an exponential increase in the flow of information in the world, and at least a noteworthy expansion of human efforts to command and control it. Developments in the exchange of information are coming faster and faster. From the first writing to the first printing was something like five thousand years; from printing to the film and electronic media, a little more than four hundred years; from broadcasting to the computer, about forty years. The very pace of these developments creates a situation wherein society has to react with increasingly short lead times to a flow of information that is not only very large but continuously larger.

Consequently it is the size and pace of information flow, rather than the nature of it, that typifies human communication today. More information is coming, faster, at cheaper rates per unit, from farther away and from more sources, through more channels, including multimedia channels, with more varied subject matter, and with focus and content that are ever briefer and more rapidly shifting.

In the growth of great production industries we have tended to lose sight of the knowledge industry that has grown up around the information professionals—preachers, teachers, writers, editors, and so forth—who performed so quietly for so many centuries. Yet the knowledge industry is now one of the largest industries in the world (see Machlup, 1962). It includes education that is becoming lifelong in economically advanced countries and requires as much as one-third of the budget of some developing countries. It includes the mass media, the printing industry, the learning materials industry, the information machine industries (including computers and recorders), the postal services, the advice services, libraries and special information services, research, advertising, and public relations. The knowledge industry now employs, if one includes education, more workers and professionals than does any other industry in the economically advanced countries, and more than does any other industry except agriculture in developing countries. It has become our chief source of news and entertainment, chief teacher, chief persuader, chief salesman.

We are therefore in the beginning of an Age of Information. The abilities to command information, to gain access to the media, to sort out and interpret the available data, to command the cognitive skills necessary to work in such a specialized age are going to be sources of power comparable to the more traditional forms of economic, political, and military power. Information may truly bulk larger in social control and social change than will armies or explosives. We have long said that knowledge is power, but now we are going to experience it in its full complexity and difficulty.

At such a time as this one, therefore, it is not sufficient to talk about what the effects of mass communication *have been;* it is necessary to project them ahead into this new kind of age in which information will play such a significant part. In the following pages, we try to sum up the ways we have so far come to think about the communication process, how it has social and psychological effects, and what those effects *now* seem to be. Then we raise a number of questions as to how these effects may be different at later stages of the Age of Information just beginning.

THE PROCESS OF EFFECT

The effect of communication on human beings and their society is not simple. No elegant statement of theory has yet been found for it. Therefore it is necessary to say something about the process before trying to sum up what we know about the effects.

Essentials of the Process

The chief elements of the communication process have been catalogued in some detail, and a number of them have been experimented with.

The most often quoted of the catalogues is Lasswell's formulation (originally in Bryson, 1948) "Who says what to whom through what channel with what effect?" This statement has launched a thousand courses and several generations of research on the source, message, audience, channel, and effect variables in human communication.

Although Lasswell himself experimented little with these variables, one of the most remarkable and persistent programs in the history of communication research did so for twenty years. This program was conducted by the talented group of psychologists gathered around Carl Hovland at Yale while Lasswell was there. They worked on the principal variables within laboratory conditions and tight experimental designs, manipulating one or two variables at a time while holding the others constant. So doing, they built up a large portion of all the "hard" knowledge we have of how the individual variables relate to the final effect.

Their books and papers are readily available (see, for example, Hovland, Lumsdaine, and Sheffield, 1949; Hovland, Janis, and Kelley, 1953; Hovland et al., 1957; Hovland and Janis, 1959; Rosenberg and Hovland, 1960). We also have several excellent reviews of the Yale research and related studies stimulated or suggested by it (for example, McGuire, 1969; Weiss, 1969). Therefore it is unnecessary to review their results again in this chapter. More useful will be some analysis of the *kind* of research findings that have been generated by this approach.

For one thing, the findings are a great deal more subtle than a short catalogue of process elements would seem to promise. Take an example from studies of the communication source. "Who" says it obviously makes a difference. Common sense, observation, simple research all agree that a source who is perceived as "credible" is more likely to be persuasive than is a less credible source, other things being equal. But to be able to work, either in practice or in research, with a proposition like that one it is necessary to ask some additional questions about the nature of credibility.

For example, what qualities in a source make for credibility? Expertise? Status? Accomplishment? Likeableness? Authority? Objectivity? Experience similar to that of the receiver? All these, doubtless, and others. But to a certain extent they interact, and contribute to or detract from the potency of each other. For example, a source of very high status or great reputation is likely to be believed, but is even more likely to be persuasive if he reveals some human failing in himself, making him more like, less superior to, his audience. In other words, a source who is a *bit* superior to his audience may be more persuasive than one who is very much superior. The "pratfall" experiments in which a high-status person was put through an embarrassing experience before his audience (see the review of some of these matters by McGuire in Pool, Schramm, et al., 1973, pp. 230 ff.), and the usefulness of telling stories belittling oneself, all support the effectiveness of not making full use of superiority. Furthermore, all of us have seen instances in which a little experience on the part of one's peers may be more credible than a lifetime of experience by one's father. There is a delicate conflict between wanting to identify one's position with that of a great man, and with a person much like oneself. Thus, on the one hand, Rogers (1973, p. 171) finds that homophily (similarity of background and experience) is usually a great advantage to a worker in a social change program, and, on the other hand, most of us have the yearning upward satirized by Groucho Marx when he said he wouldn't want to belong to any club that would accept him.

The same kind of subtlety surrounds the use of objectivity. It makes sense that a person is more likely to believe a source whom he perceives as objective, and, indeed, a number of experiments support this. For example, Walster and Festinger (1962) found that a source was more persuasive when he was *over*heard and not believed to be aware of it; and Freedman and Sears (1965) demonstrated that more persuasion took place when a source was thought to have some purpose other than persuading his audience. On the other hand, McGuire (1969) has listed a number of situations in which it is usually more effective to be open about one's persuasive intent: for example, in wooing a woman, or in advertising that deliberately flatters.

Thus, what seems like a simple and straightforward finding is not at all straightforward. It requires us to ask a number of deeper questions, and usually to find out more about other elements in the process.

An example of this is the research on message appeals. More than two thousand years ago, Aristotle set up a threefold typology of appeals—ethos, pathos, and logos, meaning that a communicator could appeal to the audience's moral principles, emotions, or logical processes. Since his time the typology has been tested, expanded, altered, and complicated, and still the state of the art offers very little that would permit us to choose an appeal as one orders up a vaccine, or a tire for an automobile. Even to decide between a rational argument or an emotional one it is necessary to know a great deal about the audience, the situation, the subject matter itself, the medium, and the source of the communication. In other words, this kind of knowledge of communication effect is *interactive*. One element in the process will have a predictable effect only in relation to the other elements, and when one studies the process in this way he can work with only a few of the countless combinations that may be encountered in practice.

Consider for a moment the studies of one kind of appeal—threat. The first experiments on fear appeals found that there was not a monotonic relationship between the amount of threat and the degree of compliance with the message. (For a review of this work on fear appeals, see Janis, 1967.) It was found that fear appeals were persuasive up to a certain degree of threat, counterproductive beyond that. The curve of effectiveness, that is to say, takes the form of an inverted *U*. Attempts to clarify this finding simply introduced more complexities. The optimum amount of threat depended on the receiver's level of anxiety, his level of self-esteem, his perception of how readily he could do something about the threat. Thus, for example, great threat might make a receiver so anxious that he would simply repress the whole message. There is also a relationship between optimum level of threat and complexity of the message. It is easier to accept simple advice to use Brushy-Wushy toothpaste for gum disease than it is to accept a message that one should have a certain kind of examination if one shows certain symptoms. Also, certains kinds of sources are more likely than others to make fear appeals effective. Thus, any prediction of the effectiveness of a threat appeal must consider personality correlates, message correlates, and source correlates within the process, as well as the appeal itself.

Many other studies of process elements have turned out the same way. Examples are primacy and recency (in certain situations there are primacy, in others recency, effects); "black" or "white" propaganda (one seems to work more effectively in some situations, not in others); implied or specific conclusions (given certain conditions it seems to be more effective to draw the intended conclusion explicitly, in others to let the audience figure it out); ignoring or answering an opponent's arguments (sometimes one, sometimes the other). This is the nature of the knowledge generated from studying process elements. It is neither simple nor straightforward, and almost invariably it is interactive with other elements in the process.

Furthermore, studies of this kind, which are as a group the most carefully designed and conducted examples of communication research, typically have used attitudes and opinions as dependent variables, persuasion as the measured effect. This is all right except that it neglects the relation of attitudes to action; or, more precisely, the relation of expressed opinions to other behavior. Often these other actions are the effects one actually desires. For example, attitudes toward cigarettes are less important to the American Cancer Society than is actual use of cigarettes. Use of contraceptives, rather than change of attitudes toward family planning, is the actual goal of a family planning campaign. If we were sure that a change in attitude is a sufficient, even a necessary, step toward a change in behavior, then we could think of such attitude research as a step toward such goals. But we are less sure of that than might be expected. Reviews like Wicker's (1969) and Festinger's (1964) find relatively few instances in the literature where behavior change has been proved to follow upon demonstrated attitude change. Indeed, the relationship has proved as often to be the other way: attitudes have been changed to fall into line with behavior. This is not to say that attitudes are unimportant or that such research is not useful—only that this relationship, like most of the other relationships we have been discussing, is a complex one. No cookbook of infallible recipes for communication effect emerges from the research on elements of the communication process, as Hans Speier pointed out nearly twenty-five years ago in "Psychological Warfare Re-examined" (Lerner, 1951).

A Process Model

It may be useful to look at one model that has been developed to try to bridge the gap between research on process elements and practical use of communication to achieve a result. This particular model (Cartwright, 1949) grew out of a psychologist's participation in campaigns to sell national savings bonds during the war of 1939–1945. When he tried to systematize his observations the result was his formulation for effective communication:

HOW COMMUNICATION HAS AN EFFECT
1. The "message" (information, facts, etc.) must reach the sense organs of the persons who are to be influenced.

1a. Total stimulus situations are accepted or rejected on the basis of an impression of their general characteristics.

1b. The categories employed by a person in characterizing stimulus situations tend to protect him from unwanted changes in his cognitive structure.

2. Having reached the sense organs, the "message" must be accepted as a part of a person's cognitive structure.

2a. Once a given "message" is received it will tend to be accepted or rejected on the basis of more general categories to which it appears to belong.

2b. The categories employed by a person in characterizing "messages" tend to protect him from unwanted changes in his cognitive structure.

2c. When a "message" is inconsistent with a person's prevailing cognitive structure it will either (a) be rejected, (b) be distorted so as to fit, or (c) produce changes in the cognitive structure.

3. To induce a given action by mass persuasion, this action must be seen by the person as a path to some goal that he has.

3a. A given action will be accepted as a path toward a goal only if the connections "fit" the person's larger cognitive structure.

3b. The more goals that are seen as attainable by a single path, the more likely it is that a person will take that path.

3c. If an action is seen as not leading to a desired goal or as leading to an undesired end, it will not be chosen.

3d. If an action is seen as leading to a desired goal, it will tend not to be chosen to the extent that easier, cheaper, or otherwise more desirable actions are also seen as leading to the same goal.

4. To induce a given action, an appropriate cognitive and motivational system must gain control of the person's behavior at a particular point in time.

4a. The more specifically defined the path of action to a goal (in an accepted motivational structure), the more likely it is that the structure will gain control of behavior.

4b. The more specifically a path of action is located in time, the more likely it is that the structure will gain control of behavior.

4c. A given motivational structure may be set in control of

behavior by placing the person in a situation requiring a decision to take, or not to take, a step of action that is a part of the structure.

Anyone who has worked in a communication campaign will recognize that Cartwright has selected essential elements of the process, and that he has not been willing to stop with attitude change. The message must be delivered, it must be accepted and internalized, and it must be perceived as a path toward some desirable action, and a person must be put into position to take this action. This is an action model rather than a catalogue.

But nevertheless it is not a simple model. For example, consider some of the information one must have in order to predict effect from this model: What categories does the person who is to be influenced use to "characterize stimulus situations," and what changes in his cognitive structure does he try to protect himself against? Under what circumstances will a message that is inconsistent with a person's cognitive structure produce a change in that structure rather than be rejected or distorted? What are the "desired goals" that a message must be made to seem to lead toward?

A model of this kind therefore requires the would-be persuader to know a great deal about the person he wishes to persuade. Given that knowledge he can manipulate his message so as to make it more likely that the subject will respond as desired. In terms of the process model, this approach emphasized the message and the audience variables. If the process model derives largely from $S{\rightarrow}R$ psychology, this one derives from cognitive psychology. It might better be called an $S{\rightarrow}O{\rightarrow}R$ model, with a great deal of attention to the mechanisms of cognitive change in O, the organism.

Mechanisms of Change

Mechanisms of cognitive change are one way that communication theorists have tried to simplify the complexities of the catalogue process model. The chief ones applied to explain communication effect have been of four kinds:

Learning. Attitudes and most social behaviors are learned; therefore anything in the message, the source, the channel, or the situation that contributes to learning should also contribute to ultimate effect. That is the theory. Consequently, attention, comprehension, and retention are necessary steps in the process of effect, and devices like reinforcement and contiguity are likely to be important components. Much of the Yale work on communication and attitude change was based on a learning approach.

Cognitive classification. Theorists who approach communication effect by the road of learning would therefore see the central mechanism as the conditioning of a new and desired response to a given stimulus. Another group of psychologists, however, would interpret the basic mechanism as changing a person's *perception* of a stimulus or a group of stimuli. Sherif and Asch are two representatives of this group (1961, 1965; 1940). The theory is that everyone has a set of value categories ("stereotypes") in his head, into which he files new information and which he changes very little; therefore, anything that would change his perception of a key stimulus so that he would file it away among the more or less favorable classifications (whichever is desired), or relate it in a desired way to existing values and concepts, would contribute to the desired effect. As McGuire cogently points out (Pool et al., p. 227), the learning approach is concerned chiefly with the response side of the process, the cognitive classification approach with the reception side.

Personality functions. The two mechanisms just mentioned are chiefly rational models. The fact that not all attitude and behavior change is rational has long been recognized. Katz used this idea in his theory of ego-defense (1960) and Adorno in his treatment of the *Authoritarian Personality* (1950). Their approaches assume that all persons have personality needs of which they themselves may not be fully aware. Thus Katz points out that individuals often change or maintain their attitudes in such a way as to defend their ego needs, and a powerful mechanism of communication effect would be to provide ways to satisfy those needs. Similarly, the best way to attack prejudice might be not directly, but by finding some other way to satisfy the personality needs now being met by the prejudiced viewpoints. The best way to stop an individual from smoking might be, not by attacking the behavior or the value directly, but by asking what function smoking serves for the individual, and then finding another way to satisfy that function.

Cognitive consistency. In the last three decades a long line of psychologists have worked on the theory that humans work hard to resolve their own internal cognitive conflicts and inconsistencies. This has been the basic approach of Heider's "strain toward inner consistency" (1958), Newcomb's "strain toward symmetry" (1953), Osgood and Tannenbaum's "congruity theory" (1957), Festinger's "theory of cognitive dissonance" (1957), and McGuire's "consistency theory" (1960). Each of these approaches assumes that man tries to set his inner house in order. If he absorbs information that does not fit his strongly held beliefs, he either distorts it to fit, represses it entirely, or changes his beliefs slightly to fit the new information. The goal of having an effect, therefore, is to introduce a message that will not be threatening enough to be rejected, not unthreatening enough merely to be distorted, but just uncomfortable enough to cause the receiver to change his own viewpoints so as to live comfortably with it. These changes may be very small, if they are in values and beliefs deeply held; larger, if they are in areas not strongly defended. But the approach has turned out to be an interesting effective one.

The value of these mechanisms is that they concentrate on processes by which change happens rather than on the elements that may be related to change. One can more easily plan a campaign or a message around a dynamic process than around a catalogue.

Toward Different Models

Although communication theorists admire the sophistication of the research on process elements and value the insights derived from mechanisms of change such as those just listed, still they have been looking for some new models. Indeed, for the last fifty years there has been a rising tide of dissatisfaction with the $S \rightarrow R$ approach, the one-way, one-time, single-effect patterns of research, and the rather mechanistic models that have been the chief ones studied in the laboratories.

The more communication has been studied under realistic conditions, the more evidence has appeared that the significant effects are not simple, direct ones. Most of them occur over a long time. Communication operates, as Klapper said (1960), "among and through a nexus of mediating factors and influences." Its long-term effects are resultants of many messages and many influences. Its most obvious effects are *other* communications. And it appears much less mechanistic as viewed in life than it does in the laboratory. That is, it does not, for the most part, seem to be something someone *does* to somebody. It is as much the property of the receiver as of the sender, and is more often an exchange than a one-way phenomenon.

Thus, since the 1920s, scholars have been backing away from the Hypodermic Needle model of communication, which conceives of a message as inserted into a receiver like a chemical. This retreat has been a slow process. Even the highly sophisticated information theory models of the 1950s (for example, Shannon, 1949; Osgood and Tannenbaum, 1957) still kept the electronic analogy. They added feedback, meaning return cues that give the sender some idea of the effectiveness of his message. They added the concepts of encoding and decoding, thereby getting away from the earlier picture of a message flowing like electrons through a wire from sender to receiver: what passed through the wire at least had to be processed at two points. Thus their concept of the flow of information was much more sophisticated than simple *transfer* (for example, the *Columbia Encyclopedia:* "Communication . . . the transfer of thoughts and messages"). Not until recent years, however, have scholars challenged the very idea of transfer: there *is* no hypodermic; *nothing* flows through the wire from sender to receiver; rather, the sender creates some communication signs, of which a receiver makes such use as he wishes. Thus for any communication to occur there must be two equal parts, a sender's act and a receiver's act.

This concept of the equality of sender and receiver in the communication process is one building block for a newer model of process. Communication is not a process in which somebody does something to someone, or in which something flows unchanged through a channel from one person to another, but rather it is a *relationship*. (For a fuller statement of this concept, see Schramm, 1973.) If one accepts this viewpoint, then he can make use of a number of social concepts that illuminate the communication relationship: What roles do the participants play in a given relationship? (For example, the roles of teacher and student obviously will lead to communication behavior different from that, say, of a lover and his lass or a salesman and prospective purchaser.) What functions is communication performing for the different participants? (Is one expecting to be entertained, to be informed, to be instructed? Is one trying to persuade, to sell, to please, or to seek information?) What customs govern the behavior within the relationship? (For example, what is the significance of the behavior of an individual who says, "How are you?" and of another who answers, "Fine!")

The relationships built around acts of communication on the part of two or a few people are part of the larger relationships of society. Communication, as Cooley said, is the means by which "human relations exist and develop" (1909). Sapir pointed out with great insight that society is not "a static structure defined by tradition," but rather "a highly intricate network of partial and complete understandings between the members of organizational units of every degree of size and complexity, ranging from a pair of lovers or a family to a league of nations or that ever increasing portion of humanity which can be reached by the press" (1935). Consequently, to study communication within society as a one-way, one-time, mechanistic event is less useful than to study it as a form of human behavior that builds, maintains, and manipulates relationships, large and small. Communication is something all people do. We can almost say it is a way people *live.* It is the fundamental process of society, without which humans could not relate to each other. And so it becomes helpful to ask what functions communication is performing in those relationships, what roles communicators are playing, what needs and values are governing communication behavior, what information is being used in what way for decisions, and what controls are upon the flow of information.

The development of our thinking about the macroprocess of communication in society has been parallel to the development of thinking about the microprocess. As people in the 1920s thought about the Hypodermic Needle model of communication, so they feared the Magic Bullets ("paper bullets" Margolin called them) of mass media propaganda and persuasion. The more that scholars looked at social communication, however, the harder they found it to see those bullets. People hit by mass communication simply refused to fall over and be properly influenced. They shook off or dodged the bullets (if any), or even caught them to braid into necklaces. Paul Lazarsfeld and his colleagues at Columbia in the late 1930s and 1940s concluded that mass communication really did not change many viewpoints in political campaigns (Lazarsfeld et al., 1948; Berelson et al., 1954), that its most evident social function was to reinforce the status quo (Lazarsfeld and Merton, 1948), and that personal influence was usually a great deal more important than mass media in affecting important beliefs and decisions (Katz and Lazarsfeld, 1964). All during this period, moreover, evidence was piling up about an *active* rather than passive audience. People were *using* communication, rather than being used *by* it. In the social process as in the microprocess, the audience was just as active as the sender. Raymond Bauer gave this conclusion a name in 1964 in a paper entitled *The Obstinate Audience,* where he summed up findings about the limited effectiveness of mass media persuasion.

Thus the building blocks of a new social model of communication are available, although no one as yet has put them together in a fully satisfying form. However, the readers of these volumes might be well advised to consider this kind of social model rather than the process model that typically has been used. It is interesting to note that whereas Harold Lasswell's distinguished essay of 1948 specified the catalogue headings that have long been used for examining the process in its minutiae, another part of that same essay may in the long run be more helpful to the understanding of communication in society. This is the passage in which he spoke of the functions of communication as surveillance, coordination, and transmission of the social heritage.

Media and Interpersonal Communication

Increased attention to communication in society has turned attention also to the relation of mass media to interpersonal communication. Several principles have emerged.

One is that they feed each other. The mass media reproduce interpersonal communication in their news, interviews, instruction, and some entertainment. On the other hand, the channels of interpersonal communication carry further, discuss, interpret, and often talk back to, what has been read, seen, or heard in the media.

Trying to account for the relatively few people who admitted to being influenced directly by the mass media in election campaigns, Lazarsfeld and his associates (1948) advanced the so-called two-step-flow hypothesis, "that ideas often flow from radio and print to opinion leaders and from these to the less active sections of the population." This seemed to be borne out by later studies of consumer campaigns and agricultural adoption (see Merton, in Lazarsfeld and Stanton, 1949; Coleman et al., 1966; Rogers, 1962). However, the more the process of information diffusion was examined, the less satisfactory the two-step flow seemed as an explanation for what was happening. For one thing, the flow did not stop with two steps: it was really a multistep flow. Again, information was carried from the mass media to other persons by a great variety of intermediaries, not necessarily opinion leaders. Third, a number of persons received information directly from the mass media, and did not pass it on to anyone. In other words, the present state of knowledge is that a great deal of information does travel to the general populace through the mass media, and some of it generates a great deal of interpersonal communication. The more interesting the information and the more gregarious and articulate the receiver, the more likely that the information will move on through personal channels. And when it does so move, it is likely to go more than two steps.

A second principle is that the methods supplement and reinforce each other. Thus, farmers learn and to some extent are persuaded by either a radio program or a guided discussion group, but when the two are combined into a rural radio forum, as in Canada, India, Togo, and elsewhere, the result is a uniquely powerful instrument. (See the review by Schramm, 1967, pp. 105 ff.) Modern politicians typically put the largest part of their budget into television, but they also try to maintain local staffs of door-to-door workers, and to see that community meetings are organized. Sociologists find that rural people most often hear of new practices or products from the media, but when these people come to the point of deciding on the innovation they usually go to their friends and advisers. (For a review of this research, see Rogers and Shoemaker, 1971.)

This comes close to being a third principle: that whereas the media may be more efficient at carrying information, interpersonal channels are more likely to carry influence. It is the point of Katz and Lazarsfeld's summary book *Personal Influence* (1955), the central implication of forty years of rural sociology, and a finding of many studies of economic and social development. But the more one examines the proposition, the more exceptions one encounters. The reason interpersonal channels are so influential is believed to be that they are two-way (one can ask questions and cross-examine, as well as listen to persuasion), that they permit a person to *seek* the advice he needs when he feels he needs it (rather than being assailed with it when the *persuader* thinks he needs it), and that they set up a personal relationship in which the decider can feel comfortable and confident (very often a relationship in which he has *previously learned* to feel at home). Yet we sometimes forget that the media carry persons and project personalities. For example, media personalities like FDR on radio, John Kennedy on television, newsmen like Edward R. Murrow, H. V. Kaltenborn, Elmer Davis, and the chief media news personalities of our own time can hardly be said not to be influential. True, their communication is one-way, but people often seek out media performers for interpretation and advice, and hence the relationship approximates two-way communication. Interviews and press conferences in the media provide a kind of surrogate two-way interchange. As a hypothesis, it might be suggested that the more one needs expertise on nonlocal matters, the more likely one is to go to the mass media for it.

Perhaps the key word is *interpretation*. Newspaper editorial writers are skeptical about how many people they can persuade, but they can interpret the news for their readers and thus set the ground for decision. Both broadcasters and print journalists think of themselves as news analysts, rather than as editorializers. On the other hand, the local political staff, the salesmen, the media evangelists make no bones about it: they are in the business of *persuading*.

An interesting note, in passing, is that the media have made rather extraordinary attempts to achieve two-way communication through talk shows, cable developments, "talk-backs" in instructional broadcasting, closed circuit video, and special programs for and by communities and minority groups.

Thus it is reasonable to believe that media news communication tends to provide a background of information, to interpret, to analyze, and to provide models of belief and behavior, and are thus indirectly influential. Personal communication tends to provide direct advice when it is sought, and to be influential and believable as only a local and friendly relationship can be.

Social Elements in the Process of Effect

To some extent all human communication is social communication, because it operates with a socially learned code, mirrors the culture, values, and beliefs of the surrounding society, and is ordinarily responded to in behavior patterns sanctioned or understood by society. The surrounding society therefore puts some limits on the kinds of effects communication can have. It is more likely to be influential when it goes along with the strongly held values of the society or suggests a slight variation, than when it deviates strongly. It is more likely to be imitated and accepted when it holds up the models and heroes of society. And it is more likely to achieve the response it wishes when the response will have social support.

Social support and social pressures are two elements in communication effect that have been both studied intensively in group experiments and observed in action. The reader probably will recall the experiments by Asch (1956) in which a subject was put into a group of stooges (who were in the pay of the experimenter) and asked to judge which of three lines was the longest. The stooges, speaking first, each gave as his opinion that line *B* was the longest. To the subject, and to any objective observer, line *B* was *not* the longest, but by the time all the stooges had given their opinions and the subject had to speak, so strong was the power to conform that the subject actually doubted his own judgment. Thirty percent of the experimental subjects went along with the stooges. Ittleson's work with the Ames illusions (1968) and Sherif's with the autokinetic effect (1965) are in the same vein.

Kurt Lewin demonstrated the power of social support in a series of experiments early in the 1940s (in Maccoby, Newcomb, and Hartley, 1958), when it was desired to persuade housewives to serve unpopular cuts of meat during wartime. When groups of housewives were brought together so that the entire group could support the decision of an individual member, then a very much higher proportion of the women were willing to go along than had been the case before the meetings. And particularly if a housewife were willing to commit herself publicly in the group, so that social pressure to keep the commitment was allied to social support from the others in the group, then the effect was very large indeed. This same strategy has been field-proved in the rural radio forum, in the animation groups of French Africa, in the Mothers Clubs of Korea, and in countless other places.

Social pressures, social support, public commitment, then, are significant social elements within the process. Still another is role playing. If an individual can be induced to play a role (write an essay, make a talk, take a position in a debate) somewhat different from his own beliefs, it has been shown over and over again that his viewpoint is likely to change in the direction of the role he has played. There are two possible explanations of this. One is that the act of stating the new arguments in public has roused some dissonance between his own beliefs and the arguments he has had to improvise, and has forced him to relieve some of the discomfort by bringing his own viewpoints more into line with what he has said. The other is that in the act of improvising he has learned and internalized some of the arguments he has had to give. Whatever the mechanism, it is likely to have some effect.

We are, therefore, actually describing another mechanism of change parallel to the learning, the conflict resolution, the need satisfaction, and the reclassification described above. The theory of this mechanism is that humans feel the need of social support and the impact of social pressure. They will tend to change, if at all, in such a way as to make them comfortable with the society around them, particularly the parts of that society they admire and value. Therefore, anything in the communication that will make them aware of social support for one position rather than another, or of social pressures to take one position rather than another, will tend to influence the direction of change, other things being equal.

Effects of the Medium Itself

We as yet have little or no general theory on the effect of media as separate from their content. The most provocative ideas on this topic have been advanced by Marshall McLuhan. Although his concepts of "hot" and "cold" media and of the differences in effect of perceiving dots on a television screen as compared with solid signs on paper or film have not stood up very well, his (and Innis's) ideas of the differences between the linear experience of print and the simultaneous experience of television and face-to-face communication proved stimulating. (See McLuhan, 1962, 1966; Innis, 1951). And in particular the statements of these two men concerning the effects of the coming of media to an oral society have illuminated some of the broader social effects of mass communication.

McLuhan's contribution, however, has been to shoot Roman candles—to stimulate thinking and insights concerning the media, particularly television and print, rather than to make theory. Few McLuhanesque experiments have been generated. It seems likely that when a systematic body of principles for the selection of media is produced, it will grow out of some less exciting observations like these:

1. Each medium uses its own code to convey information, and the nature of this code has something to do with the effect of the information carried.

For example, the code may be digital or representational. If digital, it is ordinarily presented linearly; if representational, simultaneously. (The computer has proved uncommonly adaptable by translating digital information into representational pictures.) The digital code more closely controls the content to be learned, and is capable of a high order of abstraction. The representational code presents very dense information, forces the receiver to make his own judgments as to relationship of elements in the picture, and is capable of a high order of realism. Some representational codes present moving pictures, others still; one therefore has some advantage in presenting relationships over time, the other, relationships over space. Some media codes are for the eye, some for the ear; the former can present more information in a given time, the latter are likely to command close attention and to exert more control over the pace of presenting information. Some media codes are multisensory, some not; the former are not necessarily more effective in learning or persuasion, although they are more often selected when the audience has a choice. As Broadbent and Travers have pointed out (Broadbent, 1958; Travers, 1966), only under certain conditions will a multisensory medium bring about more learning than a single-sensory one. Under certain other conditions, the two channels will interfere with, rather than supplement or reinforce, each other.

2. Each medium has a special capability and a certain cost for delivering information.

Obviously the broadcast media can more quickly deliver information over a broad area, and radio can do it at about one-fifth of the cost of television. Film and print are more permanent than radio or television. Print is a more private thing, easier to save for use by an individual. And so forth.

3. Each medium implies a certain condition of reception.

Print provides an experience for one person alone. Radio and television are for an individual or a group, usually in a home, office, automobile, or other privately controlled setting. Film usually takes its receivers into a theater audience. A reader of print controls what, when, how fast he reads. Users of the electronic and film media have the pace, the time, and the order of presentation controlled by the sender. And so on.

4. Each medium requires a certain skill of its users.

Print requires literacy. Radio requires skill in listening, and television and film require visual literacy, although we are still a long way from being able to say precisely what this is. When we are able to compare these several kinds of literacy we shall be near the point of being able to state general media theory.

This is where our understanding of the mass media is at the moment. People can learn from any medium, large or small; this we can say in confidence (for a review of the evidence, see Schramm, 1973). People probably can be persuaded by any medium. The content probably makes more difference than does the medium in both learning and persuasion; experimenters find more variance within than between the media.

Therefore, when one selects a mass medium for its effect, one is unable to draw on any grand theory, such as a finding that television is more effective than print or more persuasive than radio or brings about more learning than still pictures, or the like. Under certain conditions any of these may be true; under others, not true. It is necessary to take account of smaller factors: What does one want the medium to do? Where and how does one want the message delivered? What kind of code promises to be most effective for the content one wants to convey and for the skills the audience is presumed to have? What media are most readily available for an acceptable cost? It is unfortunate that we do not have more general guidelines.

EFFECTS OF THE PROCESS
From the Bullet Theory to the Obstinate Audience

The effects of mass media, as described in the preceding pages, have moved from the concept of the magic bullets of mass media persuasion to the concept of the obstinate audience; from a picture of a passive, defenseless audience acted upon by mass media to a picture of an active audience purposefully using communication to meet its own needs; from communication as a threat to society, to communication as the fundamental process of society.

Nevertheless, although we have overcome the irrational fear of propaganda, we have by no means discounted the social effect of mass communication. Indeed, once we have stripped the magic from it, it begins to loom larger than ever, although neither mysterious nor necessarily dangerous. Indeed, the continuing, relatively silent effects of the media may have more to do with what humans know and believe and value than have any of the paper or radio bullets that were described so noisily in the 1920s. In the following pages we deal with some of these potent but less spectacular effects.

Effect on Life-styles

One set of facts concerning media effects is on exhibition for us every day: the mass media have changed and are continuing to change our life-styles. The change is not so swift and spectacular as that brought about by the automobile, but it may turn out to be more profound because it is dealing as much with cognitive as with physical effects.

Wherever they become available, the mass media absorb an enormous amount of time. In Japan children typically become regular television viewers before the age of two. In the United States a child through the age of sixteen spends more time in toto with television than in school. An average American adult devotes somewhere near five hours a day to the mass media, and they enter into his conversation and his thinking for an additional period of time. A modern family in any country where media are readily available is likely to spend more time on media than on any other activity except work and sleeping.

These demands on time have notably affected how humans live. More than a century ago (and again in Innis and McLuhan) the privatizing effect of reading was noted. People learned by themselves rather than directly from others, and set down their ideas in private rather than talk them out in public. They turned a considerable amount of the task of storing knowledge over to print, rather than to the human memory. Printed media were largely responsible for creating knowledge institutions, the public school and the library among them. They must also have had something to do with the "inner-directedness," itself a kind of privatization, noted by Riesman et al. (1950), and the forms of privatization noted during World War II by Kris and Leites (Lerner, 1951).

The electronic media have greatly changed our use of leisure time, the arrangement of our houses, the amount we go out of our homes, the amount we talk with our neighbors. We are beginning to substitute modern communication for some of the travel to which we have become accustomed. We have let television intrude into our meal hours, become accustomed to radio as background sound for all kinds of unrelated activities, come to expect newscasts and music as we drive. We are shifting more and more of our entertainment into our own homes: films and drama and music from the theater and the music hall, athletics from the stadium and the gymnasium, and now planning for a "home education center" where lifelong learning will be more readily available than in the classroom. Riesman finds us more "other-directed," and whether we are actually any less "privatized" is a matter for discussion if not for agreement.

With the possible exception of deprivatization, these are effects evident to all of us, and it will be more productive to turn to classes of effect that are not always so evident.

The Basic Effect on Knowledge
A high proportion of all the pictures in our heads are there because of the mass media.

Almost everything we know of faraway events and places has

traveled through the media. We become so accustomed to the newspaper morning and evening, to the news bulletins and newscasts, to the newsmagazines on weekends, that we forget how much these have contributed to our images of environment.

A series of studies in the 1950s and 1960s (notably Greenberg, 1964) demonstrated that the proportion of news received by a typical individual through the mass media is related in a *U* curve to how many people are interested in the news. The fact that a neighbor child has measles is likely to come to us through interpersonal channels: its news appeal is to a small group. If our neighbor's daughter is engaged to be married, we may learn that through the media or personally: a forthcoming wedding is of wider interest than is a case of measles. Run-of-the-mill news (press conferences, court trials, meetings of the United Nations, bulletins from a distant war) is almost certain to reach us, if at all, through the media. The scope of interest of such news is wider than that of the measles case, but narrower than that of, say, the assassination of President Kennedy. When this latter news event occurred in 1963, more than 90 percent of all Americans heard of it within thirty minutes of the shooting, before the president died. Almost exactly half of these persons had heard the news from other persons, half through the media. Almost everyone who heard it through the media passed it on to someone else. Almost everyone who heard it first interpersonally then turned to one of the media for further details (Greenberg and Parker, 1964).

In other words, the pattern of news reception is like this: Events of narrow and local interest usually are reported person to person. Events of very great and demanding interest are carried both by media and interpersonally. Events whose interest is between those extremes are likely to come to us from the media, and the more interesting they are, the more likely it is that members of the media audience will pass them on to other persons.

Furthermore, a high proportion of the interpretation and analysis of news we get is now provided by the media. A complex world, distant events, and unfamiliar places increasingly demand expert interpreters. The networks are responding to a feeling of need on the part of their audiences when they bring together a group of pundits as soon as possible after, say, a policy address by the president, or election returns, to tell the audience what they think is the significance of what has happened. Sample surveys have shown again and again in recent years how deeply people trust the media, and notably the television personalities they can watch and with whom they often feel personally acquainted. How often, in recent decades, have persons in a country distant from England tuned in the BBC to find "what's really happening," or have persons in the United States tuned in a public figure or a commentator on television to see "what this news really means"!

Furthermore, a great deal of incidental learning, even more of it from entertainment than from serious material, contributes to the pictures in our heads. Social scientists have worried about the imbalance of class, wealth, and behavior portrayed in our films and television. Some foreign visitors get off the plane in New York or Los Angeles expecting to see cowboys riding the range behind the airport. Crime in our big cities is all too common, but not half so common as in television or films. The average living style in our electronic and film entertainment is far above the average in American homes. The significance of all this is that in the perception of entertainment media there is a fine line between fiction and fact; people learn some of the content, develop expectations, imitate behaviors, even though the story is only fantasy.

Thus, with or without any intention to persuade, the media still contribute to the knowledge base for values and decisions. Politicians have long been aware of the importance of this effect. When Franklin D. Roosevelt was opposed editorially by three-fourths of the newspapers who took editorial positions on the 1936 election, he laughed heartily and said that he would let them attack him in the editorial columns for six months every four years if, in the other three and one-half years, they would continue to fill their news columns with the dramatic news of the New Deal! In authoritarian countries, leaders put curbs upon the press. In more democratic countries they maintain public relations staff to get "their side" into the news, or publicly attack the news media for "imbalance" or "unfairness" in news coverage and interpretation.

The flow of news in the modern world is a delicate and complicated thing. All along the line there are gatekeepers—reporters who decide what to cover and what to write, editors who decide what to publish and how to publish it, wire editors who at various transfer points decide what is to be passed on to the ultimate users and what is to be deleted. Some is deleted and some is rewritten at every transfer point, and finally what is left comes to a newspaper or a broadcasting station that can use only a fraction of what *it* receives. It has been calculated that only 1 or 2 percent of the news reported in India ever gets to readers in Indiana (see Cutlip, 1954).

Assuming that professionalism and good intentions prevail throughout the news-gathering systems of the world, still this raises disquieting questions. What is *not* being reported that we need to know? What *viewpoints* are not being reported that we need to hear? What is being omitted because news must be gathered and written against deadlines and competition and space restrictions? Is there any systematic bias operating in the news channels and consequently being reflected in the pictures we store away in our heads?

If we think of books as mass media, consider the amount of systematic information that passes from text and reference books into our memories during our school years. This school information, for which the textbook often is the chief authority, fills our life-spaces and thereby helps to determine what kind of information will interest us later, and what we will seek in the mass media.

We ask the mass media to serve as our ears and eyes, sometimes as our voices, in distant places. We count on them to survey our environment and report it realistically to us. We accept their reports, store them away to the extent they interest us, and use them as a basis for forming attitudes, stating opinions, and taking decisions. What more important effect could we ascribe to the mass media than to say that they are largely responsible for all the pictures we have in our heads of all the environment, all the events, all the persons we cannot experience personally? We even count on them to take us to important events and bring to us important persons. As a matter of fact, who would have predicted a century ago that a large part of the population of the United States would be attending, through electronic media, the funeral of an assassinated president, the Senate hearings into a political scandal, and, each week, the quizzing of several important public figures by reporters?

Thus, quite apart from persuasion, the media are continuously responsible for a quiet effect of great power: bringing us much of our information about the world. It is not surprising that control of the news media, access to them, and their coverage and viewpoints are matters of great importance to every government, politician, business, labor union, pressure group, and any other group or individual that cares about public knowledge and its reflection in public opinion.

The Focusing of Attention and the Creation of Personalities

Another quiet powerful effect is the ability of the mass media to focus attention on events, issues, and persons.

There is nothing necessarily wrong, malicious, or harmful about this way of working. It is a natural result of the worldwide horizons of the news media and the need to select from a world of news. Furthermore, the very nature of the mass media—the front page, the large headlines, the lead stories in the newscasts, the available pictorial treatment in television news—requires that some things be emphasized over others. And the media are aware that audience attention is fleeting, that it must be caught, if at all, by carefully selecting from among the glut of events and by establishing levels of emphasis that will attract audiences to at least the more sensational stories, with the hope that their interest then will carry over to some of the less sensational ones.

The result is that people talk about what the mass media talk about, and, in general, remember about the distant world what the mass media report about it at a given time. It hardly needs saying that any person or any organization that would like to manipulate public opinion or political decisions would like to have this control over public attention. In an authoritarian system the government, the owners, or the regulatory agencies do exercise some control, and as a result the users of the media are told what their caretakers think is wise to have them know. In a relatively democratic system the safeguard against such control of attention and knowledge is the lack of monopoly control over the media and the fact that selection and emphasis usually are controlled by professional rather than political judgment. Even in a system that is not government-controlled, however, a publicity-wise politician tries to direct public attention by sensational charges or manufactured ''events'' that will be reported by the media.

But the result of this selection and emphasis is that public attention usually focuses for a phenomenally short time on any event or topic unless it directly affects the members of the audience. Thus, for example, the energy crisis stays in the news in the United States because it is a matter of daily practical concern to drivers and homeowners. What happens in Argentina or Brazil or Korea or Uganda, however, rises to the surface of the ocean of news only when something sensational happens. Then the event sinks back into the murky depths, and may never surface again even in the form of a subsequent story on later developments. Some newspapers, aware of the frustration of their viewers in trying to follow a story beyond its first exciting stage, now print columns of brief notes on ''Whatever happened to. . . .'' or ''What has happened about. . . .''

Thus the modus operandi of the news system encourages a focus of attention that flits from country to country, event to event, problem to problem, with only the briefest attention to each. The Watergate story, which remained on front pages for months, is a phenomenon among stories in this respect. Of course, it is of wide and extraordinary interest, but if there had not been the long-continued and determined effort to get at sensational facts, and, on the other side, the equally long and determined effort to keep those facts from public view, so that the *struggle over the information* became the story as much as the gradually revealed information itself, Watergate, too, might have passed into the limbo of yesterday's dimly remembered headlines. It *is* possible, therefore, to gain and hold public attention in the mass media for a very long time without monopoly control of communication, but only when it is possible to report a series of sensational and continuing events.

It is not surprising that the system tends to focus attention on sensational events. This can be explained as much in terms of human nature as of media nature, but it means that the quieter analytical story has a hard time getting attention. An observer from outer space might think that public attention would be better focused on the implications of political controls in South Korea than on the interception of a South Korean boat, or on the developing patterns in Western Europe that promise to change the nature of the Atlantic Alliance rather than on a shouting match between Mr. Kissinger and M. Jobert. He might feel that if the energy problem had been investigated a few years ago as energetically as Watergate has been studied in more recent times, we might not have been so taken by surprise when the Arab sheikhs decided to use oil as a political weapon. But this is the nature of the news flow through our media channels. Good news is not very interesting news. News that is not likely to appear in black headlines for months or years is not very interesting news. And whether good or bad, short-term in its implication, sensational or not, news is not likely to hold attention for very long. As a matter of fact, the energy crisis *was* studied twenty-five years ago, in the documents of Resources for the Future and in reports on industrial growth during the Eisenhower administration, and they were reported. But they did not make large black headlines at that time, and speedily were replaced in the news by more immediately exciting events.

One of the most striking powers of the mass media to reflect environment is the ability to focus attention on certain individuals, and, by so doing, in effect to *create* personalities. In the days of radio, every public figure knew that a "sincere" and confident voice was a priceless possession. Now, in the age of television, the ability to project an impressive personality through the picture tube is an even more prized asset. Just as pollsters have been employed for many years to find out what the public wanted to hear, so professionals are called upon today to help the candidate provide what it is thought the public wants to see. The question arises, then, whether the media are reporting or inventing a public personality. Usually there is some conflict between the urge to report and the urge to create. A political organization will be interested in *creating,* and will resist, through press conferences and interviews, the efforts of the media to penetrate through the media personality to the more basic personality.

It is possible, of course, to create an *instant* public personality through the media. For example, several members of the Watergate Committee became so well known, as a result of their performance and appearance in the committee hearings, that some of them have been talked about as candidates for high national office. A newscaster who becomes anchor man for a program with a large audience has the opportunity to become an instant public personality and to exert an influence that often he has no intention of exerting. Thirty years ago several radio newscasters and commentators, today several newscasters and analysts, and always a few columnists or by-lined writers in newspapers have been among the most trusted persons in this country—or so the polls have indicated. These are, for the most part, extremely able persons, but the question of interest to us is, how much of their influence has been the result of regular exposure, how much of native ability? The answer may well be that a certain kind of ability, a certain kind of personality lends itself to exposure in the mass media and to consequent influence.

The Effect on Decision Making: Politics

Now let us turn to some of the evidence on effects when the media are used deliberately to *manipulate* opinions and behavior.

In this section we deal mostly with the effect of the mass media on political *campaigns*. This is clearly only *one* kind of political influence the media exert. They also affect the day-to-day decision making within governments. They are a chief source of intelligence. They serve as a weathervane of opinion. They are read for advice and comment. All these enter into the decisions made by governmental departments and agencies. The number of copies of the *New York Times* delivered every day in Washington is an indicator of how significant these latter effects may be.

But the effects of mass media on political opinions and elections are more easily amenable to research and measurement, and therefore we discuss them rather than the internal effect upon governmental processes.

In so doing, it is important to distinguish, as we have done above, between the long-term knowledge and attention effects of the media and the relatively short-term effects of campaigns or events. The long-term effects—the voter's sense of what is going on that concerns political decisions, what issues are worth his attention, which persons are worth his trust and admiration —are obviously of basic importance, and they must derive largely from the mass media. But they are also extremely difficult to measure, simply because they are long-term and cumulative and almost impossible to trace directly from specific media experience to the formation of judgments.

Perhaps the most significant conclusions from studies of campaigns is how relatively little change they are able to make in long-held opinions and behavior patterns. These basic evaluations and habits are built upon the continuing input of influence from the surrounding culture, including one's friends, family, valued groups, behavior models, as well as the media. To change these significantly within a short time requires a truly traumatic event. Thus the Great Depression and the World War of 1939–1945 were instrumental in keeping the Republican party out of power in this country for twenty years. If a national election had been held in November 1973, rather than 1972, the traumatic effect of Watergate almost surely would have been seen in the votes. But fortunately there are few such events as Watergate and infrequent depressions, and all studies of attempts to manipulate political opinions and behavior through media campaigns or events indicate that (a) they attract less attention than might be expected, and certainly far less than their sponsors hope, and (b) they ordinarily do not succeed in changing many votes (for a well-known example, see Star and Hughes, 1950).

A political telethon by Senator Knowland in his campaign to be elected governor of California in 1958 (Schramm and Carter, 1959), and the nationally televised debates between John F. Kennedy and Richard M. Nixon in the presidential campaign of 1960 (Krause, ed., 1962, notably Katz and Feldman, pp. 173 ff.), both were studied in the field at the time they occurred. In the first of these studies, 563 randomly selected voters were interviewed in California. Less than 15 percent had tuned in any of the twenty-hour telethon, and only 3 voters (less than 1 percent) admitted to any change of opinion as a result (2 in the direction intended by the telethon, 1 in the contrary direction). In the second study, national survey data exist. The principal question was, who "won"? The first debate generally was regarded as the decisive one, and did indeed show the most decisive result. The figures follow.

Preference before the debate	Who did the better job in the debate?		
	Kennedy better	No choice	Nixon better
Kennedy	71%	26%	3%
Nixon	17	38	12
Undecided	26	62	45

Thus Kennedy apparently had a little advantage in these judgments, but the most interesting aspect of the results is how much the debates seemed to merely reinforce the predispositions of the audience. If voters were undecided, they were likely to be undecided between the performance of the candidates. If they were originally for Kennedy, they tended to think he won the debate; if originally for Nixon, that Nixon won. And this is about as spectacular a change as postcampaign studies have been able to measure. The conclusion of Schramm and Carter was that the Knowland telethon chiefly reinforced members of the audience in their previous voting intentions; whereas Katz and Feldman, after reviewing all the studies of the Kennedy-Nixon debates, decided that the broadcasts "resulted primarily in a strengthening of commitment to one's own party and candidate" (Schramm and Carter, 1959, p. 208).

Why should this be? Why should the later evidence be so far from supporting the earlier conclusions of psychologists and political scientists concerning the gullibility of mass media audiences? Why should such propaganda tricks as "name-calling," "glittering generalities," "bandwagon," "plain folks," "card-stacking," and so forth (see, for example, Institute of Propaganda Analysis, *The Fine Art of Propaganda: A Study of Father Coughlin's Speeches* [1939]) no longer be so threatening?

Sears and Whitney in a cogent review (see Pool et al., 1973, pp. 253 ff.) sum up the research. Perhaps the chief reason for the change is that field data that began to appear in the 1930s simply did not back up the earlier assumptions and fears. The study of Erie County in the 1940 election (Lazarsfeld, Berelson, and Gaudet, 1948) was able to demonstrate very little direct effect of influence from the mass media. Later studies of campaigns in the 1950s and 1960s, laboratory studies of attitude change, and studies of decision making within groups all found relatively little major change in behavior that could be attributed clearly to mass media. Indeed, campaign studies for the most part showed that only a small percentage of voters changed their opinions at all during the campaign, and were more likely to mention personal influence than media influence as a reason for changing. The group studies (for example, those under Kurt Lewin in the 1940s) suggested that talking it over in democratic style was more likely to result in behavior change than exposing oneself to media persuasion.

Sears and Whitney point out two probable reasons why political campaigns have not been found to be more potent. One is the relatively low level of exposure to political campaign material in the media (the politically "interested" audience sometimes has been estimated at around 30 percent). A second is the defensive mechanisms that go into action to protect an individual against change. There is some evidence of selective exposure: that is, for example, more Republicans than Democrats are likely to tune in a broadcast of a Republican rally. More important, though, is the selective *perception* of what is seen or heard or read. As Sears and Whitney note (p. 263), people are "particularly adept at avoiding acceptance of information that is discrepant from strongly held prior attitudes." Thus a voter enters a campaign with a base of knowledge and evaluations acquired over many years, with loyalties to groups, many of which hold strong political viewpoints, and with a culturally reinforced habit of voting. He tends to protect those values and behaviors. He distorts what he hears, not intentionally but nevertheless effectively, so that it fits with what he already believes. He tends to challenge the credibility of someone who challenges *his* predispositions. He typically does not enjoy political disagreement and looks for positive interpretations with which he can live comfortably. No wonder that President Roosevelt laughed when he compared the effect of six months of hostile editorials with a continuing flow of positive New Deal news!

So the general effect of political campaigns is to reinforce what would have happened anyway, despite them. But that is not the whole story, for some voters *do* change in each election (for an example, see the Pool and Abelson study of the 1960 election [1961]), and political professionals, who are the wisest and most experienced in campaigns, still put a major part of their budget into the media.

The reinforcing effect of the media is itself a major effect: every party wants to keep the faithful in line. The changes that decide a close election usually involve no more than 5 percent of the electorate. Thus it is unrealistic to expect dramatic evidence of media-related change. When we look at the evidence on the approximately 30 percent of the electorate who make much use of political campaign material in the media during a U.S. national election, and focus on the 5 percent or so who may change between August and November, then we at least can advance some reasonable hypotheses as to how the media can be used to contribute to a political effect. Sears and Whitney in the review already mentioned (1973), Lane (1962), Lang and Lang (1968), Campbell et al. (1960), among others, have approached this question thoughtfully. It is much too complex to treat in short space. But in general it seems reasonable to assume that frontal attacks on an individual's political position are less likely to be effective than are approaches that require him only to reinterpret slightly or to perceive in a different way a candidate or an issue, to bring these into closer alignment with his own perceived position. The weight of the evidence seems to be that a positive approach—for example, finding a charismatic candidate for voters to follow—is more effective than argumentative attack on a candidate or a set of opinions (although one might interpret both the Goldwater defeat of 1964 and the McGovern defeat of 1972 chiefly as *negative* reactions). If it is possible to introduce evidence that changes a voter's perception of the situation, then he may review his decision. And finally, there is some reason to think that a positive, hopeful view of the future, a promise to reduce conflict and worry, is more likely to help a candidate than for him to play Cassandra.

Effects on Decision Making: Adoption and Innovation

The decision to adopt a new practice is not, like the decision on how to vote, tied to one particular time. Nevertheless it is an all-or-none decision, it is one that affects the future behavior of the decider even more than does a vote in an election, and it resembles the voting decision in some very important ways, not the least of which is that it is an object of persuasion. For one thing, an individual comes to the decision with a lifetime of knowledge, values, and behavior patterns, which are hard to change in a short time. In the second place, the social and personal components are bound to be very important: the support or lack of support from the social groups one values, the culturally supported beliefs, the examples of persons one admires. That is to say, it is even harder, in most cases, to be a social deviate in adopting an important practice than it is in casting a vote. And finally, media and personal influences, longtime and short-term influences, are likely to be intertwined so that one must be careful not to ascribe too much influence to a media campaign.

However, the uses of mass media in adoption of change have now been studied intensively in agricultural education, family planning, and health improvements (for a few examples out of many, see Rogers and Shoemaker, 1971; Rogers, 1973; Lerner, 1958; I.I.E.P. and Unesco, 1967; and the review by Frey in Pool and Schramm, 1973). Some of the conclusions might be summed up briefly under these headings:

1. The mass media are potent, even in a relatively personal and sensitive situation like family planning, in providing the necessary information base for change.

In developing regions, the mass media, along with new roads and travel, are chiefly responsible for widening horizons, and for making known alternative ways of life. Thus they contribute to new wants and new objectives, and if the "Want: Get Ratio" is not reduced, a "revolution of rising expectations" may turn into a "revolution of rising frustrations." (See Lerner's comments, 1967, pp. 104 ff.)

In agriculture and health the mass media exhibit new practices and potential results. In family planning they help get the sensitive subject out into the open, so that people feel able to talk about it in public and to seek help if needed. In education they not only make known new opportunities but also play a more direct role by offering learning opportunities beyond the classroom and the campus.

In most developing countries radio is a chief carrier of this kind of information because it is cheap, can be operated without power lines, can overleap illiteracy, and is the principal channel to villages and rural people. Print has the advantage of permanence, and of providing a means both to practice new literacy and to use it for learning practical skills. But all the media, large or small, modern or traditional (such as, for example, puppet shows and ballads) have proved useful in furnishing the information that a potential adopter needs.

2. But when the point of decision and commitment is reached, then personal advice and influence and social support for a decision are likely to be more useful than mass media.

This is the time when friends and field workers, discussion groups such as the rural radio forum or the Korean Mothers Clubs, and community activities are especially valuable. The adopter needs to be able to seek guidance and reassurance when he wants it, and he needs to be confident of social support if he makes the decision.

One of the chief uses of mass media at this stage is for providing models of behavior, such as admired persons who are doing what the adopter is thinking of doing, or persons who have adopted and are being rewarded for it.

3. A campaign that is intended to appeal to a wide spectrum of persons and to bring about decisions for adoption among persons who are ready for it usually gains by using a number of channels of communication, both media and interpersonal.

For example, in a recent experiment in Iran (Gillespie, 1973), an intensive radio campaign brought a large number of people to the family-planning clinic. When the campaign was stopped for several months, the number fell off. Then a multimedia campaign was introduced, including field workers, radio, posters, meetings, films, and so forth. The clinic attendance went far higher than it had been with the radio campaign. This result has been duplicated frequently in other fields as well as in family planning.

4. There is very little evidence in studies of adoption and innovation that mass media are effective in changing strongly held beliefs and attitudes.

Here, as in other fields we have mentioned, it is more effective to deal with areas in which viewpoints have not hardened, or to try to bring about slight changes. A typical development campaign tries to bring about change in persons who are most ready for it, and merely to plant the seed of change in persons who would have to modify strong viewpoints in order to adopt. This is why the basic information on new alternatives, the use of models who have adopted and are being rewarded, and the incidental and unobtrusive learning from stories or novellas or other entertainment are particularly useful.

5. If adoption is to be accomplished, by the use of mass media or personal influence or whatever combination, it is necessary to provide the physical and social requirements for carrying out the decision.

This concept has been called in agriculture the "package program," meaning that a campaign of information and persuasion is insufficient by itself; a farmer must also be able to obtain the seeds he wants to plant, the fertilizer or insecticide he requires, the farm machinery he needs, a loan if his plans require it, a way to market his new crops, expert advice if he finds problems that require it, and, finally, community support and potential social rewards for what he is doing. In other words, unless the change is made to seem feasible, the most powerful media campaign in the world is not likely to persuade a potential adopter to change.

Incidental Effects on Values and Social Behavior

Now we are dealing with effects that are not, for the most part, the objective of persuasion, but nevertheless enter into the depths of the personality and the roots of social behavior.

Effects of these kinds are so shrouded in multiple and long-time causes that they are difficult to study and analyze. Most communication scholars suspect that mass media play an important part in shaping the effects, but find it hard to disentangle media effects from others.

Certain conclusions may be readily accepted. For one thing, there is no reasonable doubt that behavior which can simply be learned from the mass media and put into effect without a major challenge to values or social customs is frequently so learned. We are speaking now about behavior on the level of fads (for example, the hula hoop), or of mod language (just as an older generation learned from the radio program "Fibber McGee and Mollie" to say " 'Taint funny, McGee!" so a younger generation learns some of the favorite phrases of the counterculture). We learn something about how to dress, how to act on a date, how a living room should look, and so forth. Lerner reported his Syrian Tito saying, "The movies are like a teacher to us!" (Lerner, 1958).

We also learn something about who is worth admiring, and what kind of behavior is rewarded. Television, for example, puts in front of us a series of attractive and sometimes important persons, and offers them as models to us, whether because they have been elected to high public office, or run one hundred yards with a football, or wear a certain kind of deodorant, hair cream, or skin freshener. It offers us also a very large number of actors who perform in various antisocial ways that are intended as fantasy but seem extraordinarily realistic, and who are rewarded in ways that often prove highly attractive to younger viewers. Anyone who believes that a program or a film with thirty seconds of "crime does not pay" will keep viewers from learning the behavior that has paid so well up until those thirty seconds, should read the report of the Surgeon General's Committee on Television and Social Behavior (1972). (See also Comstock et al., [1978].)

On the basis of quite solid evidence we can say also that children and teenagers will learn antisocial behavior, in the laboratory, from seeing it on film or television (for a few examples out of many, see Bandura, Ross, and Ross, 1963; Bandura, 1965; Bandura and Walters, 1963). We emphasize, *in the laboratory*. There the evidence is clear. It is not so clear in life.

The difficulty is that the effect of a television program in the laboratory can be measured without interference from other causes or constraints. A child can see someone hitting a doll with a hammer, on a film, and be taken into the next room, where, if he wishes, he too can hit a doll with a hammer. Nothing in the room tells him he should not hit the doll, nor are there any other experiences that intervene and interfere. In life, however, violent television is only one of many experiences from which one can learn. Furthermore, there are laws against violent behavior, and policemen to enforce the laws, and people to denounce violence. There are also other people to encourage and demonstrate it. But the point is that the field is not clear. There are many influences pro and con. If someone behaves antisocially after seeing violence on television, it is probably a long time afterward, and after many other experiences and influences have intervened. True, there are cases (see Schramm, 1969) in which a viewer sees a character on television or film feed ground glass to someone else, and imitates that behavior; or sees a television burglary performed, and then performs a burglary of the same kind. But these are uncommon cases, and may well have involved disturbed or otherwise abnormal individuals. The effects that worry students of mass media are long-term ones. What is happening to values and behavior in general as a result of exposure to the mass media?

Let us take another example about which there is relatively little disagreement. When mass media come into an oral culture, that is, when a village gets radio for the first time, or some villagers learn to read and begin to receive a newspaper, profound changes can be observed in the next few years. People become interested in things that previously did not interest them. They develop different aspirations and goals. To a certain degree the power distribution tends to change: it passes from the old men who could remember the holy books, the laws, and the genealogies, to the younger men who know how things are done presently but faraway—in other words, from a time culture to a space culture. People develop more interest in taking part in government, sharing the power with the old leaders. Often culture grows more secular.

These changes have been observed in a number of places at a number of times, and it hardly can be doubted that in those situations the mass media have contributed to changing both values and behavior. But the situation is not precisely parallel to what happens in a society that is *already* a media society. Is there a *continuing* influence of the media?

From the media, during those five hours or so a day we give them, we are clearly learning a great deal. As we have already said, we store pictures in our minds that describe distant environments. We store a catalogue of persons and names. We store behaviors. And we learn something about values.

No social scientiest would doubt that this occurs. To decide exactly *what* changes in values and behavior can be ascribed to the *mass media,* however, is an almost impossible task because it requires us to separate one influence from a myriad of interlocking influences in a person's experience.

This matter has been studied most intensively in terms of the effect of television violence on children, a question that has been a matter of great concern in many countries. Japan, Britain, West Germany, and the United States all have had major studies of the problem. In the United States, two years of research and more than a million dollars of research money have gone into it since 1970, and the general conclusion of more than thirty studies is that a large amount of violence on television probably makes it more likely that violence will occur in life. (See Comstock et al., 1978.) Not many people will perform violent acts solely because of television; they learn from an entire culture that is violent. But the recent studies endorse what Leonard Berkowitz said ten years earlier:

> While it may be that television, movies, and comic books will excite anti-social conduct from only a relatively small number of people, we can also say the heavy dosage of violence in the media heightens the probability that someone in the audience will behave aggressively in a later situation (1962, p. 134).

In a sense it is a pity that most of this kind of research has been restricted to television violence and its effect on children, because there are many other questions at least as worrisome: What is being learned from the media about respect for authority? About sexual behavior? About the value of work? About the ethics of sport and fair play? About politics? About family life? About the desirability of different professions or jobs? How much of mass media time, and of television time in particular, is at least partly counterproductive because it confuses reality with fantasy?

We have asked some of the less pleasing questions. We might also suggest desirable influences of the media, beyond the horizon-widening effect discussed above. But the point is that, whether the predominant influences are good or bad, the media clearly enter into the forming of character, values, ideas, and social behavior. Although we cannot say exactly what their influence is, we can hardly doubt that it is profound.

EMERGING PROBLEMS OF EFFECT
Some Assumptions

At different levels of confidence, then, we can assume that the mass media influence our life-styles, our knowledge of the world around us and the way we differentiate that knowledge, our decisions, and our values and behaviors.

The effect on life-styles is always evident to us. The effect on knowledge is just as undeniable, although its boundaries are somewhat fuzzier and the ways we process the incoming knowledge differ widely among individuals. When the media are used in an attempt to manipulate our decisions (for example, in politics or economic and social development or advertising), they are undeniably effective in informing us, but usually less directly effective than personal communication at the time of decision; and they are most potent in a package of communication where they draw on and supplement personal influence and group support. We have little doubt, furthermore, that media experience has an incidental effect on values and behaviors, even though there is no overt attempt to exert such an effect. At the level of faddish behavior and mod language, the effect is evident though not very important. The deeper effects (for example, of violent television upon the violence of social behavior) are worrisome to most students of the subject, and there is at least some research evidence that the worries may be justified. In short-term laboratory experiments, such effects may be seen clearly. In life they are less clear, because they are mostly long-term, and are interwoven with a complex of social influences and social constraints so that the resulting behavior is almost impossible to trace back to one cause. The media contribute to such effects, but how and under what circumstances is not fully understood

There is no reason to believe that very general effects such as these will be essentially different in the new Age of Information. However, our knowledge of them will sharpen. They are likely also to reshape themselves to a degree, and thus to bulk larger or smaller in the ways we live and think and what we believe and value. Therefore, in the following section we suggest a few questions that may be worth special attention from students and observers of communication during the next decades.

We begin with a few assumptions, derived from the first section of this chapter, about the probable nature of the Age of Information:

1. The flow of information will greatly increase.
2. The pace of communication will be notably faster.
3. There will be increased dependence upon the media.
4. There will be shifts of power related to the command of information.

Given those assumptions, we suggest a few questions regarding probable extensions or modifications of mass media effect. (For a highly interesting discussion of some of these questions from a futuristic political viewpoint, see Paige, 1973.)

Will the increased flow of information—

1. *Blunt the force of the mass media as instruments of persuasion, or strengthen it?*

One might expect that an increased flow (except, perhaps, in monopoly systems) would bring about more competition for attention and hence make any one campaign or message less likely to be perceived and accepted. Similarly, a larger flow might make it more costly for any one persuader to command the relative proportion of time or space he could have had were the flow smaller. On the other hand, a considerably increased flow of information might absorb some of the time presently given to personal communication and lead to more dependence on media rather than on interpersonal channels at decision time.

2. *Decrease, or increase, the gap between the members of society who are already information-rich and information-poor?*

In other words, will the effect be toward equalizing the distribution of information, or will the rich simply grow richer as compared with the others? All existing evidence shows that the better educated, the better informed, learn more than others do from the same exposure to information, and usually are more likely to seek exposure. On the other hand, the curve of how much information one can learn and store must approach an asymptote, and therefore if the supply is very large it may indeed have an equalizing effect.

3. *Create a broader basis for rational decision making, or a broader invitation to fantasy?*

An increased flow of information supposedly will make available more news and news analysis, more information from different cultures and faraway places. On the other hand, there is no assurance that we can equate availability with absorption. The newspapers most successful in adding to circulation in recent years have tended to rely upon features, and to approach a "daily magazine" format. The commercial television networks have increased neither their offerings nor their audiences in public affairs programs, relative to entertainment, although their success with professional football, crime and adventure drama, and family comedies has been spectacular.

Will the faster pace of communication—

1. *Contribute to superficial attitudes toward problems, or toward a better-informed populace?*

On the one hand, people should be able to find out more quickly what is happening in the world, and thus be able to anticipate and perhaps contribute to policy making rather than merely be presented with policies. On the other hand, when events and figures pass so quickly through the media, when problems and stories are not followed up, the effect tends to be that of a kaleidoscope rather than a systematic view of environment. One watches the shifting colors and patterns rather than examines relationships.

2. *Disrupt information processing by giving audiences too much information to handle in a short time?*

This was Toffler's hypothesis (1970), that future shock arose from an overload—too much, too fast—that caused people to retreat from rather than to make use of the experience. On the other hand, Toffler may have overestimated the biological limitations on ability to process information.

3. *Require power centers to create special mechanisms for verification and reality testing?*

Lead time for responding to information has been a traditional need of diplomacy and negotiation. In meetings, diplomats often have welcomed the opportunity for consecutive rather than simultaneous translation, and the need to "wait for instructions." Both governments and businesses have benefited from the opportunity to consider a problem for a while before it becomes publicly known and they have to make a public response. But what will happen when the channels of public information operate as swiftly as those of governmental information, and when problems get public exposure without the traditional lead time? Will rumor, unintentional or manufactured, become a weapon? Even now, the first story, the first accusation, the first sensation is likely to get far more attention than does information that follows. Will some new methods be developed to help the media and the public, as well as the great power centers, verify facts and test reality quickly?

As societies come to depend more upon the media—

1. *What accommodation will be arrived at between the sender-oriented and the receiver-oriented delivery systems?*

As we pointed out earlier in this chapter, the spectacular developments in telecommunications (broadcasting, cable, microwave, communication satellites, laser beam transmission, and so forth) have mostly been of a nature to speed and expand the flow of information. Users, however, have been increasingly hard put to make efficient use of this abundance. Scholars and students have been overwhelmed. Laymen, reveling in their opportunities, have found it hard to get what they wanted when they wanted it. Teachers, grateful for high-quality instructional television in the classroom, have found themselves tied to its schedule and pace, rather than to the needs of their classes. This situation will have to be resolved, and presently the computer and recording machinery seem to offer the most hope for doing so.

2. *To what extent will mediated communication replace activities now carried out personally?*

Will spectator sports increasingly replace participant sports, and spectator sports increasingly find their spectators at home? Will efficient ways be found to shop or to administer businesses by television? What will be the effect on the placement of factories relative to homes? On large conferences? On travel in general?

3. *To what extent will mediated reality testing replace the traditional combination of personal experience and advice?*

Will "seeing it" in television, "hearing it" on radio, "attending" an event through the media be accepted as an adequate replacement for being there personally or relying upon a trusted adviser who has been there? And if so, what standards of reporting may be asked of the media?

4. *Will there be a shift, other things being equal, toward permissiveness, or toward a search for authority?*

The larger and more pervasive the media become, the more likely they are to be ascriptive, rather than prescriptive. Will audiences, too, become more permissive, or will they react and seek more rules and guidelines?

5. *Will there be greater similarity, or a greater diversity, of customs?*

At present there are divergent tendencies on the one hand, particularly among youth, toward sharing the same customs, the same patois, the same heroes, and so forth. On the other hand, there is an increasing effort to present distant or minority cultures in the media and elsewhere in public. Certainly we know more than previously about distant places and unfamiliar customs. Are we moving toward the "global village," or toward reinforcing the differences in villages?

6. *What important effects will there be on knowledge institutions and education?*

The trends now seem to be toward moving education more and more out of school, bringing it to people rather than people to it, and extending learning opportunities through life rather than concentrating them on young people. In this movement, the instructional media promise to play a major part, and are already doing so in the case of institutions such as the open schools and universities, and specialized extension teaching. But what accommodation will be reached between the advantages of studying together and studying at home, between the effort to meet local and individual needs for curricula and the efficiency of providing curricula centrally?

Will the shifts of power related to information—

1. *Result in widening, or in narrowing, access to the media?*

To an insecure government an increased flow of information may be potentially dangerous. Insecure governments at present, and governments that operate on an authoritarian caretaker philosophy, are extremely careful about who can say what in their media. It is likely, therefore, that the Age of Information will bring into conflict two opposing trends, one to control media access and content very carefully, the other to open the media to more spokesmen and viewpoints. In this country, the underground press, the fairness doctrine in broadcasting, the right of reply in newspapers, the movement toward providing broadcast and cable time for minorities, the talk shows on radio —all these have worked in the direction of opening the media to unofficial viewpoints. The coming flood tide of information probably will carry on this trend. What will happen when the tide hits the media gates of the more tightly controlled countries?

2. *Give media figures more influence and encourage the use of the media for advice and guidance?*

The indication is that this will happen unless the media present enough additional background material to let audiences check up more often on their pundits, simply because more voluminous, more unfamiliar, more complex information will require more expert interpretation, which is more likely to be found in the media than next door. And even if the media do present more background material, a large part of the audience still will want it predigested.

3. *Tend to create a two-class society—those able to use computers and those who are not?*

If the computer does indeed become the great communicating machine of the latter twentieth century, the ability to command and direct it will itself constitute power. A computer expert will in a sense be like a diplomat who speaks the difficult language of a powerful foreign culture, a scholar who can call upon all the memory banks in the world, and an adventurer who is exploring the far edge of the geography of knowledge. Of course, the computer, operating with natural languages, conceivably might become as common and easily used as the telephone or the phonograph, but there is likely to be a period when the computer's own logic and language, and its use as a tool of thinking, will have to be developed, and this will give a particular power to those able to work with it. A partial analogy was the early period in the history of social science when the ability to use mathematical statistics was limited to relatively few social scientists.

4. *Give political advantage to persons able to perform with professional skills on the media?*

This is the situation at present, and there is no reason to think it will be otherwise. However, a greater flow of media information will mean that audiences will see more political figures and have more to choose among. Furthermore, a greater flow of information should provide more opportunity to check up on these political media stars, to see them questioned, to hear rebuttals, to let reporters check into their statements.

5. *By turning the spotlight on political figures and public events and policies, encourage cynicism toward leaders and the processes of governing?*

This is the other side of the coin. On the one hand, the media may give preferred exposure to those among political figures who are handsome, smooth, assured media performers. On the other hand, those figures probably will be shown in greater detail, and there will be more opportunity to present and analyze their policies and accomplishments. Will the balance favor a growth of cynicism like that of the present youth culture, or an increase in the number of politicians with Academy Awards?

6. *Result in broader participation in policy making?*

It is a fascinating possibility. The spread of media and education into developing villages encourages more villagers to participate in the responsibilities of government. Will the increased depth and the wider distribution of information, in the coming age, lessen the information gap—and hence the potential power gap—between the leaders and the led? Will it bring about, not deeper cynicism as suggested above, but rather a broader desire to participate in making policy and choosing administrators of policy? And if so, are we drawing toward the time when Marx's vision of the "withering away of the state" (which as yet has shown no sign of occurring in either communist or capitalist states) might finally become a realizable possibility?

BIBLIOGRAPHY

Adorno, T. W.; Frenkel-Brunswik, E.; Levinson, D. J.; and Sanford, R. N. *The Authoritarian Personality.* New York: Harper, 1950.

Asch, S. "Studies in the Principles of Judgments and Attitudes: II. Determinants of Judgments by Group and Ego Standards." *Journal of Social Psychology,* 12 (1940):433–465.

———. "Studies of Independence and Conformity: A Minority of One Against a Unanimous Majority." *Psychological Monographs* 70 (1956):9.

Bandura, A. "Vicarious Processes: A Case of No-Trial Learning." In L. Berkowitz, ed., *Advances in Experimental Social Psychology,* vol. 2, pp. 1–55. New York: Academic Press, 1965.

———; Ross, D.; and Ross, S. A. "Imitation of Film-mediated Aggressive Models." *Journal of Abnormal and Social Psychology* 66 (1963):3–11.

———, and Walters, R. H. *Social Learning and Personality Development.* New York: Holt, Rinehart, and Winston, 1963.

Bauer, R. A. "The Obstinate Audience: The Influence Process from the Point of View of Social Communication." *American Psychologist* 19 (1964):319–328.

Berelson, B. R.; Lazarsfeld, P. F.; and McPhee, W. N. *Voting: A Study of Opinion Formation in a Presidential Election.* Chicago: University of Chicago Press, 1954.

Berkowitz, L. *Violence in the Mass Media.* In Paris-Stanford Studies in Communication. Paris: Institut Francais de Presse, University of Paris; Stanford, California: Institute for Communication Research, Stanford University, 1962.

Broadbent, D. E. *Perception and Communication.* London: Pergamon Press, 1958.

Bryson, L., ed. *The Communication of Ideas.* New York: Institute of Religious and Social Studies, 1948.

Campbell, A.; Converse, P. E.; and Miller, W. E. *The American Voter.* New York: Wiley, 1960.

Cantril, H. *The Politics of Despair.* Chap. 1, "The Nature of Our Reality Worlds." New York: Basic Books, 1968.

Cartwright, D. "Some Principles of Mass Persuasion: Selected Findings of Research on the Sale of U.S. War Bonds." *Human Relations* 2 (1949):253.

Coleman, J. S., et al. *Medical Innovation: A Diffusion Study.* Indianapolis: Bobbs-Merrill, 1966.

Comstock, George; Chaffee, Steven; Katzman, Nathan; McCombs, Maxwell; and Roberts, Donald. *Television and Human Behavior.* New York: Columbia University Press, 1978.

Cooley, C. *Social Organization,* esp. p. 61. New York: Charles Scribner's Sons, 1909.

Cutlip, W. S. "Content and Flow of AP News." *Journalism Quarterly* 31 (1954):434–446.

Festinger, L. "Behavioral Support for Opinion Change." *Public Opinion Quarterly* 28 (1964):400–414.

——. *A Theory of Cognitive Dissonance.* Evanston, Ill.: Row, Peterson, 1957.

Freedman, J. L., and Sears, D. O. "Warning, Distraction, and Resistance to Influence. *Journal of Personality and Social Psychology* 1 (1965):262–266.

Frey, F. W. "Communication and Development." In I. de S. Pool, and W. Schramm, eds., *Handbook of Communication,* pp. 337–461. Chicago: Rand McNally, 1973.

Gillespie, R. *Report on a Family Planning Campaign in Iran.* Teheran: Population Council, 1973.

Greenberg, B. S. "Person-to-Person Communication in the Diffusion of News Events." *Journalism Quarterly* 41 (1964):490–494.

——, and Parker, E. B. *The Assassination of President Kennedy.* Stanford: Stanford University Press, 1964.

Heider, F. *The Psychology of Interpersonal Relations.* New York: Wiley, 1958.

Hovland, C. I., et al., eds. *Order of Presentation in Persuasion.* New Haven: Yale University Press, 1957.

——, and Janis, I. L. *Personality and Persuasibility.* New Haven: Yale University Press, 1959.

——; Janis, I. L.; and Kelley, H. H. *Communication and Persuasion.* New Haven: Yale University Press, 1953.

——; Lumsdaine, A. A.; and Sheffield, F. D. *Experiments on Mass Communication.* Princeton: Princeton University Press, 1949.

Innis, H. *The Bias of Communication.* Toronto: University of Toronto Press, 1951.

Institute for Propaganda Analysis. *The Fine Art of Propaganda: A Study of Father Coughlin's Speeches.* New York: Harcourt, Brace, 1939.

Ittelson, William H. *The Ames Demonstrations in Perception, together with an Interpretive Manual by Adelbert Ames, Jr.* New ed. New York: Hafner Publishing Co., 1968.

Janis, I. L. "Effects of Fear Arousal on Attitude Change: Recent Developments in Theory and Experimental Research." In L. Berkowitz, ed., *Advances in Experimental Social Psychology,* pp. 166–226. New York: Academic Press, 1967.

Katz, D. "The Functional Approach to the Study of Attitudes." *Public Opinion Quarterly* 24 (1960):163–204.

Katz, E., and Lazarsfeld, P. F. *Personal Influence.* Glencoe, Ill.: Free Press, 1955.

Klapper, Joseph K. *The Effects of Mass Communication.* New York: Free Press, 1960.

Kraus, S., ed. *The Great Debates: Background, Perspective, Effects.* Bloomington: Indiana University Press, 1962.

Kris, E. and Leites, N. "Trends in 20th-Century Propaganda." In D. Lerner, ed., *Sykewar,* pp. 39–54. New York: Stewart, 1951.

Lane, R. E. *Political Ideology: Why the American Common Man Believes What He Does.* New York: Free Press, 1962.

Lang, K., and Lang, G. E. *Politics and Television.* Chicago: Quadrangle Books, 1968.

Lasswell, H. D. "The Structure and Function of Communication in Society." In L. Bryson, ed., *The Communication of Ideas,* pp. 37–51. New York: Institute for Religious and Social Studies, 1948.

Lazarsfeld, P. F.; Berelson, B. R.; and Gaudet, H. *The People's Choice.* New York: Columbia University Press, 1948.

——, and Merton, R. K. "Mass Communication, Popular Taste, and Organized Social Action." In L. Bryson, ed., *The Communication of Ideas.* New York: Institute for Religious and Social Studies, 1948.

———, and Stanton, F. N., eds. *Communication Research, 1948-49.* New York: Harper, 1949.

Lerner, D. *The Passing of Traditional Society.* Glencoe, Ill.: Free Press, 1958.

———. *Sykewar.* New York: Stewart, 1951.

———, and Schramm, Wilbur. *Communication and Change in the Developing Countries.* Honolulu: The University Press of Hawaii, 1967.

Lewin, K. "Group Decision and Social Change." In E. E. Maccoby, T. M. Newcomb, and E. E. Hartley, *Readings in Social Psychology,* pp. 197–211. New York: Holt Rinehart & Winston, 1958.

Machlup, F. *The Production and Distribution of Knowledge.* Princeton: Princeton University Press, 1962.

McGuire, W. J. "Nature of Attitudes and Attitude Change." In G. Lindzey and E. Aronson, eds., *Handbook of Social Psychology,* vol. 3, pp. 136-314. Reading, Mass.: Addison-Wesley, 1969.

———. "Persuasion, Resistance and Attitude Change." In I. de S. Pool and W. Schramm, eds., *Handbook of Communication,* pp. 216-252. Chicago: Rand McNally, 1973.

———. "A Syllogistic Analysis of Cognitive Relationships." In M. Rosenberg and C. I. Hovland, eds., *Attitude Organization and Attitude Change.* New Haven: Yale University Press, 1960.

McLuhan, M. *The Gutenberg Galaxy.* Toronto: University of Toronto Press, 1962.

———. *Understanding Media: The Extensions of Man.* New York: McGraw-Hill, 1966.

Merton, R. K. *Mass Persuasion.* New York: Harper & Row, 1946.

Newcomb, T. M. "An Approach to the Study of Communicative Acts." *Psychological Review* 60 (1953):393-404.

Osgood, C. E., and Tannenbaum, P. H. *The Measurement of Meaning.* Urbana: University of Illinois Press, 1957.

Paige, G. D. "Political Leadership in the Future Informational Society." Working paper 73-1. Social Science Research Institute, University of Hawaii, Honolulu, 1973.

Pool, Ithiel de Sola; Abelson, Robert P.; and Popham, Samuel. *Candidates, Issues, and Strategies.* 2d ed. Cambridge, Mass.: M.I.T. Press, 1965.

———, Schramm, W., et al., eds. *Handbook of Communication.* Chicago: Rand McNally, 1973.

Reisman, D.; Glazer, N.; and Denney, R. *The Lonely Crowd.* New Haven: Yale University Press, 1950.

Rogers, E. M. *Communication in Family Planning.* New York: Free Press, 1973.

———. *Diffusion of Innovations.* New York: Free Press, 1962.

———, and Bhomik, P. K. "Homophily-Heterophily: Relational Concepts for Communication Research." *Public Opinion Quarterly* 34 (1971): 523-538.

—— with Shoemaker, F. F. *Communication of Innovations: A Cross-Cultural Approach.* New York: Free Press, 1971.

Rosenberg, M. J., and Hovland, C. I. *Attitude Organization and Attitude Change.* New Haven: Yale University Press, 1960.

Sapir, E. "Communication." In *Encyclopedia of the Social Sciences,* 1st ed., vol. 4, p. 78. New York: Macmillan, 1935.

Schramm, W. *Big Media: Little Media.* Beverly Hills: Institute for Communication Research, Stanford University, 1976.

——. "The Indian Radio Rural Forum." In I.I.E.P. and UNESCO, *New Educational Media: Case Studies for Planners.* Paris: UNESCO, 1967.

——. *Men, Messages, and Media: A Look at Human Communication.* New York: Harper & Row, 1973.

——. *Motion Pictures and Real-Life Violence: What the Research Says.* Stanford: Institute for Communication Research, Stanford University, 1969.

——, and Carter, R. F. "Effectiveness of a Political Telethon." *Public Opinion Quarterly* 23 (1959):121–126.

Sears, D. O., and Whitney, R. E. "Political Persuasion." In I. de S. Pool and W. Schramm, eds., *Handbook of Communication,* pp. 253–289. Chicago: Rand McNally, 1973.

Shannon, C. E., and Weaver, W. *The Mathematical Theory of Communication.* Urbana: University of Illinois Press, 1949.

Sherif, Carolyn W.; Sherif, Muzafer; and Nebergall, R. E. *Attitudes and Attitude Change.* Philadelphia: Saunders, 1965.

Sherif, Muzafer, and Hovland, C. I. *Social Judgment.* New Haven: Yale University Press, 1961.

Star, S. A., and Hughes, H. M. "Report of an Educational Campaign: The Cincinnati Plan for the United Nations." *American Journal of Sociology* 55 (1950):398.

Surgeon General's Scientific Advisory Committee on Television and Social Behavior. *Television and Social Behavior: A Technical Report.* Washington, D.C.: Government Printing Office, 1972.

Toffler, A. *Future Shock.* New York: Random House, 1970.

Travers, R. M. W., et al. *Research and Theory Related to Audiovisual Information Transmission.* Salt Lake City: Bureau of Educational Research, University of Utah, 1966.

Walster, E. C., and Festinger, L. "The Effectiveness of Overheard Persuasive Communication." *Journal of Abnormal and Social Psychology* 68 (1962):233–241.

Weiss, W. "Effects of the Mass Media of Communications." In G. Lindzey and E. Aronson, eds., *Handbook of Social Psychology,* vol. 5, pp. 77–195. Reading, Mass.: Addison-Wesley, 1969.

Wicker, A. W. "Attitudes Versus Actions: The Relationship of Verbal and Overt Behavioral Responses to Attitude Objects." *Journal of Social Issues* 25 (1969):41–78.

10

THE SOCIAL EFFECTS
OF COMMUNICATION TECHNOLOGY

HERBERT GOLDHAMER

The revolution in communications, which owes much to the rise of semiconductor technology, is just beginning. This chapter outlines some recent and impending changes and indicates briefly some of their possible social effects. In almost every case there is considerable room for facilitation or restraint of these social effects by private and public groups. Where and how communication satellites, cable transmission systems, computers, videophones, ultramicrofiche, and various other devices will eventually fit into more comprehensive communication systems will not be simply a function of technical capabilities and cost considerations but also of public policy and of entrepreneurial and consumer pressures and choices. Once made, some of these choices may be difficult to reverse because of investments undertaken and the consequent vested interests created.[1]

Choices will also depend on technical developments in fields other than communications, for instance, transport. A message may be transmitted by a variety of communication devices or by travel and personal presence. Communications is not the only field undergoing rapid development; the total shape of the future will be determined by responses to other technologies.

Difficult as it is to forecast developments in technology, the

Originally prepared for the Russell Sage Foundation, with the assistance of Ronald Westrum.

latter's effects on society are even more hypothetical. Much of the material in this chapter is necessarily speculative. But speculation is unavoidable if intelligent discussion, research, and planning are to take place. There is too little realistic appreciation of the potential benefits of communication development and also there is too little appreciation of its difficulties and dangers.[2] The enormous amount of capital necessary to realize some of these systems, the wide range of interests that are likely to become involved, and the difficulty of changing decisions once implemented indicate the need for a wide perspective.

This chapter concentrates on devices that already exist. The communication systems of the 1980s will be based largely on devices already in use, available in the laboratory, or being tested. But it will take many years for these devices to be widely used. The 90 million televison sets and their antennas in the United States represent a consumer investment of about $21 billion. The accumulation of consumer investments of this order for new devices cannot occur overnight.

Our approach is conservative: we have avoided guessing how devices yet to be invented will affect social life. Thus, for instance, there is no mention of communication by laser, which might have important effects. The reason for this conservatism is simple: the systems described here are already being installed, and their social impact is already being felt. The comfortable sense of the remoteness of the future is inappropriate when considering data banks, cable television, ultramicrofiche, computer-implemented communication systems, "wired cities," and the like. Decisions regarding their utilization are being made now, not tomorrow.

THE TECHNOLOGICAL FOUNDATIONS OF THE COMMUNICATION REVOLUTION

The current revolution in communications is based on a large number of inventions and technological advances. Some, like the electronic computer and the transistor, are new inventions. Others, like the printed circuit, are modifications with revolutionary effects because of savings in cost, size, and weight, or improved reliability. The net effect of both new inventions and constant modifications of old ones has been a continuous flood of new and newly improved devices with each stage generally cheaper and more effective than the previous one. Even experts in the electronic field have trouble keeping up with the state of the art. For laymen and social scientists the task of understanding and keeping abreast of electronics technology is nearly insuperable. A brief discussion of some basic advances is provided here as background for understanding subsequent sections.

The Transistor

Basic to the revolution in communication technology is solid state technology, essentially the transistor using semiconductor materials, materials that in their ability to conduct electricity are intermediate between good conductors and insulators. Before the discovery of new types of semiconductors and the invention of the transistor amplifier, electronic amplification employed vacuum tubes, which were large, costly, and demanding of primary power. The first transistor was made in 1947, the result of a program at Bell Telephone Laboratories to study the properties of semiconductors. Commonly used semiconductors are germanium, silicon, and gallium arsenide. The electrical properties of semiconductors are highly sensitive to impurities. By putting controlled amounts of impurities, on the order of a few parts per million, in very pure blocks of a semiconductor material, it is possible to create devices that can duplicate the functions of the vacuum tube.

Semiconductors had been used as radio-frequency detectors and telephone rectifiers, but it was not until 1947 that the transistor amplifier was successfully developed. The transistor permitted radios, computers, and other pieces of electronic equipment to be made smaller, cheaper, and more portable. Transistors also have a smaller power consumption, are more reliable, and require no time to warm up. Solid state components gradually replaced vacuum tubes in all but a few applications. The hand-held transistor radio and hearing-aid-equipped eyeglasses, as well as the great variety of electronic "mini-snoopers" are some of the devices made possible by the transistor.

Printed Circuits

Printed circuits were first developed on a large scale after World War II. The desired connections are formed on an insulating material by either superimposing a uniform copper film and then etching it away, where no conductors are desired, or occasionally by the electroplating or vacuum deposition of a copper film, where conductors are desired. Such printed circuits are generally machine-soldered and tend to be more reliable than hand-soldered connections. Even more important, as techniques improved, the printed circuits became smaller.

The Integrated Circuit

If the connections between components could be miniaturized, why not the components themselves? In the early 1960s vacuum technology and careful control of the amount and location of impurities enabled circuits to be deposited on silicon wafers that included not only the connections but the components as well. On a single silicon wafer the size of a quarter it is now possible to have four hundred to one thousand complete circuits operating at the same time. Integrated circuits required an entirely new technology. The amount of impurities used with semiconductors had to be meticulously controlled, and a whole new range of techniques had to be developed—deposition equipment, special ovens, and the ability to lay down materials in strips 0.010 in. thick and as narrow as 0.0001 in.

Integrated circuitry (IC) was expensive at first. The original integrated circuit devices cost $250 to $600 for a single circuit; the same circuit could be produced from conventional parts for $10. But the integrated circuits were needed for specialized military applications that required light weight, small size, and minimal power consumption. Now, IC devices are mass-produced in 50,000-piece lots and sell for $2.50. IC techniques have become increasingly refined. Large-scale integration now permits placing the equivalent of hundreds of transistors on a single pinhead of silicon.

The Computer

Although the first electronic computer, ENIAC, was built at the University of Pennsylvania as recently as 1946, computer development has been so rapid, especially in the last few years, that a modern computer now seems to ENIAC what ENIAC is to an abacus. Comparing computers of 1953 and 1965, W. H. Ware notes that

> the 1953 machine weighed about 5000 lb., had a volume of 300 to 400 cu. ft., and required about 40 kilowatts of power. The contem-

porary computer [1965] is a hundredfold lighter (about 50 lb.), a thousand times smaller (about one-third cu. ft.), and requires 250 times less power (150 watts). Moreover, it has twice the storage and runs ten times as fast.[3]

The saving in size, weight, and power is the result of solid state technology and integrated circuits, as is the increase in memory storage and speed of computation. Yet progress continues so rapidly that statements about the state of the art generally have to be made in the past tense. Solid state technology and integrated circuitry appear to make the cigarette-package- or vest-pocket-sized general-purpose computer (central process) plausible in the not-too-distant future.

These technical gains have also meant economic gains. A National Academy of Science study estimates the cost of making 125 million multiplications to have progressively diminished from $12.5 million for a man working unaided, to $2.15 million for a man with a desk calculator, to $130,000 for ENIAC, $132 for IBM 7094, and $4 for CDC 6600.

Initially the principal input into computers was numbers, and the computer was required to manipulate these arithmetically to provide other numbers as outputs. Today, in contrast, computers process many nonnumerical inputs, such as in industrial production control systems. Spoken and written language and pictorial inputs facilitate the use of computers for language translation, business records, information retrieval, picture processing, medical diagnosis, chess playing, and numerous scientific tasks. Progress in processing pictorial inputs and providing pictorial outputs has been especially rapid. The development of numerous input and output devices (consoles) that make the machine and its output more accessible to the user provides for digital, alphabetic, and pictorial outputs in printed (hard copy), visual, and even oral form. Computers have not been able to produce hard-copy print-outs at the rate at which they process the inputs. But units are now available that print more than 1,000 lines per minute on paper and 3,000 lines per minute on instantly developed and viewable microfilm.

Progress has also been made in developing languages that facilitate "conversation" with the computer. Programming the computer to perform the desired tasks ("software") has advanced in several directions but primarily through the development of languages more readily learned by the user, who then allows the computer to translate this "compiler" language into the language the computer required for actual processing; and through the stockpiling of ready-made programs for operations that recur with sufficient frequency to make this stockpiling economical.

Complex programs still are difficult to write, however, and are enough of a bottleneck to have postponed some uses of computers in business because the required software was not available. Nevertheless, computers can be used effectively by persons with limited training and experience: for many uses an afternoon's instruction suffices. "Natural languages" are being developed that may permit use of the computer in more or less everyday language. And the computer's ability to respond to oral inputs and commands is not excluded in the future.

The development of input-output terminals, together with the enormously increased speed of computers, has permitted the use of communication lines to tie in a whole series of terminals to a single computer or set of computers, which thus can be shared by many users having individual terminals or consoles. This arrangement is usually referred to as an "on-line, time-shared computing system." The central computer operates fast enough so that individual users are not aware of any competition for the computer's time or of any appreciable lapse of time before the output reaches their terminal. The geographical area of such a shared computer system is as great as the available communication network (ordinarily the telephone system), although current transmission costs generally confine such systems to a radius of about two hundred miles.[4] Naturally, the sharing of a single large computer considerably reduces the cost of computer use and permits access to data banks and other computer services that otherwise would be quite out of reach for many users.

The computer is important in communication studies because its information processing abilities make it the major building block in the great array of developing communication systems. Indeed, as we note below, the distinction between computer systems and communication systems increasingly tends to be blurred.

DEVICES

The technological advances reviewed above, together with others, have permitted enormous advances to be made in a whole set of devices important for communications.[5] These devices, some of which are described below, are of two main types: transmission devices such as cables, microwave systems, and communication satellites; and input-output devices that process signals at the two ends of the communication line. Among the latter are videophone, long-range facsimile machines, and ultramicrofiche.

Cable Technology

As in most other areas of communication, developments in cable technology have increased the capacity and decreased the cost per channel. The first submarine telephone cable laid between the United States and Europe in 1956 had only 36 telephone circuits and cost $45 million to build and install. The newest transistorized cable being built between the United States and Spain will have 720 circuits at a cost of only $70–80 million.[6] Thus this cable will have a cost per circuit of only about 10 percent that of the 1956 vintage.

The cost per circuit of high-capacity terrestrial coaxial cable also has declined sharply. The "L-1" coaxial cable now in use has 2,000 voice circuits and an investment cost of 3 dollars per year per circuit-mile. In contrast, the "L-5" cable, soon to be introduced, has 81,000 voice circuits with a cost of 35 cents per year per circuit-mile.

Microwave Technology

Terrestrial microwave systems operate in the same general range of radio frequencies as do communication satellites. They use line-of-sight radio relay towers spaced twenty to fifty miles apart (depending on the terrain) to transmit communication signals. In the early postwar years they were available only to communication carriers and public utilities, but the Federal Communication Commission (FCC) now assigns frequencies within the 6–GHz and 12–GHz bands (where the gigahertz [GHz] is 1,000 MHz) for privately owned industrial microwave systems. These private systems can be used for computer data transmission, voice and message transmission, and closed-circuit television. Progress in the microwave field has been so rapid that many private companies now find it economically attractive to own and operate their own communication (microwave) system to connect widely scattered plants and offices.

Cable Television (CATV)

Cable Television distributes television programs through coaxial cables, in contrast to television broadcasting, which radiates them over the air. In 1950 in an Appalachian village, a local radio dealer rigged up a tall antenna on a nearby mountain to collect television signals because the mountains spoiled the reception of signals received by lower antennas. The wires were run from the antenna into the homes of those willing to pay a small fee. Thus began what was called "community antenna television," from which the acronym CATV sprang.

Today, CATV generally refers to distribution systems involving many building complexes and rights of way on public as well as private properties. Contemporary cables carry twelve to twenty channels, which permit more than merely relaying television signals received from local television stations. Although many cable networks use the extra channels for time signals, news headlines, or weather reports, the extra bandwidth could equally well be used to transmit programs of interest to particular neighborhoods or other limited areas. A cable system is an amazingly versatile instrument, able to relay voice signals, data signals, credit transactions, sensor signals, and in fact almost anything that one might want to send. It is precisely this versatility that makes it such an important development. Perhaps, in the future, cable will be used for all local fixed-point communication and radio will be reserved for communicating with vehicles in motion. This idea has led to the "wired cities" concept.

A wired city is an entire urban area connected by cables that might be controlled by a common carrier. Since these cables could carry nearly all signals except those to moving vehicles, the channels would be leased for telephone, data transmission, television, and the like. The financing of television programs might be done by individual subscription (pay-TV), through advertising, or by community groups who want to use the cable network for their own programs. Transmission and programming of some educational programs presumably would be financed by tax monies.

Community cable networks could be interconnected by satellite or terrestrial microwave, producing a national network of wired cities able to receive each other's television programs, voice and data transmissions, and videophone communications. It is a small jump, but with large implications, to an interconnected world.

Cable television could well become the most important communication development in the United States in the 1970s. There are several reasons for this, other than the enormous number of channels available to cable television and its ability to serve a whole host of communication purposes. Part of the excitement over cable television stems from the problems presented by conventional terrestrial broadcast televison. Although terrestrial broadcast television is at present the cheapest way of reaching very large audiences, it has the following disadvantages:

1. Signals are often of poor quality in densely populated areas, as a result of interference from other stations. Color television requires a higher-quality signal than does black and white television, because multiple images, or "ghosts," are more disturbing with color. In theory, some of these signal quality problems of terrestrial broadcasting can be solved through the installation of better rooftop antennas and the redesign of all television broadcast transmitters and home receiving sets to incorporate a change in modulation, but no really satisfactory solution is apparent at this time.

2. The variety of programs available on terrestrial broadcast television is limited. The number of commercial channels receivable by an average household in 1967 was 5.6 as compared with the potential of 20 channels on single-cable CATV. It is extremely unlikely that either conventional broadcast or direct television broadcasts from satellites will be able to match this capability in the foreseeable future.

3. There is an urgent and growing need to reserve more of the broadcast spectrum for services other than television, especially mobile radio. Available bandwidth resources already are being strained to provide communication services for police, fire, hospital, and military vehicles.

An important feature of a cable broadcasting system is its ability to provide feedback (response from viewers) via voice bandwidth lines. A single television channel on the cable, for example, can be time-shared among a thousand households. Provision of a fully two-way system requires only a minor perturbation of the one-way system, as the bandwidth for reply is small. Thus the added complexity is small and the added cost is minimal, if the reply bandwidth is furnished in the original installation.

This feedback capability could be used for many purposes. The total number of bits (see below) needed for identification and response need be only about ten to thirteen per household. A lecturer could determine whether his listeners were following him by periodically asking a question and having viewers press the answer button. A computer could read each viewer's reply and display the results in front of the lecturer. Such feedback also makes feasible a television shopping service and polling or voting from the home.

Current cables permit 20 channels of high-quality color television per cable. Typical installation charges run from $10 to $50, with monthly charges thereafter of about $5. According to National Community Television Association, Inc., toward the end of 1968, about 2,300 cable television systems were in operation with 3 million subscribers, representing about 6 percent of the 60 million households in the United States.

Videophone

Although switched[7] audiovisual systems have been in use for some thirty years (one was operated by the German post office between centers in four cities in 1935–1938), general switched systems have been available commercially only in the last few years. To date, the videophone systems in operation are only experimental. The most recent offering from Bell Telephone Laboratories is Picturephone® , a monochrome, thirty-frames-per-second system with a 5 by 5 ½ in. screen. Because its scanning is slower than that of conventional television, the picture is of lower quality. It has a "zoom" lens that can focus at distances of three to twenty feet; the latter allows showing blackboard drawings and groups of people.

While Picturephone has obvious advantages over the ordinary

telephone, it will be expensive—50 to 100 dollars just for the
fixed monthly minimum charge in addition to usage charges.
Although this may not deter commercial use, the consumer
market is likely to be small. Many in AT&T believe the service
will expand rapidly, to perhaps a million Picturephone sets in
service by 1980. For comparison, note that this is about 1 percent of the 109 million telephone sets now in service. Even this
small a penetration of the market would require an investment
of $6 billion to $10 billion, and thus would be significant compared with AT&T's $40-billion investment in current physical
plant. If penetration over the next twenty to thirty years were to
reach 10 percent of that of the telephone, the investment would
be roughly equal to the total telephone plant investment in that
period. At present, Picturephone uses a 1-MHz bandwidth
analogue signal between the subscriber and the central office,
that is, the local loop. For long-distance transmission with negligible degradation of signal quality, this signal is converted to
digital form and transmitted over a long-haul digital trunk (see
below).

Finally, someone with a Picturephone can only call someone
else with a Picturephone. Although Picturephone has genuine
utility for communication, it may, like corporate jets and computers, become a status symbol and initially be adopted even
where uneconomical.[8]

Long-Range Facsimile

The ability to send printed or written materials from one place
to another in a few minutes is important in some governmental,
business, professional, and scientific situations. To do this, one
can use either teletype, in which the document is retyped as it is
being sent, or facsimile, which transmits a photocopy. Although teletype is much cheaper, it cannot be used for drawings
or materials whose original format must be preserved. The
future of long-range facsimile service depends primarily on lowering costs. Facsimile is now transmitted over the regular telephone line, a system ill adapted to the needs of facsimile. In the
future, a digital, broadband system with electronic switching
(see below), will make facsimile transmission much more efficient.

When facsimile distribution of newspapers will become feasible is difficult to predict, but in Japan the newspaper *Asahi Shimbun* has been licensed to transmit a facsimile newspaper into homes for an experimental period. The facsimile receiving set to be used by *Asahi* subscribers is reported to be able to reproduce in six minutes a newspaper page 12½ by 18 in. on both sides of a sheet of electrostatic recording paper. *Asahi Shimbun* has stated that the facsimile receiving sets could be mass-produced for $300.

In conjunction with satellite or cable transmission, a facsimile mail system could transmit high-priority mail instantaneously from one point on the earth's surface to another, a service that could be attractive even in an era of supersonic air transport. A worldwide system would, of course, require cooperation among the post office organizations of the countries involved.

Digitalization and Switching

Engineers increasingly believe that telephone facilites should be changed from an analogue to a digital form of transmission. This means that the sound of the voice, now transmitted through continuous electrical pulses generated by the mechanical effects of sound (analogue signals), would be transmitted instead by discrete binary signals, that is, signals composed of "bits," which represent a choice between two alternatives, such as 1 or 0, "yes" or "no," and so on. (From these digital bits much more complicated signals can be constructed.) The rationale for advocating this change is fivefold: (1) digital signals are required in order to take maximum advantage of large-scale integration technology; (2) many of the kinds of signals that one would want to transmit would be digital anyway, since many devices that can be hooked to telephone systems (for example, computers) now work on a digital principle; (3) an analogue signal can be converted to a digital signal and transmitted with as little error as one desires; (4) a digital signal can much more easily be scrambled to ensure privacy; and (5) data transmission traffic is such that telephone systems may soon be swamped. A digitalized telephone system has an advantage in being able to compress information and send it in a fraction of the time it would take to send an analogue signal.

No less important than transmission of signals is switching, that is, the routing of signal traffic among a multitude of possible destinations. Digitalization offers the potential of vastly improved switching, including making switching completely electronic. Most telephone switching is now electromechanical, that is, mechanical switches have to close before the circuit can be completed, even though the switches are electronically activated.

With computers taking over the job of switching, it is natural for the same computer to serve both as a data-processing machine and as a message-switching machine. If required, the computer can store and forward messages according to established priorities. Utilizing either telephone or other communication lines, computers can initiate calls and hold "conversations" with other computers, so that the distinction between data-processing machines and a communication system is somewhat blurred. The computers of a data-processing center that services many different subscribers are at the same time message-switching and message-forwarding machines as well as data-processing instruments.

Communication Satellites

In the early 1960s it appeared that satellite systems would be quite costly in the foreseeable future and therefore attractive only for long-distance transoceanic traffic. Pessimism arose primarily from the belief that any system technically feasible in the near future would have to be of the "random orbiting" variety, that is, having a large number of satellites, each orbiting several hundred miles above the earth and requiring perhaps ninety minutes to make a complete revolution. Such a system would also require transmitting and receiving ground stations with large and expensive tracking antennas in order to follow a particular satellite, employ it as a communications relay to other stations also visible to that same satellite, and then transfer to another satellite coming into view as the previous one drops below the horizon. Thus, with a sufficiently large number of satellites in the system, any ground station would be within sight of at least one satellite at all times.

The success of the second Syncom, launched in July 1963, demonstrated the feasibility of a much more attractive system, one operating in "synchronous orbit." For this system, the satellite is placed at an altitude of about 22,000 miles above the earth's equator and its position is made virtually stationary with respect to any given point on earth. Not only does this permit a great reduction in the number of satellites required for basic global coverage (only three properly placed satellites are needed), but also elimination of the continuous tracking requirement permits use of less elaborate and less costly ground stations.

Satellites of the sort now being employed suffer a severe handicap in that their output of electrical energy is very small—the equivalent of two or three lightbulbs! It is easy to understand why large and complex terminals on earth are required to receive, amplify, and convert into usable communications such a tiny amount of energy coming from so many thousands of miles in space. The earliest satellites scattered this energy not only over the entire face of the globe "illuminated" by the satellite, but also spilled it uselessly in many directions into the vast regions of space. Fortunately, satellite antennas are being perfected to concentrate satellite energy on much smaller areas of the earth, such as western Europe and the east coast of the United States. This capability constitutes a major breakthrough because it will permit the use of much less costly earth stations. It has also greatly enhanced the feasibility of satellites for purely domestic or regional use.

In other major advances: more efficient solar cells have been designed to increase the amount of electrical power converted from the energy of the sun; improved electronics equipment has increased the efficiency of converting this electrical energy into usable communication capacity; and more powerful rocket boosters make possible the orbiting of the progressively larger and heavier satellites. Use of synchronous orbits, directive satellite antennas, and other improvements have dramatically reduced the cost per circuit, as shown below. The orbital weight of the Early Bird satellite was less than 100 pounds, and the satellite scattered its energy not only toward the earth but into space as well, and has a per-year circuit cost of $15,300. Intelsat III, by comparison, weighs a little more than 300 pounds, has a directive beam that confines the energy to the earth, and has a per-year circuit cost of about $1,450. Intelsat IV, still a few years from launching, will weigh about 1200 pounds, will have antennas to confine much of its energy to smaller regions of the earth, and will have a cost of about $500 per year per circuit. The accompanying table, based on Comsat figures, depicts these developments over the several Intelsat models.

Satellite	Year of first use	Number of voice-grade, two-way telephone circuits	Investment cost (US$) per circuit per year
Early Bird (Intelsat I)	1965	240	15,300
Intelsat II	1966	240	8,400
Intelsat III	1968	1,200	1,450
Intelsat IV	1971	6,000	500

Along with these technological advances, a global management consortium, INTELSAT, has had remarkable success in bringing together numerous countries to share the use of these satellites. Each country participates in ownership of the satellites in orbit—the "space" segment—roughly in proportion to each country's relative use, and each finances and maintains its own ground stations (shared in some cases with neighboring countries). As of 1969, more than sixty countries were members of INTELSAT; by the end of 1969 more than forty earth stations were in operation or under construction.

With these technological advances, combined with the success of INTELSAT, satellite traffic is experiencing rapid growth. In the three-year period from 1966 to 1969, the number of hours of satellite television transmission across the Atlantic grew from 66 to 666, and the number of voice and telegraph circuits rose from 63 to 941.

The utilization of satellites will depend in part on their relation to more comprehensive communication systems. Should satellites be used mainly for international telephone and television transmission? Should they be used for domestic telephone and television communication? If they are used for domestic television, should they be used to interconnect cable television systems, or to broadcast directly?

Let us look at the last of these questions first. If cable television achieves much of its potential and if satellites are used to connect cable television networks, why is there any interest in direct-broadcast satellites?

Even if cable television systems interconnected by satellite reached all households with television sets, they still would not reach those individuals who are mobile and those who are outdoors, for example, at the beach or camping. (Some, of course, would consider this an advantage.) Terrestrial television broadcast generally does not provide a good signal to such groups, nor could it be expected to do so economically. A broadcast satellite could reach just about everyone everywhere and perhaps could do so economically. In any case, of more importance than reaching mobile vacationers is reaching rural residents. If cables provide large numbers of channels combined with high-quality signals to much of the urban population, the provision of an analogous service for the remainder of the population will become important. In time, this latter purpose may be the primary justification for a domestic direct-broadcast satellite. Terrestrial broadcasting may interfere with direct satellite broadcasting, but this problem may be solved through the use of special techniques.

The use of satellites for international connections is attractive because of the low cost per circuit of satellites as compared with that of long submarine cables. Although satellites have a short life, on the order of a few years, and have a tendency to cease functioning suddenly, short satellite lifetimes of between five and ten years are not entirely a disadvantage, as the satellites can be amortized quickly and replaced by more modern equipment. Current regulations force satellites to split their business with cables. Recent heavy investment in the latter is thus being protected against satellite competition.

Whether satellites will be used for domestic interconnection depends to a large degree on economies of scale that future systems are likely to achieve. Satellites have to be compared with terrestrial microwave and cables as a way of getting messages and broadcasts from one place to another. The most likely use of U.S. domestic satellites in the near future may be for the distribution of network television (as in the USSR and in the Canadian system now under construction) and for emergency replacement of analogue and digital traffic made inoperative by outages or overloads of terrestrial facilites. One of its most important eventual uses, however, may be to interconnect the thousands of cable television systems and thus to provide a number of networks.

Ultramicrofiche

Ultramicrofiche (UMF) is a microform-printing process that allows as many as thirty-two hundred 8½ by 11 in. pages to be put on a 4 by 6 in. card, usually transparent.[9] These cards (fiche) are inserted in a reader, which projects the page to slightly greater than normal size on a screen. The fiche is durable and rigid, being laminated, and is inexpensive (royalties ignored) when compared with the books the fiche contains. UMF offers an effective way to miniaturize libraries. A library of one hundred thousand volumes on UMF has the cubic content of about three filing cases.

The special readers that UMF requires are expected to cost somewhat more than five hundred dollars in large-quantity orders. Some readers are portable (about the size of an attaché case) and permit rapid positioning to the desired material. It is likely that costs will drop considerably in the future, just as the costs of microfiche readers are dropping. The U.S. Office of Education, which supplies some six million microfiche of research documents annually, is financing a project to develop a portable, low-cost microfiche reader.

Commercially produced collections of ultramicrofiche libraries are already being advertised. The first Encyclopaedia Britannica collection, comprising twenty thousand volumes, is to be available in 1970. It will include only material on which there is no copyright problem, either because it is too old for copyright to apply or has been especially developed by Encyclopaedia Britannica. Other collections are planned. National Cash Register is advertising several collections in the social sciences, humanities, physical sciences, and various professional fields.

Competing modes of reproducing the printed page are being developed. The Columbia Broadcasting System has announced the development, in conjunction with a number of European enterprises, of a film cartridge with micro-images, which, when connected with a home television set, will make about five hundred books with an average length of fifty thousand words, available in a single cartridge of film tentatively priced at fifty dollars. (The CBS statement did not refer to copyright questions.)

Micro-images are of interest not only for the reproduction of books. Combined with high-speed retrieval and display instruments, they enable enormous savings in storage for business, governmental, professional, and scientific documents.

The reduction of material to such small dimensions also has important implications for information transmission and transportation. Images can be transmitted to distant screens if desired and a hard-copy version produced. But when data can be reduced to so compact a form, such cheap, old-fashioned modes of transmittal as air mail and messenger boy take on new interest.

SOCIAL EFFECTS
Education

The school and the teacher, and, through the teacher, books, have been the principal means for the young to acquire knowledge and cognitive skills such as arithmetic and reading. The advent of electronic communications (radio, television), especially as supplemented by satellite and cable transmission, has added new sources to these traditional ones. Nonetheless, the one-way character of mass communication makes it more suitable for assimilation of information than for learning that requires performance. If and when two-way communication with computers is available in the home, the school no longer will have a monopoly on instruction in cognitive skills. To be sure, the school also will use computers, but computer-assisted instruction will not be confined to the schoolroom.

In the meantime, the contribution of children to adult activities has been reduced as the child's labor and as economic activities generally in the home have declined. At the same time, the teaching of nonacademic tasks (for example, driving a car) and the process of socialization have increasingly been transferred from the home to the peer group and the school. Just as children have become less important for many adult activities, so adults have lost some importance for children. In part this is a result of communication technology, principally television, which has subtracted some of the child's time from other activities, such as interaction with other persons, especially adults.[10]

Reduction of interaction between the child and adults is not necessarily bad. This depends on the relative quality of the socialization that replaces the missing parental influence. Replacement appears to be principally through peer socialization in the school and outside.

One consequence of the changes in communication technology may be that schools and other formal institutions will provide more and more nonacademic training and less and less traditional academic instruction. Schools certainly will remain necessary for setting standards and motivating children to seek out information or to learn certain skills; but the explicit teaching function of the school—at least of the teacher—in the traditional academic subjects may be reduced. The balance between school and other environments in fulfilling this function will in part depend on how barren or rich the child's nonschool environment is.

One of the most problematic aspects of growing up for many adolescents today is entrance into a productive adult role. The family's ability to help in the transition has declined, and the school's has not correspondingly increased. The school very likely will become increasingly involved in guidance and counseling, and this may depend greatly upon electronic means. Even today, schools that have adopted flexible scheduling of the school's activites have ordinarily found it necessary to use computer scheduling. As the school's activites and student choices increase, this dependence also will rise. Simulation and games, some of which are likely to be computer-based, may be developed to help adolescents choose a career, train for management positions, and perform other adult roles. Both information and cognitive skills may be learned as by-products of this performance training. The principal function of the schools will be not to provide the information, but to organize and manage "the games," to furnish, in effect, the settings in which performance learning will take place.

The school likely will offer more work-study programs, community projects, and action programs. As it encompasses more of the child's socialization, the school (or some other formal organization) will become more nearly a community, with members in responsible interaction with each other, in contrast to the type of adolescent community (now found in many secondary schools) that is purely informal, has few collective goals, and thus has few norms by which to induce personal responsiblity. Socialization in these schools consequently is based on continuous social competition for position, which may undermine rather than develop a sense of responsibility. The emergence of schools that will develop a sense of responsibility is not at all apparent at present, and it may well be that they will not evolve in this direction. Nonetheless, the ability of future communication devices in the home to provide some of the services now performed by teachers in the schoolroom suggests that the school will have more time available to undertake the child's socialization. If it does not do so, both the school and the nonschool environment may undergo stress as the latter becomes less and less able to fulfill the socialization function.

The availability in the home and school of, say, eighty cable television channels, satellite-cable connections, and direct broadcasting from satellites could reduce dependence on a physically present instructor. Introduction of the computer to instruct but more especially to drill, correct, and examine would reduce this dependence even further. Technical capability does not by itself guarentee application. However, the incentives for industrial and commercial enterprises to promote new devices and services virtually ensure that they are not overlooked. Indeed, a premature or misguided application of them may be stimulated, especially in fields such as education, where political influence is not unimportant and where the value of alternative expenditures is not easily established. Professional educational interests also are affected by the new possibilities, and may be expected to influence the pace and the direction of developments. A further incentive for the introduction of such innovations would be the hope of mitigating the effects of teacher shortages (both numerical and qualitative) and rising costs of education.

In the short run, cost considerations may dampen enthusiasm for television- and computer-assisted instruction and favor instead the educational uses of radio. Compared with television, radio conserves bandwidth, and its dollar costs are a fraction of television costs. In addition, radio more effectively uses scarce talent for the preparation of good educational programs. Finally, in a number of educational uses, radio seems to have as great instructional effectiveness as television.[11] But all these comparisons, especially the last, need additional research, as indeed do so many other questions in education that take on new dimensions in the context of electronically assisted education.

The computer, cable television, and satellites will combine to make education a more continuous process than it is now. Changing technology and rapid advances in science indicate the need for continuing adult education for all levels of workers, managers, and professionals. The computer, probably the most flexible tool ever invented by man, has especially increased the need for individuals who can accept a high degree of change in their way of life. Fortunately, man is the most flexible and re-programmable of the animals; and fortunately too, as communication technology creates a need for retraining, it also provides at the same time new ways of doing it. One illustration of a process that no doubt will become widespread is the Medical Television Network in California, which provides professional television programs for doctors and nurses.[12]

The future availability of, say, eighty cable television channels and radio in the ghetto could compensate in homes and schools for teacher shortages and inadequate educational investments. Adult education also would benefit. Many people now on welfare are given the choice of staying at home to take care of children or working at jobs for low pay and paying a baby-sitter to take care of children. Multiple-channel cable television would allow them to train while at home for better jobs. Under these conditions, welfare schemes might be able to develop incentives for self-education.

More attention has been devoted to the potential benefits of communication technology for less developed countries than for underprivileged areas in the United States. The use of educational television (and radio via satellites for adults and school children in foreign rural villages) has been much discussed. Educational television has been used to good effect in Colombia, American Samoa, and India. A new program for India involving direct television broadcasting to village receiving stations is planned for 1972 and is based on technical improvements that will permit the village stations to be equipped at an estimated cost of five hundred dollars or possibly less for the quantities expected to be produced.

Although it seems almost certain that such programs will spread to many parts of the world and will have considerable impact on children's education and on community life, this will not be without difficulties and perhaps setbacks. Serious problems arise in the use of television that have less to do with the use of satellites than with the supporting ground facilities. Personnel must be trained and motivated to use television properly. Equipment must be properly installed and maintained. Financial support must be forthcoming from a variety of governmental bureaus that often have little effective liaison. And, of course, the programs themselves must be produced. Were the countries involved willing to cooperate in the task of educational programming, the preparation of suitable programs might be a relatively minor problem. In fact, most countries hesitate to employ educational programs produced elsewhere. They want to maintain complete control over what is shown to their own students, and this requires them to bear the full burden of its cost. Investigation might provide means to overcome these resistances.

Bringing educational television into the village square and the village school will not, of course, spare less developed countries with only primitive educational facilities the expenditures to encourage students to stay in school by providing schoolrooms, transportation, meals, and other services as well as educational programs. It is desirable to remind ourselves that television can furnish only a part of the total educational effort.

The satellite, cable television, and the computer are not the only communication devices important for education. At higher educational levels and for the general public, the availability of ultramicrofiche libraries and readers can make general and specialized reading materials far more accessible. Just as microfilm has enabled scholars to read manuscripts held in distant libraries, so microfiche can bring entire libraries of a hundred thousand or a million volumes to places with limited library resources. Such a development illustrates the decreasing dependence of persons on the facilities of a particular location. Just as a student may, through satellite and cable television, receive instruction from educators in any part of the world rather than simply from "his" university, so the reader is released from dependence on local library resources or the need to travel to libraries in distant places. The student equipped with a personal, portable reader or with one accessible in his dormitory or library could be given with his course registration one, two, or three microfiche that would contain a large part of his course reading material. The easy availability of this material conceivably might induce a greater interest in humanistic and scientific literature than does a queue in the university library.

Political Behavior

As communications improve, so do the conditions for both centralization and decentralization of administration over larger areas. Although the command and control capabilities of current communications have reached the point where virtually a state of any geographical size under any political system may be at least technologically feasible, it is another matter whether this is true for any population size. As population increases, the "choreography" needed to coordinate a given level of freedom of choice seems to increase exponentially. This means that as population grows, the information and communication requirements for maintaining a given level of freedom (for most acceptable definitions of freedom) may increase as rapidly as or perhaps more rapidly than improvements in communication technology. Without modern communication technology, it no longer would be feasible to contemplate the success of political systems involving a large amount of decentralized free choice.

As computer networks and "time-sharing for the masses" grow, it will be possible to organize political districts on other than geographical lines. It may be possible to have an even more pluralistic society than we do now, with each individual participating in many roles and associations.

Of more immediate interest is the relation of communication technology to the voting system and the electoral process. Computerized voting systems already exist, as does the possibility of cheating in computerized vote counting. The danger of this is made all the greater by irresponsible statements of technicians in the computer companies who dismiss these dangers, perhaps because they interfere with the sale of computerized systems.[13]

An immediate improvement could be effected in computerized voting by standardizing voting machinery over the whole country, and by introducing an easy way to split one's ticket. Undoubtedly, many biases, attributable to differences in voting machines and listing procedures, currently affect voting results from state to state and from municipality to municipality.

The future availability of a cable television feedback channel in individual homes or on neighborhood computer consoles will facilitate holding "instant referenda." Complicated preferential voting schemes also will be technically feasible. In countries like France and Israel, with many parties and frequent runoff voting, the politically useful period of bargaining that takes place after an indecisive first round may be abolished in favor of an almost immediate second round or in favor of various complicated preferential voting schemes.

In many societies there are voters who take politics seriously, are fairly well informed, and have a clear position on a number of political questions. They are to some extent analogous to the intelligent buyer in economic theory. They have well-formed preferences and are well informed about available choices. Although the degree of influence of this class of voters is not at all clearly established, what influence it has probably depends on time lags in the political system that allow its influence a chance to operate on other sectors of the society. Communication technology may soon make it possible to shorten or eliminate time lags in the political process. Unless precautions are taken, this might reduce the amount of political discussion and the influence of thoughtful people over the more volatile sectors of the public.

There is a growing trend among candidates for political office to use sophisticated techniques to determine what image will best appeal to a given section of the electorate. Most candidates feel that general appeals are not likely to be persuasive in urban areas of great social diversity. To many candidates, the task of communicating with this electorate seems very difficult indeed. Campaigning today increasingly focuses on groups that might prove crucial to the candidate's victory. Census data, past election behavior, public opinion research, and a wealth of semipublic personal data (such as credit ratings, credit cards, magazine subscriptions, drivers' licenses, and housing) have been computerized for many electoral districts. By applying this information intelligently, candidates can use a variety of media to make specialized appeals that emphasize those aspects of a candidate's image that each target group is likely to find most attractive and persuasive.

The current art of computerizing personal data for political appeals focuses on two techniques, each involving different media. The first technique combines the use of computers and available data about the electorate with information obtained from advertising agencies about the television-channel and radio-station preferences of the various ethnic, education-income, and occupation groups in a given area.

The second strategy uses computerized personal data to generate a set of tapes, each of which contains a list of names selected according to some mix of variables. For example, one might isolate by name all the people in Los Angeles who subscribe to The New Republic, earn more than fifteen thousand dollars annually, and have a Diners Club credit card.[14] If some aspect of a candidate is believed attractive to such people or if a credible appeal can be created for the group, the candidate can write a letter for this type of person and send copies to all of them living in the Los Angeles area. The number of different letters and hence the number of different name tapes that will be generated will depend, of course, on the candidate's awareness of the different types of groups and of the appropriate political appeals for each. (Naturally, one has to be careful about sending contradictory types of letters to the same person.) An impression of personalization can be conveyed by having the computer printer insert the recipient's name in his copy of the form letter.

In the future, as cable television channels become more specialized, it will be possible to use different appeals to different channels, each appeal designed with a particular audience in mind. This might prove considerably more effective than the broadly based and vague appeals often necessary when addressing present television audiences.

Campaign strategists argue that the use of data banks in conjunction with different media allows politicians to return to the more personal communication with their constituents of earlier times. This may be true in one sense, but is inaccurate in another. The data bank does lead campaign managers to focus on the differences among groups in the population and to evaluate their relevance for elections. Perhaps politicians now have a more accurate view of the electorate and of policy options. However, no personal contact is involved in the use of data banks and the mass media. Feedback occurs only in a very gross, if definite, form: votes.

Computerization of data and its linkage to the mass media

have increased the cost of election campaigning. No serious candidate in an urban contest can forego the use of data banks and mass-media appeals, as the competitive advantage to the opponent would be too great. Yet the cost of these techniques is truly staggering to anyone without access to the type of financing usually asociated with major business investments.[15] These high costs may make candidates more responsive to their backers, even though much of the money is spent to create the illusion of close communication with and responsiveness to the voters rather than to special interests.

It is wrong, however, to represent the new technology as primarily a force for evil. The availability of multichannel cable television and later mass access to data banks hold the possibility of a better-informed electorate. However, the local programming that multichannel cable television makes possible requires not only the technological capability but also the interest and desire of local groups to create the programs and maintain standards. Similarly, future access to politically useful data banks will not be of service unless the files of the data bank have been stocked by nonpartisan or multipartisan personnel and unless incentives and capabilities exist for their use.

Multichannel television and data bank access will allow greater attention to be paid to local or other narrowly restricted interests. Satellite relays and direct broadcasts from satellites will, on the other hand, provide the means to reach broader and more distant audiences. Already, because of the transistor radio, many peasants throughout the world know more about world or national politics than they do about political events in their own immediate district.

The inexpensiveness, sturdiness, and portability of the transistor radio make it attractive to populations whose only prior contact with radio was a loudspeaker wired to a radio in some prominent local place. To the greater privacy of listening made possible by the transistor radio has been added a greater choice of programs as a result of an increase in the number of transmitters, which makes jamming and other forms of censorship more difficult. Radio range now can be measured in thousands of miles, whereas the range of television broadcasting is only in tens of miles. Broadcast satellites sending television signals directly to home receivers (and not to a local relay broadcasting

station) will provide television broadcasting that is more difficult to censor.

The increasing speed with which the mass media disseminate
news often means that information reaches the general public
and political leaders at the same time. The latter thus can be
questioned about, or asked to act upon, information that has
just reached them, or, in some cases, may not yet have reached
them. On the other hand, the new communication technology
enables political leaders and administrators to react faster to a
crisis. Groups can confer more quickly if they need only get to a
special "secured" telephone than if they have to go to Washington. The time required to contact a person will decrease with
advanced paging systems, that is, through pocket devices. Of
course, it is not only crises that require consultation among political leaders and officials. The Metropolitan Regional Council
of New York is currently trying to establish a two-way closed-
circuit microwave system to connect twenty-seven urban and
suburban municipalities. This television network would enable
local, state, and federal officials of the region to meet regularly,
without traveling, to discuss regional problems.

Consultation with those who serve them is important for
higher bureaucratic officials, but the pressure of time, the an-
noyance of travel, and the restricted access of different bureaucratic levels to each other make such consultation difficult.
Future communication systems, especially the television screen,
will make it easier for those at the top to confer with their aides
and with those whom they otherwise might not see. Here, as in
many spheres, technological possibilities have to be coupled
with appropriate organizational design and incentives.

Crime, Security, and Privacy

Considerable attention has been devoted to the use of new electronic and communication devices to combat crime and less to
the opportunities these advances have created for new crimes or
new methods of committing old crimes. We have already noted
above the possibility of manipulating computerized systems for
counting votes. In January 1969 the Department of Justice con-
fiscated shipments from Las Vegas to Haiti of electronic equipment designed for a different form of cheating, remote radio
controls for roulette and other gambling equipment that permit

the gaming table to "do everything but reach into the player's pocket and remove his money." A witness has testified before the New York State Joint Legislative Committee on Crime that criminal elements operating on Wall Street were recruiting better-educated people who knew "how to steal with an I.B.M. machine." The use of time-shared computers by corporations and other entities raises questions of improper access to important corporate information by criminal elements or by competitors (the two categories are, of course, not mutually exclusive). The availability of so much information in so compact a form and the possibility of altering operations on them raise similar questions, even where the information is processed on an enterprise's own computer equipment. Code systems have been devised that restrict access to computer data and computer operations to persons possessing the requisite code. These codes have been further differentiated to permit different persons access to different parts of the data system and computer operations. Although computer companies and service centers sound confident about the ability of their systems to maintain confidentiality, it is by no means clear that current schemes provide adequate protection. And probably it will not be clear until we have a better picture of the types of crimes and the size of gains that unauthorized access to computer systems will permit. Unauthorized access can be made not only at the computer system proper but also at transmission lines along which computer or other data are transmitted. Scrambling and descrambling as currently practiced are not necessarily adequate protection. Safeguards against unauthorized tampering with computer operations and communication lines, if at all feasible, may require physical redesign of these systems and not simply software and other subsequent security measures.

Enthusiasts for the "cashless and checkless society" of the future seem equally confident that the individual's code for receiving and making payments via computers can be maintained inviolate. Of course, a system of computerized transactions in place of currency and checks (and perhaps bonds and stocks) need not be perfectly secure to work. The counterfeiting of currency and stock shares and the forging of checks today may be a greater source of loss than future criminal penetration of computer transactions.[16] It is difficult to devise entirely new crimes, but the centralization of records and fiscal operations and the possibility of easier concealment of criminal activity may in the future increase the scale of crimes and also the safety of some types of criminal activity.

The new electronic equipment has indeed served to fight crime. The greater speed of police and private reaction to an actual or potential crime, the instant availability of large bodies of data, and the increased possibilities of surveillance of public and private places probably will make some types of criminal activity more hazardous.

The FBI maintains a large fingerprint data bank that is accessible by telecommunications all over the country. Several states have developed or are developing similar data banks. A police agency can send a facsimile of a fingerprint to the central data file in less than a minute. Thus, a person stopped for speeding may be discovered to be wanted on a felony charge. For most practical purposes, monitoring systems combined with data banks could at some point in the future do away with anonymity. A national identification system similar to that used by some European countries, coupled with a computerized data bank, would facilitate surveillance of criminals—or anyone else.

Many commercial firms use to monitor checks a computerized system that is so fast that forgers are caught while trying to cash their checks. Gas station attendants in some parts of the country are now able to make an instant check on credit cards presented to them and determine whether the card has been stolen or whether its owner is delinquent.[17]

The New York State Intelligence and Identification System (NYSIIS) data bank is a significant innovation. It unites the information possessed by the various law enforcement agencies, such as the police, the courts, penal institutions, and parole boards. Information is safeguarded to the extent that an agency furnishing information can specify the agencies that may have access to it. The NYSIIS facilities for telecommunications provide various degrees of security, depending on the sensitivity of the information being conveyed.

Although instant identification systems will make it easier to apprehend criminals, mistakes in the system could lead to false arrests and embarassments. Many feel that records of arrests not ending in convictions should be dropped from the files that will be transmitted to, for instance, the civil services in regard to job applications. Safeguards are also necessary to ensure that statistical data systems are not used as intelligence systems, either by officials or by others who might seek access to government records.

It is reasonable to expect an increase in the surveillance of public places. Television cameras commonly are seen surveying activities in industrial plants, banks, and high-traffic stores, and undoubtedly such monitoring will be extended to a variety of public places. The police, for instance, may wish to survey street corners, parks, or other areas. Traffic surveillance through radar already has become routine. Data banks have been used in conjunction with license plate checks to provide instant identification of scofflaws. Managers of large apartment buildings and commercial establishments may wish to cover entryways, hallways, stairwells, or elevators, either to restrict access by "undesirables" or to observe the conduct of employees or residents for various purposes.

Surveillance as an anticrime measure is likely to increase the invasion of privacy and erosion of anonymity already threatened by other developments. Communication technology obviously makes access to private information easier. Sensor technology already has had a major impact on privacy and security. A "shotgun" microphone can pick up conversations several hundred feet away. Conversations in a room can be picked up from outside through sound vibrations from the window panes. There are myriad ways to "bug" a room. Telephones can be inconspicuously turned into microphones to record nontelephonic conversations occurring in the same room.

Governments, the police, and private organizations in the near future will have heightened information-gathering abilities, both to query records about individuals and groups and in the range and sensitivity of their physical sensors. Having sensors available does not necessarily mean that they will be used, but surveillance abilities will be great even if sensor technology remains at the present state of the art, which is rather unlikely. Nor can private recreational snooping be precluded. The use of television and other sensors to watch the baby or the back yard or to monitor the front door has led to other uses of a less utilitarian character.

Technology now makes feasible computerized credit systems, which usually assume that a person's past behavior is the best indication of his present and future behavior. As one's past becomes accessible to others, one may be less able to disregard it, and be forced to "live it down." As credit becomes more common, so do the records of its use. These records reveal the places we stayed, things we bought, entertainment we purchased, calls we made, and so forth.

The more information accumulated, the more valuable it usually becomes. Statistical data banks developed by the government pose important questions. The proposed national data bank for the Bureau of the Census has become the subject of controversy over what will go into it and who will have access to it. The proposed system will combine into a single store information from the twenty governmental agencies that now maintain large data banks. At present there is a regulation that all governmental agency data must be computer-compatible, so some coordination already exists. A national data bank may be of great use to social scientists and to the government, and it would permit large savings by eliminating costly duplication. However, although designed for statistical studies, it may be difficult to exclude its use as an intelligence system by overzealous officials and unauthorized private persons who may or may not have criminal intentions. Credit bureau and police intelligence data banks raise similar questions. To be sure, the latter can, for example, be used to justify "instant bail," in cases where a suspect is apprehended and his data file indicates he can be released on his own recognizance. But they can also be used for questionable purposes.

Heretofore, public and private spying has been limited by personnel costs; a few agents or persons cannot watch everything. The computer, however, can monitor a great number of sensors simultaneously and therefore economically. Depending on how sophisticated its recognition abilities are (and these will become increasingly more acute), the computer can be programmed to select objects, words, and actions that are of interest to the programmer. Car license plates are an elementary example. The computer can record location and other data for selected license numbers and alert the human monitors.

Different temperaments view these developments differently; probably it will take considerable analysis and finally experience to judge more accurately whether the optimists or the alarmists have the better case.

Economic Life

Developments in communication technology can be expected to have a great effect both on business organization and operations and on consumer shopping practices. Changes in business are already occurring and no doubt will proceed more rapidly than will those in consumer behavior. The latter requires the spread of communication devices on a scale that is not likely to occur for a number of years.

Business Organization. Many scenarios of the future envisage businessmen inundated by information. It is more likely, however, that executives, at least, will get less raw data and more information in useful summary form. This information will be available not only in the familiar computer print-out but also in a number of computer-generated graphic displays. The significance of this for centralization or decentralization of business administration and control still is a controversial subject.

One effect of the general-purpose animal, man, working with the general-purpose machine, the computer, will be to reinforce existing tendencies for the corporation, and probably the trade union, to become multipurpose, or to extend themselves over a broader range; for example, an automobile company may become a transportation company. Contemporary management technology may encourage the entrepreneur and business manager to broaden the scope of their activity beyond what originally seemed feasible or desirable.

It is likely that communication devices soon will play an important role in reducing administrative and especially distribution costs, as they already have in reducing production costs. To be sure, the effectiveness of enthusiastically proclaimed "total management systems," made possible by computer and communication technology, will depend on intellectual advances in the construction of models relevant to corporate decision making and to an understanding of the total economy. Management is likely to develop corporation policy more self-consciously, simply because businessmen will want to derive maximum advantage from the data-storage and data-processing capabilities of the computer-communications system.

In the past, the conduct of certain business enterprises seemed to be possible only through a concentration of men and paper in the same building, in the same urban area, or in the same city. The huge office buildings with which we are familiar represent one form of this concentration. Where this concentration does not in itself provide opportunities for face-to-face contact, intercity and international travel provide businessmen and professional groups with the temporarily required degree of concentration. The larger part of airline space is occupied by business passengers. The new communication systems are likely to affect both the permanent forms of business concentration and the temporary concentrations created by travel. Videophone and switched audiovisual communication systems in general are likely to reduce the need for business and professional travel, at least where such travel is not considerably stimulated by obvious additional reasons having little to do with business or professional necessities. Videophone will not only reduce interurban and intraurban travel, it can also reduce traveling along the corridors for intraoffice business. When Westinghouse introduced Picturephones experimentally into its New York and Pittsburgh offices, it found that people used them to talk to colleagues down the hallway, as well as to more distant associates. Westinghouse and Union Carbide trials apparently indicate that Picturephone tends to restrict conversation to the immediate subject that motivated the call and reduces informal extensions of the time and subjects of conversation that occur during face-to-face office visits. Whether this is good or bad is another matter, although there is a tendency to interpret the results as an increase in efficiency.

Facsimile reproduction, ultramicrofiche, and data transmission capabilities in general will provide additional incentives for remaining where one is. These various communication systems permit quick reaction to pressing problems: conferences can be arranged with participants who are scattered about the country or the world, and relevant background information, in hard copy or visual display, can be provided to everyone within minutes. What effect this will have on the quality of rapport and thought is difficult to say, but certainly it is likely to conserve the energy and time involved in travel. Naturally, a willingness to substitute audiovisual for face-to-face communication will develop slowly until present limitations in both cost and viewing give way to the cheaper and far more adequate widescreen, color-television switched networks of the future.

It is possible, indeed likely, that the use of the new communication systems for avoiding business travel may be of secondary importance compared with their effect on the daily journey to work. And, indeed, just as airline and transportation executives are becoming sensitive to the effect communication technology may have on business and private air travel, so automobile manufacturers are already alert to the impact of communications on the journey to work, which at present is a major reason for the purchase and use of motor vehicles. For some professionals and for some businessmen, the availability of computer consoles and communication terminals in the home has already led to an increase in the amount of business transacted from the home, reducing the amount transacted from the place of business. Some businesses have provided their personnel with home terminals that permit them to transmit orders and other data to the company's computers, which then automatically prepare shipping orders, invoices, and loading instructions and record inventory changes. Sales and other personnel thus are freed from the need to return to the office to prepare written reports.

The pace of these developments will be affected by the availability of personnel to implement the array of alternative futures. Twenty years ago the computer field did not exist. Since then new jobs at all levels have been and still are being created. Some jobs have been of relatively short duration. The programmer of today is considerably different from the programmer of fifteen years ago. Keypunchers may shortly suffer technological obsolescence. Our ability to distinguish between computer personnel and communication personnel is declining. Experience of the last few years indicates that the demand has constantly outstripped the supply. The bottleneck in people may occur in completely unexpected areas. Within a few years, the lack of telephone or television engineers may slow technological applications more than will the lack of programmers.

Marketing and Shopping. In the future, marketing is likely to change in several ways. Over the near term, cable television will be the main agent of change. In a longer period, say, twenty to thirty years, it will be switched audiovisual and computer systems.

Cable television offers several possibilities. A large number of channels (say, forty to four hundred) and local programming will decrease the cost of advertising broadcasts. At the same time, it will be possible to provide for a reaction, including a signal to purchase, using the narrowband feedback link. One or more local advertising channels could be established with a regular schedule of product offerings. This would allow mutually interested advertisers and consumers a better chance of contact. There are many ways, technically, of getting a signal from the home to the advertiser to tell him which people have ordered his product. The costs of doing this are so modest that if political obstacles to such systems were removed tomorrow, within ten years there could well be a great change in advertising and shopping practices.[18] In any event, business and institutional buyers are likely to lead the way toward electronic shopping.

The truly radical innovations in marketing will come with the widespread use of switched audiovisual systems and time-shared home computer consoles. This will make possible a great deal of shopping without leaving the home. It will be possible to "videophone" a particular store, have a product displayed, and discuss its merits with the salesperson. Alternatively, one might consult the computer, which could act as a much more efficient and vastly more detailed set of "Yellow Pages." The home console could display or print out names of stores, product specifications, and other information that might be required. Various products and brands would be visually displayed for the consumer, who then could order immediately via his console or else phone a particular store for more detailed visual inspection and final purchase, which would be charged against his central, computerized bank account. It is unlikely that electronic shopping will entirely replace direct shopping, which, after all, serves purposes other than simply acquiring merchandise. Besides, buying often involves senses other than vision and hearing. Nonetheless, in the future, electronic shopping undoubtedly will make a large dent in the amount of private and public transport required for shopping, and thus will reinforce the communications-versus-transportation competition already noted in connection with business travel and the daily journey to work.

As the cost of information processing decreases and its speed increases, the consumer may have greater opportunities to obtain merchandise suited to his particular needs and specifications. The computer control of manufacturing processes makes it possible to change settings on machines without the manual adjustment of each control. Extension of this computer control to permit on-line changes in product specifications will make customized products cheaper. For some products, customization may become the rule rather than the exception.

Regulation

Regulatory problems arise in connection with two types of communication enterprises: common-carrier companies providing point-to-point communications (telephone and telegraph) and companies engaged in mass communications (radio and television broadcasting). Since communication satellites and coaxial cables can be used for both point-to-point and broadcast communications, it is increasingly difficult to keep these two types of communication services separate. Governmental regulation of communications will need to deal with entities whose communication functions are more diverse than at present. Similarly, the separation of private and common-carrier communication systems is no longer clear-cut. Private microwave systems received an important stimulus when the Federal Communications Commission ruled in the Carterfone proceedings (1968) that "foreign attachments" to telephones were permissible, thus facilitating the tie-in of private microwave systems to common-carrier telephone lines.

Spectrum Allocation. One of the most serious regulatory problems at present concerns the allocation of the electromagnetic spectrum, which is becoming very crowded in some urban areas. The UHF portion of the spectrum is useful for television broadcasting, landline microwave, satellite-ground communications, and mobile radio. But the UHF television broadcasting stations have made large investments in their equipment, and have been supported by the Federal Communications Commission; it may be difficult to get spectrum space now allocated to UHF television stations reallocated for other purposes. Ultimately, however, radio communication over the air may be reserved for communication with vehicles,[19] and most other transmissions may take place through cables. In the meantime, competing demands for the spectrum will continue to increase rapidly in the near future.[20]

As satellites and their capacities multiply, new spectrum allocation problems will arise, requiring international cooperation and regulation. Satellites in synchronous orbits are confined to a narrow band around the earth; two satellites employing the same radio frequency and placed too close together in the equatorial plane cannot be separated by the ground antenna beams and thus can interfere with each other. Since a minimum distance must be maintained between adjacent satellites, only a limited number of orbital positions are available around the world. As traffic expands, considerable regulation may be required.

Satellites may interfere also with terrestrial systems (for example, microwave facilities) when both systems attempt to share the same frequency. Unless satellite ground stations are properly located and shielded, or unless precautions are taken at microwave relay sites, serious interference may occur. Careful design and cooperation in the "reasonable" allocation of radio frequencies can prevent these problems from being too serious.

Costs and Rate Structures. A conflict exists between exploiting the efficiencies of large-scale systems and satisfying the specialized needs of particular countries and regions. Large reductions in cost per circuit are afforded by using satellites that have high capacities. But high capacities are, in most cases, far greater than can be fully used by single countries. The rationale for INTELSAT was to develop high-capacity systems on a global basis so that member countries could take full advantage of their economies. However, separate satellite systems are being considered to satisfy more specialized needs and to permit closer control by the particular country or regions involved. For example, satellite systems are being considered in the United States to transmit television programming from central locations to broadcasting stations around the country. Canada and Europe also have talked about such systems.[21] If they can be operated without harm to the basic global system, it is all to the good. But if domestic or regional systems grow to large proportions, they could seriously disrupt traffic for the global system, and a multitude of separate, competing satellite systems could emerge—each small, each high-cost on a per-circuit basis, and together denying the countries the efficiency of a large-scale shared operation. Clearly, international cooperation will be required if satellite technology is to be fully exploited for the public benefit.

Rate structures and regulatory principles can either encourage or discourage the development and introduction of new communication technology. It is commonly the case throughout the world today that the underlying costs of performing a given, specific communication service, such as a particular telephone call between New York and London, may bear little relation to the price paid by the person placing that particular call. The reason for this is that a "composite" price or rate structure usually is employed, which reflects the cost of both new and old technology and routes of both low-traffic density and high-traffic density. This practice arises for two principal reasons: (1) When a particular telephone call is routed between two points, it may use a variety of old and new faciles and the particular route may depend on a number of random factors. For example, a call between New York and London might go over either cable or satellite and, if over cable, over either the very newest or the one laid in 1956. It is generally argued that the cost of placing the telephone call ought to reflect an average of all of the costs of the whole network and mix of facilities. (2) It is widely held that certain services ought to subsidize others in the interests of the general welfare. Revenues from high-density urban traffic sometimes are used to help support the less profitable rural routes in the interest of developing a broad, nationwide communication network. Similarly, profits from international traffic sometimes help to support domestic services. Composite pricing and subsidization will continue to be major elements in cost policy in the communication field. Nevertheless, it may be possible in the future to relate prices more closely to specific costs in order to enable new technologies to reap greater benefit from their cost savings and thus promote their development and use more effectively.

Cable Television. Cable television involves a host of regulatory problems. At present the most controversial is cable television's actual and potential competition with terrestrial broadcast television, especially UHF. Because cable television re-sends signals that are copyrighted, but is not required to pay copyright royalties (see below), the cable television importation of signals into an area well served by local broadcasting stations can provide "unfair" competition. As one response to this threat, the FCC has generally not permitted cable television systems to bring distant television signals into the largest one hundred metropolitan areas (where more than eighty percent of the population live). However, a preliminary vote by the FCC in May 1970 seems to presage more or less unlimited importation of out-of-town programs in cable television systems.[22] The present television industry is threatened also by the desire of the cable companies to originate television programs over their own cable systems and by attempts to promote pay-television. One response to the problem of cable competition might be to make the cable system a common carrier, open to anyone willing to buy time and including special provisions for educational and public-service broadcasting.

Changes are occurring so rapidly in cable television technology that a certain amount of regulation of or perhaps cooperation among involved parties will be needed to prevent wasteful developments. In two or three years a single cable television cable will be able to carry forty channels at little additional cost. In ten years or more, one hundred channels on a single cable are likely. If four of the new twenty-channel cables, together with their amplifiers, were installed in a single duct in one operation, it would be possible to have an eighty-channel television system tomorrow. Economical expansion, or even development at a much slower rate, requires planning and regulation of installations, especially underground ducts, to permit the latter to take not only television cables but also expanded underground installations for telephone, power, gas, and water. It may soon become standard practice to install underground broadband cables during the construction of new housing tracts, as in the Columbia, Maryland, development. Large economies would be possible if several cables were installed initially even though they were not used immediately.

The components of cable television systems, produced by many small firms, lack standardization, and the installation of systems often is of low quality. It is not at all clear that regulation is the solution to such problems, but efforts to prevent the hodgepodge that now exists among the twenty-three hundred cable television systems from occurring on a larger scale in the future are indicated, as some interconnecting of cable television systems is almost certain to occur.

Regulation of Computer Services. The computer services—information storage, retrieval, and processing—are not now regulated. Indeed, the extraordinary development of the computer field may be the result of the absence of governmental regulation and the stimulus of a very vigorous competition. The provision of transmission services by companies that provide computer services will raise regulatory problems in the computer field. The lack of adequate data transmission facilities may soon become a serious bottleneck in national data processing. Since the needs of data processors, who now use telephone lines, are significantly different from those of the average telephone user, present regulatory policy already is proving inadequate. This will become increasingly the case as firms whose data needs are small operate through an inexpensive access terminal and simply lease computation from a large computer facility center.

There is a reason other than its communication services that may warrant the regulation of the computer facility center, namely, the protection of private data from eavesdropping and criminal manipulation. A first step in getting more adequate protection will be to destroy the myth that adequate protection already exists. The licensing of computer executives, programmers, repair and maintenance men, and designers responsible for computer operations may become necessary, but obviously cannot in itself guarantee the inviolacy of the computer system. Appropriate legal measures and improved basic design also will be needed to provide greater security.

Copyright. In June 1968 the U.S. Supreme Court held that cable television operators who capture television signals and transmit them by cable to subscribers are not subject to copyright liability under the law.[23]

Facsimile transmission and microform reproduction of copyrighted materials involve interesting legal questions that are not likely to be resolved until these new devices for symbol storage and transmission of printed data have become fully developed and more widely used. The U.S. Copyright Act protects the right of the copyright holder "to print, reprint, publish, copy, and vend the copyrighted work." This applies also to audiovisual materials, for example, filmstrips. The microform reproduction of copyrighted materials covers several different cases: (1) printed books in collections held by private individuals and corporations or by private and public libraries may be copied on microform (in a few or many copies), and such copies made available to the general public, and (2) copyrighted materials may be reproduced by microform for commercial sale. Either case involves a technical copyright violation, although publishers and authors tend to ignore infringements made by the single-copy, noncommercial reproduction of their materials. That publishers are indeed concerned, however, about the spread of this practice, is indicated by the following somewhat hysterical warning appearing in a 1968 book:

> All rights reserved. Except for use in a review, the reproduction or utilization of this work in any form or by any electronic, mechanical, or any other means, now known or hereafter invented, including photocopying and recording, and in any information storage and retrieval system is forbidden without the written permission of the publisher.[24]

A way may be found, under the law, to protect authors and publishers and the public interest without making the further development of microform libraries too expensive. For the time being, the complex technology involved in ultramicrofiche (UMF) and the high cost of production will probably prevent UMF piracy of copyrighted publications. If and when more accessible technology and lower costs enter the picture, the evasion of royalty payments may become a more serious issue.

One feature of microfiche development may be a renewed emphasis on the classics, where, in this context, a classic is a book whose copyright has expired.

Censorship. Any communication raises questions of possible censorship, formal or informal. The future availability of one hundred, two hundred, three hundred, or four hundred television channels will raise new questions. Many programs may be produced by local or other groups who have access to the cable system as an inexpensive public utility. Perhaps the rich variety of programs thus made possible by a super-multichannel television system will reduce problems of "equal time." Because, however, for many persons the right to say what they think does not always imply a similar privilege for those who have different views, the involvement of the public in the production or sponsorship of television programs may raise political passions difficult to regulate. Educational television may be no less controversial. Multichannel television can vastly extend opportunities in the home to study languages, pottery, plumbing, astronomy, astrology, sex technique, religion, and higher mathematics. There is no doubt that it will be possible to provide a great part of a university education and much vocational training through skillful use of the facilities that will be available in the home. But it is not clear that controversies over the content of education in schools and universities will disappear when these contents are transferred to the television screen. Nor is it certain that all groups in the society will be happy to accept increased access to television by astrologers, scientologists, and other elements of dubious repute whose ability to manipulate human apprehensions may be limited chiefly by the possible fragmentation of future television audiences rather than by the force of competing views. In any event, whether or not regulation of content occurs, it is likely that various groups in the society will seek to have such regulatory action taken.

Living

In a number of specific areas, some of which have been reviewed above, it is possible to see the blurred outlines of the impending future. It is not easy, however, to capture from them an image of what the communication revolution will mean for the character and quality of life in the 1980s, difficult in any case to envisage without considering other important changes. We know, now, much about the speed and cost of storing, transmitting, and manipulating signals; something about the increased variety of contents and applications that will be possible; but little about the quality, from various standpoints, of what will be transmitted or the human attributes or social conditions required for these contents to be effectively produced, used, and enjoyed. Some of the more enthusiastic accounts of the future tend to ignore the amount of individual determination, discipline, and energy needed to extract the projected cultural benefits from the materials that may be made available by the communication explosion.

A review of today's television fare might make the vision of a 100- or 200-channel television system paralyze all thought. There is no reason, however, for an increase in some of the parameters of a system necessarily to produce a deterioration in system outputs. In fact, an increased number of television channels implies an increased specialization of programs and consequently, for particular groups, programs of increased relevance and utility. Increased specialization also suggests that many types of talents and enthusiasms that now contribute little or nothing to television or other public programs may have greater opportunity for expression. Perhaps this will permit an increase in programs without a decrease in quality. It is true, nonetheless, that technique sometimes dominates content (as in some teacher training), and it cannot be assumed that programs for rose cultivators, chess enthusiasts, or stitchery connoisseurs will not sacrifice some substantive appeal in order to conform to prevailing habits and dicta of specialists in presentational technique.[25]

It is not clear who is going to pay for all these programs, not that future costs of production and dissemination need be very high, at least compared with present costs. The interest in who will foot the bill derives from its relevance for who will have access to and control over the television screen. Presumably, many programs with an explicit or formal educational and job-training content will be paid for by public authorities, private educational institutions, or possibly industrial and commercial groups. Popular entertainment may continue to be dominated by commercial sponsors who want to keep a name before the public, with additional commercially (or consumer) sponsored channels providing shopping or buyers' services with greater product specification and less medicine-man or soft-sell advertising. Many religious, political, hobby, and cultural programs probably will be sponsored by private groups whose resources may not have to be too great to acquire time on multichannel cable television. Any serious attempt to forecast the financial structure of cable television including pay-television, will need to consider its evolution through a number of different technological and economic stages, and also a host of political-regulatory issues. Here the point is simply to emphasize that predictions of the character and quality of future communication contents require a prior or accompanying scenario of the economic structure and regulatory practices affecting communication enterprises.

The ability to carry on an increasing amount of educational, business, and professional activity, shopping, and spectator entertainment in the home, together with lessened requirements for business travel, suggests more opportunities in the future for families to be together in the home and a decline in other kinds of togetherness. There will be some obvious sources of resistance to this development, which an affluent society may overcome in part by increasing the size of living units to provide greater privacy and by installing more television screens in the household to accommodate the multitude of choices and tastes.[26] Projections about increased family togetherness, like many other guesses based on a single dimension of change, tend to presuppose a continuation of other basic characteristics of social life. In fact, other developments, for example, increased income, greater familiarity with other parts of the world, and lessened costs of travel, might encourage family dispersal. Developments in communication technology suggest, then, not that family togetherness necessarily will increase, but simply that there will be greater incentives to conduct various activities in the home.

The ability of communication devices to lessen dependence on face-to-face relations raises questions about the losses and gains sustained thereby. Personal relations presumably still will involve direct contact, although the pen-pal may give way to the videophone-pal. The more extreme cases of substitution of machines for face-to-face contact presumably will occur not in social relations but in business and some types of professional services. In the future, economy of travel and professional time increasingly will dictate the use of computers and communication devices in place of direct contact between the professional person and client. Already, Massachusetts General Hospital in Boston has set up a "telemedicine system" with Logan Airport, which permits direct consultation over a television channel about the medical problems of airport personnel that do not warrant immediate hospitalization.

Whatever can be electronically recorded, such as pulse, EKG, blood pressure, and temperature, also can be stored and transmitted. The automation of diagnostic information will mean the storage of and rapid access to audiovisual medical records, and the ability to transmit them quickly wherever they may be needed, a great advantage in areas where only medical technicians are available. These records will also be useful in medical education, including the continuing education of physicians.

Monitoring of patients often is unsatisfactory in a large hospital, especially when there is a shortage of staff. Serious changes in a patient's condition often fail to be noticed until too late, even by the most dedicated nurses. The computer already has become an important adjunct in the collection, processing, synthesis, and display of hospital patient data, not as a substitute for medical personnel but as an amplifier of the staff's abilities.

Of course, professional services are not confined to the analysis and dispensing of technical information. The minister, the doctor, and the lawyer not only furnish advice but sustain hope and give consolation to people in personal crisis. The non-human element in the electronically aided practice of medicine indeed will deprive people of some of the psychological comforts provided by the doctor, although the popular esteem for and awe of the computer may inspire in some patients as much confidence and comfort as does the time-pressed and fallible doctor. Besides, the computer-aided doctor may be able to spend more time attending to the patient's psyche, although it is not at all clear that professional, financial, or other incentives for this will exist. In any case, telecommunications and the computer will make available to him the help of specialists and bodies of information and analysis that should improve his professional services and enable him to share with the computer the esteem of his patients.[27]

Some of the applications of communication-computer technology to professional services may be enjoyed first by low-income groups, as improved professional services for these groups might otherwise be difficult to assure. On the other hand, the home devices of the future, especially audiovisual two-way communication with home computer consoles and print-out terminals, initially will be the playthings, the status symbols, and finally the useful home appliances of the well-to-do. If having these devices in the home confers, as some believe, a marked educational, cultural, or economic benefit, then an interim advantage to the well-to-do will thereby ensue. It is difficult to predict just when these devices will be available at a price that will permit mass consumption.

There are, of course, plenty of enterprising persons eager to bring to the less educated or the more easily put-upon members of our society the benefits of computer technology by providing them with computerized horoscopes, social partners, and life mates. The breakdown of machines in these areas or the fallibility of the advice they dispense are not likely to occasion severe social crises. However, a large dependence of some social systems on computer-communication technology could lead to major difficulties in the event of electronic errors or because the human servants of the machine are not up to their jobs.

It is not clear whether a future world of time-shared computer systems will require that most individuals have a higher level of education and intelligence than today. Mass literacy was needed for the development of societies such as the United States, but perhaps a world divided between a small elite and a multitude of relatively ignorant workers is again in the making. On the one hand, chances for a genuinely literate society would appear to be improved by the developing communication systems. But the effects that an increasingly complex technology will have on requirements for and standards of individual performance are not self-evident. With improved audiovisual communications and automated correction systems, literacy may become less important for many activities. An optimistic view is that any additional sophisticated service available in the society is a gain for the individual. A pessimistic view considers the possibility that society might evolve into a situation with users on one side and system designers, producers, and manipulators on the other side. It has been said of the United States Navy Logistics System that it was a system designed by geniuses to be run by idiots. True or not, this at least succinctly states one possible form of the developer-user relationship.

The data banks and interlinked computer systems that may be used by individual householders in perhaps the next twenty years will change by orders of magnitude every few years. Human beings, on the other hand, are not going to change by orders of magnitude every few years. We already see a whole series of elaborate games called ''blame the computer'' if anything goes wrong. Often it is quite legitimate to blame the computer; often it is not.

It is by no means clear what the consequences are of supplying a greater and greater number of people with tools whose implications they scarcely understand. A communication device that does not merely transmit information, like the telephone, but is capable of manipulating information, like the computer, poses problems far more difficult than have been faced before. Many areas of apparently legitimate scientific or administrative activity may be able to flourish in an arbitrary manner, with hundreds of thousands of users all thinking that somebody else is "minding the store" at the data base. Many of them will be thinking, "There are intelligent people somewhere in the system who really understand what is going on and who have got everything arranged so that the service is just right for me." Perhaps there is an upper limit to the degree of complexity a system can tolerate before breaking down, unless the individuals operating and using it have themselves changed as much as the systems they use.

RESEARCH IMPLICATIONS

Almost every paragraph of this chapter implies or raises research problems whose character and significance, at least in broad outline, are almost self-evident. To restate these paragraphs in the form of explicit research questions is hardly necessary. The number of scientific and policy questions raised by communication developments is so great, however, that an attempt to suggest a few guidelines for research seems desirable.

Given the rate of development in the communication field, research begun now is going to be less effective in guiding policy than it might have been if begun earlier. Still, better late than never. The moral, however, is fairly clear: study of developments that may not occur in full measure for another decade or so should not be deferred. Otherwise, in five or ten years we may again regret the failure to have begun research earlier. Research planning, then, should encompass not only matters of immediate concern but problems and issues where time permits a more deliberate and longer-term study.

Important decisions on regulatory matters are now under discussion, and public and private action may be taken before the consequences of alternative steps have been adequately investigated or have penetrated public consciousness. For this reason some of these subjects deserve priority, particularly those where legislative and regulatory actions are likely to be more or less irreversible, either because of the political commitments that a decision once taken creates or because the action (or lack of it) leads to investments by private and public agencies that can be reversed later only at considerable cost. Of the host of regulatory problems already on the docket, none may be more important than the development of cable television into a common-carrier public utility and the establishment of "ground rules" for access to cable television by private commercial, private noncommercial, and public groups.

Current regulatory and legislative issues are not, of course, the only ones to which investigation should address itself as soon as possible. A number of issues need investigation precisely because they have not yet been subjected to regulatory action or debate. One such issue is safeguarding the privacy of data banks and transmission lines and preventing criminal manipulation of computer-communication systems.

This particular example illustrates very well the need, in some fields of communication research, for a combination of different skills. Regulatory and legislative safeguards of communication-computer systems can be devised and evaluated only in the context of possible design changes in computer and communication equipment, in the context of different forms of organization of the communication-computer service industries, and in the light of an imaginative construction of criminal possibilities based on a knowledge of criminal practices, corporation practices, and future computer operations and applications. The talents required include those of the computer-communication engineer, the sociologist, the economist, the lawyer, and the political scientist. Nevertheless, some issues are amenable to separate investigation, and need only a modest amount of consultation or knowledge of related facets.

It is sometimes not recognized by persons anxious to lighten the burden of the decision maker that one of the most useful forms of policy research is not devising lines of action or evaluating alternative choices but rather providing a better understanding of how the world works or is likely to work under given circumstances. Despite prejudices to the contrary, some private and public decision makers are capable of making intelligent decisions by themselves, provided specialists in the relevant sciences are able to take off enough time from their policy-advisory activities to do some research that will provide decision makers with a better understanding of the world. "Nonpolicy" research, that is, old-fashioned scientific investigation, is in some situations the most urgently needed form of policy research. Even where decisions require the delicate balancing of numerous factors and where only advanced techniques are capable of achieving a nonarbitrary result, a prior stock of theoretical and empirical knowledge is required if the decision-making techniques are not to grind on empty air. The moral of this for communication research is evident. A better understanding is needed of probable individual and group responses to a variety of hypothetical future communication situations.

There is an evident difficulty about investigating behavior in future hypothetical circumstances: the difficulty of making these studies empirical.[28] Nonetheless, in a manner of speaking, empirical investigation of the future is possible. First, some communication-computer situations of the future have analogues in the past and in the present, and second, in other cases the future situation already is present in an incipient form and thus is available for empirical study. The effects that radio and television have had on "family togetherness" are not irrelevant for understanding what is likely to happen in the years to come, although obviously studies of the past and present cannot be mechanically extrapolated to the future. Similarly, current public responses to cultural and educational television programs are not irrelevant for a better understanding of what a future communication-inspired cultural explosion might involve. This does not mean that existing research on these matters suffices for analysis of the future. Much past research may be relevant. But the main point is that with a clearly specified future hypothetical situation in mind it is possible to do new studies in the present designed specifically to exploit those aspects of the present most relevant for understanding—not the present—but the future. This will sometimes require design features at variance with usual social science research practice.

As noted above, in a number of areas the "future" is already with us. "Electronic crimes" no doubt are going to have a long and complicated history difficult now to foresee. Nonetheless such crimes already exist and their study already has provided some preview of the future. Videophones and closed circuit conference television also are in use, however limited, permitting study of some of the consequences that will not be fully evident for another decade of substituting audiovisual for face-to-face contact. Similarly, computer-assisted education and microfiche libraries already exist, and intelligent extrapolation of early findings can be a useful guide to the future.

Another case in which the future is in some measure available for study in the present is the data bank. This illustration is particularly relevant to social scientists, as the data bank is not simply a part of the society they study; it is a device that they themselves employ in a professional capacity. The data bank raises, among others, questions concerning a possible divorce between the selection, categorization, and stocking of data, and their later retrieval and use. The type of data stored and the manner in which they are stored may shape the questions asked of them, which generally is not a desirable sequence in scientific or even administrative contexts. Those who use the data bank may become progressively less capable of or more uninterested in taking responsibility for the data they use ("that's someone else's job") and in verifying its accuracy or, more important, its real relevance. In some administrative and scientific areas this division of labor could become dangerous; one can easily imagine a whole hierarchy of outputs, each level of which is progressively farther away from and increasingly corrupted by the data base on which it rests. In some cases, consequences will ensue that may suggest that all is not well and impel corrective action. This may or may not come early enough to prevent some intellectual or administrative disasters. Nor does it seem impossible that the data bank system will develop self-sealing devices that will make errors and the consequences of errors almost impossible to detect. The empirical study of the problems raised here in so alarmist a form does not have to be deferred to the future. The data bank in its scientific and administrative applications already exists, and research on these early applications can tell us a good deal about some of the problems that will occur in the future and the manner in which responses, or nonresponses, to them develop.

Social science also has a professional stake in ultramicrofiche applications to social science literature and education. The commercial development of social science collections on ultramicrofiche evidently could be a notable gain for social science study and instruction. It would be unfortunate, however, if the commercially developed collections are not of a professionally suitable quality or character. No one will have to buy them, of course, but commercial initiative in the field may lead to the use of instructional material over whose selection social science educators have had little or no control. These problems exist for other professional groups as well. Ultramicrofiche is, of course, not only significant for its relation to these professional interests; it is a field of first-rate importance in communication studies. And again, it is a field in which the future already is available for study in incipient form in the present.

Opportunities to study the future in the present are considerably increased by being alert to current communication developments in different countries. Thus, for instance, home facsimile newspaper reception presumably will be available for study in Japan before it is available for study in the United States. Even where the stage of technological application is much the same in different countries, the variations in social, economic, or cultural contexts may permit a better theoretical and empirical understanding of the social effects of technology and thereby a far more effective forecast of the likely future course of development in various communication fields.

The social effects of the new communication technologies presumably will be studied mostly by different types of social scientists. Engineers and physical scientists will not, of course, forego their right to contribute, as they already have, to the study of social effects as well as to a better understanding of the technologies themselves. But social scientists are hardly likely to allow this interesting field to be preempted by their colleagues in the engineering sciences. This imposes on social scientists the obligation to acquire a fuller understanding than they generally possess of the relevant basic scientific findings and their engineering applications. This is not because the social scientist will be working without the collaboration of the engineer, but rather because effective collaboration and also the ability to take intellectual initiatives require a sufficient knowledge of technology to permit useful conversation between the engineer and the social scientist. Some social scientists are going to have to apprentice themselves for a while to engineering groups if they wish to acquire a sound understanding of technological developments as a foundation for an imaginative construction and study of future social changes. Association with engineers may have a bonus effect in improving the morale of social scientists. Social scientists readily envisage dangers in approaching changes; engineers mostly see exciting vistas where goodness and efficiency conquer.

Inferences from past experience, theoretical knowledge, specially designed research in the present to throw light on situations not yet existent, and the use of incipient futures to study more developed and later stages, almost certainly can improve our understanding of what changes in communication technology can and will mean for the social life of the next decade or two. Still, we should be prepared to concede that on many questions research will not enable us to speak very confidently. Nonetheless, even in these cases, the very attempt to understand the future and to trace out possible paths of social development will ease our adaptation to the path that finally emerges.

NOTES

1. The transoceanic Atlantic cable using vacuum tube amplifiers that was installed in 1956 was assumed to have a service life of twenty years for calculating depreciation. The useful technical life of that cable now is expected to be about forty years. The new transoceanic submarine cables using transistor amplifiers also are to be depreciated over twenty years. As the amplifiers are being designed to eliminate primary failure mechanisms, the new cables in fact may have a useful technical, but not necessarily economic, life of one hundred years. This, of course, does not preclude such systems seeming obsolete within the next twenty years compared with the performance of satellite systems.

2. To confine attention for the moment to purely technical and economic difficulties: if 1 percent of the households in the country were to have Picturephone® (a trade name), twice the current channel capacity would be required, since Picturephone requires one hundred times the channel capacity of the ordinary telephone.

3. Willis H. Ware, *Future Computer Technology and Its Impact*, P–3279 (Santa Monica: Rand Corporation, March 1966), p. 12.

4. Of course, some data uses are sufficiently important to bear costs of

transmission over much greater distances. And the different time zones create different times of peak load. Thus, the transmission of some kinds of data across the Atlantic may be warranted.

5. The transmission of signals electronically requires the use of a certain portion of the electromagnetic spectrum. The amount of spectrum required to transmit a given signal is called the bandwidth, which is measured in such units as kilocycles per second or megacycles per second. A megacycle is equal to 1,000 kilocycles. Kilocycles per second and megacycles per second are shortened, respectively, to kilohertz (kHz) and megahertz (MHz). For instance, a telephone channel requires a bandwidth of about 3 kHz for each direction, or 6 kHz for a two-way circuit; a television channel occupies a band 6 MHz wide. Thus, a cable that carries five thousand voice circuits can carry only five television channels. To transmit music at high fidelity requires 10 to 20 kHz or about four to six times the bandwidth used in one-way voice communication. Bandwidth for analogue signals is related to the information rate for digital signals. Information rate is measured in binary digits, or bits, transmitted per second. The greater the bandwidth of the analogue signal or the higher the information rate for digital signals, the greater the cost for transmission.

6. The transistor amplifiers of the cable repeat or amplify the signal along the cable and thus offset the attenuation due to cable losses.

7. A switched system is one that is capable of routing traffic among a multitude of possible destinations (see below).

8. The Bell telephone system now provides Picturephone service between New York, Washington, and Chicago. Users, however, must go to special Bell terminals in each city. Two days' advance notice is required. The New York–Washington rate is currently $8.00 for the first three minutes and $2.50 per minute thereafter.

9. This is the current commercially available capability. National Cash Register has, however, produced a 1,245-page Bible on an area 1.5 inches square. Microfiche, as distinguished from ultramicrofiche, reproduces about sixty to one hundred pages on a 4 by 6 in. fiche.

10. One qualification immediately is evident: television may provide two-dimensional adults instead of three-dimensional adults as socializing personages. Even so, because of the inability of television personalities to respond individually to the viewer, we can hardly speak of them as substituting for adults in the home or in the "real" environment.

11. Radio can, of course, also be combined with visual aids (slides, film strips, printed materials), which are sent to the student or the school in advance of the broadcast, as in France.

12. By being scrambled, these programs are limited to the medical profession; they are descrambled at the reception end, usually hospitals, as the descrambler is still fairly expensive.

13. Recently, computer experts from the Rand Corporation, Santa Monica,

and the University of California at Los Angeles, in a private exercise, formed themselves into offensive (cheating) and defensive (detecting) teams to test the possibility of cheating and detecting cheating in the counting of votes in computerized systems. In all tests the offensive or cheating teams were able to win.

14. Apart from other considerations, these practices raise questions about the invasion of privacy.

15. For example, the primary and runoff campaigns of Thomas Bradley, the losing candidate in Los Angeles's 1969 mayoralty election, cost $1.1 million, $631,000 of which were communication costs. At the end of his campaign, Bradley's election committee was nearly $300,000 in debt.

16. Obviously there are problems involved here other than crime: the legal status of transactions with no supporting paper; and the individual's degree of confidence in the infallibility of the computer system.

17. This ability to check on lost or stolen credit cards does not prevent, and in fact may have encouraged, the criminal duplication of legitimate cards by penetration of the security system of plants producing the cards.

18. Of course, direct selling on television is practiced today in the sense that people are given a phone number and can call in an order for something that has just been advertised. Enabling the cable television subscriber to push a button may not have much additional impact. However, the amount and detail of advertising on, say, an eighty-channel cable television system could make a great difference.

19. Mobile radio includes radio for police, fire, hospital, military, and various other public-service vehicles, as well as an increasingly large number of commercial and private ones. In 1967 there were about 2.5 million mobile transmitters, excluding those operated by the common-carriers.

20. Bandwidth problems are not limited to signals that are propagated through the air, as in broadcasting. Picturephone now is designed to use a 1-MHz analogue bandwidth over the ordinary telephone wires between the subscribers and their local telephone central offices. This is not compatible with the 6-MHz channel bandwidths used for commercial television. Over the next thirty years, Picturephone may grow to represent a capital investment of $50 billion or more, and the investment in cable television could be almost as much.

21. Canada has set up a new department of communications at the cabinet level; has created a new corporation, Telesat, to operate its satellite system; and is proceeding rapidly toward an operational capability.

22. If implemented, this plan would divert 5 percent of the income of cable companies for educational programming, would require cable companies to pay a certain percentage of their income to copyright owners, and would permit local high-frequency stations to receive revenue from the local advertising that replaces commercials on imported programs.

23. *Fortnightly Corp.* v. *United Artists Television, Inc.*, 392 U.S. 390 (1967). In another case, the Court did decide that the FCC had jurisdiction to regulate cable television. The commission's regulatory actions have, in effect, limited the growth of cable television. See, however, the above reference to recent FCC action.

24. Ernst Kjellberg and Gösta Säflund, *Greek and Roman Art* (New York: Thomas Y. Crowell Company, 1968).

25. A trivial example: One can observe on some noncommercial stations announcements made in the same theatrical voice and style of the circus barker and the street-corner huckster common among announcers on commercial stations. Apparently on noncommercial as well as commercial programs, failure to achieve a dramatic note in prosaic statements implies an absence of professional expertise.

26. In the longer-term future, these choices, it is useful to recall, also will include hard-copy and display materials on console screens as outputs from newspaper and other subscription services and in response to interrogations of data banks and other computer services. The ability in the home to have audiovisual contact with people outside the home may have some effect on family togetherness, just as does the young adolescent on the phone today.

27. There is, perhaps, a tendency to expect a greater impact of some technological applications than past experience warrants. Has the doctor's substitution of the electrocardiogram for the laying on of hands and the stethoscope reduced rapport with his patients? Is there a great difference between being wired to a computer and being wired to an electrocardiograph? Of course, if the doctor largely steps out of the picture, a decisive difference occurs.

28. Of course, if the relevant sciences provide reasonably well verified theories, then by varying the parameters according to different assumptions about the future we could derive some useful inferences. Unfortunately, in only a few relevant areas is theory this well developed. Still, social developments are rarely so discontinuous that a good social scientist cannot usefully apply his knowledge to analysis of the future.

THE SYMBOLIC INSTRUMENT
RETROSPECTS AND PROSPECTS

11

THE HISTORIC PAST
OF THE UNCONSCIOUS

ANDREW ROLLE

We do not usually think of the historian as an expert who tries to communicate the meaning of the past to those who live in the present. That this is, in fact, his heaviest responsibility as custodian of the human record is often overlooked by historians themselves. Mastery of the art of historical communication involves interpreting many interlocking activities. These include man's myths and arts, technology, social conditions, folklore, mass movements, discoveries, institutional history, political and economic ideology, the roles of individual leaders, and other intricate aspects of the past. Just below the surface of all these many activities lie the motives and phantasy systems of those who carried them out—a major concern of this chapter.

In examining the ways in which historians have communicated knowledge of the past to their contemporaries we shall focus primarily upon political history. Although my essay occasionally mentions literary and religious motivation in the past, relatively little attention is given here to the history of artistic achievement, supported as it is by a rich psychoanalytic literature. Similarly, only passing scrutiny is paid to the problem of warfare and its etiology. To treat these and other factors would lengthen an already quite extensive contribution to this book. Yet the reader should be aware of the constraints which the author has placed upon this particular piece.

Our task is to show how the communication of man's past has been based upon incomplete, conscious-level analysis. In fact, man has deceived himself by propagandizing his past. His very intellect is distortive. For there is more than one plane of historical reality. Beneath the patterned world which we historians normally portray lie motives rooted in the unconscious mind. Understanding of these vitalities plunges us into that repressed behavior which stems from man's neolithic origins. Out of such dark, prehistoric beginnings emerged some of our most primal phantasies. Our record reflects a primordial time when man lived in caves and forests by the rule of tooth, claw, and club. And this biological inheritance continues to affect human conduct.

An important group of unconscious phenomena are not, however, primitive. These originate in a specific historic milieu, but become intrapsychic constructs. Some thinking is communicated to us by the structure and vocabulary of the language we use and unconsciously follow within our cultures. Only occasionally, however, do unconscious phenomena come to the surface of history, sometimes disguised as symbol or myth. Carl Jung called these archaic forms of mental imagery "archetypes" buried latently in man's "collective unconscious."[1]

Communication, influenced by feeling and mood, occurs both consciously and unconsciously. A society projects underlying tensions onto its institutions and people. Yet the city-states and urban civilizations of our Western cultures are based upon conscious-level, goal-oriented constructs. Underlying the seemingly planned political institutions and economies of the historical state are forces, leaders, and classes that have become dominant in a society via manipulation of unconscious drives. By raising these obscured factors to the level of consciousness we may "update" (strange as the term seems) the past.

In this sense the improvement of historical communication gives historians a chance to influence the future. As we historians identify the underlying motivations of supposedly rational civilizations we enlarge the range of solutions available to decision makers, beyond what seems current or novel. By viewing man's missed opportunities the interpretation of unconscious conflicts becomes functional as well as historical. Indeed such "history" offers us all emancipation from past errors.[2]

As Freud and Jung suggested, the unconscious is ideally

analyzed within the paradigms of personal behavior. Individual personality in history, therefore, provides our best prospect for uncovering the subsurface interplay of both propaganda and communication, including deliberate manipulation. My task here is to deal also with how individuals within groups are affected by the unconscious. When appropriate I refer to specific leaders and to those they led. But first we must examine some of the broader implications of how we historians put history together.

Conditioning has clouded our vision of subsurface factors, limiting us to "rational," conscious-level interpretations. The historian of the future will be better able to test this "conscious organization" of human life. He will want to compare the present state of a civilization with its tribal origins in order to see how and why submergent individuals and groups assumed power. Via new insight procedures he may effect what Harold Lasswell has termed as "creative rearrangement" of data.

Institutions sometimes emerge that are gripped by the power of man's unconscious life, not by his conscious will. His laws as well as his art are based, in part, upon cultural symbolisms that reflect the unconscious. The law, once thought to have accumulated in response to societal needs, we now perceive as reflecting urges buried far below the scaffolding of legal precedence. Since Montesquieu's *L'esprit des lois* (1748), man's legal record no longer can be viewed as a rationalistic abstraction responding to his need for justice and reason alone. Important memory traces, or "primordial images," must also be explained, though they seem as complex as the individual id, ego, and superego.

Although men are desperate to know their inner natures, most persons (including historians) have become alienated from their unconscious feelings. Indeed, our major societies have long insisted that personal feelings are too subjective to be validated. Only quite recently have a few historians admitted that "unconscious reality" helps to explain history and that in stressful times confusing emotions well up that are determinative and that must be analyzed. Collective intolerance, delusions, vindictive warfare, genocide, and hysteria have generally gone unrecorded. Yet overt behavior, nakedly observed, forms only the outer layer of existence, cloaking the intents and disguises of personalities, events, and epochs.

At this stage in the development of psychohistory, if we insist

upon exact validation of unconscious motives we cut ourselves
off from forms of truth more closely related to art than to science. In the measurement of the unconscious, rigorous research
designs are not fully useful. Knowledgeable scholars simply assume the existence of an unconscious with a symbolic language
quite different from that once believed to have shaped the great
rational systems of Western culture.

One can scarcely fathom the accumulation of myth, illogic,
and even "magic" that clutters human history—impinging unconsciously upon the present. Historians have been left mainly
letters and memoirs that describe mostly conscious activities.
We can, nevertheless, discern what "goes on underneath"
when behavior follows known aberrational pathways, as with
Adolph Hitler's hysterical paranoia. The historian cannot hope
to be so successful in analyzing every leader or society. But we
may begin by extrapolating what underlies the behavior of children. Their motives are usually simpler to diagnose than those
of adults. The child who says too often that he does not fear the
dark resembles the adult who indulges in wishful thinking to
protect his ego. Another child may insist upon many rituals to
control his impulses. So may an adult with a handwashing compulsion. What underlies surface behavior must remain conjec-
tural without analytic tools. Hence the attraction of psychoanalysis and of other behavioral disciplines that enable us to
reexamine the lives of historical figures too often treated as the
"playthings of destiny."

The "facts" of history partly depend upon the moods and
mores of the society in which they are later explained. What
Ernst Kris called a "cover memory" takes over. Solidified gossip
passes as history. Men rationalize the contradictions in their history as well as in their lives. Names, dates, and "facts" are convenience, but they are not the only "reality." A phantasy is a
patched-up story of what we imagine to have happened. To isolate historical "truth" hinges partly on who sees it, and under
what circumstances. We know that there are "truths" other
than the ones we hold dear.

At the conscious level, deep-seated anxieties have not ordinarily been allowed to disturb man's social order. Only in times
of emergency—as during floods, famines, or revolutions—do
subsurface forces burst into consciousness. Most often order has
been the watchword of man's historic consciousness. Conform-

ity to existing mores has been aggressively enforced—whether symbolically in the authoritarian monuments of a Rome erected by the Caesars or in the Middle Ages when secular buildings were not to be built above the eaves of cathedrals. The rationalized voice of God and Emperor has drowned out the unconscious voice of man. More recently the symbolisms of mechanical authority have continued to crush our fragile intrapsychic selves. As a result, a mythic construct, a caricature of man's "inner history," has emerged. Our "outer history," thus, is the record we all take at face value. But its thin veneer covers a deep and unfathomable subworld only barely touched by historians, ancient or modern. This subjective underworld, like Henri Bergson's life-force, remains mostly a mystery.

The recasting of man's "inner record" depends upon recognizing a hidden self that is biologically-based, easily repressed, and overcome by disorienting role conflict. Abraham H. Maslow has written about that inner core which embraces "basic needs, capacities, talents, anatomical equipment, physiological or temperamental balances, prenatal and natal injuries," as well as other historic traumas. As our inner core contacts the outside world it begins to grow into a "self." But this instinctoid self may be killed off. Humans no longer have instincts like that of animals, "powerful unmistakeable inner voices which tell them unequivocally what to do, when, where, how and with whom. All that we have left are instinct-remnants. And, furthermore, these are weak, subtle and delicate, very easily drowned out by learning, by cultural expectations, by fear, by disapproval. . . ."[3]

If historians have too little heeded the role of an instinctoid unconscious it is because its workings remain mysterious in all branches of knowledge. Among its hard-to-interpret and mercurial variables are aggression, fear, frustration, guilt, ambiguity in a search for selfhood, loneliness, anger, pride, sadism, the role of accident, and love versus hate. Not always apparent are the ways in which men have acted from hidden motives, or in protest, or by devious protection of their egos. Largely unexplored, for example, is the role of repression and resistance in history.

Let us see if we can isolate the role of repression in a society. But, first, an observation or two about group versus individual characteristics. When we think of "group unconsciousness" it is usually in terms of a tribe, society, region, nation, or community collectivity. To speak of the plural behavior of a nation as similar to that of an individual is to be partly metaphorical, for we can reconstruct national character only in relation to a country's dominant attributes. Some individual traits do, however, carry over as aggregate characteristics. In small and uncomplicated societies especially, homogeneous culture values are more easily measured.

The older a society, the more unconscious conditioning has occurred. Taboos and restrictions erected by its high priests lead to underlying frustrations (and irrationality) in most societies. The culture of India, for example, exhibits considerable instability, partly because the mass of its population cannot readily accept new values or innovations. India, furthermore, is one of those complicated societies where widely different layers of social attainment coincide. On the one hand a highly educated, semi-Oxonian elite presides over a teeming culture in which there remain (quite literally) remnants of the stone age. This piling of layer upon layer of social stratification causes researchers great problems of interpretation. Running through the spectrum of Indian life are unconscious factors that remind one of those ancient (often priest-ridden) societies in which people were instructed for centuries as to what they should believe.

Persons who deviated from established patterns in the most authoritative of such cultures risked being called heretical, even treasonable. Unconscious guilt is, therefore, apt to make the individual who contemplates change feel unworthy of the approval of both his ancestors and his own generation. He is exhorted to recall that old ways are "tried and true." Furthermore, the middle and lower classes tend toward self-righteousness about their social immobility. A lower-middle-class morality exercises extraordinary group restraints.

Countries so economically poor that they cannot afford experimentation fear risk-taking. When survival is at stake (especially in times of famine or war) neither deviance nor social experimentation is allowable. Leaders minimize group expectations. Security of life comes before any consideration of changes. Superego (conscience) thinking does not encourage casting aside sacred folk beliefs revered since time out of mind.

Ingrained patterns rooted in unconsciousness play a disproportionately big role in agrarian and sedentary cultures. Such societies (as among the Indians of the American Southwest) may long remain relatively unexposed to outside influences. Little technology or expertise, therefore, is available to cushion a community against floods or famines. Under the restraints of medicine men or shamans such a people may react quite violently to change outside a narrow range of prescribed experience. Emotional insularity requires that these primitive societies stand fast against imagined dangers. The same spirit, incidentally, may characterize the restorationist urges of political rightists in advanced societies. The Colons of France, the John Birchites of America (not to speak of the Ku Klux Klan), and the emperor worshippers of Japan all desire to remain "whole" or "one with the past."

The more primitive the culture, the more dangerous it becomes to defy its superego formations. To strive for the "new" is considered a form of deviance in some older communities. A clan conscience and collective superego dictates what changes seem rational enough to accept. Via the superego each society transmits concepts of right and wrong to successive generations of children, a process we will discuss later in detail.

This systemic group conscience helps to explain why so stable and tight a society as eighteenth-century England produced such an unusual number of "great eccentrics." Their behavior provided a safety valve, opened to relieve the stifling elitist conformity and class stratification in which the secure country gentry lived. Meanwhile, the priest-ridden and decayed nobility of Spain and Italy had no such leeway—which helped to cut off the Latin societies from moderation in favor of static, indeed stagnant, behavior patterns.

Today men seem to search for the roots of that individualistic homeland which the Greeks knew in their small city-states or which the Florentines and other Italians experienced during the Renaissance. Our mass societies, instead, have become places in which one lives anonymously—rather than the personalized *polis* of the ancient world. The Greeks, clustered around a primitive *agora* or forum, knew both their political leaders and their thinkers personally. Relatively intact smallish societies (such as Athens or Switzerland) thus found it easier to achieve psychological unity than did our teeming Protean cultures. The

result has been a growing confusion in the belief systems of
mass societies and resultant frustration of the individual. Rarely
in heterogeneous mass societies (and mostly in times of emergency, as in wartime Britain, or in the United States after the
death of President Kennedy) do a people pull together in a
spirit that resembles the warm and loyal associations between
comrades in arms under fire on the battlefield. It usually takes a
threat from outside by a dreaded enemy to arouse inspirational
courage, as in Periclean Athens or Churchillian London. The
emotional unity of similarly motivated people has become a
rarity in the fragmented societies of the twentieth century. It
almost seems necessary for deep insecurity to occur (especially
when linked to patriotism) before a government can inspire
self-preservational and instinctual renunciation of chaos.

Man remains ill at ease about this kind of history, partly
because (as in his daily life) he has troweled over what he senses
to be an illogical world. The mysterious forces that govern his
unmanageable subworld constitute a jungle which he neither
likes nor understands. At times man seems to teeter on the edge
of the unconscious, harboring latent aggressions, imprisoned by
myth. Freud once said that man is both more base and more no-
ble than he realizes, an ambivalence like Robert Louis Stevenson's portrayal of Dr. Jekyll, whose transfiguration seemed to
well up out of a subwaking self. Stevenson portrayed Jekyll's
''lower'' soul as brutal, irrational, and cruel. As compared with
the considerate Mr. Hyde, he emerged as a sometime criminal
who, at the nadir of his passions, lacked all self-control.

When the inner world of a person or of a society becomes
separated from outer reality, pathological problems emerge.
Codification of such nonlogical phenomena has never really
been achieved. Written history constantly reflects attitudes shot
through with facile conscious-level concept formation. Yet
man's ''inner life'' is always with us. It helps to distinguish us
from subhuman species, and its effect on man's history remains
incalculable.

Each society represses or ''forgets'' its most painful memories. But, as with individuals, ideas suppressed by religious,
political, or social systems accumulate. They fester as an unconscious residue, almost guiltlike, until a latent imagery of neuroses or dreams allows these disguised impulses to escape from

the prisonry of our unconscious life. A release of anxious tensions must occur, whether by liberating what Freud called libidinal energy or by resort to violence. We are most familiar with intraspecific killing via terroristic wars, yet mass insecurity, national hatreds and class prejudice may also result from the oversocialization demanded by a society, sometimes in the name of patriotism. Throughout history, however damaging the consequences, emancipation of the force of the psyche has been an unspoken demand. In exchange, man has gained daily equilibrium. Somehow, for us to survive, our deepest fears and yearnings must be articulated, no matter how disguised or camouflaged. As General De Gaulle once told André Malraux: "People want history to resemble them or at least to resemble their dreams. Happily, they sometimes have great dreams."

Although censorship separates conscious-level activity from the unconscious, clinical experience indicates that man is motivated much more by the drives and memories of his unconscious self than by factors of which he is aware. The term "underlying consciousness" may be more acceptable to the historian than the word "unconscious."

Validation of the existence of an unconscious mind has been difficult to achieve. In 1968 two researchers reported discovery of a "brain wave correlate" of unconscious mental processes. Measurable fluctuations in electrical activity go on while a person is thinking unconsciously. Before this discovery the notion of the unconscious was a useful clinical hypothesis for which there was no direct evidence.[4] In 1966, at a Leningrad laboratory, Russian scientists also believed they had established beyond doubt (a) that man possesses a sixth sense, (b) that it is activated by special brain radiations, (c) that the mentally ill perceive it most clearly, (d) that it resembles the telepathy through which animals communicate, and (e) that its discovery is as momentous as that of atomic energy.[5]

The historical unconscious could be likened to that nightworld which we each experience. It stands in vivid contrast to one's daytime routinized existence, which demands duty, order, sobriety, and thrift, based on the work ethic. In our dreams a florid, dramatic, intense, and passionate universe comes alive that is suppressed as we reach a waking stage of "reason."

Benjamin Lee Whorf and Émile Durkheim have demonstrated how conscious culture impinges upon the individual. They point out that acculturation firmly imprints its patterns and standards on both persons and groups. Durkheim writes of "collective consciousness" whose imprinting effects may become unconscious. Zevedei Barbu has also shown how societies in different ages of history (like individuals) develop specific personalities. Social factors may force the individual to have the illusion of freedom; actually he follows the unconscious dictates of his culture. In 1949 the anthropologist Edward Sapir was one of the first to realize that Jung's collective archetypes deposited in our primordial unconscious only part of the historical pattern transmitted by the culture in which one lives.[6]

Theodor Meynert, Freud's teacher, once observed: "Appearance is not identical with the essence of things." Freud, Jung, and their successors saw the unconscious mind as the central part of man's emotional life, whether expressed as neuroses or in dreams. As a man of reason, Freud at first also distrusted the unmeasurable—as do historians, trained to deal with validatable facts. Unconscious mental activity, harboring latent aggressions, hostilities, and hatreds, remains unfathomable for most of us. Yet all these factors continue to influence human behavior. (We are all familiar with daily stock market reports that read "Among leading groups of industrials, *emotional selling* carried the Dow-Jones averages to closing lows.")

Psychoanalysts, by using the case method that historians so prize, have delved into unconscious infantile sexuality, the child's oedipal situation, and the interpretation of dreams. They have discovered similarities among the thought patterns of children and savages as well as of man's unconscious mind. In Freud's words, "the inhibitions or even inability to deal with life, of people dominated by neurosis are a very important factor in human society. The neurosis may be regarded as a direct expression of a 'fixation' to an early period of their past." Conflict within men thus may influence their history as much as does environment. In fact, historical events may be fashioned to cope with buried anxieties. Habit becomes controlling in the lives of individuals, as William James pointed out.

Man's "inner nature" persists "underground, unconsciously, even though denied and repressed. Like the voice of the intellect, it speaks softly but it *will* be heard even if in a distorted form. That is, it has a dynamic face of its own, pressing always for open, uninhibited expression. Effort must be used in its suppression or repression from which fatigue can result."[7] This inner force seems to be part of an urge from which people derive their own identity, and "if this essential core (inner nature) of the person is frustrated or suppressed, sickness results, sometimes in obvious forms, sometimes in subtle and devious forms, sometimes immediately, sometimes later."[8] Unresolved childhood fears and phantasies rankle in the unconscious mind, interfering with a person's functioning at a later stage. The complementary processes of introjection and projection continue to affect the unconscious life of maladjusted adults, influencing the societies in which they dwell.

Erik Erikson has characterized the fuzzy borderland between history and psychology as a "compost heap of today's interdisciplinary efforts," but also as a hyphenated area that promises "to fertilize new fields and to produce future flowers of new methodological clarity."[9] We cannot, he writes, leave history to nonclinical observers and to professional historians alone. For these nobly "immerse themselves into the very disguises, rationalizations, and idealizations of the historical process from which it should be their business to separate themselves."[10]

The historian must not deny the existence of "inner man" and "outer man." These, symbolically, may be history's equivalents to science's outer space and inner space. In examining both microcosms and macrocosms, are the "laws of history" only outer constructs put together by historians working with supposedly objective but incomplete evidence? How much of what we consider rational is, indeed, rationalization? Could we call some historical findings the "echoes of life" rather than life itself? For example, overt conduct (such as criminal activity) may mask a deeper conflict, which causes a person to act in a given way.

Let us now try to record, albeit briefly, "the historic past of the unconscious," giving attention first to its outcroppings in antiquity. The ancient Mediterranean cultures lived within two psychic worlds simultaneously. They combined realities in the present with supernatural fears. This still occurs among primitive folk. At one level of his mind a savage may seem omnipotent, his world "divided into two forces—a benevolent power which would give everything for nothing, and a malevolent, which would deprive him of even life itself."[11]

For the Greeks, too, it seemed natural to experience life on an emotional as well as heroic scale. As their history seemed quixotic and variable, the Greek chroniclers dwelt in a world of superstitions, traditions, and legends. Divine possession could render "psychological man," his eyes full of unreason and rage, quite powerless. The Greek gods were man-centered, and divine acts were not separate from the life of man.

Herodotus began the skepticism that would take historians away from the unconscious in the life of man. Rationalization would thereafter help men to justify primitive behavior toward each other.[12] A generation after Herodotus, Thucydides cultivated an even more definable historical accuracy, including the sifting of evidence.[13] Yet Thucydides saw the human record in terms of an underlying power and greed that shaped men's motives. History was the scene of mankind's cowardice as well as of his idealism, of man's treachery as much as of his generosity and folly. Depending upon the degree of stress, even stable leaders might display anxiety, irritability, or depression, or act upon superstition. Thucydides once recorded that Nicias threw away a chance for the Athenian army to escape from Syracuse by delaying a retreat in order to avert an eclipse.

One may liken the Greek search for historical truth to rummaging in a house with a basement. Unconscious, astonishing ideas were stored down there, some of which were not so accessible or usable as in times past. In the basement was a subterranean labyrinth, a ruin of former times whose artifacts lay forgotten; the ancients prowled about it as do today's psychiatrists, biologists, and anthropologists. In the basement lived *Psyche,* whom the Greeks credited with intuition.

The Greeks understood that we see only a small portion of reality. Both their playwrights and their historians utilized the illusive and mysterious inner core of man as well as his outer nature. They gave high importance to the immortality of the soul, to omens, to the fates, and to man's "humours." E. R. Dodds considers that the word "irrationalist" describes Euripides better than any other term, stressing the power, wonder, and peril of the nonrational Greek ethos.[14]

The Greeks also realized what Jung was to point out two thousand years later—that at least half of man's life is spent in sleeping and dreaming. Consciousness, they believed, has its roots in that realm. Jung was to maintain that "the unconscious operates in and out of waking existence." He observed: "No one doubts the importance of conscious experience; why then should we question the importance of unconscious happenings?"[15]

The Greek *ate* was a state of mind, an unexplainable fate that temporarily clouded or confused normal consciousness. The belief in psychic intervention by daemons and other strange forces allowed one to project unbearable feelings of guilt onto an external power, even onto a god.[16] *Menos* was yet another sort of "psychic intervention," celebrated by Homer in the *Iliad*. Via the concept of *menos* the goddess Athena could put a physical strength, or new state of being, into the chest of a warrior. This mysterious energy gave such a leader the confidence to win that could only be termed supernatural.

In the Greek world of *ate* and *menos* Plato (whose reputation, like that of Socrates, is rooted in rational skepticism) also made room for the indefinable. Anticipating Freudian dream theories, Plato's *Timaeus* explains how dreams are "perceived by the irrational soul as images reflected on the smooth surface of the liver. . . ."[17] Aeschylus, too, recognized the importance of dream interpretation. The Greeks, like the ancient Indians, devised "dream books" for this purpose. Plato averred that men were "anchored in the life of feeling, which is part of our humanity and they cannot surrender it. . . ."[18]

The role of the historical unconscious was to change with the advent of Christianity. Indeed, Christianity represented a kind of emergence of consciousness. As the Middle Ages replaced ancient times, a shift in religious perceptions accompanied this change. Unlike the Greek and Roman gods, the medieval God had no human foibles. He was a punishing deity bound to weaken the faith that man could know himself. The medieval world cared passionately about the search for truth; but its sense of evidence was different from ours. Priests, thus, arose to decipher God's wishes, invoking the aid of saints and miracles to stave off disease and to exorcise the devil and his works.

The men who lived in those intermediate centuries before the dawn of modern times appear curiously remote. We see figures who look mutely out at us from gold-encircled mosaics and ikons, static in appearance, helpless, and two-dimensional. These men did not occupy the center of life's stage. Their god did. With the Greek message of individuality submerged, men came to be relegated to the outermost wings of the stage. Just as the ancients had blamed unknowable misfortunes upon the fates, daemons, and furies, medieval man ascribed plagues and floods to his fall from grace. Before his fall, man was made perfect in the image of God "in the light of his mind," as the Elizabethan writer Richard Bostocke maintained as late as 1585.[19]

From Shakespeare onward, "psychological man" came to be depicted in terms of a "tripartite soul" that reminds one of Freud's id, ego, and superego. Plato, too, had spoken of a three-layered soul, one strata of which was a potentially evil subsoul. Plato had recognized the irrationality of these various souls, connected with wickedness in man.[20] The Elizabethans called the "lowest level of soul" the "vegetative or quickening soul." It had to do with reproduction, elimination, and all the muscular, physiological needs of man. There was nothing evil or sinful about this soul. Rather, it had something in common with the instincts of animals. A second level of soul the Elizabethans called the "sensitive or sensible soul," which included the faculties of knowing, perceiving, and apprehending through the five senses. Man also held these characteristics in common with animals, except that creativity and imagination (nonanimal traits) formed part of this second "soul." The third or highest soul the Elizabethans labeled intellectual or rational power. Here man was supreme among the animals. When his three subsouls functioned harmoniously together, the Elizabethans considered man to be happiest. However, when man bypassed the top level of soul he was damned by pleasure, and by the passions of murder, hate, and jealousy.[21]

Descartes, and Roger Bacon before him, had urged the substitution of empirical observation for theological or dogmatic scrutiny of man's memory, thoughts, and emotions. Descartes, known primarily as a mathematician, also dissected bodies. He saw the nerves as tubes that siphoned off animal spirits into man's brain in a rough approximation of the "reflex action" of the nerves, separating man's nature into two kinds of reality, physical and mental.[22]

Renaissance man had doubted that mankind would again rise to the level of the ancients, and he had venerated the glories of antiquity. But, as the concept of progress grew in popularity, Francis Bacon came to see history as passing through decided cycles of improvement. Conscious-level explanations of man's record accompanied skepticism over divine providence's role in humanity's march toward perfectability. Men saw their age as better than what ancient or medieval folk had ever known. This doctrine of progress became the very creed of eighteenth-century rationalists.[23]

Man's concept of history, like his view of himself, thus changed from the sacred to the profane. As historians substituted intellectualization for emotion, the restatement of myth, conjecture, and tradition was replaced by the quest for verifiability. Count Claude Henri de Saint Simon, looking back upon the course of history, saw man as increasingly perfectible. He contended that there were two major eras in mankind's development. The first was a primitive period of theological conjecture; the second (important in extinguishing the role of the unconscious) was one of "positive knowledge," beginning with Bacon and Descartes.

Yet the rationalist historian Edward Gibbon wrote in his memoirs that "the most essential and important" part of a biographer's job was to discover and to report the "private life" of an individual. Following the French Revolution, Anquetil du Peron returned from India with a collection of fascinating writings called the *Upanishads*. These gave Europeans their first modern insights into the secret and nonrational mind of the East, but the effect on Western historians was peripheral.

Instead, at least from Vico's time onward, a rational pseudo-scientific history grew. As late as the first half of the nineteenth century we find relatively little psychological understanding in the writings of historians; they saw man as largely explainable along political lines. He could, in effect, control his actions, and therefore, his destiny. This concept, anchored upon the drab bedrock of Ludwig Von Ranke's German historical method, became dominant. A relentless search for brute, objective "facts" was sanctified as the "true" methodology for history.

Rather than openly defying Ranke's exaltation of conscious-level, rational history, those historians who differed with him

substituted only cultural or intellectual factors for political
ones. German *Historismus,* as a result, encouraged a continuing
failure to get at unconscious motivation. Only occasionally did a
David Hume treat emotional behavior as a motive for historical
events, believing that man's "passion for glory is always warped
and varied according to the particular taste or disposition of the
mind on which it falls."

In the second half of the nineteenth century Wilhelm Dilthey, a forerunner of the psychological approach to history,
joined the great historian of the Renaissance Jacob Burckhardt
in suggesting different ways to study man other than via the
"scientific" historicism then so popular in Germany. In a pre-
Freudian setting, Dilthey (whose works still remain mostly un-
translated) proposed an embryo psychology for history. This was
to be both descriptive and analytic as well as focused upon "inner man." Dilthey wanted historians introspectively to examine
empathy and imagination, to seek out man's psychological and
sociological past as well as his political history. Dilthey hoped to
move beyond the economic motivations to which Marx had introduced historians. For Dilthey, the life of the mind was an
historical product. He was interested in the discrepancy between
what men believed they were doing and what they actually did.
His dualism was not too different from conscious versus unconscious motivation, the interaction of the real and the imaginary.
Dilthey's work did not blunt Ranke's powerful influence. But
the idea of underlying causes for man's action had not entirely
died.[24]

Across the channel from Germany, the English historian
W. E. H. Lecky moved haphazardly in the same direction. In
1856, commenting prophetically about the value for history of
repressed dreams, Lecky maintained that "certain facts remain
hidden in the mind" and that

> only by a strong act of volition they can be recalled . . . but it is
> now fully established that a multitude of events which are so com-
> pletely forgotten that no effort of will can revive them, and that
> their statement calls up no reminiscence, may nevertheless, be, so
> to speak, imbedded in the memory, and may be reproduced which
> the mind had pursued, but of which we are entirely unconscious.[25]

For decades, however, eighteenth-century conscious-level notions of man's relation to the universe pervaded the study of his

behavior. The physical sciences provided the models by which the invariants of physics went virtually unchallenged until Darwinian biology suggested that individual species differed from one another in origin and historical development. By 1880 social theorists began to turn to biological models as the disunity of knowledge made earlier physicalistic promises of a conscious unity seem unrealizable. The old rationalist physics had been, furthermore, nonexperimental, featuring the bias of stability.

The nineteenth century finally spawned a romantic revolt against rationalism, a dethroning of pure reason, a rediscovery of the unconscious psyche. Faith in the reasonableness of man gave way to fascination with his passions and instinctual remnants. In literature especially, man's internal depth was to become a major preoccupation of Stendhal, Flaubert, De Maupassant, Dostoevski, Shaw, and Ibsen. As the sun set on the Age of Reason, skepticism about conscious-level assumptions coincided with an era of advancing mechanization. Pessimism grew concerning man's capacity to see his problems rationally. Wide differences of opinion erupted about how to solve society's ills; a raw, nihilistic individualism encouraged upheavals in artistic, philosophical, and theological canons as well.

In the 1890s, the German historian Karl Lamprecht put forth the concept that each major period possesses a dominant "collective psychology," similar to a dominant trait in an individual. Influenced by Auguste Comte and by the psychologist Wilhelm Wundt, Lamprecht was a devotee of *Kulturgeschichte,* a broader cultural history than Ranke's. He believed that urgent causal factors led men from one way of thinking in a particular age into another. Lamprecht was interested not only in psychological factors but also in economics and culture.

In Paris Marcel Proust, fascinated by a brilliant but dying culture, became its metaphysician in that supreme imaginative creation, *A la Recherche du Temps Perdu.* Vienna and Europe were about to be exposed to the ideas of Sigmund Freud. Napoleon III had called the Austrian empire *"un cadavre."* Was not the decaying society of its capital, Vienna, a fitting place to produce critics who saw the old order as increasingly irrelevant? The same declining Austria-Hungary of Freud saw the appearance of the talented and young Arthur Schnitzler, Hugo von Hofmannsthal, and other sensitive and alert intellectuals who

sought to understand the impending collapse of the social order
that shaped their lives. As educated Jews in a position of dependency, they gave voice to unconscious realities that went beyond
the ideology and sloganry of a declining Hapsburg monarchy.[26]
Other Viennese in that lost society, Franz Kafka in literature,
Max Reinhardt in the theater, and Gustav Mahler in music, depicted a complex subworld of absurdity and paradox shot
through with aimless futility. An astute critic of that era has
suggested that "cultural fatigue is sometimes preceded by a
kind of euphoria, a last flare-up, which forecasts the impending
collapse."[27]

FREUD AND THE UNCONSCIOUS

In *fin de siecle* Vienna, Freud's generation faced a world in
which family life was breaking down and in which empires were
decaying. Religious and sexual ambivalence provided a new interest in unconscious motivation through the use of symbol,
myth, and allegory. But the Victorian denial of sex encouraged
physical scientists to resist reductionist explanations of behavior. Historians, too, were slow to detach themselves from traditional conscious-level views of reality.

Freud's conceptualization of psychoanalysis resembled Columbus's epoch-making voyage to America. It culminated in
lifting "psychotherapy from an almost entirely intuitive art to
a semi-scientific procedure, had its roots in man's total
phylogeny. . . ."[28] Yet Freud's major biographer described
psychoanalysis as "simply the study of the processes of which we
are unaware, of what for the sake of brevity, we call the unconscious, by the free association technique of analyzing observable
phenomena of transference and resistance."[29]

Reaffirming Lamprecht's observations, Freud believed that
"the inhibitions or even inability to deal with life of people
dominated by neurosis are a very important factor in human society." A society (quite unconsciously) can thus be as neurotic
as an individual. Like individual men, it too can become a creature of passion rather than of reason. An outmoded, archaic
heritage, Freud believed, afflicts man, irrationally and nonre-
flectively, much as instincts control animals. For men, and perhaps for nations as well, that heritage survives in Jung's "collective unconscious,"[30] passing on both thought and behavior

("culture") from one generation to another, reflecting the unconscious taboos by which the individual is socialized.

For Freudians the unconscious represented psychic realities that involved primitive processes, in contrast to those approved by consciousness. Freud equipped his theory with an explanation of how unacceptable sexual and aggressive impulses came into one's life as disguised symbols. As a member of a generation of repressed Victorians, he saw forbidden infantile sexuality as a major explanation of a society's most complicated behavior, just as neurosis was "a direct expression of a 'fixation' to an early period of their past."[31]

Although Freud's historical and anthropological contributions remained mostly poeticized evocation, poignantly stated but difficult to verify, there is a grandeur in his concepts that "has not received the attention it deserves from historians."[32] The religious philosopher Sören Kierkegaard wrote in a similar vein long before; yet full realization of how emotion conditioned history began with Freud. He did not invent the unconscious mind. But he made it an operational concept by applying it to therapy, although "the idea of unconscious mental processes was, in many of its aspects, conceivable around 1700, topical around 1800, and became effective around 1900." The imaginative sociologist Karl Mannheim soon applied the concept of an unconscious mind to the seminal formulation that generational forces were at work during specific historical periods. Participation by a generation in a "common destiny" moved investigators closer to understanding the responses of persons who had experienced the same traumas and crises in life.[33]

Freud's *Civilization and its Discontents* (1929) put forth the notion that societies grew at the price of instinctual denial and repression, that civilization demands subjugation of human drives in exchange for cultural achievement. Man developed intellect at the expense of passion. Freud saw excessive sexual taboos as stunting man's fullest emotional growth while delusional religion kept him from achieving ideal maturity. This repression, Freud argued, had produced a basic neurosis, causing misery for the whole human race. Because there is a limit, Freud believed, beyond which most people "cannot comply with the demands of civilization," one must "include the influence of civilization among the determinants of neurosis. It is . . . easy for a barbarian to be healthy; for a civilized man the task is hard."[34]

Freud did not counsel poetic license in dealing with the unconscious, and he believed that novelists like Charles Dickens made overrated and too sharp distinctions "between virtue and vice which [do] not exist in life."[35] Because a social novelist has different motives than the search for truth, Freud's sympathies lay with the more scrupulous historians. Like them, he deplored simplistic interpretations of why and how men once acted.

Beyond Dickens and Dostoevski, novelists increasingly came to terms with the unconscious. In America these included Hawthorne, Melville, Poe, Whitman, Edith Wharton, and Henry James. Their work obliquely affected historical thought. Although the drama of Ibsen, Pirandello, Shaw, and Wilde may not have influenced historians directly, it too had an impact. As these playwrights scrutinized human motives, they viewed man as a victim of ambivalent and contradictory moods and goals. The late Victorian age saw a growing sympathy with Wilde and Shaw in parting the veil of self-deceptive respectability behind which psychological dishonesty had been concealed. To glorify the past by unbelievable rationalizations was really to falsify history, a hypocritical conspiracy against the truth. To shield man from his true nature was to depict his battles and wars as heroic epics, as wilful glorifications of the past.

Now critics saw man as still a drive-centered beast. They no longer chose to comfort society by denying that history was fraught with violence or that "both ruler and ruled indulge in the same need for self-justification," that each represses "self-seeking tendencies in order to live up to some kind of moral standards."[36]

Freud inferred that, in the future, historical specialists, aided by psychoanalysis, might unravel past group neuroses and thereby comprehend what motivated a society. By penetrating the symbolic content of unconscious behavior the psychohistorian could interpret latent material into the language of consciousness. The only hope of reforming a society that had neurotically deflected its libidinal drives away from socially useful ends was for it to acquire knowledge of man's hidden unconscious past. In studying primitive cultures Freud saw resemblances to the psychology of neurotics in the Western world. A society's totemisms and taboos, Freud maintained, are rooted in the Oedipus complex, which he considered the basis of neurosis. Neurotic man, like the savage, flees from "dissatisfying reality to a more pleasurable world of phantasy," further estranging himself from other human beings and institutions.

Freud was harsh concerning one of these institutions—organized religion. In a scarcely charitable book, *The Future of an Illusion,* he depicted religion as a childish defense against society's insecurity by an appeal to magical incantations. For Freud, a mass obsessional neurosis was at the heart of religion. As Philip Rieff has characterized it: "The pious are simply the neurotics of another culture epoch. Penance was analogized to obsessional acts."[37] Thus, for Freud, a nun telling her beads would be little different from a neurotic counting the buttons on his shirt.

Related to the perversions of religion was exploitation of the individual by the use of an evolutionary invention, guilt. Freud once called man's sense of guilt "the most important problem in our culture." Whether we label it guilt, conscience, or superego, the phenomenon becomes a dynamic controller of behavior. Individuals and societies alike are damaged by their continuing sense of shame at having offended and broken rules, morals, or taboos of family, tribe, or state. At the heart of this phenomenon is our infantile fear that we will no longer be loved. "None of us," writes one analyst, "relishes the idea of harboring a neurosis, because of its origin in an unconscious sense of guilt."[38] One's feelings of guilt may be increased or decreased by ridicule, denial, or projection onto others. Man historically has craved some form of release from guilt. Once people were ready to admit guilt about so simple a matter as not going to church on Sundays. Today we frequently encounter admission but also suppression of such guilt. Yet guilt, especially "true" guilt, cannot be obliterated by denial. "True guilt is guilt at the obligation one owes to oneself to be oneself, to actualize oneself," according to R. D. Laing. "False guilt is guilt felt at not being what other people feel one ought to be or assume that one is."[39]

Guilt remains intact in the case of a nation as well as of an individual. One thinks of the discernible feelings of the French over defeats at the hands of the Germans in 1870, 1918, and 1940. Similarly, in both England and France frequent references were publicly made to the allied "sell-out" of Czechoslovakia after the 1938 Munich agreement. As an English psychiatrist puts it: "Whether it was or was not possible to defend Czechoslovakia at that time, there is no doubt that most of us, at least unconsciously, felt a moral obligation to challenge the aggressor, and that our failure to do so aroused a great deal of unconscious guilt."[40] There followed the well-known defenses of denial of one's obligation, transference of responsibility (to France or the United States), or putting the blame onto the object of guilt (Czechoslovakia herself). But guilt feelings were not thereby extinguished. There is evidence that the modern Mexican nation has never gotten over the guilt of having lost the Mexican War to Yankee invaders who stormed the walls of Mexico City's Chapultepec Castle in 1845.

A once powerful country can suffer unconscious guilt over its abuse of nationalism in forcing superior rule over native peoples, as is the case of some modern English critics of their colonial past. The American South has, similarly, been spoken of as harboring latent guilt over its subjugation of the black culture, imported in slavery from Africa. At times national guilt feelings can become so aroused that a wanton aggressor power will defend itself against them by deluding its people into the belief that it is being attacked, a primitive device for the relief of anxiety.

The killing of fairly likable monarchs, including Charles I of England, Louis XVI of France, and Nicholas II of Russia, generated "enormous quantities of unconscious guilt." Although weak and obstinate, none of these rulers was personally cruel. Collective guilt over killing a father symbol, even in the case of the youthful President Kennedy, is sometimes so great that it goes unacknowledged or is suppressed. As with revolutionists who have killed off a king, historians may, instead, "overstress the vices of the royalists and the virtues of the revolutionaries." In a way, the historian thereby is forced to defend himself unconsciously against past feelings of guilt by others.[41]

One of Freud's most controversial (and odd) books, *Moses and Monotheism* (1939), produced additional insights on the origins of guilt. Specialists have criticised *Moses and Mono-*

theism as an historical work. Freud had no such illusions. He originally entitled it *The Man Moses, An Historical Novel*, about which he wrote: "It won't stand up to my own criticism. I need more certainty and I should not like to endanger the final formula. . . . so we will put it aside." On another occasion he was equally self-critical of his vision of Moses: "I am no good at historical romances. Let us leave them to Thomas Mann." Freud also wrote that the historical roots of the Moses story were "not solid enough to serve as a basis for my invaluable piece of insight."[42] Freud's speculative reconstructions of man's primal crime, as enunciated in his *Totem and Taboo* (1913), have also fallen into oblivion, mostly because he had to leave unprovable connecting threads hanging loosely. Just as anthropologists and sociologists resisted Freud's interpretations of sexual motivation, his absolutist explanations offended relativists. Conversely, we historians could argue that the anthropologists are too concerned with social patterning and not enough with the role of individuals in a culture.

The full reconstruction of man's primal record (from patricide to civilization) that Freud hoped for has proved to be all but impossible. This portion of his work has been suspended, if not discarded. The environment in which his notion of society was formed restricted Freud's view of anthropological man. His biological premises, too, have been superseded by new studies of animal aggressivity, territoriality, and metabolism. Freud was, paradoxically, a brilliant logician, yet given to some metapsychological speculations that were not wholly provable.

Although Freud's anthropology and biology may be dated, and although we quarrel with some of his precepts, from the start the Freudian technique had impressive possibilities within it for the historian, showing us how unconscious forces are constantly at work in our daily life. No matter how irrational or distorted man's acts appeared to be, Freud claimed that man always could find some underlying logic to them. Even paranoiacs, who distort reality severely, had their reasons for doing this. Simply to distinguish between mentally healthy and ill persons was a practical step forward in our understanding of man in society.

Although psychoanalysis has moved beyond Freud's formulations, a modern authority on schizophrenia reminds us that the "tripartite model of the Ego, Super-ego, and Id has proven the most useful and most encompassing working construct advanced to date for the understanding, prediction, and control of behavior."[43]

Had Freud not been so immersed in the treatment of patients, he might well have made other adaptations of his theory of psychoanalysis to history. He might have compared the way in which neurotics hide their emotions with the way dominant groups in a society also seek to obscure their history. Guilt about a nation's past may, indeed, encourage an "establishment history" that is bound to be critical of challenges to its elitist principles.

Long before Freud, of course, there were more than muted challenges to the belief that history rested upon solid, rational foundations. The writings of Schopenhauer, Nietzsche, Bergson, and William James all had acknowledged undercurrents in man's "stream of consciousness." Kierkegaard believed that man had lost touch with his inner nature. Unconscious drives under the facade of reasonableness thus were overdue to be probed, as James complained: "The recesses of feeling, the darker, blinder strata of character, are the only places in the world in which we catch real fact in the making." Marx, Comte, and Sorel also made serious inroads upon the belief that human action could, somehow, be divorced from emotion. As the twentieth century dawned, everywhere evident were forces that would foment resentments over restrictive dogmas, rituals, and social myths.

The Italian sociologist Vilfredo Pareto, too, dwelt upon the significance of unconscious factors in discerning those destructive repressed forces that so frequently influence group power. Pareto, however, used crude sociological terminology to describe how man rationalized his divided self. In France, Taine and Renan also showed an interest in the psychological interpretation of historical events. In England, Graham Wallas's *Human Nature in Politics* (1909) stressed the relation between thought and feeling, distrusting man's pure reason. Ludwig Feuerbach in Germany also joined in the attack upon conventional rationality, turning from Hegelianism to a philosophy stressing man's reabsorption by nature. Consciousness became, really, a consciousness of the infinite universe. Max Nordau went so far as to suggest that historians served the interests of the ruling classes by hiding the true natural forces behind events, distorting history in the name of objectivity.[44]

Lying near the heart of historical reappraisal there arose the concept that things were simply not what they seemed to be. No man appeared to function as one piece of flesh, blood, and mind. Split into parts, man was moved by fears and memories over which he had little control. These seemed remote, were not easily perceived, and were governed by forces derived from his complex internal nature. Although part of the physical universe, he internalized that world.

The new mass societies thus dissented from the bourgeois standards of Europe and America. By the twentieth century an authoritarian nihilism raged as the Marxian and Hegelian dialectics took their course. Terms like egoistic, self-centered, and irrationalist cropped up to describe man's isolation and alienation from his culture. An outburst of subsurface feelings and intuitive images threw into question the old faith in a manageable, stable, and perfectible life on earth. The new world of Comte, Darwin, Nietzsche, Schopenhauer, and Freud offered historians confusing evidence that man's conscious past had scarcely been a rational one.

Although an outwardly stable Victorian society troweled over unconscious insecurity, revolutionary "misfits" emerged to demand a leadership role. We now know what was not realized seventy-five years ago—that unconscious human hatreds may be expressed internally as anxiety or depression. They may also be displaced externally as prejudice or warfare. The fact that our century has seen so marked a deterioration of international relations, with defeatist substitutions of violence for order, reminds us that the destruction of life by mass riots or mechanized warfare frequently has been governed by unconscious forces. While Freud, Jung, and Adler turned their expanding knowledge of emotionality toward the treatment of individual patients, the political theorists Pareto and Gaetano Mosca wished to reconstruct whole societies (in the opposite direction) along scientific-materialist lines. Later, Mussolini, influenced by them, would become a quack doctor whose fascist corporate state poisoned his patients and those of his follower, Hitler.

In the twentieth century man's most civilized societies acquiesced in cruel acts of mechanized hostility, as if to affirm that "intellect plays a role subordinate to that of the blind and irrational emotions." This, because man "is not yet a fully domesticated animal."[45] In the light of obvious subterranean patterns for men's actions and thoughts, the old "name, fact, and date history" seemed steadily less relevant. Henceforth historians began not to treat all psychological findings as leprous. After World War I Sir Lewis Namier attributed history to something other than man's professed motives. Namier called man's historical sense "an intuitive understanding of how things do not happen." He believed, with Freud, that the reasons men give for their actions are rationalizations that cloak deeper purposes. His research focused upon the individual lives of almost two thousand members of the English Parliaments. "Namierization" came to mean the substitution of accurate personal details for vague political generalizations. Behind every idea or theory Namier saw a man, elusive and difficult to comprehend. Such a person's ideas or public behavior could be a mere rationalization of subsurface anxieties. For example, a revolutionary figure was found, in some cases, to be rebelling against his father. Namier considered knowledge of the unconscious as important to history as mathematics to astronomy. Without attention to psychological motivation, history became one-dimensional.[46]

More recently, the contemporary Rumanian-born philosopher E. M. Cioran has spoken of pure reason as "the rust of our vitality" and of historical study as the "terror of chronology." Both, he writes, lead us to separate consciousness from ultimate reality. Cioran thinks that supposedly air-tight philosophical systems inevitably fail men. He believes that man perpetuates almost instinctual prejudices that resist scrutiny and "withstand reasoning and proof"—truth being "based on the undemonstrable and unverifiable."[47]

Jung once wrote about man's insistence upon overestimating the value of pure reason:

> Most of my patients knew the deeper truth, but did not live by it. And why did they not live it? Because of that bias which makes us all put the ego in the centre of our lives—and this bias comes from the overvaluation of consciousness. . . . Unfortunately we keep

blundering along in the same dogmatic way, as if what we call the real were not equally full of illusion. . . . It cannot be compassed by the rational concepts of consciousness anymore than life itself.[48]

THE POST-FREUDIAN UNCONSCIOUS

Let us now consider some of the broader determinants of the historic unconscious that flowed from Freud's investigations. These include discovery of a most useful language of myths, symbols, and dream analysis in discerning underlying historical motivation. Although dead people cannot be psychoanalyzed and there can be no response from absent persons, humans do record their dreams. A dream repeatedly encountered in our culture can be applied to the past. Dreams may reflect that ongoing past which continues to live in the present "within the superego of each member of society."[49]

A dream can tell us much that a society sought to hide. Dreams do not record conscious thoughts, but reveal unconscious motives and pressures disguised by daily censorship. Concealed beneath their manifest content are latent meanings, sometimes even more confused by secondary elaboration, or reconstruction of the dream in waking life. Dreams deal with the emotional core of things, and symbolism pervades their content. The phallic symbol of the snake, often associated with Freudian analysis, also appears in the dreams of persons in non-Western societies. Dreams of the faeces, usually associated with wealth or money, recur in both advanced and primitive cultures. One's dreams may include technological symbols, for example the airplane. Mechanical flight has greatly influenced recent history; dreams about flying have been connected with a desire to master one's environment. Psychiatrists have, in fact, related the airplane's development to man's irrational urge to overcome an earth-centered existence, rather than to his sense of utility or scientific curiosity.[50]

The documentary value of a dream depends in part upon when it is recorded. If it is written down immediately, conscious-level material will not so likely intrude upon one's memory. In the 1930s a German journalist began to collect more than three hundred political dreams of nazi victims. A great number of persons were plagued by similar dreams during the period of the Third Reich.

German Jews dreamt repeatedly of being shot, martyred, scalped, of running for their lives, of having their teeth knocked out, of being humiliated. But their dreams were also full of disguises in the form of parables, paradoxes, and parodies. These dreams were preponderantly about persecution rather than about self-assertion. They illustrated how a totalitarian state can prevent people from leading private lives even in their dreams. For the nazis succeeded in destroying the ability of people to restore their emotional strength through dreaming.[51]

There is a generational consistency not only in dreams but in "the structure, functioning and development of human personality." This "makes it possible for a biographer to work effectively on the basis of data which would not suffice for the purpose of the psychoanalyst." The historian fortunately is "spared the difficult task of attempting to alter the subject's personality," but he can take advantage of the many thousands of complex cases studied by psychiatrists and psychoanalysts to help reconstruct "unconscious history."[52]

Wider understanding of Jung's theory of the collective unconscious has been delayed in part because he used inapplicable definitions to explain how man's psyche "does not operate along the lines of our accustomed rationality." Jung's symbolic language reached beyond logic to encompass nonrational functioning. His use of symbols, archetypes, and mythology is an attempt to decipher the unconscious behavior that supports the world of consciousness. Life's pattern of wholeness he saw in man's repressed secret language of symbol and myth. Myths become so firmly established that they cannot be easily undone, thus "the roots of the myth stretch into the unconscious."[53]

Yet the development of an individual personality or that of a society can be traced through what Jung called individuation, a partly historical process. For Jung considered that "the psyche does not reveal itself in the doctor's consulting room, but above all in the wide world, as well as in the depths of history." He believed that "just as human anatomy has a long evolution behind it, the psychology of modern man depends upon its historical roots, and can only be judged by its ethnological variants."[54] Over a series of generations it is possible to accumulate and to record meaningful cultural attributes, including gestures, expressions, smiles of approval, head and eye movements, glances, voiced disapprovals, smells, and signals. There is a veritable psychology of gestures that the historian has never seriously utilized, attributes that accompany a "collective unconscious" passed on from generation to generation. Freud, like Jung, spoke of "memory traces of the experiences of former generations."

Jung saw the collective unconscious as "a deeper stratum of the unconscious than the personal unconscious," influenced by inherited remnants. Thus our own history determines how we experience life, our brain itself having been "shaped and influenced by the remote experiences of mankind." For Jung, "it was the mental processes in our ancestors that created the paths," man's tendency to see life as he has been conditioned by the past being "archetypal."⁵⁵

How can the historian take account of a "collective unconscious?" Corroboration by anthropological evidence is difficult. Furthermore, parapsychological phenomena threaten established viewpoints and challenge the "consciously-arrived-at views" of social scientists who remain blocked toward new ways of seeing and knowing.

Future historians of the unconscious may be able to rely upon broad categories *(Gestalten)*. Already in widespread use within psychological circles, these include neurosis, schizophrenia, and paranoia. The Greek physician Galen had sought to classify humans according to psychological types. Today the categories that he called sanguine, phlegmatic, choleric, and melancholic seem naive. Much later, the artist Albrecht Dürer laid down virtually the same classification. These terms have become a regular part of our speech, refined and updated by Jung's work with psychological types. Jung became convinced that each of us is essentially an *introvert* or an *extrovert*. Also, Jung identified four functions: thinking, feeling, intuition, and sensation, by means of which we express ourselves, be we introvert or extrovert. The term used best and most often describes a person's major tendency, according to Jung.

Jung's *Psychological Types* (London, 1923) traces the historical influence of extroverted and introverted thought in the Western and the Oriental worlds. The outgoing, well-adjusted organizer whom society calls an extrovert has most often been associated with the material and technical development of

Europe and America. Conversely, spiritual wealth, but material poverty, appear natural to the introverted, inward-looking spirit of the East. (William Blake is an exemplar of the introverted and intuitive artist and poet in a Western setting.) .

Jung, furthermore, considered the Hindus "notoriously weak" in rational exposition. The Orient as a whole was "not interested in appealing to reason." He also, incidentally, believed that the Greeks thought with their hearts, rather than their heads, as did other ancient peoples.[56]

As to behavior, rough social categories gradually emerged, including peasants, city workers, artists, scholars, warriors, and professional people. In writing their history it is not enough to establish that certain people belong in particular niches. Man cannot be fully described by physical categories. The mental attributes that accompany physiognomy are also important. For this reason, Ivan Pavlov's laboratory experiments with animals led him to focus upon personality types, based upon their reflex reactions to stimuli.

Adler did not believe in such "typification" of past behavior. He considered each person unique as a human being. Yet he divided people into four types of "life-style." Adler made several modifications of Freud's concepts that are relevant to historians of the unconscious. His explanations of individual and group neurosis in terms of drives for power grew out of insight into man's attempts to cope with feelings of inferiority as the ego is overwhelmed by compensation for these *sentiments d'incompletude*. Deep feelings of inferiority may lead to character disorders that become crucial for the history of the world, if we concede that a Hitler or a Lee Harvey Oswald possessed disabilities that surfaced as aggressivity. A major source of mental illness, although not its only source, is frustration of basic human needs and overreaction in the pursuit of power over others. Adler even saw the sex drive as "determined by the goal of totality or superiority. We must always interpret abnormal sexual tendencies as expressions of the entire style of life, looking for the deeper movements which underlie them."[57]

Examination of the loneliness and alienation that have become prevalent in the Western world permeated the writings of the first generation of Freudians. Later cultural psychoanalysts refined unconscious behavioral theory: Karen Horney, with her descriptions of feminine neurotics; Harry Stack Sullivan, with his interpersonal constructs; Erik Erikson, with his probing of ego function; and Erich Fromm, with his analyses of authority in recent history.

AUTHORITY AND GROUP UNCONSCIOUSNESS

Fromm saw social processes as inseparable from psychological motivations within the individual and "the context of the culture which molds him."[58] Yet, for *homo politicus,* the defense of ego may revolve around "desire to control the motives of others, methods varying from violence to wheedling, and success in securing communal recognition."[59] Fromm stresses how man seeks relatedness to his fellows at the price of individuality. At the heart of this observation lies the magnetic power of dictatorship. On a national scale, loneliness and alienation can lead men to submit to that authoritarian power which gave rise to the nazis.

In the twentieth century one senses the anomie that has become man's fate in Western culture. It produces an ambivalence between excessive consciousness (rationality) and unconsciousness (nonexplainable). An authoritarian irrationality can, in fact, be foisted upon anxious societies in the name of collective order. The supposedly rational order of fascism or of communist economic determinism is actually a rationalization of rigid ideological belief systems, a disguising of unconscious factors for perverted purposes.

Knowledge of more than conscious-level behavior is thus necessary to understand the disturbances of a Hitler's use of the unconscious. Early in life he somehow unconsciously connected his mother's death from an "overdose" of morphine to his own "gassing" in World War I. In each case mother and son were treated by "Jewish doctors," whom he associated with "poisonous" and "cancerous" vapors. In Hitler's mind both episodes were escalated into a national drama in which Jews were poisoning the body politic of the German people. He must, therefore, be the savior of Germany against a hidden conspiracy. Hitler's "tortured and sick mind became convinced that the Jewish people were his personal enemy. The reason why he believed *that* lies in the murky realms of the unconscious and the irrational."[60]

As an outgrowth of his own insecurities, a leader can mobilize latent unreason, illusion, and ignorance. One thinks also of the Soviet terror after 1917, or of the deadlocked Arab-Jewish struggle in the Middle East.

There was, however, no more startling example of the manipulation of the unconscious mind than that practiced by the nazis. Hitler's effect upon some Germans was almost one of daemonic possession. As many as thirty thousand persons once stood in the rain for hours at Nuremberg Stadium awaiting the arrival of their frequently tardy leader, chanting "Wir wollen unsern lieben Führer" ("We want our beloved leader"). Repeated exposure to arousal phenomena may so sensitize individuals that they lose contact with reality. Acute excitement and emotional discontinuity lead to an almost unconscious state of surrender.

Both Freud and Gustave Le Bon had wondered why men behaved so much more irrationally in groups than as individuals. Freud's *Group Psychology and the Analysis of the Ego* suggested that this is because group behavior is basically regressive. Men, like children, are willing to renounce civic obedience in the name of the group. Power over group irrationality, Freud explained, could fall into the hands of a leader-father-surrogate who "needs no logical adjustment in his arguments: he must paint in the most forcible colours, he must exaggerate, and he must repeat the same thing again and again. . . ."

Under the nazis, European "civilization" provided a fragile barrier against the bestialities of mass arrests and incarceration in concentration camps. Did men have an unconscious need for punishment of their fellow humans? And why? Was it because ruthlessness expresses concealed anxiety? The group can be made "as intolerant as it is obedient to authority." In such an atmosphere the group, which respects force, comes to look upon kindness "as a form of weakness. What it demands of its heroes is strength, or even violence." The group, wrote Freud (1921), "wants to be ruled and oppressed and to fear its masters. Groups have never thirsted after truth. They demand illusions and cannot do without them." Within the security of the group, men—obedient to mass authority—can regress to an earlier state of dependent infancy. By setting aside the demands of one's individual superego, "group norms can support delinquent conduct which private consciences could not tolerate."[61]

Freud distrusted the long-run effects of revolutionary groups, and their anarchical tendencies. Coercive social systems he saw as repeatedly overthrown, only to be succeeded by other authoritarian institutions or regimes. He saw the "mob mind" as ruled by the hypnotic spell of a primal father, whom the hordes followed blindly and obediently, as if they wanted to submit to his authority—a veritable flight of the soul. The nazi tyranny exemplified the extreme "archaic and irrational ties to the primal horde leader."[62] "Panic states" could follow loss of a key leader. Under stress of panic, which, Freud observed, "often breaks out on the most trivial occasions," people could go berserk, being incapable of tolerating frustration and delays, and could regress to childish states of disorganisation. One recalls the mass fear that gripped rural prerevolutionary France or postearthquake San Francisco in 1906, when normal leadership collapsed.

Even when there is no emergency, Aldous Huxley observes in his *The Devils of Loudun* (1952), man has a deep-seated urge for self-transcendence. He may satisfy this by alcohol, sex, drugs, or by fleeing toward collective manias. The individual who seeks to transcend himself in a crowd gains absolvence from past guilts and future fears by what Huxley calls "herd-intoxication." Identification with a cause, religious or political, offers escape. As a member of some patriotic or revivalist group, one can achieve the "blissful consciousness of being someone else." Adler, too, noted how neurotics disguise their inadequacies by making "causes" responsible, thereby reassuring themselves of their personal worth. To join a mass movement or to worship an idol becomes a flight from selfhood. The more excited the mob, the more complete the frenzy of escape and, sometimes, hypnotic transcendence.

Among object-fixated, self-righteous persons, deep emotions well up to justify individual violence and collective warfare. Seemingly lost causes, like the Confederate secession from the Union, can be sustained for generations by a subjective militancy based upon feelings of self-love, pride, and glory.[63]

The *actions* of groups may not be wiser or more rational than those of individuals. Jung said about large groups that to preserve their entity they must stress the adaptation of their members, cultivating average, rather than unusual, qualities. The larger the group, he reasoned, the more stupid it is likely to become. Even a group of highly intelligent people usually acts at a lower level of intelligence than its individual members.[64]

The tendency toward conformity is strengthened when a community is threatened, from without or from within. Then "the herd huddles together and becomes more intolerant than ever of 'cranky' opinion."[65] While much social history has been written since George Lefebvre's pioneer work on crowds in the 1920s, historians seem content to focus on who made up the crowd in history, not upon its motives for action.

> Being primitive, the group is characteristically impetuous, irritable, changeable. It is often convinced of its near omnipotence. It is credulous, suggestible, intolerant, and prone to violence. Generally conservative, it coddles traditions and self-fortifying illusions. Dominated by a collective subconsciousness, it is given to extremes in ethical conduct and matters of sentiment. The group's intellectual capacities are invariably lower than are the individual member's.[66]

A nation may manage its relations with other nations in ways that spring from the unconscious. One authority on foreign policy believes it is "the primary task of rationality in politics . . . to understand and handle irrationality." Still others find the foreign policy of most countries shot through with habitual patterns of unreason. For example, on the one hand the Germans conspired to bring about the Bolshevik revolution in order to do away with monarchical government in Russia; on the other hand they did not foresee that the same revolutionary fervor would spread, albeit in communist forms. These protest movements ultimately helped to cause the military defeat of their own kaiser. After World War I "the victorious western allies treated the new German government as though it had caused the war. . . ." Instead of propping up the Weimar Republic (a democracy they had helped to establish), the allies irrationally insisted upon viewing the new and fragile "German democracy as potentially hostile, similar to the regime it had superseded." Other instances of "irrationality" in the conduct of foreign relations may grow out of nationalism, ignorance of local conditions, lack of information, misinterpretation of fragmentary data, prejudice, or simple wrongheadedness. Nonpsychiatric origins thus may influence a nation's conduct in directions contrary to existing conditions.[67]

Related to crowd behavior is the phenomenon of revolution, with which our own age has been unusually afflicted. Here, again, knowledge of the unconscious helps us to understand the revolutionary syndrome. There is evidence that some revolutionists harbor unresolved oedipal problems and that their anally regressed materialism can be self-defeating. E. Victor Wolfenstein's study of Gandhi, Lenin, and Trotsky maintains that a "revolutionary personality" is one who "had an unusually ambivalent relationship with his father," and that a potential revolutionist's "conflict with paternal authority must be alive and unresolvable in the family context as adolescence draws to a close."

Revolutionists are seldom nonviolent. An act of violence is a break with the historic order, an explosive attempt to reshape that order, sometimes out of a sense of despair. Violence transforms creative energy into brute force. A crowd is energized into a howling mob. A coward becomes a murderer; to detroy, to smash, to burn becomes fused with the neurotic urges of people who have contempt for others, and even for themselves. Dostoevski reaffirmed this for us in *The Possessed.*

A few generations ago historians believed that revolutionary crowds were composed primarily of riffraff, ne'er-do-wells, drifters, and other misfits. Recent studies of crowd behavior have given us a different view of the French Revolution and similar outbreaks. Those respectable middle-class leaders, as well as liberal aristocrats, shopkeepers, and small merchants *(bourgeoisie),* who joined the mobs on the streets of Paris in 1789 and 1848 hardly corresponded to the *canaille* depicted by Taine and earlier writers. Fused together contagiously by revolutionary concepts, the so-called dregs of a society can temporarily join its elite in forcing social, economic, or political change. And this fusion-phenomenon is, in part, unconsciously motivated.[68]

Unacknowledged desires, excluded from man's consciousness except in dreams or daydreams, may take the form of moral uneasiness whose outlet is fanatical devotion to a political or religious cause as people "act out" Jung's repressed "collective unconscious." We conveniently forget early traumas, substituting deceptive constructs (often via transference and reidentification) concerning sex, motherhood, family, and other elements of daily life. What may be socially unacceptable thus becomes

buried. Yet, lost in the unconscious are archetypes that once
may have exercised a powerful influence. For some neurotics it
is as though their signals had gotten twisted, as they took refuge
in paradoxical feelings of flight or fight.

CHILDHOOD AND CULTURE

Yet another aspect of the historic unconscious concerns
childhood and family life. One could speak of the childhood of
nations, those formative periods when the role of a country is
shaped by its national experience. With nations, as with children, only slowly have historians accepted the finding that disturbed behavior has sometimes resulted from flawed earlier settings. Although family errors (some of them embarrassing) are
difficult to pinpoint, within the family each generation learns
to hold a culture's values in common (or to misconstrue them).
The family, despite its weakening in modern times, has been
more long lasting than have changing laws and fragile governments.

As we turn somewhat away from the state as a unit of inquiry,
greater attention is bound to be given to the nuclear family, a
universal form of social organization. Long-term transformation
of the family in Western culture lies at the heart of historical
behavior. The family is the one core upon which most civilizations have rested, and the loyalty that men have given the family has been nearly unique.

Unconsciously, a child's fears may well up within the family
setting, with little surface explanation of their origins. Melanie
Klein reconstructed those infantile phantasies in children (after
their later breakdowns) that bore virtually no resemblance to
early "real" experiences. She suggested that these irrational ter-
rors were based on fear of punishment for forbidden desires and
linked with a biological inheritance carried into historic times.
Freud believed these childhood phantasies come from primitive
conflicting feelings about parents. For example, young boys
sometimes displace those feelings from their fathers onto animals, thereby externalizing inner conflict. (See Freud's study of
"Little Hans.")

Jung also considered the problem of why the members of a
family react differently to life's obstacles and challenges:
"Why, in a neurotic family, does one child react with hysteria,

another with a compulsion neurosis, the third with a psychosis, and the fourth apparently not at all?'' This choice of neurotic style "robs the parental complex of all aetiological meaning and shifts the enquiry to the reacting individual and his special disposition."[69] Family life has a certain randomness about it. A dissenter or an eccentric exists in most families. On the American scene "a solid Middle Western family of farmers for three generations produces a free thinker and radical who becomes a schoolteacher; the son of an immigrant labor leader becomes a staunch Republican; the son of an orthodox rabbi, a frivolous columnist of a New York periodical."[70]

The historian must look also at the roles of an only child or of first-born siblings or of children born into a large family. Suggestive are the birth order of individual children, their adjustment (or lack of it) to reality, and the irregularities that may grow out of a child's adjustment to his parent's distorted demands.

Male and female identification with the father affects relations with later authority figures—teachers, employers, government officials. If a society places a high value upon authority, it becomes especially difficult to work out child-father identifications. They may remain unresolved within both family and other culture groups.

The early Freudians saw the primal father as both scourge and strength, yet considered the family the prototype of man's most binding relationships. They located emotional disturbances within the vortex of family existence, as expressed in Freud's "psychopathology of everyday life." Jung viewed succeeding generations as acting out the repressed wishes of their parents. Dormant or repressed yearnings, he reasoned, were realized in subsequent times, but their origin was within childhood.

In relation to the unconscious mind the family provides an important setting in which rivalries, confusion, or cohesiveness develops. The myth of family can capture the child's imagination, especially if he feels insecure about his origins. The phenomenon called "family romance" had a great influence, for example, upon Joseph Conrad, who looked back to a golden childhood that he had been denied by flight from his native Poland. In other cases the child creates a phantasy that he has been adopted from a more famous lineage than he sees in his parents. These awful people cannot really be his parents. He, therefore, creates a mythical, more romantic and dramatic, family to take their place.

Sometimes problems emerge from living within the bower of a famous family like the Roosevelts, the Adams family, the Beechers, or the Kennedys. One can consult the youthful diary of Charles Francis Adams to get the feel of what it was like to be the son of John Quincy Adams: "To judge by the amount of study being given to the subject in the 20th century, the problem of growing up in the Adams family was one of the most unusual and difficult feats a human being could be called on to perform in the 18th or 19th centuries." Charles Francis Adams' diary documents his "painfully slow start toward mastery of himself and thereby toward his important place in the diplomatic, political, and cultural history of his country and his central place in the Adams story for half a century."[71] He and his son, that notable man of letters Henry Adams, became bound up in an inner-connected web of aspiration as well as frustration. Robert F. Kennedy once spoke of the need to battle one's way to the top as a member of his large family of individualists.

Another phenomenon that may occur among "political families" is the creation of an almost unconscious dynastic succession, such as characterized the Borgias in Italy. In America modified political succession also occurred among the Adams, Roosevelt, La Follette, Taft, Kennedy, and Lodge families. Unconscious identification with the father's career shaped some private emotional needs—for good or ill—within the bower of these families, alongside social processes.

LEADERSHIP AND THE UNCONSCIOUS

Twenty years ago Harold Lasswell pioneered in utilizing the "insight interview" to discover unconscious motivation in political leaders. He, like Freud, saw how early childhood is the locus of formative defenses against subsurface "strategies devised by the individual in an effort to harness his anxieties and to avoid situations in which they might have severely disruptive effects."[72]

Lasswell and his followers found public leaders high or low in their unconscious need to affiliate with power. Politicians are conservative, authoritarian, and open or closed minded. We know that some have been misanthropes, intolerant of ambiguity, and provincial, as well as introverted, narcissistic, and filled with dependency needs. The Lasswellians have increased the attention paid to the inner-directed and other-directed typology of David Riesman, and to optimism, pessimism, altruism, or exhibitionist versus apathetic characteristics, as well as to sadism, masochism, and manic-depressive behavior.[73]

Politics, for some leaders, has been a way to gain deference; for others it has allowed them to overcome a low estimate of themselves, or isolation, loneliness, and resentment of authority. Rebelliousness toward conformity may take the form of radical or unconventional behavior. Unconscious craving to command respect is sometimes related to an almost compulsive revolt against established authority. Each leader must, somehow, cut the binding ties of parental control, frequently via repressed hatred for the father.

Although at the conscious level the leader can never admit such matters, one sees his fear of the unconscious repeatedly. Consider how some politicians shy away from subsurface emotional topics. If they can do so, the shrewdest of them shun discussions of war and criminal punishment (which mask aggression), or religion and communism (which plumb intrapsychic tensions), or birth control and obscenity legislation (matters of sexuality). These are socially dangerous and threatening subjects that draw disproportionately volatile responses from constituents because they touch troublesome unconscious forces.[74]

Although some behavior of political figures may be ego-defensive, the historian must remain open to nonreductive explanations. Not all political motivation is related to defense of ego.

Beyond group motivation in history, therefore, lies the rich field of individual behavior. We need to know much more about how renowned persons respond to stress. Do they, as in the case of President Franklin D. Roosevelt, after his poliomyolitis attack at Campobello, reshape their lives to meet new conditions? Or, as in the case of San Francisco's "Emperor Norton," do they resort to neurotic, schizophrenic, or paranoiac behavior? What unconscious factors caused America's first secretary of defense, James Forrestal, to leap to his death from the Bethesda Naval Hospital?

Even among relatively "healthy minded" leaders, unconscious needs may move them toward politics, as with two arch-
antagonists, Alexander Hamilton and Thomas Jefferson. Both
looked to a living father symbol, Washington, for emotional
support and guidance in rivalry and crisis. The brave but by no
means brilliant Washington, in turn, may himself have moved
toward political leadership in order to satisfy unconscious
needs.[75] The personalities of Generals Washington, Grant, and
Eisenhower played a part in their choice of political as well as
military involvements.

There are, of course, limits to "psychologizing" past leadership. Although personality is the reason some men go into politics, a society's institutions also determine what kinds of people
lead it, as do events. During the French Revolution no single
leader could have eliminated the social issues that gave rise to
Mirabeau, Robespierre, or Napoleon. Had these leaders not
been available, others would have taken their places. As long as
great public needs remained unsatisfied, the revolutionary
movement in France would have continued. Obsolete political
institutions were as significant as emotions in determining what
took place. At times, the possibility of the individual influencing the fate of a culture may be great. Yet the leader cannot
turn back the clock concerning social forces. Lamprecht once
said that Bismarck, even at the height of his powers, could not
keep Germany from moving toward a socialized economy. Thus
the extent of a leader's influence is determined by the organization of a society, and by the forces within it. There would have
been no Presidents Grant or Eisenhower without the United
States Army and two crucial wars. Quite possibly there would
have been no F.D.R. and J.F.K. presidencies without Harvard,
radio, and television. No Harry Truman and Lyndon Johnson
would have emerged as presidents without the United States
Senate and the deaths of their predecessors.

Erikson suggests that, in the case of five reform-minded
innovators—Luther, Gandhi, Kierkegaard, Wilson, and Elea-
nor Roosevelt—they exhibited a low self-esteem that led them
toward greater compassion for their fellow humans.[76] In appearance, size, and physical attraction both Gandhi and Mrs. Roosevelt may have felt inferior. But a definite, perhaps compensatory, moral and spiritual "superiority" ran through their

careers. As to Wilson, a low self-estimate churned up feelings of inadequacy, for which he overcompensated, developing an unwillingness to share power, to take advice, to delegate responsibility, or to inform others while seeking to impose personal order upon his environment.[77] Feelings of unimportance become euphoria, as if to transcend former weakness and inadequacy.

The search for motive may lead one down some strange alleyways. A leader's personal associations may be based upon guilt, and an unconscious need for self-punishment. This could have been the case with King Leopold of Belgium, whose inner difficulties helped to determine the course his country took during World War II. A recent analysis of Leopold's actions shows how his neutralist foreign policy was related to hyperpersonal as well as to strictly political factors. While it is possible to overstress the importance of single events (especially those far removed from childhood), personal motives may become political ones.

Leopold, like his father, Albert, affirmed Belgium's neutrality as a cardinal assumption from which he would never swerve. Leopold admired Albert's conduct during World War I, when the son had been an impressionable young man. He had also been shocked by his father's death in a grisly mountain accident in 1934. Two years later, barely eighteen months after his own accession, Leopold's beautiful wife, Queen Astrid, also had been killed in a mountain auto collision at Küssnacht, with Leopold at the wheel of their car. Leopold apparently suffered, first from unconscious oedipal guilt over a childhood death wish against his father. This became translated into a duty to carry out the father's will, long after a policy of neutrality was advantageous to Belgium. Second, the death of his equally popular wife at his own hands threw him into deep grief. Leopold's premonition of a sudden, staggering German *Blitzkrieg* can be compared to the *choc* which the earlier auto accident had produced. He determined to meet all these crises alone, disregarding the advice of his ministers, who wanted Belgium to join the allies in fighting off the nazis. Rudolph Binion traces the similarities between the death of Leopold's queen and the impending "death" of Belgium. For both events Leopold wished to be held blameless. He treated these tragedies as essentially personal ones for which he must assume direct responsibility, refusing to abandon either his country or the memory of his queen. Thus "the skill with which Leopold III, haunted by the private tragedy of Küssnacht, unconsciously continued its repetition as a Belgian national tragedy was downright uncanny. Unobtrusively, he imposed his purposes on successive governments until May 25, 1940—even then his failure served his further purposes." Leopold seems to have consciously imitated his father at the same time he was unconsciously reliving the Küssnacht tragedy.[78]

Adrift amid the frustrations and barbarisms of an age such as that in which we live, some creative leaders virtually doom themselves to unhappiness. One thinks of Harold Nicolson, a diplomat with high credentials, the author of eight books, once a member of the English Parliament and the confidant of Churchill. Yet Nicolson's memoirs reveal that he always considered himself an outsider. His diaries are riddled with self-doubt, almost to the point of a decayed self-esteem.[79] Such persons can be overwhelmed by a sense of stagnation and decadence about what they seek in life. This can result, as it did with Luther, in that imbalance that psychiatrists call manic-depressive.[80]

There is a practical reason why it is important to analyze the unconscious drives of political leaders. Great men exercise a decisive influence upon history. To fathom the motivations of persons who seek political power is related to the very process of how mankind has been led in the past and may be governed in the future. Erikson reminds us of the complexities involved:

> Whether or not mankind can afford its great men, sickness and all, is another question. Before we can even approach it we must first learn to recognize the afflictions of our favorite heroes, as well as the madness in those great men whom we could do without. For . . . the influence of the men we elect, support, or tolerate can indeed . . . be felt beyond the third and fourth generation.[81]

The role of leaders was increasingly seen as related to "ego psychology," a concept pioneered by Heinz Hartmann, Anna Freud, Ernst Kris, and Erikson. Their studies lifted Freud's concept of the ego out of the position of a battleground between id (or instinct) and superego (or conscience). His drive-oriented analysis had stressed the potential injuriousness of both id and overly active superego. Erikson did not focus only upon stages of development rooted in early life. He showed how a personality may continue to unfold as an adult, responding to society's "organ modes." Erikson's studies of Luther and Gandhi did not invoke the dubious authority of narrow specialists. He avoided the fictional comfort of precision while crossing the borders of history, medicine, theology, philology, anthropology, and sociology.

It is a long leap from considering a leader's past acts to describing the reasons for those acts. Before jumping that chasm, caution and tentativeness are necessary, for it is hard enough to understand the motives of living men. Yet the historian does know at least part of what was once said about a dead leader or by him, even though the records may be mute concerning key points. Much of that kind of information, however, was oral, and thus lost to posterity. Yet, given good sources, the historian may gain a better grasp of what occurred than did even a man's contemporaries, for they "were imprisoned in their time as we are in ours, and they could not fully grasp the significance of what was happening before their eyes; they were also imprisoned in space, and could not grasp the significance of distant events."[82]

Although Erikson's *Luther* has been attacked as paying too little attention to nonpsychological details, it corrected the writing of an earlier historian who, surprisingly, overpsychologized Luther. This reputable scholar, Preserved Smith, was fascinated by Freudian notions, but his analysis of Luther reflected his own Puritan background. (Smith was intrigued by a possible relationship between masturbation and Luther's sense of guilt.) Historians who so misuse popular psychology undermine the credibility of unconscious evidence as much as do psychologists who use history uncritically.

Among the factors which Erikson considered important in a leader like Luther were active remnants of childhood repression, his loves and rages, and those things that make a leader feel guilty, ashamed, and mistrustful but that are dissipated by the recuperation of dreaming and sleeping. He also examined Luther's brooding despair, the unhappiness of childhood caused by excessive parental harshness (displaced obsessively upon God as an avenger), and that *angustus* (anxiety) by which a person feels hemmed in or choked up. Erikson analyzed suspiciousness, obsessive scrupulosity, sadism, and preoccupation with dirtying and infectious thoughts—factors frequently linked together. Luther's early predictions that his "speaking impulsively" would lead to a "judgment day" were also connected with his rustic provinciality, in contrast to Luther's grand conscious-level expansiveness.

Serious unconscious anxieties may cause procrastination, a conscious-level phenomenon with underlying causes. The historian can perceive avoidance of decision making in leaders as different in personality and time as Queen Elizabeth I, President Abraham Lincoln, or Hitler. A latent rigidity could have influenced an irresolute and habitually tardy Hitler's failure to invade England as much as did strategic considerations. Repeatedly, the Hamlet-like Hitler entered into periods of rumination before undertaking a new course of action. About Hitler's indecision over the invasion of Poland, Alan Bullock has written: "At every crisis in his career—in 1932, in June, 1934, September, 1938, as much as now—he had found it difficult to make up his mind, hesitating, listening first to one, then to another, argument, waiting for some sudden impulse to carry him forward." [83] One would need to examine childhood patterns of behavior carefully before venturing an explanation of such procrastination. In Hitler's case it was not unconscious indecision alone that kept him from crossing the channel. He was bound by the past, in a determination to avoid the costly errors of World War I. In 1914 General von Moltke had been stopped at the Marne River in France by his excessive attention to English forces on his flanks. In 1940 Hitler stopped his panzer tanks at Dunkirk, allowing the British to escape from his own flank on the Somme.

We know that some disturbed persons shun freedom of choice or promises of release from the prisonry of their daily lives. Conservative routine becomes a form of personal salvation. Konrad Lorenz has observed that some animal habits become so ingrained that they cannot be broken without a creature being stricken by fear. Anxiety is painful, and routine flight is one way to allay anxious feelings. [84] Procrastination, a form of escape, may be connected with this need.

Procrastination is only one characteristic that the historian may encounter. The narcissistic personality appears and reappears in history, just as he does in daily life. A few of the distinguishing characteristics include a self-centered and rather continuous search for approval which may get distorted as a need for disapproval. Regression to infantile narcissism sometimes leads persons to react to the present in unbalanced childish ways. Adversity is countered by defensive childhood phantasies that continue to rule the adult. Early disruptions in the life of the child may terminate in deep character weaknesses that feature ego-defenses sometimes expressed as phobias. The narcissistic character may grasp at "safety" even if it is an unreliable straw. Dependency needs make it imperative that the patient act out and share his childhood excitations.[85]

Political assassinations remind the historian of how unconscious delusion, hallucination, and confusion of reality can alter historical events. Individuals on the fringes, or outside normally organized society, seem to provide a pool from which assassins come. Some of these reflect displaced lower-middle-class uneasiness about the future. In a society like the United States, where rapid change is hard to control, angered individuals spring up who are too rigid and maladjusted to accept. And those leaders who preach the need for change create both hatred and fear in the minds of such reactionaries. Violence becomes a response to imagined threat. In frustration, malcontents strike out against such harbingers of change as the charismatic Kennedys, who seemed to be leading America toward threatening readjustments in a confusing technological environment.[86]

Other assassins may have unfulfilled sex drives, perhaps accompanied by alienation and envy. As they slide toward despair, their deranged minds can no longer deflect the unconscious wish to destroy authority figures (Freud's primal fathers). Since the time of Brutus these frustrated men have reacted like animals in a cage. From Lincoln's time to the present the killers of major American figures—Booth, Guiteau, Czolgosz, Oswald, and Sirhan—all suffered from a sense of being blocked in life. Obsessed by complex fixations, their emotions exploded. Whatever the unconscious cause, their violence interrupted national historical patterns and affected the lives of countless persons.[87]

As we have suggested, historians are sometimes in a better position than a man's contemporaries to interpret underlying motives. "If in the past a writer unconsciously attributed motive to irrational impulses, it would have done him no good to formulate his unconscious assumption, for scholarly knowledge of the workings of the human mind ended at the limits of rationality, but today we know enough about the nature of the unconscious to be able to some degree to evaluate our hunches about unconscious motivation."[88]

Can the need for unconscious documentary evidence concerning individuals long since dead ever be met? Yes. Gustave Flaubert left behind thirteen volumes of correspondence, each containing some six hundred pages. He frequently wrote to several individuals during the same day. He also left behind diaries and a complete archive of letters with George Sand of a candid, personal nature. Flaubert's autobiographical writings are, furthermore, highly self-revelatory. Only our need to perfect analytic skill stands in the way of a model reconstruction of unconscious motivation in the case of Flaubert. Proust, too, left behind some four thousand letters that are remarkable in communicating his living presence. The survival of personal documents that reflect the unconscious sometimes depends upon circumstance. Although Henry Adams destroyed his diaries following his wife's suicide, the journals of William Byrd II are full of material for the discovery of motivation. The writings and correspondence of the Italian revolutionary leader Giuseppe Mazzini run to more than one hundred volumes.

The imaginative writings of novelists provide further images that can be mined concerning inner feelings. The books of Jean Paul Sartre, for example, are full of images of an internal world toward which its author turns, sickened by the viscous, chaotic nature of external existence.

Jean Delay, an internationally renowned psychiatrist, has given us perhaps more accurate professional information about the homosexuality of André Gide than even Gide could have known. Delay had the help of journals and memoirs into which Gide poured out intimate sexual thoughts over a period of sixty years. Gide's desperate attempts at self-understanding also spilled over into confessional letters to cousins, uncles, aunts, and, above all, to his mother.[89]

A writer often uses letters or a diary as a device for resolving inscrutable unconscious tensions. The diary of Anais Nin became so pervasive a part of her life that she sought the counsel of Otto Rank in order to understand its tyrannical demands upon her. These inner conflicts may be productive in a literary sense, but destructive psychologically, as with Walt Whitman and Ernest Hemingway. Letters may become a means by which personal failures and the inability to sustain close relationships are rationalized to others. Thomas Wolfe's letters show us a genuine transference of emotion from his mother's charisma (the dominant figure in his life) to his writing. The punishing silences of his mother had a discernible effect upon Wolfe's work.

Is man—past or present—ever fully capable of knowing what motivates unconscious behavior? André Malraux's book *Man's Fate (La Condition Humaine)* has as its premise the idea that man, utterly alone, never fully knows his ''condition.'' A few may manage to reach momentary understanding of themselves, but this is fleeting and even illusory. Cut off like Christ in the agony of crucifixion, it is as though the soul itself has been severed from the life source, the *élan vital*. Humans, rather than face the fact that they cannot know their inner natures, writes Malraux, patch up a scaffolding. This creates a measure of comfort in overcoming anxiety and loneliness. To confront the brute fact of one's aloneness is almost beyond man. To Malraux, existentialism means awareness of this aloneness. He considers it rare to find a thinking person able to ''live his condition.''

Just as drama has come to stress an inner ''theater of being,'' pitched at the level of internal experience, the future craft of history will concern itself with the unconscious struggles of the past. If there are really no self-evident rules in the universe, why should there be conscious-level rules in history? Specific conventions in drama, religion, and science appear to be dead or dying. Many psychiatrists would insist that, without attention to unconscious factors, one looks at life as through a glass darkly and one is apt to see a reflection of a reflection rather than the truth. There may be a lesson for historians in all of this.

CONCLUSIONS

Man still searches to discover his unconscious identity. To seek out this real self in the past becomes, in fact, a way to depict the present. Peter Drucker has called our complex times the age of discontinuity. But, in a sense, the emotional life of man—his truly personal history—has been a perennial record of fragmentation. History, as a centralizing discipline, is uniquely suited to describing man's total selfhood. History is concerned with what it means to be a human being, inwardly as well as outwardly.

As we have seen, Freud was not alone in seeking the importance of the unconscious. Artists, too, have shown us how the arts are to society what dreams are to the individual—projections of underlying mental states. Experimenters as different as Hieronymus Bosch and, later, James Joyce, Gertrude Stein, Pablo Picasso, Salvador Dali, the Dadaists, and the surrealists suggested that new forms of truth may erupt out of man's unconscious. Some of their symbolisms resemble the free-association material unearthed by psychoanalysis. Dreams, symbols, and myths make up the underlying process that artists tap, inspiring art forms that are partly a nonvolitional reflection of unconscious impulses.[90]

The enlargement of historical method may eventually occur in the same way that the arts have recently evolved as inarticulate forms. From the late nineteenth century onward, artists created not only new aesthetics but devised the media and techniques necessary to express them. The ideological backgrounds that encouraged such developments ranged from the Romantic revolt to the advance of technology. Arnold Schönberg, for example, vastly expanded standard harmonic theory. He not only reflected the times in which he lived but moved music beyond a system of articulate, consciously heard chords in a manner that resembled the psychoanalytic unearthing of conscious thought. Classical polyphony thereby gave way to a new musical approach.

Picasso has striven to rearrange art forms so that his views of people are multidimensional, combining internal conditions as well as external states—the whole viewed at differing times. Picasso (like Lasswell) speaks of rearranging reality to arouse "a new emotion in the mind of the viewer, because it momentarily disturbs his customary way of defining what he sees. It would be very easy to do these things by traditional methods, but this way I can engage the mind of the viewer in a direction that he hadn't foreseen and make him re-discover things he had forgotten."[91]

Anton Ehrenzweig believes that such inarticulate thoughts as pervade dreams, reveries, daydreams, jokes, and creative vision originate in the lower layers of the mind, rather than in its more rational cortex.[92] Primitive art, which sometimes resembles the dream in structure, reminds one both of infantile and of unconscious minds. Such insights go beyond normal cultural explanations of societal change.

The approach that Freud originally propounded cannot provide us with complete answers to why men or societies evolved in a given way. It can, however, give historians, in the words of Marc Bloch, "nothing more nor less than a perspective whose legitimacy is proved by its fruitfulness, but which must be supplemented by other perspectives. . . ."[93] If the historian can overcome "resistances," partly historic in nature, new insights may burst forth to which he once was blind. We cannot reset the stage of history, call back its actors, or ask what motivated them. Even if we could, they would not necessarily know what it was that made them act. Yet tomorrow's historians will wish to probe conscious and unconscious impulses, especially repetitive ones.

Historians have a responsibility to utilize the exciting new methods that become available seriatim. We possess more verifiable data into the unconscious than ever did Thucydides, Dilthey, or Freud. It is no longer quite so becoming to deny the relationship between man's inner thoughts and outer acts, although we have been trained to interpret only the conscious, or public, circumstances of a man, a crowd of men, or a nation.

There are, of course, pitfalls to probing the unconscious. Such research must be as cautious as it is emancipative. Continued attention must be paid to verifiability. This is a major stricture to be imposed upon one's findings. Regrettably the 1920s, which saw the fashion of lay psychological analysis raging, spawned amateurs who exercised irresponsible freedom. Whereas today's analysts spend months exploring the neuroses of living people, the lay biographers of the twenties quickly made up their minds concerning the psychoses of Lincoln or George III. Snap judgments leaped to the pens of the Lytton Stracheys, Philip Guedallas, and Emil Ludwigs. The Strachey era of iconoclasm sought to trace the origins of Charlotte Brönte's genius, to examine the alleged lesbianism of Margaret Fuller, the psychosexual infantilism of Swift, and the anal-sadistic impotence of Carlyle. From 1920 to 1940, especially, biographers intrigued by the Adlerian dicta of inferiority complexes, power madness, sublimation, defense mechanisms, and compensation, scavenged history in search of subjects onto which they could affix pretailored conclusions. Although unable to cross-examine a dead author, biographers misused the Freudian technique of examination via free association. Inexpert biographers wrote as though their subjects were only slightly affected by historical, geographical, or economic conditions. Queen Victoria, General Gordon, Wellington, Napoleon, Byron, and Disraeli appeared in highly lacquered books as leaders who shaped the times in which they lived. The times seldom made the men. Overstressing individuality, "Stracheyism" featured those controversial, subsurface matters in which people frequently become enmeshed; the historical events that also shape man's life and society took second place. But, these writers who reposed so great a faith in the intuitive approach also mocked the "littleness" in men. At the same time they dealt with what they believed was the inner spirit and tried to reconstruct conflicts, tensions, ambitions, and passions, crowding out political, economic, or social factors. Because the historian, trained in accuracy, deeply resents the mistakes of the amateur, he has developed a caution toward unconscious factors that is understandable. Living with the human record, he becomes time's arbiter, the measurer of its pace, of its ebb and flow. But this demands a delicacy operative below the surface, whatever irrational factors creep into the reconstructed story. Writers untrained in history are not apt to grasp psychohistorical subtleties that relate to periodicity and ambience. As a result, they sometimes reach startling irrelevant conclusions.

In searching for unconscious motivation we must acknowledge that we are denied the great tool of the psychoanalyst, the unstructured personal interview, in which unconscious motives are usually revealed. We must, therefore, learn to live with indefiniteness and to concentrate upon maximizing certain ranges of evidence. Yet, by making careful use of letters, diaries, and memoirs, as well as of screened recollections, the historian can go a long way toward reconstructing motives. Word-association techniques, medical records, and computer research can also prove helpful. On the other hand, we may never fully recover the "inner reasons" why a person, group, or nation acted in a deviant or "normal" way. We may be forced to settle for indirect insights. This sort of approach does not offer the statistical validative security of econometrics. For man is perverse.

As a result of the devaluation of emotion, important insights have been lost in the reconstruction of historical events. American and English historians of recent times have produced writings steeped in excessive rationalism. Overstressing abstraction, they have underestimated the ways in which feelings influence history.

There are no watertight compartments of the mind. Thoughts ebb and flow like waves that break on a sandy beach. Jung made the point that the search for rational precision robs mental activity of that feeling which, by nature, belongs to it. Extroverted thought concentrates on objects and imposes a discipline that becomes its very limitation. Persons mesmerized by "facts" cannot see beyond a set of details. Thought "becomes clogged by a mass of undigested material, and tries hard," says Jung, "to escape from this dilemma by artificial simplifications —by inventing formulae and concepts which appear to give coherence to what is really disconnected." This is not to say that a Darwin (who gave a marvelous order and meaning to masses of collected data) was not fully creative. It is the lesser thinkers who produce what Jung called "more and more facts, until there is a mountain of material, often of doubtful value." They often, furthermore, avoid inference, causing a loss of perception.

Historians are criticized for clinging unimaginatively to conscious-level causation. We also stand accused of simplistic analyses partly derived from our caution. Just as in physics and philosophy logical inconsistency has become more acceptable, so should historians take into account heretofore unexplainable complexity in history. In science the rational Newtonian universe has given way to contradictory, yet functional, efficacy. This accommodation to the psychologically complex in history should provide us with the sort of insights that scientists enjoy in discerning that matter in motion often acts indifferently to rational processes. Modern life, too, is seen increasingly as a universe of constant change, development, novelty, innovation, defiance of the immutable and even of the "logic" of the past.

By thinking in terms of unconscious motivation historians can incorporate formerly inaccessible insights, clarifying past obscurities. For those who wish to probe unreasonable behavior in man's past, even minimal self-instruction can widen one's vistas. If historical methods have become jaded, it is time to move toward new models, to produce a more humane view of history. In searching out the roots of unconscious behavior the historian can continue to utilize all those skills which he has perfected since the time of Herodotus. Fuller knowledge of the unconscious may one day revise our most basic assumptions about the underlying nature of man's history.[94]

NOTES

1. One of the most convincing collections of evidence of a historically continuous "collective unconscious," based upon gestures, smiles, grimaces, and other bodily functions, are the photographic studies of both humans and animals in Hans Hass, *The Human Animal* (New York, 1970).

2. There is evidence that modern mass societies do not use even their volitional consciousness to full capacity. Low self-esteem seems to dissipate the problem-solving capabilities of our technology into wasteful gadgetry.

3. Abraham H. Maslow, *Toward a Psychology of Being* (New York, 1962), pp. 178–189.

4. This first relationship ever to be statistically supported is complicated to explain, being based upon electrocortical stimulus responses. Brain waves measured by Electroencephalograph (EEG) are named Alpha, Beta, and Delta. The first has been associated with creative and meditative thought, the second with excitation and emotion, and the third, a low-frequency wave, with sleep. Recent experiments indicate that, in the absence of a conscious discrimination process, there may be present an electrocortical discrimination (on the unconscious level) related to differences in stimulus content revealed in verbal associations. The average response (measured by an electroencephalogram) was coded for both conscious and unconscious processes. Thirteen subjects were exposed to visual stimuli flashed on a tachistoscope. Average responses were recorded on an electroencephalograph. The experimental stimuli consisted of a pen and knee in a detailed pictorial representation and another in abstract form. Subjects were exposed to 60 stimulations, 30 for each pictorial image, in a pattern of .001 second, .030 second, and .001 second, respectively. After each block of 10 stimuli, the subject closed his eyes and described as fully as possible what he had seen. See Howard Shevrin and Dean E. Fritzler, "Visual Evoked Response Correlates of Unconscious Mental

Processes," *Science*, July 1968, pp. 295–298; and *Menninger Perspective*, October–November 1970, p. 16.

5. See Sheila Ostrander and Lynn Schroeder, *Psychic Discoveries Behind the Iron Curtain* (Englewood Cliffs, N.J., 1970).

6. See Silvano Arieti, *The Intra-Psychic Self* (New York, 1967), pp. 169–170 and Zevedei Barbu, *Problems of Historical Psychology* (New York, 1964), *passim*.

7. Maslow, *Psychology of Being*, p. 180.

8. Ibid., p. 181.

9. Erik Erikson, *Young Man Luther: A Study of Psychoanalysis and History* (New York, 1958), p. 16.

10. Ibid., p. 20.

11. E. R. Dodds, *The Greeks and the Irrational* (Berkeley, 1951), p. 264.

12. The gradual replacement of mythological by rational thinking among the Greeks is discussed in Wilhelm Nestle, *Vom Mythos zum Logos* (Stuttgart, 1942). See also Chester G. Spirit Starr, *The Awakening of the Greek Historical Spirit* (New York, 1968), which focuses upon the period 700–450 B.C.

13. See F. M. Cornford, *Thucydides Mythistoricus* (London, 1907).

14. Dodds, *The Greeks and the Irrational*, focuses upon ancient preoccupations with phenomena that seem inexplicable in rational terms.

15. Carl Jung, *Modern Man in Search of a Soul* (New York, 1933), p. 15.

16. The momentary insanities of *ate* and *menos* remind one of that East Indian phenomenon described in Aubrey Menon's *The Prevalence of Witches*. See Dodds, *The Greeks and the Irrational*, pp. 5, 17–18, 65–67, 139, 184, for details; and also George Rosen, *Madness in Society* (New York, 1969), pp. 114–115, 119–120; and Emma J. Edelstein and Ludwig Edelstein, *Asclepius: A Collection and Interpretation of the Testimonials*, 2 vols. (Baltimore, 1945). As early as the Greek Archaic age, one sees what the anthropologist Ruth Benedict discerned in various "shame cultures," genuine displacement behavior institutionalized.

17. Dodds, *The Greeks and the Irrational*, pp. 120, 131.

18. Ibid., p. 210.

19. Bostocke, *The Differences Between the Auncient Phisicke and the Latter Phisicke* (London, 1585).

20. See G. M. A. Grube, *Plato's Thought* (London, 1935), pp. 129–149; Dodds, *The Greeks and the Irrational*, p. 227.

21. See James E. Phillips, "The Tempest and the Renaissance Idea of Man," in *Shakespeare 400* (New York, 1964), pp. 148–150.

22. Gardner Murphy, *Psychological Thought From Pythagoras to Freud* (New York, 1968), p. 81.

23. See J. B. Bury, *The Idea of Progress: An Inquiry into Its Origin and Growth* (London, 1920); also F. S. Marvin, *Progress and History* (Oxford, 1916), p. 14.

24. See Herbert A. Hodges, *The Philosophy of Wilhelm Dilthey* (London, 1952) and *Wilhelm Dilthey* (New York, 1944).

25. W. E. H. Lecky, *History of the Rise and Influence of the Spirit of Rationalism in Europe* (London, 1865), vol. 2, p. 102.

26. Erich Fromm, *Sigmund Freud's Mission* (New York, 1959), p. 4.

27. Gerhard Masur, *Prophets of Yesterday: Studies in European Culture, 1890-1914* (New York, 1966), pp. 298, 452.

28. C. P. Oberndorf, *A History of Psychoanalysis in America* (New York, 1964), p. 227.

29. Ernest Jones, quoted in Oberndorf, *History of Psychoanalysis*, p. 242.

30. Sigmund Freud, *Moses and Monotheism* (London, 1949), p. 16.

31. Freud, *Moses and Monotheism* (New York, 1939), p. 96.

32. Masur, *Prophets*, p. 315.

33. L. L. Whyte, *The Unconscious Before Freud* (London, 1962), p. 16; Karl Mannheim, "The Sociological Problem of Generations," in Paul Kecskemeti, ed., *Essays on the Sociology of Knowledge* (London, 1952), p. 320.

34. See James Strachey, ed., *Standard Edition of the Complete Psychological Works of Sigmund Freud* (London, 1951-), vol. 23, p. 185 and vol. 9, p. 191.

35. Ernest Jones, *The Life and Work of Sigmund Freud* (New York, 1953), vol. 1, p. 174.

36. Franz Alexander, *This Age of Unreason* (Philadelphia, 1942), pp. 118-119, develops the concept.

37. Philip Rieff, "History, Psychoanalysis, and the Social Sciences," *Ethics* 63 (January 1953):107-120.

38. Oberndorf, *History of Psychoanalysis*, p. 144.

39. R. D. Laing, *Self and Others* (London, 1969), p. 133.

40. R. E. Money-Kyrle, *Psychoanalysis and Politics* (New York, 1951), p. 171.

41. Ibid., pp. 164-165.

42. Jones, *Sigmund Freud*, vol. 3, pp. 193-194. For Freud's views on the origins of society, see Philip Rieff, "Authority of the Past: Sickness and Society in Freud's Thought," *Social Research* 21 (Winter 1954):428-450.

43. Leopold Bellak, *Schizophrenia, a Review of the Syndrome* (New York, 1966), p. 6.

44. See Max Nordau, *The Conventional Lies of Mankind* (Chicago, 1884), and *The Interpretation of History* (London, 1910).

45. Alexander, *Age of Unreason*, pp. 22-38.

46. Lady Namier, his widow, describes Sir Lewis's fascination with so "brillant, indispensable, unreliable or exasperating" a character as Charles Townshend, who became the subject of a fragmented psychoanalytic biography by her husband and John Brooke. See also Howard R. Wolf, "British Fathers and Sons, 1773-1913: From Filial Submissiveness to Creativity," *Psychoanalytic Review*, 1965.

47. These notions are developed in E. M. Cioran's *The Temptation to Exist* (Chicago, 1968) and in his *The Fall Into Time* (Chicago, 1970).

48. C. G. Jung, *Modern Man in Search of a Soul*, pp. 70, 73.

49. Paul Roazen, *Freud: Political and Social Thought* (New York, 1968), p. 276.

50. The meaning of dreams in various cultures is discussed in G. E. von Grunebaum and Roger Callois, eds., *The Dream and Human Societies* (Berkeley, 1966); see also Alexander, *Age of Unreason,* p. 204, and Erich Fromm, *The Forgotten Language: An Introduction to the Understanding of Fairy Tales and Myths* (New York, 1951), p. 7.

51. Charlotte Beradt, *The Third Reich of Dreams* (Chicago, 1966), pp. 11–18.

52. Alexander L. George and Juliette L. George, *Woodrow Wilson and Colonel House* (New York, 1964), p. vi; Kurt Eissler, "Freud and the Psychoanalysis of History," *Journal of the American Psychoanalytic Association* 11 (October 1963):678. It may be possible to study dreams in such a way as to reveal a person's or a society's most deeply hidden thoughts. A letter from Woodrow Wilson to his wife, when he was president of Princeton University, is illustrative. In 1910 he had gone to Bermuda in a state of exhaustion, about which he wrote: "I did not realize until I got here how hard hit my nerves have been by the happenings of the past month. Almost at once the *days* began to afford me relief, but the nights distressed me. The trouble latent in my mind came out in my dreams. Not till last night did the distress—the struggle all night with college foes, the sessions of hostile trustees, the confused war of argument and insinuation—cease." Quoted in Sigmund Freud and William C. Bullitt, *Woodrow Wilson, A Psychological Study* (New York, 1966), p. 138. A psychiatrist-anthropologist has noted the "striking correspondence between dreams of people who are being analyzed, phantasies of psychotics, and beliefs or myths of people in quite different cultures." See Géza Róheim, *Psychoanalysis and Anthropology: Culture, Personality and the Unconscious* (New York, 1950), p. 361.

53. Robert Waelder, "Psychoanalysis and History," *The Psychoanalytic Interpretation of History,* ed. Benjamin B. Wolman (New York, 1971), p. 16.

54. Quoted in Frieda Fordham, *An Introduction to Jung's Psychology* (London, 1953), p. 10.

55. Ibid., pp. 23–24.

56. Miguel Serrano, *C. G. Jung and Herman Hesse: A Record of Two Friendships* (New York, 1968).

57. Alfred Adler, *Problems of Neurosis: A Book of Case Histories,* ed. Philip Mairet (New York, 1964), p. 15.

58. Erich Fromm, *Escape from Freedom* (New York, 1941), p. 8.

59. Harold Lasswell, *Psychopathology and Politics* (New York, 1960), p. 52. Other writings that concern the relationship of the ego and achievement (not only in politics) are by Heinz Hartmann, Ernst Kris, Rudolph Loewens-

tein, Anna Freud, Fred Greenstein, Martha Wolfenstein, and Gilbert Kliman.

60. I am indebted to Rudolph Binion for part of this interpretation. See also Robert G. L. Waite, "Adolf Hitler's Anti-Semitism: A Study in History and Psychoanalysis," in Benjamin B. Wolman, ed., *The Psychoanalytic Interpretation of History* (New York, 1971), pp. 215–216.

61. Strachey, *Standard Edition of the Works of Sigmund Freud,* vol. 18, pp. 70, 78–80.

62. Jacob Arlow, *The Legacy of Sigmund Freud* (New York, 1956), pp. 86–87.

63. Arnold Rogow, "Psychiatry, History, and Political Science: Notes on an Emergent Synthesis," in Judd Marmor, ed., *Modern Psychoanalysis* (New York, 1968).

64. Fordham, *Introduction,* p. 118.

65. Rupert Crawshay-Williams, *The Comforts of Unreason* (London, 1947), p. 28.

66. This is a paraphrasing of Freud's ideas as derived from Gustave Le Bon's *Psychologie des foules* (1895): quoted from Thomas Johnson, *Freud and Political Thought* (New York, 1965), p. 42.

67. Stefan T. Possony, "Foreign Policy and Rationality," *Orbis* 12 (Spring 1968):132–160.

68. See especially George Rude, *The Crowd in the French Revolution* (London, 1959), pp. 232, 239, and his *The Crowd in History* (New York, 1966); also Franklin S. Klaf, "Napoleon and the Grand Army of 1812: A Study of Group Psychology," *Psychoanalytic Quarterly,* 1960.

69. Jung, *Modern Man in Search of a Soul,* pp. 80–81.

70. Alexander, *Age of Unreason,* p. 236.

71. L. H. Butterfield, *Diary of Charles Francis Adams,* (Cambridge, 1968), vol. 3, p. xxii.

72. Harold Lasswell, *Power and Personality* (New York, 1948); Alexander L. George and Juliette L. George, *Woodrow Wilson and Colonel House* (New York, 1964), pp. 318–319.

73. J. David Singer, "Man and World Politics: The Psycho-Cultural Interface," *Journal of Social Issues* 24 (July 1968):135.

74. Fred Greenstein, "The Impact of Personality on Politics: An Attempt to Clear Away Underbrush," *American Political Science Review* 61 (September 1967):640.

75. Carl Binger, "Conflicts in the Life of Thomas Jefferson," *American Journal of Psychiatry* 125 (February 1969):1098–1107.

76. Alexander L. George, "Power as a Compensatory Value for Political Leaders," *Journal of Social Issues* 24 (July 1968):33.

77. Ibid., p. 37.

78. Rudolph Binion, "Repeat Performance: A Psychohistorical Study of Leopold III and Belgian Neutrality," *History and Theory* 8 (1969):213–259.

79. Harold Nicolson, *Diaries and Letters, 1930–1939,* ed. Nigel Nicolson (New York, 1966).

80. Erikson, *Young Man Luther,* pp. 254–261.

81. Ibid., p. 149.

82. William Willcox, "Historical Research Through A Biographer's Eyes," in Donald E. Thackrey, ed., *Research: Definitions and Reflections* (Ann Arbor, 1967), p. 13.

83. Allan Bullock, *Hitler: A Study in Tyranny* (New York, 1962), p. 480.

84. Fredrick S. Perls, "Gestalt Therapy and Human Potentialities," in *Explorations in Human Potentialities* (New York, 1966), pp. 1–2; Konrad Lorenz, *On Aggression* (New York, 1966), pp. 70–71.

85. Remarks of Anna Freud on a paper entitled "The Analysis of a Young Woman Previously Analyzed in Adolescence," 8 July 1970, Hampstead Child Therapy Clinic, London.

86. Sidney J. Slomich and Robert E. Kantor, "Social Pathology of Political Assassination," *Bulletin of the Atomic Scientists* 25 (March 1969):9–12. Robert E. Kantor and William G. Herron, "Paranoia and High Office," *Mental Hygiene* 52 (October 1968):508–511.

87. See Martha Wolfenstein and Gilbert Kliman, eds., *Children and the Death of a President* (New York, 1967).

88. David Potter in Louis Gottschall et al., eds., *Generalizations in the Writing of History* (Chicago, 1963), pp. 191–192.

89. Jean Delay, *The Youth of André Gide,* trans. and abridged (Chicago, 1963).

90. See Stanley Burnshaw, *The Seamless Web* (London, 1970), and Walter Abell, *The Collective Dream in Art: A Psycho-Historical Theory of Culture . . .* (New York, 1966).

91. Quoted in Francoise Gilot, *Life with Picasso* (London, 1966), p. 311.

92. In addition to Anton Ehrenzweig, *The Psycho-Analysis of Artistic Vision and Hearing* (New York, 1965), the rich literature on the unconscious in art includes Abell, *Collective Dream in Art,* and Ernst Kris, *Psychoanalytic Explorations in Art* (New York, 1964).

93. Marc Bloch, *The Historian's Craft* (New York, 1954), p. 150.

94. In addition to the work of Lasswell and Erikson, a growing historical literature on the role of the unconscious mind includes: Norman O. Brown, *Life Against Death* (Middletown, Conn., 1959), Zevedei Barbu, *Problems of Historical Psychology* (New York, 1960), Fred Weinstein and Gerald M. Platt, *The Wish to be Free* (Berkeley, 1969), Herbert Marcuse, *Eros and Civilization* (Boston, 1956), Rudolph Binion, *Frau Lou, Nietzsche's Wayward Disciple* (Princeton, 1968), Brigid Brophy, *Black Ship to Hell* (New York, 1962), Alexander and Margaret Mitscherlich, *The Inability to Mourn,* and Alexander Mitscherlich, *Society Without the Father* (New York, 1969). Following upon William Langer's 1957 presidential address to the American Historical Association, Bruce Mazlish also called attention to the possibilities of psychohistory

in a book of readings entitled *Psychoanalysis and History* (Englewood Cliffs, 1963). See the imaginative work of Peter Loewenberg in "The Psychohistorical Origins of the Nazi Youth Cohort," *American Historical Review* 76 (December 1971):1457–1502, as well as his "The Unsuccessful Adolescence of Heinrich Himmler," in the same journal (June 1971):612– 614; also his analysis of Theodore Herzl in Benjamin B. Wolman, ed., *The Psychoanalytic Interpretation of History* (New York, 1971), pp. 150–191. The present chapter is part of a larger study tentatively entitled "The Irrational and History."

12

SOCIAL SCIENCE AND THE COLLECTIVIZATION OF HUBRIS

JOSEPH J. SPENGLER

> The university had been able to repulse all of its
> enemies save those that its own hubris had created
> within its ranks.
>
> Robert A. Nisbet, *The Degradation of the
> Academic Dogma*

> The underlying cause of our problem [the dollar
> crisis]—described by some as "the arrogance of
> power"—remains with us. . . . Our global involve-
> ments must be more realistically proportioned to
> our resources.
>
> Robert Lekachman, "Hubris and the Dollar,"
> *The New Leader*

> The most instructive revelation may be how little
> faith the leaders had in those they led—a classic case
> of the arrogance of the powerful.
>
> "Pentagon Papers: The Secret War," *Time*

> Economists have much to be modest about [and]
> much to be sad about.
>
> W. R. Allen, in Randall W. Hinshaw,
> *The Economics of International Adjustment*

In ancient times the *I Ching*'s counsel to man not to press
beyond "his own limitations" seems to have been widely supported. The Greek poet Pindar described "unattainable aspirations" as a source of "madness";[1] and Plato warned against giving "too great power to anything" or "too much authority to
the mind" lest "everything [be] overthrown."[2] In recent times,
however, advantage has been associated with man's meeting
challenges, even those of his own making, and with his overreaching himself, though not too immoderately. The injunc-

tion against immoderate overreaching is more likely to be honored in the breach in an age of highly concentrated power.[3]

As the epigraphs to this chapter suggest, concern with immoderateness or arrogance—what the ancient Greeks called *hubris*—may again be developing in the realm of applied natural and social science. For, as will be indicated, not only have policies of overreaching imposed heavy costs on the public at large; repeated failure is threatening also to undermine man's inclination to overreach even with moderation, heretofore a principal source of progress. Of this we have evidence in the emergence of a fin de siècle mood that threatens to blanket out support not only of the "technology of haste" and futurologists' dreams of tomorrow's "endless horizons,"[4] but also of science as well. Indeed, there is danger that man, finding the growth of knowledge unequal to removing his ignorance and curing his ills, may slacken in his search for ways out.[5] In this essay I deal with the growing recognition of hubris, its adverse effects, and the means to its control, especially in the economic world. For purposes of illustration I use mainly American data, for it is in the United States more than elsewhere that hubris now flourishes.

EARLY MANIFESTATIONS OF HUBRIS
Although hubris is of ancient vintage, it was among the Greeks, anticipators of modern unfettered inquiry if not also of unfettered application of the results of inquiry, that hubris found greatest condemnation. The hubris, or arrogant and unwarranted pride, of which they wrote permeated mainly individual, not collective, behavior. It was an evil of which the individual was guilty, but he was capable of inflicting widespread injury only when he was a powerful individual, as was Xerxes.[6] Hubris was considered to be destructive of the cardinal virtues—courage, temperance, justice, and wisdom—of their unity and balance, all essential to political stability and the good life. According to this view, anticipated in the traditional wisdom of Greece and subsequently stressed in her belletristic and philosophical literature (for example, Homer, Herodotus, Aeschylus, Thucydides, Plato), hubris was the "chief sin," the principal fountain of bad judgment and disaster, the main source of political instability, and (later writers believed) the cause of the destruction of the imperial power of Athens.[7]

The doctrine of the four virtues passed into Christendom and with it condemnation of hubris, or its Latin equivalent, *superbia*.[8] It received little or no attention from such sects as the Gnostics, some of whose virtues are remindful of those regnant today among the lumpenintelligentsia.[9] Eventually St. Thomas Aquinas described "pride" as "the movement by which the will is borne towards ends beyond its real limits," as "primarily the revolt of being against its own nature; it is the permanent and deliberate refusal to accept its own limitations."[10] He condemned excessive pride in general, but did not link its ill effects closely with the behavior of scientists as such. Several centuries later, Erasmus hinted at such an outcome, though hardly at its possibly collective form and without reference to still nonexisting social scientists.

In *The Praise of Folly*, Erasmus ridiculed what verged on hubris among contemporary "scientists" and theologians. Of these scientists, men concerned with the physical rather than the social world, Erasmus observed that "they feel that they are the only men with any wisdom, and all other men float about as shadows. . . . They postulate causes . . . as if they had exclusive knowledge about the secrets of nature, designer of elements, or as if they visited us directly from the council of the gods"; and of the theologians that "they draw exact pictures of every part of hell, as though they had spent many years in that region. . . . It is their claim that it is beyond the station of sacred discourse to be obliged to adhere to the rules of grammarians. . . . They share this honor with most intellectuals."[11]

Greek, Roman, medieval, and even early modern writers found the ill effects of hubris to be incident in the main upon the excessively arrogant individual. Ill effects were more widely incident only when hubris animated political or military leaders to overreach themselves and visit misfortune upon their followers. Outside the military realm, hubris could at first become a source of misfortune only in the area of theology, since theologians were relatively numerous and identified with the Universal Church, which in turn had behind it the apparatus of the state; and on occasion they could direct this apparatus against the welfare of the common man, as they did in the age of the Crusades against the Saracens and the world of Islam. At that time scientists still had too little skill as scientists and, though they sometimes were organized in guilds, too little collective power to be driven by hubris to generate harm. Only the Devil's Apprentice was capable along these lines, and even he was without a hypothetical counterpart in the as yet uncultivated social sciences.

Foundations for the emergence of a "scientistic hubris" began to be laid within the century succeeding the death of Erasmus. Francis Bacon, perhaps more than any other writer, developed the view that knowledge is power and that science bestows power. A scientistic hubris could not, however, come into being until the natural sciences and mathematics had made great discoveries possible and thus played a John-the-Baptist role to a social science still in the preparturition stage. These critical discoveries came in the age and aftermath of Newton, in a late eighteenth- and early nineteenth-century France that lacked the leavening influence of a Locke and a Burke. The leading product of this exuberance, the École Polytechnique, not merely generated interest in science, engineering, and machines as well as confidence in the omnipotence of pure science and the efficacy of engineering organization; it also gave rise to a feeling "that there were no limits to the powers of the human mind and to the extent to which man could hope to harness and control all the forces which so far had threatened and intimidated him." For, as Hayek has observed, "never will man penetrate deeper into error than when he is continuing on the road which has led him to success."[12] In the school's heyday, however, its influence, though not confined to natural scientists, had but limited impact upon social scientists as such.

The philosophy that permeated the École Polytechnique did, however, exercise considerable influence upon those with an interest in social planning and/or an approach founded upon historicism. The most influential of these were Saint-Simon and Auguste Comte together with their associates and some of those in what became the Hegelian tradition.[13] While it may be said that hubris affected some of these individuals, the state had not yet become economically powerful enough, nor had these individuals acquired sufficient analytical and administrative leverage within the apparatus of the state, to affect the community very adversely. Moreover, their numbers were both few and counterbalanced by economists in the tradition of Smith and Say, a tradition subsequently reinforced by the approach of Karl Menger and his associates. Furthermore, professional economists continued to be too few in number and too uninfluential to foment a hubris-oriented intellectual climate.

POSTCLASSICAL DEVELOPMENTS

Even in the late nineteenth century the place occupied by social science in the realm of science was too unimpressive to generate hubris at the individual level or make possible its collectivization. The changes that took place in and after the closing years of this century, though not confined to the United States, were more intense and rapid here than elsewhere. American experience therefore epitomizes the changes that took place. It is correct to say that here, as elsewhere, social scientists, among them economists, never on top, were hardly on tap until shortly before or during World War I. Social scientists did, however, play a role in rising governmental agencies (the Bureau of the Census, for example, was established in 1903) and found demands for their skills emanating from the inability of progressivist reformers to solve the problems to which they directed attention.[14] Until then, and perhaps even then, social scientists did little more than survive in an atmosphere of what Lord Durham might have called ''benign neglect'' and with the boundaries of the respective social sciences still only vaguely defined.

The status of social science was influenced in part by that of natural science, but not greatly until the turn of the century. For, as Henry Adams reports, only then did men become conscious of the replacement of a slowly rising curve of scientific progress by a ''law of acceleration,'' that could, by 1938, produce ''a world that sensitive and timid creatures could regard without a shudder,''[15] one from which the ''one great emperor —Coal'' might be dethroned by fissionable and fusionable materials.[16]

Whereas today full-time intellectuals in America are said to number about one million—five thousand times as many as in Periclean Athens[17]—their number was small around 1900. Moreover, those who were active had not yet attained the power to support effectively social scientists whom they believed capable of developing a civilization to which eventually modern literature was to become increasingly hostile.[18] The annual number of college graduates was low—twenty-seven thousand in 1900—with the fraction of persons of college age who went to college not rising above 3 percent until about 1890 and above 5 percent until about 1910. Furthermore, as late as 1900, intellectuals had not yet recovered from the impact of specialization and the resulting atomization of their formerly detached and universalist outlook into a multiplicity of outlooks, particularly those associated with Marxism, fascism, and progressivism.[19] Of adherents to these, the most relevant to the present discussion is "the intellectual as progressive"; for it is he who places complete trust in science, the ballot box, "the march of history," social engineering, and now futurology, always in a utopian context that overemphasizes technological solutions and neglects the constraints flowing both from the individual and from the social structure as such. Only occasionally are the dangers of wisdom stressed.[20]

The Great Depression of the 1930s, together with the resulting increase in public employment, augmented the demand for economists and their number increased. They could not acquire much influence and administrative leverage, however, until macroeconomics of Keynesian and post-Keynesian vintage had come into being and general acceptance, and governments had assumed a great deal of responsibility, particularly for maintaining so-called full employment. Only then could hubris begin to flourish among economists. Neither Walras nor Marshall fathered hubris. It was Keynes who made possible the rise of an economic mandarinate, together with an intellectual climate conducive to hubris and its capacity for generating negative as well as favorable externalities.

Growth of social scientists in number, especially after 1945, has strengthened other forces favorable to hubris, at least insofar as the spirit of tribalism has tended to hold in check critical discussion of professional incapacity. Ever more outlets for their wares were found in industry (about one-sixth of whose Ph.D.'s are social scientists),[21] in government (with federal social-science employment increasing 54 percent in 1960–1968), and in education—outlets made possible in part by a 124 percent increase in GNP between 1949 and 1969. Social science doctorates increased 135 percent in 1960–1969, and social science doctoral candidates, 144 percent in 1960–1968.[22] It is anticipated that the annual number of social science doctoral degrees, 1,716 in 1958, will be 8,946 by 1977, more than the society can absorb.[23]

Increase in the number of social scientists has been accompanied by a great increase in the number of social science journals and articles, so many that the flow of print now obscures as well as facilitates the flow of essential information, too often treated as if it were a free good.[24] Indeed, a conscientious scholar sometimes finds himself in the position of Pavlov's dog, so battered with printed stimuli that he hardly knows where to turn. Hence, most articles, whether useful or not, are virtually forgotten within a few years, thus producing little effect beyond providing the author with what might be called "occupational therapy."

Increase in the number of social scientists has also been accompanied by a marked growth in the financial support of social science research, though not by a corresponding amount of analytical progress and information suited to solve man's ills, social and otherwise. After all, at least some "research" is carried on mainly to enable the social scientist to increase his income and reduce his teaching load; much of it deals with trivia, is informed by little imagination, and is of little relevance beyond the pretense that it could prove socially useful. It is largely confined to quantitative inquiry into observable behavioral regularities, to the neglect both of other sources of information and of intermediate variables that condition degrees of regularity and seldom are to be gotten at with the instruments of a single discipline. It tends to remain under the empire of a self-sustaining elite which, with the assistance of governmental and foundation funds, controls the perimeters of inquiry, at least on the part of those in search of support, status, and promotion, and thereby transforms what should be quality-enforcing rules into rules making for licensure, monopoly, and thought control. Up to now, however, social scientists have not been able effectively to wrap themselves in the white robes of serendipity.

HUBRIS EMERGES: NATURAL SCIENCE
Social science, economics in particular, has benefited greatly, at least until recently, from the post-1945 aura that has surrounded natural science. Never in its history have the kudos of science, together with its support, and its self-confidence, been so great. Up to now, therefore, science has easily survived the growing hostility of the once friendly intellectual, by now becoming angry at the alleged misuse of science by some of those coming to Washington in the Camelot invasion of 1960 or dis-

turbed at his own inability to fathom or appreciate a "culture" narrowly pragmatic and in the pay of the Leviathan. Science survives in part, of course, because its critics, often contemptuous of those whom Joseph Kraft has called "ordinary Americans" and "middle America" (and whom intellectuals have sometimes regarded as aspirants to a "pornutopia"),[25] have aroused a reciprocal and offsetting contempt at the hands of the "common man."

Growth of expenditure upon "research and development," much of it inspired by Sputnik and thermonuclear competition (as evidenced by the fact that about one-half of this expenditure has been defense-space related), may serve as an index of the increasing importance attached to science, especially natural science and engineering.[26] This expenditure, essentially exclusive of outlay upon capital, increased in the aggregate (in real terms) about 7.6 percent per year between 1955 and 1970, but with real outlay upon "basic" research growing even faster, close to 10.5 percent per year. Meanwhile, gross national product rose only about 3.4 percent per year. Since 1967, however, money expenditure upon basic research as well as upon "research and development" has not quite kept pace with rising prices. Of these funds, about 55 percent have been of federal origin. Accordingly, the slowing down of federal expenditure, together with inflation, has been reducing the *real* support of science in recent years.

The share of social science in federal as in public plus private funds devoted to "research and development" is minuscule even though social scientists constituted about one-fifth of all scientists and engineers in 1969 and about 9 percent of the scientists employed by the federal government in the 1960s. Of the federal funds devoted to "research" in 1960 and 1968, the share of the social sciences was that of Lazarus, under 2 percent and 3.6 percent, respectively. Of the funds devoted to "research and development," just over 1 percent went to social science in 1968.

Having become accustomed to a high rate of increase in the *real* support available for research—about 20 percent per year even in social science in 1963–1968—scientists are experiencing a sense of intense deprivation at the failure of this support to grow in recent years, together with the collapse of aerospace and defense-related outlets for their activities. Adjustment is proving much more difficult, of course, for natural scientists, who, unlike social scientists, have not been hardened by having had to live on support at a more Spartan level.

This sense of deprivation has in turn aroused protest and concern. It is insisted that, in our internecine world, survival depends upon scientific progress, a goal made ever harder to attain by the rapidity with which research apparatus becomes obsolete and the ineffectiveness with which this apparatus is used,[27] a state of affairs especially characteristic of educational, medical, governmental, and other undertakings not subject to the discipline of the market. The "public policy doctrine of academic science," however, remains boosterish and "vainglorious" as it has become "for too many years";[28] and support continues to be given to the view that the federal government must support science lest unemployment develop.

Exaggerated as well as arrogant claims are made, sometimes in such a manner that the cause of the scientists is weakened.[29] For example, it has been alleged that discoveries made over a period of five years in so-called space medicine have "relieved human misery" more than those "made in medicine in the preceding fifty."[30] It is said that within thirty years the share of expenditure upon research and development could profitably run as high as 25–50 percent of the gross national product; that each Ph.D. (in science) generates 100 jobs; that, contrary to fact, science accounts for a very large share of the increase in national output.[31] To claims of this sort are added the Delphic forecasts of futurologists who make book on man's prospective problems and options as of (say) the year 2000. The questionable allocation of funds is ignored, as when the federal government in 1965 spent $1.5 billion on medical research compared with over $7.5 billion on space-oriented "research," including manned moon flights that cost about twenty times as much as unmanned flights.[32]

Exaggerated and cost-disregarding claims can be interpreted only as manifesting both a great deal of hubris and a threat to the state's support of the social scientist; for the latter cannot back up the rhetoric of his submissions with thermonuclear credentials at a time when close to half of all federal support of science remains defense- and space-oriented. The now common argument for more and more scientific personnel recalls the argument of the mercantilists when they reasoned as if the elasticity of a country's demand for gold were almost infinite, with this demand flowing in ever larger measure from the state.

The potential danger lurking in exaggerated scientific and technological claims may assume manifold form; it has found expression recently in the collapse of Rolls-Royce, caught in "the trap of technological pride" that led it to undertake commitments far beyond its resources: "The Rolls-Royce collapse is a tale of illusions on every side—illusions of technological omnicompetence by Rolls-Royce, of export grandeur by the British government, and of driving a hard bargain by Lockheed." The lessons to be learned have been had at a very high price:

> A government can be too eager for exports. For a buyer like Lockheed, the lowest price is not necessarily the best deal, because a delivery failure by a crucial supplier can involve both in calamity. Most important, perhaps, men who think themselves so much the masters of complex technology that they can control its costs and timing may be riding for a shattering fall.[33]

Unfortunately many critics fail to distinguish between science viewed as an instrument and the uses to which science is put. As a result, science and scientists are condemned by those who object to uses to which it is put. The manifestation of hubris by natural scientists probably contributes to this unfavorable reaction and what has become a "senseless war on science."[34]

HUBRIS EMERGES: SOCIAL SCIENCE

Hubris becomes a matter of concern only insofar as its adverse consequences affect others than the hubris-animated source of these effects. Should these effects be entirely incident upon their agent and hence self-regarding, there is no occasion for public concern. Unfortunately, hubris may give rise to externalities, often predominantly adverse and usually incident upon uncompensated victims. These effects, moreover, tend to be accentuated in a society such as America by both state and nonstate agencies. In the past hubris was seldom an occasion for alarm, for is was unaccompanied by externalities. This is largely true even today of natural science. For, while the findings of the natural scientist can be misapplied, they are less likely to be so than are the findings of the social scientist, which tend to become policy oriented. As J. M. Clark observed in contrasting discoveries of natural science with those of social science, discovery of the theory of relativity made no "perceptible difference to the man driving a car or operating a lathe."[35] In contrast, the social scientist, if he obtains public power directly or through the instrument of policies based upon his theories and models, can inflict adverse externalities on many people. Social science, in short, is more externality prone than natural science, in part because it is "relevance" prone.[36]

Since 1945, two major changes have taken place: the ascendance of the apparatus of state over the individual and lesser collectives, and the infiltration of social science, together with its practitioners, into the apparatus of state—oblivious to the moral of Aesop's fable about the fate of the frogs who made a king stork possible or to the apparent decline of Liebermanism in a Soviet Union dominated by military "metal eaters." The ascendancy of the state, initially facilitated by war, ever favorable to the concentration and mobilization of economic power,[37] has since been facilitated by ideology and that accessibility to personal power which many anticipate from enlargement of the overall role of the state. Indicative of the increasing role of the state is the rise of the ratio of total governmental expenditure to national income, from 11.9 percent in 1929 to 39.1 percent in 1970, a level much above the fraction (about 14 percent) of the nation's assets under public ownership.[38]

Indicative also is A. Cairncross's comment on Eric Roll's *The World after Keynes,*

> respecting the limitations of economics in the face of the issues described. Less and less is being left to the market and more and more requires the intervention of government and other agencies whose operations are not circumscribed like the market by economic factors, but are shot through with politics, administrative convenience or feasibility, and a whole range of psycho-social considerations. . . . Judgment about issues rests on the view one takes of the wisdom and potency of government action and of the likelihood that the failure of governments will bring into play more automatic and sometimes more powerful market forces.[39]

Indicative of growing confidence in the contribution of economists to public policy was the assumption by the federal government, under the Employment Act of 1946, of the management of national economic policy "to promote maximum employment, production, and purchasing power"—a commitment inspired by Keynes's *General Theory* and one that some economists believed realizable, given the technical competence and the empirical and political capacity of at least some members of the profession. Less confidence has been manifest in social scientists other than economists, yet they too have been upgraded—political scientists by growing interest in governmental processes and structures, sociologists by growing concern respecting urban, welfare, and race-connected problems, and both by the "need [of economists] for a partnership with other disciplines in tackling" many issues.[40] Moreover, steps are under way to produce an annual social report parallel to the annual report of the Council of Economic Advisers, though some fear such a social report would embody governmentally sanctioned value judgments that belong within the domain of the individual.[41]

Social science, unfortunately for policy makers, presents much more difficult problems than does inorganic or even organic science. The number of variables and parameters involved is much greater, and the microcosm to be subjected to analysis is seldom so separable from systems of which the microcosm is a part. The counsel of the social scientist needs, therefore, to be much more qualified than that of the natural scientist. The transmutation of even careful and complete social science findings into terms of policy tends to result in dangerously simple instruments. Thus, Tilford Gaines, commenting on the source of a consistent pattern of errors in forecast models, described it as "the undue importance the models attach to changes in fiscal and monetary policies," because these are "subject to the manipulation of the policy authorities" though not "so uniquely able to generate a multiplicative impact upon total economic activity" as the policy makers assume. Daniel Patrick Moynihan is correct, therefore, in describing the tendency to oversimplify as "the great single temptation of our time" and "the great corrupter," much as Jacob Burckhardt foresaw.[42]

Let us illustrate Moynihan's observation by writing

$$O = f(V_i,\ W_i,\ U_i,\ P_i)$$

where O denotes response or mode of behavior, V_i designates the variables of which a social scientist takes note, W_i denotes important neglected variables, U_i denotes variables that are both neglected and unimportant, and P_i denotes parameters (which condition response to variables and most of which are susceptible to change over time). Policy respecting O and based solely on V_i tends to be inadequate and may produce unintended and adverse effects. Moreover, the effects of policy, when they are adverse, may be observed only quite long after a policy has been introduced, given the slowness with which feedbacks are registered and reacted to, particularly when bureaucrats are arbitrary and arrogant. The resulting dangers, especially pronounced in a society dominated by oligopoly and big trade unions, were anticipated in 1947 by J. M. Clark in his comments on "After Keynes What?"[43]

In his presidential address to the 1970 annual meeting of the American Economic Association, W. Leontief took cognizance of the state of economic analysis and its adequacy for the tasks to which it is being put:

> The consistently indifferent performance in practical applications is in fact a symptom of a fundamental imbalance in the present state of our discipline. The weak and all too slowly growing empirical foundation clearly cannot support the proliferating superstructure of pure, or should I say, speculative economic theory.[44]

Presumably, what Leontief observes is equally applicable to practitioners of other social science disciplines. Representative is their contribution to the development of our almost miraculously defective welfare system.

The performance of the American economy since the establishment of the president's Council of Advisers might prove illustrative if contrasted closely with the advice (if any) given by the council to the president. Crude comparison of the period 1904–1929 with 1945–1970[45] indicates little improvement in the overall level of employment and a not much higher rate of increase in average output. The most striking difference is the increasing tendency of the American economy to inflation and all the evils and immoralities associated with inflation. Between 1904 and 1929, the consumer price index rose about 89 percent, and between 1945 and 1970, about 115 percent. Of this inflation virtually all was war-connected in the earlier period whereas only something like three-fifths was war-connected in the later period when uncurbed speculative activity as well as governmental fiscal and monetary policy contributed to inflation. Very little effort has been made, however, to reimburse those defrauded by government-created inflation, much of it intended to cure short-term unemployment (with about one half running four weeks or less) and much of it the product of man-made barriers to employment—of unwillingness to change jobs, of unattractive tradeoffs between work and relief, and perhaps of entry into the labor force with unreal expectations and small intent to find employment. There is little assurance that inflation will generate the increase in employment sought in the United States or the economic development sought in economically lagging countries. Indeed, as R. A. Mundell points out, inflation causes unemployment in the United States and undermines that country's economic power and standing.[46]

Even as war and governmental whim create an unstable economy, often too dependent upon highly specialized and inflexible industries (such as the aerospace industry) that tend to collapse upon withdrawal of support, so does inflation generate an unstable economy prone to shrink upon withdrawal of its unnatural and necessarily transitory stimulus. In contrast, when the public sector is small and every decision maker free to make the most of his flexible, disposable, and usually market-oriented resources, the flow of expenditure is relatively stable and continuous, especially in economies with low rates of population growth and reduced emphasis upon nonconsumables.

The dangers lurking in the public sector are great, for that sector is under the empire of whim, unwarranted confidence in the cybernetic capacity of governmental bureaucrats, and the search of politicians for survival in a politically Hobbesian world. Not surprisingly, therefore, according to one study the public sector "has been the major source of cyclical instability," while monetary policy has served to exacerbate inflationary pressures.[47] Confidence in federal management of the national economic framework, whipped up by the New Frontiersmen and their fellow travelers in the early 1960s, has since been dissipated. "The late Sixties," writes Max Ways, "brought another round of disillusionment," great inflation, high unemployment, and no growth, "a combination that had been considered improbable under almost any set of policies."[48] Even the integrity of policy makers is called into question by the report of a close student of the political scene to the effect that he finds it profitable to base his speculative undertakings in the market on the supposition that an American president always begins pump priming in the third year of his administration in order to stimulate employment and his party's chances at election time.[49]

The dangers that lurk in turning control of economies over to simplistic disciples of dead philosophers cannot be matched by those lurking in policies advocated by sociologists and political scientists, again in disregard of the complexity of the societal system and subsystems to which the latter would apply policies transmuted out of a few selected and imperfectly representative observations. All can, however, contribute to a climate of opinion insensitive to costs, externalities, and many relevant elements, processes, functional relations, and underlying concerns.[50] Such insensitivity is partly responsible, however, for the passage of the educational legislation of the 1960s, now found largely to have failed. It probably contributed to the steady conversion of Sweden's "middle way" into a stasis-ridden society, and, one author suggests, "con" game masquerading as a welfare state.[51]

CONTROLLING HUBRIS

Guarding society against the evil effects of hubris calls for corrective action, particularly by social scientists themselves, for the recurrence of the adverse effects of unwise policies imputed to social scientists could destroy confidence in their skills and thus deprive society of what it badly needs. There is need for at least three courses of action. The first need, now probably the least attainable of major needs, consists in modification of the political structure. Decentralization of economic and political authority and decision making would be most effective. It would deprive hubris, wherever it developed, of most of its leverage and capacity for harm, particularly if decision makers remained subject to an effective system of penalties and rewards as well as to disciplining tests of performance—conditions that are consistent with the realization of objectives of countrywide impact. A reversal of the centralizing trends under way for nearly three centuries thus is indicated, together with the cybernetizing of vast, insensitive, and ever-expanding federal bureaucratic structures (such as the Department of Defense) and the diminution of the national managerial and fiscal role of the state, currently lauded by social scientists as well as by subjective proletarians and lumpen intelligentsia. There is need, second, to immunize social and other scientists against hubris, though not by shortening the scientific reach more than its grasp. This can be done in two ways: (a) by stressing the empirical bases, mechanisms, and complexities of the systems through which policies must be carried out, together with the heavy social costs associated with ill-conceived policies; and (b) by emphasizing the inadequacies of the social sciences, particularly in respect to their capacity to generate effective problem-solving techniques.[52] Third, foundations and other suppliers of research funds can contribute notably by allowing more support to imaginative research and inquiry and less to pedestrian and expensive quantitative trivia, by demanding *real* evidence of policy potential when research is defended on such ground, and by weakening the control currently exercised over social-science practice and policy by a self-extending "elite."

Max Ways notes the need for "a public temper both more humble and more resolute."[53] Improvement in the communication of information between the scientific community and the underlying population could stimulate feedback, making for greater responsibility in both quarters. Such improvement needs to assume at least two forms, improvement in terminology and increase in the relevance of "information." "Semantic aphasia . . . habitual and prolonged abuse of words," common to all social science, needs to be given up.[54] Mathematical models need to map more closely upon the real world. Witness K. E. Boulding's description of a recent magnum opus on economic growth as an "interesting mathematical exercise, which throws very little light on the conditions of any real world."[55] It has even been implied that while economists proclaim cures for many nonexistent diseases, they are able to cope with few that do, in fact, afflict man. Thus F. H. Hahn writes that "there is something scandalous in the spectacle of so many people refining the analysis of economic states which they give no reason to suppose will ever, or have ever, come about." Moreover, they mislead people to believe that they "actually know how an economy is to be controlled. . . . It is an unsatisfactory and slightly dishonest state of affairs."[56]

Given improvement in the communication of social science information and more realistic assessment of the comparative serendipity component of social science, the pressure of the market for the wares of social science will greatly reduce its affliction with hubris. Adeptness at modest communication of useful knowledge is bound to increase in utilitarian significance as the public at large becomes increasingly aware that social scientists are writing in too great measure for each other—taking in each other's esoteric verbal wash, so to speak. Having become aware of this state of affairs, philanthropoids, agents of the state, and currently captive audiences will demand a greater return on their investment in social science. The resulting outcome, especially the resulting increase in serviceability, should augment the overall demand for the services of social scientists and allow them to displace products of law schools and engineering-oriented planner factories from areas of public and private need. These areas are often badly served by engineers who neglect the sensitivity of man to the market and the system of penalties and rewards, by lawyers with their emphasis upon the adversary principle, unempirical descendant of the duel and the ordeal,[57] and by what Richard Hofstadter described as "a massive adversary culture," one making for conflict when what is needed, as Kenneth Boulding has observed, is greater recourse to self-correcting mechanisms.[58] Needed also is aesthetic sensibility and awareness of the best of what the world community of man has produced over the centuries.

NOTES

1. Pindar, *Nem.*, XI, 47.

2. Plato, *Laws*, III, 691.

3. A. O. Hirschman, *Development Projects Observed* (Washington, D.C., 1967), chap. 1; Arnold J. Toynbee, *A Study of History* (London, 1939), esp. vols. 1–6.

4. Cf. Bentley Glass, "Science: Endless Horizons or Golden Age," *Science* 171 (1971):23–29.

5. Max Ways, "Don't We Know Enough To Make Better Public Policies?" *Fortune*, April 1971, pp. 64 ff. See also Reinhard Bendix, *Embattled Reason* (New York, 1970), p. 348.

6. According to Herodotus, VII, 10, Artabanus warned Xerxes (much as able generals have warned Western politicians against military ventures in Asia) against undertaking the conquest of Greece.

7. See C. M. Bowra, *The Greek Experience* (New York, 1959), chap. 4, esp. pp. 99–101; W. R. Agard, *The Greek Mind* (New York, 1957), p. 68.

8. John Ferguson, *Moral Values in the Ancient World* (London, 1958), chap. 3, pp. 46–51.

9. See Hans Jonas, *The Gnostic Religion* (Boston, 1958), pt. 3; R. M. Grant, *Gnosticism and Early Christianity*, 2d ed. (New York, 1966), chap. 1.

10. Etienne Gilson, *The Christian Philosophy of St. Thomas Aquinas* (New York, 1956), pp. 299–300, 483, nn. 57–58.

11. Erasmus, *The Praise of Folly* (1517), in John P. Dolan, ed., *The Essential Erasmus* (New York, 1964), pp. 142, 147.

12. F. A. Hayek, "The Source of the Scientific Hubris: L'Ecole Polytechnique," in *The Counter-Revolution of Science* (Glencoe, 1952), pp. 105–116, esp. 105, 110, 112.

13. See the illuminating account in Hayek, pt. 2. See also E. Halévy, *The Era of Tyrannies* (New York, 1965), pp. 21–104.

14. See Gene M. Lyons, *The Uneasy Partnership* (New York, 1969), chap. 2. On how little attention economists as economists commanded among formulators of policy, see Joseph J. Spengler, "Evolution of Public-Utility Industry Regulation: Economists and other Determinants," *South African Journal of Economics* 37 (1969):3–31. On the progress of professionalization, see G. J. Stigler, *Essays in the History of Economics* (Chicago, 1965), chap. 3.

15. Henry Adams, *The Education of Henry Adams* (New York, 1905; New York, 1931), chap. 35 and p. 415.

16. On when coal will be displaced, see M. K. Hubbert's paper in Harry Foreman, ed., *Nuclear Power and the Public* (Minneapolis, 1970).

17. These estimates, attributed to George Stigler, appear in the unsigned article "The Flourishing Intellectuals," *Time*, 21 May 1965, p. 32.

18. For example, see Lionel Trilling, *Beyond Culture* (New York, 1965), p. 3.

19. See Thomas Molnar, *The Decline of the Intellectual* (New York, 1961); G. B. de Huszar, ed., *The Intellectuals* (Glencoe, 1960).

20. For example, see E. M. Cioran, *The Fall Into Time* (New York, 1970). Anthony Downs argues that many problems, especially urban ones, are social rather than technological; Downs, "New Directions for Urban Research," *Technology Review* 73 (1971):26–35.

21. See Matthew Radom, *The Social Scientist in American Industry* (New Brunswick, 1970); compare this with D. C. Pelz and F. M. Andrews, *Scientists in Organizations* (New York, 1966).

22. A series of ten books, each on one social science, comprising *The Behavioral and Social Sciences Survey* (Englewood Cliffs, 1967–1969) and prepared under the auspices of the National Academy of Sciences and the Social Science Research Council, has been issued recently. See also *The Behavioral and Social Sciences: Outlook and Needs* (Englewood Cliffs, 1969), issued jointly by the National Academy of Sciences and the Social Science Research Council.

23. Ibid., pp. 312–313. On deceleration in the growth of markets for

Ph.D.'s, see A. M. Cartter, "Scientific Manpower for 1970–1985," *Science* 172 (1971):132–140.

24. Some of the problems are discussed in *Communication System and Resources in the Behavioral Sciences,* Publication 1575, National Academy of Sciences (Washington, D.C., 1967). See also Bentley Glass, *The Timely and the Timeless* (New York, 1970), and D. J. de Solla Price, *Science Since Babylon* (New Haven, 1961).

25. See Kraft's discussion of "intellectuals" in his column that appeared on the *Durham Sun's* editorial page, 9 December 1968. See also Arthur Koestler, *The Sleepwalkers* (New York, 1959).

26. The data presented are taken or derived from U.S. Bureau of the Census, *Statistical Abstract of the United States: 1970* (Washington, D.C., 1970).

27. See H. A. Krebs, "The Goals of Science," *Proceedings of the American Philosophical Society* 115 (1971):1–3.

28. Harold Orlans, "Science And Polity, Or How Much Knowledge Does A Nation Need?" *Proceedings of the American Philosophical Society* 115 (1971):4–9, esp. 4. On "disgusting publicity and propaganda" in support of science, see Erwin Chargoff, "Preface to a Grammar of Biology, *Science* 172 (1971):637–642.

29. P. M. Boffey reports that governmental personnel interested in helping scientists gain higher funding for science found "that the ineptness and arrogance of scientists made them ineffective allies" in these efforts. See Boffey, "Science Policy," *Science* 171 (1971):874. It is said that "leaders of aerospace sometimes displayed an unconscious arrogance, in their case the arrogance of commanding an elite knowledge"; "Aerospace: The Troubled Blue Yonder," *Time,* 5 April 1971, p. 91. L. M. Branscomb, director of the National Bureau of Standards, writes: "Many people feel that humanity is threatened by the *vanity* of those who believe only good can come from so thoroughly satisfying a process as scientific creativity"; Branscomb, "Taming Technology," *Science* (1971):972 (my italics). See also J. R. Pierce's editorial, "A Time to Take Stock," *Science* 171 (1971).

30. This statement was made in 1966 by a high government official; see the letter of Warren Weaver, in *Science* 171 (1971):752.

31. See Orlans, "Science and Polity." "More research expenditures do not seem to lead to more technical progress," L. C. Thurow concludes; Thurow, "Research, Technical Progress and Economic Growth," *Technology Review* 73 (1971):44–52.

32. This estimate is reported by Warren Weaver in his letter in *Science* 171 (1971):752. The spacemen who would escape the confines of the earth do not, of course, find the greater outlay uneconomic.

33. "Rolls-Royce: The Trap of Technological Pride," *Time,* 22 February 1971, pp. 84, 86. See also the article "Aerospace," in *Time,* p. 91.

34. L. Lessing, "The Senseless War on Science," *Fortune,* March 1971, pp. 88 ff. See also Branscomb, "Taming Technology."

35. J. M. Clark, *Alternative to Serfdom* (New York, 1960), p. 112.

36. On the propensity of economists to be "relevant," see Rand Guffey, "Econ. 101. . . ." *Wall Street Journal,* 22 March 1971, p. 1.

37. For example, see Halévy, pp. 265–285. See also F. A. Hayek, *The Road to Serfdom* (Chicago, 1944), chaps. 12, 13; and on the costs of central- ized planning, P. J. D. Wiles, "Economic Activation, Planning, and the So- cial Order," in Bertram Gross, ed., *Action Under Planning* (New York, 1967), pp. 138–185. For what was often an unfashionable albeit prescient view, see Ely Devons, *Papers on Planning and Economic Management,* ed. A. Cairncross (Manchester, 1970).

38. On ownership, see D. A. Flagg and Virginia G. Flagg, "An Empirical Application of Measures of Socialism to Different Nations," *Western Eco- nomic Journal* 8 (1970):233–240.

39. Eric Roll, *The World after Keynes* (New York, 1968), reviewed by A. Cairncross, *Economic Journal* 80 (1970):111. See also A. Leijonhufvud, *On Keynesian Economics and the Economics of Keynes* (New York, 1968), esp. pts. 1 and 6.

40. Quotation from A. Cairncross, *Economic Journal* 80 (1970):111. Cairncross has in view not an "interdisciplinary economics" but the need to resort to several disciplines when one alone does not supply the answer. See R. L. Heilbroner, "On the Limited 'Relevance' of Economics," *Public Inter- est,* no. 21 (1970):80–93; R. M. Solow, "Science and Ideology in Econom- ics," ibid.:94–107. On the reluctance of economists to give adequate weight to technology, see P. M. Boffey, "Technology and World Trade: Is There Cause for Alarm?" *Science* 172 (1971):37–41.

41. See U.S. Dept. of Health, Education, and Welfare, *Toward a Social Report* (Washington, D.C., 1969).

42. See Gaines's monthly "Economic Report," issued by Manufacturers Hanover Trust Co. (New York), March 1971, p. 1; for Moynihan's remarks, see Ways, "Don't We Know Enough," p. 118.

43. Clark, *Alternative,* chap. 4. On the insensitivity of big governmental organizations, see Robert Moses, "Does Federal Reorganization Matter?" *Wall Street Journal,* 9 April 1971, p. 4. On deficit finance in the 1930s, see J. R. Davis, "Chicago Economists, Deficit Budgets, and the Early 1930's," *American Economic Review* 58 (1968):476–482.

44. W. Leontief, "Theoretical Assumptions and Nonobserved Facts," *American Economic Review* 61 (March 1971):1.

45. Output and employment data are from the *Annual Report of the Council of Advisers,* February 1971, pp. 19–22.

46. R. A. Mundell, *The Dollar and The Policy Mix: 1971,* Essays in Inter- national Finance, no. 85 (Princeton, May 1971). See also H. G. Johnson, "Is Inflation the Inevitable Price of Rapid Development or a Retarding Factor in Economic Growth?" *Malayan Economic Review* 11 (1966):22–28; G. S. Dor-

rance, "The Effect of Inflation on Economic Development," *International Monetary Fund Staff Papers,* March 1963, pp. 25–31; Arthur Burns, "The Basis for Lasting Prosperity," *Monthly Review* of the Federal Reserve Bank of Richmond, January 1971, pp. 2–7; Leijonhufvud, *Keynesian Economics.*

47. Paul W. McCracken, "Economic Policy in the Age of the Employment Act," in I. H. Siegel, ed., *Manpower Tomorrow: Prospects and Priorities* (New York, 1967), pp. 73–86, esp. 74, 77.

48. Ways, "Don't We Know Enough," p. 66.

49. "Allen's Law," *Time,* 15 February 1971, p. 14.

50. On such disregard, see E. J. Mishan, *The Costs of Economic Growth* (New York, 1967), and *Welfare Economics* (New York, 1964).

51. "Caught in the Middle," *Barron's,* 1 March 1971, pp. 1, 8.

52. See Joseph J. Spengler, "Is Social Science Ready?" *Social Science Quarterly* 50 (1969):449–468; also the many accounts of the failure of economists to contribute effectively to the solution of problems confronting underdeveloped countries, such as S. Wellisz, "Lessons of Twenty Years of Planning in Developing Countries," *Economica* 38 (1971):121–135. See also representative pieces in G. M. Meier, ed., *Leading Issues in Economic Development,* 2d ed. (New York, 1970); also C. P. Snow, *Public Affairs* (New York, 1971).

53. Ways, "Don't We Know Enough," p. 128.

54. Melvin Maddocks, "The Limitations of Language," *Time,* 8 March 1971, pp. 36–37. See also Joseph J. Spengler, "Notes on the International Transmission of Economic Ideas," *History of Political Economy* 2 (1970):133–151; W. G. Bennis, "The Failure and Promise of the Social Sciences," *Technology Review,* October–November 1970, pp. 39–42; Paul Halmos, "Social Science and Social Change," *Ethics* 69 (1959):102–119; Gunnar Myrdal, *Asian Drama* (New York, 1968), vol. 3, pp. 1839–1842. Many critiques of the use of ambiguous or ineffective language could be cited.

55. K. E. Boulding, review in the *Journal of Economic Literature* 7 (1969):1162. Cf. G. C. Harcourt's review in ibid. 9 (1971):92.

56. F. H. Hahn, "Some Adjustment Problems," *Econometrica* 38 (1970):1–2.

57. See Joseph J. Spengler, "Cost of Specialization in a Service Economy," *Social Science Quarterly* 51 (1970):237–262, esp. 248–249, 257, 259–261.

58. See the *Bulletin of the American Academy of Arts and Sciences* 24 (1971):16–17, reporting an address by Daniel P. Moynihan together with comments by Boulding.

13

THE EMERGING SOCIAL STRUCTURE OF THE WORLD

Alex Inkeles

In the second half of the twentieth century, laymen and professional intellectuals alike frequently have expressed the sense that the relationship of all of us, all humankind, to each other and to our world, has been undergoing a series of profound changes. We seem to be living in one of those rare historical eras in which a progressive quantitative process becomes a qualitative transformation. Even when, in more sober moments, we recognize that we are yet far from being there, we have the unmistakable sense that we are definitely set off on some new trajectory, and that we are not merely launched but are already well along toward an only vaguely identified destination. The widespread diffusion of this sense of a new, emergent global interrelatedness is expressed in numerous ideas, slogans, and catchphrases that have wide currency, such as "world government," "the global village," "spaceship earth," "the biosphere," and the ubiquitous cartoon of a crowded globe with a lighted fuse protruding from one end, the whole labeled "the world population bomb." Although the pervasiveness of the response to this emergent situation certainly tells us that some-

This paper, orginally prepared for the present volume, was presented at the International Political Science Association meetings at Montreal, 20–23 August 1973. The creative research assistance of Dean Nielsen is gratefully acknowledged.

thing is happening, its diversity highlights our confusion as to exactly *what* it is that is happening.

Obviously the issue is one that is going to occupy us for a long time to come. Indeed, it is of such fundamental significance that our future welfare, perhaps our survival, will depend on our ability initially to understand and subsequently to guide the processes of change in which we are caught up. Consciousness and concern about this process at the community and national level have become so widespread as to be commonplace and even banal. But it should give us pause—perhaps it is even cause for alarm—that so little attention is being paid to the problem of social change at the global level, at least when one expresses the amount of that attention as a proportion of the time the world's specialists in sociology and political economy spend on other scientific problems and issues. Moreover, such attention as the issue gets is usually sporadic, the methods applied eclectic, the data of dubious validity and reliability, and the "mode of analysis" casual and unsystematic. It will require a great and concerted effort over many years to rectify our inadequacies in this regard. Of the several tasks that lie before us, it seems to me that one of the most critical, especially at this early stage in our work, is that of clarifying our basic concepts. It is to that end I plan to devote a large part of this chapter. I shall, as well, make a few forays into the empirical realm, not so much to make a convincing case about the facts as to illustrate and test the usefulness of some of the conceptual distinctions I feel it is important to introduce.

A SET OF BASIC CONCEPTS AND A HISTORICAL EXCURSUS

If we are moving toward a new condition, it will be helpful to have some sense of what that condition may be. Otherwise, it is logically impossible to tell whether or not we indeed are more closely approximating it. Some reflection on the matter makes it immediately apparent that there is not only one end state toward which we may be moving; rather, there are several. Moreover, we should recognize also that we *start* not from one position, but in fact from several, depending on the unit of action from whose perspective we view the situation. Some brief excursions into definition and a clarification of basic concepts are therefore indispensable to further discourse on the matter.

What is most distinctive about the problem before us is that it moves us beyond even the largest customary unit of social analysis, namely, the nation-state, to focus on the entire human population of the globe. Of that population, and the social units in which it is organized, we are asking: what kind of socio-cultural system did it constitute in the past, what character does it have in the last quarter of the twentieth century, what are its current emergent properties, and what will be its probable future characteristics?

Given this perspective, we might well have framed our investigation in the terms common to the analysis of social systems as large and complex as the nation-state. Thus, we might inquire into the structure of stratification among the units; the nature, if any, of the overarching legal system; the social consequences of the economic subsystem; and the extent of shared values, norms, and behaviorial dispositions. Although this approach would be legitimate, and no doubt revealing, I have chosen instead to rely on a different set of concepts which I feel is better suited for dealing with the distinctiveness of the problem at hand. This set of categories seems less to presume that the world does indeed share what can meaningfully be described as "*a* system of social action." At the same time, it does not exclude consideration of important themes such as stratification and the sharing of norms.

Autarky

Autarky exists when a set of people share a more or less completely self-contained and self-sustaining sociocultural system. The condition does not necessarily assume physical isolation, although such isolation is often associated with autarky. Rather, to meet the test of autarky, a system should be such that if all other forms of human and social life were suddenly to disappear, the remaining system would have a high probability of continuing to propagate itself in much the same form it had before the cataclysm overtook everyone else. This condition is most easily met by small and isolated communities, for example, tribes living on isolated Pacific atolls or high mountains. Mere isolation, however, is not enough to guarantee the condition of autarky. A particular type of social structure and economy is essential. A group that depended on other tribes for a basic commodity of life such as salt, or an indispensable and unsubstitutable instrument for gathering food such as a trap, or which was obliged regularly to come together with others to permit exogamous marriages, would to that degree be less able to satisfy the requirement of autarky. Thus, an Eskimo family wandering in full isolation for months across the arctic wastes in search of food is not an autarky, since functions critical to maintaining the long-term system of action of the group require that its members periodically come together with other similar physically isolated families to exchange brides and perform certain religious and communal services essential to the continuation of the sociocultural system of the tribe. An Eskimo tribe as a whole, however, might well qualify as an autarkic social system.

Although small and isolated groups with simple social systems and primitive economies may predominate among autarkies, such systems are also found at the other end of the scale of size. Units at the level of the nation-state may achieve a high degree of autarky. Thus, Japan, Soviet Russia, and Communist China, at various periods in their history, more or less totally sealed their borders and strove to achieve complex goals of social reorganization while relying almost exclusively on resources and ideas internal to their respective sociopolitical systems.

Interconnectedness, Dependence, and Interdependence

Moving away from autarky, we encounter various degrees of interconnectedness and dependence. The terms refer to similar but not identical conditions. *Interconnectedness* refers to the volume or frequency of communication, interaction, or exchange between two sociocultural systems. It is most often expressed in the exchange of goods and services, that is, in trade, as when tribes living in the hills grow tea that they exchange in regular markets for rice grown by culturally distinct tribes living in the lowland valleys.

Substantial interconnectedness suggests, and may lead to, but is not a sufficient condition for *dependence*. Dependence refers to reliance on an item of exchange that is more or less indispensable to the survival of the system or systems engaging in the exchange. A system experiencing such dependence would to that degree be unable to achieve or maintain autarky.[1]

In a system of exchange, however, the implications of the exchange are not the same for all the units participating. The salt given by system *A* in exchange for the jade beads of system *B* may be vital to the physical continuity of *B*, whereas the beads may easily be replaced in *A* by some other means of ornamenting the dress used in tribal dances. *A* and *B* therefore are interconnected, but not interdependent. *B* is dependent on *A*, but *A* is not dependent on *B*. To illustrate from the contemporary world, Japan and the United States each manifest an extremely complex pattern of interconnectedness with other countries. In the case of the United States, however, the means are available for continuing the current American system basically intact without relying on these ties. Japan, not possessed of domestic sources of coal and iron ore, to say nothing of oil, could not possibly continue as a major industrial producer without its external trade. Japanese interconnectedness therefore is also extreme dependency, whereas American interconnectedness, while extensive, is manifested by a system that is, overall, so far autonomous as to have high potential for attaining a condition of autarky.[2]

Integration and Hegemony

Integration is a step beyond interdependence. It represents a condition in which formerly autonomous units have more or less permanently surrendered vital functions to another, more extended unit while still retaining a substantial number of other vital functions. Integration therefore may apply to only a given institution, to a subset of institutions such as the economic or political, or to a series of major institutional complexes. Thus, two neighboring states may adopt a joint customs arrangement with regard to third parties and suspend such formalities for all goods passing between the two states, while each yet maintains a separate parliament, executive, police force, tax system, and the like. For example, the princely states of India after independence were largely, although not totally, integrated into the new national state while retaining some degree of distinctness. In time we may expect this integration to become complete, and these units of the system will become indistinguishable from all the other subdivisions of the Indian state.

Integration may, of course, be either voluntary or imposed. Thus, the total integration of the colonies in the former British

Empire was, with few exceptions, a result of the imposition of force, whereas the participation of most of the ex-colonies in the Commonwealth was largely voluntary, perhaps because it involved a lesser degree of integration. Integration imposed by force may be treated as a special case, designated as *hegemony*. It was the predominant mode of integration in the past, and its history has not yet run its course, although we may hope that voluntary integration will be the predominant mode in the future.

Convergence

Integration sometimes presupposes and often leads to similarities in political form, in social organization, or in cultural patterns, but such similarities are neither a necessary nor a sufficient condition for integration. Where social units start from diverse positions on some scale of organization, sociopolitical structure, or culture, and then move toward some more common form on the given dimension, the process is labeled *convergence*. Just as integration may occur without convergence, as in the relations of an imperial center and its colonies, so convergence may occur without any substantial degree of integration. Thus, the Soviet Union and the United States may become more alike in their urbanization, dependence on scientific research and technological innovation, and development of a delinquent subculture among the *jeunesse dorée,* without any substantial movement toward greater integration of the two political systems.

A Historical Excursus

Having elaborated our basic set of concepts, at least in preliminary form, we now should test their serviceability. Ideally, this test would require application to a number of historical periods. Indeed, it would have been preferable to make this test by applying the concepts to at least four periods: prehistory, the era of Greco-Roman dominance, the medieval period, and the premodern world scene. The limits on the space allotted for this particular essay, however, oblige us to restrict ourselves to a single application, in this case the earliest relevant period, namely, prehistory.

Before undertaking this exploration, however, it seems appropriate to pause long enough for one general note of caution concerning the severe limits on our ability to generalize, which constrain us the moment we move from the nation-state or the culture region to the global level of analysis. Throughout much of recorded history, different areas of the world were at quite different stages of development, especially so far as the level of technology and of political integration are concerned. The earth was divided into a series of different worlds, each with its own character as a subworld. Moreover, for much of human history some of these subworlds were mutually in total ignorance of the existence of each other. Great Incan and Mayan empires rose and fell without having any awareness of Europe, just as Europe was totally unaware of those empires. Of course, it is precisely the fact that such complete isolation and insulation is no longer possible that distinguishes the modern era. Knowing that, however, does not settle for us the question as to whether, in dealing with such periods, it really is appropriate to treat the world as one unit, or whether it should be treated as a series of discrete subworlds, for each of which we need to test, separately, the extent to which the elements within it enjoyed autarky, were independent, converged on a common model, and so on. It seems both more consistent with the theoretical orientation of this particular presentation and more consonant with practical constraints, to maintain here a focus on the world as a single system. Applying our concepts to the prehistorical period, approximately between 10,000 and 5000 B.C., we may say the following of the world at that time:

Autarky was extremely high, which is to say of course that dependence was very low. Hunting and gathering, herding, and limited agriculture permitted relatively self-contained, self-supporting communities.

Interconnectedness was minimal. Most groups had contact only with immediately adjacent groups; exchange was limited to a small number of less than vital commodities; interchange of persons, customs, ideas, and technology was extremely selective. Although pottery, animal husbandry, and some cultivated plants gradually diffused, the norm seemed to be total avoidance where possible, and sporadic, brief, and limited engagement where unavoidable.

Integration rarely was the outcome of such connections as were established. Populations often were nomadic or in other ways in motion, which reduced the length of contact between groups below the term optimal for integration. In addition, the groups coming into juxtaposition often were extremely disparate, as illustrated in a later historical period by the relations between the settled, cliff-dwelling, almost "urban" Hopi, and nomadic herders such as the Navajo. The barriers to the integration of such groups were very great. Moreover, limits on the technical capacity of rulers, above all with regard to communication, minimized the prospect of establishing political *hegemony,* and hence further reduced the attainment of other forms of integration.

Convergence. It is a curious feature of the prehistorical period that despite maximal autarky and minimal interconnectedness and integration, convergence was quite substantial. Probably the most important manifestation of the similarity which most societies displayed in that period was in their level of technology. That technology, in turn, evidently established constraints which influenced institutional patterns, thus ensuring the existence of certain very broad similarities in the social organization of late stone-age and early bronze-age societies.

Our image of the standing of the prehistorical period on the seven dimensions of our analytic scheme, reducing our characterization of each to a key word or phrase, may be summarized as follows:

Autarky	High
Interconnectedness	Minimal
Dependence	Extremely limited
Interdependence	Virtually none
Integration	Virtually none
Hegemony	Minimal and sporadic
Convergence	Considerable similarity in technology; modest in other forms of culture

Once we move into the historical era, we quickly discover how difficult it is to avoid being ethnocentric. For example, if

we elect to represent early history by the period from 200 B.C. to
A.D. 200, the temptation for an individual in the European historical tradition is to treat it automatically as the era dominated
by Greek culture and the Roman Empire. From the perspective
of an Asian, however, it might more appropriately be seen as
the period of the flourishing of the great Han dynasties. Going
either back or forward, the specific actors would change, but the
pattern would remain the same. The tendency for vast parts of
the global population to become organized in great territorial
hegemonies marks a sharp break dividing the historical period
from prehistory. These hegemonies were generally concentrated
in, although not absolutely limited to distinct, even if broad,
culture areas, and were generally organized and dominated by a
particular dynamic subgroup within the area. They were possible only after widely diffused, settled agriculture made available large surpluses of grain and labor. But they depended at
least as much on technological advances such as irrigation, improved navigation at sea, systems of imperial roads such as those
built by Darius for the Achaemenid Empire, and the development of cavalry and a reliable iron sword. Equally critical was
the development of new forms of political and military organization, including the means for collecting and allocating the
surplus food and human services that became available.

Within the limits of each of these subworlds, and notably
within the area of Roman dominance, *autarky* was greatly reduced, *interconnectedness* and *interdependence* became much
more extensive, and, despite a high degree of cultural diversity
in the hinterlands, a *convergence* toward a common metropolitan culture was strongly manifested.

In the global system as a whole, however, the tendencies were
different. The characteristic of the world system was that it was
multicentered. Each of the major subworlds, such as Rome and
China, manifested a high degree of *autarky*. *Interconnectedness*
between the major subworlds was relatively minor, limited to a
few trade routes mainly carrying specialized commodities, particularly luxury goods not at all vital to the economy or social
structure of either party to the exchange. In brief, neither dependence nor interdependence was manifested between these
subworlds. Finally, *divergence* rather than congruence was the
norm in the elaboration of social and cultural forms. In this era,

each of the subworlds greatly elaborated forms of stratification, of architecture and art, and of religion, starting from different points and following principles of internal coherence that moved them in ever more divergent directions. The phrase "a typical resident of the world" is a much less meaningful concept when applied to this period than it was when applied to the prehistorical era.

We have come forward partway through history, although by great leaps and bounds, with at least some basis for concluding that our small repertoire of concepts provides a reasonably serviceable instrument for characterizing the global social system at any one time. Thus assured, we may turn to our analysis of the current modern period, which is to be the main object of our analysis.

THE RECENT MODERN ERA

At some point after the medieval period in Europe, the world entered upon a new and unprecedented era of interconnectedness. No precise moment or event can claim unambiguous priority in defining the start of this era; appropriate candidates might be Marco Polo's visit to Asia in the last quarter of the thirteenth century or Columbus's discovery of the New World. In any event, after a slow beginning lasting several hundred years, the rate of interchange among individuals, institutions, and societies began to grow at an exceedingly rapid rate.

In characterizing the modern era, one is greatly tempted to see a relatively sharp break with much of what had gone before in human history. To the Western imagination, this temptation is reinforced by the image of the Dark Ages, exaggerated perhaps, but on the whole correctly perceived as one of stagnation and even retrogression on many dimensions of human endeavor. But even if we use as our standard the centuries that witnessed the remarkable burgeoning of the Roman Empire, we must be struck by how little that was fundamentally new was added to knowledge or to mankind's stock of basic resources. The Romans may have been great innovators, but they were mediocre inventors. And of this small set of inventions they sometimes took but little advantage, as in the case of the waterwheel.[3] By contrast, what is archetypical of the modern era, and in particular of the industrial system, is the great flood of new materials, technique, knowledge, and institutions, coupled with an explosive growth in the production and diffusion of people, goods, services, ideas, and relationships. In many respects the facts are staggering.

Probably the most dramatic changes have come about through the growth of population. Thus, the modern era, although representing less than one-tenth of 1 percent of the time man has been on the earth, has produced about one-quarter of all the human beings who ever lived on this globe.[4] Not only are the numbers vastly larger, but per capita consumption has increased enormously. As a result, the world's supply of nonreplenishable resources is being consumed at an incredible rate. We may fault Meadows and the Club of Rome on one or another of their projections, but it is difficult to disprove their contention that in many respects the modern era has become the era of exponential growth.[5] Such growth is one of the most fundamental facts of our time. To deny it is ridiculous, even though embracing it uncritically is foolish. Social reality is much too complicated to permit one to summarize it in a single statistic, or to represent it adequately by a single concept. That becomes fully apparent when one examines some of the evidence bearing on the issue of the interconnectedness of the modern world.

Interconnectedness

A very large number of indicators may be drawn on to prove that the national institutions and populations that comprise world society have been very rapidly increasing the degree of their interconnectedness over the last half-century. Among many indicators of this trend, we may point to the following:[6]

University-level students abroad: The number of students studying outside their own country approximately doubled between 1960 and 1969, rising from 239,000 to 477,000. This continued a pattern that had been in evidence at least since 1950. Over that longer period of time, the annual increase in the number of students studying abroad was in excess of 7 percent a year.[7]

Foreign mail: Between 1938 and 1970 the volume of foreign mail sent and received by forty reporting countries increased almost seven times. The annual rate of increase was some 6 percent per year.[8]

International telephonic and telegraphic communication: Closely paralleling the pattern manifested by the mails, a marked increase is shown in the frequency of electronic communication across national boundaries. The number of telegrams sent abroad in 1970 was more than two and a half times that for 1938, indicating an annual increase rate of 3 percent per year.[9] Moreover, there was a much higher rate of increase in the frequency of international telephone calls, conservatively estimated at 15 percent per year in the decade of the sixties.[10] Putting all the evidence together, we may safely assume that the total of international wired and wireless exchanges combined has increased at a rate sufficient to ensure at least a doubling every decade.

International tourist travel: From 1954 to 1970, the twenty-six main "tourist-receiving" countries experienced a surge from 26 to 106 million visits, indicating an increase of about 8.7 percent per year. This did not come about merely because the affluent were flooding the more exotic corners of the globe. For example, in this same period the interchange between Europe and the United States, accounting for a large part of all tourism, also increased at a rate in excess of 7 percent per year.[11]

World trade: Commerce between nation-states increased tenfold between 1938 and 1969. In each of the three decades it approximately doubled, indicating an annual increase of about 7 percent.[12] Increases expressed in value terms, as these are, should perhaps be discounted to allow for inflation. But even expressing the value of world trade in constant 1963 prices, the three-decade period still yields an annual rate of increase of about 5 percent.[13]

Direct capital investment abroad: United States data, the most readily available, show a change in the rate of investment, from about $1 billion or $2 billion in 1946–1952 to $3 billion by 1963, and then to $8 billion by 1971. Even allowing for inflation, the amount of such investment clearly at least doubled within the last decade.[14] Data on the rest of the world, still being studied, are expected to show comparable patterns.

International nongovernmental organizations (INGOs): From around 1850, when some five or ten INGOs were founded in each quinquenniad, the number founded rose to more than 300 per quinquenniad by 1950. From 1954 to 1968, the rate of increase in the total number of such organizations was about 5 percent per year.[15] Moreover, a study of the congresses and conferences sponsored by these organizations presumably would show an equal and more likely a higher rate of participation by groups and individuals than is indicated when participation is measured on the basis of the number of "organizations" involved.

International governmental organizations (IGOs): In general, membership in such organizations increased substantially after World War II. In the United Nations, for example, the rate of membership increase from 1945 to 1970 was 3.6 percent per annum; for UNESCO it was 6.4 percent. Some of the specialized organizations, such as GATT, experienced an annual membership increase of more than 10 percent.[16]

The pattern manifested in these figures is unmistakable and indeed rather remarkable in its consistency. Over a wide range of systems of exchange we find evidence for rapid acceleration in the development of ties linking nations, their institutional components, and the individuals who populate them. The abundance and complexity of the networks that interconnect the world's population are, and for some time have been, growing at a phenomenal rate. With some variation according to the specific indicator used, recent decades reveal a general tendency for many forms of human interconnectedness across national boundaries to be doubling every ten years.[17]

Obviously, there are many quite serious defects in the available data, which will take a long time to correct. There are also some anomalous findings that may be hard to explain. In addition, summary figures on average rates such as those given obviously must conceal a great deal of variation in the degree to which different nations and people are participating in this increased connectivity. The variation by no means is obvious; indeed, there are some marked surprises in store for anyone who will carefully examine the detailed statistics.

For example, not wealth but the size of the population best predicts the dependence of countries on foreign trade. The proportion of GNP represented by trade rises from a mere 10 percent in countries of more than 100 million to almost 80 percent in countries of less than 1 million.[18] In the utilization of telegraphic communication directed abroad, the less developed countries actually have been gaining markedly on the more developed, as their rate of increase of the use of such means of communication was 4.3 percent, against 2 percent for the advanced countries, between 1938 and 1970.[19] There is also a contrast between tourists, who mainly stem from the wealthier countries, and students, who are sent abroad to study mainly by poorer countries. Only a relatively small proportion of the students of the wealthier countries studies abroad.[20]

All these anomalies, if such they be, surely have sensible explanations, and could be discussed at length.[21] Some of these issues will, in fact, be further dealt with below. At this point, however, I must limit myself to calling attention to the complexities. That, however, does not gainsay the main thrust of the data.

Faced, then, with the evident facts of such rapid growth of interconnectedness, one must inevitably wonder what the long-term implications of this process will be. Can and will the expansion of connectedness go on indefinitely? If not, what are the limits on further expansion? And, whether the expansion continues or must come to a halt at some more or less definable point, what will the resultant world system be like?

First, we should acknowledge the obvious fact that worldwide connectivity cannot continue to grow indefinitely. Indeed, for some forms of interchange we can specify absolute ceilings and practical limits on further expansion. For example, the increase in membership in the United Nations from 1950 to 1970 was clearly determined by a set of unique historical circumstances. Even if a number of the currently less well-integrated nations were to break up into several separate sovereign states where only one existed before, the earlier rate of increase in UN membership would not be sustained. On the other hand, there is no obvious limit on the rate of participation by individuals and subgroups in international nongovernmental organizations. As there are billions of people who do not yet participate in any way, and much more involvement is possible on the part of those already active, we could well have a doubling of participation every decade for a very long period indeed. Overall, the situation evidently is complex, with objectively defined limits balanced against forces making for probable long-term increases.

The case of university students studying abroad illustrates the complexity of the issue. First, we must acknowledge that obviously there is a theoretical point beyond which it would become impossible to maintain the high rate of increase in study abroad which the world experienced in recent decades. It is, however, equally obvious that, with only 2 percent of all university students studying abroad, we are very far from reaching that theoretical limit.[22] We may well wonder, therefore, whether more practical considerations do not hold some promise of stemming the tide.

We can, indeed, identify certain forces that should act, over time, to reduce the number of students studying abroad. As we shall see below in the discussion of dependence, the tendency to send university students abroad to study is related to the availability of domestic training facilities. In very small countries, such facilities most likely always will be limited to a few important fields. In the larger national communities, however, a greater number of places over a wider range of subjects is likely to become available within the country as each increases its wealth and develops a fuller array of domestic institutions for advanced training. Indeed, it is precisely because the wealth and the institutional resources of almost all countries are increasing, however much less rapidly and less equitably than we might hope, that we can expect most countries to find it possible, in time, to train their students at home.

The attainment of this stage of development by most of the currently less developed countries could lead the *proportion* of students studying abroad, and in time perhaps even their *absolute* number, to become stabilized, and the numbers and proportions might even begin to decline absolutely. Such trends actually already can be observed in specified fields, such as engineering and medicine, which with each passing year, account for a smaller percentage of the students studying abroad.[23]

On the other hand, the issue is complicated by the prospect that, as countries increase in wealth, the students who now go abroad out of necessity may increasingly be replaced by those who go to foreign countries because it is presumed to be "broadening." That has been the chief reason for study abroad by the more affluent, and there are no grounds for assuming that the idea will not appeal also to those whose higher income is of more recent vintage. In other words, if the supply of discretionary income keeps up with or surpasses the diminution in the pressures of practical necessity, a decline in the proportion of students studying abroad may be quite long in coming.

Having now acknowledged the observed, the practical, and the theoretical limits on indefinite exponential growth, we nevertheless must report our impression that many indicators of interconnectivity have no obvious saturation point. In any event, most indicators are very far from having reached the point where growth must stop. On the contrary, the fact that on many indicators the less developed countries show a tendency toward acceleration in the rate at which they become connected to the outside world gives reason to assume that the trends we noted still have much momentum.[24] Most of the indicators we have identified respond to the growth in wealth. And wealth, however unevenly distributed, is increasing in *most countries,* and in some *segments* of all countries. We may therefore confidently expect the next thirty, and perhaps the next fifty, years to be characterized by the increasing connectivity of the world population.

Interdependence

Interconnectedness may suggest, but does not necessarily define, interdependence. Dependence exists where a service, commodity, or resource obtained from abroad is relatively vital and not easily substitutable. Interdependence exists where there is a relatively equal or balanced exchange of such goods. If country *A* has good coking coal while country *B* has ore, and each makes its own steel, they are interdependent in the steel-making process. If capital is in surplus and can find no profitable investment in *C,* whereas *D* has rich and potentially profitable resources and no capital, an exchange between them may also indicate a basic interdependence.

How much of the observed interconnectedness reported above also represents some approximation of this type of interdependence cannot be stated with precision. Indeed, one may easily be misled into assuming that all increases in interconnectedness also mean increased interdependence, when they actually represent nothing of the kind. Take, for example, the exchange of students among countries. As noted above, the *number* of students studying abroad has been rising by more than 7 percent per year. The absolute number of interconnections therefore will double every decade. To assert *interdependence,* however, we should be able to show that such exchanges serve functions not permitting ready or efficient substitution. Alas, that assertion cannot be made, as, of the world's university student body, less than 2 percent study abroad. It is clear, therefore, that despite steeply rising *interconnectivity* in absolute numbers, most countries are *not* linked with others in a system of interdependence so far as the education of university students is concerned.[25]

There are probably many other forms of exchange and interconnectedness that also do not involve a substantial element of interdependence. Take, for example, the tourist flow between the more developed countries. For many years Japan was the favorite goal for American tourists to Asia, even though few Japanese came to the United States. Then, in a short span of time, the number of tourists coming from Japan to the United States, and particularly to Hawaii, rose from about fifteen thousand to more than three hundred thousand.[26] This counterflow perhaps was some slight help in adjusting the balance of trade between the United States and Japan. Beyond that, however, the exchange of several million tourists between these two countries can hardly be assumed to have been terribly important to the life of either. We had interconnectedness without interdependence.

Nevertheless, the world does offer a number of examples of true interdependence, which provide some basis for asserting that in recent decades there has been a real increase in that phenomenon. Probably the best example—certainly the best-documented case—is that of world trade.

Nations, especially nation-states, are driven to trade by the limits on autarky and by the demands of efficiency. It is the rare nation indeed that can find within its boundaries all the material it needs, and it is the exceptional producer who can find a large enough market within one state's population to permit an efficient scale of production. The contrast with the task of educating students is striking. Belgium can educate virtually all of its university students at home, but within the confines of its limited territory it can find but the smallest part of the material necessary to operate a modern industrial civilization, and only a tiny market for its industrial output. Hence, Belgium must trade so extensively that such trade equals three-fourths of its GNP. That is, of course, a rather high proportion, but not unusual. Of 79 countries tabulated by Taylor and Hudson for 1965, the median proportion of GNP represented by trade was 34 percent.[27] In sharp contrast, students studying abroad represented only 4 percent of all university enrollees in the median case for 119 countries.[28]

But what of the future? Will this particular kind of interdependence in trade increase? As small nations are more forced to trade, and as more and more of the new nations are in the category of "mini-states," one might expect the importance of trade relative to GNP to rise. One would be led to the same conclusion on the basis of the increasing industrialization of the world, since industralization seems to be a great stimulus to trade.[29] There are, of course, countervailing trends that might work against the success of this reasonable prediction. For example, national economic policies increasingly apply pressure for import substitution, fostering the manufacture of products within the country in which they are to be sold. In one way, that means less international trade. However, this practice may reduce one type of import only to require another; for example, the assembled auto, previously imported whole, is now being replaced by imports of steel, rubber, copper, chrome, and the like.

It turns out, somewhat to our surprise, that the available data for seventy-nine countries show very little recent change in the median proportion which trade represents of GNP, the figures being 37 percent in 1959 and 34 percent in 1965.[30] This reflects a very high degree of interdependence.[31] By contrast, consider the situation in earlier times. Certainly the Roman era was impressive for the bulk and variety of commodities exchanged, yet how sobering it is to realize that in the first century B.C. the number of caravans annually crossing from China to Europe via Russia was perhaps one dozen each year.[32] Even allowing for more extensive commerce by sea, external trade must have represented a negligible proportion of GNP in these systems.

Beyond trade, it is likely that the national science establishment of all countries would be seriously hampered, and might indeed be rendered relatively sterile in all but the largest nations, were it not for the continuous interchange of ideas and personnel among the several countries important for scientific productivity. Great literature probably would continue to be produced by authors, and vital new paintings by painters, if we cut off all international contacts among creative artists around the world, but a substantial case can be made for the critical role such exchange plays in stimulating and sustaining innovation and vitality in aesthetic creation.

In science, as in trade and capital flows, the giants, such as the United States and the USSR, probably are least interdependent with the world system; curiously enough, though, it is precisely these two giants that seem most consistently and forcefully to impinge on the development of all the rest of the world.[33]

Dependence

If the earlier example of tourist exchanges between the United States and Japan had involved Jamaica, Mexico, or Spain rather than Japan, the matter would have appeared in quite a different light. Not because tourism would mean more for the United States, obviously, but rather because it would be so much more vital for the countries receiving the tourists.[34] Exchanges vital to one partner but of relatively casual significance for a second define situations of dependency for the former.

In the nature of the case, the poorer or so-called less developed countries most often find themselves in the position of such dependency. Curiously, the situation most commonly cited to illustrate such dependency—that in which these countries seem limited to selling raw materials in exchange for finished industrial products from the advanced countries—is more nearly a situation of interdependence than of strict dependence.[35] Nevertheless, there is plenty of evidence of the pervasive dependence of the overwhelming majority of the less developed countries. They are dependent on the more advanced countries for all manner of more sophisticated machinery, including complex machines of war; for scientific knowledge of all sorts and the related training of specialists in a host of fields; for the technical and organizational know-how vital to large-scale, complex productive enterprises; and for the investment capital essential to purchase, borrow, rent, or otherwise employ those resources.

Again, the situation may be vividly illustrated by the statistics on students sent abroad to study. In 1968, less than a thousand students from North America went to study full time in South America, but more than ten thousand went in the opposite direction. For Asia, the contrast was even more dramatic, as sixty-three thousand students came from Asia to North America, compared with only about a thousand North Americans studying in Asia.[36] These exchanges are wildly disproportionate not only in absolute numbers but in terms of the ratio that students studying abroad represent of all university students enrolled at home. Less than 1 percent of North American students study abroad, as do slightly more than 1 percent of European students. By contrast, Africa and the Arab states were, as late as 1968, obliged to send 15 and 19 percent, respectively, of their students abroad for university-level education.[37] It is evident, then, that many of the smaller and poorer nations are heavily dependent in this respect.

The dependency is all the more obvious if we examine particular fields, especially the scientific and technical. For most of the youths from the advantaged countries the act of going abroad is an indulgence; they usually could do as well at home. For comparable students from the less developed countries going abroad may be an absolute necessity—the only way to obtain the desired training. This is reflected in the distribution of specialties chosen by students studying abroad. In 1966 almost two-thirds of all North Americans studying abroad took "arts" subjects, whereas some 55 percent of students from the developing countries were studying the more applied and critical fields of science, engineering, medicine, and agriculture.[38] The dependence is even more evident when we consider the contribution that study abroad makes to the supply of critically needed specialists in the composition of their respective professions in certain countries. Thus, in 1966 some 28 percent of Africa's science students were obtaining their training abroad, as against a mere 0.3 percent of North American students of science seeking *their* training abroad.[39]

Integration

Progressively increasing interconnectedness and high levels of interdependence might well be expected to serve as preconditions, even as stimulants, for increasing integration. In actual fact, the extraordinary increases in interconnectedness and interdependence that humankind has experienced since World

War II have not been reflected in any really substantial increase in the integration of national states into a united world political system. While the growth curve for interconnectedness has been exponential, the curve for integration has been at best linear, and many more conservative observers would insist that it be shown as more or less flat, with a few small peaks to reflect events such as the creation of the European Economic Community or other regional agencies.

Even these organizations are, of course, extremely limited in their powers. Meantime, most of the agencies of the United Nations and of UNESCO, while serving extremely valuable functions in setting standards, gathering statistics, and channeling aid, have in fact not succeeded in securing the surrender of virtually any important function or other element of sovereignty from the individual nation-states. Indeed, the multiplication of nation-states, including island mini-states, emerging as new sovereignties out of the elements of dissolving colonial empires, had by 1970 brought us to a condition such that the degree of integration of the world system probably was substantially less, on balance, than it had been in 1900. There is therefore not much basis for challenging the assessment of Phillipe de Seynes, the UN under-secretary for economic and social affairs, who asserted that as late as 1972 we still lived in ''an almost anarchical world community with a mosaic of states as yet bound together only by the most general notion of solidarity and with an international system in which the area of clearly recognized common interests is still small [and] the possibility of central planning immediately conjures up new uncertainties, specifically the fear of manipulation by the powerful.''[40]

Convergence

We now come to the consideration of convergence, an issue that seems to be particularly vexing to social scientists. Much of the difficulty of dealing with this problem stems from the failure to distinguish with sufficient precision the different elements of a very complex situation. A minimum list of such elements should include the following:

1. Modes of production and patterns of resource utilization
2. Institutional arrays and institutional forms
3. Structures or patterns of social relationships

4. Systems of popular attitudes, values, and behavior
5. Systems of political and economic control

As these elements may change not only at different speeds but may actually move in opposite directions, the prospects for seemingly contradictory conclusions are substantial.

The following summary position on the issues may be offered:

1. *Modes of production and patterns of resource allocation.* In this respect the general movement is unmistakable and often seems almost inexorable. Indeed, the key to all other issues in the convergence debate may lie precisely here. Marion Levy proposes that we judge modernization by the propensity to utilize inanimate sources of power. By that standard all nations certainly are converging toward a common model, albeit at enormously different rates. The uses of power may, however, be only a crude indicator of a more fundamental process, that of increasing dependence on science and the resultant technology. This conception permits us to appreciate the importance of objects utilizing little power, such as transistors and desk computers, as well as the significance of the chemical-biological revolution symbolized by inoculation and "the pill" in human biology, and by miracle rice, insecticides, and fertilizers in agriculture.

Different societies may play quite different roles as producers of new knowledge of this sort, and they may differ greatly in the speed with which they more or less fully adopt and utilize the products of new technology. Nevertheless, the increasing dependence of all societies on that technology and its products, and the incorporation of all peoples into the network of their influence, is unmistakable. Electronic communication, scientific medicine, rapid transit, and computerized record keeping are a few of the outstanding examples of this wide diffusion.

2. *Institutional arrays, forms, and processes.* One of the hallmarks of modern or developed societies is the presence of a fairly standard array of institutional structures and the wide diffusion of the forms and processes characteristic of their operation. The key element in the transformation so many societies are experiencing consists in increasing differentiation and specialization, arising as a response to steady technological change and growing human interconnectedness. This process of differentia-

tion leads to the burgeoning of new institutions. Within these new institutions, in turn, rational-technical bureaucratic forms of administration tend to diffuse and come to predominate.

Medieval society could reasonably be encompassed by reference to the state, the church, the military, the town and its special classes, the manor, and the peasant villages. In modern society we confront, by contrast, a vast array of institutions previously unknown or existing in only very rudimentary form, but each now fully elaborated with its own character and special forms. The king's chancellery becomes a host of governmental ministries; the pursuit and dissemination of knowledge moves from being a subordinate concern of the church to being the specialized responsibility of a vast array of academies of science, research institutes, universities, and schools; and so on, across many realms encompassing medicine, law, insurance, trade, production, recreation, and leisure. Furthermore, within all these newly elaborated institutions there is a strong tendency to establish rational bureaucratic modes of organization.

The process is, of course, full of vicissitudes, and in many cases what actually is achieved by way of developing an efficient organization is very far from the Weberian model or the canons set by the Harvard School of Business Administration. Neither should one ignore countermovements designed to increase decentralization and to minimize bureaucratization, tendencies we cannot pause to discuss. Nevertheless, the main thrust toward bureaucratization and the rationalization of administration is not to be denied. In substantial degree the world *is* being cast in the Weberian mold.

3. *Structure and patterns of social relationships.* We have in mind here such cultural and structural subsystems as the kinship system, the class structure, and the patterning of leisure-time activity. The basic issue for convergence theory is to assess how far the increasing similarity in modes of production and their associated institutional forms and processes encourages the development of concomitant similarities in sociocultural subsystems. Substantial and rather convincing documentation is available indicating that worldwide family patterns are converging on a norm common to urban-industrial societies.[41] There is equally extensive evidence to sustain the argument that the stratification systems of all large-scale complex societies have

come to resemble each other in many essential respects.[42] Although the facts are less well documented, a case can probably also be made for convergence in the use of leisure within comparable segments of urban-industrial societies.[43]

Of course, all of the facts and alleged facts need to be critically assessed. In addition, the same mode of analysis should be extended to other features of the cultural subsystem, such as religion, to ascertain how far, if at all, comparable tendencies may be discerned there. Certainly we must anticipate that there will be some aspects of the cultural systems shared by particular national and subnational populations that will be completely, and others that will be at least relatively, immune to standardization, despite strong pressure exerted by other elements of the social system. On balance, however, I see no way to deny that some elements of the cultural system of national populations are manifesting a considerable tendency toward convergence as the nations move along the continuum leading them to the status of advanced industrial societies.

4. *Systems of popular attitudes, values, and behavior.* In 1960, in a paper called "Industrial Man," I demonstrated that in a variety of realms there was a similar *structure* of attitudes and values manifested by the population of a diverse set of developed and developing countries.[44] It is important to stress that the similarity was not in the *average* opinion, but rather in the *distribution* of opinion across the stratification system. The populations were alike only in that the structure of opinion in all cases was similar, with certain views and orientations becoming either more or less frequent as one went up or down the scale of education, occupational prestige, and the like. The theoretical explanation for these patterns was that the differentiated life experience of people in different strata of large-scale complex societies generated a standardized differentiation of response. This idea subsequently was tested more systematically in my cross-national research on individual modernization. There I was able to demonstrate, quite unambiguously I believe, that in six quite diverse developing nations each increment of increasing contact with modern institutions moved men a corresponding degree along a composite scale of modern attitudes and values.[45]

I read this evidence as arguing strongly that, as human life ex-

perience becomes more alike, attitudes, values, and basic dispositions also will become more alike. However, this should not
be interpreted as meaning that *all* men will become psychically
alike. Clearly, if the theory I enunciated is correct, all people
will not become alike so long as there are patterns of social differentiation *within* national populations. Moreover, the fact
that men may become more alike should not obscure the fact
that their having started from quite different initial positions
still may leave them quite dissimilar even after they have moved
a substantial distance toward some common norm.

Finally, it should not be forgotten that I posit movement
toward a common norm only on certain aspects of modern industrial and organizational experience, as identified by the syndrome of individual modernity. There are clearly many other
realms of attitude and value that are independent of the industrial organizational complex common to advanced nations. The
influence of cultural traditions or national history may more
strongly affect attitudes concerning democracy, social distance,
and stratification. Thus, the attitudes of the citizens of Australia and England on these issues may be widely divergent despite
the fact that the two nations share the same broad cultural tradition and that both qualify as modern complex societies. The
features held in common by the two societies evidently are less
effective in influencing the attitudes in question than are the
facts of the pioneering tradition in Australia and the low-status
origins of the original settlers there.

5. *Systems of political and economic control.* We have in
mind here the nature of the state, and the organization and distribution of power, along with the mode of its exercise. It is over
this dimension that the greatest disagreement, and perhaps the
greatest misunderstanding, has been manifested in the course
of the debate about convergence. The evident durability of the
Soviet system after more than fifty years has surely confounded
the prediction of those who, some thirty years ago, asserted that
the Soviet and the American systems were going to converge on
some common position.[46] Indeed, the increasing divergence of
China from the Soviet Union, so far as concerns the sharing of a
common socioeconomic system, must give pause to those who
assumed that, at least within the so-called socialist half of the
world, a common social order surely would be emerging. Out-

side the socialist world the situation is comparable. Despite an extraordinary degree of *decentralization,* the United States continues to display most of the standard attainments of modernity that are also manifested by an equally *centralized* France, with the system of each in fact having had its origin in premodern times.

Therefore, anyone who insists that the emergence of a common standard of economic and political organization for modern nation-states is inevitable must be prepared to acknowledge that this outcome can be expected to arrive only after a span to be calculated in centuries rather than decades. And, I fear, he must be prepared to face a very difficult task in specifying whether the common system that presumably will emerge will be more like that of the United States or that of the Soviet Union, or some variant altogether distinct from these.

Some will argue that all these models focused on the nation-state are obsolete, and urge us to recognize the multinational corporation as having transcendent significance in its impact on the existing modes of political and economic organization of the world system. They see this new form of social organization as exercising economic power on a scale of magnitude and coordination so great as to make its heads more powerful than any set of national rulers—indeed, to make them the cadre of a new form of world government. Against this image, however, one must balance the evidence of continuing and effective exercise of the ultimate power of the state in forcing such entities to adapt their policy to national interests or else suffer a set of consequences ranging up to exclusion from the territory of a given state, and, ultimately, to total confiscation.

All this is not to say there is no process truly common to all the states of the modern world. I believe there is. That common feature is the growing power of the state to control the lives of its citizens. That process is, of course, most dramatic in those parts of the world where a central state apparatus previously was either weak or nonexistent. I believe, however, that the same tendency is manifest also in countries such as the United States, which have a long history of organized government, but in which we are experiencing a new tendency in the progressive penetration of systems of central control into more and more aspects of individual life.[47] Whether this is a long-term trend toward which all humankind is converging, or whether the process is reversible in countries that attain a sufficiently high degree of development, I find very difficult to decide.

To sum up my position on the convergence issue, there is evidence of a strong tendency for all nations to move toward increasing utilization of modes of production based on inanimate power, resting in turn on modern technology and applied science. Managing this type of system, as well as coping with the new demands that populations impose for special goods and services, encourages the elaboration everywhere of new institutional forms intended to deal with them, rather consistently foster the incorporation of the population into new roles and patterns of role relationship; in turn, the latter directly or indirectly shape the structure of human relations in matters of class, kinship, leisure, and the like. This new structure of relations in part is produced by, and in part induces, new attitudes and values, forming the complex or syndrome we may identify as modern and postmodern.[48] This, in turn, brings the individuals occupying similar statuses in different societies much closer than commonly was the case in earlier times.

All of these processes are, however, subject to countervailing and contradictory trends that greatly mute the force of the tendency toward the emergence of a uniform world culture. One of the most important of these brakes on the process of homogenization lies in the distinctive cultural traditions which different national populations bring to the contemporary situation, and in the array of historically determined institutional arrangements with which they enter the contemporary era. These traditions and forms seem remarkably adaptable, and a high degree of variability in economic and political arrangements seems compatible with the management of a modern industrial society. Finally, despite the uniformity of the pressures and the consistency of the trends we observe, we should not lose sight of the enormous range over which the world's nation-states are spread on the various dimensions of development. Unless some unforeseen event causes the advanced nations to halt their further development while the others catch up, we can count on a very large amount of diversity throughout the world for at least another century.

NOTES

1. There is another related and currently very popular use of the term "dependence," which gives prime emphasis to the ability of a nation-state to make decisions about its internal development relatively free of the dominant and/or domineering pressure of more powerful states or economic systems. Thus, contemporary radical political-economists make a great deal of the "dependence" of the Latin American and other less developed countries on the greater political and economic power of the U.S. government, on "international capital," and on multinational corporations. The concept is also used to describe cultural phenomena, epitomized by the dominance of products like *Coca Cola,* which displace indigenous beverages, or systems of American empirical social research, which are charged with inhibiting the development of distinctive national systems of social analysis. See Suzanne Bodenheimer, "Dependency and Imperialism: The Roots of Underdevelopment in Latin America," in K. T. Fann and Donald D. Hodges, *Readings in U.S. Imperialism* (Boston: Porter Sargent, 1971); James D. Cockcroft, André G. Frank, and Dale L. Johnson, eds., *Dependence and Underdevelopment: Latin America's Political Economy* (New York: Anchor, 1972); Arghiri Emmanuel, *Unequal Exchange* (New York: Monthly Review Press, 1972); John D. Esseks, "Economic Dependence and Political Development in the New African States," *Journal of Politics* 33 (November 1971); Irving L. Horowitz, *The Three Worlds of Development* (New York: Oxford University Press, 1966); and Henry Magdoff, *The Age of Imperialism* (New York: Monthly Review Press, 1966).

2. The diversity of basic materials to be found within the boundaries of the United States is well known. It is helpful, however, also to see the contrast expressed in statistical terms. For the United States, foreign trade (in 1965) was only 7.3 percent of GNP, whereas for Japan it was 20 percent and for Singapore 238 percent. See Charles L. Taylor and Michael C. Hudson, *World Handbook of Political and Social Indicators,* 2d ed. (New Haven: Yale University Press, 1972), pp. 372–377.

3. The water mill was one of the few, and certainly one of the most important, mechanical inventions introduced in Hellenic times. Yet Childe reports that a century after Christ such mills were hardly more common than a century before. See Gordon Childe, *What Happened in History* (Baltimore: Penguin Books, 1942), pp. 235, 251–253. I am indebted to Keith Hopkins for the distinction between Roman invention and Roman innovation, i.e., the adoption and adaptation of the inventions of others.

4. Nathan Keyfitz of Harvard University estimates that 69 billion people have lived on earth since the beginning of the human race. Of this total, roughly 18 billion, or 26 percent, have lived on earth during the past 300 years; 3 billion, or 4 percent, are living on earth now. See Keyfitz, "How

Many People Have Lived on the Earth," *Demography* 3 (1966):581–582. We estimated the span of human habitation on earth to be 300,000 years, which yield our calculation that the modern era, covering some 300 years, equals .1 percent of the span of human occupancy of the globe. Keyfitz took the period of human habitation to cover one million years. Using that base would, of course, make the modern era an even smaller fragment of the span of human habitation on earth.

5. Donella H. Meadows and others, *The Limits of Growth* (New York: Universe Books, 1972).

6. The figures for percentage of annual increase given in this chapter were almost all computed by us from relatively crude time series, and therefore should be considered only approximate. In most cases only summary figures for two points in time were available to us, sometimes thirty or more years apart. Obviously, within so great a span the actual annual rate could have varied greatly from year to year and decade to decade. In cases where we could obtain more detailed time series, we checked to verify that the rates of increase had been more or less uniform over the longer span before computing a per annum rate of increase. Thus, we did not compute such a rate-of-increase figure for direct U.S. investment abroad for the *total period* from 1946 to 1971, because the years from 1946 to 1952 were relatively stable, whereas there was a sharp upturn from 1963 to 1971.

The formula used to calculate annual rates of increase takes beginning year and ending year figures and derives the yearly rate of growth in the following manner:

$$ r = \frac{1}{T \log_e} \frac{f(t)}{f(o)} $$

T=Total time elapsed
$f(t)$=figure at ending year
$f(o)$=figure at beginning year

This formula has been checked by use after the fact where appropriate, and in most cases has proven to be quite accurate. In fact, if anything, there is a slight conservative bias in our growth rate statistics. Discrepancies probably do arise because (1) the table we have been using gives natural logarithms ($\log_e$) to five significant figures only, and thus contains a certain amount of statistical error; (2) the assumption behind the use of the natural log is that "interest" is compounded constantly, i.e., that the number of times a year that the interest is compounded is taken to the mathematical limit; (3) there is an assumption that the value of the variable increases at a constant rate over the time period.

7. *United Nations Statistical Yearbook 1971* (New York: Statistical Office

of the United Nations, 1972), p. 78; UNESCO, *Statistics of Students Abroad 1962–1968* (Paris: UNESCO, 1972), pp. 19–21.

8. Figures are from forty countries listed in the *United Nations Statistical Yearbooks* for 1955 and 1971 for which there were data for years 1938 and 1970.

9. Figures computed on the basis of data found in *United Nations Statistical Yearbooks* for 1955 and 1971.

10. Between 1963 and 1970 the number of overseas telephone calls from the United States increased by about 25 percent per year (*World's Telephones* [New York: American Telephone and Telegraph, January 1970]). Data for other countries are not at hand, but it seems reasonable to assume that, at least for the other developed countries, rates of increase have not been much lower. Moreover, the United States alone accounts for a very large share of all the world's telephonic communication. To assume a worldwide increase in international telephonic communication of 15 percent therefore seems conservative.

11. Figures computed on the basis of data found in *United Nations Statistical Yearbooks* for 1955 and 1971. Annual increase of tourists used in these calculations include Belgium, Denmark, France, Germany, Ireland, Italy, Netherlands, Switzerland, and the United Kingdom as countries of origin. The omission of some European countries results in an underestimation of absolute numbers of tourists going from Europe to the United States. This omission, however, is not likely to affect the percentages of change reported.

12. *United Nations Statistical Yearbook 1970*, p. 402.

13. Calculated from data in *United Nations Yearbook 1972*, table 12, p. 43, for the years 1938–1971.

14. Figures taken from U.S. Department of Commerce, Bureau of Economic Analysis, *Survey of Current Business* (Washington, D.C., 1973).

15. Kjell Skjelsbaek, ''The Growth of Nongovernmental Organizations in the Twentieth Century,'' *International Organization* 25 (Summer 1971): 420–443.

16. Percentages computed on the basis of data reported in Moshe Y. Sachs, ed., *World Encyclopedia of the Nations* (New York: Harper and Row, 1960 and 1971).

17. The measures of increasing interconnectedness presented here are almost all absolute rather than relative or proportional. They indicate the number of ties extant, rather than the proportion of all countries, institutions, or individuals having such ties. As world population is increasing substantially, even holding constant the average degree of connectivity would obviously yield a significant increase in the absolute *number* of connections to be observed year by year. Therefore, some downward adjustment of our figures on connectivity should be made on a systematic basis. Nevertheless, the adjustment would not lead to a dramatic reinterpretation of the facts, because world

population has grown at a rate of only some 2 percent per annum, whereas most of the interconnections we noted increased at a rate of better than 7 percent per annum.

18. Based on figures reported in Taylor and Hudson (n. 2), pp. 372–377. By our calculation, the percentage of GNP represented by trade falls regularly as the population of a country increases. Median percentages are as follows: less than 1 million population, 78 percent; 1 to 10 million, 43 percent; 10 to 50 million, 33 percent; 50 to 100 million, 26 percent; more than 100 million, 10 percent of GNP.

19. Based on figures from *United Nations Statistical Yearbooks* for 1955 and 1971. Developed countries in these calculations included most European countries, the United States, Canada, Japan, Australia, and New Zealand. Less developed countries included the following few for which complete data were available: Angola, Morocco, Mozambique, Tunisia, India, Indonesia, Lebanon, Syria, Turkey, Argentina, and Paraguay.

20. All data on student exchanges are from United Nations sources, especially UNESCO (n. 7).

21. For example, the reason less developed countries are gaining on the more developed ones in the use of the telegraph can probably be explained by the fact that the more advanced are switching to the long-distance telephone, a more modern, rapid, and flexible form of communication. That would certainly seem to be indicated by the fact that the number of foreign telegrams sent out from the United States remained more or less the same in most years between 1963 and 1970, whereas the number of telephone calls abroad placed from the United States increased at better than 25 percent per year (see *United Nations Statistical Yearbook 1972,* and *The World's Telephones,* n. 10).

22. See UNESCO (n. 7), p. 30. If we assume a condition in which *all* young people went as far as the university, and make the further unlikely assumption that all university students would customarily be sent outside the country for advanced training, we have designed a situation such that in time no further increase in the number of students studying abroad could be attained unless the population of young people could be expanded by a rapid rise in births. Moreover, such expansion of the supply of young people could hardly occur at a rate of more than 2 or 3 percent per year, whereas the current and recent past rate of expansion in foreign study has run at 7 or 8 percent per year. Thus, with a stable rate of population growth, the *rate of increase* in students studying abroad could be brought as low as zero, even though the frequency of interchange of students was at 100 percent, i.e., saturation, with all students studying outside their home country.

This hypothetical example may give some satisfaction to our need to find some way of showing that exponential growth has clearly definable limits; we must nevertheless acknowledge that it is improbable that the conditions specified will be reached in the near, or even the distant, future.

23.   Percent of All Foreign Students Enrolled in Medicine
and Engineering, 1962–1968

	1962	1966	1968
Medicine	16.2	13.5	12.7
Engineering	19.5	18.1	17.8

Excerpted from UNESCO (n. 7), table 21, p. 47, which gives the field of study of all students studying abroad from 117 countries.

24. For example, UN statistics show the following: in foreign mail received, twenty less developed countries show an average annual gain of 7.3 percent from 1938 to 1970. In comparison, twenty developed countries show an average annual gain of only 3.7 percent. In foreign telegrams sent, twelve less developed countries show an average annual increase of 4.3 percent from 1938 to 1970, while twenty-two developed countries averaged only 2.0 percent. These statistics are complemented by telephone use data. Between 1967 and 1971, telephones in use increased 61.4 percent in Asia as compared with only 37 percent in Europe.

25. This is, of course, not to gainsay the fact that some countries are relatively heavily dependent on foreign universities to train their specialists in certain fields. For some evidence, see the section on *dependence* below.

26. The *United Nations Statistical Yearbook* for 1972 shows that in 1953 tourists from Japan to the United States numbered about 17,000. By 1971 the figure was 313,000. The 1953 figure included tourists from Korea, which, if omitted, would probably leave us a figure closer to the 15,000 mentioned in the text. The press reports an enormous surge of additional Japanese tourists to Hawaii in 1973. Some estimates place that flow at an increase of more than 100,000 in a single year.

27. This subset of 79 countries was selected from the full set of 124 presented by Taylor and Hudson (n. 2), in order to facilitate a comparison with figures for 1959 that had been presented by Bruce M. Russett and others, *World Handbook of Political and Social Indicators* (New Haven: Yale University Press, 1964). Results of the comparison will appear below. The full set of 124 countries presented by Taylor and Hudson shows the median proportion of trade to GNP to be 39 percent. The figures on trade as a percentage of GNP, cited above, are not meant to reflect total world trade as a proportion of total world GNP. Since many small countries that enter our set have high ratios of trade to GNP and relatively *small* GNPs, the median percentage figure we give is bound to be considerably greater than the ratio of total world trade to world GNP. This is especially true when one considers that the countries with the highest GNPs (U.S., U.S.S.R.) show figures for the proportion of trade to GNP that are below 10 percent. World trade as a proportion of world GNP can be roughly estimated from UN statistics. Considering market

economies only, the proportion of worldwide imports to worldwide GNP in 1963 was roughly 10 percent. By 1970 this figure had risen to nearly 12 percent. Figures based on *United Nations Statistical Yearbook 1972,* tables 146 and 188.

28. *United Nations Statistical Yearbook 1971,* pp. 460–463.

29. One basis for this conclusion is the fact that trade *within* the set of industrialized countries is much more intense than is trade either *between* industrialized and nonindustrialized sets or *within* the subset of the nonindustrialized. A more direct test of the hypothesis presented required that we compare the increases in trade with the increase in industrialization for specific countries. We selected eleven countries on the basis of availability of data, geographic spread, and variation in the degree to which their industrialization increased between 1948 and 1970. For those eleven we then compared the increase in industrialization with the increase in the value of exports over the same period. The rank-order correlation of the two sets of figures was .67, indicating a close correspondence between the two types of growth. At the top of the list, Japan's industrialization index increased 25.8 times (1963=100), and her trade increased by 20 percent per year; at the bottom of the list, Algeria's industrialization index increased only 1.1 times, and her exports by only 4 percent per year.

30. Figures for countries found in Russett (n. 27), as well as in Taylor and Hudson (n. 2).

31. Again we call attention to the fact that thus approaching the association of trade to GNP by country gives an impression of greater interdependence than one would derive by contemplating only the fact that the value of worldwide exports as a proportion of worldwide GNP is in the much more modest range of 10–12 percent.

32. Childe (n. 3), p. 239.

33. It is fascinating to apply this notion of potential autarky in trade and science to the realm of art. Some critics would assert that all the important sources of real creativity in art are found outside these giants, and that if they were not interconnected with the rest of the world, they would soon become artistic wastelands.

34. These assertions are confirmed by the fact that in 1970 tourism accounted for 8.1 percent, 5.6 percent, and 4.5 percent of the national income in Jamaica, Spain, and Mexico, respectively. By comparison, in the same year foreign tourist receipts accounted for a mere .3 percent of the national income of the United States and .1 percent of that of Japan (based on tables 157 and 187, *United Nations Statistical Yearbook 1972*).

35. If the point were not obvious when this sentence was first written in August 1973, it must surely have become obvious since then as a result of the Arab oil embargo and the resultant worldwide energy crisis.

36. UNESCO (n. 7), p. 33.

37. Ibid., p. 30.

38. Ibid., p. 55.

39. Ibid., p. 57.

40. De Seynes, "Prospects for a Future Whole World," *International Organization* 26 (Winter 1972):6.

41. See William J. Goode, *World Revolution and Family Patterns* (New York: Free Press, 1963).

42. Reinhard Bendix and Seymour Lipset, *Class, Status, and Power,* 2d. ed (New York: Free Press, 1966); see especially in this volume Robert W. Hodge, Donald J. Treiman, and Peter H. Rossi, "A Comparative Study of Occupational Prestige."

43. See Alexander Szalai, *The Use of Time: Daily Activity of Urban and Suburban Population in Twelve Countries* (The Hague: Mouton, 1973).

44. Inkeles, "Industrial Man: The Relation of Status to Experience, Perception, and Value," *American Journal of Sociology,* vol. 64 (July 1960).

45. Alex Inkeles and David H. Smith, *Becoming Modern* (Cambridge: Harvard University Press, 1974).

46. Inkeles, *Social Change in Soviet Russia* (Cambridge: Harvard University Press, 1968); see especially chap. 20, "Russia and the United States: A Problem in Comparative Sociology."

47. It may be argued that increasing affluence actually has had the effect of greatly increasing freedom of choice for the average individual in the United States. The issue is certainly debatable, but it is not the one to which the text is addressed. Rather, the text refers to the ever-widening regulation by the state of matters previously left to individual resolution. For example, we started with each person obliged to look to his retirement as best he can, but in time we have arrived at government social security payments obligatory for most people and increasing government regulation of previously private retirement plans worked out by corporations, unions, and other organizations. Under these new conditions, individuals may be more secure financially, but they also operate within a wider and more penetrating network of regulation and control.

48. The nature of the "postmodern" man is a challenging subject which I must unfortunately bypass here. It is a topic to which I will return in a later and fuller exposition of the ideas presented in this paper.

14

THE FUTURE OF WORLD COMMUNICATION AND PROPAGANDA

Harold D. Lasswell

I

The introduction to the first volume of this series ended with the statement that the new technology that created the first operational "world communication network" poses drastic problems for students of communication and propaganda as shaping forces in world history. We are less concerned with foretelling the future than with stengthening the propensity of thoughtful and responsible persons to approach the threats and opportunities of the emerging world determined to reshape communication technology in ways that satisfy and contribute to the satisfaction of human values.

Scrutiny of the past sharpens awareness of the role of the symbolic instrument as an accelerator of history, especially following the invention of printing from movable type and its application in the West. Among later innovations, the telegraph and cable, radio, and television have been cumulatively effective. With all deference to the impact of technology, we do not exaggerate its influence. An intensifying demand to communicate became a mobilizer of concerted action for political, economic, and other value goals. Communication continued to be pursued for its own sake. From Western Europe and the Americas the new instruments and demands were carried to Asia, Africa, and Oceania, where they stepped up the pace and influenced the direction of history.

To assert that the timing of history was affected carries with it the implication that what was likely to happen later happened sooner. More is implied than that messages passed more quickly from one person or group to another. The principal point is that the factors that shape history were differently aligned. Since the future thrust of history is influenced by changes in the relationship of these factors, a variably accelerated agenda is a modified agenda.

We begin our consideration of future developments by imagining that the principal trends of world communication and propaganda will continue much as they have in the recent past. It is manifestly unsatisfactory to leave it at that, for contradictory trends are bound to converge and therefore to clash with each other. By drawing upon the available stock of scientific knowledge, estimates can be made of how these coming conflicts are likely to be resolved. Cases in point are the new nationalisms of Africa. The strength of tribal loyalties may prevent a new national loyalty from gaining intense support. The new nation also may be threatened simultaneously by outside pressure from political entities that attract the allegiance of disaffected elements who come to believe that they will have more security and opportunity as members of a unit larger than the initial state. If we extrapolate these conflicting tendencies into the future, assuming that the larger units are the most attractive, it is plausible to predict that, barring catastrophe, the peoples of the globe will eventually acquiesce in propaganda on behalf of a public order of planetary scope.

A "construct" of this kind is open to reservations whose net effect is to emphasize the strength of many factors—including mechanisms of communication—that probably will slow down or threaten the hypothetical result. In Daniel Lerner's terms, a key factor in the recent past that will affect the future is "the revolution of rising expectations." When we examine the relationship of this revolution to national unity, the results appear to be equivocal. The short-run effect may be to promote the consolidation of hitherto divided peoples into a new nation; or, on the contrary, the impact may be to initiate secession from a larger empire. We have less experience with a "revolution of rising frustrations" (again in Lerner's words), though indications are that the short-run results also may be contradictory.

In any case, we concur with those who believe that the primary aim of a future-oriented exercise is less to prophesy than, in
Dennis Gabor's phrase, to "invent" what comes later. The act
of considering the shape of things to come is itself an event that
is not without effect on ensuing events. One result of imagining
a possible development is to strengthen individual and collective determination to expedite its occurrence or, on the contrary, to stave it off as long as is practicable. We are impressed
by the fact that the act of taking the future as a policy problem
has sometimes ignited a flash of creativity that introduced into
the emerging configuration an objective or strategy that was
previously unformulated. The contemporary challenge is to
constitute a policy process that reconsiders the common goals of
man, reexamines the trends of achievement, and both invents
and applies policies that are most likely to optimize the realization of value goals.

II

When we project the future technology of communication, one
statement at least would seem to be beyond serious dispute.
*Since contemporary technology is capable of almost instantane-
ous transmission of messages around the globe, a ceiling has
been reached that will remain unchanged unless qualitative innovations are introduced.* We are not discussing at this point
the factors that affect the spread or restriction on a global scale
of advanced technologies that are only partly applied.

It is not out of the question to imagine a truly qualitative innovation, such as the direct transmission of messages from mind
to mind with no mediating channel. As research stands at present, it is impossible to obtain agreement on whether or when
this change will come about.

Another possible source of drastic innovation is no less speculative. The reference is to communication with advanced forms
of life in other solar or galactic systems. The challenge would be
to find workable means of discourse, and to formulate inclusive
goals and strategies.

Two other contingencies—also "outrageous"—deserve to be
mentioned. One relates to "machines" and assumes they will
be perfected to a point that allows them to simulate the size and
appearance of human beings, and to acquire inner processes of

sufficient complexity and indeterminateness to allow them to engage in equivalents to "learning" and the experiencing of "emotion."

The other contingency is the experimental development of forms of life equal to or superior to man's intelligence and his other attributes. The discovery of the "genetic information code" by Crick and Watson has released a wave of research whose practitioners expect to achieve great things in the next few decades.

The principal virtue of thinking about novel possibilities is to underline the importance of viewing the accessible world not as a completed source of empirical experience but as a sample state of possible systems.

III

Returning to less "outrageous hypotheses," we consider two contrasting projections of the future of mass communication. *One "construct" assumes a relatively smooth sequence of mutual influencing and change. The other depicts a zigzag course, accepting important levels of conflict.*

The script that assumes a smooth course of development emphasizes the continuing growth of global interdependence. An interdependent relationship is not restricted to such cross-boundary movements as trading or visiting. It also implies taking one another into account irrespective of activities that reach across boundary lines. The participants continually estimate how they will be affected by any policy of the other. In political matters the key estimates relate to the making of war or peace, or to any other decision that requires public authority and control. Estimates may refer to every institutional process of value shaping or sharing. Therefore references may be to the cultivation of enlightenment either in mass media or scientific installations. Possibly the allusion is to policies of wealth production and distribution, or to safety, health, and other forms of well-being. Expectations may include policies relating to educational and aesthetic, familial, class, or ethical affairs.

The future presented in the evolutionary model can be expected to pass through an interrelated sequence of communication phenomena. A common zone of *attention* is already a reality among the elite elements of the nation-states of the globe.

The audience of the future will include broader strata of the mid-elite and the rank and file, and will have exposure to images of man and environment that are at once more frequent and detailed, and inclusive of the attention zone itself.

People who pay attention to events in any nation begin to entertain judgments about them, and to utter opinions in the hope of affecting, at least in some measure, what goes on. A world *opinion* zone can be expected to emerge and gain strength. The inhabitants of the earth who learn of events in New York, Moscow, or Peking will eventually give voice to their opinions. They will tend to disregard the legal technicalities that are supposed to limit policy participation to those who are members of the state.

Perpetually interacting with zones of attention and opinion are the zones of *action* that include participants in the world community who engage in transnational acts. Travel and trade are among the activities that have long functioned on a global scale.

Zones of action include networks of more or less inclusive *organization*. In part this is a consequence of competition and conflict, and the economics that result from adapting interests to one another. Much more than intergovernmental relations are at stake; every value-institution sector is partially organized. Satellite technology, for instance, calls for structures of communication that, if not fully official, at least are able to transcend national frontiers. Transnational corporations are a well-recognized feature of world economy. Both private and public organizations are specialized to safety, health, and other well-being outcomes. A vast network is devoted to transmitting and evaluating skill in vocational, professional, and aesthetic matters. Prestige structures cross boundary lines, as do organizations specialized to religion and ethics. Families, fraternities, and other institutions of individual love and group loyalty may pay scant heed to national limits.

It is in reference to identity and loyalty that the future of world communication must evolve in a particular manner if a comprehensive system of world public order is to become a reality. In addition to the zones of attention, opinion, action, and organization, a zone of *identity* is essential. Included will be persons who possess an active sense of belonging to the "nation of man" without losing their attachment to lesser identities within the whole. The primary ego of each individual is capable of achieving a "self-system" composed of symbolic ties with many egos.

The "smooth" trajectory of the sequence outlined above is in many ways deceptive, for it contains no hint of the magnitude of the changes required to achieve a unified world order. The dimensions of the transformations called for can be made explicit by examining a conflictful, zigzag model of world communication. At root such a "construct" postulates that the disunited, militant, and apprehensive world of today continues into the future. If we are to reach a trustworthy estimate of the strength of the forces that must be altered before the world arena can be modified, it is helpful to question why, given the degree of global interdependence already achieved, the world community remains basically divided against itself.

A partial answer is forthcoming when we look into the *mechanisms of self-maintenance* presently available to the global system. Among the symbolic factors that help to perpetuate the traditional state of affairs is the *expectation of violence*. It is not necessary to love violence to accept the assertion that future wars are likely. Political leaders who would prefer to allow their military defenses to deteriorate and to contribute to an international security force are deterred from doing so by political rivals who are likely to accuse them of negligence or treason. It is undeniable that interstate confrontations *may* take place, and that inclusive institutions of public order, like the United Nations, have as yet neither won world confidence nor attained notable efficiency as instruments of peaceful conflict resolution. Formal education and informal socialization combine to create a structure of acquiescence among young and old in measures of national security.

The basic condition that favors the successful transmission of the central myth of the state is a monopoly of attention. In big states, at least, attention is absorbed by current events, past memories, and expressions of future purpose. The exclusiveness of a national self is sustained by absorption with the self.

The implication is not that opportunities to receive public messages from other countries or to travel abroad are totally ignored. Foreign intelligence is regularly obtained by members of the community who live abroad. Diplomats and soldiers, businessmen, physicians, students, artists, and tourists collectively scrutinize the external environment. To some extent everyone is affected by the *mechanism of self-reference.* When a person is exposed to a new environment his attention swings back to the experiences and attributes of the self. The ordinary tourist is a good example: if he sees that motor cars are driven on the left side of the road, he thinks immediately of "how we do it at home." A similar sequence occurs in reference to food, clothes, and every other aspect of the situation.

While the self-reference mechanism has the immediate effect of maintaining the original predispositions of an individual, eventual outcomes may differ. By connecting the new with the old it is possible to maintain a sense of continuity—of identity —while undergoing exposure to novel environments.

If progress is to continue toward an inclusive system of public order and if the retarding effect of the self-reference mechanism is to be overcome, the zone of world identity must be in a flourishing condition. In this connection we commend attention to an often-reported feature in the growth of more inclusive identities. It may be that the individuals or groups who are undergoing an identity change may not be aware of what is happening until the transformation is well along. Neighborhood and provincial loyalties may be more fully conscious and "more real" to the individuals involved than is their sense of belonging to a new nation-state. It may be with surprise that citizens find themselves shocked and resentful of any suggestion that the larger union ought to be dissolved, or that the authority of the new nation should be curtailed. Analysis shows that over the years some thoughts have gradually become "unthinkable" and some ideas "unspeakable." Cognitive maps have been unobtrusively revised to sustain the view that net value indulgences depend on sustaining the institutions of a larger, in this case a national, "self."[1]

The evolution of an inclusive world identity is a combined rational and nonrational process. Curiosity and the continuing search for information are nonrational in the sense that they are rooted in impulses whose presence depends on the genetic constitution. In this sense the dynamics of public order are lodged in "human nature," even though after birth human nature must be modified in interaction with other human beings.

In the broadest terms the social process directs basic impulses toward acceptable modes of expression. In the political sector impulses are displaced from primary objects in the intimate circle to public objects, and rationalized in the common interest.

If an inclusive world public order is to be achieved, it will be necessary to expedite the discovery of an inclusive identity by enough decision makers in the world arena who control a sufficient supply of base values to consolidate and defend constitutive institutions that are powerful enough to protect themselves against coercive challenge. World integration will be signalized by the progressive development of comprehensive zones of attention, opinion, action, organization, and identity.

IV

The rise of the symbolic in world history carries with it *the progressive subordination of change to the impacts of communication*. The formation and execution of policy, which is mainly a symbolic activity, implicates ever-widening configurations of man and environment.

One of the most consequential changes is *the attenuating spatial connection between policy activity and the processing of resources*. The shift is a result of the impact of science-based technology on energy and materials. Chemists discovered or synthesized new materials with which to expedite the transmission of energy or to perpetuate the forms that appeared when energy was applied. Running water or wind, among the traditional supplements to biological energizers, has been far outdistanced by steam, oil, electricity, and nuclear power.

The commitment of people to geographical sites of energy and raw materials was sharply reduced as human energy became a declining fraction of all the energy in use. With the aid of a relatively small labor force, it was possible to extract coal, petroleum, and metals from their original locations, and to route them, or any other energy or material, through lengthening chains of operation to their ultimate destinations. In consequence finishing industries multiplied and clustered in cities where they were close to workers, customers, and policy agencies.

The specific technology of communication expedited the process outlined above. A ''sign'' is a resource that is adapted to the task of making a symbolic reference. As a rule the amount of material or of energy that is required by a particular sign is small. We do not, of course, overlook such exceptions as giant steles or huge memorializing edifices. Typically a specific "bit" of information is miniscule if the infrastructure is built to transmit by telegraph, cable, radio, or television.

The process by which policy becomes spatially attenuated from resource sites or behavioral operations is exemplified by the military. As Hans Speier pointed out, as technology became more sophisticated a top commander was no longer compelled to follow a battle or a war game from a seat in the saddle. Top commanders sit in chairs at remote headquarters where the action can be followed on maps, charts, radio, and television. During an intercrisis period, headquarters are located where easy communication is possible with politicians, businessmen, research workers, and other symbol handlers and managers.

In the economic process the policy makers who communicate with one another specialize on the choice of plant location, layout, and production routine; or on financing, merchandising, personnel administration, law, public relations, research, development, and so on.

The proliferation of forums in politics, economics, or any other sector of society is at once a consequence and a condition of intellectual (symbolic) differentiation. In the management of personnel, for instance, the growth of a new profession leads to the introduction of new actors, routines, and situations in the sequence of operations that relate to individuals. Doctrines and procedures evolve for the handling of recruitment, promotion, discipline, and other characteristic features of the process.

The attenuating space relationship between resources and policy has fostered a specific architectural form in the central cities of industrializing countries.[2] This is the high-rise office building. Expanded reliance on communication brings with it a need for both personal and impersonal channels to serve as agents for the transmission, storage, and retrieval of messages. Every participant who exercises a discretionary role at each policy phase brings with him a bevy of clerks and a cluster of files to backstop the postal messengers, telephones, telegraphs, interviews, and conferences employed in policy formation and execution.

Every office building can be conceived of as a stack of shelves for communicators (executives, professionals, subexecutives) and their equipment. As the stacks rise floor upon floor, and competition for lot space intensifies, the consequences irradiate the urban environment. Whether in New York, London, Moscow, or Tokyo, the complaints are remarkably similar: traffic congestion, housing shortages, air and water pollution, urban sprawl, and ugliness.

As the sign revolution enters a new phase, the general picture may be modified. The first step in the sign revolution was to accelerate the centralization of policy processes in supercities. The giant transformation that is now under way is associated with the rise of computer technology. In principle, computer networks can be used to integrate a policy process whose phases can complement one another without requiring a few centrally located structures. *The new technology makes it possible to share with anyone at any desired location a picture of the total context of any operation, including the several phases of policy.* The coal vein that tied man to the mine face, the waterwheel that bound the spinner to the mill, the blast furnace that kept the puddler close to the heat, or even the libraries, files, and clerks who kept the manager or the researcher tied down in their vicinity, are no longer the determiners of location. We appear to be at the threshold of the epoch in which, as microcomputers evolve, universal and complementary networks of information deliver their messages to the focus of attention of an interested party wherever he may be found.

The implication is contextuality of perspective and space-free access to contextual maps. Computer technology provides a means of achieving a policy process open to influence at every step by the opportunity to perceive any specific detail in the setting of an inclusive map of value goals, trends, conditions, projections, and alternatives. Evidently the supercentralizing, superconcentrating trends that were fostered by the early phases of the sign revolution are of lessening importance.

V

The *style* as well as the policy content of communication will affect the future. Style is the arrangement of the signs and symbols of which a communication is composed. *Expressive* styles are focused on skillful communication as an end in itself. *In-*

strumental styles, by contrast, subordinate the arrangement of communicative elements to the realization of other values.

The elements of a sequence of communication can be resolved into two fundamental categories: *symbols, signs.* In schematic terms we think of a completed act as a sequence of events that characteristically begins in impulse and subjectivity and proceeds to expression. The moods and images are the symbols; the use of words and word-substitutes are the signs.

When an act of communication is a scope value, an end in itself, the culminating outcome is perceived as symbol and sign arrangements for their own sake. The styles of communication may be classified in many ways for many purposes. One useful classification notes that sign and symbol patterns vary from *parsimony* to *opulence.* The essential criterion is the degree to which they are restricted to the minimum necessary for comprehension. Although shouting may gratify some inner need of the shouter to dramatize his existence to himself, the noise may not be essential to alert a respondent to the fact that a traveler is coming up the lane.

The calm tones of the BBC political broadcasters established a prototype for a parsimonious style of radio broadcasting at a time when it was customary in many quarters to blow the man down. The scientific community has imposed a discipline on its writers that applies canons of parsimony to the dissemination of scientific knowledge. The only conscious purpose was audience comprehension; superfluous words or ''mere speculation'' were discouraged. The demand to make economic transactions quickly comprehensible led to market quotations, which masterfully exemplify what is possible in condensed reporting. Many pharmaceutical notations and insignia are rooted in early civilization. In sports reporting we are familiar with the parsimoniousness of a box score and, in contrast, the ebullience of a feature writer. In educational administration, uniform class schedules may consolidate the control of a bureaucratic structure over large districts. For untold generations, emblems of identity have been employed as means of focusing mass sentiment on people or objects certified according to rank. The cross or the crescent may designate an agent or an object specialized to rectitude in the positive or negative sense of religion, ethics, or criminality.

In the future *the parsimonious style will continue to function as long as the demand continues (1) for human experience to be speedily shared, or (2) for concerted action to be taken on a large scale without delay.*

The projection is not that parsimonious styles will increase at the expense of opulent styles. It is conceivable that the motives expressed in the latter may multiply as rapidly as the former. *Styles may very well run the gamut between extremes of opulence and parsimoniousness.*

In this connection it is illuminating to consider the future of the public buildings specialized to the requirements of government, law, and politics. These buildings do much more than provide space in which the various functions of government are housed. They communicate: they convey messages to those who are exposed to either their exterior or interior dimensions. For example, the walls of ancient cities transmit many messages to many audiences. To a potential enemy they said, or were designed to say, that "you have no prospect of defeating us by force; don't embark on a costly and hopeless enterprise." To the inhabitants the principal message was compounded of security, identity, and pride. In some circumstances the communicative function may gain the upper hand and result in public edifices that compromise a military or other operational purpose. For instance, the role of stone masonry as an expressive medium appears to have attained such value priority in ancient Peru that political stability was undermined by the burden of labor and taxation. Dynasties have inflated the iconic (communicative) function of a complex of palaces until the weight of governmental exactions provoked succession or rebellion. We know that the symbolic inflation of public buildings beyond the limits of economic prudence is no monopoly of dynasties or aristocracies. In the United States we are familiar with dilapidated structures that connote failures of expectation on the part of rival towns and cities to become the seat of a county courthouse or the capital of a state.

As recognition of world identity emerges, we foresee a growing demand to stabilize and to celebrate a satisfactory world public order. With the partial exception of nomadic cultures, man is accustomed to expand the iconic function of public structures as an expression of collective honor and as an enduring means of obtaining and transmitting acquiescence to the public order.

Whether or not the resource environment is transformed into an artifact as a result of collective effort, it exercises a standardizing impact on perspectives. A physical object—especially a towering one—is *there,* and initially generates the expectation that it will remain. Hence the intense demand for monumentality (an opulent style even when unembellished) that marks the emergence and consolidation of a new culture, class, interest group, or personality. The monumental style, which our study of the past has so often mentioned, becomes a common experience for all whose focus of attention is directed toward imposing structures.

It is true that in some circumstances a new elite or mass may be strongly disposed to reject the opulent style of a regime perceived as oppressive. Palaces and memorials are razed to the ground, and the first substitutes may be improvised. A revolution in the name of democratic ideology may return to "simplicity" (allegedly of the Greeks, for instance) and construct or reconstruct their legislatures, executive buildings, and courthouses accordingly. If the body politic stabilizes and survives, the expected sequence is for public buildings to return to more lavish use of material and more embellished modes of decoration. Our image of the future is in no way incompatible with the view that fluctuations are possible (and in fact likely) in the level of participation sought and realized at various times and places; or in the acceptance of any given set of limits, or nonlimits, on the growth of a member of the world community. An enduring public order cannot be an utterly rigid system; and wherever variability is found it will continue to find expression in styles that emphasize different mixes of the parsimonious and the opulent. Outcomes are continually affected by the competition and conflict among those who become devoted to particular patterns of style criteria, and who form coalitions of artists and laymen in official or nonofficial positions.

VI

As world interdependence encourages long-term tendencies toward a unified and differentiated world order, the iconic function of the earth will itself be more widely perceived and more assiduously cultivated. Already we are aware of the halting steps that have been taken to develop subcenters on various continents where international operations are sited. The silhouettes of the UN buildings in New York seem to be achieving primacy as an image of the organized world in competition with the palace at The Hague or the former League of Nations buildings at Geneva. Very likely they are achieving design primacy as well.

If we conceive of architecture as the symbolic and factual creation of enclosures, it is evident that enclosures range from single rooms to clusters of rooms, and from particular buildings and compounds to towns, regions, and superregions.[3] Evidently we are in the early phases of perceiving the iconic function of Earth itself. This process has been enormously stimulated by the self-reference effect of looking back at the planet Earth from outer space. In imagination our eyes are the eyes of the astronauts and their photographing equipment. The new vision of Earth provides a rounded backdrop for every static or mobile object in our vicinity. These local spots are ordered into an enlarging perspective that is "ours." We are in the early stages of retouching our conceptual maps, and of imagining ways to augment the variety and the significance of Earth and its growing brood of artificial satellites. The resymbolization of Earth in the media of painting and sculpture is already in progress. The economies of design that shaped rocket launchers, rockets, and space ships are becoming primary themes for the imaginative grand designs that are likely, over time, to modify the iconic aspect of Earth from whatever standpoint it is experienced.

It is perhaps valid to infer that man will continue to be affected in the future as in the past by both primitive and sophisticated images of his body. These images are individual and multiindividual. We are especially aware of the influence of the solitary body-figure on cave painting and eventually on building plans. The physical facts were well observed and simplified even in the early days of culture. The self-reference is unmistakable when a circle with two dots and a slit for the face surmounts a straight line that forks into a short pair of lines near the top and into a longer pair at the lower end. The masculine reference is obvious of a short, slanted potency line where the long line forks at the bottom. Similarly, the female allusion is clear of two small circles near the top of the central line and a larger pregnancy circle farther down.

Our many-bodied social images are expressed in sculptured

circles and in elaborate constructions, like Stonehenge, that relate man to the celestial sphere, and particularly to the sun. The zodiac is the product of a cumulative collective imagination that insists on projecting human and other forms of life, individually or in groups, on the cosmic habitat.

The rearranging of Earth and its satellites into a "factual" and a "symbolic" enclosure will no doubt persist and contribute to maintaining a fundamental core of identity with our self-images. The face of Earth, when perceived as a face, can be further adapted to the image by evolving a composition of dots and great circle lines that represent the head, the source of the intelligence that is recomposing the relationship of this planet to its solar and galactic environment. The principal locations are likely to be the orbiting and returning facilities that are specialized to space operations. Artificial satellites are a lattice constituting a canopy of mobile units whose paths can be timed and placed to reinforce a sense of identity and achievement. Self-reference designs eventually will affect the arrangement of the principal exiting trails that avoid or touch artificial and natural objects and provide "upright" vents for crude power objects and symbols, such as rockets and ships.

Among the strategies that expedite these developments is the cultivation of small configurations of experience that enable the viewer-participant to orient himself in the cosmic context of past, present, and future events. A "social planetarium" can be adapted to neighborhoods, cities, and larger territories.[4] It can have at its disposal all the audio-visual modes of vivid presentation, and mobilize both nonprofessional and professional participation in initiating and revising the exhibits.

The planetarium idea was originated by astronomers as a means of popular education in science. The viewer is introduced to models and maps of the earth among the stars and satellites. The presentations replay past trends and project future developments; or they delineate a model that expounds current scientific explanations.

A social planetarium can be constructed on a scale that ranges from a modest chamber to a complex of rooms and buildings. Retracing "Homo sapiens" as a form of life calls for information about his origin and spread. As man is a "culture-inventing" form, his institutions can be classified and described according to the value-outcome whose realization they are specialized to foster. As will be recognized from preceding pages, we use eight terms as a classificatory convenience in examining the value institutions of any social context, whether the scope is global, transglobal, or subglobal (power, enlightenment, wealth, well-being, skill, affection, respect, rectitude). Participants in the social process interact continually with one another, and with the "resource environment," which implicates transsurface, surface, and subsurface phenomena.

A social planetarium will be most illuminating to its audiences if it presents the past, present, and future flow of events in alternative versions. This acknowledges the fact that scholars who are educated in different environments usually differ in their interpretations of the dynamics of society. An advantage of the planetarium conception is that it provides a recurring experience for the spectator-participant that enables him to arrive at less parochial and more disciplined judgments than he otherwise would make. If it is inexpedient for intergovernmental structures to administer planetarium facilities, private organizations can be mobilized for the purpose. Civic order is both a supplement and a partial alternative to public order.

VII

Among the critical factors to be estimated in projecting the role of communication and propaganda is the relative advantage afforded by the symbolic instrument to political elites. The maximization principle suggests the trite inference that decision makers give preference to the symbolic instrument when they expect to obtain net advantages from its use. We have seen that among the characteristics of the symbolic instrument from which it gains a competitive advantage in many situations are the *rapidity, parsimony,* and *realism* that result from the management of signs and symbols as means of sharing common experiences and of mobilizing common action on a large scale. We foresee that the *communication and propaganda instrument will be of increasing political importance in the immediate future.* Over the longer term, the situation is more problematic.

Consider the fundamental dimensions of communication. A communication system is parsimonious in the sense that it substitutes specialized channels or messages for more elaborate somatic, behavioral, or environmental means of obtaining results. Instead of finding it necessary to walk or run in order to touch the environment, the sensory system, which is a specialized communication network, provides the signs that initiate the symbols of reference to objects at a distance, thereby rendering it feasible to perceive them as opportunities for value indulgence or threats of deprivation. The use of visual, sound, and other receptors is parsimonious in a triple sense. They are compact and sparing of energy inside the body. As remarked above, the receptors often make it unnecessary to move the body to test the environment. They may also utilize information channels built outside the body (such as installations on the moon or in orbit). Once installed, these channels save the resources otherwise required for subsequent trips.

Under various circumstances the distinctive features of the symbolic instrument cease to yield net political advantages, and presumably give way to alternative means. For instance, the rapidity and parsimony of communication may introduce or spread political tendencies that undermine the system with which an established order identifies itself. The communication instrument would appear to be particularly dependent upon the vigilance of authority, for indoctrination is not necessarily a job that is done "once and for all." It is always essential to consider the creativity of individuals, as well as to allow for a changing correlation of impulse and sentiment whose effect may be to undermine routine commitments.

In view of the far-reaching consequences of interdependence, it is in no sense certain that established elites will be able to use public education and information to maintain the degree of support that they require, and in crises symbolic instruments will be supplemented and supplanted by instruments whose main reliance is on physical coercion.

We offer an additional forecast about the nature and use of coercive instruments. We concur with those who predict a vast expansion of the chemical and biological sciences and who expect this explosive development to generate a body of knowledge and procedures of application that will enrich the arsenal of coercive devices at the disposal of power elites. Eventually it may be possible to use drugs on a large scale to standardize popular acquiescence in an established order. Most decisive of all, mastery of the genetic code may result in the permanent submission of a new class of "slaves." Preconditioning probably can occur before birth, and the individuality that has hitherto defeated all standardizing processes of socialization may at last be deprived of its capability as a threat to self-perpetuating castes.

It should be reiterated that we do not view any construct of the future as presenting an inevitable outcome. *The essential proposition is that if man's potential for dignity and creativeness is to be realized, the symbolic instrument must be used to keep alive the pluralism of authority and control that prevents the absolutization of political power.*

VIII

In coming years the study of communication, where societies are relatively open, will deepen the insight of the population into the patterns of continuity that link personal development with society and history. Methods are now available that, with small investment of time, connect present perspectives with the "forgotten" perspectives of earlier years. The hypothesis has long been stated, for instance, that the personal dynamics of politics is to be found in the displacement of impulses of the individual from objects in the early primary circle to public personalities, doctrines, issues, and operational procedures. It is now feasible to use short interview procedures to disclose the specific displacements, for example, from early family members to presidential candidates and other public figures.[5] In principle, these methods can be applied in a global network to intensify the understanding of the results obtained from conventional survey and content analysis research.

It is apparent that the information gathered by "intensive" interviewing may be used by professional manipulators to manage public response. The same information, however, can be made accessible to participating persons, and can contribute to self-understanding and the making of choices to continue or discontinue particular perspectives.

Self-knowledge is a means of realizing continuities within experience and of undermining the sense of alienation that comes from seeming discontinuity. The findings of communications research, as made available, can be expected to aid the progressive reorientation of individuals in relation to personal development, society, and history.

NOTES

1. An illuminating historical case study by Richard L. Merritt is *The Growth of American Community, 1735–1775* (New Haven: Yale University Press, 1965).

2. For detail, see, for instance, Peter Hall, *The World Cities* (New York: McGraw-Hill Book Co., 1966).

3. This characterization has much in common with Suzanne Langer, *Feeling and Form* (New York: Scribner, 1953).

4. See my discussion of "Strategies of Inquiry: The Rational Use of Observation," in Daniel Lerner, ed., *The Human Meaning of Social Sciences* (New York: Meridian Books, 1959), pp. 89–113.

5. See Steven R. Brown, "Intensive Analysis in Political Research," *Political Methodology* 1 (1974):1–25.

CONTRIBUTORS

W. PHILLIPS DAVISON received a Ph.D. in sociology from Columbia University in 1954. Since 1965 he has been professor of sociology and journalism at Columbia. His works include *International Political Communication* (1965) and *Mass Communications and Conflict Resolution* (1974).

ITHIEL DE SOLA POOL received a Ph.D. in political science from the University of Chicago in 1952. He is professor of political science at MIT, where he also serves as director of the research program in international communication at the Center for International Studies. His works include *Candidates, Issues and Strategies* (1965), *The Prestige Press* (1970), and *Talking Back: Citizen Feedback and Cable Technology* (1973).

HERBERT GOLDHAMER (1907–1979) received a Ph.D. in sociology from the University of Chicago in 1938. He taught at Stanford and the University of Chicago before becoming a senior staff member of the Rand Corporation in 1948. His works include *Process and Effects of Mass Communication* (1971) and *The Foreign Powers in Latin America* (1972).

ALEX INKELES received his Ph.D. from Columbia University and taught at Harvard from 1952 to 1971. He is currently Margaret Jacks

Professor of Education and Sociology at Stanford. His works include *Public Opinion in Soviet Russia* (1950) and *Social Change in Soviet Russia* (1968).

LEWIS M. KILLIAN received a Ph.D. in sociology from the University of Chicago in 1949 and taught at the University of Oklahoma and Florida State University. Since 1969 he has been professor of sociology at the University of Massachusetts, Amherst. His works include *Collective Behavior* (1957, rev. 1972), *Racial Crisis in America* (1964), and *White Southerners* (1971).

HAROLD D. LASSWELL (1902–1978), one of the foremost political theorists of our time, is perhaps best known for his development of the "policy sciences," a fusion of law, political science, sociology, and psychology into one overarching discipline dealing with public choice and decision making. He received his Ph.D. in political science from the University of Chicago in 1926 and in later years was Edward J. Phelps Professor of Law and Political Science at Yale and co-director of the Policy Sciences Center in New York City.

L. JOHN MARTIN received a Ph.D. in political science from the University of Minnesota in 1955. He is professor of journalism at the University of Maryland, the author of *International Propaganda* (1958), and co-editor of *Propaganda in International Affairs* (1971) and *Role of the Mass Media in American Politics* (1976).

ARNOLD A. ROGOW received a Ph.D. in political science from Princeton University in 1953. He taught at the University of Iowa, Haverford College, and Stanford before becoming graduate professor of political science at the City College of New York. His works include *Politics, Personality, and Social Science in the Twentieth Century* (1969) and *Psychiatrists* (1971).

ANDREW ROLLE received a Ph.D. in American history at UCLA in 1952. He is Robert Glass Cleland Professor of History at Occidental College. His works include *California: A History* (1963), *The Immigrant Upraised* (1968), and *The American Italians* (1972).

WILBUR SCHRAMM received a Ph.D. in American civilization from the University of Iowa in 1932. He taught at Iowa, the University of Illinois, and Stanford before joining the East-West Communication Institute, of which he was formerly director, at the East-West Center in Honolulu. His works include *Science of Human Communication* (1963), *Process and Effects of Mass Communications* (1971), *Men, Messages and Media* (1973), and *Communication and Change* (1976).

JOSEPH J. SPENGLER received a Ph.D. in economics from Ohio State University in 1930. He is James B. Duke Professor of Economics at Duke University and the author of *Population Economics* (1972) and *Population and America's Future* (1975).

JEROME B. WIESNER first became associated with MIT in 1942 as a staff member of the radiation laboratory. In due course he became professor of electrical engineering, director of the electronics research laboratory, dean of science, provost, and, from 1971 to 1979, president of the institution. From 1961 to 1964 he served as director of the Office of Science and Technology at the White House. His works include *Where Science and Politics Meet* (1964).

INDEX